Religion, State and Society
in the Transformations
of the Twentieth Century

Gerhard Besier

Studien zur Kirchlichen Zeitgeschichte
Studies in Contemporary Church History

herausgegeben von/edited by

Prof. Dr. Dr. Gerhard Besier (Universität Dresden)
Prof. Dr. Andrea Strübind (Universität Oldenburg)

Band/Volume 1

LIT

Religion, State and Society in the Transformations of the Twentieth Century

Modernization, Innovation and Decline

Gerhard Besier

LIT

Gedruckt auf alterungsbeständigem Werkdruckpapier entsprechend
ANSI Z3948   DIN ISO 9706

Cover Picture: Cavert and Michelfelder, two American Church Officers,
arriving at Stuttgart by a Military Jeep, October 1945

Bibliographic information published by the Deutsche Nationalbibliothek
The Deutsche Nationalbibliothek lists this publication in the Deutsche
Nationalbibliografie; detailed bibliographic data are available in the Internet at
http://dnb.d-nb.de.

ISBN 978-3-8258-0980-5

A catalogue record for this book is available from the British Library

© LIT VERLAG Dr. W. Hopf Berlin 2008
Auslieferung/Verlagskontakt:
Fresnostr. 2   48159 Münster
Tel. +49 (0)251–62 03 20   Fax +49 (0)251–23 19 72
e-Mail: lit@lit-verlag.de   http://www.lit-verlag.de

Distributed in the UK by: Global Book Marketing, 99B Wallis Rd, London, E9 5LN
Phone: +44 (0) 20 8533 5800 – Fax: +44 (0) 1600 775 663
http://www.centralbooks.co.uk/acatalog/search.html

Distributed in North America by:

Transaction Publishers
New Brunswick (U.S.A.) and London (U.K.)

Transaction Publishers
Rutgers University
35 Berrue Circle
Piscataway, NJ 08854

Phone: +1 (732) 445 - 2280
Fax: + 1 (732) 445 - 3138
for orders (U. S. only):
toll free (888) 999 - 6778
e-mail:
orders@transactionspub.com

Preface

As a matter of course, the established churches and religious communities were both passively and actively involved in the transition processes of the twentieth century. This volume is about their role. The articles discuss the high importance of the enlightenment for the secularization process and the development of a modern culture in which church and state are separate. In such societies religiously neutral governments and courts deal strictly with the different denominations according to the principle of equality. Theocracies, which act according to religious principles, are not able to develop in this manner. The European political and religious cultures during the time following the French Revolution were based on the principle of separation. This, of course, did not keep many European states from using the services of the Christian religion at will – and vice versa.

The short, but influential missions-history of the German Empire consisted of the imperial European powers' attempts to force the Central European Culture on Africans, Asians, and other peoples in order to make them more "significant" Europeans. The state churches cooperated in these efforts wholeheartedly by trying to impose Christianity on the people.

Churches and their pastors also played an important part in the implementation of the "political religion" of nationalism. In order to make up for the amount of spontaneous persuasive power that the biblical worldview had lost, national liberal and nationalist pastors tried to make their religion attractive again using nationalist slogans and to awaken political-religious emotions in this way.

German Protestantism was also deeply involved in the two German dictatorships – National Socialism as well as the Communist regime of the German Democratic Republic. In both cases, the church leadership worked closely with the repressive systems and tried to win the people over to the dictatorships' ideologies. On the other hand, religious opposition played a comparatively marginal role.

The churches of other countries, especially the Federal Council of the Churches of Christ in America and its successor organization tried not to sever their contacts with the German churches and did their best to understand the change that National Socialism was enacting in Europe. For a long time the USSR was considered the least humane dictatorship. Many American groups shared the German churches' strictly anti-Communist attitudes, which clouded their judgment regarding "anti-Communist" National Socialism. It was not until the war that attitudes in America began to change at the grassroots level. Of course, the completely different religious and political circumstances in the USA also stood in the way of a deeper understanding of the German situation throughout the course of the entire German-American discourse.

In places where Protestants were a minority group, for example in Spain, where Francoism was supported by the Catholic church, there were lively conflicts between protestant pastors and the Fascist regimes in Germany and Spain because the denominational minority had been repressed by the "Catholic" dictatorship in Southern Europe.

In Germany itself, competition also arose to the National Socialist inclined portion of majority Protestantism, such as that which was developed and maintained by Heinrich Himmler and his SS. Often the SS was also supported not only by the population in general but also by religious officials in their attempts to establish a "new religion". In this way it was possible to use old cathedrals such as the one in Braunschweig or Quedlinburg as cult memorials for the neo-pagan religion.

After the Second World War the U.S.'s churches were extremely involved in the European transition process, especially in that of West Germany. By providing financial and spiritual aid, above all through an invitational program for leading German clergy, the American denominations tried to influence the previously nationalistic course of German Protestantism and to democratize the German churches.

During the Cold War Christian religious communities were often used as political pawns. Church leaders, mostly in the name of "real socialist" concerns, entire churches, and even the World Council of Churches in Geneva took sides and declared political goals especially compatible with the wishes of the Gospel. After the collapse of the Eastern Bloc, therefore, a serious controversy developed regarding the direction of Protestantism in the second half of the twentieth century.

In summation, the transformation process, in which the Christian religion was involved and, in part, actively aided, did not increase its credibility in Europe. Quite the contrary: the history of the religious transition process is – with a few exceptions such as that of Poland – a history of the de-christianizing of Europe. This is just one of many ways in which Europe differs from the United States.

Washington D.C., October 2007   Gerhard Besier

Contents

8   *Contents*

Religion and Politics in Dictatorships and Democracies from the Enlightenment to the Present*

If one wants to understand the mentality of Europeans, one must investigate European history since the Enlightenment.[1] The Enlightenment was the period in the eighteenth century, during which people placed a particular emphasis on the clarity of their understanding. In this epoch they expressed a strong desire for a clear and accurate way of thinking. Additionally prejudices, superstition and fanaticism were no longer to obfuscate one's mind. They saw this as an act of self-deliverance, implying the will to use one's mind. "Think for yourself" was the maxim of Enlightenment. Of course it is not only a question of the autonomy of thinking but also of the self-determination of one's action. It was not only about the individual because the Enlightenment intended to instruct all of humanity, qualify them for a critical approach to life and free them for liberty. The enlightenment of others presupposes one's own enlightenment. All of this sounds quite abstract but at the time very tangible things were questioned, such as the abolition of torture, witch trials and slavery, as well as the attainment of political and civil rights, the advancement of women in society, the education of useful citizens and the improvement of the rural economy.

All in all the Enlightenment was a reform movement. It pointed to a general renewal. This required something that appeared scandalous to some contemporaries: tolerance.[2] Every citizen should have a right to believe whatever he or she wanted, thus the state and the state church should no longer determine the conviction of human beings. This implied a second change in that a human being ought to be understood as an individual. He or she is not to be defined merely as a member of a collective. Their personal convictions are to be given priority, not those of the community to which they belong (i. e. country, language, etc.).

There are three causes of the Enlightenment. Firstly, the old feudal society was decaying and a new social class, the bourgeoisie, arose. Secondly, with changed social behaviour, religious behaviour consequently also changed. The Christian worldview crumbled because modern science made it look incredible. Human beings could no longer believe in a three-level medieval world, which consisted of heaven, earth and hell. Thirdly, the human's image of himself changed. God was no longer at the centre of thoughts and activities but instead humans saw themselves as the centre of this world. They were no longer an object, through which the real subject, i. e. God, acted but they could take responsibility for their actions themselves and did not have to answer for their deeds to an entity outside of their own world.

---

* First published in *RSG* 5 (2004), 113–125. This paper was read on the occasion of a visit from Iraqi scholars of political sciences to the State Chancellery of Saxony in Dresden (Germany) on 16 February 2004.

What provoked this development? The former elites in the form of the nobility could not cope with the changes in the world. They tried to preserve the old structures through violence, however religious and civil wars destroyed the traditional system. The strongest influence was exerted by the sciences. Knowledge was decreasingly understood as an insight from fixed principles but was now grounded on experience, i. e. observation and from these observations new paradigms were drawn.

However, in Great Britain the culture of relying on experience was much older. The victory of the exact and applied research in nature had already begun in the last third of the seventeenth century and the Society for Improving Natural Knowledge had been established in 1662. Pure natural observation (John Locke) was associated with the conviction that the individual has a moral sense within himself, which qualifies him for ethical action (Lord Shaftesbury). Despite the failure of the Protestant "Puritan Revolution" and the blood-shedding civil wars (1642–1659), a pluralistic society with different value systems developed from this movement. Alongside the state church, a number of religious communities (gathered churches), which were based on a voluntary covenant, came into being. Soon after during the Glorious Revolution of 1688 both parties of the British Parliament made the conscious decision to no longer be sheep-like victims of murderous religious wars. They sent King James II, who was there by the grace of God, into exile and proclaimed another king, William of Orange. The new king was obliged to give up the idea of being an absolute monarch but became a constitutional monarch, i. e. a king by the grace of the people. In the "Bill of Rights" of 1689 the monarchy was given a constitutional basis. As a result dictation by the state and church came to an end. The reformers implemented a liberalisation programme, which created equality before the law for all citizens, political stability by the division of powers, religious tolerance, freedom of opinion and the press, as well as the protection of property. Political pragmatism, a long experience with parliament, and a deeply rooted aversion to religious and political tenets have since then protected Great Britain from dictatorships.

It took France a century longer to attain a constitution. The oppression, which had up until then accumulated, produced a political radicalism that was unique in Europe. In 1789 a violent revolution erupted. The people refused to be dependant either on an all-powerful king or on God. The new magical word was "constitution", which was intended as a network of laws that were to guarantee legal certainty. Laws appeared to be an effective way of improving the world. God, according to the new understanding of the people, had perhaps formerly created the world but he did not intervene in present events. Thus in this world human beings have to act for themselves. This change in thought was articulated by the term "human rights" (*droits de l'homme*). The road to safety no longer led through God but through the human being. The human being experiences what he recognises in nature by using his reason. This also had consequences on the form of government because the simple subject became a citizen. He did not need an all-powerful king invested by God and as such the king had no place in this new worldview. At first the king was demoted and given the title "Chief of the Executive", then in 1793 the Republic was proclaimed.

Constitutionalism was now becoming a kind of Holy Scripture. Christianity, as personified in the clerics of the Roman-Catholic Church, was resisted. The old religion was regarded as an instrument of repression. For the first time the notion of a "political religion" developed in Europe. The political concerns of the Republic were expressed in religious words. The revolution promoted a "messianic conception of politics"[3] and the people began to focus on life in this world. Traditional Christian piety rapidly decreased and people no longer concerned themselves with the salvation of their souls. Nor were they prepared to continue to make financial contributions to symbolic places of religion, especially church buildings. A deep contempt towards the clergy ensued. The de-Christianisation of the population increased and was supported by the state. In 1795 the division of state and church was regulated by legal means. Laicism or secularisation, which consigned religion purely to the private sphere, became a determining influence on the life of most French people and it is still evident today.

Compared to Great Britain and France the Enlightenment in Germany seems more apologetic, less politically but more culturally accentuated.[4] However, there can be no doubt that religious criticism also led to a change in people's beliefs. Religion lost its credibility and its sphere of influence diminished. The formerly uniform worldview disintegrated and instead of just one worldview, there were now several. The pluralisation of worldviews and also of religious convictions had begun. An important prerequisite for this development was already to be found in mid-sixteenth century. Since Protestantism seceded from the Roman-Catholic Church, religion in the West was never united again. Then there were at least two ways to salvation, via Protestantism or via Catholicism. Both approaches confronted each other irreconcilably and were the cause of numerous wars. This is why with the advent of the new sciences and the new worldview, which accompanied them, people began to detach themselves from the old paradigm.

Over time the goals of the Enlightenment did not endure. There were counter-movements and corrections. But a return to the old views of God, the world and the human being was no longer possible. In this respect religious people lived in a double world, on the one hand they believed in the Bible and on the other hand in their daily lives as physicians, lawyers or natural scientists they kept to the rules of the modern world. The interpretation of the world by the different religions did not embrace reality as a whole. Gradually modern sciences ousted religion from a growing number of areas in a person's life.

The philosophers of the Enlightenment were mistaken in believing that freedom, virtue, happiness and benefits for the human being could be attained by reason alone. It was only discovered much later that the individual is not a solely rational being. His emotions and his behaviour are not always guided by reason, although he would like to give this impression. In retrospect he construes sensible reasons for his unreasonable behaviour. However, it was Schleiermacher who, at the end of the eighteenth and beginning of the nineteenth century brought feelings into the equation. He asserted that religion was neither thinking nor acting, but a feeling.[5]

In the following nineteenth century, several attempts were undertaken to achieve a higher synthesis of sensibility and sense, which started from the assump-

tion that the essence of reality could not be captured by reason alone but that belief and emotion also determined reality. However, there was no consensus on the
consistence of this "over-reason". Through religious pluralisation religious societies emerged, which were not under the auspices of a state. In the formation of
such societies the Protestant Methodists played a special role. The Methodists
hardly argued rationally but fanned the flames of emotion at mass events. In the
process they developed organisational techniques, which would later be used by
political parties. Small leading groups operated in larger districts while paid itin-
erant preachers and missionary venture groups travelled across the country. These
functions were later taken over by the cadres, agents and functionaries in political parties. Instead of a stirring missionary sermon, convincing demagogy was
used.

Several political parties developed out of free amalgamations and independently from the state and the mainstream churches. They represented value systems,
which had partially but considerably detached themselves from the churches and
were now in competition with them. The spectrum of these parties emerged clearly in Central Europe during the revolution of 1848. Conservatism[6], political
Catholicism and Liberalism can be named as the three main directions. The
Conservatives wanted to build a strong, monarchic state on a Christian basis.
Political Catholicism struggled for the emancipation of Catholic citizens in states
ruled by Protestants, who considered the Catholic way of life to be backward. In
their view people should be "delivered" from the Catholic superstition and become integrated into the progressive national community. The most potent new
political worldview was Liberalism. For Europeans the nineteenth century is considered as the century of Liberalism. No other ideology was able to develop such
an effective vigour. Even so, in Central Europe, especially in Germany, Liberalism
still remained weak. The country was economically underdeveloped and its democratic institutions were weak whereas the bureaucratically controlled state was
strong. Even without a broad basis in society, the powerful state exerted a certain
fascination on the Liberals. Occasionally it seemed as if Liberalism was having
great success but soon it lost popularity again. Against this backdrop Liberalism
drew attention away from economic and political liberties and directed it towards
the conciliation of nation and state by ascribing itself a national mission within
the framework of this task.

Nationalism, i. e. the aspiration for national unity, had always been an element
of German Liberalism. As a result of the impact of the unification of the German
Reich in 1871[7], national political aims and their ideological justification were ever
more important to Liberalism. Nationalism, which linked national greatness to
the individual citizen, developed into the most important political force.[8] At the
same time a growing fascination with power politics developed during the last two
decades of the nineteenth century and the first decade of the twentieth century.
Most of the National Liberals sympathised with the many associations that advocated a large fleet, a national policy of world power and German colonial possessions. This ideology was based on the concept that the German nation was sur-
rounded by enemies and must defend herself in order to fulfil her historical
destiny. In order to realise this aim the National Liberals formed a coalition with

the Conservatives. Protestantism also supported these endeavours by shaping the people and the nation ever increasingly into sacred entities, thus rendering political aims holy. At the very time when the credibility of Protestantism was waning[9] its leaders turned to the mobilisation of nationalist emotions. Religion and nation should combine in a way so that national feelings were to support religious institutions as places that preached nationalism. At around the turn of the century even the left-liberal parties turned to nationalism and supported the policy of worldwide acceptance and expansion. The myth of nationalism seemed to unite all patriotic powers i. e. the Conservatives, Liberals and Protestantism.[10] The climax of this collective surge of nationalism was the so-called "August 1914 experience" at the beginning of World War One. Once again Protestantism placed itself willingly at the disposure of the national cause.

At that time the advocates of nationalism believed that the heterogeneous society had turned into the homogeneous community. This Romantic idea of the end of all social, cultural and ideological conflicts was to play a fateful role in the subsequent years when it was used to justify the Nazi propaganda behind the unifying figure of Adolf Hitler. Only too late would the Germans learn that conflicts of all kinds are part and parcel of an open society and what really counts is reaching constructive compromises between opposing interests.

There was only one faction that refused to join this choir and was therefore defamed as an "enemy of the empire". This group was the Social Democrats. In the working class movement religion initially had a certain importance. However, the "national religion" of Protestantism, which claimed to be Christian and approved of the authoritarian state, soon led to a growing distance to the Social Democrats. As a result of their fundamental criticism of religion in their party programmes in the years 1875 and 1891 the Social Democrats declared that religion was a "private matter". At the same time the social democratic milieu developed its own rituals and social forms of expression for the main rites of passage (births, weddings, deaths, etc.). This civil subculture rivalled traditional religiosity and formed its own alternative culture with religious meanings. The estrangement of the Social Democrats from Liberalism was, similar to the case of religion, the result of the strategies for the exclusion of Socialism, in which the Liberals readily enough took part.[11]

The First World War shook European civilisation to its very foundations. The brutality reached its peak in the war and just prior to it in the form of colonialism, especially in the case of the genocides[12] in South West Africa and Armenia. This dissolved the self-image of an advanced civilisation with fitting moral and humanitarian ethics. The de-individualisation and collectivisation destroyed the system of values based on individual rights. The national culture of religious and political Liberalism lost all credibility. An intense sense of crisis and the feeling that something completely new must now begin captivated people's minds. In Russia a completely new model of a one-party dictatorship developed through totalitarian Socialism.[13]

Europe's landscape was dramatically changed by the Treaty of Versailles. Eleven new states emerged from the ruins of the three collapsed Empires of Russia, Germany, and Austria-Hungary. But with the exception of Czechoslovakia these eleven democratically constituted states, which were established by the victorious powers, were only able to survive for a few years.[14] The nations were consumed by authoritarian or totalitarian regimes. Democratic parliamentarian systems only proved to be stable in those states, which had won the war or were established before 1914. States with less than five political parties proved to be especially stable. In the northern European countries the established parliamentary democracies, despite all the economic and social crises, managed to survive. Nevertheless, at the end of the nineteen-twenties and the beginning of the nineteen-thirties the dictatorship appeared as the victorious political system in Europe. People trusted them to solve their recurrent political, economic and national crises. In comparison parliamentary democracy looked extremely weak.

In Germany the Social Democrats emerged as the strongest political power after the revolution of 1918. They did not want to endanger their hard-won democratisation by importing a Communist "Soviet republic". The Weimar Constitution from 11 August 1919 foresaw an increase of people's rights by anchoring basic rights in the constitution and by allowing the people's participation in politics through petitions and referenda. The Protestant state church ceased to exist because the constitution contained a provision for the separation of state and church. However, both the mainstream churches, the Protestants as well as the Catholics, retained many of their privileges and still enjoyed some protection from the state in regard to small religious communities, which could now proselytise freely. Although it was obliged to cooperate with the republican state, Protestantism kept a distanced position towards the new form of government. The Protestant leaders agreed too frequently with the nationalist agitators that this system, which had been imported from the West, was alien to the German mind. Many Protestants longed for a strong, authoritarian state with a Christian and monarchical basis, whereas German Catholicism and the Catholic party undoubtedly supported the Weimar democracy. But in other European countries such as Poland, Portugal, Italy, Austria, and Spain the Catholic social teachings along with a decidedly anti-Socialist course, were the ideological basis for the authoritarian dictatorships.[15]

At the beginning of the nineteen-thirties the political parties in Germany were unable to form coalitions with positive parliamentary majorities. The governments were thus appointed by the Reich President on the basis of emergency decrees. At the end of January 1933 after a long hesitation the President appointed Adolf Hitler, chairman of the largest party, the National Socialist Party, as Reich Chancellor. No sooner had he attained power, which he incidentally accomplished in a completely legal manner, than he embarked on the destruction of the whole democratic edifice. Hitler was a fanatic; his sense of mission culminated in the form of apocalyptic delusions and it was his aim to free Germany followed by the whole of Europe from the "international Jewry". He demonised the stereotype of Judaism until it represented plain evil and he claimed the Jewry was making use of Liberalism and Parliamentarism as different guises to hide under. In other aspects German National Socialism had much in common with Italian Fascism, i. e. the strong condemnation of Liberalism and Marxism, an excessive nationalism, the cult of manhood, violence and death, the fascination with mass mobilisation and the charismatic role played by the leader.[16] Both movements fanned the flames of fear of a Communist revolution and offered "salvation" from Bolshevism.

Hitler made use of a sacral form of speech. Many Protestants were enthusiastic about his movement and applauded him.[17] The Catholics more prudently thought they might be able to arrive at a legal arrangement with Hitler and in that way be able to protect their Church and social Catholicism. From the ranks of the Protestants the group of so-called "German Christians" attempted to promote an alliance between Christianity and National Socialism.[18] Nevertheless the Nazis were not prepared to set limits on their ideological demand for total control. Thus from the mid-thirties onwards they refused to cooperate with the "German Christians", even though the latter aspired to close collaboration. Due to its worldview the ideology of National Socialism may also be classed as a "political religion" or a "surrogate religion".[19]

A small minority of Christians and clergy were opposed to the totalitarian claims of National Socialism, although not against the regime as such. When the political and military resistance movement against the Nazi regime finally emerged, it did not express any desire to re-establish the Weimar constitution. If these men had succeeded in overthrowing Hitler, most of them wanted to establish an authoritarian state. Much of what is said about the German resistance movement is a myth.[20]

Germany's capitulation in May 1945 ended the dictatorship in the western part of the country. Under the control of and with the economic support of the western Allies the Germans established a democratic constitutional state in the West, which economically prospered (e. g. the "economic miracle" or *Wirtschaftswunder*) and was soon integrated among the western countries.[21] During the so-called "Cold War" West Germany took her place within the western alliance. Germany's most eastern territories were assigned to Poland by the Allies and in what was formerly the central region of Germany the Soviets shaped a socialist dictatorship.

The Soviet dictator Stalin was hardly better than Hitler. Barely 30 years had passed since the Russian Revolution and the Soviets were now occupying the country, from which their ideological hopes had originated. In Lenin's view the Russian Revolution and the International Revolution were inextricably linked to each other. According to his firm conviction the Russian Revolution could not triumph without the World Revolution, which he expected to originate in Germany. However, the Germans had opted for racist National Socialism and not for the Bolshevik class state. The October Revolution of 1917 turned out to be an exception in the history of world revolutions. This remained the case until 1945 because the Soviet Union was, despite the war, unable to leave its politically isolated and unique position. After the war this began to change as the Soviet Union viciously and violently transformed its surrounding states into Socialist People's Republics. As a result thousands were killed or died of hunger and exhaustion in concentration camps. After Stalin's death in 1953 the totalitarian system became less repressive on certain issues, however, basic human rights such as the freedom of movement and religious freedom were still not granted. The state party and the organs of the government constituted a unity. The tight surveillance network of secret service, spies and informers greatly reduced the personal liberty of the individual.

Those Germans living in the Soviet occupation zone experienced a direct change from Nazi to Stalinist dictatorship. Over several generations, between 1933 and 1989, these people knew nothing but dictatorships. The socialist dictatorship laid claim to the entire human being. The Christian religion, just as all religions, was restricted and suppressed. Instead the party was the church and the writings of Marx and Lenin were considered as "holy scriptures".

In contrast to the situation in 1933 when the Nazis had come to power, the Protestant movement in East Germany was decidedly opposed to Bolshevism. Nevertheless the longer the dictatorship lasted and the more the Germans living in the socialist German Democratic Republic were cordoned off from West Germany, the more the will to maintain an oppositional stance slackened. After the erection of the Berlin Wall in 1961 the church leaders generally accommodated the regime to some extent. They now saw themselves as the "Church within Socialism", which identified itself with "our state" and the "humanitarian achievements" of the dictatorship. Sometimes they even reproached the West German churches for being too rich, having fraternised with "capitalism" and as such no longer being the "real church".

Socialist dictatorships and their churches exerted a strange attraction on the at the time so-called "Third World". The Americans occasionally spoke of the "Socialistic gospel". Many states in the "Third World" despised the western "Capitalist" countries and formed alliances with the Soviet Union and its satellite states. Often these "Third World" countries were also ruled by dictators, who exploited their subjects. Some of these countries even called themselves "Socialist". The common feature, which connected all these countries, was their inability to change into functioning liberal democracies.

At the end of the nineteen-eighties and the beginning of the nineties the Socialist eastern bloc collapsed. Economic factors were the main cause of this and in some countries the population expressed its dissatisfaction by fleeing to the West. A number of Christians and clerics also played a role in opposition movements, however defiantly entire "churches" were not involved. As Marianne Birthler, the head of the archives of the former GDR secret service, remarked in 2003: "Today, many boast that they were part of the Protestant Church and its peace movement."[22] However, she added that there had been only a few parishes, which had dared to foster an oppositional attitude. Today we call it the "peaceful revolution" but it was probably not a revolution at all. But this is a taboo. A taboo, though, is something we should not accept in an open society.

The reunification of the Federal Republic of Germany and the German Democratic Republic (GDR) was, at least superficially, quickly implemented. Yet even today there are distinct divisions between the East and the West due to the different mentalities, which developed over the decades of separation. In the old GDR there was a shortage of everything. But this was administered in a way that allowed the majority to believe they had everything they needed, for example everybody was employed, although not everybody really had work. Similar to the period after the Second World War we observe that a certain nostalgia is being propagated. After the collapse of the Nazi dictatorship some people claimed: "Not everything was bad under Hitler!" Comparable statements were repeated during the nineties in those countries, which formerly belonged to the Soviet sphere of power: "Not everything was bad during Socialism!" The same is true for the former East Germany.

Why is this so? In a dictatorship the life of the people is regimented, in so far as they are told what they should and may do. This has the function of relieving people of decision-making. However, life in a liberal state is full of risks and people are expected to organise their own lives. The constitutional state only builds a frame, within which the individual is to freely develop. Of course an individual may fail in regard to the demands that he is faced with in a complex society. Thus there is a social net that catches people, who have lost their job, become sick or who are otherwise reliant on support. Nevertheless the idea of an individual underlying the liberal democracy assumes that everybody should take their fate in their own hands, that they love their own freedom and the free society in which they live so much, that they will accept the obligation of striving for it.

This state of mind is not given haphazardly and by no means in Germany. Many people in this country prefer personal safety to freedom and would like the state to take over a large amount of responsibility. The state should to guarantee that they are protected. A rich state is able to extensively succumb to desire, which explains the elaborate social system in the Federal Republic that is intended to prevent people from suffering all social ills. On top of the social system there are the social insurance schemes, which offer protection from all possible risks in life. However, social systems of this kind are expensive and the state must demand increasing taxes in order to satisfy the security needs. The economy suffers from these expectations and the people become dissatisfied because of the high costs. This is today's problem thus we must modify the social state and make it viable at a lower cost. People must take on more responsibility for their lives but this does not stop the phenomenon that in periods of economic crisis many people develop fears and long for a strong state, sometimes even for a strong charismatic leader.[23] Periods, in which the economy is weak, are periods of probation for democracy. It now remains to be seen whether people have learnt to appreciate the Liberal state. Those, who had employment in the GDR but are unemployed today, may want the old dictatorship back but the value of life in freedom must be made clear even to them. The democratic constitutional state needs emancipated citizens, who are capable of responsible cooperation and thinking. Such a state depends on well-educated citizens. The establishment of a democracy and even more importantly the stability of a democracy demand a democratic education. Without schools, universities and political education the democratic constitutional state is unable to develop or maintain its appeal.

And religion? In most democratic constitutional states there is a separation of state and church by law. Whatever a citizen believes and which ideology he stands for is his affair alone so long as these beliefs do not infringe on other laws. Neither civil disadvantages nor advantages should result from his religious conviction. Religious freedom is one of the great liberties of the free peoples in this world. Without religious freedom other liberties are also at risk. Those who do not en-joy the freedom to believe what they want without danger and to live according to their belief, are not really free. This is why religious freedom is also called the "First Liberty". A state may support the religions of its country but it must not grant special privileges to one religious community and thus disadvantage other denominations.

Keeping to these principles is important, however, it is also especially difficult in countries, where one religion has been predominant for centuries and does not tolerate other religions or allow them grow. This problem is not completely unknown in Germany.[24] In other countries, such as Russia, the problem presents itself even more severely. The Russian-Orthodox Church would like to have the status of a privileged state church and would possibly not tolerate any other denomination in the country.[25] In France, where there is a strict separatist model, religion is a private matter and may not appear in the public sphere of society. For this reason the French Parliament passed a law in February 2004 forbidding pupils and students to wear ostensibly religious symbols in state schools. This ban affects Christians, Muslims, Jews, and members of other religions alike. Meanwhile uncertainty prevails in Germany because some federal states only want to forbid the Muslim headscarf for women because they claim this is not an exclusively religious symbol. In this argumentation they have forgotten that Christian symbols throughout European history were also not simply mere religious symbols.[26] Situations of this kind require civic commitment and are challenging to the constitutional state thus a public debate is necessary. A democratic political civilisation cannot exist without public controversies. According to the constitution and the actual experience of the people the Federal Republic of Germany is not a "Christian state" but a secular one. These are the values that need to be defended, i. e. not the Christian tradition but the Liberal, enlightened, constitutional state with its tolerant openness towards civil plurality. Either the Germans are prepared to progress further on the way towards a multi-denominational and multi-cultural society, which they themselves chose to take, or they must follow France's approach and consequently ban any sign of religiosity from the public sphere. There is no possibility of a third way in modern societies. In a democracy it is important to debate these questions. The propositions of the Enlightenment remain fundamental to us, i. e. think for yourself, act for yourself and be critical! Let myths and legends be disenchanted and above all recognise that blind obedience to the authorities is not a democratic virtue.

Notes

1 Cf. William Reginald Ward, Christianity under the Ancient Regime 1648–1789, Cambridge 1999.
2 Cf. Rainer Forst, Toleranz im Konflikt. Geschichte, Gehalt und Gegenwart eines umstrittenen Begriffs, Frankfurt am Main 2003.
3 François Furet, The Passing of an Illusion. The Idea of Communism in the Twentieth Century, Chicago-London 1999, 32.
4 Cf. Thomas P. Saine, The Problem of Being Modern or The German Pursuit of Enlightenment from Leibniz to the French Revolution, Detroit 1997. See also Mary Fulbrook, A Concise History of Germany, 2nd ed., Cambridge 2004, 84 ff.
5 Cf. Gerhard Besier, s. v. 'Schleiermacher', in Roy Domenica and Mark Hanley (eds), An Encyclopaedia of Modern Christian Politics, Westport 2006, 494–495.
6 Cf. Larry Eugene Jones and James Retallack (eds), Between Reform, Reaction, and Resistance. Studies in the History of German Conservatism from 1789 to 1945, Providence-Oxford 1993.
7 Cf. Margaret Lavinia Anderson, Practicing Democracy. Elections and Political Culture in Imperial Germany, Princeton 2000.
8 Cf. Hedda Gramley, Propheten des deutschen Nationalismus. Theologen, Historiker und Nationalökonomen (1848–1880), Frankfurt am Main 2001.
9 Cf. Hugh McLeod and Werner Ustorf (eds), The Decline of Christendom in Western Europe, 1750–2000, Cambridge 2003.
10 Cf. Rainer Hering, Konstruierte Nation. Der Alldeutsche Verband 1890 bis 1939, Hamburg 2003.
11 Cf. Sebastian Prüfer, Sozialismus statt Religion. Die deutsche Sozialdemokratie vor der religiösen Frage 1863–1890, Göttingen 2002.
12 Cf. Steven L. B. Jensen (ed.), Genocide: Cases, Comparisons and Contemporary Debates (The Danish Centre for Holocaust and Genocide Studies), Copenhagen 2003.
13 Cf. Paul Brooker, Non-Democratic Regimes. Theory, Government and Politics, New York 2000.
14 Cf. Gerhard Besier/Katarzyna Stokłosa, Das Europa der Diktaturen. Eine neue Geschichte des 20. Jahrhunderts, Munich 2006.
15 Cf. Fulvio De Giorgi, 'Linguaggi militari e mobilitazione cattolica nell'Italia fascista' [Militärischer Sprachgebrauch und katholische Mobilisierung im faschistischen Italien], Contemporanea 5 (2002), 253–286. Gerhard Besier/Francesca Piombo, The Holy See and Hitler's Germany, Basingstoke 2007.
16 Cf. Raymond Aron, Machiavel et les tyrannies modernes, Paris 1993; Stanley Payne, A History of Fascism 1914–45, London 1995.
17 Cf. Gerhard Besier, '70 Years after Machtergreifung', in this volume.
18 Cf. John S. Conway, 'Totalitarianism and Theology', in Humanitas. The Journal of the George Bell Institute 4 (2002), 89–103.
19 Cf. Raymond Aron, 'Bureaucratie et fanatisme', in idem, Chroniques de guerre. La France Libre, 1940–1945, Paris 1990.
20 Cf. Maurice Philipp Remy, Mythos Widerstand, Munich 2004; Gerd R. Ueberschär (ed.), NS-Verbrechen und der militärische Widerstand gegen Hitler, Darmstadt 2000.
21 Cf. Edmund Spevack, Allied Control and German Freedom. American Political and Ideological Influences on the Framing of the Western German Basic Law [Grundgesetz], Münster 2001.
22 Quoted from ideaSpektrum 41/2003, 12.
23 "Using Weber's concept of a charismatic prophet it can be posited that contemporary fundamentalisms arise out of the convergence of deeply alienating crises and dislocations ... with the emergence of charismatic prophetic personalities ... ." David Zeidan, The Resurgence of Religion. A Comparative Study of Selected Themes in Christian and Islamic Fundamentalist Discourses, Leiden-Boston 2003, 6. Cf. Max Weber, Wirtschaft und Gesellschaft. Grundriss der verstehenden Soziologie, Studienausgabe,

5th rev. edition, ed. by Johannes Winckelmann, Tübingen 1980, ch. IX: Herrschafts-soziologie.

24 Cf. Gerhard Besier and Erwin K. Scheuch (eds), The New Inquisitors, Bergisch-Gladbach 2003.

25 Cf. Elena Miroshnikova, 'A Comparative Analysis of State-Church Relations and Civil Religion in Russia and Germany', in Derek H. Davis and Gerhard Besier (eds), International Perspectives on Freedom and Equality of Religious Belief, Waco 2000, 155–167; Kathrin Behrens, Die Russische Orthodoxe Kirche: Segen für die "Neuen Zaren"? Religion und Politik im postsowjetischen Russland (1991–2000), Paderborn 2002.

26 Cf. J. Harold Ellens (ed.), The Destructive Power of Religion. Violence in Judaism, Christianity and Islam, 4 vols, Westport-London 2004.

Mission and Colonialism in Friedrich Fabri's (1824–1891) Thinking*

I. Biographical sketch

Friedrich Gotthardt Karl Ernst Fabri was born on 12 June 1824 in Schweinfurt, where his father was a professor in a secondary preparatory school, later a pastor. After 1836 his father was ordained the Dean of the church in Würzburg, where he died in 1866. Fabri senior was a faithful mediating theologian and, therefore, profoundly sceptical of the upcoming emphasis on the Lutheran Confession. After finishing secondary school, Fabri studied theology in Erlangen and Berlin between 1841 and 1845. When applying for the theological examinations he mentioned that his academic teachers included Ranke, Schelling, Steffens, Ritter, Neander and Marheinecke. Why he did not mention Hengstenberg and Theremin, with whom he had also studied, is unknown. One thing is certain: while in Erlangen he was especially influenced by Karl von Raumer. Even later on in his life he was to recall this acquaintance with gratitude. When his father, who had participated in the Wartburg Festival, suggested that Friedrich join the Bubenreuther fraternity, to which he had also been a member, Friedrich agreed. Between 1841 and 1845 a number of young people belonged to this society, who were later to play an important role in politics. Some were later to become members of the Bavarian Parliament: Michael Schoberth, Franz Ferdinand Seitz and Friedrich Strobel, for example. Otto Freiherr von und zu Aufseß was later a member of the Reichstag. Ludwig Karl James Aegidi, university professor in Erlangen and a honorary member of the Bubenreuther society since 1858, played an important role after 1871 in the department of foreign affairs and was a founding member of the Independent-Conservative Party. In 1846, Fabri attended seminary in Munich to study homiletics. He became City Vicar of Würzburg in 1848 and taught religion at the agricultural and vocational school. In 1851, he received a call to the post of pastor in Bonnland near Würzburg. In the same year in Bonnland he married the daughter of a wealthy farming family from Southern Hanover (died 1888). Four of their eight children died. The "Constitution in accordance with the teaching and law of the Protestants" (1840), written by Friedrich Julius Stahl, had a substantial influence among many German Lutherans and was also of great significance for the young pastor Friedrich Fabri. After all, he was interested in becoming acquainted with the leading men in the church-political discussions. This interest can especially be seen in his personal acquaintance with August Vilmar and in his correspondence with Hengstenberg, whom he addressed as "most honourable Sir and Friend". In 1857, Friedrich Fabri succeeded Wall-

*   First published in Torben Christensen and William R. Hutchison (eds), *Missionary Ideologies in the Imperialist Era: 1880-1920. Papers from the Durham Consultation 1981*, Århus 1982, 84–93.

mann and joined the Rheinish Mission (*Rheinische Mission*). Although the comittee's first choice, Auberlen from Basel, had declined, he suggested his personal friend Fabri as a good candidate. For Fabri the call had come "totally unexpected and as a surprise". The decision to accept the position meant an enormous adjustment for Fabri, who until then had had little contact with missions. In addition he had to adjust to some "unusual experiences" since the mission advocated church union by consensus and as such took a confessional stance that was quite different from his own. The commission tried to deal with extreme positions by viewing the different confessions in purely historical terms. This was in line with what Fabri also believed but it caused even more tension at this time. Fabri desired to prevent a split in the mission society and his diplomatic strength was shown by his ability to bring about unity in the year 1860. Now "church union" was understood as meaning "confederation": in other words as a mere administrative unit. In a letter to Hengstenberg he wrote in this respect: "I had come with the best intentions for unity, but was soon convinced that reasons of justice and truth alone, considering the unusual development of our mission, precluded our holding on to and insisting on the specific reasons for unity." Between January and August of 1871 Fabri was a member of the Staff of the Strasbourg governor von Bismarck-Bohlen, where he worked as an advisor on church matters. However, the reorganisation of church relationships in Alsace-Lorraine did not come about because of the resistance from the liberal and pro-French Protestant society, which finally forced the governour to resign. This resignation also spelled the end of Fabri's assignment. In 1884 Fabri retired from the Mission, ostensibly because of age and his inability to fill the position adequately. In October 1889, he was made honorary professor of the Protestant theological department at the University of Bonn. However, he only rarely took advantage of this privilege. On 18 July 1891 Fabri died in Würzburg at the age of sixty-seven. Fabri's effectiveness had not been limited to his activities as a pastor and inspector of missions. Especially from 1866 on he had published several articles dealing with the relationship and reorganisation of church and state. His sound judgment and knowledge in these matters was far ahead of anything being done and suggested in literature of theology, law and politics. But he was also quite influential in the development of colonial politics. Especially his publication "Does Germany need Colonies?" (1879) gave an impetus to a colonial movement. He demanded with detailed suggestions that an office be established for dealing with these matters, suggesting more justice for the indigenous population and concern for the economic and political improvement of the colonies. His recommendations impressed Bismarck. In his detailed remarks he used language and concepts of early imperialism, including the term "human materials" for example. A group of prominent evangelical pastors was convinced that Germany had an important position in history and as such had received a direct mission for the German people. In this group Fabri held a position somewhere between the generation of Wilhelm Hoffmann (general superintendent in Berlin) and Paul Rohrbach. Nevertheless, in writings dealing with charity organisations and housing development in urban industrial sections, this versatile man showed an interest in social programmes for the homeland.

II.   The theological thought of Friedrich Fabri

1.   The universal-theological outline of history

a) The fight against materialism

By 1856 Fabri had already entered the heated worldview debate by publishing his "letters against materialism". The discussion focused on the progressive and general philosophy of thinkers such as Darwin and Lyell that was strongly propagated by D. F. Strauss. Three years earlier he had already published an anonymous article that called the modern natural science and history "the most dangerous ... enemy ... of the Christian truth in the present time". The "Babel-like world alliance" of materialist philosophies and historical immanentism was ruining youth and releasing sensuality in the masses: it destroyed all science. Against this perceived decline, Fabri demanded that "biblical metaphysics" should be established in order to confront these growing materialistic worldviews and their axiomatic presuppositions. This "biblical metaphysic", which was grounded on basic concepts of Holy Scripture, should be capable "to penetrate to a total view, a *philosophia sacra* that was to be filled with life, in that one would use known principles of insight and research the areas of nature and the spirit".

b) The sensus communis – the agent of general revelation of God

Fabri confesses that he had "been starving for some deep and living streams that would come out of the divine Word" – and had found in the writings of theosophical men a guide for a better and more comprehensive understanding of the Bible. Hence Fabri adopted the speculative "generative" method of Oetinger. This method tried, similar to a key, to unlock the basic concepts of the Bible by placing them into an organic relationship so that they could be disclosed both deductively and inductively. This key, which was found by way of a speculative method, would need to conform to the Scripture; otherwise a new key would be required to do more justice to the real form of the divine Word. Traditional exegesis was not adequate to uncover the spiritual treasures of Holy Scripture because according to Oetinger, "there are thoughts, which are not directly expressed in the Bible, but are nevertheless silently presupposed throughout". In allowing the biblically-grounded system of divine truth to be disclosed in its fundamental principles, *ex fide* and *ex ratione,* by methods of "combination, contextualisation and comparison of passages of Scripture", Oetinger had adhered to the *philosophia sacra* that Fabri had longed for. It might more precisely be called "theosophy" because God is himself the goal, centre and beginning of all philosophical knowledge. This God, who dwells in the subject, who recognises him, as well as in the word that provides the "identity of subject and object of thought and being". Such an insight is not only a thinking process but it fills the entire life and existence of the one who is philosophising and this by way of the *sensus communis*, the instrument of recognition, which all men have that connects them to God. Fabri took over Oetinger's teaching of the "general feeling of truth" with all its formulations. With Auberlen he knew full well that he would be in open conflict with the church's teaching on original sin, which does not allow any natural knowledge of God. He quotes Auberlen favourably: "We recognise that the *sensus communis* finds in all pure humanity, in nature in its widest sense, in science, in the state and society generally the revelation of the ever-present God and his wisdom; he is the gathering place and source of life for all that which is humanly true, beautiful and good, for the original and incommunicable seeing, grasping, experiencing of the Living and Godly in it, as far as this is possible for natural man. But in this the *sensus communis* propels us to Christ, who had this divine sense of life 'in its most pleasant form', and through his spirit it receives its fullest consecration. The revelation in Christ is not a break with that which was until now, but an enhancement and a completion."

c) World history as revelation of Salvation History
Using the thought of Oetinger, Fabri applies the *sensus communis* not only to the areas of academics and ethics, but also to history. In line with Hamann, for whom all history of personal experience as well as world historical occurrences were foretelling Transcendence and the place of revelation of God's action, Fabri fully accepted the theology of the history of salvation, to which Auberlen was committed. In, with and under the occurrences of world history, salvation history is revealed. Here God's action is not seen as a creative intervention, but rather as a continuous follow-up according to the laws of earthly forms of life. "The gathering, spreading and preparation of God's kingdom in this time is a progressive process of life which cannot be stopped: every period of time has its task, but also its limit, beyond which few will be permitted to gaze." The original unity of mankind and history was destroyed due to the pride of man and the Tower of Babel; the miracle of Pentecost on the other hand predicts how in the apocalyptical period the End will bring back the Beginning. From this perspective we can grasp the meaning and goal of the neglected message in all proclamations of the Gospel to the heathen: the uncovering of the secret of the *one* humanity. History, which is understood as prophetic and therefore a supplement in a sensible and necessary way to the prophecy of the Word, provides for the onlooker a higher vantage point from which to see world history with composure and objective distance – he knows the beginning and destiny of all that will happen – he can overlook it all and can interpret it accordingly. This position, almost at the side of God as it were, does not allow the historian of salvation history to take a direct part in ideological dissent, but instead demands an increased engagement in the world, which receives its justification from the teaching of *sensus communis*. This position is crucial for the establishment of a political ethic and explains Fabri's ecclesiastic political postures and decisions, which in particular revealed his impartial and practical suggestions for solutions. The criteria for his presentations are taken from the notion of God's plan of salvation. Here not only the work of culture and the ethical arrangements is mapped out but also the replacement of the Christian state by a non-theistic one. All of this has its place in the eternal kingdom as it approaches consummation under God's governance.

d) The rejection of the teachings of orthodoxy

The discovery of history within theology has its analogy in a comprehensive critique of the static scholastic wisdom and doctrinal teaching of orthodoxy, which ignored everyday experiences. Orthodoxy used the Bible as a lifeless book of learning instead of viewing it as the living and revelatory report of history. "The angry dogmatic, with all of his subtleties and uncountable disputes and heresy hunts, which angered the world and the brothers in belief, did not permit an undiluted and pure taste of the Word of God, and happened under the cover of a simplistic, hidden, pompous self-glorification" (Fabri). The more one discerns God's revelation in history, where future salvation events are foreshadowed in historical occurrences, the more one is free to view one's position objectively and calmly in the process of examining strongly held confessional differences. For Fabri "Scripture was enough"; his vision of the church in the future knew neither a confessional stance nor a confessional constraint. The end was as the beginning.

e) Fabri's understanding of the church

"The only acceptable concept of the church that is valid for all times is the one which the Lord himself has given in Matthew 18." Here Fabri narrows the understanding of the church to its periodically actualised promise, which is a constant from eternity to eternity. The empirical church in its continuity (which is to say its apostolicity), is taken up in the relativity of the passing of time. The real and invisible church is confronted with the "interim church", which is nothing more than a gathering place. The church of the apocalyptic period can already be recognised in its "deeds", and in this respect the congregation of Philadelphia (Revelation 3,7 ff.) is an example, which knew neither a constitution with a bishop, a consistory nor a Presbyterian form. In the history of God's kingdom the work of mission has a prophetic and revelatory character for the church of the future. Indeed, the mission congregation is like a parable of the hidden and eschatological "Philadelphia". Here Fabri departs from the formulation of CA VII: the Proclamation of the Gospel and the dispensing of the sacraments. At no time may the "deeds" of the church be the basis upon which it is recognised.

2.   The theological relationship to the "ethical and irenic direction" of the Netherlands

In the foreword to Chantepie de la Saussaye's writings, Fabri explains his friendly relationship with the Dutch theologians by comparing it to the "relationship of two characters engaged in the battle of life". Under the encouragement and influence of la Saussaye, Fabri's text was published in Dutch with the title "The sensus communis". In his foreword la Saussaye remarked that "this booklet is definitely for the orthodox and not for those who, in aberrant contrast to them hold that the general feeling for truth is superior to the Spirit of truth, and who thus misunderstand the necessity of regeneration or understand it to imply natural development". La Saussaye as a representative of "ethical beginnings" and Fabri make common cause against their orthodox Protestant partners in faith. The latter, who were informed by classical and reformative views, were convinced that even the slightest reduction of the concept of justification was unsound, since the forensic motive was an inseparable part of the salvation wrought by Christ. One of la Saussaye's students, J. H. Gunning, was also a dear friend of Fabri. Gunning declared in his "Leven en Werken" that it was impossible to discuss anything with Fabri "without thereby being enlightened".

III.   Applying the theological and basic insights to questions of the day

1.   The basic outline of a teaching on missions based on philosophy of history (1859)

a) The first ideas of Zinzendorf as starting point for the theory of mission
Fabri considered expressly the single conversion, i. e. using the example of the New Testament to establish "first-born congregations" among as many people as possible, as the goal of all missionary activity. There was little time left until the eschaton forbade in principle the conversion of nations, but it was not entirely beyond the realm of possibility. In addition Fabri's historical perspective led him to assert that the heathen nations clearly lacked "the necessary natural vitality" to establish their own churches.

b) The contribution of the theology of the kingdom to the method of missions
Only after establishing the *heilsgeschichtliche* [i. e., related to the history of salvation] locus of mission within God's plan of the kingdom could the task and function of its mission among the heathen be presented according to the Scripture. The Scripture teaches and experience strengthens the understanding that the structure of the history of the kingdom is grounded on and has received its decisive turn from the eleventh chapter of Genesis. Here mankind destroyed itself with its own pride, and the primordial common "consciousness of God and humanity" was shattered. "Every nation and every group of nations since Babel has its own form that penetrates and permeates the consciousness of its people and that at the present time will be broken through not by whole nations, but only by some from all nations who enter through Christ into the new and divine birth, both morally and spiritually." Within this biblical and historical framework, all of God's deeds in salvation history and the basic lines of mission are to be seen. While Pentecost did not provide a spiritual unity in this life for all nations, it can be regarded as a prophecy and pledge of the great day to come. The attempt to Christianise whole nations would mean to oppose the historical development of God's kingdom.

c) The world-historical significance of Europe as an argument for single conversion
Fabri was convinced that those who suggested a "people's church" (*Volkskirche*; state church) for heathen nations had forgotten that according to the witness of

the biblical Apocalypse the countries of the Roman empire were to remain the "centre and ... vehicle of world history and world events". Fabri found it also rather strange to think that people from India and China could accomplish something on their own that would be deemed "important for the Church and politics". Should the Gospel be accepted in some other land and reproduced in the fashion of that land, it would have undesired consequences. Establishing a new world centre would mean declaring biblical prophecy a hoax.

2.   The relationship of mission and colonialism

a) The mission as vehicle of culture

The teaching of *sensus communis* makes it possible to connect the act of proclamation with the ethical order as well as with all cultural endeavours. In the Mediterranean region, Christianity is the creator and shaper of culture. It is difficult to overestimate the values that arrived in the Occident due to the penetration and mutual influence of Christianity and culture. Therefore, a separation of the two realms is neither desirable nor seemingly possible. The implication is that the reception of Christianity not only engenders new and creative powers for one's own cultural endeavours; the reception of European culture is also the beginning of Christianisation! Therefore, it was possible for Fabri to assert that "the steady, ongoing victory of European culture will also mean the beginning of the Christianisation of the nations, for the present mission work among them is essentially the groundbreaking for the coming decision".

b) Orderly political conditions as prerequisite for a successful mission

In his pathbreaking book dealing with colonialism "Does Germany need colonies?" (1879), Fabri distinguishes between his interests in mission and colonialism: for a German colonial initiative one only need cite the economic and ethnic-political reasons. However, one notices that his motives for action bring about an increasingly questionable mixture of Gospel and civilisation, of missionary strategy and colonial politics. The history of mission in Borneo (i. e. the rebellion of the Dayaks in Borneo 1859) and in Southwest Africa (the tribal wars between Hereros and Hottentots) showed that total anarchy made positive work impossible. Fabri came to the conclusion that a mutual endeavour or the success of mission and colonial expansion "is something that is in the providential order". The missionary was neither to involve himself in it nor consciously oppose it. In most cases such a development was actually to be considered good for mission. "After all the work of mission is at its safest in the colonies and it is without doubt most effective in those places, where the missionaries share the nationality of those who rule the land." Fabri thus encouraged the programme of a national colonial mission; an idea, which was to henceforth guide and rule his thought.

3.   Consequences of Fabri's activities for mission and colonial politics

a) The Rheinish missionary society
Because of Fabri's pro-colonial statements, the "German Colonial Society" considered him as the "father of the German colonial movement". Both the "Society
for German Colonisation" and the forerunner of the "Pan-German Society" – the
"General German Society" – considered him to be "the pioneer of German colonial politics". Still, with this anti-revival concept he risked a division within the
Rheinish mission, which actually occurred under the leadership of the long-time
pioneer of the Herero mission, C. H. Hahn. In 1869, a separate missionary trade
society of the Rheinish mission was established in line with the flourishing example of the Basel mission. The financial risk thus introduced became so burden-
some that it bankrupted the missionary trade society, which led to Fabri's departure in 1884. This missionary trade understood itself as a Christian variation of
current exploitative colonial trade practices. But the more profitable a missionary trade society wanted to be, the more it was forced to use methods of colonial
trade (avoiding of course any trafficking in weapons and alcohol). After 1879,
Fabri had more frequent contact with colonial propaganda, with the "West-Ger-
man Society" and with big industry and its representatives, than with his own missionary section, whose trust he lost as a result. A further problem was his steady
concurrence with the colonial theoretician Hübbe-Schleiden and similar thinkers.
Two of his sons eventually went to work for colonial societies. It became almost
impossible to withstand the critique from his fellow workers and the mission representatives. Clearly he had become both the victim of his own immense labour
and the victim of his all-too-expansive plans for a synthesis of social, colonial, political, commercial and emigration issues. Following his departure, the Rheinish
mission resumed its "neutral and expectant position" and "separation of mission
and civilisation".

b) Fabri and Bismarck
It was hardly an easy task to direct trade capital into political responsibility for
colonialist purposes because banks and industry only grudgingly relinquished capital. Bismarck was not at all ready to make concessions to those who wanted radical expansion, such as the "German Colonial Society" and others. Even though
Fabri had also thought about expansion, he held a key position in several organisations and thus could offer Bismarck interesting advice and provide contacts to
the German Colonial Society, the German East-Africa Society and the German
anti-slavery movement; he could also provide contacts to the national-liberal and
centrist politicians. Bismarck had to learn that Fabri's willingness to work for him
was matched by a will that could also mean opposition to the chancellor. Determining the economic urgency of transatlantic expansion was important for both
men, as was the recognition of the possibility, the intention and ability to use it
in arguments of internal politics. They did not agree in their basic understanding
of "colonial" politics and their estimation of its importance in relation to European politics of unity, let alone Fabri's later writings on emigration. While Fabri
warned Bismarck of the political consequences of doing colonial politics on the

side, whether within or across the oceans, Bismarck suggested that Fabri's concerns were "secondary". Bismarck rightly recognised Fabri's overestimation of the politics of colonialism. Even so, he came to appreciate Fabri's warning of the consequences for domestic and parliamentary politics of dealing with the colonial question as if it were an afterthought. Bismarck's mistake was, therefore, that in spite of exploiting the talents of this discreet advisor, mediator, man of propaganda and sensor of public opinion, he failed to take him seriously.

Thus all German endeavours to establish a colonial empire failed. Nevertheless, the Germans were spared the painful process of de-colonisation that other European nations had to undergo. Only in the limited groups gathered around the merchant Lüderitz from Bremen a small colonial "elite" gathered. On the basis of Darwinist racial teachings this elite encouraged what was later to become the illusion of the German "master-race" (*Herrenvolk*).

References:

Klaus J. Bade, *Friedrich Fabri und der Imperialismus in der Bismarckzeit: Revolution – Depression – Expansion*, Freiburg i. Br. 1975.

Gerhard Besier, 'Das kirchenpolitische Denken Friedrich Fabris auf dem Hintergrund der staatskirchlichen Geschehnisse im 19. Jahrhundert', in *Zeitschrift für bayrische Kirchengeschichte* 46 (1977), 173–238.

Gerhard Besier, *Preußische Kirchenpolitik in der Bismarckära. Die Diskussion in Staat und Evangelischer Kirche um eine Neuordnung der kirchlichen Verhältnisse Preußens zwischen 1866 und 1872* (Veröffentlichungen der Historischen Kommission zu Berlin 49), Berlin-New York 1980.

Gerhard Besier, 'Mission und Kolonialismus im Preußen der Wilhelminischen Ära', in *Kirchliche Zeitgeschichte* 5 (1992), 239–253.

Hans Beyer, 'Friedrich Fabri über Nationalstaat und kirchliche Eigenständigkeit, Mission und Imperialismus', in *Zeitschrift für bayrische Kirchengeschichte* 30 (1961), 70–97.

Karl Hammer, *Weltmission und Kolonialismus. Sendungsideen des 19. Jahrhunderts im Konflikt*, Munich 1978.

Walter Mogk, *Paul Rohrbach und das 'Größere Deutschland'. Ethischer Imperialismus im Wilhelminischen Zeitalter. Ein Beitrag zur Geschichte des Kulturprotestantismus*, Munich 1973.

Wolfgang R. Schmidt, *Mission, Kirche und Reich Gottes bei Friedrich Fabri*, Wuppertal-Barmen 1965.

Theo Sundermeier, *Mission, Bekenntnis und Kirche. Missionstheologische Probleme des 19. Jahrhunderts bei C. H. Hahn*, Wuppertal-Barmen 1967.

Further references, as well as lists of writings, articles and speeches by Fabri, are to be found in the works listed above.

Nationalism of Pastors and the Authoritarian State. Political "Cultures of Belief" in German Protestantism during the 1920s and 1930s*

I.   Protestant Mentalities in Bourgeois Circles and Milieus

In different regions of Germany, at the latest in the 1890s, a process of urban and rural camp or rather milieu formation took place with a peculiar denominational character and conservative, anti-modern reflexes.[1] However, in the areas it dominated, Protestantism did not acquire the importance that Catholicism had in "its" regions.[2] Differences in denomination were an important criterion for an idea of collective identity.[3] Borne by opinion leaders of aristocratic, academic, bourgeois, craftsmen, or farming provenance, a community of like-minded people was established – to preserve what had been well tested – in a broad national network of associations and clubs that still continued to diversify. Home clubs, often organised by teachers to maintain domestic customs and traditions, developed. A few examples include patriotic warrior and comrade clubs that brought veterans together and facilitated collective remembrance of past military actions complete with all their symbols and legends. Gymnastic clubs and choral societies were revived, and served as places where – in addition to the at first implicitly and later explicitly split Christianity[4] – internal and external separation from the opponent contributed to the ferment of the group formation process. Fleet and colonial unions, often linked to missionary companies of a "new" kind, sprang up like weeds beginning in the 1880s. They were another way to separate oneself from other nations and denominations.[5] These unions served as a "community-making"[6] brace that reached beyond the socio-economic group differences of Art and Science Associations of the educated classes, or exclusive sport clubs such as "fatherland"-oriented associations. Protestant chaplains reinforced these national-conservative, ideological patterns of analysis through their partly social-romanticist aspirations in these subcultures. From a biblical, anti-modern, and Socialist-averse position, these chaplains (especially in rural regions) condemned modern, liberal city-life with its individualist and pluralist tendencies and spewed rhetoric against a general decline in customs and beliefs, and against contempt for Christian norms.[7] In cities, on the contrary, it was possible for old-liberal, intellectual-bourgeois circles to connect with liberal priesthoods and theologians and, thereby, to form a bourgeois-shaped culture network. In these milieus especially, the belief in the German fatherland's superior Protestant position and its Protestant imperial status in the world were unquestionable.[8] The possibility of cooperation

*   First published in German as 'Pastorennationalismus und autoritärer Staat. Politische "Glaubenskulturen" im deutschen Protestantismus während der 20er und 30er Jahre' in *RSG* 4 (2003), 7–40.

between conservative and liberal pastors, especially in issues concerning socio-political and social-moral matters, did indeed exist as long as the cultural-political space was accepted as the limited realm in which action would take place.[9] "Boundaries of hatred" or "inner-Protestant cultural fights", if any at all had existed in Berlin or elsewhere until 1914[10], lost their significance after 1918 or underwent a transformation. When these boundaries ceased to exist, Lutherans, Liberals and German Christians formed enduring alliances against the pastors movement of "Word-of-God-theology", which marginalised culture, or came together over what would soon be the all-imposing "peoples-missionary" (*volksmissionarisch*) claim. This claim aimed not only to strengthen parochial Protestantism, but also explicitly included its secular world vision within the national frame of the German state[11] and its overseas possessions. Friedrich Naumann regarded the formation of associations as a result of the altered socio-economic conditions as well as of the emancipation claims of wide sections of society, and encouraged Christians to "pervade all such associations with Christian spirit and Christian personality"[12] in the *Monatsblätter für innere Mission* in 1894.

In addition to the secular clubs and associations in Wilhelmine-political style, a similar model of Protestant sponsorship[13] gradually prospered as a clear imitation of this organisation model[14], which indeed also could not compare to the network of Catholic associations[15]. The Protestants' competitive relationship with the already existing socio-moral milieus of ultramontane Catholicism and atheistic Socialism forced Protestants to form closer alliances in the realm of regional church institutions[16] and in the establishment of a differentiated union system. According to the views held in Protestant circles, the Social Democratic milieu[17] consisted mainly of Protestants gone astray – a circumstance that intensified the rivalry over who would win over the working class[18].

Apart from the Inner Mission[19], whose growth did stagnate in certain phases[20], the *Evangelischer Bund zur Wahrung der deutsch-protestantischen Interessen* (Protestant Union to safeguard German Protestant interests, EB) was the leading Protestant association with 90,000 members (1893) in 900 groups[21]. The practical Theologian and New Testament biblical scholar from Halle, Willibald Beyschlag, and most of his brothers in mind belonged to the church's moderate national-liberal Central Party (*Mittelpartei*)[22]. For them, the "nationalist position [was] highly self-evident; to be a nationalist [was] a holy duty"[23]. After the *Kulturkampf*[24] was settled, these circles thought that nationalism and Protestantism were seriously threatened by "the Catholicising policies of Bismarck as the ruler"[25]. They regarded "Romanism" as "the enemy"[26]. Faced with the "powerful unity of Rome", they wanted to create an equally powerful alliance of "German Protestant Christianity", which was still divided and whose constituent parts were constantly at odds with one another. They also wanted to "improve the Christian-Protestant community's awareness regarding the indifference and materialism of the time"[27]. Due to the vibrant life of its associations – monthly meetings in local groups were standard, but weekly get-togethers were also not uncommon – the EB grew rapidly: in 1898 it numbered 100,000 members; in 1904, 240,000 and in 1914, 510,000.[28] After the socio-economic and ethical crises in the aftermath of World War I, the association was able to stabilise by 1927 with 300,000 members in 2,800 branch associations.[29] The so-called Wartburg Programme of 1921, which had proclaimed the "collective consciousness of sensible men and women who considered themselves German and Protestant"[30], became the authoritative text at the time of its inception[31]. "The Protestant Alliance has declared that it is its task to help the Protestant ideology become a force in public life again, that the Protestant sense of duty and Protestant feeling of responsibility penetrate all of our peoples' circles, religious and political, social and economic, and thereby contribute to the elevation of our national character and public life."[32] As a mass organisation designed especially for the middle class, the EB functioned at times as a national-liberal "electoral-aid club" in its fight against the Centre.[33] In addition to the Centre, the other main enemy was Social Democracy; both were apostrophised as "Reich enemies".[34] Aside from its contacts with, above all, national-liberal and conservative political parties, the EB also collaborated with "national" unions.[35] In regard to the EB's multiple memberships, it is clear that the EB exerted considerable influence on the forming of political opinions.

To help threatened Protestant congregations in Catholic environments, the *Gustav-Adolf-Verein* (GAV) was founded, an entity which was first established as a foundation in 1832/33. The aftermath of the First World War caused the association to develop into a kind of Protestant welfare organisation for the preservation of the German nationality in bordering countries and foreign states. In 1927, the association consisted of 44 main associations, 1,341 branch associations, 509 women's associations and 4 student associations.[36] That same year, the GAV's total income was 1,852,198 RM (*Reichsmark*).[37] At the main assemblies "the strong sense of community was always quite an experience"[38]. The "German national feeling"[39] was also traditionally maintained at these meetings. In 1889, the GAV already included 6.7 % of all Protestants from Baden with its 40,000 members. Roughly one-third of all of Baden's Protestant households, therefore, were influenced by the association's "force of milieu formation".[40] It is striking that the social support-groups of the evolving milieus were somewhat more scattered than Synod memberships were. In 1876, in spite of the unquestionable dominance of the bourgeoisie, 7.2 % of the GAV side association's members in Oldenburg were still small business owners and master craftsmen; 1.9 % were workers, 0.6 % farmers.[41]

Apart from these two major associations "in the service of the Protestant church"[42], there was a large number of smaller associations supporting scattered Protestant minorities including the *Evangelisch-Kirchlicher Hilfsverein* (Protestant Churchly Welfare Organisation), the *Deutscher Evangelischer Volksbund* (German Protestant Peoples Union), the *Reichselternbund* (Reichs Parents Union), associations for religious art and chants, as well as associations for Christian missions among the Jews. The *Evangelisch-Kirchlicher Hilfsverein* was founded to win over "masses [in large cities] that had been alienated by the church". Above all, it supported the church's struggle against "poor moral-religious conditions in cities as well as in the countryside"[43]. The establishment of this organisation was set in motion at the so-called Berlin Waldersee Meeting.[44] The association's mobilisation of laymen to do religious work in communities and its encouragement in the organisation of Protestant women's welfare were especially significant.[45] The

Deutscher Evangelischer Volksbund for Christian public missions was founded in 1911 and sought to personally involve church members in Christian public missions as well as to unite those willing to do so in one organisation. The union, which consisted of approximately 200 local branches with 120,000 members in 1929, was designed to enact a comprehensive mobilisation of "the biblical-moral vitality still remaining in the German people", to "clarify in an orderly fashion devout Protestant Christianity's duties with respect to the whole nation" in order to be able to "fight purposefully against anti-Christian ideologies and ways of life", "establish and spread a German Protestant people's press based on Christian national ideas", to conduct "socio-ethical schooling and to be socially active in general".[46] The union arranged a meeting of all union associations annually in conjunction with German Protestant people's day. After the EB and the *Gustav-Adolf-Verein*, the *Deutscher Evangelischer Volksbund* represents the third strongest German Protestant association. All three associations thought and acted in a way that was shaped by a liberal, collectively Protestant, nationalist and anti-Catholic viewpoint. After 1918 and in connection with the implementation of Socialist policies in school, a powerful parents' movement (by protestant standards) evolved, which had its beginnings in the 19th century.[47] The chief of the Protestant press union in Germany, August Hinderer[48], united the various regional parents' unions in a nation-wide alliance – the *Reichsverband evangelischer Eltern- und Volksbünde* (Reich Alliance of Protestant Parents' and People's Unions) (also called *Reichs-elternbund*). Only a year after its formation, the alliance could already count two million members. The association demonstrated its predominance with the annual *Reichselterntag* (Reich Parents Day), while the *Reichserziehungswochen* (Reich Education Weeks), which were arranged in every part of the Reich, gave helpful suggestions "on deepening the quality of domestic upbringing and on enlarging the people's community"[49]. In connection with the various drafts of school laws, the parents' union fought to obtain Protestant schools and against the emergence of Christian comprehensive schools.

Many pastors participated in the establishment of these associations – mostly as individuals, not as official representatives of their established regional churches, which mostly viewed these "secondary religious" fields of work with a great deal of suspicion and occasionally integrated them in their official structure.[50] In some associations like the social charitable *Badischer Landesverband für Innere Mission* (Baden Regional Association for Inner Mission), "roughly two thirds of the members"[51] consisted of pastors. Due to multiple memberships in secular and religious associations, chaplains often had cross connections, which created a horizontal flow of information and, therefore, formed the precursors to networks.[52] They had a double-function in creating Protestant-tinted milieus: they represented the milieu's core and functioned as milieu managers.[53] Even though rectory self-recruitment was consistently decreasing and the pastor profession was a route increasingly taken by social climbers after the turn of the century, pastors' sons still formed the dynastic nucleus of the whole with a representation of one-third of all pastors, who lived in a milieu that was close to the state.[54] Protestant chaplains in the *Verband deutscher evangelischer Pfarrvereine* (Union of German Protestant pastors' associations) had possessed a professional-political union representation on a supra-regional level since 1892.[55] In 1923, this entity included about 15,300 of the 18,000 ministers.[56] The association defended the interests of the clerical class on a regional and national level against the background of a gradual loss of social relevance[57] by emphasising equal social security coverage similar to the one afforded to lawyers and gym teachers who worked for the state. According to the pastors, only an equal academic education and an analogous income went along with the necessary social prestige, which for the sake of their fundamental "cultural responsibilities" should not lag behind that of comparable professions.[58] Annual pastor conferences and the circulation of a main periodical, *Deutsches Pfarrerblatt* (German Pastors' Paper), cultivated the formation of this subculture's collective identity and self-esteem and increased its influence in bourgeois society by continuously discussing such characteristic "mentality themes". In the light of pastors' traditionally strong position in parishes, church administration and the leadership structures of associated Protestantism, their attitudes, behaviours and stances on certain issues took on a class and opinion-shaping function to a degree that should not be underestimated. It was no longer the handed-down Revelationist positivism of their in the meantime radically historicised, and therefore relativised, religion[59] that determined the self-conception of these pastors, but rather a deep belief in the national cultural meaning of Protestantism. Even conservatives gradually became "modern positivists" in order to maintain a link to the contemporary understanding of reality. This was due mostly to the verisimilitudinous pressure of historical critique that lasted until 1914.[60] In an "apologetic courting of modernity"[61], they constructed a political-conservative theology in which the orders of creation of family, people and fatherland (nation) evolved as central covenant categories in "the [coming] realm of God". The more time passed, the more this trend would prove to be the predominant force in religion and politics as compared to liberal and traditional conservative positions. Its mental reserves, which were continually revitalised, even in the development of prejudice, were directed against Catholicism. After the *Kulturkampf,* this was especially the case in places where, because of the prevailing mono-denominational structure, actual Catholicism scarcely appeared.[62] Where denominationally mixed conditions prevailed, one could act out one's animosity[63] by reciprocally breaching religious holidays and particular religious customs – for example by carting stinking manure through the village and noisily cracking the whip on such occasions.[64] No other mental disposition would soak in so deeply, or be able to manifest itself for such a long period of time in the Protestant milieu as anti-Catholicism did. Even if on different levels, not being Catholic constituted a close relationship between pastors, believers and milieu Protestants. "The split and tension between denominations was one of the fundamental, unexceptional and vital realities of German life. Among such born Protestants displaying a more simple nature the no-longer proper Protestantism shrank to become anti-Catholicism; both then kept each other alive: because one was born a Protestant, one remained anti-Catholic, and because one was anti-Catholic, one felt 'Protestant'."[65] As a society-forming order and cultural power, Protestantism also remained with those who had already turned their backs to it as a system of faith. Those who, like the Social Democrats during the school debates in 1918/19, questioned this general consensus of Protestant culture had to expect considerable resistance. Thus, this experience among pastors reinforced the high valuation of national Protestant civil culture as a societal ferment that rose beyond spiritual means. Despite the occasionally ambivalent emotional frame of mind of conservative pastors facing the antagonism of church-hostile circles, which was directed against Catholics as well as Protestants, most of the time, if it was about supporting the Centre for instance, in terms of the general Protestant mentality, they decided for the anti-Catholic option.[66]

In 1918/19, in addition to modernity, which with its permanent pluralising nature was already perceived as a crisis by many ministers, the until then state-hegemonic national-Protestant culture was threatened with marginalisation.[67] In their eyes, the conservative Protestant brand of cultural Christianity suddenly seemed threatened on many fronts. Many Protestant circles regarded the First World War as a cultural-religious fight between the "*Heiliges Deutsches Reich Evangelischer Nation*"[68] (Holy German Empire of a Protestant nation), which evolved in the form of a founding myth in 1870/71, and the "Romanism" of ultramontane and Gallican provenance. After the *Kulturkampf*[69], Luther-Germany had, for the second time – and seemingly irrevocably – lost the war for Protestant morale.[70] It had to resign as the dominant interpretation-giving elite. It was these Protestant circles that regarded not only political Catholicism with its Centre Party, but also a new flourishing cultural Catholicism as the winners.[71] The people felt existentially affected, a condition that was not limited to the intellectual part of the cultural industry, but also affected people in their everyday lives, for example in the tightening of Catholic intermarriage rights in the *Codex juris Canonici* of 1917/18.[72] The political arm of Catholicism, the Centre Party, even formed coalitions with the atheist Socialist workers' party, whose church-averse "subculture"[73] would soon become the hegemonic "leading culture" of the republic. Did liberal Jewish circles not also contribute to this revolutionary subversion and encourage moral decline in large cities by their cynical relativisation of all national-Protestant values? During the Weimar Republic these denominational stereotypes became even more rigid and were enriched by individual sets of bogeymen. So, for example, a Protestant clergyman ranted during a GAV celebration that "Russian and Roman spirits" were about to "tear down what Protestant collective will" had "created".[74] And at an annual EB celebration Russian Bolshevism and Roman "pseudo-Christianity" were declared the two main enemies of Protestantism.

What had already become apparent in the two previous decades and had been interrupted by the "Spirit of 1914"[75] in a way that gave people hope but turned out to be short-lived, became an irrevocable reality in 1919: Modernity with its peculiar shimmering ambivalence, its pluralist nature and manifold centres of gravity had conspicuously caught up with German Protestantism. The terms mirroring the experience of life in those days, which were continually restated with new descriptions and always borne-out by new experience, were "crisis", "decline" and "decadence". Indignant and ashamed of the humiliation it had suffered, Protestantism looked upon the past longingly and took advantage of every opportunity that was offered it for a restitution of old conditions. The DNVP, Hindenburg and the presidential dictatorship owed a large proportion of their clientele to such attitudes, which were solidified through subjective experience – in contrast to the objective reality under constitutional church law and its protection of and the privileges it afforded to the traditional church[76]. Only minority subcultures from the Protestant large-scale milieu found their way into the democratic DVP and DDP.[77] The DNVP established a "professional committee" for its Protestant clergymen in 1919, and a Protestant Reich committee in 1921.[78] In 1922, the DDP tried a similar integration with its "democratic friends of the church" subcommittee. In an appeal during the December elections of 1924, the DNVP assured the people that: "Our party will stay what it was: monarchic and traditional, Christian and social. Our goals will remain like our name: German and national ... . And our will is stronger than ever: to create a Germany free of Jewish dominance and French dominance, free of a parliamentary clique and of capitalist democratic rule ... ."[79] The great majority of the Protestant priesthood agreed with this programme wholeheartedly. Since there were no spiritual advisors to the national and provincial government as there had been in the Kaiser's days, pastors now had to carry out their own political campaigns to at least maintain what was left of their world of bourgeois culture and to rescue the German-Protestant national identity. Bruno Doehring, the last chaplain of Wilhelm II's court and a master of political-religious symbolism, showed his colleagues what impact he could still have as a preacher in the Berlin Cathedral and as a delegate in the Reich parliament (*Reichstag*).[80] As time wore on, church leaders increasingly dealt with the considerable difficulties involved in leading political lives, but often proved indecisive or could only gain some acceptance. Moreover, they had different measures with respect to their pastors' party work as shown by the examples of Doehring on the one hand and of Heinz Kappes and Erwin Eckert on the other.[81]

By the beginning of the 1920s, Protestantism was already unable to carry out the social functions held vacant for it by the state, and carried out a fatal misattribution of its marginalisation due to inappropriate appraisals of its situation. Above all, these misattributions were directed at the strange democratic "system", as well as expressed in stereotypes of the "other" that included Catholicism, Socialism, the Jews and smaller religious denominations. Set against this background, the process of cultivating and forming the Protestant milieu, which was catching up with its rival, took place in a hectic, radical fashion. The milieu exhibited a clear tendency towards religious-politicising. It was not about constructive compromises, pragmatic solutions, but rather, in word and deed, about "redemption" from circumstances that were considered smothering. Therefore, associated Protestantism as well as the regional churches were involved in the social conflicts of that time, with the latter trying to camouflage their political options by employing generalised common welfare rhetoric. But even when one had to come to terms with the powers of the republic[82] or even cooperated with them on the basis of national interest[83], a "rational republicanism" (at the most) developed, while one still supported polarisation and discrimination on other levels. Protestant associations were required to be in harmony with the affine "movements" in order to remain capable of making cultural-political connections and to be able to become active again in the people's mission in the claimed breadth of the people's church. In 1928, Otto Dibelius[84] observed: If there is talk about religious matters at church conferences, you can expect respectful, maybe even curious listeners. "The spirits become vivid, as if incited by a blow, though if the political field is touched upon. Then everybody feels involved. Then comes the heckling ... political desire rules everything."[85] It was absolutely possible to syn-thesise a comprehensive experience from these disparate perceptions, namely a mixture of religious ideologies and political issues. This amalgamation was like-wise applied to Germany's political culture of belief long before 1918: "Ideo-logising and concomitant emotionalising of political antagonisms were normal; pragmatism and the acceptance of compromises were hard to come by ... . After the religious connections of Protestantism started to fade, there was a tendency towards political welfare myths and substitute theologies."[86] Not only Nipperdey but also Hans-Ulrich Wehler[87], Michael Stürmer[88], Heinrich August Winkler[89] and Wolfgang Altgeld have characterised this phenomenon of the German Reich's nationalism[90] as a "political religion", "secular substitute religion"[91] or "church substitute".[92] Peter Berghoff points at the tense relationship that evolved because the "construction of a political collective", an artefact, had come un-hinged from the "traditional construct of transcendence" on the one hand, but on the other hand – due to the need of embodiment in transcendence and the need for "religious legitimisation"[93] with a consistent spiritual matrix[94] – imme-diately carried out a re-sacralisation whose original myths were people, nation and race.[95] The re-nationalisation as an outcome of the First World War led to national homogenisation[96] on the one hand, as was the case in Germany, and to serious tensions between the population's majority and the minorities on the oth-er, as was the case in Poland[97]. In both cases, the features that divided people in-cluding ethnic group, language, and race were also experienced in the religious dimension. This is where Protestantism had an opportunity to establish a connec-tion. It strived – as a consequence of the mutual emancipation of church and state, which accompanied the process of its social marginalisation – to proceed with a re-politicisation of religiousness. This procedure referred to the same ori-gin myths, which were presented as part of the "orders of creation". It came in handy for Protestantism during this reconstruction process that functional, i. e. integrating forces in the process of developing collective constructs, were depend-ent on "collective ideals" with religious dimensions.[98]

II.   Church life, religion and piety in "cults" and communities of similar ideologies

Statistics about the way of enacting church life – attending service and the Lord's Supper, baptism, weddings, funerals, joining and leaving the church – have been seen as an indicator of actual religiosity and have been systematically registered since the last third of the 19th century. Lucian Hölscher has repeatedly drawn at-tention to the problem of implying that external perceptions of churchly rituals are a reflection of internal religious attitudes.[99] Then again, he rightly noted that social organisations could not exist over a long period of time without ritual expressions. It is probably due in part to this idea that, in article 137 of the Weimar Constitution of 1919, legislators enabled those religious communities to achieve corporate status, which offer "through the constitution and the number of their associates the warranty of their duration".[100] Apart from external appearances, religions are neither sociologically nor legally comprehensible. "Basically religiosity is ... – at least as a social appearance, not only understood as a personal attitude – always dependent on collective manifestation."[101] The importance of rituals to individuals is hard to evaluate afterwards, for a survey among the participants is no longer possible.[102] One can work, on historical levels, on the collective importance of church rituals in their social and religious dimensions against a backdrop of statistical information and their embedding within society. Participating or not participating in church rituals does not necessarily lead to a definite conclusion. The motives for external religious behaviour can be traced back to different circumstances, which can differ considerably in different regions.[103] Such data, though, provides essential parameters for quantitative-based interpretations of historical mentalities. On an average statistic scale, a progressive decline of the participation in church life can be determined during the period of the Weimar Republic.[104] "The enormously large number of church resignations in the first years after the war did decrease during the 1920s, but selectively shot up repeatedly, and generally increased by 1930."[105] In addition to a decline in the number of Christian burials, one can also speak of an obvious decline in church life. The participation in the Lord's Supper decreased by circa 3 % between 1918 and 1932[106], in the same period the number of baptisms compared to the number of births decreased by about 2 %[107] and the number of Protestant marriages and weddings even declined by over 10 %[108]. The sum of all resignations per year varied between 314,005 (1920) and 83,020 (1924).[109] Between 1919 and 1932, on average 191,868 Protestants left the church every year. A minority joined one of the smaller religious circles or ideological communities. However, from then on, most of them belonged to a growing sub-culture of "milieu Protestants" that did not have any denominational connection.

Empirical social research on churches, which originated between 1890 and 1914[110], investigated these and other phenomena of open or latent dissociation from the church by examining the frequency of church attendance[111] and carried out standardised group-interviews about the "religious world in the minds of proletarian youth"[112]. It executed – with catastrophic results – surveys on the state of knowledge about the Bible and Christian creeds[113], and analysed the broad indifference towards Christian belief – now not only among the workers but also among intellectuals. It was because of this research that the myth that the lack of interest in religious issues was class based was finally shattered.[114] "A Doctor of Philosophy and a Doctor of Political Science in my borough resigned from the church", Gerhard Jacobi wrote in his *Tagebuch eines Großstadtpfarrers* ("Diary of a metropolitan pastor"). "On the one hand I am relieved that these totally non-religious intellectuals have finally started to resign and therefore show that they do not get anything out of the church and do not care about it. On the other hand, though, it is still a breaking away from the people's church which I do love, after all."[115] The proud self-conception of intellectual cultural Protestantism was hit, more than by the Socialists' and organised free-thinkers' manifest hostility towards the church, by the attitude of such bourgeois classes, "which oscillate between indifference, strangeness and more or less favourable toleration"[116]. He commented on this as the "great religious trouble of the present"[117].

Considering this development, which was already looming, and its often blunt description, it is understandable that official reports from the *Kirchliches Jahrbuch* about the "church's contemporary situation" and "church life" were brimming with pessimistic tones.[118] Yet, it is notable how much Protestantism considered itself an integral part of society as a whole. In the analysis, the bad state of the people's church and of the Protestant associations, which also had to suffer harsh membership losses, was only considered a symptom of the miserable state of the people as a whole. Johannes Schneider lamented in July 1919: "We have lost the war ... the national humiliation is beyond example. We have overestimated our powers. God wants to lead us back to self-awareness and humbleness. ... If many people throw away their Christian belief, as the brawlers want, we will be desperately poor. ... Never before was the church's responsibility, which can be put in the words 'strengthen what wants to die', so serious and so hard and so large as now."[119] Then again, Protestantism remains absent whenever people talk about the "great mistake[s]" of the "old regiment[s]"[120]. In point of fact, the "loyal work of the church"[121] could not fill the chasm between city and countryside, and Protestantism had to helplessly watch "the decline of moral public life" that occurred because of incapable politicians. Immorality and the "spiritual lowness of our people" formed a picture of sorrow. "Every free building-space in Berlin will soon become a fairground, where a bustling activity of the lowest sort will unfold as part of the 'culture of the big city'. Movie theatres are overcrowded and in fact, the more indecent their features are, the more overfilled they become. The athletes' races and wrestling fights attract people by the thousands"[122], while the churches remained empty. "The church's circumstances suffered quite a bit due to the illness of the public's mind."[123] Schneider denounces "those who carried out the political overthrow"[124] as the moral transgressors against the German people. Admittedly, this "ethical moral decline" had been looming for years. "The desired decline in the birth rate became a people's sin ... . The death of a hundred thousand who should have become procreators was God's retaliation. ... No one had a greater obligation to spread awareness about these blind times than the church."[125] In the months after the revolution a "great flood of hatred for religion, which had been brewing hidden in the depths of society for a long time"[126], threatened to bury the church. But, "the fact that church loyalty on an unforeseen scale came about, was among the few sparks of light in these dark times."[127] It was with this and similar reports that a new myth was born: the already-foundering people recall the source of their spiritual power and in fact find their way back to the "true 'peoples' church'", which had emerged "from the old 'state church'".[128] But this repeatedly invoked renewal of people and church in the midst of German National Protestantism failed to materialise. Protestantism saw the alleviation of church resignations that began in many places as the cause of the "newly awoken church resignation movement"[129]. According to the Hamburg Church Resignation Law of 21 December 1918, for example, it sufficed to announce one's resignation verbally or in writing at the registry office to make one's resignation valid. There was no time required to reconsider the decision.[130] From the church's perspective, the propaganda of many free-spirit groups was responsible for many church members taking this step. In the first decade of the 20th century, the "cultural associations" that had emerged from these circles united in the Weimar cartel to become a greater union, which forwarded a modern cultural policy through which the state would be freed of religion and the church freed of nationalism.[131] Cultural associations associated with the bourgeois left cooperated with the Social Democrats in cultural-political actions such as the Organised Church Resignation Movement, which was organised because of a planned inclusion of religion in schools and church-tax legislation.[132] Such agitations came less from an anti-religious resentment, as the church leadership suspected, but more from the wish to have a laicist, emancipated transformation of society. "The hoped-for de-politicising of religion would at the same time lead to a subjectification of religious commitment."[133] A second wave in 1912/14 followed the first wave of church resignations in 1906/08, but eventually faded out.[134] Both waves led to tremendous irritations in church circles, though. Among the landowning religious establishment, which was already in a weakened condition, the third wave of 1918/19 increased the uncertainty and led to an all-out fear for the group's existence[135], a fear expressed in extraordinarily aggressive polemics. This was due to the fact that the issue of church taxes was raised again. Considering the overall tax burden, this could become a serious reason for resigning.[136] In view of the formation of an ideological counterculture, the church surely did not fear acutely heterogeneous subcultures. By 1914, former pastor and later Social Democrat Paul Gröhe was already warning his party about a free-religious substitute religion within the frame of an "exceedingly blurry ... bourgeois cultural movement"[137]; at about the same time pedagogic reformer Ludwig Gurlitt was forwarding the *Komitee Konfessionslos* (Non-denominational Committee), which was founded in 1910/11. It was a religious-national reformation on a Germanic foundation.[138]

Well-organised Protestants undertook a series of measures to combat alleged threats by free-spiritual, free-thinking and other competing groups[139]. The multiplicity of apologetic associations within the sphere of the Inner Mission, which had emerged at the turn of the century, experienced organisational tightening, coordination and differentiation. In the course of this re-structuring, the Inner Mission central-committee established apologetics – in addition to evangelism – as part of public missions.[140] In autumn 1921, the committee appointed Christian theologian Carl Gunther Schweitzer, who was of Jewish descent, a full time apologist at the newly institutionalised "Apologetic Centre" (AC). The centre's personnel were constantly expanded and the Protestant unions were simulated and supported on a local[141] as well as on regional levels (networks were formed). However, there was also harsh competition between the Protestants.[142] Until his resignation in 1932, Schweitzer favoured the modern concepts of communication technology and mass psychology. In addition to "explicitly influencing public life"[143] through a series of popular lectures, posters, press articles, and brochures that were propagandistic in their character, the "material collecting point" and the "observation service" gained tremendous importance through "people of trust", "ideological weeks", apologetic schooling, broadcasting work[144] and even motion pictures.[145] Diversification of the religious-ideological scene, which was considered a "cultural crisis", needed to be approached with an offensively lectured "Protestant ideological doctrine". The cultural productivity of Christianity, which was considered the highest form of religion, was to be focused upon. Instead of the "pastor-church", a church that campaigned and communicated and had a wide missionary base, was supposed to develop. It was by these means, that a sort of disavowal was carried out towards the "foreign" culture of devoutness[146], the "sects"[147] that came from the British-American west. An effective containment of general church alienation as result of de-Christianisation was not achieved. Just as little as other cultural-Protestant initiatives, the AC was unable to exert religious influence on secularised culture.

Though widespread protective measures were taken, the Christian rhythm of life quietly disintegrated. The church reacted to this by continuously lamenting "dying Sunday" as well as the disregard for "holding [Sunday and the holy days] sacred." "Public amusement, sports events, races and similar things destroy the entire peace of Sundays during the service times."[148] At the end of the 1920s, the modern "weekend"-phenomenon developed, accompanied by escapes from the cities into nature.[149] Appointing weekend-pastors failed to stop these migrations.[150] The church was still able to document its great social influence through other initiatives such as scheduling shop closing times earlier in observance of Christmas, censoring "dirty and trashy movies"[151], or the "blasphemy paragraph"[152], but most of these legislative actions did not bring people back into the churches and exerted very little influence on their lifestyles. In describing this development, reports in the *Kirchliche Zeitlage*, a religious periodical[153], used the terms "secularisation" or "secularism" with a pejorative connotation. This phenomenon is described as a voluntary process of removing Christian influences from the "public" sphere. Compared to this, non-church circles saw the cause of secularisation – which sociologists like Emile Durkheim and Max Weber[154] isolated as the basic concept – in a descriptively displayed, long-lasting trend of social transformation, in the course of which religion has lost one stronghold after another to the modern world, which is represented by science, rationality and bureaucracy.[155] The former religious identity of the public, represented as a whole, included a decreasing number of areas of life and from then on, as a very highly-subjective, denominational partial identity, possessed a very limited, functional purpose.

The religious and ideological pluralism that was introduced to the bourgeois milieu in the 1890s (at the latest), but had been driven back decisively, could unfold almost completely uninhibited in the new, denominationally neutral Weimar State[156], and that also occurred in the form of closer unions. Those who did not actively take part in the external Christian majority-culture experienced almost no social disadvantages. From the Protestant point of view, this religious pluralism was overwhelmingly regarded negatively as a loss of orientation, a threat to the German soul and as a loss of its collective identity to all sorts of political substitute religions, mystic, occultist, eschatological, national-religious, free-thinking and other esoteric movements.[157] Genuine theological reasons for the defence against non-mainline religiousness played a minor part, which can be seen among other things in Hermann Priebe's 1929 book *Kirchliches Handbuch für die evangelische Gemeinde*, where Free Churches, which were closely related to the Protestant regional church – Methodists, Baptists and others –, are discussed in one chapter with the "sects" and "ideological communities". The Free Churches "could [indeed] not stifle the feeling of satisfaction" they had about the legislative situation of the state church, because they expected that they "from now on did not have to suffer under the reign of the regional church anymore".[158] Despite the fact that they had very different religious-ideological preferences, most of these small religious subcultures shared an intense community-life, but did not draw any socio-politically relevant solutions from their teachings and did not appeal to political actions. Moreover, they settled in positions at the outskirts of society and did not include more than 300,000 members.[159] However, many of these groups were involved in difficult missionary work, especially in publication activities and personal address in order to spread their ideas and, in part, achieved surprising results. This was especially the case for the belief-community of the Serious Bible-researchers [as Jehovah's Witnesses called themselves at that time], who within eight years were able to increase their membership six fold and in 1926 already had 22,535 members.[160] Even though this totally eschatological-oriented religious community acted decidedly abstinent, Protestantism had a special aversion to them, because on a sheerly religious level no other group questioned it with more determination – namely as subsystem of an only "nominal Christianity". "Their attitude towards the church is more hostile than that of any other sect", Priebe wrote. They "agitate the masses to fight against the church and demand for them to leave it"[161].

The "national (*völkisch*) religious communities"[162] and *Deutschgläubigen* (German believers) movements – which had also developed in Wilhelmine society[163] –, on the other hand, combined their critique of the churches and their propaganda of a heroic Arian religious belief regarding German origins with political aims, which were expressed by a close interplay between religion and nationalism. Their ethnic ideology targeted modernity, internationalism, Socialism, and the "West", and had distinct racist characteristics. These groups blanketed the country with anti-democratic publicity, and were not only fundamentally responsible for the mixing of religion, ideology, and politics, but also increased the polarity that existed between different political-religious positions towards the end of the Weimar Republic. They were very popular with the German youth-movement, which was looking for a communal experience with a neo-Romantic, anti-Enlightenment, anti-liberal and national-ethnological (*national-völkisch*) foundation. In contrast to most of the other "sects" and ideological circles, the *völkisch* religious communities were, in principle, positively acknowledged in Priebe's Handbook for the Protestant Community: It is a movement mostly carried-out by the youth, "which in place of international aims and values have national ones, bursting with love for the German ethnicity and the desire to free the [German] people from their miserable situation: the ethnic [*völkisch*] movement, due to its nationalist position wants to remove everything foreign and un-German and wants to build a life-community of the German people upon the foundation of a German-Germanic ideology."[164] In making this well-meaning assessment and the following strictly-neutral portrait of different groups such as the *Germanische Glaubensgemeinschaft*, Artur Dinter's anti-Semitic *Geistchristliche Religiònsgemeinschaft* or the *Tanneberg-Bund* of Erich Ludendorff (former General quarter master of the imperial army) and his wife Mathilde von Kemnitz, Priebe refers to the publications of the Apologetic Centre in Spandau.[165] Actually, apologetic work in the twenties focused on religious competitors in a more narrow sense. "It was only with the beginning of the 1930s that political religions began to enter the AC's field of view."[166] But, at the beginning of the Third Reich, the fight against "sects" and free-thinkers was also a focus for the AC – partly in cooperation with the Nazi regime.[167]

III.   Protestantism and "Political Religion"

"Interest in political religions is experiencing a renaissance in several countries."[168] In Germany a broad research project – initiated and led by Hans Maier – developed in the 1990s within the subject area of "totalitarianism and political religion", which combines both concepts.[169] While totalitarianism approaches[170], like Hannah Arendt's historical-philosophical theory[171] and Carl Joachim Friedrich's structural power concept[172], try to show through ideologically focused or classification models the terrorist "nature" or rather the characteristics of totalitarianism against the democratic-theoretic background of universal human rights in their repressive, autonomy-limiting form[173], the religious approach can bring forth the fascinating ideological sides of such dictatorships.[174] An "un-deserved compliment" to totalitarian dictatorships, as Hannah Arendt feared in 1953[175], should of course not be connected to the concept of "political religion", but rather to a broadening of the explanatory perspective as to why people affirm such regimes. Moreover, the content-related "religious" criteria contradict the formalism-objection that opponents of the totalitarianism-comparison tend to have.[176] The results of the Maier research project[177], documented in two volumes at the time of this writing, reflect the ambivalence of "political religions": On the one hand, they display "phenomena similar to religions", on the other hand they behave in a "decidedly anti-church" and "anti-religious" manner.[178] "We therefore have both", Hans Maier wrote in the introduction to the second volume, "a distinct religious language, many formalities of the religious and church history – and at the same time an anti-religious face of modern totalitarianism."[179] Because of this double-sidedness and the different perceptions of religion it is still hard to say if the totalitarian systems of the 20th century can be correctly labelled "political religions".[180] For the Israeli historian Jacob Talmon, historical research on "political Messianism" has to lead to historical-religious and theological perspectives, in order to use the Jewish-Christian Messianism in "its best and most original form" as a measurement for its secular post-formation.[181]

"Religious exaltation" in different forms that can envelop hundreds of thousands people in waves of overexcited piety[182] and which at the beginning of the 20th century inspired the then young discipline of religious psychology in Germany[183], also has a psychological-physiological aspect. Brain researchers have been studying religious stimulation for several years.[184] The results of their research of neural structures up to the present day include isolating a characteristic pattern in the cerebral cortex during religious experiences, which on the one hand shows increased, on the other hand, decreased neural action. Since this pattern appeared with Buddhists as well as Franciscans it would be obvious to include "political religions" in the comparison of neuronal processes, particularly since evident parallels exist in the fields of rituals and social interaction, norms, and taboos. It is possible that the astounding commonalities that exist between religious belief forms and systems, which are also present in the psychological-physiological field, may also be extended to apply to political ideologies as well.

Since the 1930s, Nationalism, Fascism, National Socialism and Socialism have been characterised as "political religions" by philosophers and sociologists in exile.[185] If collective excited states, or even enthusiastic mass-movements[186], are indications of religious lifestyles, then one can determine transferences of this state that were made from official, religiously cool Protestantism to nationalism. During the evidential experiences under such emotional circumstances, which included a frank affirmation of suggestive explanations of their world, the followers experienced a foment of sense, coming to terms with contingency and a fulfilment of their deep longing for simplicity and homogeneity. Nationalism took the place of traditional national Protestantism, with its action-oriented function of integrating an entire society in the emotional, interpretational and cognitive realms. A number of subcultures of the Christian milieu, not least of all in the interest of the people's church or missions among the people, ennobled Nationalism as affirmed "national Protestantism" and therefore wanted to "re-Christianise" it. Since the beginning of the 19th century, such an amalgamation in the field of religious "experience" could principally be realised in the form of increasingly programmatic concepts of cultural-Protestant theologies.[187] This symbiosis could indeed only work as long as nationalism hesitated to emancipate itself from Christianity. Pastors also experienced an enthusiasm in the fatherland's environment of wallowing and politicising, which was present neither in themselves nor in their parish members when they executed their doctrinally imbued church piety. The formation of a national-religious synthesis was a long-lasting, reciprocal culture-stripping process, in the course of which old sacred images[188], symbols[189], linguistic signs and ritual actions, were gradually transferred to nationalism.[190] Thus, over generations a sort of "national-Protestant mentality" was able to crystallise, which proved resistant to the altering of theological paradigms.[191] In their emotional-religious misery, a portion of the Confessing Church even sought refuge in Catholic religiosity.[192] As time wore on, religiously stuffed nationalism faced an increasingly ischemic Protestantism, which had exploited its biblical basis in service to people and nation in such a manner that an increasing gap of credibility had appeared.

A good example of the mix of national and Protestant terms, images and myths, but also one that illustrates the problems of crossing the line and veering into the totalitarian realm is the *Christlich-deutsche Bewegung* (CdB), which was established at the end of 1930 with a conservative identity. Bruno Doehring, who was responsible for the CdB's theological direction[193], wanted to establish a mutual relationship – namely to show "the church the way to the people, and our people the way to the church".[194] Such dreams forged a connection with the national-missionary methods of his predecessor, Adolf Stoecker. Stoecker also wanted to renew and strengthen the "Christian-German character" of the nation with suitable political and public missionary methods.[195] An essential basis for this concept was the known symbiosis between political and Christian nationalism. Despite the enormous efforts made in Victoria von Dirksen's parlour, where this circle met, the district leader of Berlin Joseph Goebbels was unable to persuade all personalities to cooperate with the NSDAP on a sustained basis. In October 1931, Doehring had indeed lent the *Harzburger Front* some political-religious resplendence with his "marvellous preaching"[196] and "a few pithy words"[197], but he now had doubts about the one-sided national socialist course of the CdB, because National Socialism put "the party before the fatherland"[198]. Heinrich Rendtorff, the Bishop of Mecklenburg, who was a recent addition to the CdB, also declared war upon the "unreal nationalism that was threatening to swallow the real one".[199] The situation escalated and caused the national socialist wing of the CdB to break off from the main wing.[200] The national socialists left the movement and committed themselves to the construction of the *Deutsche Christen* (DC) belief movement. Friedrich Wieneke, one of their protagonists with a theologically liberal background, formulated his concept of synthesis as follows in 1931: "But The Lord did not send the saviour to abolish previous creational order, but to pierce flesh and blood with his holy spirit. Swastika and Holy Cross are therefore not contradictory ... . The first speaks of the natural gift created for us by God, the other of the historical spiritual power of redeeming love that God placed in nature. ... We believe that experience of the Napoleonic Wars was also a Christian experience that surely does not have to hide from the peace-apostles of this weak and effeminate present ... . The Lord Jesus never spoke of 'general love of man', but of charity that in light of current political affairs would surely mean the love of the German customs and traditions."[201]

The Protestant "experience of 1933" seemed to be of just as much importance as the Napoleonic Wars, the founding of the Reich in 1879/71 and August 1914, and even acted as the final fulfilment of the yearning for unity.[202] Many preachers of the younger generations compensated for their contingent experiences by undergoing a restoration of personal sense in life, the rule of godly justice, during the political upheaval. But it soon became apparent that the National Socialist movement would eventually want to emancipate itself from Christianity and propagate its own ideology. The new "people's community" could manage without a people's church and tried to further suppress the church's outdated validity claims. To prevent this development from occurring and to preserve the people's church, large parts of Protestantism desperately tried to come up with more and more new ideological compromises – with the regime as well as other competing subcultures. This was the case for the DC church authorities in Brunswick, Hamburg and Schleswig-Holstein, for the "intact" Lutheran church authorities in Hanover, Stuttgart, and Munich, for the Reich movement DC and for Union-Protestantism, especially the *Evangelischer Bund*, the *Gustav-Adolf-Verein* and the *Reichsbund der Deutschen Evangelischen Pfarrervereine*.[203] The loss of the "people's church", of "people's Protestantism" was more traumatic for such circles than any other solution. The only exceptions were sub-milieus of the determined wing of the Confessing Church (*Bekennende Kirche*, BK). Their Reich Brothers Council (*Reichsbruderrat*) also "did not want to [form] a sect or a 'nook church' [*Winkel-kirche*]", but to "proclaim the Gospel in the midst of our nation".[204] But against the backdrop of National Socialist policies regarding religion, the way into the "Free-Church" did not appear to be a totally unacceptable alternative for such groups. While the DC saw themselves as a traditional, non-dogmatic, national religious "men's movement" of the German awakening, which aptly "Germanised" Christian religion for their contemporaries, the BK seemed more a slave-to-tradition, orthodox, bible-based, feminine piety movement.[205] The anti-clerical polemics of the DC, not least of which were directed against competitors within the church, corresponded more to the feeling of a majority of church-absent Protestants. These milieu-Protestants wanted, in general, to be good National Socialists, but because of socialised similarities did not want to turn their back on the church either. Their attitudes and beliefs corresponded more or less with those of the DC movement, without officially being members of this group. National Protestantism with its anti-Jewish, anti-Semitic, anti-western emotions had long ago become a civil religion.[206] "As a civil religion, National Protestantism was able to gain certain advantages for Protestant churches. The amalgamation of Protestantism and nationalism seemed to broaden the appeal of the churches as German society secularised."[207] But the flip side of this success story was the gradual hollowing out of Christian beliefs and the continual decrease in reserves necessary to combat extreme nationalist ideologies. The consequences of this development would become apparent when National Socialism said farewell to National Protestant interpretation patterns. Instead of renewing civil religion and taking it to new heights, which would have been advantageous for both parties, as many Protestants had expected, the NS-regime destroyed the old symbiosis of nationalism and Protestantism. The important break between the National Protestant civil religion and the political religion of National Socialism occurred between autumn 1934 and autumn 1937.[208] It began with the forced withdrawal of pastors and theology students from Nazi SS units and ended with the refusal to grant NSDAP membership to candidates from the same target group.[209] At the same time a wave of church-resignations occurred in 1937, which with 317,980 resignations was much higher than the one of 1919/20.[210] The exclusion of all theologians from the Nazi movement was not only an unprecedented act of humiliation, it also announced the abysmal social collapse of the Protestant milieu and accelerated disintegration on one hand and the emergence of "sectarian" movements within their own ranks on the other. Between 1937 and 1939, a state enforced removal of denominations from public life followed, a process to which Protestant subcultures of German-Christian provenance had contributed. The only satisfaction that could be gained by the affected social milieus was in seeing that National Socialism was unable to develop a cohesive concept[211] from its heterogeneous ideological ideas, its utopias, myths, cults and celebrations.[212] Hitler and his god of providence merely worked as the integration force in this ideological tangle.[213] Around 1937, Hitler's "charismatic legitimacy" also took over the traditional, conservative National Protestant basis.[214]

Notes

1   Cf. on this Jochen-Christoph Kaiser, 'Die Formierung des protestantischen Milieus. Konfessionelle Vergesellschaftung im 19. Jahrhundert', in Olaf Blaschke/Frank-Michael Kuhlemann (eds), Religion im Kaiserreich. Milieus – Mentalitäten – Krisen, Gütersloh 1996, 257–289.

2   So among others Thomas Nipperdey, Deutsche Geschichte 1866–1918, vol. 1: Arbeitswelt und Bürgergeist, Munich 1994, 439 ff., 480 ff.; Frank Bösch, Das konservative Milieu. Vereinskultur und lokale Sammelpunkte in ost- und westdeutschen Regionen (1900–1960), Göttingen 2002, 31.

3   Cf. Manfred Kittel, 'Konfessioneller Konflikt und politische Kultur in der Weimarer Republik', in Olaf Blaschke (ed.), Deutschland zwischen 1800 und 1970: ein zweites konfessionelles Zeitalter, Göttingen 2002, 243–297.

4   Cf. Kittel, Konfessioneller Konflikt (op. cit. note 3), 263.

5   Cf. Gerhard Besier, 'Mission and Colonialism in Friedrich Fabri's (1824–1891) Thinking', in this volume.

6   For the definition of *Vergemeinschaftung* (community-making) cf. Max Weber, Wirtschaft und Gesellschaft. Studienausgabe, Tübingen 1972, 21.

7   Cf. Wolfgang Pyta, Dorfgemeinschaft und Parteipolitik 1918–1933. Die Verschränkung von Milieu und Parteien in den protestantischen Landgebieten Deutschlands in der Weimarer Republik (Beiträge zur Geschichte des Parlamentarismus und der politischen Parteien 106), Düsseldorf 1996.

8   Cf. Gerhard Besier, Die Mittwochsgesellschaft im Kaiserreich, Berlin 1990.

9   Cf. Dietmar von Reeken, Kirchen im Umbruch zur Moderne. Milieubildungsprozesse im nordwestdeutschen Protestantismus 1849–1914 (Religiöse Kulturen der Moderne, vol. 9), Gütersloh 1999, 187 ff.; Frank-Michael Kuhlemann, Bürgerlichkeit und Religion. Zur Sozial- und Mentalitätsgeschichte der evangelischen Pfarrer in Baden 1860–1914 (Bürgertum, vol. 20), Göttingen 2001, 348 ff.

10   Cf. Gangolf Hübinger, Kulturprotestantismus und Politik. Zum Verhältnis von Liberalismus und Protestantismus im wilhelminischen Deutschland, Tübingen 1994, 297 ff.

11   On the common, conservative as well as liberal nationalism of pastors, cf. Frank-Michael Kuhlemann, 'Pastorennationalismus in Deutschland im 19. Jahrhundert – Befunde und Perspektiven in Deutschland', in Heinz-Gerhard Haupt/Dieter Langewiesche (eds), Nation und Religion in deutscher Geschichte, Frankfurt a. M.-New York 2001, 548–601.

12   Quoted after Kuhlemann, Bürgerlichkeit und Religion (op. cit. note 9), 436.

13   For the example of Hessen cf. Siegfried Weichlein, Sozialmilieus und politische Kultur in der Weimarer Republik. Lebenswelt, Vereinskultur, Politik in Hessen, Göttingen 1996, 62 ff., who also points at the stable denominational situation between 1871 and 1933 (ibid. 39 ff.). An analogue development of club cultures can be shown at the establishment of political and church parties who considering their contents strongly tended towards each other. See for the example of Prussia Gerhard Besier, 'Die Evangelische Kirche der altpreußischen Union [APU] im Weimarer Staat', in idem/Eckard

Lessing (eds), Die Geschichte der Evangelischen Kirche der Union, vol. 3, Leipzig 1999, 35–210, here 79 ff., 187 ff.
14 Cf. Thomas Nipperdey, 'Verein als soziale Struktur im späten 18. und frühen 19. Jahrhundert', in Hartmut Boockmann et al. (eds), Geschichtswissenschaft und Vereinswesen im 19. Jahrhundert. Beiträge zur Geschichte historischer Forschung in Deutschland, Göttingen 1972, 1–44, esp. 4.
15 Cf. Heinz Hürten, Deutsche Katholiken 1918 bis 1945, Paderborn 1992, 119 ff.; Weichlein, Sozialmilieus (op. cit. note 13), 67.
16 Cf. Besier, APU im Weimarer Staat (op. cit. note 13), 76 ff.
17 Cf. Sebastian Prüfer, Sozialismus als Religion. Die deutsche Sozialdemokratie vor der religiösen Frage 1863–1890, Göttingen 2002.
18 See on this Reeken, Kirchen (op. cit. note 9), 357 ff.
19 See on this Volker Herrmann/Jochen-Christoph Kaiser/Theodor Strohm (eds), Bibliographie zur Geschichte der deutschen evangelischen Diakonie im 19. und 20. Jahrhundert, Stuttgart 1997.
20 On the development of the Inner Mission, its classic social-deaconry tasks and its position towards the "social issue" on a regional level see Dietrich Höroldt, 'Der Rheinische Provinzialausschuß für Innere Mission im Zeitalter von Hochindustrialisierung und Urbanisierung (1871–1914)', in Reinhard Witschke (ed.), Diakonie bewegt. 150 Jahre Innere Mission und Diakonie im Rheinland, Köln 1999, 25–58, here: 33.
21 Cf. Walter Fleischmann-Bisten/Heiner Grote, Protestanten auf dem Wege. Geschichte des Evangelischen Bundes, Göttingen 1986, 24; Armin Müller-Dreier, Konfession in Politik, Gesellschaft und Kultur des Kaiserreiches. Der evangelische Bund 1886–1914 (Religiöse Kulturen der Moderne, vol. 7), Gütersloh 1998, 79 ff.
22 Cf. Besier, APU im Weimarer Staat (op. cit. note 13), 79 ff.
23 So Gottfried Maron, in idem (ed.), Evangelisch und Ökumenisch. Beiträge zum 100-jährigen Bestehen des Evangelischen Bundes, Göttingen 1986, 25.
24 Cf. Gerhard Besier, 'Kulturkampf', in Joachim Rogge/Gerhard Ruhbach (eds), Geschichte der evangelischen Kirche der Union, vol. 2, Leipzig 1994, 196–216, 247–257.
25 So Willibald Beyschlag in his autobiography: Erinnerungen und Erfahrungen der reiferen Jahre, vol. 2, Halle 1899, 543.
26 Call for establishment of 15 January 1887, quoted after Fleischmann-Bisten/Grote, Protestanten (op. cit. note 21), 15.
27 Ibid.
28 Cf. Hermann Priebe, Kirchliches Handbuch für die evangelische Gemeinde unter besonderer Berücksichtigung der Evangelischen Kirche der altpreußischen Union, Berlin ³1929, 342.
29 Ibid. Cf. Weichlein, Sozialmilieus (op. cit. note 13), 208 f.
30 Quoted after Priebe, Kirchliches Handbuch (op. cit. note 28), 343.
31 See Walter Fleischmann-Bisten, Der Evangelische Bund in der Weimarer Republik und im sogenannten Dritten Reich, Frankfurt a. M.-Bern-New York-Paris, 149 ff.
32 Quoted after Priebe, Kirchliches Handbuch (op. cit. note 28), 343.
33 Cf. Müller-Dreier, EB (op. cit. note 21), 480 ff., 516 ff.
34 Cf. ibid. 494 ff.
35 Cf. ibid. 502 ff.
36 Priebe, Kirchliches Handbuch (op. cit. note 28), 338.
37 On the development of the GAV during the Weimar times see Kirchliches Jahrbuch, 1919, 254–259.
38 So Walter Birnbaum, Die freien Organisationen der Deutschen Evangelischen Kirche, Stuttgart 1939, 35.
39 Ibid. Cf. in total also Hermann Wolfgang Beyer, Die Geschichte des Gustav-Adolf-Vereins in ihren kirchen- und geistesgeschichtlichen Zusammenhängen, Göttingen 1932; Gottfried Beck (ed.), Im Dienste der Diaspora. 150 Jahre Gustav-Adolf-Werk im Rheinland, Köln 1993.
40 So Kuhlemann, Bürgerlichkeit und Religion (op. cit. note 9), 211 f.

41   Cf. Reeken, Kirchen (op. cit. note 9), 169, 174 f.
42   So the definition by Priebe, Kirchliches Handbuch (op. cit. note 28), X.
43   Quote from the statutes, quoted in Priebe, Kirchliches Handbuch (op. cit. note 28), 345.
44   Cf. Gerhard Besier, 'Kirchliche Theologen. Die Provinzkirche in der Politik der Alt-preußischen Union (1861–1918)', in Gerd Heinreich (ed.), Tausend Jahre Kirche in Berlin-Brandenburg, Berlin 1999, 527–560, here: 530 ff.
45   Cf. Nipperdey, Deutsche Geschichte, vol. 1 (op. cit. note 2), 480; Ursula Baumann, 'Religion und Emanzipation. Konfessionelle Frauenbewegung in Deutschland 1900–1933', in Irmtraud Götz von Olenhusen et al. (eds), Frauen unter dem Patriarchat der Kirchen. Katholikinnen und Protestantinnen im 19. und 20. Jahrhundert (KuG 7), Stuttgart 1995, 89–119.
46   Ibid. 347.
47   On the dispute over the schools in North West Germany see Reeken, Kirchen (op. cit. note 9), 261 ff.
48   Cf. epd media no. 48, 24 June 2002, 25.
49   Priebe, Kirchliches Handbuch (op. cit. note 28), 350. On the history of the term "peoples community" (*Volksgemeinschaft*) see Cornelia Schmitz-Berning, Vokabular des Nationalsozialismus, Berlin-New York 1998, 654 ff.
50   Stefan Grotefeld gives an example for the "churching" (*Verkirchlichung*) of the German branch of the entirely ecumenically orientated *Weltbund für Freundschaftsarbeit der Kirchen* (World Alliance for International Friendship through the Churches), in 'Friedensförderung durch internationale Freundschaftsarbeit der Kirchen von 1919 bis 1933. Das Beispiel der deutschen Weltbundvereinigung', in Kirchliche Zeitgeschichte 4 (1991), 46–72.
51   Kuhlemann, Bürgerlichkeit und Religion (op. cit. note 9), 216.
52   On the mutual relations framework between religious and political Liberalism cf. Kuhlemann, Bürgerlichkeit und Religion (op. cit. note 9), 225 ff.
53   So Reeken, Kirchen (op. cit. note 9), 154 ff.
54   Cf. Oliver Janz, Bürger besonderer Art. Evangelische Pfarrer in Preußen 1850–1914, Berlin 1994, 96 ff.; Kuhlemann, Bürgerlichkeit und Religion (op. cit. note 9), 121 f.
55   For the memberships development on a regional level on the Prussian example see Janz, Bürger (op. cit. note 54), 324 ff.; for the *Hannoverscher Pfarrerverein* (Hanoverian Pastors' Association) see Reeken, Kirchen (op. cit. note 9), 157.
56   Priebe, Kirchliches Handbuch (op. cit. note 28), 122. In 1907, already three quarters of all Protestant chaplains were organised in pastors' associations. Janz, Bürger (op. cit. note 54), 325.
57   Cf. Janz, Bürger (op. cit. note 54), 317 ff. This is one of the main reasons for Janz to speak of the de-civication (*Entbürgerlichung*) of the priesthood. Cf. Kuhlemann, Bürgerlichkeit und Religion (op. cit. note 9), 116 ff., passim.
58   Cf. Kuhlemann, Bürgerlichkeit und Religion (op. cit. note 9), 353 ff.
59   Cf. James Thrower, Religion. The Classical Theories, Edinburgh 1999. Religion as experience (op. cit., 49 ff.), religion as psychological construct (op. cit., 161 ff.) and religion as social construct (op. cit., 161 ff.) determined the creation of paradigms until the twenties.
60   Cf. Kuhlemann, Bürgerlichkeit und Religion (op. cit. note 9), 353 ff.
61   So Nipperdey, Deutsche Geschichte, vol. 1 (op. cit. note 2), 475 ff.
62   Cf. Reeken, Kirchen (op. cit. note 9), 351 ff.
63   Cf. Kuhlemann, Bürgerlichkeit und Religion (op. cit. note 9), 291 f.
64   Cf. Kittel, Konfessioneller Konflikt (op. cit. note 3), 257.
65   Nipperdey, Deutsche Geschichte, vol. 1 (op. cit. note 2), 529.
66   Cf. Besier, APU im Weimarer Staat (op. cit. note 13), 57. See also Kuhlemann, Bürgerlichkeit und Religion (op. cit. note 9), 307 ff., 348 ff.
67   Cf. Besier, APU im Weimarer Staat (op. cit. note 14), 187 ff.

68 That is how Stoecker in 1871 once hailed the empire's establishment. Cf. Walter Frank, Hofprediger Adolf Stoecker und die christlichsoziale Bewegung, Hamburg ²1935, 27 f. On the mental overcoming of the French Revolution through the military victory of Germany 1870/71 cf. also Heinrich August Winkler, Germany: The Long Road West, vol. 1: 1789–1933, Oxford 2006, 192 ff.

69 Different from the first volume of Nipperdey's "Deutsche Geschichte", where he contents with the heading "Die Katholiken" ("The Catholics") (op. cit. note 2, 428), it reads in the 1988 pre-publication of the chapter on religion "Sieg des Ultramontanismus" ("Victory of Ultramontanism") (Thomas Nipperdey, Religion im Umbruch. Deutschland 1879–1918, München 1988, 9). The following text remained unchanged.

70 Cf. Kittel, Konfessioneller Konflikt (op. cit. note 3), 247 f. Cf. with this the term coined by Nipperdey, *Moralprotestantismus* (Moral Protestantism) (Deutsche Geschichte, vol. 1 [op. cit. note 2], 475). Reeken, Kirchen (op. cit. note 9), 220 ff.

71 Cf. Albrecht Langner, 'Weimarer Kulturkatholizismus und interkonfessionelle Probleme', in Anton Rauscher (ed.), Probleme des Konfessionalismus in Deutschland seit 1800, Paderborn 1984, 71–115; Hürten, Deutsche Katholiken (op. cit. note 15), esp. 144 ff.

72 Cf. Kittel, Konfessioneller Konflikt (op. cit. note 3), 258 ff.

73 Cf. Prüfer, Sozialismus statt Religion (op. cit. note 17), 101 ff.

74 This one and the following example by Thomas Fandel, Konfession und Nationalsozialismus. Evangelische und katholische Pfarrer in der Pfalz 1930–1939, Paderborn 1997, 94.

75 Cf. Jeffery Verhey, Der "Geist von 1914" und die Erfindung der Volksgemeinschaft, Hamburg 2000, esp. 355 ff. As myth of the "national community", of the re-establishment of social unity, this "spirit" indeed lived on in the different spectra of political Weimar.

76 Cf. Besier, APU im Weimarer Staat (op. cit. note 14), 58 ff.

77 Cf. e. g. Matthias Wolfes, 'Die Demokratiefähigkeit liberaler Theologen. Ein Beitrag zum Verhältnis des Protestantismus zur Weimarer Republik', in Rüdiger vom Bruch (ed.) Friedrich Naumann in seiner Zeit, Berlin-New York 2000, 287–314.

78 Cf. Norbert Friedrich, '"National, Sozial, Christlich". Der Evangelische Reichsausschuß der Deutschnationalen Volkspartei in der Weimarer Republik', in Kirchliche Zeitgeschichte 6 (1993), 290–311; idem, "Die christlich-soziale Fahne empor!" Reinhard Mumm und die christlich-soziale Bewegung (KuG 14), Stuttgart 1997, esp. 219 ff.

79 Quoted after Hans Fenske, Deutsche Parteigeschichte. Von den Anfängen bis zur Gegenwart, Paderborn 1994, 168

80 Cf. Gerhard Besier, 'Der Dom in der Weimarer Republik und im Dritten Reich', in Der Berliner Dom. Zur Zeitgeschichte der Gegenwart der Oberpfarr- und Domkirche zu Berlin, Berlin 2001, 197–209.

81 Cf. Friedrich Martin Balzer/Gert Wendelborn, "Wir sind keine stummen Hunde." Heinz Kappes (1893–1988). Christ und Sozialist in der Weimarer Republik, Bonn 1994; see also Gerhard Besier, '"Ihm wurde die Fähigkeit aberkannt, zu den Prüfungen der Landeskirche in Baden zugelassen zu werden." Albert Böhler (1908–1990) – Heidelberger Theologiestudent, Religiöser Sozialist und deutscher Emigrant', in Heide-Marie Lauterer et al. (eds), Geschichte und Politik. Festschrift Soell, Heidelberg 2004, 79–122.

82 This, so Jochen-Christoph Kaiser ('Die Formierung des protestantischen Milieus. Konfessionelle Vergesellschaftung im 19. Jahrhundert', in Olaf Blaschke/Frank-Michael Kuhlemann [eds], Religion im Kaiserreich. Milieus – Mentalitäten – Krisen [Religiöse Kulturen der Moderne 2], Gütersloh 1996, 257–289, here: 286) was especially the case for financial reasons in inner missions.

83 Cf. the examples of cooperation: Expropriation of the Sovereigns (*Fürstenenteignung*), the Revaluation Movement (*Aufwertungsbewegung*) and the Ruhr Iron Conflict (*Ruhreisenstreit*) by Besier, Die APU im Weimarer Staat (op. cit. note 13), 170 ff.

84   See on Dibelius, who's influence on protestantism in the Weimar Republic can not be underestimated, Hartmut Fritz, Otto Dibelius. Ein Kirchenmann in der Zeit zwischen Monarchie und Diktatur, Göttingen 1998.
85   Otto Dibelius, Nachspiel. Eine Aussprache mit den Freunden und Kritikern des 'Jahrhunderts der Kirche', Berlin 1928, 91.
86   So Nipperdey, Deutsche Geschichte, vol. 1 (op. cit. note 2), 530. Wolfgang Beutin (in Peter Dinzelbacher [ed.], Europäische Mentalitätsgeschichte. Hauptthemen in Einzeldarstellungen, Stuttgart 1993, 150), writes summing up: "The religiousness, the way it was propagated by the administrative church and the way it was vastly absorbed by the public from the 19th to the first half of the 20th century, is best characterised through its amalgamation with secular politics."
87   Hans-Ulrich Wehler, Deutsche Gesellschaftsgeschichte, vol. 3, München 1995, 938 ff.
88   Michael Stürmer, Das ruhelose Reich. Deutschland 1866–1918, Berlin 1983, 15, 406.
89   Heinrich August Winkler (ed.), Nationalismus, Königstein/Ts. 1978, 6. On the change of meaning of the "national confession" after 1878/79, cf. Winkler, Germany: The Long Road, 213 ff. (op. cit. note 68).
90   Cf. Hedda Gramley, Propheten des deutschen Nationalismus. Theologen, Historiker und Nationalökonomen (1848–1880), Frankfurt a. M.-New York 2001.
91   Cf. Wolfgang Altgeld, Katholizismus, Protestantismus, Judentum. Über religiös begründete Gegensätze und nationalreligiöse Ideen in der Geschichte des Nationalismus, Mainz 1992, 166.
92   Cf. on this Peter Walkenhorst, 'Nationalismus als "politische Religion"? Zur religiösen Dimension nationalistischer Ideologie im Kaiserreich', in Blaschke/Kuhlemann (eds), Religion im Kaiserreich (op. cit. note 82), 503–529; Frank Becker, 'Konfessionelle Nationsbilder im Deutschen Kaiserreich', in Haupt/Langewiesche (eds), Nation und Religion (op. cit. note 11), 389–418, esp. 415 ff.
93   Cf. Peter L. Berger, Zur Dialektik von Religion und Gesellschaft, Frankfurt a. M. 1988, 87.
94   Cf. Thomas Luckmann, Die unsichtbare Religion, Frankfurt a. M. 1991, 93.
95   Peter Berghoff, Der Tod des politischen Kollektivs. Politische Religion und das Sterben und Töten für Volk, Nation und Rasse, Berlin 1997, 78 f.
96   Cf. Dieter Gosewinkel, Einbürgern und ausschließen. Die Nationalisierung der Staatsangehörigkeit vom Deutschen Bund bis zur Bundesrepublik Deutschland, Göttingen 2001, esp. 340 ff.
97   Cf. Gerhard Besier, 'Die Evangelische Kirche der altpreußischen Union, die Ökumene und die Protestanten in Westpolen', in Kirchliche Zeitgeschichte 15 (2002), 86–127.
98   Cf. Emile Durkheim, Die elementaren Formen religiösen Lebens, Frankfurt a. M. ³1984, 561 ff.
99   Cf. Lucian Hölscher (ed.), Datenatlas zur religiösen Geographie im protestantischen Deutschland. Von der Mitte des 19. Jahrhunderts bis zum Zweiten Weltkrieg, vol. 1, Berlin-New York 2001, 4 ff.
100 Cf. Gerhard Anschütz, Die Verfassung des Deutschen Reiches vom 11. August 1919. Ein Kommentar für Wissenschaft und Praxis, Berlin ¹⁴1933, 629, 646 f.
101 Hölscher, Datenatlas, vol. 1 (op. cit. note 99), 5.
102 For tests on measuring Christian religiousness in the present cf. e. g. Robert Kecskes/ Christof Wolf, 'Christliche Religiosität. Konzepte, Indikatoren, Meßinstrumente', in Kölner Zeitschrift für Soziologie und Sozialpsychologie 45 (1993), 270–287.
103 On the regional incline of Protestant churchliness cf. Hölscher, Datenatlas, vol. 1 (op. cit. note 99), 18 f.
104 Cf. Johannes-Georg Sternberg, Kirchenaustritte in Preußen 1847 bis 1933 im Lichte der kirchlichen Publizistik als Anfrage an die evangelische Kirche, Bochum 1992.
105 Hölscher, Datenatlas, vol. 1 (op. cit. note 99), 16.
106 Cf. Hölscher, Datenatlas, vol. 4 (op. cit. note 99), 696.
107 Ibid. 699.
108 Ibid. 700.

109 Ibid. 703 f.
110 Cf. Jörg Kniffka, Das kirchliche Leben in Berlin-Ost in der Mitte der Zwanziger Jahre. Eine Untersuchung der kirchlichen Teilnahme und ihrer Motivation in evangelischen Arbeitergemeinden von 1924–1927, Münster 1972, 11.
111 On the *Soziale Arbeitsgemeinschaft Berlin-Ost* (S.A.G.), which performed such studies, see Stefan Grotefeld, Friedrich Siegmund-Schultze. Ein deutscher Ökumeniker und christlicher Pazifist (Heidelberger Untersuchungen zu Widerstand, Judenverfolgung und Kirchenkampf im Dritten Reich, vol. 7), Gütersloh 1995, 73 ff.; Kordula Schlösser-Kost, Evangelische Kirche und soziale Fragen 1918–1933 (Schriftenreihe des Vereins für Rheinische Kirchengeschichte, vol. 120), Köln 1996, 92 ff.
112 Günther Dehn, Die religiöse Gedankenwelt der Proletarierjugend, Berlin (1923) [2]1924.
113 Cf. Paul Piechowski, Proletarischer Glaube in sozialistischen und kommunistischen Selbstzeugnissen, Berlin [3]1928.
114 Cf. Günter Kehrer, 'Soziale Klassen und Religion in der Weimarer Republik', in Hubert Cancik (ed.), Religions- und Geistesgeschichte der Weimarer Republik, Düsseldorf 1982, 67–89.
115 Gerhard Jacobi, Tagebuch eines Großstadtpfarrers. Briefe an einen Freund, Berlin (1929) [8]1930, 67.
116 Kirchliches Jahrbuch, 1932, 14.
117 Kirchliches Jahrbuch, 1932, 19.
118 On the Prussian area see my analysis 'APU im Weimarer Staat' (op. cit. note 13), 1919 ff.
119 Kirchliches Jahrbuch, 1919, 307 f.
120 Ibid. 309.
121 Ibid. 311.
122 Ibid.
123 Ibid. 314.
124 Ibid. 318.
125 Ibid. 320.
126 Ibid. 321.
127 Ibid. 323 f.
128 Ibid. 323.
129 Ibid. 329.
130 Kirchliches Jahrbuch, 1920, 332.
131 Cf. Frank Simon-Ritz, Die Organisation einer Weltanschauung. Die freigeistige Bewegung im Wilheminischen Deutschland (Religiöse Kulturen der Moderne, vol. 5), Gütersloh 1997, esp. 154 ff., 166 ff.
132 Cf. Prüfer, Sozialismus statt Religion (op. cit. note 17), 223 ff.
133 Simon-Ritz, Die Organisation einer Weltanschauung (op. cit. note 131), 202.
134 Cf. Jochen-Christoph Kaiser, 'Sozialdemokratie und praktische Religionskritik. Das Beispiel der Kirchenaustrittsbewegung 1878–1914', in Archiv für Sozialgeschichte 22 (1982), 268–298; idem, Arbeiterbewegung und organisierte Religionskritik. Proletarische Freidenkerverbände in Kaiserreich und Weimarer Republik, Stuttgart 1981, 352.
135 Cf. e. g. Paul Scheurlen, Die Sekten der Gegenwart, Stuttgart [2]1921, 5.
136 Cf. Kirchliches Jahrbuch, 1920, 333 f.
137 Cf. Kaiser, Sozialdemokratie (op. cit. note 134), 289 ff.
138 Cf. Simon-Ritz, Die Organisation einer Weltanschauung (op. cit. note 131), 206 ff.
139 For details see Horst Reller et al. (eds), Handbuch Religiöse Gemeinschaften und Weltanschauungen, Gütersloh [5]2000.
140 Cf. on this and on the following Harald Iber, 'Die Apologetische Centrale und der Central-Ausschuß für Innere Mission. Zur Geschichte der Apologetischen Centrale bis 1934', in Theodor Strohm/Jörg Thierfelder (eds), Diakonie im "Dritten Reich",

Heidelberg 1990, 108–124; Matthias Pöhlmann, Kampf der Geister. Die Publizistik der Apologetischen Centrale (1921–1937), Stuttgart 1998, 55 ff.

141 On the apologetic works of the EB see Fleischmann-Bisten, EB (op. cit. note 21), 215.

142 On the *Wittenberger Forschungsheim für Weltanschauungskunde* [Wittenberg Institute for Research on Ideologies] see Pöhlmann, Kampf der Geister (op. cit. note 140), 88 ff.; Besier, APU im Weimarer Staat (op. cit. note 13), 198 f.

143 Pöhlmann, Kampf der Geister (op. cit. note 140), 66.

144 Cf. Rolf Schieder, Religion im Radio. Protestantische Rundfunkarbeit in der Weimarer Republik und im Dritten Reich, Stuttgart 1995, esp. 94 f., 127 f.

145 Cf. on this and on the following Carl Gunther Schweitzer, Antworten des Glaubens. Handbuch der neuen Apologetik, Berlin ²1929.

146 Cf. the article by the liberal theologian Otto Baumgarten about "Englishness in church life", in Die Religion in Geschichte und Gegenwart¹ vol. 2, col. 337–339.

147 Cf. Carl Gunther Schweitzer (ed.), Das religiöse Deutschland der Gegenwart. Ein Handbuch für jedermann, vol. 1: Der allgemein-religiöse Kreis, Berlin 1928.

148 Kirchliches Jahrbuch, 1925, 551; cf. Schlösser-Kost, Evangelische Kirche und Soziale Frage (op. cit. note 111), 199 ff.

149 Cf. Kirchliches Jahrbuch, 1929; Detlef Peukert, Die Weimarer Republik. Krisenjahre der klassischen Moderne, Frankfurt a. M. 1987, 177.

150 Cf. Oskar Goehling, Feiern auf Fahrt. Erfahrungen und Versuche kirchlicher Wochenendarbeit und Betreuung von Ausflüglern aller Art, Berlin 1929; Herbert Jagow, 'Das Wochenende', in Kirchlich-Soziale Blätter, no. 5/6, 1929. Cf. also Hermann Schäfer (ed.), Am siebten Tag. Geschichte des Sonntags, Bonn 2002, esp. 28 ff.

151 Cf. Almuth Püschel, 'Die Einflußnahme von Institutionen der evangelischen Kirche auf die den Film betreffende Gesetzgebung in der Weimarer Republik 1919/20', in J. C. Kaiser/M. Greschat (eds), Sozialer Protestantismus und Sozialstaat. Diakonie und Wohlfahrtspflege in Deutschland 1890 bis 1918, Stuttgart 1996, 423–435.

152 Strafgesetzbuch [criminal code], § 166.

153 Cf. i. e. Kirchliches Jahrbuch, 1930, 446 ff.

154 Impressive is Weber's statement of "breaking the spell on the world": Max Weber, 'Die Protestantische Ethik und der Geist des Kapitalismus (1920)', in Gesammelte Aufsätze zur Religionssoziologie I, Tübingen ⁸1986, 94, 114.

155 Cf. Hartmut Lehmann (ed.), Säkularisierung, Dechristianisierung, Rechristianisierung im neuzeitlichen Europa, Göttingen 1997; idem, 'Zwischen Dechristianisierung und Rechristianisierung. Fragen und Anmerkungen zur Bedeutung des Christentums in Europa und Nordamerika im 19. und 20. Jahrhundert', in Kirchliche Zeitgeschichte 11 (1998), 156–168; idem, Protestantisches Christentum im Prozess der Säkularisierung, Göttingen 2001; Jeffrey Cox, 'Secularization and Other Master Narratives of Religion in Modern Europe', in Kirchliche Zeitgeschichte 14 (2001), 24–35; Michel Lagrée, Durkheim, Weber et Troeltsch, un siècle après, in op. cit., 49–60; Hugh McLeod, Secularisation in Western Europe, 1848–1914, London 2000, 1 ff.

156 Cf. the Reich president's decree of 28 March 1931 to fight political rioting; with its help the state could act against Jehovah's Witnesses. Cf. Detlef Garbe, Zwischen Widerstand und Martyrium. Die Zeugen Jehovas im "Dritten Reich", München ⁴1999, 42, 82 f. See also Pöhlmann, Kampf der Geister (op. cit. note 140), 214 f.

157 Cf. Friedrich Heer, 'Weimar – Ein religiöser und weltanschaulicher Leerraum', in Cancik (ed.), Religions- und Geistesgeschichte (op. cit. note 114), 31–48, esp. 32 ff.

158 So the Wahrheitszeuge 1918, quoted after Erich Geldbach, Freikirchen – Erbe, Gestalt und Wirkung (Bensheimer Hefte 70), Göttingen 1989, 161.

159 Cf. Priebe, Kirchliches Handbuch (op. cit. note 28), 418 ff.

160 Cf. Garbe, Zwischen Widerstand und Martyrium (op. cit. note 156), 58 f.

161 Priebe, Kirchliches Handbuch (op. cit. note 28), 444.

162 So ibid. 459.

163 Cf. Uwe Puschner, Die völkische Bewegung im Kaiserreich. Sprache – Rasse – Religion, Darmstadt 2001.

164 Priebe, Kirchliches Handbuch (op. cit. note 28), 459.
165 Ibid. 461.
166 So Pöhlmann, Kampf der Geister (op. cit. note 140), 140.
167 Ibid. 213 ff.
168 So Michael Burleigh, Das Zeitalter des Nationalsozialismus. Eine Gesamtdarstellung, Frankfurt a. M. 2000, 25. See also Philippe Burrin, 'Political Religion. The Relevance of a Concept', in History and Memory 9 (1997), 321–352; Wolfgang Hardtwig, 'Political Religion in Modern Germany, Reflections on Nationalism, Socialism, and National Socialism', in GHI Bulletin 28 (2001), 3–27.
169 See also Wolfgang Dierker (Himmlers Glaubenskrieger. Der Sicherheitsdienst der SS und seine Religionspolitik 1933–1941, Paderborn 2002, 535–549), who analyses the "specific correlation between ideology and usage" (540) empirically by the religion policies of the SD and tries to interpret his solutions with the figure of "political religion" (esp. 545 ff.).
170 See Eckhard Jesse, 'Die Totalitarismusforschung und ihre Repräsentanten. Konzeptionen von Carl J. Friedrich, Hannah Arendt, Eric Voegelin, Ernst Nolte und Karl Dietrich Bracher', in Aus Politik und Zeitgeschichte. Beilage zur Wochenzeitung "Das Parlament" B 20/1998, 3–46. Critical on that: Simon Tormey, Making Sense of Tyranny. Interpretations of Totalitarianism, Manchester-New York 1995, 38–63.
171 Cf. Hannah Arendt, 'Ideologie und Terror. Eine neue Staatsform', in Bruno Seidel/ Siegfried Jenker (eds), Wege der Totalitarismusforschung (Wege der Forschung 140), Darmstadt 1968, 64–85B. For a critical approach see Simon Tormey, Making sense of tyranny. Interpretations of Totalitarianism, Manchester-New York 1995, 38–63.
172 Cf. Carl Joachim Friedrich/Zbigniew Brzezinski, 'Die allgemeinen Merkmale der totalitären Diktatur', in Eckard Jesse (ed.), Totalitarismus im 20. Jahrhundert. Eine Bilanz der internationalen Forschung, Baden-Baden 1996, 225–236. Critical on the Friedrich-Brzezinski-Approach: Tormey, Making sense (op. cit. note 171), 69–99.
173 See also the approaches by Leonard Schapiro (Totalitarianism, London-Basingstoke, 1972) and Karl-Dietrich Bracher ('Der umstrittene Totalitarismus. Erfahrung und Aktualität [1973]', in idem, Zeitgeschichtliche Kontroversen. Um Faschismus, Totalitarismus, Demokratie, München ⁵1984, 34–62).
174 "The ascent of totalitarian movements and dictatorships is difficult to imagine without the means of ideological seduction, which is – in its total dimension – only possible by means of the promise of an ideology enhanced to a political faith, or even a political religion." Karl-Dietrich Bracher, Die totalitäre Erfahrung, München 1987, 196.
175 Hannah Arendt, 'Religion und Politik', in idem, Zwischen Vergangenheit und Zukunft. Übungen im politischen Denken I, ed. by Ursula Ludz, München 1994, 305–326, here: 308.
176 Cf. Jesse (ed.), Die Totalitarismusforschung (op. cit. note 170), 16 f.; Markus Huttner, Totalitarismus und säkulare Religionen. Zur Frühgeschichte totalitarismuskritischer Begriffs- und Theoriebildung in Großbritannien, Bonn 1999, 91 f.
177 Hans Maier (ed.), "Totalitarismus" und "politische Religionen". Konzepte des Diktaturvergleichs (Görres-Gesellschaft zur Pflege der Wissenschaft. Politik- und kommunikationswissenschaftliche Veröffentlichungen der Görres-Gesellschaft 16), vol. 1, Paderborn 1996; idem/Michael Schäfer (eds), Totalitarismus und politische Religionen, vol. 2, Paderborn 1997; vol. 3, Deutungsgeschichte und Theorie, appeared in print in 2003.
178 So Hans Maier, in idem/Schäfer, Totalitarismus (op. cit. note 177), 13.
179 Cf. op. cit. note 13. On totalitarianism see also Jesse (ed.), Totalitarismus (op. cit. note 172), esp. 12, 28 f., 118 f.
180 Cf. for example the different point of view of Hans Mommsen and Julius H. Schoeps in regard to National Socialism, e. g. in Gerhard Besier (ed.), Zwischen "nationaler Revolution" und militärischer Aggression. Transformationen in Kirche und Gesellschaft 1934–1939, München 2000, 43-4-63. See also Hans Maier, 'Deutungen tota-

litärer Herrschaft 1919-1989', in Vierteljahrshefte für Zeitgeschichte 50 (2002), 349-366.

181 Jacob Talmon, Politischer Messianismus. Die romantische Phase, Köln-Opladen 1936, 467. Cf. in general Klaus Hornung, 'Politischer Messianismus. Jacob Talmon und die Genesis der totalitären Diktatur', in idem, Die offene Flanke der Freiheit. Studien zum Totalitarismus im 20. Jahrhundert, Frankfurt a. M. 2001, 39-84.

182 Cf. Christoph Ribbat, Religiöse Erregung. Protestantische Schwärmer im Kaiserreich, Frankfurt a. M.-New York 1996.

183 On the "Zeitschrift für Religionspsychologie", which was founded in 1907, see ibid. 197 ff.

184 Cf. Andrew Newberg/Eugene d'Aquili/Vince Rause, Why God won't go away. Brain Science and the Biology of Belief, New York 2001. See also Harald Welzer, Das kommunikative Gedächtnis. Eine Theorie der Erinnerung, München 2002; Stefan Klein, Die Glücksformel oder Wie gute Gefühle entstehen, Reinbek bei Hamburg 2002; Johann Grolle, 'Hotline zum Himmel', in Der Spiegel 21/2002, 190-201; Wolf Singer, 'Wahrnehmen, Erinnern, Vergessen. Über den Nutzen der Hirnforschung für die Geschichtswissenschaft', in Frankfurter Allgemeine Zeitung no. 226, 28. Sept. 2000, 10.

185 On the classical concepts of Eric Voegelin, Raymon Aron and Frederick A. Voigt see Eric Voegelin, Die Politischen Religionen (Wien 1938; Stockhom-Berlin ²1939), ed. by Peter J. Opitz, München 1993; Dietmar Herz, ,Die politischen Religionen im Werk Eric Voegelins', in Hans Maier, Totalitarismus und Politische Religion, vol. 1 (op. cit. note 177), 191-209; Hans-Christof Kraus, ,Eric Voegelin redivivus? Politische Wissenschaft als Politische Theologie', in Michael Ley/Julius H. Schoeps (eds), Der Nationalsozialismus als politische Religion, Bodenheim 1997, 74-88; Huttner, Totalitarismus und säkulare Religionen (op. cit. note 176), 145 ff.; Michael Henkel, Konservativismus im politischen Denken Eric Voegelins. Überlegungen zum Problem der Verortung seines Ansatzes, München 2001, esp. 9 ff. In 1939, Raymond Aron spoke of „political religions", in 1944 of „secular religions". Cf. on this Brigitte Gess, ,Die Totalitarismuskonzeption von Raymond Aron und Hannah Arendt', in Maier (ed.), Totalitarismus und Politische Religion (op. cit. note 177), 264-274, esp. 265 f.; Harald Seubert, 'Erinnerung an den "Engagierten Beobachter" in veränderter Zeit. Über Raymond Aron als Theoretiker des Totalitarismus und der nuklearen Weltlage', in Maier/Schäfer (eds), "Totalitarismus" und "politische Religionen" (op. cit. note 177), 311-361.

186 Cf. already George L. Mosse, Nationalisierung der Massen. Politische Symbolik und Massenbewegungen von den Napoleonischen Kriegen bis zum Dritten Reich, Frankfurt a. M. 1993, esp. 91 ff.

187 Cf. Arlie J. Hoover, The Gospel of Nationalism. German Patriotic Preaching from Napoleon to Versailles, Stuttgart 1986; idem, God, Germany, and Britain in the Great War. A Study in Clerical Nationalism, New York 1989; Hartmut Lehmann, 'The Germans as a Chosen People. Old Testament Themes in German Nationalism', in German Studies Review 14 (1991), 261-274.

188 Cf. Hans Maier, 'Die Politischen Religionen und die Bilder', in Historische Zeitschrift, Beiheft 33, 2002, 485-507.

189 Cf. Luckmann, Die unsichtbare Religion (op. cit. note 94), 175 f.

190 This process is not limited to Germany. See, e. g., on Sweden, Kjell Blückert, The Church as Nation, Frankfurt a. M. 2000. For the USA, cf. Martin E. Marty, Pilgrims in Their Own Land. 500 Years of Religion in America, New York-London 1985; Rolf Schieder, Civil Religion. Die religiöse Dimension der politischen Kultur, Gütersloh 1987; Eugene F. Hemrick, One Nation Under God. Religious Symbols, Quotes, and Images in Our Nation's Capital, Huntington 2001. On cultural conceptualising systems (*Sinngebungssysteme*), which provide among others religions in the form of communicative acting, cf. Clifford Geertz, Dichte Beschreibung. Beiträge zum Verstehen kultureller Systeme, Frankfurt a. M. ⁴1995, esp. 49 ff.

191 Cf. on this Manfred Gailus, Protestantismus und Nationalsozialismus. Studien zur nationalsozialistischen Durchdringung des protestantischen Sozialmilieus in Berlin,
Köln 2001, 52 ff.

192 Cf. Gerhard Besier, Die Kirchen und das Dritte Reich, vol. 3: Spaltungen und Abwehrkämpfe 1934–1937, Berlin-München 2001, 276 f.

193 Cf. on this as well as on the following Christoph Weiling, Die "Christlich-deutsche
Bewegung". Eine Studie zum konservativen Protestantismus in der Weimarer Republik, Göttingen 1998, here: 26.

194 Bruno Doehring, Krieg und Kirche, Berlin 1919, 71.

195 Cf. Weiling, CdB (op. cit. note 193), 106 f.

196 Letter Dommes to Wilhelm II, quoted according to op. cit. note 140.

197 Der Reichsbote, quoted according to ibid.

198 Bruno Doehring, Die Fehlleitung der nationalen Bewegung durch Adolf Hitler. Aus
seiner Weltanschauung erklärt, Berlin, no year [1932], 8.

199 Quoted according to Weiling, CdB (op. cit. note 193), 160.

200 On the rapprochement of the CdB and National Socialism cf. ibid. 289 ff.

201 Friedrich Wieneke, Christentum und Nationalsozialismus (Aussprache-Schrift der
Christlich-deutschen Bewegung), Küstrin-Neustadt ²1931, 38 f.

202 Cf. Kurt Salamun, 'Demokratische Kultur und anti-demokratisches Denken. Vorbe-
merkungen zur demokratischen Kultur', in idem (ed.), Geistige Tendenzen der Zeit.
Perspektiven der Weltanschauungstheorie und Kulturphilosophie, Frankfurt a. M. et
al. 1996, 151–165, here: 153 ff.

203 Cf. Besier, Die Kirchen und das Dritte Reich (op. cit. note 192), 653 f.

204 Ibid. 652.

205 Cf. Doris Bergen, Twisted Cross. The German Christian Movement in the Third Reich,
Chapel Hill-London 1996, esp. 119 ff.; Gailus, Protestantismus (op. cit. note 191),
652 ff.

206 See for the term "civil religion" Hermann Lübbe, Religion nach der Aufklärung, Graz-
Wien-Köln 1986, 306 ff.; Rolf Schieder, Civil Religion (op. cit. note 190), esp. 74 ff.
To explain quasi-religious phenomena in Italian fascism, Emilio Gentile (The Sacralisation of Politics in Fascist Italy [London 1996]) does not speak of the paradigm of
"political religion", but of "civil religion". See also idem, 'The Sacralisation of Politics.
Definitions, Interpretations and Reflections on the Question of Secular Religion and
Totalitarism', in Totalitarian Movements and Political Religion 1 (2000), 18–55; Stephen R. Di Rienzo, 'The Non-Optional Basis of Religion', in Totalitarian Movements
and Political Religion 3 (2002), 75–98.

207 Daniel R. Borg, 'German National Protestantism as a Civil Religion', in Menachem
Mor (ed.), International Perspectives on Church and State, Omaha 1993, 255–267,
quote: 258.

208 Cf. Besier, Die Kirchen und das Dritte Reich (op. cit. note 192), 215 ff.

209 Cf. Gerhard Besier, 'Die Heidelberger Theologische Fakultät unter dem Nationalsozialismus', in Wolfgang U. Eckart/Volker Sellin/Eike Wolgast (eds), Die Ruprecht-Karls-
Universität Heidelberg im Nationalsozialismus, Heidelberg 2004, 173–260.

210 Cf. Hölscher, Datenatlas, vol. 4 (op. cit. note 99), 704.

211 Cf. Frank-Lothar Kroll, Utopie als Ideologie. Geschichtsdenken und politisches
Handeln im Dritten Reich, Paderborn 1998; Claus-Ekkehard Bärsch, Die politische
Religion des Nationalsozialismus, München ²2002.

212 Cf. Besier, Die Kirchen und das Dritte Reich (op. cit. note 192), 241 ff.

213 Cf. on this Martin Rissmann, Hitlers Gott. Vorsehungsglaube und Sendungsbewusst-
sein des deutschen Diktators, Zürich 2001.

214 M. Rainer Lepsius, 'Das Modell der charismatischen Herrschaft und seine Anwend-
barkeit auf den "Führerstaat" Adolf Hitlers', in idem, Demokratie in Deutschland.
Soziologisch-historische Konstellationsanalysen, Göttingen 1993, 95–118, here: 117.

Seventy Years after "Machtergreifung".
The German Churches' Political Stance 1933–2003*

Churches and religious communities in 1933

When Hitler seized power Germany was practically bi-denominational country. Approximately 63 percent of the population (in figures 39.5 million) were members of the Protestant state churches and 32 percent (24.5 million) were Roman Catholics. Of the smaller religious and ideological groups, the Jewish communities were the largest with an total of 0.8 percent of the population (or half a million believers).[1] There were considerable differences in mentality between the two largest denominations. While Roman Catholicism had ceased being the "Church of the Empire" after the decline of the Holy Roman Empire in 1806 and independent from state protection it had developed into a strong power in society paired with solid milieus[2], Protestantism first experienced the division of Church and state at the beginning of the Weimar Republic. Neither before 1918 nor after did Protestantism manage to create mass structures to rival those of the Catholics. There was no "Protestant party" and Protestant associations could not be compared with Catholic organisations neither in size nor internal consistency.[3] A socialist subculture, which was quite heterogeneous in itself, contributed considerably to loosen religious bonds, especially in milieus with a Protestant background. The majority of people did not adopt the Socialist rites of passage, however, they distanced themselves from those, which the churches offered. The Church's complaint about the "dying Sunday" pointed to the fact that after the constitutional division of Church and state many people no longer felt obliged to go to church.[4] Nevertheless this process of distancing oneself from the Church had already begun in the last third of the nineteenth century and would gain more ground.

The National Socialist movement as a hope of new departures for the churches

Both for the ideologically indifferent and for the official representatives of the churches the National Socialist movement appeared to offer great hope. Some saw in it a modern response to the crisis of the day and looked to a new future under vigorous Nazi leadership. On the other hand many bishops and lay members of the Church establishment counted on a state-supported re-Christianisa-

*   Paper delivered at the University of Notre Dame (Indiana, USA) and at the University of Lund (Sweden) in spring 2002. The text was first published in *KZG/CCH* 16 (2003), 463–487.

tion and trusted that the conditions as they existed before 1919 would be restored. Both believed that the unifying factor of religion was vital for Germany's political future.[5]

Hitler won support from the churches with his government's declaration on 23 March 1933, which contained far-reaching assurances to the churches calling them the "most important factors for the preservation of our ethnicity". Protestants particularly were reminded of the "spirit of 1914" and were gratified to see growing numbers of church-goers. They presumed the churches would be included in the "national revolution" in the weeks that followed 30 January 1933. The vast majority was not affected by the measures taken against political, ideological and religious minorities and therefore took a rather indifferent stance towards their persecution. The new government's clear breaches of human rights raised no critique from the churches. Indeed many Protestants welcomed the restrictions of fundamental rights and viewed the harsh measures for the development of the dictatorship as a step to the reestablishment of law and order.[6]

In the declaration on 28 March 1933 the Catholic episcopacy recanted its condemnations of National Socialism, which it had expressed in previous years. Catholicism had a significantly smaller problem with National Socialism because believers and theologians were hardly affected by this "political religion". With the help of the Reich Concordat and by assuming a diplomatic position the Catholic Church believed it would be able to defend its rights even under a dictatorship.[7] The "anti-bolshevism" stance, which it shared with National Socialism, was for both churches an important factor in the ideological and political consensus.

Attempts to synthesize Christianity and National Socialism

A Protestant group attempted to create an assimilation of National Socialism and Christianity even before Hitler has seized power. These were the so-called German Christians (*Deutsche Christen*, DC). This new ideology had multiple sources. The *völkische Bewegung* ('national' or 'ethnic' movement), which appeared in the last third of the nineteenth century, played a significant role.[8] The younger generation of pastors were greatly influenced by this *völkisch* and national body of thought.[9] Even the majority of the small opposition group from Confessing Church (*Bekennende Kirche*, BK) within the Church was of the opinion that National Socialism had created a political system, which was appropriate for the Germans. They only wanted to keep the Church out of the hands of those Nazis, who advocated state control, a position which would soon prove illusory. Although the German Christians (DC) were also a minority, it may be assumed that the majority of Church members, who were not very close to the Church shared the vast part of the German Christians' convictions. The readiness to be obedient to state authorities and an opportunistic philosophy of survival played their parts. Had the more radical Nazis not continually distanced themselves from the DC and expelled them with ever increasing determination from their own "movement", a final victory of the DC-movement and the creation of a "national church" may have resulted. After all the decline of the "Confessing Church" after 1938 was obvious. The so-called "intact" churches of Hanover, Württemberg and Bavaria were more ready to compromise than the "destroyed" Prussian churches.[10] Whereas the former did not want to endanger their status, the latter had nothing left to lose. This deserves to be interpreted beyond inter-Protestant denominational differences.

The privileged position of the churches in post-war Germany

The end of Second World War led to the breakdown of German society, with the exception of the churches. The Western Allies were aware that the churches had heavily compromised themselves, but they were convinced that due to the conditions in their own countries that a democratic society could not be built without Christianity. This is why they granted privileges to the churches and gave them much scope for renewed activity. However, under pressure from the Allies both the major churches had to draft an admission of guilt. From then on the Stuttgart Declaration of Guilt issued in October 1945 was a notable document but it caused considerable objections in many Protestant circles.[11] Much more welcome was the attempt made by the churches to see themselves as resistance organizations, which was an interpretation strongly supported by the early post-war historiography of the Confessing Church.[12] Within Protestantism the old dispute among Lutherans and United Protestants revived in summer 1945. In order to circumvent this problem the traditional structures of the state churches were maintained and reforms were mostly foregone.[13]

On the larger scale Protestants and Catholics were united in a common negative stance towards the Allies' military occupation policies. In their struggle against denazification they withdrew to a position of legal positivism, which made all efforts of the Allies appear as vindictive legislation. Furthermore, they frequently explained their own former positive attitudes towards National Socialism as venial, comprehensible political errors in reason and pleaded for an end to all attempts to brand Germans with collective guilt.[14] With this interpretation the Church leadership responded to the expectations of Church members and improved their social reputation. Yet, there was no lasting "movement of return to the churches". The number of people joining the churches reached its peak in 1946. In 1949, however, 86,000 people left the Church compared to 43,000 new members. Thus after a brief interruption the erosion of folk Protestantism continued. The Roman Catholic Church was initially spared this erosion but in the nineteen-sixties its sphere also began to shrink.

Churches and Church policy in the GDR

In 1949 as the GDR was established, 80.5 percent of the population were members of the Protestant Church, whereas by 1989 the figure had sunk to a mere 23 percent while the level of people leaving the Church remained high until the mid-nineteen-seventies, the low points were reached in 1958 and 1975. From the mid-nineteen-seventies the numbers of leavers sank or was balanced out by people joining the Church. After the collapse of the GDR the number of leavers once again increased.[15] The Roman Catholic Church found itself in a classical minority position. Due to the refugees from the former East German regions (now belonging to Poland) and the Sudetenland, the number of Catholics increased from 4.7 percent to 13.9 percent between 1945 and 1949, but by 1954 it had dropped by a third because of further migration and people emigrating. In 1989 only 4.5 percent of the population were Catholics.[16]

Two of the eight Protestant state churches and seven Catholic dioceses (*Jurisdiktionsbezirke*) on the territory of the GDR suffered severe losses of territories and members due to the new frontier with Poland along the rivers Oder and Neiße. These political factors caused substantial reassessments in Church policy and required special efforts for the necessary restructuring. Even in 1945 the "Conference of Eastern Churches" was established, from 1951 it was known as the "Conference of Governing Bodies of the Protestant Churches in the territory of the GDR" (*Konferenz der Kirchenleitungen*, KKL).[17] After the establishment of both German states the Catholic Church also established a regional bishops' board on the territory of the GDR, which was called "Berlin Conference of Diocesan Authorities" (*Berliner Ordinarienkonferenz*, BOK).[18]

The Soviet Military Administration (SMAD), which ruled Eastern Germany at that time, initially gave the churches free reign. The SED (Socialist Unity Party), which was established through the forced unification of the Communist (KPD) and Social Democratic (SPD) Parties in February 1946, originally expressed its tolerance and will to cooperate with religious convictions and churches. This behaviour, which was mainly motivated by tactical reasons, was based on the basic principles, which were formulated since 1944 by the "working group for religious questions" of the National Committee For A Free Germany (*Nationales Komitee Freies Deutschland*, NKFD) in the USSR.[19] After 1945 some clergymen in the NKFD had a secondary function as secret informants to the Soviet and later in the GDR secret service. In 1947 the "Department for Church, Christendom and Religion" was integrated in the party structure[20], while from 1949 on Walter Ulbricht's "Small Secretariat" or some ad-hoc commissions of the Politburo were appointed to treat Church questions. In 1950 a department for "Churches and Religious Questions" was established within the SED State Administration[21], which was made an independent department in 1954[22]. The leaders of the Eastern Christian Democratic Union (CDU) also appointed a "Main Department on Church Questions".[23] From the beginning the State Security Department (*Ministerium für Staatssicherheit*, MfS) i. e. the Secret Service of East Germany, which was established in 1950, worked for the SED on Church issues.[24] The "political police" K5, which came into existence in 1947 and worked closely with the Soviet

Committee for a Free Germany, had already been dealing with Church questions.[25] Still in 1950 the "Main Department for Contact with the Churches" was instituted under the rule of Otto Nuschke, the Deputy Minister President and Chairman of the CDU. This department remained active until Nuschke's death in 1957, however, it gradually lost importance.[26] During the entire existence of the GDR the SED was convinced. due to its ideological principles, that the churches would eventually die out. The only matter of discussion over the years was the idea of how the state-Church relationship, which was expected to be time limited, should be organised.

. The first and only summit meeting (*"Spitzengespräch"*) between representatives of the state and churches of both denominations took place in April 1950, with the aim of ending the Church's opposition to the Communist developments in society. Minister-president Otto Grotewohl, Walther Ulbricht, Otto Nuschke and MfS-Minister Wilhelm Zaisser among others took part as representatives of the state. This meeting only achieved a temporary respite[27], which was destroyed by the forced Stalinization in 1952/53[28]. After Stalin's death the SED gave up its policy of repression against the "Youth Communities" and "Protestant Student Communities" at the beginning of 1953. A second summit meeting with representatives from the Protestant churches ended with the issuing of a communiqué stating that the conflict was over.[29] However, in 1954 the atheist youth consecration ceremony enactment caused a new escalation. The so-called youth consecration ceremony (*Jugendweihe*) was a secular rite of passage, which was offered by the state and was intended for children of about 13 or 14 years of age. Its aim was to gradually offer a substitute for religious rites such as communion and confirmation, which were maintained by the churches. This aim was almost achieved, if one considers that to date, about 13 years after the fall of the GDR, the majority of young East Germans prefer the youth consecration ceremony to its religious equivalent.[30]

In the spring of 1957 the office of the "State Secretary for Church Questions" replaced Nuschke's "main department".[31] In a third summit meeting on 21 July 1958 the representatives of the Protestant Church declared that they acknowledged the development towards Socialism in the GDR ("Church within Socialism").[32] Prior to these talks the state had managed to drive a wedge between the leaders of the Protestant churches by finding certain individuals, who were ready to cooperate with the regime, such as the Bishop of Thuringia, Moritz Mitzenheim.[33] Furthermore, the State Security Department (MfS) had started to successfully infiltrate the churches up to the level of bishop with "unofficial collaborators" (IMs). After building the Berlin Wall in 1961 the SED Party wanted to split the Protestant national umbrella organisation, the Confederation of Protestant Churches of Germany (*Evangelische Kirche in Deutschland*, EKD). In 1967 the EKD Synod still rejected this demand[34], but the basis of discussion changed when a new GDR constitution was introduced in 1968[35]. When the Federation of Protestant Churches in the GDR (*Bund der Evangelischen Kirchen in der DDR*, BEK) was established[36], a new phase in state-Church relations began, the highpoints of which were marked by the fourth summit meeting of BEK chairman Bishop Albrecht Schönherr and state President Erich Honecker on 6 March

1978[37] and the agreement for cooperation between state and Church during the (500th) Martin Luther anniversary year in 1983[38]. An example of the poor way of "solving" conflicts during this period is the appeasement policy followed when dealing with the suicide of pastor Oskar Brüsewitz in 1976, who burnt himself to death in protest about the lack of religious freedom in the GDR.[39] After having criticized the West German state-Church-relationship in connection with the rearmament policy in 1983[40], in 1984/85 BEK Chairman Bishop Johannes Hempel could speak of a "fundamental trust", which existed between the Church and state in the GDR.[41] However, soon after Hempel's summit meeting with Honecker in mid-February 1985[42] the tensions between state and Church grew stronger once again because of the opposition groups, who gathered on the fringes of the churches and the repressions directed against them. Nevertheless, leading members of the BEK still stood up for a democratically renewed GDR, however then and even after 1989 their vision was of a socialist state.[43]

In contrast to the Protestants the Catholic Church kept a clear distance from the SED state until 1974. Despite the bishops' resistance Pope Paul VI opted for a policy of détente in 1974.[44] In 1976 an independent Berlin board of bishops was established.[45] However, the separation from West German Catholicism, which was already planned, was never fulfilled in the end thanks to the new pope. Pope John Paul II was a decided adversary of the Eastern bloc.[46]

The division of the Protestant Church in Germany

Against the backdrop of the Cold War the SED regime in East Germany tried to force the eastern member churches to leave the EKD, the VELKD (Union of Lutheran Churches) and the EKU (United Churches formerly in Prussia). The treaty signed by the EKD and the western Federal Republic of Germany in 1957 concerning pastoral care in the armed forces was the occasion for the German Democratic Republic (GDR) to demand the division of these organisations.[47] The GDR's state secretariat for Church questions, which was established on 1 April 1957 and led by Werner Eggerath (1957–1960), Hans Seigewasser (1960–1979), Klaus Gysi (1979–1988) and Kurt Löffler (1988–1989), received orders to only maintain contact with the eight churches existing within the boundaries of the GDR.[48] On 17 May 1958 GDR Minister President Otto Grotewohl cut diplomatic contacts with the EKD's appointee for the GDR, Heinrich Grüber.[49] In 1962 one year after the building of the Berlin Wall, the Conference of Governing Bodies of the Protestant Churches in GDR (abbreviated as KKL – *Konferenz der Kirchenleitungen*), instituted its own office in East Berlin, which was run by the young Church lawyer, Manfred Stolpe.[50] In 1967 the Politburo of the Communist SED party, which ruled East Germany, insisted on the existence of two divided German nations and refused to grant any legitimacy to a "pan-German" Protestant Church organisation (EKD). In the same year the EKD synod in Fürstenwalde refused to consent to the GDR government's demand for dividing and possibly disbanding the EKD.[51] However, the Protestant student communities (*Evange-*

lische Studentengemeinden, ESG) and the Work Group of Protestant Youth (*Arbeits-gemeinschaft der evangelischen Jugend*, AEJ) split in 1967.[52] One of the causes, alongside the structural impediments to any cooperation, was the one-sided political indoctrination of young people.

However, against the backdrop of the new GDR constitution of 1968, Bishop Moritz Mitzenheim of Thuringia declared on 29 February 1968: "The state boundaries of GDR also constitute the limits for an organisation of the churches."[53] Without any prior consultation with their western partner churches the eastern churches of the VELKD (Union of Lutheran Churches) left the organisation in order to form the separate VELKDDR in 1968.[54] In 1969 the establishment of the Federation of Protestant Churches in the GDR (*Bund der Evangelischen Kirchen in der DDR*, BEK) followed. This was an organisation totally independent from the (western) EKD.[55] However, the official recognition of the BEK by the SED state did not occur until 24 February 1971.[56] A reason for this delay may have been article 4, paragraph 4 of the constitution of the BEK, which stated: "The Federation acknowledges a special union of the entire Protestant Christianity in Germany."[57] As a kind of contradiction to this affirmation of unity, attempts were made to give theological reasons for this institutional detachment from the EKD. A peculiar interpretation of the theological theories proposed by Karl Barth and Dietrich Bonhoeffer, as well as of the so-called *"Darmstädter Wort"*, the Declaration of Darmstadt of 1947, which acknowledged the mistakes made by the Protestant churches during the Third Reich, served this purpose.[58] In addition to the slogans "Church for the others" and "community of witness and service", the ambivalent expression "Church within Socialism" was used.[59] When trying to shape a theological profile of the BEK, the theologians in question profited from differing concepts of what a Church is, as could be seen in the rival views expressed in German Protestantism since 1949. The BEK saw itself ever increasingly as the true "Confessing Church", which however was being scorned on by the West. Some theologians from the Federal Republic and from the ecumenical movement agreed with this estimation, thus reinforcing this self-assessment.[60] In this regard the western EKD seemed to be a rich façade organisation that was bound to capitalism and militarism, preserving only a few spiritual qualities.

Yet at the same time substantial ties between the east and west branches of the EKD remained. The western EKD continued to give strong financial and manifold support to its sister organisation.[61] The western churches subsidized their eastern partners in a variety of ways, despite the differences of political view, which were often openly expressed. For example, in order to promote such closer relations both at the parish and regional level a so-called "advisory board", consisting of members of both federations, was engaged in 1969[62], followed by an additional "consultation board" in 1980[63]. The protocols of their meetings document the ambivalence of closeness and at the same time a growing estrangement. Despite this, subsidies for the maintenance of partner parishes as well as for building costs and even for the "rescue" of Church personnel in danger from the GDR's secret police, were paid for by the western churches to the GDR.

Plans for a reform of the state churches and for the formation of a "United Protestant Church of the GDR" (*Vereinigte Evangelische Kirche in der DDR*, VEK), which had been on the table since the end of the nineteen-seventies, failed due to the opposition of some individual land churches.[64] However, this discussion led to a self-dissolution of the VELKDDR.[65] After the fall of the GDR in 1989 some representatives of the EKD and BEK declared their desire for a re-unification of state and Church in the Loccum declaration on 17 January 1990.[66] On the other hand some left-wing church representatives sought to present an alternative strategy, for example as expressed in the "Berlin Declaration" on 9 February 1990.[67] Nevertheless these opinions were ignored and the re-unification process took place faster than expected. It was essentially completed by June 1991.[68]

On the history of a change: "Church within socialism"

The re-organisation of the eight eastern state churches in the Federation of Protestant Churches in the GDR (BEK) at the end of the nineteen-sixties was followed by a theological "reconsideration". The result of which was the ambiguous expression "a Church within socialism". This expression seemed ideal as a central category of an ecclesiological theory because it allowed different self and external descriptions and thus enabled both the SED state and the churches to follow a flexible policy. However, this undefined expression was motivated and limited by the (contemporary) historical and ideological frame of the "first German socialist" constitution of 1968. The state secretary for Church questions in the GDR, Hans Seigewasser, proclaimed the principle that the Church policy had to submit itself to general politics for the benefit of a full development of the "socialist human society".[69] Although some theologians (H. J. Fränkel) expressed a substantial critique of the expression "socialist" and of its actual meaning during the GDR-dictatorship the conference of the bishops of the Protestant Churches in the GDR declared on 15 February 1968: "As citizens of a socialist state, we face the task of manifesting socialism as a more just form of co-existence."[70] This self-assessment was regarded as an important phase on the "path" towards a "learning process". There had already been some bench marks. For example, a common declaration from the state and the Church in 1958 stated: "They [that is, the Christians in the GDR] respect the development toward socialism and contribute to a peaceful establishment of everyday life."[71] In his formulation on the "foundations of the relationship between state and church" from 1962 Manfred Stolpe, the architect of the BEK, had already used the expression "Church within socialism" in describing this relationship.[72] The concept of socialism was definitely integrated in the Church's teachings during the Federal Synod of Eisenach in 1971.[73] From then on many BEK-theologians adopted this propagandistic key expression from their political-social surroundings without reflecting that within the structure taught by the Communist SED, it was granted metaphysical qualities. By doing this they did not put the spiritual autonomy of the Church at the centre of their ecclesiology, but instead a semantic participation in the officially established political reality. As the social context gained a normative quality, some parts of the Church only managed to see the reality of the GDR in a distorted way, namely through its own official self-definition.

At the time Protestantism in the Federal Republic was also considerably influenced by the ideas of social democracy. This gave rise to a considerable debate on the question whether Christians should be socialists. These tendencies were motivated by a perception of guilt towards the poor and those deprived of their rights in the past (see, for example, the Darmstadt Declaration of 1947). Furthermore, the churches of the GDR attempted to disprove the manipulative suspicion of the state that they were acting as a "fifth column" of the "class enemy". Although a steady approximation of the BEK to the terminology and semantics of the "real socialist" ideology was undeniable, the SED state had no reason to rejoice in it because some BEK theologians claimed that they had a right to give further impulses to the future more democratic development of socialism due to their accommodation of the socialist surroundings. One of the protagonists of this theological direction was the future Provost of Erfurt, Heino Falcke, who against the backdrop of the "Theology of the Word of God" supported an "improvable [form of] socialism" (*"verbesserlicher Sozialismus"*).[74] However, such views were not shared by all. Several theologians, as a consequence of the repressive measures taken by the SED regime against the churches, questioned the use of the "compromising metaphor" (Planer-Friedrich) "Church within socialism".[75] These doubters were increasingly more vocal from the beginning of 1988. But not it was until the collapse of 1989 that Bishop W. Leich (from Thuringia) was the first bishop to openly reject the "idea of socialism" (*"Sozialismus-Begriff"*).[76]

The ecclesiastic-political development in the Federal Republic of Germany

The growing affinity of eastern EKD member churches with Socialism cannot be properly understood without considering the analogous developments in western churches and in the ecumenical movement of Geneva.[77] The post-war re-structuring of the Social Democratic Party (*Sozialdemokratische Partei Deutschlands*, SPD) and the emergence of a new elite, which was basically concluded by the Godesberg party conference of 1959, resulted in a fundamental consensus between the two main parties as to the social-political significance of the two mainstream churches.[78] From the mid-nineteen-sixties onwards the Christian-Democratic Union (*Christlich-Demokratische Union*, CDU) no longer enjoyed the support of the majority of the Protestant Church. Due to the above-mentioned change of elite the SPD became a "Protestant Party" (Willy Brandt) and remained so until the mid-nineteen-eighties. By the early nineteen-nineties the Catholic Church still registered a certain affinity with the CDU/CSU (Union of Christian Democrats and Christian Socialists). However, following the peace and ecology debates in the nineteen-eighties parts of the Protestant Church and the Green Party moved closer together, thus splitting sympathies in the centre-left wing. In characterizing the closeness or distance of a Church to a political party the attitudes

of Church officials are significant. The voting habits of citizens with denominational ties show that they did not and do not generally follow the mental gymnas-
tics of their bishops, Church presidents and pastors. The growing distinctions of
church milieus and the mental distance between the leaders and the people of
the Church has not been without consequences. Principally, one must note that
all these socio-political transformations hardly affected the status of Free Churches, Christian "Special Associations" and so-called "sects". They remained on the
social periphery and due to latent reservations they had to put up with many professional disadvantages.[79]

From 1969 one could no longer ignore the gradual departure of Christians
from the two mainstream churches. At the same time commissioners for sect issues in the mainstream churches increased their apologetic activity against so-
called "youth cults". Since 1969 the Protestant Church has carried out official
polls every ten years in order to record the way of thinking, feelings and actions
of Church members. However, these churches are experiencing the loss of members, while new religious groups and secular providers of life-counselling services are gaining ground. The inner emaciation of the mainstream churches, particularly the Protestant Church could force politicians to reconsider the privileged
position of the churches, even though the legal status of the churches under public law, as written in the 1949 constitution, is not endangered. A minority church
will no longer be able to play, as hitherto, a unique and privileged role in shaping
society. Instead it will have to gain recognition for its arguments in pluralistic discourse with other social groups. Thereby, much will depend on the persuasive-
ness of its arguments. The two smaller coalition parties, the Free Democratic
Party (*Freie Demokratische Partei*, FDP) and *Bündnis 90/Die Grünen*, have considerable political potential, as they speak in favour of a clear separation of state and
Church. The more external power the churches lose due to their declining number of members, the more influence will be gained by members of these parties
and by liberal sceptics of the national church. The Protestant Church now attempts to counteract this development with personal political contacts. This explains why, for example, in 1997 Edzard Schmidt-Jortzig (FDP), then the Federal
Minister of Justice, and Antje Vollmer (*Bündnis-Grüne*), the Vice-President of the
Federal Parliament, were appointed to the new Synod of the Protestant Church
in Germany. It remains to be seen whether this archaic diplomatic technique, i. e.
politics through personal contacts, will lead to success.

It can be clearly seen how the established religious institutions during the nineteenth and twentieth centuries lost their power of attraction. At the same time
the emotional power of political surrogate religions in Germany grew. Exaggerated nationalism, undiminished personality cult (Bismarck, Hindenburg, Lenin,
Hitler, Stalin), Socialism and National Socialism were political movements that
took over the role of a religious revival and veneration of the saints. Likewise, the
peace movement of the nineteen-eighties, the human rights movement and the
environmental movement also showed unmistakably religious traits. The fact that
the larger religious associations curried favour with these movements, indeed
sometimes claiming to be the original creators of these ideas, does not change
their position as tolerated free-riders, who were pityingly smiled at and even de-

spised. The Protestant Church has achieved an enormous amount of inner emaciation. In 1950 it had 43 million members, whereas now there are 26.6 million. Berlin-Brandenburg has fewer people going to Church on a regular basis than people, who work for the deaconry and Church. According to some polls[80], up to a third of clerics themselves do not accept the fundamentals of Christian belief: i. e. the Holy Scripture, Jesus Christ as God's son and salvation. The believers notice this inner discrepancy, are mystified and turn away from the Church. According to the findings of the Allensbach Opinion Research Institute only a minority of Germans, namely 39 percent have the impression that the churches seek to "convince people of belief". For a number of years, at least a third of people interviewed in relevant opinion polls declare that they do not have confidence in the churches. This is understandable considering the churches' history and their significant number of political and theological misadventures. The churches are facing the danger of a demographic over-aging well above that of the general population. All of this does not encourage a good prognosis for the German state churches. On the other hand there is evidence that the Christian belief will survive the state-like German religious institutions, since for years opinion polls have been noting a development, which may be summed up as "yes to belief, no to the Church". This could be, even in Germany, the era of small Free Churches and religious communities.

History of mentalities: problems of the church reunification in 1989/91

In late summer of 1989 the unstable GDR dictatorship expected some positive assertions from the Protestant Church on its relationship with the regime during the twenty-year history of the Church Federation.[81] Few were forthcoming. Yet, even in West Germany there were some churchmen, such as the editor of the magazine "Young Church" (*Junge Kirche*), who expressed their support "in principle, solidarity with the GDR".[82] Bishops and general superintendents of churches in the GDR admonished those attempting to leave East Germany to stay in the country, although they also pointed out the regime's lack of preparedness to enact reforms. Yet despite their criticism the clergymen praised certain achievements of GDR socialism saying they were worth keeping and they were worth staying in the country for. The "social securing of the basic needs of life", "the priority of the responsibility for peace in foreign policy [of the GDR]", "the anti-fascist commitment of our country" and "the basic socialist matter of concern, of sharing the toll and the fruits of work with each other", were among the factors selected for praise.[83] However, during the latter half of 1989 due to the ensuing political developments increasingly obvious tensions grew amongst the leaders of the Conference of Church Governing Bodies in the GDR. By the beginning of 1990 the issue of national reunification was on everyone's mind. On the one hand, Bishop Christoph Demke of the Province of Saxony[84] and General Superintendent Günter Krusche of Berlin strongly rejected the idea of German re-unification. But others, such as Bishop Werner Leich of Thuringia[85], welcomed this development. From the sequence of events during that period we can conclude that the discussion on German unification or re-unification preceded the discussion about re-unifying the churches and might even be considered its pre-condition. Among some East German clergymen there was a clear "dismissive attitude towards that twaddle of re-unification"[86]. Not only those taking a positive position towards the GDR state such as Demke, but also those who massively criticised the regime, such as Bishop Gottfried Forck of Berlin-Brandenburg[87], wanted to preserve the "option for socialism"[88].

After Egon Krenz replaced Erich Honecker as the general secretary of the SED on 18 October 1989 he intensified contacts with the Conference of Governing Church Bodies and tried to find a harmonious new beginning with them on the basis of a changed Socialism.[89] Again, the bishops were divided in their reactions. Whereas some placed great hopes in the new policy of dialogue, others remained sceptical. The breach of the Berlin Wall on 9 November 1989 created a new situation in so far as it became clear that, despite all appeals, the people were flocking to the West. On 28 November the West German Chancellor, Helmut Kohl, presented a program on the Federal German policy consisting of ten points to the West German Parliament. Its aim was the re-unification of both countries.[90] In Dresden on 19 December Chancellor Kohl and GDR Minister President Hans Modrow announced a union by treaty [*Vertragsgemeinschaft*] of both German states for the spring of 1990.

At the end of November 1989 the Church leaders in the GDR, including Christoph Demke, Günter Krusche and Pastor Friedrich Schorlemmer, signed an appeal "For our country", in which they demanded "a socialist alternative to the Federal Republic"[91]. They warned the readers that a "selling off of our material and moral values is starting and sooner or later the German Democratic Republic will be taken". Finally, they appealed to the population: "We can still go back to our anti-fascist and humanist ideals that we once started from." The BEK board on "Church and Society" criticized this one-sided view of things but pointed to the differences in mentality, which had arisen between the East and the West, and advised against "precocious plan[s] and aim[s] of a governmental unification of the Germans"[92]. The chief administrative officer (*Konsistorialpräsident*) of the Protestant Church of Berlin-Brandenburg, Manfred Stolpe, like Demke, still belonged to those, who wished to preserve a separate GDR state. In contrast the population in general in the "Monday demonstrations" voiced increasingly determined demands to join (*anschließen*) the Federal Republic.

The expression "joining" (*"Anschluss"*) is in German a word with a negative connotation of a forced political union like the annexation of Austria by Nazi Germany in 1938 and was first used by the Church-journalist, Reinhard Henkys, during his speech to the leading committees of both the EKD and the BEK in mid-January 1990 at Loccum monastery (close to Hanover). What precisely was discussed during this meeting remains a mystery. In any case the declaration that "both German states are growing together" and that "the special union of the entire Protestant Christianity in Germany should also find a suitable expression through a [united] Church"[93], cannot have been motivated by Henkys's speech.

This Loccum text had already been formulated earlier "after a controversial debate and was not unanimous". Especially economic obligations were probably negotiated by the EKD Council and the Eastern member churches. As a direct reaction to the Loccum declaration an Ecumenical Action Circle (*Ökumenischer Initiativkreis*) published the "Berlin Declaration of Christians from both states" on 9 February 1990, which was signed among others by Provost Heino Falcke (of Erfurt), Pastor Ulrich Duchrow (of Heidelberg), Joachim Garstecki (of East Berlin) and Konrad Raiser (of Bochum). This declaration opposed the "wrong signals" of Loccum, by which were meant both the efforts to re-establish German state unity and to re-establish the EKD as sole Protestant umbrella organisation. The "misleading alternative of capitalism and socialism" should be "avoided", since the process of conciliation had shown that "neither system was able to offer a solution to the question of survival of humanity and of the earth". Especially, in this situation "the experience of the 'Church within a socialist society' [should] not be denied in order to get back to an imaginary 'normal everyday life'"[94].

These sentences are evidence of the uneasiness among many leftist intellectuals in East and West Germany. Both the state and Church reunification were not brought about as new mergers among equals, taking into account the different developments of both German partial states, but as a mere joining (*"Anschluss"*) of the Eastern part to the heavily criticized structures already existing in West Germany. Through this all the positive ideas on the achievements of East Germany cultivated up to then in the East as well as in the West, proved to be illusions. Nothing in the state system of the GDR, nor in the East German Church Federation was to be preserved in the new era. The "progress" made under socialist premises had to give way to a "conservative-bourgeois restoration". This procedure could be interpreted as a collective humiliation, and gave rise to a sense of polarization between Western and Eastern elites, which resulted in vehement controversies among intellectuals in both states and Church federations.[95] Some Western sub-cultures also saw themselves deprived of their hopes of building a "third way" between East and West.[96] The east-west antagonisms were of course also stirred up by those individuals, whose former collaborative activities for the GDR led them correctly to feel threatened by the re-unification process, or who had profited under that system as highly privileged agents of the regime. Among them were several professors of theology and personalities from the governing bodies of the churches.

As was revealed in 1990 about five percent of the members of the church assemblies, administrative officers and bishops were serving as officers of the State Security Department in special deployment (OibE) or as Unofficial Collaborators (IM) in different categories.[97] Finally, the parallel procedure of state and Church *"Anschluss"* was bound to create the impression that there was also an analogy between the SED state and the East German Church Federation (BEK). Bishop Martin Kruse of West Berlin tried to counter this impression in the council meeting in February 1990 by stressing that it was the SED state, which had gone bankrupt not the East German Church Federation.[98]

From the justifications of the Conference of Church Governing Bodies following the Loccum Declaration, we may deduce that this declaration was written and published on the "suggestion" of the Western EKD-representatives.[99] At any rate it was not possible to convince the new BEK-synod at the end of February 1990 to adopt this declaration officially, although this council was prepared to give overall support to the process of unification of the churches. Demke's election as Leich's successor, despite having been arranged long in advance, now seemed to be a positive signal for those criticizing Church re-unification. In the meetings of the KKL at the end of April 1990 the resistance grew against a simple re-integration of the Eastern member churches in the EKD.[100] However, the general approval for a simple reunification by public opinion in both the political and ecclesiastical spheres was irresistible. After the East German parliamentary elections (*Volkskammerwahlen*) in March 1990, Demke appealed to Hans Modrow, who remained Minister President in charge to have the files of the state security (*Stasi*) sealed from the public. Demke went on: "A denunciation of individuals because of an alleged collaboration with the state security service should, in my opinion, not be permitted."[101]

The imminent currency unification aggravated the economic problems of the Eastern Church Federation and its member churches. At the end of May 1990 the EKD committed herself to "a certain silent support"[102], but these circumstances of course increased the dependence on the Western churches. Nevertheless, the Common Commission of Federation and EKD in Iserlohn decided on the unification of the churches, but was still uncertain whether the GDR state churches should simply join the EKD or whether a new Federation should be established. They reckoned with a period until the end of January 1993.[103] Among other things, some special arrangements had to be made for the Eastern member churches regarding the introduction of Church taxes to be collected by the state, the introduction of a religious education curriculum for all the schools and especially of a contract for pastoral care in the armed forces.[104]

Things happened fast because of the impending currency reform due to take place on 1 July. This led leading Church lawyers to believe they could wait no longer for the results of the negotiations of the Common Commission of BEK and EKD. Contrary to the ideas of some Eastern representatives, they wanted a "unification on the basis of the Constitution of the EKD". An integration of the Eastern Church Federation into the EKD seemed legally impossible.[105] At the end of August 1990 the KKL voted for "a quick establishment for the membership of the Eastern Federation churches in the EKD"[106]. At the same time Martin Heckel, a church lawyer from Tübingen, presented his expert opinion, which favoured the absorption of the eastern churches into the western organisation and the abandonment of the BEK.[107] In mid September 1990 the juridical committee of the EKD synod adopted Heckel's expert opinion.[108] The unification law of the EKD[109] merely reactivated the old EKD membership rights of the Eastern churches, which had never been cancelled but simply downplayed or sidestepped by the constitution of the Eastern Church Federation. This procedure left the number of members of the EKD untouched and did not require a common consent of all EKD member churches. This law "[stayed] below the level of agreement of the EKD constitution"[110]. The legal solution avoided modifications to the EKD constitution, however, it completed the unavoidable impression of an

Anschluss, from an ultra-legal point of view, for those members of the Eastern churches, who had been expecting a totally new Federation or at least a merger of both Federations.[111] The law having established the East German Church Federation in 1969[112] was inconsistent to this solution and therefore ignored. These circumstances and especially the dissolution of the East German Federation were bound to reinforce painful impressions[113] and caused resentment among the losers, especially since in the arguments put forward by the Western speakers great importance was given to the argument that the 1969 settlement had been imposed on the eastern churches and thus lead to a "forced Church Federation"[114].

The last BEK synod before German re-unification in September 1990 dealt with the question of how far the churches in the GDR "helped actually and sometimes also willingly to stabilize the state and thus the dominating system" among other issues.[115] From 22 to 24 February 1991 the BEK synod met one last time, parallel to the EKD synod. The futile attempts of Western clergymen failed to make the legal facts appear less brutal through acts of appeasement.[116] Rosemarie Cynkiewicz, the chairwoman of the Eastern BEK synod, criticized the EKD for not being willing to "use the situation as a chance for creating something new together"[117]. Along with eight synod members she voted against the BEK unification law and one member abstained.[118] The first general EKD synod met in June 1991 in Coburg after the Conference of Church Governing Bodies had met for the last time. Due to the reservations in the Eastern part it is understandable that the act of unification in Coburg took place "without major festivities, without any special expressions of gratitude"[119]. The next task was to consider the unification of the divided Protestant Church of Berlin-Brandenburg[120], where one half of the Church in West Berlin had been entirely separated from the other half in East Berlin for thirty years. So too the question arose of how to repeal the division of the Evangelical Church of the Union (EKU, the former Prussian state church)[121] and whether to welcome the restoration of the United Lutheran Church in Germany (VELKD)[122]. It must be said that the leitmotif of these changes was to seek a return to the situation at the end of the nineteen-sixties.[123] (The common elaboration of a new constitution for the Protestant Church in Berlin-Brandenburg, which was completed in 1995, changed nothing.)

Thus it can be no surprise that despite the legally correct merger the existing tensions did not decrease but even grew in some areas. The argument on the employment status of military chaplains continued until the EKD synod in Amberg in November 2001. Although ten years have passed in the meantime, it remains uncertain whether the synods of the Protestant Church in Berlin-Brandenburg or the Church Province of Saxony will accept the arrangement for employing the approximately 30 military chaplains from the Eastern member churches as non-permanent federal civil servants.[124] If we consider the atmosphere in society in general, of which the churches are only a small part, we find that the differences of mentality in East and West have hardly diminished over the last ten years. Inner re-unification has made little progress.[125]

It was not only the re-unification of the churches but the demographic and economic changes brought about by the large numbers of people leaving the churches[126], as well as the increase in aging Church members, and a dramatic decrease of Church taxes, which forced German Protestantism to consider several reforms of structures. Since the mid nineteen-nineties a merger of some state churches as well as a reduction of the traditional church "umbrella organisations" has been considered. In 2001 church tax income amounted to 4.25 Billion Euro and membership constituted 26,601,000 believers. But assessments say in the next generation there will be a 50 percent decrease in tax paying Church members. The repercussions for the legally-established Church structures are bound to be severe.

The problem of contemporary Church historiography

The undeniable affinity of vast parts of German Protestantism with the National Socialist state remains a heavy burden. For decades Church historians and publicists have struggled to come to terms with this legacy. The undeniable fact that many churchmen in the eastern churches collaborated with the socialist dictatorship has also had catastrophic consequences for the image of the Protestant Church in Germany. That is why the Protestant Churches by largely avoiding the problem of the State Security Department (*Stasi*) attempt to offer evidence that during the period of the GDR's existence they were engaged in a considerable number of opposition activities, which followed the pattern established in the immediate post-1945 period. By assigning a large number of doctoral dissertations, which were partly subsidised with Church stipends this version can be expected to maintain the dominant position in historiography. On the other hand there is no doubt that, since the nineteen-sixties there has been a strong affinity in some sections of German Protestantism with several socialist utopian views and that since the nineteen-eighties in connection with NATO's two-track decision some clear convergences with "real existing socialism" in the GDR could be perceived. The efforts of some Protestant historians to describe the collapsed GDR regime as something other than a purely totalitarian regime must be also be examined against this backdrop. Furthermore, by stressing the differences between the Nazi regime and the SED regime these authors are trying to give at least a partial correction to the view that the GDR was a criminal dictatorship, which lacked rule of law. However, given the continuing separation of mentalities between east and west it is clear that the task of coming to terms with the churches' experiences in the GDR is far from complete and will likely occupy a prominent position in historiography over the next few years.

In contrast to the large number of books and articles dealing with the churches of the GDR the historiography of the western members of the EKD has been relatively sparse. For the immediate post-war years, we have seen a plethora of excellent collections of documents and monographs. But the years of the Bonn Republic from 1949–1989 are still largely unexplored ground. And this despite the fact that both major denominations established their own separate commissions for contemporary Church history in the nineteen-fifties. However, their publications have chiefly concentrated on the earlier, much disputed periods of the twentieth century. Furthermore, these endeavours are highly denominational in tone and none of them has sought to bring a wider ecumenical or international dimension to these commissions' labours. All the more notable therefore was the initiative taken in the late nineteen-eighties to bring together a group of scholars of various nationalities and denominations in order to try and search for a larger dimension in the writing of contemporary Church history. The conferences of this group have deliberately sought to relate German experiences to those of other countries, such as the Scandinavian countries, Poland, France and Italy. The findings are printed in the journal *Kirchliche Zeitgeschichte*, which can be regarded as the leading publication in this field. Nevertheless, the historiography of the German churches for the foreseeable future is likely to remain, as the ecclesiastical structures of the churches themselves, highly denominational in character. Coming to terms with the convoluted legacy of the recent German past still presents scholars in this field with numerous still-to-be-fulfilled challenges.

Notes

1   Cf. Jürgen W. Falter, Hitlers Wähler, Munich 1991, 169.
2   Cf. Heinz Hürten, Kurze Geschichte des deutschen Katholizismus 1800–1960, Mainz 1986; idem, Deutsche Katholiken 1918–1945, Paderborn 1992.
3   Cf. Kurt Nowak, Evangelische Kirche und Weimarer Republik. Zum politischen Weg des deutschen Protestantismus zwischen 1918 und 1932 (AKGW 7), Göttingen-Weimar, ²1988.
4   Cf. Gerhard Besier, 'Dogmatische Neuansätze, praktisch-ethische Kontroversen und praktisch-theologisches Handeln in Kirche und Universitätstheologe', in idem/Eckhard Lessing (eds), Die Geschichte der Evangelischen Kirche der Union, vol. 3: Trennung von Staat und Kirche. Kirchlich-politische Krisen. Erneuerung kirchlicher Gemeinschaft (1918–1992), Leipzig 1999, 142–210, here: 191–205.
5   Cf. Klaus Scholder, Die Kirchen und das Dritte Reich, vol. 1: Vorgeschichte und Zeit der Illusionen 1918–1934, Frankfurt/M -Berlin-Wien 1977, 277 ff.
6   Cf. Scholder, Die Kirchen und das Dritte Reich (op. cit. note 5), 286–299.
7   Ibid. 300–321, 482–524.
8   Cf. Uwe Puschner, Die völkische Bewegung im wilhelminischen Kaiserreich. Sprache – Rasse – Religion, Darmstadt 2001.
9   Cf. Doris L. Bergen, Twisted Cross. The German Christian Movement in the Third Reich, Chapel Hill 1996; Kurt Meier, Die Deutschen Christen. Das Bild einer Bewegung im Kirchenkampf des Dritten Reiches (AGK.E 3), Halle/Saale-Göttingen 1964.
10   Cf. Heinrich W. Grosse/Hans Otte/Joachim Perels (eds), Bewahren ohne Bekennen? Die hannoversche Landeskirche im Nationalsozialismus, Hannover 1996; Gerhard Schäfer (ed.), Die Evangelische Landeskirche in Württemberg und der Nationalsozialismus. Eine Dokumentation zum Kirchenkampf, 6 vols, Stuttgart 1971–1986; Björn Mensing, Pfarrer und Nationalsozialismus. Geschichte einer Verstrickung am Beispiel der Evangelisch-Lutherischen Kirche in Bayern (AKZG B 26), Göttingen 1998. On Prussia, cf. Besier/Lessing (eds), Geschichte (op. cit. note 4), ch. VII. Gerhard Besier deals with the development from the end of 1934 to 1937 in his book: Die Kirchen und das Dritte Reich. Spaltungen und Abwehrkämpfe, Berlin-Munich 2001.
11   Cf. Gerhard Besier/Gerhard Sauter, Wie Christen ihre Schuld bekennen. Die Stuttgarter Erklärung 1945, Göttingen 1985.

12 Cf. Gerhard Besier, Kirche, Politik und Gesellschaft im 20. Jahrhundert (Enzyklopädie deutscher Geschichte 56), Munich 2000, 62 f.

13 Cf. Gerhard Besier/Hartmut Ludwig/Jörg Thierfelder (eds), Der Kompromiß von Treysa. Die Entstehung der Evangelischen Kirche in Deutschland, EKD, 1945. Eine Dokumentation (Schriftenreihe der Pädagogischen Hochschule Heidelberg 24), Weinheim 1995; Annemarie Smith-von Osten, Von Treysa 1945 bis Eisenach 1948. Zur Geschichte der Grundordnung der Evangelischen Kirche in Deutschland (AKZG B 9), Göttingen 1981.

14 Cf. Clemens Vollnhals, Entnazifizierung und Selbstreinigung im Urteil der evangelischen Kirche. Dokumente und Reflexionen (SKZG 8), Munich 1989; idem, Evangelische Kirche und Entnazifizierung 1945–1949. Die Last der nationalsozialistischen Vergangenheit (Studien zur Zeitgeschichte 36), Munich 1989; Gerhard Besier, "Selbstreinigung" unter britischer Besatzungsherrschaft. Die Evangelisch-lutherische Landeskirche Hannovers und ihr Landesbischof Marahrens 1945–1947 (SKGNS 27), Göttingen 1986.

15 Cf. Herbert Heinecke, Konfession und Politik in der DDR. Das Wechselverhältnis von Kirche und Staat im Vergleich zwischen evangelischer und katholischer Kirche, Leipzig 2002, 275–277; Gerhard Besier, Konzern Kirche. Das Evangelium und die Macht des Geldes, Neuhausen-Stuttgart 1997, 195 f.

16 Cf. Heinecke, Konfession und Politik in der DDR (op. cit. note 15), 158–161.

17 Cf. Gerhard Besier, Der SED-Staat und die Kirche, vol. 1: Der Weg in die Anpassung, Munich 1993, 28. Cf. on its history Michael Kühne, Die Protokolle der Ostkirchenkonferenz von 1945–1950, Göttingen 2005.

18 Cf. Bernd Schäfer, Staat und katholische Kirche in der DDR (Schriften des Hannah-Arendt-Instituts für Totalitarismusforschung 8), Köln-Weimar-Wien, [2]1999.

19 Cf. Gerhard Besier, 'Kommunistische Religionspolitik und kirchlicher Neuanfang 1945/46', in Hartmut Mehringer/Michael Schwartz/Hermann Wentker (eds), Deutschland im internationalen Kräftefeld und die sowjetische Besatzungszone (1945/46), Munich 1999, 121–145.

20 Cf. Schäfer, Staat und katholische Kirche in der DDR (op. cit. note 18), 34.

21 Ibid. 35 f.

22 Cf. Besier, Der SED-Staat und die Kirche, vol. 1 (op. cit. note 18), 177 f.

23 Cf. Hermann Wentker, 'Die kirchenpolitische Abteilung der Ost-CDU: Organisation, Wirkungsweise und personelle Besetzung', in Clemens Vollnhals (ed.), Die Kirchenpolitik von SED und Staatssicherheit. Eine Zwischenbilanz (Analysen und Dokumente), Berlin 1996, 159–189.

24 Cf. Vollnhals, 'Die kirchenpolitische Abteilung des Ministeriums für Staatssicherheit' (op. cit. note 23), 79–119.

25 Cf. Gerhard Besier/Stephan Wolf (eds), "Pfarrer, Christen und Katholiken". Das Ministerium für Staatssicherheit der ehemaligen DDR und die Kirchen (Historisch-Theologische Studien zum 19. und 20. Jahrhundert [Quellen] 1), Neukirchen-Vluyn, [2]1992, 3.

26 Cf. Besier, Der SED-Staat und die Kirche, vol. 1 (op. cit. note 18); Andreas Schalück, Eine Agentur der Kirchen im Staatsapparat? Otto Nuschke und die Hauptabteilung "Verbindung zu den Kirchen" 1949–1953 (Studien des Forschungsverbundes SED-Staat an der Freien Universität Berlin), Berlin 1999.

27 Cf. Besier, Der SED-Staat und die Kirche (op. cit. note 25), 74–77.

28 Ibid. 106–125.

29 Ibid. 125–139.

30 Ibid. 178 f.; passim; Detlef Urban/Hans Willi Weinzen, Jugend ohne Bekenntnis? 30 Jahre Konfirmation und Jugendweihe im anderen Deutschland 1954–1984, Berlin (West) 1984; Christian Fischer, Wir haben euer Gelöbnis vernommen. Konfirmation und Jugendweihe im Spannungsfeld. Ein Beispiel für den Einfluss gesellschaftlicher Verhältnisse auf praktisch-theologische Argumentationen in der DDR (1949–1978), Leipzig 1998; Susann Illing, Die Jugendweihe im Wandel der Zeit – ein Fest der

Jugend oder ostdeutsche Familientradition? Vorgeschichte – Hintergründe – Bedeutung vor und nach 1990, Stuttgart 2000; Albrecht Döhnert, Jugendweihe zwischen Familie, Politik und Religion. Studien zum Fortbestand der Jugendweihe nach 1989 und die Konfirmationspraxis der Kirchen (AptTh 19), Leipzig 2000; Anselma Gallinat, Negotiating Culture and Belonging in Eastern Germany. The Case of the Jugendweihe. A Secular Coming-of-Age Ritual, Thesis (Ph.D.), Durham 2002.

31 Cf. Besier, Der SED-Staat und die Kirche (op. cit. note 25), 220 ff.

32 Ibid. 261–291.

33 Cf. Gerhard Besier, 'Aus der Resistenz in die Kooperation. Der "Thüringer Weg" zur "Kirche im Sozialismus"', in Günter Heydemann/Lothar Kettenacker (eds), Kirchen in der Diktatur, Göttingen 1993, 182–212; Clemens Vollnhals, 'Oberkirchenrat Gerhard Lotz und das Ministerium für Staatssicherheit. Zur IM-Akte "Karl"', in Deutschland Archiv 27 (1994), 332–336.

34 Cf. Besier, Der SED-Staat und die Kirche, vol. 1 (op. cit. note 18), 628–645.

35 Ibid. 645 ff.

36 Ibid. 694–722; idem, Der SED-Staat und die Kirche, vol. 2: Die Vision vom "Dritten Weg", Berlin-Frankfurt/M. 1995, ch. 1.

37 Ibid. (vol. 2), ch. 2.

38 Ibid. 333–336; passim; idem, Der SED-Staat und die Kirche, vol. 3: Höhenflug und Absturz, Berlin-Frankfurt/M. 1995, ch. 1, passim.

39 Cf. Helmut Müller-Enbergs/Wolfgang Stock/Marco Wiesner, Das Fanal. Das Opfer des Pfarrers Brüsewitz aus Rippicha und die evangelische Kirche, Münster 1999.

40 Cf. Gerhard Besier, Der SED-Staat und die Kirche, vol. 3 (op. cit. note 38), 38 f., 519.

41 Ibid. 71–79, 94–102.

42 Ibid. 116–125.

43 Cf. Besier, Kirche, Gesellschaft und Politik im 20. Jahrhundert (op. cit. note 12), 53–57.

44 Cf. Schäfer, Staat und katholische Kirche in der DDR (op. cit. note 18), 313–316.

45 Ibid. 316.

46 Ibid. 319–321.

47 Cf. Besier, Der SED-Staat und die Kirche, vol. 1 (op. cit. note 18), 216–240.

48 Ibid. 220.

49 Ibid. 260.

50 Cf. Manfred Stolpe, Schwieriger Aufbruch, Berlin 1992, esp. 143 ff.; Ralf Georg Reuth, Die 'Gauck-Recherche' und die Dokumente zum 'Falle Stolpe', Berlin 1992; Klaus Roßberg/Peter Richter, Das Kreuz mit dem Kreuz. Ein Leben zwischen Staatssicherheit und Kirche, Berlin 1996, 84 ff.

51 Cf. Besier, Der SED-Staat und die Kirche, vol. 1 (op. cit. note 18), 628–644.

52 On this cf. Claudia Lepp, 'Die evangelische Kirche als "Klammer" im geteilten Deutschland. Rollenerwartung und Rollenwandel 1948 bis 1969', in Joachim Mehlhausen/Leonore Siegele-Wenschkewitz (eds), Zwei Staaten – zwei Kirchen? Evangelische Kirche im geteilten Deutschland. Ergebnisse und Tendenzen der Forschung, Leipzig 2000, 66–84, here: 81 f.; Klaus-Dieter Kaiser, 'Gemeinsame Verantwortung. Zur Geschichte der Trennung der Evangelischen Studentengemeinden 1967', in Peer Pasternack (ed.), Hochschule & Kirche. Theologie & Politik. Besichtigung eines Beziehungsgeflechts in der DDR, Berlin 1996, 297–307.

53 Cf. Besier, Der SED-Staat und die Kirche, vol. 2 (op. cit. note 36), 21.

54 Cf. idem, op. cit. note 18 (vol. 1), 697 f.; idem, op. cit. note 36 (vol. 2), 29 ff.

55 Ibid. (vol. 2), ch. 1.

56 Ibid. 41–55.

57 Ibid. 120.

58 Cf. Hartmut Ludwig/Hans Prolingheuer/Albrecht Schönherr, In die Irre gegangen? Das Darmstädter Wort in Geschichte und Gegenwart, Berlin 1997.

59 Cf. Wolfgang Thumser, Kirche im Sozialismus. Geschichte, Bedeutung und Funktion einer ekklesiologischen Formel, Tübingen 1996. – In his paper 'Zur Geschichte des

Atheismus in der DDR' (Beiträge zur Geschichte der Arbeiterbewegung 43, 2001, 72–83, here: 81, note 25), Hans Lutter highligts what Stolpe said during a "dialog" event at the Humboldt University in Berlin on 16 Feb. 1989: "The political approach for this formulation [Church within socialism] is the consent of the socialist society."

60 On this ecumenical aspect see Gerhard Besier/Armin Boyens/Gerhard Lindemann, Nationaler Protestantismus und Ökumenische Bewegung. Kirchliches Handeln im Kalten Krieg (1945–1990), Berlin 1999, esp. 312 ff.

61 Cf. Besier, Der SED-Staat und die Kirche, vol. 1 (op. cit. note 18), 240 ff., 537 ff.; idem, vol. 2 (op. cit. note 36), 511 ff. See also Wolfgang Brinkschulte/Hans Jörgen Gerlach/Thomas Heise, Freikaufgewinnler. Die Mitverdiener im Westen, Frankfurt/M.-Berlin 1993.

62 Cf. Besier, Der SED-Staat und die Kirche, vol. 2 (op. cit. note 36), 120.

63 Cf. Walter Hammer/Uwe-Peter Heidingsfeld (eds), Die Konsultationen. Ein Ausdruck der "besonderen Gemeinschaft" zwischen der EKD und dem BEK in den Jahren 1980 bis 1990, Hanover 1995.

64 Cf. Holger Kremser, Der Rechtsstatus der evangelischen Kirchen in der DDR und die neue Einheit der EKD, Tübingen 1993, 146–150; Besier, Der SED-Staat und die Kirche, vol. 2 (op. cit. note 36), 326 ff.

65 Cf. Kremser, Der Rechtsstatus der evangelischen Kirchen (op. cit. note 64), 144; Besier, Der SED-Staat und die Kirche, vol. 3 (op. cit. note 38), 317 f.

66 Cf. epd-ZA no. 13 of 18 Jan. 1990, 1 f.

67 Cf. epd-ZA no. 35 of 19 Feb. 1990, 13.

68 Cf. Kremser, Der Rechtsstatus der evangelischen Kirchen (op. cit. note 64).

69 Cf. e. g. Reinhard Henkys (ed.), Bund der Evangelischen Kirchen in der DDR (epd.D 1), Witten-Frankfurt-Berlin 1970, 135–143.

70 Besier, Der SED-Staat und die Kirche, vol. 1 (op. cit. note 18), 657 f.

71 Ibid. 280.

72 Ibid. 514–516, here: 515.

73 Cf. Besier, Der SED-Staat und die Kirche, vol. 2 (op. cit. note 36), 55 f., 131–133, 261–284.

74 Ibid. 60–64.

75 Cf. Goetz Planer-Friedrich, 'Kirche im Sozialismus? Eine Kompromiß-Metapher hat ausgedient', in Evangelische Kommentare 21 (1988), 503–505.

76 Cf. Besier, Der SED-Staat und die Kirche, vol. 3 (op. cit. note 38), 369 f.

77 Cf. Besier/Boyens/Lindemann, Nationaler Protestantismus und Ökumenische Bewegung (op. cit. note 60).

78 Cf. Peter Lösche/Franz Walter, Die SPD. Klassenpartei – Volkspartei – Quotenpartei, Darmstadt 1992; Franz Walter, Die SPD. Vom Proletariat zur Neuen Mitte, Berlin 2002.

79 For this and the following section cf. Besier, Konzern Kirche (op. cit. note 15), passim.

80 Cf. Klaus-Peter Jörns, Die neuen Gesichter Gottes, Munich 1997.

81 Cf. Besier, Der SED-Staat und die Kirche, vol. 3 (op. cit. note 38), 413.

82 Ibid.

83 Letter from Christoph Demke to collaborators and members of his parish at the end of August 1989, in epd-Dok. 44/1989, 39.

84 Cf. Hagen Findeis/Detlef Pollack (eds), Bischöfe und Repräsentanten der evangelischen Kirchen in der DDR über ihr Leben. 17 Interviews, Berlin 1999, 586–621.

85 Cf. Werner Leich, Wechselnde Horizonte. Mein Leben in vier politischen Systemen, Wuppertal-Zürich 1992, 269 ff.; Findeis/Pollack, Bischöfe und Repräsentanten (op. cit. note 84), 322–355.

86 According to Christoph Stier of the consultation board at end of September 1989 quoted from Besier, Der SED-Staat und die Kirche, vol. 3 (op. cit. note 38), 433. See also the warning issued by the East Berlin weekly newspaper Die Kirche about "reunification euphoria", epd-ZA no. 32 of 14 Feb. 1990, 3 f.

87 Cf. Gerhard Besier, 'Zum Tod von Altbischof Gottfried Forck', in Jahrbuch für Berlin-Brandenburgische Kirchengeschichte 61 (1997), 225 f.; Findeis/Pollack, Bischöfe und Repräsentanten, 286–321.

88 Quoted after Besier, Der SED-Staat und die Kirche, vol. 3 (op. cit. note 38), 434.

89 Ibid. 448.

90 Cf. Helmut Kohl: "Ich wollte Deutschlands Einheit." Dargestellt von Kai Dieckmann und Ralf Georg Reuth, Berlin 1996, 157 ff.

91 Neues Deutschland from 29 Nov. 1989.

92 Quoted from Besier, Der SED-Staat und die Kirche, vol. 3 (op. cit. note 38), 459.

93 Ibid. 464.

94 epd-ZA no. 35 of 19 Feb. 1990, 13.

95 Cf. e. g. the book by pastor and head of the Land Central of Political Education in Potsdam, Hans-J. Misselwitz, Nicht länger mit dem Gesicht nach Westen. Das neue Selbstbewußtsein der Ostdeutschen, Bonn 1996.

96 Cf. Norbert Sommer (ed.), Der Traum aber bleibt. Sozialismus und christliche Hoffnung. Eine Zwischenbilanz, Berlin 1992. This book contains a circular from the then head (Präses) of the Protestant Church in Rhineland, Peter Beier (ibid. 44–49), who pleaded for maintenance of socialism as an "unforsakeable human achievement" ("unaufgebbares Humanum") and to stop the "cheap attacks against socialism" ("wohlfeile Sozialismusschelte"). Cf. also Peter Beier, Am Morgen der Freiheit. Eine Streitschrift, Neukirchen-Vluyn 1995.

97 On the President of Consistory, Detlef Hammer (OibE) cf. Harald Schultze/Waltraud Zachhuber, Spionage gegen eine Kirchenleitung. – Hammer – Stasi-Offizier im Konsistorium Magdeburg. Gespräche, Dokumente, Recherchen, Kommentare, Evangelisches Büro Magdeburg, no year [1995]; on the member of the Church Assembly Hans-Joachim Weber (IM "Bastler"), President of Consistory Martin Harder (IM "Dr. Wintzer"), member of the Church Assembly Siegfried Plath (IM "Hiller"), member of the Church Assembly Christoph Ehricht (IM "Ingolf Seidel"), Church Head (Präses) Dietrich Affeld (IM "Dietrich") and Bishop Horst Gienke (IM "Orion") cf. Rahel von Saß, Der "Greifswalder Weg". Die DDR-Kirchenpolitik und die Evangelische Landeskirche Greifswald 1980 bis 1989, Schwerin 1998. The author concludes: "Except for two people, the complete leadership of the Church was in the hands of two district collaborators of the MfS [Department of State Security] and their superior officials" (ibid. 34). On Bishops Hans-Joachim Fränkel (IM "Bruder") and Joachim Rogge (IM "Ferdinand") as well as other employees of the church district of Görlitz cf. Roland Brauckmann/Christoph Bunzel, Rückblick. Die evangelische Kirche des Görlitzer Kirchengebietes, die Einflußnahme des MfS und der DDR-Staat 1970–1994, Görlitz 1995; on the members of the Church Council of Thüringen, Gerhard Lotz, cf. Vollnhals, 'Oberkirchenrat' (op. cit. note 33). On the situation of the Church of Thüringen and its Bishop, Ingo Braecklein (IM "Ingo"), see Walter Schilling, 'Die "Bearbeitung" der Landeskirche Thüringen durch das MfS', in Clemens Vollnhals (ed.), Die Kirchenpolitik von SED und Staatssicherheit. Eine Zwischenbilanz, Berlin ²1997, 211–266. In 1997, Vollnhals cautiously estimated the "statistical burden" of Church employees at "about five percent, more at higher levels", cf. idea-Dokumentation 1/1997: 'Erfahrungen aus zwei Diktaturen in Deutschland und unsere politische Verantwortung im demokratischen Rechtsstaat heute', 68. On the inner-church consistory view of the situation and differing numbers cf. Kirchliches Jahrbuch 1996, Gütersloh 2000, 285–407 (Harald Schultze). On the problematics of the MfS in the old (western) Federal Republic cf. Hubertus Knabe, Die unterwanderte Republik. Stasi im Westen, Berlin 1999, esp. 261 ff. ('Kirchen').

98 Quoted from Besier, Der SED-Staat und die Kirche, vol. 3 (op. cit. note 38), 467.

99 Ibid. 468.

100 Ibid. 470.

101 Ibid. 471.

102 Ibid. 472.

103 Cf. epd-ZA no. 103 of 30 May 1990, 1 ff.

104 Cf. also Peter Müller, 'Kirche nach der Wende. Die Vereinigung der deutschen Staaten und ihre kirchenrechtlichen Konsequenzen', in Gerhard Rau/Hans-Richard Reuter/ Klaus Schlaich (eds), Das Recht der Kirche, vol. 3: Zur Praxis des Kirchenrechts, Gütersloh 1994, 450–492.

105 Cf. Kremser, Der Rechtsstatus der evangelischen Kirchen (op. cit. note 64), 115 ff.

106 Quoted from Besier, Der SED-Staat und die Kirche, vol. 3 (op. cit. note 38), 476.

107 Cf. Martin Heckel, Die Vereinigung der evangelischen Kirchen in Deutschland, Tübingen 1990.

108 Cf. op. cit. note 107, 47 ff.

109 Amtsblatt der EKD, 1991, 89 ff.

110 Kremser, Der Rechtsstatus der evangelischen Kirche (op. cit. note 64), 123.

111 Ibid. 115.

112 Ibid. 124 f., 128.

113 The volume edited by Demke et al. on instructions of the Council of the EKD, Zwischen Anpassung und Verweigerung. Dokumente aus der Arbeit des Bundes der Evangelischen Kirchen in der DDR, Leipzig ²1995, esp. 121–169, must be considered against this backdrop. Alongside the attempt to make the BEK work's known by documenting it, this book contains the extra-juridical expression of "the 'special community' with the EKD".

114 Quoted from Kremser, Der Rechtsstatus der evangelischen Kirche (op. cit. note 64), 127.

115 epd-ZA no. 184 of 24 Sep. 1990, 3 ff.

116 The president of the EKD Synod and former SPD-party politician Jürgen Schmude declared: "Nothing will return to the same as before. But then no one had this aim. The Protestant Church in the GDR has unique experiences during the period of division. It proved its worth in a way, which will play a role for the way the future common EKD will see itself. But the former EKD of the Federal Republic has also developed itself and gained further stronger clarity about its tasks. The common EKD will be based on of all this.", cf. idea no. 15 of 18 Feb. 1991, 1.

117 epd-ZA no. 37 of 21 Feb. 1991, 6.

118 epd-ZA no. 39 of 25 Feb. 1991, 1.

119 Kirchliches Jahrbuch 1990/91, Gütersloh 1995, 330 (comment by W.-D. Hauschild).

120 Cf. Kremser, Der Rechtsstatus der evangelischen Kirche (op. cit. note 64), 138–141.

121 Ibid. 137 f.

122 Ibid. 141 f.

123 Cf. Gerhard Besier, '"Kirche im Sozialismus". Transformation einer Großinstitution (1969 bis 1990)', in Gerd Heinrich (ed.), Tausend Jahre Kirche in Berlin-Brandenburg, Berlin 1999, 843–974 (with the main focus on Berlin-Brandenburg); Peter Maser, 'Ohne große Feierlichkeit, ohne besondere Bekundungen der Dankbarkeit. Anmerkungen zum Weg der evangelischen Kirchen in die Einheit', in Wolfgang Thierse/Ilse Spittmann-Rühle/Johannes L. Kuppe (eds), Zehn Jahre Deutsche Einheit. Eine Bilanz, Bonn 2000, 195–206; Werner Radatz/Friedrich Winter (eds), Geteilte Einheit. Die Evangelische Kirche Berlin Brandenburg 1961 bis 1990, Berlin 2000, esp. 74 ff.; Friedrich Winter, Die Evangelische Kirche der Union und die Deutsche Demokratische Republik. Beziehungen und Wirkungen, Berlin 2001, esp. 346 ff.

124 Cf. Frankfurter Allgemeine Zeitung no. 259 of 7 Nov. 2001, 4.

125 Cf. on this the caustic description given by Friedrich Wilhelm Graf, 'Der deutsche Protestantismus nach der Wiedervereinigung', in Andreas Wirsching (ed.), Die Bundesrepublik Deutschland nach der Wiedervereinigung. Eine interdisziplinäre Bilanz, Munich 2000, 99–114, here: 110 f.

126 Cf. idea-Spektrum 45/2001, 19.

"The friends ... in America need to know the truth ... ." The German Churches in the Opinion of the United States (1933–1941)*

Introduction

Whereas the nineteenth century saw customarily little interest from European churches in ecclesiastical development in the United States, American denominations constantly looked to Europe and, with a certain respect, observed both the theological and ecclesiastical-political paths of the mother churches they had only too often had to leave behind as a result of their wish for religious freedom and confessional, inspirational piety not being granted. The First World War was subsequently viewed by North American daughter churches as a definitive change in the direction of the spiritual tide: it was no longer the Europeans who provided the Americans with theological stimuli, rather now the latter who, in a reversal of roles, were charged with re-Christianising the crusty state church structures of the Old World in a type of "great awakening". Armed with this missionary self-confidence, which was able to draw on energy in the form of Christian comfort, the great grandchildren of those who had previously been religiously displaced returned to the European stage and sought to reanimate the old religions with new spirituality and morals. These missionary efforts in the immediate aftermath of the War were continued during the 1920s, though a gradual trend towards a religious retreat from Europe began to emerge.[1] At the beginning of the Third Reich a curious situation arose. Could it be that the Americans could once again take lessons from the Germans?

The following essay aims to present the stances of the somewhat conservative American Lutheran Church, the liberal American Federation of Churches, specialists from the U. S. Department of State for Germany and German churches themselves. The opinions of the institutions mentioned can only be understood if the conditions under which their opinions were formed are given mention. This includes above all the prevailing situation at the time in the United States itself. It must also not be neglected that the destructive downfall of German National Socialism and Italian Fascism was not obvious to observers at the start of the Second World War.[2]

* First published in German as '"The friends ... in America need to know the truth ... ." Die deutschen Kirchen im Urteil der Vereinigten Staaten (1933–1941)', in *Jahrbuch des historischen Kollegs* [München] (1998), 23–76.

1.   Germany and the German Churches in the opinion of the Lutheran Church in America and Mainline Protestantism

The Executive Committee of the Lutheran World Convention met in Hanover between 8 and 18 November 1933.[3] Executive Secretary Ralph H. Long[4] (1882–
1948) and Lars W. Boe (1875–1942), president of St Olaf College in Northfield,
Minnesota, travelled there on behalf of the North American National Lutheran
Council[5], which represented around 4.8 million confirmed Christians in America[6]. Boe, an American of Norwegian descent with an excellent command of the
German language, came, like Long, from the American Lutheran Conference[7],
which had been founded in 1930. Both Americans were visibly agitated by August
Marahrens[8], the Hanoverian Regional Bishop, and received the distinct impression that he was not informing them fully about actual church-political circumstances in Germany. "Under Bishop Marahrens we went around like some mealy-
mouthed fools when we were in Germany", wrote Boe one year later, incensed by
the meeting in Hanover.[9] On the other hand, the Americans found the Bavarian
Regional Bishop Hans Meiser[10] to make an excellent impression, and saw him as
a worthy Executive Committee successor to the Saxon Regional Bishop Ihmels,
who had died in June 1933[11]. Marahrens had joined the Committee in place of
Wilhelm Freiherr von Pechmann[12], who had retired, and rose to the level of First
Vice-President of the Lutheran World Convention.

In his January 1934 report to the president of the Lutheran World Convention,
John A. Morehead (1867–1936), who had not travelled to Germany due to illness,
Boe arrived at an astonishing self-correction of his assessment of the German situation, a correction which he acknowledged himself[13]: "In regard to the situation
in Germany as a whole I come back worth a picture differing very much from
that which I had when I went over." He initially stressed the fundamental depen-
dency of all churches on the ecumenical, social and political changes in their respective countries. In this regard, he emphasised the catastrophic situation of the
Lutheran Church in the USSR[14], and in particular the Ukraine. Bearing in mind
the circumstances in Russia, he was not able to take Marahrens' somewhat grim
point of view seriously. "I have the impression that Bishop Marahrens felt very
keenly the difficulties of the situation in Germany and feared some of the developments, and for that reason was rather hesitant."[15] In his opinion, however, the
judgement of "Jewish world propaganda" was giving the Americans a "distorted
view"[16]. He also deemed British, French and American reports to be characterised
by an entirely "anti-German stance".

"In order to understand fully the developments that have taken place a man will have
to know something of the situation that confronted the German people six or eight
months ago. They were much nearer to absolute chaos and dissolution as a people
than we in America can understand and appreciate. The communist party was making great inroads and especially among the younger generation, which saw no way out
of increasing difficulties than to destroy the whole system. Conditions were becoming impossible. Many a professional and business man had to take his turn marching
in front of his home and place of business to protect his family and property. The general situation is the logical result, in my estimation, of the provisions of the Treaty of

Versailles, which first of all placed all the guilt for the war upon the German people and, secondly, put them in a place of inequality as far as the rest of the nations were concerned. Then there is a third factor which partially has been modified, that of the reparations imposed upon the German nation. What is interpreted in America as preparation for war, the marching up and down the streets of the cities of Germany by old and younger men in uniform, does not indicate that they are in favor of war, but that they are supporting whole heartedly the program of Hitler, who, by the way, is not the 'boor' that he is made out to be in the English and American papers. But it may become a cause for war if the neighboring nations put a wrong interpretation upon what is being done. There are those who do not like the people of the United States of America, who insist that we too are preparing for war because we have thousands of our young men in camps throughout the country supposedly to give them employment. It is difficult to convince some of the anti-Americans of the fact that we are simply trying to deal with an unemployment situation ... . In campaign and election that took place in the midst of the meeting of the committee, the slogan was 'equality and peace with honor', an equality that can be reached either by the disarmament of the other nations or permission being given for Germany to arm. Peace with honour includes a revision of the Treaty of Versailles as far as the guilt proposition is concerned. It was fortunate that we could travel into Italy immediately after being in Germany because there we could see the second stage of what is taking place in Germany. Hitler is following the technique of Mussolini. He again undoubtedly is using the techniques worked out by the Russian Revolution in handling the masses. There is this distinction between the Italian, German, and Russian Revolutions. In Russia the revolution aimed to destroy all that was old, while in Italy and Germany they aim to preserve for future use everything that comes down from former days ... . He [i. e. Hitler] places the emphasis upon purity of race and blood and one can easily understand the philosophy of Hitler when one remembers that he comes out from the mix-up of races in the old Austro-Hungarian Empire. There too he undoubtedly got his anti-Jewish attitude which found fertile ground because of the developments these last years in the German Empire. There is no question but there are many individual instances of injustice being done to the Jew today in the attempt which is being consistently made to 'ration the Jew' ... . There is law and order in Germany today, but there is also a great deal of fear because Hitler and his administration are digging back into industrial and political conditions to punish, on the one side, because of the injustices that have been done by financial and political leaders and, on the other, to rectify the very evident inequalities that have manifested themselves. Not only Jews are found in the concentration camps of Germany. There are many Germans of noble blood, but little is said about them. The Jew, on the other hand, knows how to dramatize his sufferings and we hear, therefore, relatively more about the injustice being done to him than the people of other races. There is a danger that they may go too far and still one cannot help but wish sometimes that we would have something more than fine 'senatorial investigations' in this country, which leave the leaders of the financial world unpunished and in possession of their ill-gotten gains. The aim in America by these investigations, as I understand it, is to hold up these men, who have been unfaithful to their trust, to the scorn of a public that more often envies them for the special opportunities they have had. I have the feeling that there is a fundamental balance in the German people that will curb any tendency to go too far in this direction ... . The leaders of the Lutheran and Reformed Churches and of the *Unierte Kirche* were the ones who drew up the constitution for the German Church and they made every attempt to preserve the Confessions of the Reformation in their integrity ... the deciding factor, in my estimation, in this, as well as in other matters where things are turning out well, is the good, fundamental Christian common sense of the German people themselves. The developments which have taken place since our leaving Germany have all been in the direction that was indicated at the time we left. Out of it all I take courage to express the hope, and it is a strong one, that the Lutherans, as well as the Reformed Churches of Germany, will have a greater appreciation of the Bible and of the Confessions of the Reformation than they have had before, and that the Church has been awakened and has become conscious of its responsibility towards the whole people ... . In many respects it is a second reformation, though this time it is a reformation in spirit more than anything else. I can only hope and pray that out of the difficulties we have in America will come something of the same character."[17]

Boe's report is simply a snapshot taken at the end of the first year of Hitler's rule, and corresponds to a large extent with the impression gained from American journalists' interviews of German theologians at the time.[18] Nonetheless, the *Deutsche Christen* (DC) staged their rally at the Berlin Sports Palace on 13 November 1933 (*Berliner Sportpalastkundgebung*) whilst the meeting in Hanover was taking place, and shortly afterwards, on 17 November, the members of the Lutheran Executive Committee travelled to Berlin and were welcomed by *Reichsbischof* Ludwig Müller, who assured them that the Reformist denomination would remain intact and the so-called "Aryan clause" would not be introduced into the church.[19] The Executive Committee refrained from publicly criticising the persecution of the Jews and even the Aryan clauses.

Corrections to this take on the situation followed rapidly and were influenced in particular by Nordic Lutheranism[20], despite its considerable reservations where the Brethren Council wing of the Confessional Church – as well as Karl Barth and his Word-of-God theology – were concerned[21]. It was against this backdrop that Boe wrote the following to Morehead as early as 9 April 1934: "Whatever we may think of the Jews, there is no question but that an anti-Jewish attitude such as is manifesting itself in Germany is un-Christian, un-Scriptural and against the very things that Martin Luther stood for."[22] He simultaneously challenged Morehead to support the protest of the Swedish Archbishop Eidem.[23] He subsequently felt deep regret that the Americans and Scandinavians had granted the presidency of the Lutheran World Convention to the Germans rather than bestowing it on the Swedes.[24]

Nonetheless, in his report of January 1934, Boe had mentioned aspects which were firmly rooted in the conservative American Protestantism mentality. This was, therefore, certainly not an isolated case or "blind spot" in terms of Boe's perceptive ability.[25] It was only the tough political and ecclesiastical-political facts of the following years which were to bring about an extremely gradual change in stance in the Protestant milieu.[26] In this way, for example, the politics of conformity exercised towards the Lutheran national churches and the treatment of Bishops Meiser and Wurm led to a harsh telegram of disapproval being sent to Hitler by Frederick H. Knubel (1870–1945), the president of the somewhat more liberal United Lutheran Church in America.[27]

American Judaism – there were 4.7 million Jews in the United States at the time – enjoyed little support from conservative Christian subgroups. On the contrary: a large number of declared opponents who suggested that the economic collapse in the USA was a consequence of conspiratorial Jewish machinations came from the Christian milieu, the message being delivered in part by the newly popular medium of radio.[28] In personal letters Long justified the prevailing silence within American Lutheranism on the repression of Lutherans under dictatorships by way of a socio-psychological boomerang effect, which he illustrated using Jewish protests as an example: "The Jews have protested here in this country ... the treatment of their brethren in Germany but I fear that it has not helped the cause because there is growing a tendency right here in America against the Jews which might not be so evident had these great public demonstrations and the publicity, which accompanied them, been omitted."[29]

According to opinion polls, anti-Semitism in the United States actually reached its peak between 1938 and 1945.[30] Half of Americans were of the opinion that Jews held "too much power" in the USA, with 20 % even responding that they would sympathise with an anti-Semitic campaign. As the efforts of many American Jews to find help for their persecuted fellow Jews in Europe were linked to the principles of Zionism – where other than Palestine should these people without a homeland flee? – they were even suspected by patriotic Protestants of being untrustworthy Americans.[31] Ultra-conservative Protestantism in America did, however, support the Zionist movement, as it saw the fulfilment of God's original will in the colonisation of Israel by the Jewish refugees.[32]

Pronounced anti-Communism due to religious persecution in the USSR[33] and complaints regarding circumstances in the USA itself – which were seen as desperate and even corrupt – make it clear that the judgement passed on Germany and Italy was influenced by the domestic situation in the USA[34]. This was also valid in the case of the positive assessment of the church situation in Germany, with 1933 seeing various denominations in the USA speaking of not only an ecumenical but also a "religious depression"[35] in the country where, according to the legends of the founding fathers, God's own people lived (i. e. the United States)[36].

Comments made by Charles Macfarland, the former general secretary of the Federal Council, who spent a three-week period in October-November 1933 travelling through Germany, showed that it was not only the conservative Protestants, but also Mainline churches in the liberal Federal Council who were able to take positives from the German dictatorship despite some criticism of it.[37] In March 1933, the Federal Council had published a sensational statement against the persecution of Jews in which had caused national sensitivity and unanimous indignation on the part of German Protestantism, although American Christians had seen a link between their call and self-incrimination due to racial discrimination in their own country.[38] Seven months later, Macfarland was still able to arrange an audience with Hitler.[39] Although Karl Barth had attempted to instruct him as clearly as possible on the church situation in Germany during a prior preparatory meeting, Macfarland, with the domestic conflict between liberals and evangelicals in mind, presumed that there were two church groupings of approximately equal strength and of radical or conservative orientation, between which negotiation in the interests of church unity was necessary.[40] This goal corresponded exactly with the concerns of the Federal Council. During his conversation with Hitler, Macfarland even received the impression that the *Reichskanzler* himself would be ready to carry out such negotiations.[41] "Probably no one but Chancellor Hitler himself has any chance of securing any real harmony and it may be feared that he was uninformed too long. As mentioned elsewhere, it was evident that the facts which I frankly conveyed to him had not been adequately realised by him ... . His motives [scil. to interfere in church affairs] have undoubtedly been good and he has acted at all times in the interests of the church, people and nation, as he saw and conceived them."[42]

At the beginning of September 1933, and therefore still under the effect of a recently-completed trip to Germany, Henry Smith Leiper, a Congregationalist minister and the Federal Council's Foreign Secretary, wrote to a colleague that the German situation was subject to fundamental misinterpretation abroad.[43] He was led to observe that many grim accounts did not correspond with the truth of the situation. Of course it was possible for German clergyman to travel to ecumenical meetings. No, churches were not subject to enforced conformity, rather searching for internal unity[44] and yes, the victory of the *Deutsche Christen* was based on the wishes of the majority of Protestant Christians and not on vote manipulation. As a Congregationalist he had some doubts as to whether or not a church really needed to be led by the "spiritual elite". Before he left Berlin, he bought the "New York Times" and read a stinging attack on Hitler's "Mein Kampf" and American publishers who had made the book available in the United States, thereby confirming the freedom of the press in Germany.

Parallels between the assessment of Boe, a conservative Lutheran, and Leiper, a liberal Congregationalist, cannot go unnoticed and show, even if only as snapshots, the misinterpretations which were still possible based on circumstances in Germany in 1933/34. By the end of the 1930s, Leiper had arrived at another point of view, not least because of his exchanges with Dietrich Bonhoeffer.[45] The influence that German theologians had in the United States must, however, be considered rather low. For instance, Paul Tillich lectured as a "relative unknown" at the Union Theological Seminary, New York, between 1933 and 1948.[46]

Between 1934 and 1938, the Federal Council and some of its member churches formulated a variety of peace prayers, appeals and resolutions, the majority of which expressed deep concern over the church situation in Germany and the violence being directed towards Jews.[47] Authors showed their profound support for the battle being fought by the Confessional Church[48] on numerous occasions, and appealed to all parties involved to stand up for world peace. However, these statements remained unknown not only to the Germans, but also to the majority of the American public[49]. They tended to perform the function of coordination between their authors and the determination of ecclesiastical-political guidelines.

At the end of 1935, the new general secretary of the Federal Council, Henry Smith Leiper, spoke with undersecretary Stahn and church affairs advisor Dudzus at the Reich Church Ministry. At the beginning and the end of their conversation, the American underlined that his visit was on a friendly basis and designed to contribute to mutual understanding between the respective parties. This notwith-standing, he used the conversation to question his partners on the reasons for the forced retirement of respected professors of theology[50], the position of the *Reichs-bischof* and the duties of Kerrl, the Reich Minister for Churches. He received no satisfactory answer and was referred to the activities of the new minister, who, ac-cording to Dudzus "disposes of a deep theological knowledge"[51].

On the 27 September 1935, ten days after the passing of the Nuremberg Race Laws, the Federal Council selected a three-man commission which was to pre-pare a manifesto on German racism.[52] The group was unable to find a consen-sus, and therefore needed to be enlarged. It finally formulated a compromise pa-per at the end of November, which adjudged National-Socialist racial doctrine as a false, heathen doctrine from the point of view of Christian belief.[53]

Christmas 1937 saw an official Federal Council direct an appeal to American Christians and request help for refugees. Refugees were defined as "the Christian German refugees who are all victims of the cruel laws against all 'non-Aryan' and who are classified as 'non-Aryans' if they have even a Jewish grandfather's blood in their veins"[54].

With its statements having received hardly any attention for five years, spring 1938 saw the Federal Council's publication of an "open letter to the Christians of the world", in which it made a statement on the prevailing situation at German churches.[55] The direct cause of this document was the trial of Martin Niemöller and not the treatment of the Jews.[56] It is only in the second paragraph that the following observation is made: "In National-Socialist Germany, where the war de-clared on Jews has aroused the moral indignation of the Christian world for some time now, an undeclared war is in progress on the Christian church itself, both Protestant and Catholic." Circumstances in Germany were typically compared with those prevailing in the Soviet Union. "It is only with deep pain that we point to increasing evidence that the behaviour of the National Socialists is becoming ever more similar to that of the Communists where the treatment of Christians and the Christian religion is concerned." The letter ends with an appeal to the "Christian powers of the world" to help those who are "forced to flee". The re-sponse from the "official representative ... of Christian churches within Germany" – signed on behalf of the official Reich Church by the head of the Church Foreign Ministry, Bishop Theodor Heckel[57] – came in a tone of deep indignation, accus-ing the Federal Council of both complete "ignorance of the public situation at churches in Germany" in their judgement, and, in their defamation of the National Socialist state, of engaging in the un-Christian alienation of both peo-ples. The statement came down severely on "an equation of our churches with Roman Catholic politics" and against the comparison of the "constructive Nation-al Socialist development with the godless, destructive Soviet system and their per-secution of Christians and the blood and tears it brings with it". The following sentence shows that the compilers of the statement were well-versed in the inter-nal discussions among American churches: "We ask the men of the American Federation of Churches when they have ever called upon the Christians of the world to fight against Bolshevist Russia?" This was grist to the mill of the critics of the Federal Council within the United States.[58] Neither the Germans nor the Americans heard anything of the Federal Council's retort.[59]

A few months later, on his return journey from the second meeting of the Council of Russian Orthodox Churches Abroad, which had sat in Sremski Kralovci (Yugoslavia) from 14 to 24 August 1938, Archbishop Vitaly (New York) of the Russian Orthodox Church in America visited Berlin.[60] During his stay he spoke about National Socialist religious politics in decidedly friendly fashion. "The promotion of the Orthodox Church by the German government has been noticed by a wide number of people in America. He himself [scil. Vitaly] has repeatedly pointed to this in order to demonstrate that there is no persecution of churches in Germany, despite the frequent claims to the contrary by anti-German press in America."[61]

The spring of 1939 saw some sections of the German Protestant Church entering into yet closer union with National Socialist ideology. The Godesberg Declaration had been published on 6 April 1939, having been signed by eleven German Christian church leaders with a national church stance.[62] It stated that "suitable-to-type National Socialist *Weltanschauung*" was to be viewed as the continuation of the "ideological-political side" of Martin Luther's work.[63]

One month later, the Lutheran Churches of America came to a resolution on the current church situation which, though very carefully-worded, addressed the politics of violence followed by National Socialism and the persecution of the Jews.[64] However, during the 1939 meeting of the Executive Committee of the Lutheran World Convention in Waldenburg[65] a mention of this resolution was struck from the minutes on the basis that it was directed at the churches' own congregations, and not to the churches of the World Convention.

2.   The religious, political and societal situation in the USA as a basis for the assessment of the German situation

Whereas the two national churches in Germany were not able to assert themselves in legal, material and quantitative terms[66] – and this despite the transition from the monarchy to the Weimar Republic and the Freethought Movement – the USA of the 1920s saw not only societal upheaval but also fundamental changes to its religious landscape. Traditional Mainline churches had to come to terms with stagnating – if not decreasing – memberships, whilst non-traditional churches and former religious fringe groups of somewhat fundamentalist dispositions witnessed rapid growth which strengthened during the Depression.[67]

It is therefore no coincidence that it was the successors to the old colonial churches – Presbyterians[68], Episcopalians[69], and Congregationalists[70] and then also the Methodists[71], Baptists[72] and Disciples of Christ[73] – which formed the pillars of the Federal Council of Churches of Christ in America[74], which was founded in 1908. This federation of churches was designed to help the old denominations with crisis management and guide them towards cooperation with each other.[75] The representation of churches from the countries of origin of non-

English-speaking immigrants – Lutherans, Reformists and others – was significantly weaker. Understanding of the federation was highly varied; whereas some saw it as a binding association, other denominations only considered it to be an advisory body. Despite the establishment of the American Federation of Churches in 1908, America's Protestants had held to their traditional denominational separation until the end of the First World War. This separation could not always be explained from a religious point of view, and was primarily the result of cultural influences.

In the 1920s, fundamentalist movements both within and outside of the traditional denominations[76] ensured that liberal mainstream Protestantism focussed on shared theological basics, as it needed to assert itself against the explosive growth in this pious stance and set out religious norms for a "nation under God". Though 1941 saw "Newsweek" describing the Federal Council as having "a virtual monopoly" on American Protestantism, growing dissent from the large Protestant denominations underlined the power of the new religious alternatives.

The creation of fundamentalist and evangelical alliances at the start of the 1940s increased institutional pressure to unify on the Mainline churches within the Federal Council. 1942 saw the formation of the neo-evangelical National Association of Evangelists.[77] In 1943, the evangelicals set up an office in Washington, D. C. in order to be able to exert greater pressure on the U. S. government.[78] Their first highlight in terms of official government recognition came in 1953, when President Eisenhower received an evangelical delegation at the White House in order to discuss moral and religious bases for American liberties.

The founding of the Association was, of course, not only directed against the liberal Federal Council, but also against the old fundamentalists and their American Council of Christian Churches, which was set up in 1941. The evangelicals' association split the fundamentalist camp into moderate modernist evangelicals and intransigent, feudal fundamentalists.[79] Their militant representatives – John R. Rice, Bob Jones Sr. and Carl McIntire – saw the evangelicals' approach as a "sell off" of biblical-fundamentalist positions. They also found it completely incomprehensible that the evangelicals could countenance membership of both the National Association and the Federal Council. McIntire, a leading member of the Bible Presbyterian Church, had hastily founded the American Council as he wanted to pre-empt the Federal Council's planned founding of the National Council of Churches.[80]

There were also fierce debates between modernist and conservative forces within individual denominations, for example within Lutheranism. Only the United Lutheran Church of America (ULCA) worked together with the Federal Council, whilst the majority of the other Lutheran Churches adopted negative stances towards federational trends.[81] The Lutheran synods of Iowa, Ohio and Buffalo formed the American Lutheran Church[82] in August 1930 and the American Lutheran Conference in the following October[83]. The Missouri synod argued with even greater biblicism than these Lutherans, and insisted on being handled as an exclusive body. As soon as immigrant churches united (and for the first time) they lost their specific national backgrounds and went through a process of Americanisation in terms of culture and language. This led to significant feelings of uncertainty. Doctrinaire commitments, some of which exhibited fundamentalist features[84], were supposed to cushion lifestyle destabilisation. Confessional dissociations, for instance between Lutheran Churches and non-Lutheran Churches, gained new importance as differentiation and identification criteria. 1934 saw the founding of a general American Christian Committee for German Refugees[85] and their invitation to work in its general committee[86]. His answer stated that the National Lutheran Council had been helping persecuted Lutherans on a worldwide scale since its inception, and that he therefore did not deem it wise for him to join the general committee.[87] In mid-July 1938, American Lutherans did, however, reach an agreement with the American Committee for Christian German Refugees in order to ease the emigration of persecuted Lutherans in Germany to the USA.[88]

Not only in religious terms, but also in socio-economic and domestic and foreign political terms, the 1920s ended and the 1930s began with wide-reaching social upheaval. A "fog of despair"[89] spread over the entire country, also affecting the churches[90]. The stock market crash of 1929 disconcerted the American people for many more reasons than just the financial consequences. Under profound shock, it appeared to many Americans that the political, social and economic systems of the United States had collapsed like a house of cards. This was to be followed by the 1932 collapse of international payments in Europe, which lead to a second, catastrophic depression in the USA. By spring 1933, the number of unemployed persons had risen to fourteen to fifteen million people – almost a third of all employed persons. Respect for representative parliamentary democracy as a form of government dropped considerably, as the impression had arisen that it was not capable of coping with a crisis on this scale. Some intellectuals began to sympathise with the Communist ideology, with the clergy also orienting itself further to the left. On the other hand, fewer than fifty ministers tended towards the Communist Party.[91] Despite some economic upturns the Great depression effectively continued until 1941.[92]

In September 1931, Japan took advantage of the weakness of the USA and Europe and occupied southern Manchuria. Encouraged by silence on the part of the USA, Great Britain and the League of Nations, they took the rest of Manchuria in January 1932 and created the puppet state of Manchukuo.[93] Once the League of Nations had finally adjudged Japan's action to be unlawful, the 27 March 1932 saw the aggressor's announcement of its withdrawal from the League of Nations.

This general upheaval led to the 1932 presidential election victory of the Democrat Franklin D. Roosevelt (1882–1945) over the incumbent, the Republican Herbert C. Hoover (1874–1964). When Roosevelt took office on 4 March 1933, the country was in a desperate social and economic situation. The new president had the difficult task of overcoming the "great crisis" ahead of him, made no easier by the fact that the institutional machine had also crumbled. His New Deal social action plan included nothing less than the extensive reconstruction of American society with the help of dirigiste state emergency and reform measures. Some of these interventions showed structural similarities with the efforts being made in Europe. In order to get the unemployed off the streets, for example, a large job creation programme – only ended by the USA's entry into the Second World War – was set up. A type of voluntary community service was established. Instructed by officers and working for a daily wage of one Dollar, the ranks of this "unemployed army" planted forests, created national parks, regulated rivers, dried out swamps and built 664,000 miles of new road, 77,000 bridges and 285 airports. Unlike his German counterpart, Roosevelt had to find compromises with political opponents, which reduced the effectiveness of his reform programme. As such, and also due to the related reduction in his power, resistance from the old elite[94] and dissatisfaction among the population grew, even though Roosevelt's measures had led to significant improvement of the situation within a year. Roosevelt's programme did not go far enough for some social radicals, who had a not-insignificant number of ministers among their leaders. According to opinion polls[95], their animosity towards the financial world was occasionally mixed with anti-Semitic undertones[96] and was popular enough to have endangered a Democrat victory in the congressional mid-terms in autumn 1934. It must be taken into account, after all, that a wave of severe strikes had shaken the country that year. Socio-radical criticism during the second phase of the New Deal prompted Roosevelt to make a "swing to the left" in 1935, which took the form of comprehensive social legislation. This change of course led to accusations of Roosevelt being the "unofficial Comintern candidate" during the 1936 presidential campaign. The Republican vice-presidential candidate went as far as to say that the Roosevelt administration wanted to usher America towards Moscow.[97] Roosevelt's opponents were predominantly conservative Protestants, sections of the Roman Catholic hierarchy and various anti-Semitic groups. This, of course, did not prevent Roosevelt from writing charming letters to conservative churches, informing them on his take on the political situation and asking them for advice and support.[98] The Protestant opposition also maintained contact to the previous president[99], who had both claimed in 1932 that Roosevelt was a Marxist or a Socialist[100], and, in his "Speeches on the American Way", denounced the politics of the New Deal as a route to fascism or socialism[101]. Roosevelt's most vehement opponents even accused him of wanting to make himself the "dictator of America"[102]. Despite such attacks – which were, in this case, unfounded – Roosevelt and his party achieved landslide victories in both houses of Congress in the 1936 elections.

In terms of foreign policy, the neutrality laws passed between 1935 and 1937 severely restricted the Roosevelt administration's room for manoeuvre and strengthened the position of the non-interventionists and isolationists.[103] There were also insurmountable differences between the liberal Federal Council and President Roosevelt where the safeguarding of absolute neutrality and the avoidance of a policy of military strength were concerned. Roosevelt received address after address from the group imploring him either to refrain from allowing military manoeuvres in the Pacific in order to avoid provoking Japan[104] or to forego building up the Navy, as they believed that armament would threaten peace[105].

The USA's recognition of the USSR and the establishment of diplomatic relations on 16 November 1933 had remained free of economic and political consequences.[106] The same applied to church politics. In the spring of 1934, the

American Lutherans attempted – without success – to benefit from the resultant new possibilities by trying to support persecuted Lutherans in the USSR via the Soviet embassy and the State Department.[107] The route via the German Lutherans and the German embassy, on the other hand, was so successful that August 1934 saw Morehead making a renewed call to Marahrens, the Hanoverian Regional Bishop, to approach the Russian authorities via the German embassy on behalf of the Lutheran Church in Russia.[108] Almost at the same time he did, however, also write to the Swedish Lutheran Per Pehrsson, stating that he feared that the situation of Lutherans in Russia (who were seen as a colonial church[109]) would worsen due to the anti-Communist propaganda being carried out by Hitler's Germany, and that it would no longer be possible for the German embassy to aid their harassed fellow Lutherans in the USSR as they had been able to in the past[110]. Yet, it turned out that Morehead was wrong: in cooperation with the German Foreign Ministry, the Lutheran World Convention was able to bring about commutation by the Soviet administration of the death sentences of three Lutheran Pastors who had been exiled to Siberia.[111]

Against the backdrop of circumstances in the Soviet Union, it was not only the Germans who distinguished between fundamental appreciation of the National Socialist regime on the one hand and its resistance to the protection of church autonomy on the other.[112] As the Danish Lutheran Jørgensen wrote to the Americans: "We foreigners, we who have seen how much the Führer has done for Germany, ... are faced with a dilemma: we want to help German Lutheranism – but are in danger of working against the German state!"[113]

The peculiar status of German Lutherans in the Lutheran World Convention also becomes obvious in case of the election of Marahrens to the position of president at the Third Lutheran World Convention (held in Paris in October 1935)[114], which came in spite of the fact that American and Nordic Lutherans had repeatedly voiced reservations in the run-up to the event[115]. Furthermore, the newly-created position of general secretary was bestowed upon the Hanoverian Lutheran Hanns Lilje[116] and based in Berlin. This came despite Jørgensen's urgent warnings against this course of action in a confidential letter to Long, which referred to the national reservations of Lutherans from other European countries[117]. The formal selection of Lilje, who had supported Marahrens even before being called to office, took place during the meeting of the Executive Committee in New York (September/October 1936) – a meeting the representatives of Nordic countries were unable to participate in. According to the newly-elected Lilje, the "great and joyful resolution of the American members of the Executive Committee was definitive"[118] to his election. There were certainly also practical reasons: as Marahrens had risen to the rank of president, it was reasonable to select an executive secretary who enjoyed his trust and was based somewhere geographically close to him. It was not only the media who paid great attention to the three German delegates – Marahrens, Meiser and Lilje – during their American visit.[119] President Roosevelt sent the guests a welcome telegraph and even granted them a special audience at the White House, thereby underlining the importance of German-American church relations.

The division of the organisation into three sections ("regional groups")[120] agreed in 1935 saw the American (and Nordic) Lutherans gain greater institutional independence from Central Europe, and was, to a certain extent at least, a church-political counterpart to the general foreign policy of isolationism being followed by the USA[121].

In the assessment of the Methodist Bishop Ivan Lee Holt, occasional president of the Federal Council, the economic depression had hit the institutionalised social gospel[122] of the social-liberal American Federation of Churches far harder than it had the conservatives. All romantic hope of the "one nation" scenario, under which new social order, justice, equal rights to education and middle-class affluence were to have reigned, as well as ecumenical dreams of peaceful co-existence of peoples, races and religions, had been destroyed.[123] Both the inter-faith dialogue which had been initiated by the Presbyterians – and included the Jews and the Roman Catholics[124] – and the National Conference of Christians and Jews, which had been founded in 1927[125], slid into a serious crisis. "Relations between many Jews and Christians were strained because non-Jews did not come up with much by way of help for Jews seeking refuge from Hitler."[126] A confidential report delivered by an American pastor illustrates just how excellently the American churches were informed concerning the persecution of the Jews. The report made the following warning fourteen days before the passing of the Nuremberg Race Laws: "We must reckon with the possibility of pogroms in Germany in the near future."[127] As part of his appeal to the churches to roll out a campaign of widespread diplomacy in order to prevent the pogrom, he indicated the number of those in potentially-affected circles. In contrast to the critical self-assessment of American efforts provided by church historians such as Marty[128], however, it is to be mentioned that numerous committees and societies formed during the following years in order to collect money and lead complex negotiations to facilitate the emigration of persecuted Jews and Christians from Germany[129]. Admittedly, there were also considerable differences between the Federal Council and the National Lutheran Council in these matters. This did not help to push forward work on behalf of the persecuted[130] – 70 to 80 % of whom were Lutherans[131]. A further problem came in the form of immigration quotas enforced by the U. S. authorities, which, once immigration quotas had been exhausted, would only allow preachers of Jewish descent into the country who could prove that they had a definite position in a parish.[132] A prior encumbrance on relations between Christians and Jews in America arose out of the situation whereby the International Mission Council, which operated its own department for the conversion of Jews, had accused the liberal Federal Council's Committee on Goodwill Between Jews and Christians, which was less enthusiastic where missionary work was concerned, of not doing enough to save Jewish souls.[133]

Searching for a "new Protestant strategy"[134], liberal ministers preached from the pulpit on the severe economic problems faced by the country, and were forced to look on with the realisation that in doing this they were subjecting their churches to a new test: the threat of schism no longer only came as a result of theological disputes, but also as a result of economic issues[135]. The following was published on 28 September 1935 in a circular for business people: "The Federal

Council of Churches of Christ is the most hypocritical of the subversive organizations ... . It is said to be largely financed by communistic radicals."[136] A memorandum from the Navy's secret service section, which was quoted from in
Congress in mid-September 1935, was even more severe. According to their information the Federal Council was an organisation "giving 'aid and comfort to the
Communist movement and party'"[137]. This matter developed into a scandal, with
Roosevelt having to receive church delegations and ensure them that he har-
boured no distrust for the activities of the Federal Council whatsoever. It is said
that the Army was instructed to make no further comments on civil organisations.

Such accusations were naturally without any factual basis, however these political misunderstandings still showed that the liberal Mainline churches had not
succeeded in reacting to socio-economic problems in a specific religious way.
Their leading personalities supported the New Deal's social programmes and
therefore Roosevelt's domestic politics.[138] Despite their votes against and their reporting on the persecution of the Jews[139], as well as their reporting on the oppression of German churches under the National Socialist regime, it was these same
liberal church circles that were against the Roosevelt's preparedness approach to
foreign policy, as they feared that military defence programmes would endanger
peace. In particular, influential associations of combined radical-pacifist powers
both within and outside of the Federal Council rejected all forms of military conflict, therefore splitting their churches and church groupings along a fault line.[140]

Perhaps the most controversial episode involving the Federal Council and the
White House came at the end of 1939, when Roosevelt chose the Protestant
Myron C. Taylor as his personal representative in the Vatican.[141] Cardinal Secretary of State Pacelli was elected Pope on 2 March. Both Congress and the House
of Representatives had passed appropriate resolutions on the death of Pius XI and
adjourned their negotiations for one day.[142] Roosevelt had sent Joseph P. Kennedy, the ambassador in London at the time, to the enthroning of Pius XII as his
representative.[143] Roosevelt – the holder of an honorary doctorate at the Catholic
Notre Dame University since 1935 – had consulted Cardinal Francis Spellman[144]
before taking this series of diplomatic steps in order to ensure that his actions
would ensure continued productive relations with both the Vatican and the domestic Catholic population, which numbered 21,403,000 believers[145]. Catholicism
was one of the President's strongest sources of support both in terms of domestic and foreign policy, as his social policy conformed to Catholic social doctrine
and had repercussions amongst the republican-Protestant elite above all other
groups.[146] The Catholics supported Roosevelt's policy of preparedness with few exceptions.[147] Spellman had been considered an intermediary between Washington
and Rome since his accompaniment of the Cardinal State Secretary on his trip
around America and visit to the White House in 1936.[148] Roosevelt had obviously completely underestimated the vehemence and solidarity with which American
Protestantism – internally at loggerheads but united in its anti-Catholicism[149] –
would react to this collective infringement on its feelings of cultural superiority
and supposed danger to democracy[150]. The Protestant camp had been watching
the rising influence of Roman Catholicism on the Roosevelt administration for
years.[151] Until 1933, "Protestantism is America's 'only natural religion'" had re-

mained uncontradicted.[152] All large Protestant denominations – and even the Federal Council[153] – used verbal and written representations to attempt to make Roosevelt recall the special envoy. This was to no avail. Roosevelt did, however, make reassuring statements indicating that this was a time-restricted measure and moreover that it was linked to Taylor as an individual.[154] Yet American Protestantism remained sceptical and followed all announcements on this subject with great interest.[155] The weakest protests came from the American Lutherans[156], as they had to be conscious of the fact that the failure of their fellow Lutherans in Germany had literally pushed Roosevelt and his search for allies into the arms of Rome. The same applied to a lesser extent where church-political circumstances in the United States were concerned. In contrast with American Lutheranism, Cardinal George Mundelein (Chicago) was among the most vehement critics of church and race politics under the National Socialist regime.[157] At a May 1937 priests' conference, he publicly described Hitler as an "inept paper hanger"[158].

Jørgensen, American Lutheranism's main informant with regard to the German churches, wrote the following at the end of 1937: "The Catholic churches – and the Pope in particular – speak out in harsh opposition to the [German] regime. Our friends, on the other hand, are, as is typical to the Lutheran way, submissive to the powers that be. They are shocked and anxious, however, and they are silent. They wish to stand firm on the Creed, but only speak out actively with great caution."[159] Almost a year later in November 1938, Jørgensen was even more devastating in his assessment of German Lutherans: "Our friends, and Marahrens first and foremost, waste no opportunity to show that they are subjects loyal to the Führer. They saluted him, for example, when *Anschluss* agreements annexed Austria and the Sudetenland to the Reich."[160]

It was less the annexations and rather the *Reichspogromnacht* of 9/10 November 1938 which brought about a swing in public opinion in the United States, whereby disgust at the appalling acts carried out by Germans again deflected potential sympathy for the Jews. Sylvester C. Michelfelder of the St Paul's Evangelical Church, Ohio, wrote the following to Long in New York: "I think that the sympathies of many people are turning away from the German people. The persecution of the Jews has made martyrs out of the Jews. Personally I regret this very much. It will take many years for the German people to recapture some of the good feelings that existed just a few years ago."[161]

The second decisive drop in support followed the signing of the Hitler-Stalin Pact on 23 August 1939.[162] Hardly any arguments remained which either the religious right or the religious left could use in favour of their respective, supposedly better dictatorship.[163] On the contrary: public opinion tended towards the opinion of those who saw both regime types as closely similar and were no longer able to find any grounds at all to support either system. This view did not, however, foster readiness to intervene. The American declaration of neutrality on 1 September 1939 corresponded with opinion polls, which showed that 96.5 % of the population wanted to refrain from entering the War.[164] The American clergy reflected the popular stance. The liberal Protestants of the Mainline churches in particular stuck with their "no more war" stance of the 1920s[165], and set up the "Ministers No War Committee" as late as 1941[166]. The extent to which opinions can endure despite the emergence of facts which refute them was exhibited by the discussion of the 1940 book "The Trojan Horse in America"[167], in which the Committee published its investigations into radical political groups in the United States. Whereas Catholics paid greater attention to Communist activities and judged them severely, liberal Protestants tended towards a more lenient assessment of the Communists than the National Socialists, combining this stance with anti-Catholic attitudes.[168]

Towards the end of 1940, liberal theologians grouped around Reinhold Niebuhr, Henry Van Dusen and Francis P. Miller, founded the anti-isolationist oriented journal "Christianity and Crisis", which was designed as a counterweight to the neutral voice of liberal Protestantism, the "Christian Century".[169] The Federal Council also created a commission designed "to study the bases of a just and durable peace". This commission put together a handbook containing principles for sustainable post-war order. The lawyer John Foster Dulles, a member of the Presbyterian Church and a politician in the interventionist wing of the Republican Party, was the chairman of this commission.[170] He was among the most prominent lay people in the Federal Council and had participated in the planning of the foundation of the World Council of Churches in Oxford in 1937. He was also to play an important role at the full meeting of the Ecumenical Council in Amsterdam in 1948.[171]

3.   The German Churches in the opinion of the State Department (1933–1941)

The American administration continued to receive bulletins on Germany and the German churches until 1941, and not only from Christian denominations and Minister Stewart W. Herman of the American Churches in Berlin.[172] Dossiers from the Berlin embassy also arrived regularly in Washington, D. C.[173] Herman, incidentally, sent his reports and correspondence with American Lutherans using both the embassy's letterhead and diplomatic post in order to circumvent German mail surveillance.[174]

The State Department received detailed reports, analyses and assessments on the German church situation from the consulate general in Berlin (which also drew on local reports from the consulates in Munich, Stuttgart, Cologne, Bremen, Hamburg and, later, Vienna) on an almost weekly basis. These statements were based on the evaluation of confidential information and published texts and comments. They were accompanied by translations of key German texts in order that Washington could make its own interpretation of the situation independent from the opinion of the embassy staff. The diplomatic accounts were fundamentally different to those of observers from the clergy. They refrained from speculative comments, stayed strictly non-denominational and were extraordinarily sober in their judgements and free from any sort of hopes or wishes with regard to future development. It is not possible to determine the denomination of the author from the reports. Infringements on religious freedom were described down to the last detail, with numbers of detained ministers, levels of total fines imposed and publication bans on church pamphlets registered. Of particular note in comparison with the religious accounts was the realistic characterisation of Hitler himself.[175] On 24 July 1935, the embassy reported on fresh radical Nazi operations, commenting on proceedings:

"Certain ... individuals ..., particularly Church authorities who feel the pressure of circumstances, regard Hitler and Göring as being the prisoners of radicals such as Goebbels, Rosenberg, and especially Himmler, who possesses inordinate power as leader of the SS. As may be seen from the enclosed memorandum there is no doubt about the determination of extreme Party circles to proceed with what they call liquidation of the Jewish and Church problems ... . What appears to be an obvious camouflage to divert attention from internal friction is the prominence given in the press to events abroad, particularly the current disorders in Ireland. Trouble in all parts of the world are seized upon, and the United States is not spared with such a remark as that appearing in the *B. Z.* [*Berliner Zeitung*] on July 24, that 'daily the cases of Negro lynching become more frequent' a theme treated with variations in the Nazi *Angriff* and the *Völkischer Beobachter*."[176]

As a result of this diplomatic reporting, a clearer and noticeably more sinister picture emerged than the one being painted by conservative Protestants in the USA in particular. It seems that the Protestant church had better contact to the uncompromising wing of the Confessional Church than to moderate Lutheranism and the "neutrals". The American embassy had received the Pentecost Memorandum issued by the 2nd Provisional Directorate of the Confessional Church on 28 May 1936 a few days before its publication, and was therefore not surprised at its publication in the Anglo-American press.[177] Despite reports coming in on the stance of the Confessional Church, it was the differences between the Protestant and Catholic churches in terms of their powers of resistance against the National Socialist regime which were emphasised. The following was written in mid-February 1937: "The Roman Catholic on the other hand are better organized and are inspired apparently by a more active belief, Catholic feeling being still vigorous enough to produce the demonstrations reported in recent issues."[178]

In particular, the encyclical *Mit brennender Sorge* (With Burning Sorrow) issued by Pius XI (1922–1939) on 14 March 1937 was seen by the embassy as a beacon to devout Christians of both denominations.[179] On the other hand, diplomats also observed the growing dissociation of the population from traditional churches and an ever-clearer number of citizens turning to the political religion of National Socialism.[180]

The Berlin embassy collected reports and information from all across the Reich in connection with the *Reichspogromnacht* on 9/10 November 1938. Although this material meant that the American administration was faced with the full magnitude of the brutality used, the reports also included other impressions. It is thus that the following was said about the Germans: "Many feel ashamed of and criticise the persecution of the Jews, which is regarded unnecessary and highly unwise from an international point of view."[181] In another report it read: "They are deeply shocked and repelled by the physical excesses against the Jews."[182]

The violence directed against the Jews and the suppression of the churches were seen as a success by the radical National Socialist powers, such as Goebbels and Himmler, and as a defeat by moderate groups, which appeared to include Göring and Schacht.[183]

Since mid-1937, the State Department had attempted to use its embassies in order to create an analysis of German church politics in comparison with European standards, with London and Rome the key benchmarks. Discrete support to efforts being made by the Vatican was provided via diplomatic channels in order to influence Mussolini and ask him to mediate in the German state versus church conflict.[184] These attempts ended after Hitler's visit to Rome in May 1938[185], especially as messages from the Warsaw embassy at the start of December 1938 reinforced the impression that Hitler intended to use methods similar to those he had employed against the Jews against the Catholics as well. These messages came from Burckhardt, the High Commissioner of Danzig.[186] They corresponded with confidential reports which had been passed to the Polish Foreign Minister, Józef Beck (1894–1944).[187] In his response to questions from the American ambassador, Beck was of the opinion that Cardinal Hlond[188], who had repeatedly been mentioned as a potential successor to Pius XI, would have hardly any chance as a candidate due to his Polish nationality. The death of Pius XI triggered busy activity in terms of publicity and diplomacy. He had been an uncompromising opponent of National Socialist Germany and fascist Italy. The selection of his successor appeared to offer an opportunity to instigate positive change in the relationship between state and church in Germany, especially as relations had worsened significantly during the previous two years.[189] The American embassy shared this opinion.[190] In the race to curry favour with the Vatican, the democratic states, and the USA in particular, therefore, made sure that there was no lack of attention towards the Curia. After Pacelli's election on 2 March 1939, the new pontiff made efforts to improve diplomatic relations, including those with Berlin[191], which caused a temporary period of détente in church circumstances in Germany[192]. On the other hand, the annexation of the remaining areas of Czechoslovakia on 15 March 1939 sparked various church-led initiatives designed to put the German dictatorship in its place and rescue peace. Although these initiatives did not take Roman Catholicism as their starting point, they definitely secured a leading role for Pius XII.[193]

The ambassadorial reports reflected the dynamic development in Central Europe. They may explain why it was that the Roosevelt administration was so much quicker (i. e. around mid-1937) than the American churches and the American population as a whole to arrive at the realisation that the humanisation of the National Socialist regime could no longer be expected and that National Socialism was a real threat to the existence of Christian churches, Judaism and world peace.

4.   Germany, America and the Churches of both countries during the "Phony War" (1939–1941)

On 22 September 1939, the Federal Council discussed the drafting of a statement by American churches on the European war. In it, the Federation of Churches once again reinforced its determination to do everything possible to keep America out of the military conflict. They saw it as America's duty to alleviate the suffering caused by the war and to work towards stable peace. Those responsible for the war were mentioned unmistakeably: "In appraising the present situation some of us put the emphasis upon the fact that one party to the conflict has committed an act of aggression against another people and unjustly invaded its territory. Others of us put the emphasis upon the futility of war as a method of establishing justice or defending democracy."[194]

In the version of "Call to the Churches" ratified on 6 October 1939, however, it was stated that: "Every land has some share in the common guilt and the Christians in every land have followed their Master only 'after off'." The appeal to churches to defend freedom of conscience, freedom of the press, freedom of speech and freedom to preach indicated a certain taking of sides in itself.[195] On 10 November 1939, Roosevelt received a delegation from the Federal Council, who handed him a letter.[196] The President's assurances that he wished to keep the United States out of the war were welcomed by the Federal Council both in writing and verbally. The Federal Council also expressed a desire to see America accept a higher degree of responsibility for the creation of a just and brotherly world.

In mid-May 1940, the Federal Council debated a telegram which had arrived from Visser't Hooft, the General Secretary of the nascent Ecumenical Council of Churches in Geneva.[197] The Dutchman had described Hitler's victories as a catastrophe, and asked the Americans whether or not they really wanted to stand by as a large section of the world was subjected to both the loss of the possibility to behave as a Christian and the destruction of the ecumenical movement.[198] Adolf Keller had also sent a telegram: "Where is America? We need your help and prayers more than ever."[199] Both obviously expected that the American churches would move away from their neutrality stance. Yet though the Federal Council's statement condemned the infringement of the neutrality of the Benelux nations and the bondage of churches in Germany, it remained silent on America's own neutrality. In a statement made on 21 July 1940 on the churches' stance on the world crisis, the Federal Council supported the ecumenical community but illustrated once again American desire for neutrality.[200] The Federal Council demonstrated both ecumenical community and neutrality during the visits it paid to churches of all denominations and from all countries engaged in the war. A Federal Council delegation visited Berlin in mid-January 1940, and was honoured by Bishop Heckel with a lavish reception, which was also attended by the American ambassador.[201]

Simultaneous to this, the embassy was reporting that the "confessional front" had slid into the background, that its synods were no longer meeting and that their organisation had collapsed to a large extent. Thanks to its strict organisation, the Catholic Church was in relatively good shape when compared to the paralysed state of Protestantism, particularly as state pressure on both churches appeared to have been reduced. At the end of February 1940, the embassy made the following judgement on the alliance between Germany and the USSR: "It has already unquestionably hardened the opposition to National Socialism of many devout churchmen, both Protestant and Catholic, who on grounds of doctrine alone are shocked by Germany's new friendship with a frankly atheistic regime."[202] The shock of an alliance with Communist Russia was yet to face American spirituality.[203]

The fact that American public opinion viewed the dictatorships in Italy and Germany differently to the Communist regime in the USSR[204] up until the outbreak of war is verified by the work of the House Committee on Un-American Activities. From its inception, the Committee devoted itself to the uncovering of Communist infiltration in the machines of the Roosevelt administration. On the other hand, associations such as the *Bund der Freunde des Neuen Deutschland* (Friends of New Germany), the German-American Bund[205] and other groups which were more or less sympathetic to National Socialist ideology and fought Roosevelt's "Jew Deal" got off lightly to a large extent[206]. The lack of readiness to amend immigration quotas to the benefit of Jewish refugees from Europe indicated how little desire there was to deal with their desperate situation in Germany.[207] People with strongly anti-Semitic views were to be found among the isolationists[208] – who fought against American intervention right until the end – in particular[209]. In terms of political debate this element served to shift all neutrals towards National Socialist supporters.[210]

Although the Ku Klux Klan had lost since past the high point of its powers by the end of the 1930s, it must not go unnoticed that it was still highly visible in the South and Mid-West. According to the way it saw itself it was a Protestant movement protecting white America against the threats posed by of Catholics, blacks and Jews. Its members were reputed to be highly moral, were amongst the most steadfast of churchgoers and were led by Protestant preachers on a not-too-infrequent basis.[211] Due to their common aims there were often links and defections between them and the new radical right-wing movements.[212]

Even after the beginning of the Second World War, the varying assessment of both dictatorships in conservative church circles prevailed for some time. At the end of September 1939, Jørgensen reported to the Americans on the church situation in Poland. Although he was able to report on dead and deported ministers, bishops and professors in the German-occupied area of Poland, he came to the conclusion: "Yet the circumstances of Poles in the German-occupied area of Poland are almost heavenly when compared to those of those unfortunate enough to find themselves under Russian authority."[213] On 5 September 1939, Long directed an address to American Lutherans in which he expressed fears for the future of "world Lutheranism" in view of the war. Whereas he took no stance whatsoever on the warring nations and their national churches, this was not the case when it came to the Soviet Union: "Russia has been a great blackout spot in the world so far as Christianity is concerned. Whether it will continue as such after the war is concluded no one knows. It may be that God will make use of this catastrophe to open up the vast empire of Russia to the Gospel."[214]

As late as the end of June 1940, Long expressed the following in an internal report for the American Lutheran Church: "The probability is, although it cannot be confirmed, that in that part of Poland now occupied by Germany the Roman Catholic Churches are able to continue their services, but that in the eastern half which is now under Russian domination the Churches have been liquidated."[215]

Roosevelt and the circles around him tended towards a contrary assessment of the European dictatorships clearly against the tide of public opinion in the USA until the outbreak of war. It is likely that the information arriving from the Berlin embassy was responsible for this, as it was lacking in neither clarity nor precision where the persecution of the Jews was concerned. Nonetheless, February 1940 saw the State Department ignore calls from the American embassy to make a public statement on the ongoing atrocities. Their reasoning was that it would be a mistake at that point in time "to take such action ..., either in the form of a public statement by the president or a note to the German Government"[216], as this would have represented intervention into the internal affairs of another state. They also believed that the Allies would have seen such a statement as a condemnation of Germany and exploited it politically.[217]

The diplomatic reports of 1940/41 included detailed records of existing ghettos, insufficient medical supplies, epidemics, hunger and death among those within their boundaries. The State Department also received exact indications on the deportation of German and European Jews. A Berlin diplomatic attaché provided a shocking report on the situation in Czechoslovakia on 22 November 1940. The report included the unusually emotional comment of "God spare the western world from this new order!"[218]. February and March 1941 saw reports arriving at the State Department detailing the execution of "deportation programme" moving Viennese Jews to Poland. Acting on the recommendation of the embassy, the State Department denied the American Jewish Welfare Organisation access to this data, despite the fact that they had requested that such information be passed on to them.[219] In September 1941, the Berlin embassy reported that a large proportion of Berlin residents were sympathetic to wearers of the Star of David and exhibited awkward embarrassment due to their treatment.[220] Reports on the deportation of thousands of Berlin Jews to Poland followed in the months thereafter.[221]

Also in September 1941 – the month in which it became compulsory for Jews in Germany to wear the yellow star – the Federal Council ratified a statement on anti-Semitism in America: "Recent evidence of anti-Jewish prejudice in our own country compels us to speak again a word of solemn warning to the nation. Divisiveness on religious or racial grounds is a portentous menace to American democracy. If one group be made the target of attack today, the same spirit of intolerance may be visited on another group tomorrow and the rights and liberties of every group thus be put in jeopardy."[222] In spite of the atrocities being carried out by Germans on the Jews of Europe, it was necessary for the Federal Council to make a solemn statement denouncing anti-Semitism in their own country as un-American and un-Christian.

On 3 September 1941, the American President wrote to Pope Pius XII that he believed the Russian dictatorship and the survival of Russia to be less dangerous to the safety of other nations and "to religion, to the church as such" than the German form of dictatorship. "In so far as I am informed", stated Roosevelt, "churches in Russia are open. I believe there is a real possibility that Russia may as a result of the present conflict recognize freedom of religion in Russia."[223] "Furthermore, it is my belief that the leaders of all churches in the United States should recognize these facts clearly and should not close their eyes to these basic questions and by their present attitude on this question directly assist Germany in her present objectives."[224]

The American President demanded (in the form of a public press publication) and received a corresponding statement of religious freedom from the Kremlin on 4 October 1941.[225] The Kremlin's statement recapitulated exactly those convictions on the state of religious freedom in Russia which Roosevelt had already expressed. Although the Great Patriotic War had indeed led to cooperation between the Russian Orthodox Church and the Communist state, such far-reaching comments were hardly justified.[226] Even if this meant that the Vatican could hardly follow this point of view in terms of its content – and found it impossible to believe that the American President could be so badly informed on the situation in USSR – Roosevelt achieved his intended aim: Rome did not hinder America's provision of war aid to the pressurised USSR[227] and also helped to soften anti-Soviet opposition among American Catholics[228]. At Roosevelt's request, Pius XII interpreted the fundamental statements made in the encyclical *Divini Redemptoris*[229] issued by Pius XI in February 1937 – which had not only condemned Communism but also prohibited any cooperation with Communists – as not referring to the Russian people[230]. Monsignor Tardini wrote to Cicognani, the apostolic envoy in Washington, on 20 September 1941:

"Besides, it is evident that with the encyclical 'Divini Redemptoris' the Holy Father only wanted to condemn atheist communism and not the Russian people, towards whom he in the same document expressed himself in a paternal and compassionate tone. Those observations are obvious and easily comprehensible, however, for reasons Your Excellency will not ignore, they cannot be brought forward authoritatively by the 'Osservatore Romano' and even less by the Holy See and in the name of the Holy See. Your Excellency, on an appropriate occasion, could communicate this openly and confidentially to Monsignor Mooney or other bishops who might enquire about this subject, warning them all that if they wanted to make use of this information they would have to do it without involving the Holy See."[231]

After highly confidential consultations between Cicognani and Monsignor Mooney, the Archbishop of Detroit, and the General Secretary of the National Catholic Welfare Conference, Michael Ready, all three agreed that the Archbishop of Cincinnati, John T. McNicholas, was best suited to make a corresponding public statement. McNicholas immediately showed his willingness to participate and directed a pastoral letter to the congregation of his archdiocese. He gave the release to press services for dissemination and arranged for his colleagues, such as the Archbishop of Chicago, to make positive comments on the pastoral letter. In his report to the Vatican dated 29 October 1941, Cicognani wrote about the structure of the argumentation used in the pastoral letter: "After having advised the believers to charity and tolerance in regard to political opinions, Monsignor McNicholas reminded of those parts of the Encyclicals of His Holiness Pius XI on Germany and the distinction between Nazism and the German people contained therein; he went on with similar considerations regarding the Soviet regime and the Russian people; then he examined the discussed paragraph of the Encyclical 'Divini Redemptoris' by putting it into the right context and concluding that it cannot be applied in this moment of armed conflict."[232]

The assessment of religious freedom in the Soviet Union made public by Roosevelt himself during a "for the record" comment at an October 1941 press conference[233] also called the Federal Council into action. The liberal Protestants used a published statement and a discussion with their President in an attempt to explain the difference between religious freedom in America and the freedom of religious expression detailed under Article 124 of the Soviet Constitution to both the President and the American public. "President Roosevelt's interest in religious freedom, as emphasized on several occasions, merits deep appreciation, but it is hoped that he will not be misled into assuming that the freedom which is guaranteed under the Russian Constitution has any real resemblance to the religious freedom which we have known in America. If he can help to interpret to Russia the meaning of religious freedom in the full American sense, he will earn the gratitude of all men of Christian insight and conviction."[234]

They had either not understood – or did not want to understand – that their President had voiced his opinion on the religious circumstances in a country which needed to be accepted by the American people as a World War ally.[235] Yet as soon as two weeks after that statement, 1,000 prominent Protestants made an appeal supporting Roosevelt's aid programme for the USSR[236], whilst the Federal Council assured the President of its loyalty in an address made shortly after the USA entered the war[237]. A careful cooperation which contrasted with the enthusiastic allegiance exhibited by churches during the First World War and was fittingly known as "a cautious patriotism"[238] began[239]. This was nothing different to the behaviour which the American embassy had noticed among German pastors in February 1940: "On the whole, it would appear that many, if not the great majority, of the Protestant pastors support Germany's cause in the present war, if not with fervour then at least with acquiescence."[240]

Summary

Both the churches and the government of the United States were informed on internal circumstances in National Socialist Germany to a high degree of accuracy. They collected information through various channels and interpreted it correctly for the most part.[241] The initially positive judgment on circumstances in Germany after Hitler took power needs to be viewed against the background of the situation in the United States itself. Parliamentary democracy appeared incompetent when it came to reacting appropriately to the comprehensive collapse of American society which saw political and religious depressions follow the economic Depression. Many conservative Protestants believed that Roosevelt and his social legislation, which was rejected as "un-American", were setting an inevitable course towards socialism. His acceptance and implicit upgrading of Roman Catholicism awoke feelings of cultural inferiority which were strong enough after the start of the war to engender the feeling that the Catholics could emerge victorious from the war.

In contrast with the USA's democracy, which was seen as ailing, Europe was witness to two types of dictatorship, with the Italian fascists and German National Socialists on one side and the Stalinist Communists on the other. As a result of information passed to it by the Russian Orthodox Church in Exile[242] and the Lutheran Church since the October Revolution, the United States had had exact knowledge of religious persecution in the Soviet Union and the high number of victims it had claimed[243]. In comparison with this scenario, the much younger Italian and German dictatorships, which were constantly uttered in the same breath, did not only seem successful in an economic and law and order sense, but also somewhat more restrained when it came to the treatment of churches. American churches were divided with regard to the disputes between the Brethren Council wing of the Confessional Church and moderate to neutral Lutheranism. Fundamentalist, evangelical or confessional-oriented denominations saw and rejected radical political tendencies in Karl Barth and his followers. In the case of the liberal Mainline Churches aligned to the Federal Council there appeared to be greater appreciation of the theological concerns of the Brethren Council of the Confessional Church. However, as all groups involved in the struggle between church and state initially stressed their loyalty to the National Socialist state and the German Lutherans tended to report to foreigners on political conflict with the state in a somewhat cautious fashion, the impression that these were only temporary disputes prevailed for a lengthy period. The anti-Semitic slogans and acts of violence used by the National Socialist state met with at least partial anti-Semitic sentiment in America. Though the majority of these groups – which were often from Christian backgrounds – condemned the use of violence, they did back the suppression of Jewish influence in American society and were completely against an increase in the immigration quota.

As can be seen from opinion polls carried out at the time, it was only the Niemöller trial in the spring of 1938, the *Reichspogromnacht* in November 1938, the Hitler-Stalin Pact and the beginning of the war in autumn 1939 which brought about fundamental changes to the prevailing mood in American churches and American society as a whole.[244] Nonetheless, despite the slow realisation that the National Socialist regime was also a dictatorship worthy of loathing, it was not until 1941 that Stalinism and Hitlerism were seen in terms of completely negative equality. Even the 1939/40 rejection of both dictatorships and the desire to defeat the Axis powers was not enough to convince the American public to back the entry of the USA into the war. In the case of the liberal Mainline Churches, the rejection of the war also played an important role in ecumenical-pacifistic thought.

The Germans were not always forthcoming with the truth requested so insistently and repeatedly by America.[245] Within the mix of fascination and disgust which America showed for the National Socialist dictatorship – a mix that varied according to the specific point in time – there lay a moment of uncertainty which sometimes represented a significant restriction on the powers of judgment of the American people and their churches.

(Translation: Peter Welchman)

Notes

1   Cf. Adolf Keller, Amerikanisches Christentum – heute, Zollikon-Zurich 1943, 415 ff.; Ernst Benz, Kirchengeschichte in ökumenischer Sicht, Leiden-Cologne 1961, 75 ff. Also see Hartmut Lehmann, Alte und neue Welt in wechselseitiger Sicht, Göttingen 1995. On the twenties see Carmen Müller, Weimar im Blick der USA. Amerikanische Auslandskorrespondenten und öffentliche Meinung zwischen Perzeption und Realität (Studien zur Geschichte, Politik und Gesellschaft Nordamerikas 7), Münster 1997.

2   Stewart W. Herman, an American pastor, attempted to explain in his book "It's Your Souls We Want", which was published in 1942, why the American public did not recognise the radical change in 1933 and its meaning for the churches. He names as considerable factors the separation of state and church in the USA on the one hand and on the other the hardly overcome state church tradition in Germany.

3   Cf. Protocol of the conference of the executive committee in Hanover (dated 30 Mar. 1934 and signed by Marahrens and Jørgensen), in Archive of the Evangelical Lutheran Church in America (AELCA), Chicago, Best. Lutheran World Convention (LWC) 1/1, Minutes and Reports 1921–1947, Box 2, Folder 14, 1933. See Kurt Schmidt-Clausen, Vom Lutherischen Weltkonvent zum Lutherischen Weltbund. Geschichte des Lutherischen Weltkonventes 1923–1947 (Die lutherische Kirche, Geschichte und Gestalten 2), Gütersloh 1976, 139, 168 ff.; Armin Boyens, 'Luthertum im Zeitalter der Diktatoren. Der Lutherische Weltkonvent 1923–1947', in Ulrich Duchrow (ed.), Zwei Reiche und Regimente. Ideologie oder evangelische Orientierung? Internationale Fall- und Hintergrundstudien zur Theologie und Praxis lutherischer Kirchen im 20. Jahrhundert (SEE 13), Gütersloh 1977, 241–272; Verantwortung für die Kirche. Stenographische Aufzeichnungen und Mitschriften von Landesbischof Hans Meiser 1933–1935 (AKZG, A 1), vol. 1, revised by Hannelore Braun and Carsten Nicolaisen, Göttingen 1985, 122–124.

4   Long came from the Joint Synod of Ohio, which became a member of the American Lutheran Church in 1930. This Church in turn belonged to the American Lutheran Conference, which was founded in 1930. Cf. E. Clifford Nelson, The Rise of World Lutheranism. An American Perspective, Philadelphia 1982, 267 ff.

5   Cf. Frederick K. Wentz, Lutherans in Concert: The Story of the National Lutheran Council 1918–1966, Minneapolis 1968; Naomi Frost, Golden Visions, Broken Dreams: A Short History of the Lutheran Council in the U.S.A., New York 1987.

6   At the meeting of the executive committee in Hanover in 1933, Bow and Long said the number of confirmed members was 4,784,795. Cf. Protocol of the conference, AELCA, Chicago, Best. LWC 1/1, Minutes and Reports 1921–1947, Box 2, Folder 14, 1933.

7   Cf. Martin E. Marty, Modern American Religion, vol. 2: The Noise of Conflict (1919–1941), Chicago 1991, 211. The Joint Ohio Synod, the Norwegian Lutheran Church, the Iowa Synod, the Augustana Synod, the Lutheran Free Church and the United

Danish Church belonged to the American Lutheran Conference. See also E. Clifford
Nelson, The Lutherans in North America, Philadelphia 1980, 443 ff.

8   Marahrens reported in Hanover on "The spiritual side of the national revolution",
which he characterised as an ideology consisting of ideal religious belief and as standing in contrast to humanism and liberalism. He formulated it as a problem from the
viewpoint of the church: "National Socialism is religiously as well as politically positive, but it is at the same time a battlefield for the conflicts between Christianity and
ideology. The totalitarian claim of the state and the excessive value of race imply the
danger of gaining absolute validity and in this case are the exact opposite to the universal claim of God and the universality of Christianity." [self-translation] Cf. Protocol
of the conference of the executive committee in Hanover, AELCA, Chicago, Best.
LWC 1/1, Minutes and Reports 1921–1947, Box 2, Folder 14, 1933. Cf. Hanns Lilje,
'Präsident des Lutherischen Weltkonvents', in Walter Ködderitz (ed.), D. Marahrens.
Pastor pastorum zwischen zwei Weltkriegen, Hanover 1952, 128–130; Eberhard
Klügel, Die lutherische Landskirche Hannovers und ihr Bischof 1933–1945, vol. 1,
Berlin-Hamburg 1964, 31, 219.

9   Boe to Morehead, on 1 Sept. 1934, AELCA, Chicago, Best. LWC 1/2, Correspondence
File 1921–47, Box 21.

10   Cf. Hans Meiser, Kirche, Kampf und Christusglaube. Anfechtungen eines Luthera-
ners, ed. by Fritz and Gertrud Meiser, Munich 1982; Johanna Haberer (ed.), Er liebte
seine Kirche. Bischof Hans Meiser und die bayerische Landeskirche im Nationalsozialismus, Munich 1996.

11   The positive impression of Meiser remained throughout the years. On 5 Oct. 1936, Boe
wrote to Rev. Stubb: "I would like to have a little showing to honour the man in Germany that I respect most today." Cf. AELCA, Chicago, Best. NLC 2/3/1, Executive
Director Ralph H. Long Files 1930–47, Box 4.

12   Cf. Friedrich Wilhelm Kantzenbach, Widerstand und Solidarität der Christen in
Deutschland 1933–1945. Eine Dokumentation zum Kirchenkampf aus den Papieren
des D. Wilhelm Freiherrn von Pechmann, Neustadt/Aisch 1971, 120 f., 161, 183 f.,
205 f. Pechmann left the permanent committee of the Lutheran World Convent because Morehead with the support of the Scandinavians stood for a second period
although it was Ihmels' turn (ibid. 184). To the controversies between Ihmels and
Morehead cf. Hanns Kerner, Luthertum und ökomenische Bewegung für praktisches
Christentum 1919–1926 (Die lutherische Kirche, Geschichte und Gestalten 5),
Gütersloh 1983, 272 ff. Cf. also Nelson, The Rise of World Lutheranism (op. cit.
note 4), 262 ff.

13   Boe to Morehead on 5 Jan. 1934, AELCA, Chicago, Best. NLC 1/2, Correspondence
File 1921–47, Box 21. Long had the same experience, which he wrote to Boe on 13
Mar. 1934: "You recall that we had a certain picture in mind when we went over last
November but came back with an entirely different picture of this situation. Now I am
wondering if it is as bad as is generally reported." Cf. AELCA, Chicago, Best. NCL
2/3/1, Executive Director Ralph H. Long General Files 1930–1937, Box 2. Cf. as well:
Ralph H. Long, 'Wither in Germany', in The Lutheran, 28 Dec. 1933. Also see the
German press report from 16 Nov. 1933 with the title "Deutschland kämpft für uns
alle" [Germany fights for us all], in which the foreigners positively expressed themselves on National Socialist Germany. Since 1934, Long gave detailed reports on the
situation in Germany to individuals, parishes or churches. Long's reports stood out
because of his excellent expert knowledge. Cf. AELCA, Chicago, Best. NCL 2/3/1,
Executive Director Ralph H. Long General Files 1930–1937, Box 3. His 'Impressions'
on the meetings of the executive committee of the Lutheran World Convent in Hanover are also to be found there. A letter from TIME to Long on 6 Aug. 1936 reveals that
the TIME article of 10 Aug. 1936 on the stance of the church towards Hitler had been
realised with Long's help. Cf. AELCA, Chicago, Best. NLC 2/3/1, Executive Director
Ralph H. Long, Files 1930–47, Box 3.

14   On the help of the world Lutherans for the Lutherans in the USSR cf. Nelson, The Rise of World Lutheranism (op. cit. note 4), 264 ff.

15   Boe to Morehead on 5 Jan. 1934, AELCA, Chicago, Best. NLC 1/2, Correspondence File 1921–47, Box 21.

16   "The more I studied the situation, the more I became convinced that Jewish world propaganda is giving us a distorted picture." (op. cit. note 15). On 14 May 1933, the "American League for the Defence of Jewish Rights" under the leadership of the lawyer Samuel Untermeyer and Rabbi Stephen S. Wise in New York organised a boycott of German goods. According to the report from 27 Sep. 1934 from the German embassy, not only Jewish groups took part in the boycott; the Federal Council of Churches of Christ was particularly mentioned, cf. Politisches Archiv des Auswärtigen Amtes, Bonn [Pol. AA], Kult. VI A, Ev. Angelegenheiten 2, Bd. 7. According to the report from the third Jewish world conference in August 1934, apart from the American Jews "more than 20 millions other Americans, including millions of members of catholic and protestant churches" also supported the boycott.

17   Boe to Morehead on 5 Jan. 1934, AELCA, Chicago, Best. NLC 1/2, Correspondence File 1921–47, Box 21.

18   Cf. AELCA, Chicago, Best. NLC 2/3/1, Executive Director Ralph H. Long, General Files 1930–1947, Box 2. Also see William S. Shirer, Berlin Diary. The Journal of a Foreign Correspondent 1934–1947, Boston-Toronto 1941. German edition: Jürgen Schebera (ed.), Berliner Tagebuch, Aufzeichnungen 1934–1941, Leipzig-Weimar 1991.

19   Cf. Report on the short, 35 minutes long reception in the protocol of the conference of the LWC executive committee in Hanover, AELCA, Chicago, Best. LWC1/1, Minutes and Reports 1921–1947, Box 2, Folder 14, 1933. Cf. Thomas Martin Schneider, Reichsbischof Ludwig Müller. Eine Untersuchung zu Leben, Werk und Persönlichkeit (AKZG, B 19), Göttingen 1993, in particular 165 (Suspension of the Aryan Article on 16 Jan. 1933.) Schneider did not mention the reception for the executive committee of the LWC.

20   On 5 May 1934, Morehead asked Alfred Th. Jørgensen (Copenhagen) to give a detailed opinion of the situation in Germany. On 11 Aug. 1934, Jørgensen wrote to Morehead, Boe and Per Pehrsson (Gothenburg): "The situation of the Church in Germany has now become so serious that we cannot wait any longer with our plan." In a letter from Jørgensen to Morehead from 5 Oct. 1934 it reads: "Every day brings new communications about the terrible situation in Germany." On 1 Oct. 1934, Jørgensen had written to the Inspecteur Ecclésiastique, Pasteur H. Boury (Paris): "Vous savez que la situation en Allemagne est terrible." ["You know that the situation in Germany is terrible."] AELCA, Chicago, Best. NLC 1/2 Correspondence File 1921–47, Box 21. Long made a similar request of Pehrsson for information on the developments in Germany on 13 Jan. 1934, AELCA, Chicago, Best. NLC 2/3/1 General Files 1930–1937, Box 2. Also see Nelson, The Rise of World Lutheranism (op. cit. note 4), 341 ff.

21   Cf. e. g. Jørgensen's letters to the members of the executive committee of the Lutheran World Convent outside of Germany dated 27 May 1937 and 5 Nov. 1938, AELCA, Chicago, Best. LWC 1/3, Correspondence File 1936–47, Box 1. In the latter letter it reads: "As important as Barth is as a dogmatist, he is equally dangerous as an ecclesiastic politician. Therefore his books are banned in Germany." On 14 Feb. 1939, he wrote to the same group: "'The provisional leadership', to be exact Pastors Müller and Albertz among other Berlin pastors, are only the leadership of the union followers, in particular the Reformed Church, which is heavily influenced by Barth. Karl Barth as an ecclesiastic politician has become a dangerous man, he attacks the German government ruthlessly and without understanding." [self-translation] AELCA, Chicago, Best. LWC 1/3, Correspondence Files 1936–47, Box 2. Cf. in contrast Jens Holger Schjørring, Ökumenische Perspektiven des deutschen Kirchenkampfes, Leiden 1985, 82 ff. Schjørring shows that Eidem and Ammundsen in 1936 certainly tended to have sympathy for the *Dahlemiten* and were sceptical of the Lutheran Church of Germany.

To the situation of the Nordic churches during Hitler's reign also see Kirken, Krisen og Krigen [Church, Crisis and Conflict], ed. by Stein Ugelvik Larsen and Ingun Montgomery, Bergen-Oslo-Tromsö 1982, and Carsten Nicolaisen (ed.), Nordische und deutsche Kirchen im 20. Jahrhundert. Referate auf der internationalen Arbeitstagung in Sandbjerg, Denmark (AKZG B 13), Göttingen 1982; Jens Holger Schjørring, 'Nordisches Luthertum und Antisemitismus', in Jochen-Christoph Kaiser and Martin Greschat (eds), Der Holocaust und die Protestanten. Analysen einer Verstrickung (KoGe 1), Frankfurt a. M. 1988, 120–150, esp. 135 ff. Jens Holger Schjørring, 'Nordisches Luthertum zur Zeit des Zweiten Weltkrieges', in Joachim Mehlhausen (ed.), ... und über Barmen hinaus. Festschrift Carsten Nicolaisen, Göttingen 1995, 386–401. Long quoted the view of Jørgensen to a large extent. On 17 Nov. 1938, he wrote to Rev. Roscoe B. Fischer: "Barth is an important person as a dogmatician, but it is felt that he is dangerous as a church politician. His books have been proscribed in Germany." AELCA, Chicago, Best. NLC 2/3/1, Executive Director Ralph H. Long, General Files 1930–1947, Box 5.

22 Boe to Morehead on 9 Apr. 1934, AELCA, Chicago, Best. NLC 1/2, Correspondence File 1921–46, Box 21.

23 Cf. Eino Murtorinne, Erzbischof Eidem zum deutschen Kirchenkampf 1933–34, Helsinki 1968.

24 In a letter to Long on 28 Mar. 1934, Boe justifiably made Marahrens responsible for the end of the Berlin Bishop's reception with Hitler, cf. Klaus Scholder, Die Kirchen und das Dritte Reich, vol. 2, Frankfurt a. M.-Berlin [2]1988, 59 ff.: "The man that I blame for much of this is Bishop Marahrens whom we both know could have dominated the situation if it had been handled right from the beginning." Two sentences later he wrote: "I can see now where we made one mistake at Hanover and that was to let it be understood that the Germans were next on the presidium. I do not know whether or not I spoke to you about it, but I did write to Dr Jørgensen before the meeting that I thought by all means that the presidium should next go to the Swedes, or to the Scandinavian countries." AELCA, Chicago, Best. NLC 2/3/1, Executive Director Ralph H. Long, General Files 1930–1947, Box 2.

25 This is contrary to Nelson, who after the Munich meeting of the executive committee in November 1934 and in connection to Boe's thank you letter to Meiser dated 13 December 1934, interpreted Boe's judgement as lacking understanding for the Church political situation, cf. Nelson, The Rise of World Lutheranism (op. cit. note 4), 273. Boe's letter to Morehead from 5 Jan. 1934 was briefly mentioned only once (ibid. 272).

26 Ibid. 341 ff.

27 Ibid. 272. In the same year, the American Lutheran Church also gave a message to the Lutheran Church in Germany, cf. Minutes of the American Lutheran Church Convention at Waverly, Iowa, 1934, 239, quoted according to Long to Sheatsley on 7 Apr. 1938, AELCA, Chicago, Best. NLC 2/3/1, Executive Director Ralph H. Long, General Files 1930–1947, Box 5.

28 Cf. Martin E. Marty, Pilgrims in their own Land. 500 Years of Religion in America, New York 1985, 396 ff.

29 Letter from Long to Simen on 8 May 1934, AELCA, Chicago, Best. NLC 2/3/1, General Files 1930–1937, Box 2.

30 Cf. the Roper opinion poll, quoted from Michael Berenbaum, The World Must Know. The History of the Holocaust as told in the United States Holocaust Memorial Museum, Boston-New York-Toronto-London 1993, 57. See also the failure of the legal initiative of the New York senator Robert Wagner and the member of Congress from Massachusetts, Edith Rogers. Both of them had campaigned in February 1939 to allow 20,000 Jewish children under the age of 14 to travel to the United States as a special contingent; the costs would be borne by private entities. The law failed before it even reached the two houses. A prominent example of the lacking inclination of the Americans to raise the immigration contingent is the odyssey of the luxury liner St.

Louis from the Hamburg-America Line in 1939 (ibid. 57 f.). In an official report from June 1998, the US-State Department allowed that "America's response to the early stages of the slaughter of European Jews was largely one of indifference". According to this report only 21,000 refugees from Europe were taken in by America during the war. Cf. U. S. and Allied Wartime and Postwar Relations and Negotiations with Argentina, Portugal, Spain, Sweden and Turkey on looted Gold and German External Asserts and U. S. Concerns about the Fate of the Wartime Ustasha Treasury, coordinated by Stuart E. Eizenstat, Washington 1998, 9.

31   Cf. Marty, Modern American Religion, vol. 3: Under God, indivisible (1941–1960), Chicago 1996, 54 ff., 59. Against this backdrop, all attempts (the conference in Evian in July 1938, the conference in Bermuda in April 1942) to actively support the persecuted Jews was deemed to failure because the governments of democratic states, above all the USA, were hardly able to offer help due to the anti-Semitic mood among their home population. Cf. Henry L. Feingold, The Politics of Rescue. The Roosevelt Administration and the Holocaust 1938–1945, New Brunswick, NJ 1970, 22 ff., 167 ff.; Patrick J. Hearden, Roosevelt Confronts Hitler. America's Entry into World War II, Dekalb, Ill. 1987, 112 ff. However, Hearden also draws attention to the fact that Jewish bankers in the Anglo-American world also showed little inclination to undertake the financial burden of saving the European Jews (ibid. 116 f.).

32   Cf. Marty, Modern American Religion, vol. 3 (op. cit. note 31), 59, 63. Also see Richard V. Pierard, 'Varieties of anti-Semitic Responses to the Holocaust within American Conservative Protestantism', in Remembering the Future. Jews and Christians during and after the Holocaust. These papers were presented at an International Scholar's Conference held in Oxford 10–13 July 1988. Oxford-New York 1988, 447–460.

33   Cf. the letter from the State Department to Morehead on 3 Mar. 1933, in which in connection with the fate of the Lutheran Priest Richard Mayer from the Ukraine is stated that the American government could do nothing, "which would result in the improvement of the situation of the clergy and the congregations of the Christian churches in Russia". AELCA, Chicago, Best. NLC 1/2, Correspondence File 1921–47, Box 21. On 16 Apr. 1934, Morehead wrote to Boe, "the problem of Russia has reached a critical stage and we are under the necessity of making decisions in regard to any possible action looking to the alleviation of pressure upon the Evangelical Lutheran Church in Russia, its institutions, pastors and people. Believe me, it is the biggest church problem with which any of us have ever been confronted". (loc. cit.) Compared to this the church problems in Germany, which are dealt with in the same letter, appear a lot less worrying. Cf. on Soviet religious policy Manfred Hildermeier, Geschichte der Sowjetunion 1917–1991. Entstehung und Niedergang des ersten sozialistischen Staates, Munich 1998, 328 ff., 580 ff.

34   On 24 Nov. 1934, Long wrote to E. Harry Schirmer (Columbia): "In a number of the European countries, even including France, the issue is becoming a definitive alternative between Communism and National Socialism. ... National Socialism is Germany's answer to communism just as Facistism [sic!] is Italy's answer. ... The influence upon our own country would, of course, be much less but in the final analysis we cannot escape the conclusion that if other nations adopt it [i. e. National Socialism] as a suitable form of government it must eventually have considerable influence upon us, especially if we are threatened by communism or something similar to it." AELCA, Chicago, Best. NLC 2/3/1, General Files 1930–1937, Box 2.

35   Nelson, The Lutherans in North America (op. cit. note 7), 454, also see Robert T. Handy, The American Religious Depression 1925–1935, Philadelphia 1968.

36   Cf. Ulrike Brunotte, 'Puritanismus und Pioniergeist. Die Faszination der Wilderness als Herausforderung für den amerikanischen Protestantismus', in KZG 7 (1994), 44–58.

37   From 1921 to 1930, Charles Macfarland was FCC General Secretary. He was followed in 1930 by Samuel McCrea Cavert. See on this William J. Schmidt, Architect of Unity:

A Biography of Samuel McCrea Cavert, New York 1978, 46 ff., 237 ff. Cf. also Charles Macfarland, The New Church and the New Germany, New York 1934, also see the report of the American ambassadors William E. Dodd and J. C. Whites (US ambassador to Berlin) to the state department on 8 Nov. 1933 and 16 Nov. 1933 regarding Macfarland's visit, National Achieves [NA] at College Park, MD (Archives II) Washington, D. C., RG 59, 862.404/35 and 36. In the latter report it reads: "Macfarland ... visited Chancellor Hitler some weeks ago and informed him that the American Protestant denominations would view with regret any harsh treatment of the dissenting pastors. The Chancellor is said to have consented to receive representatives of the protesting clergy, but it is not believed that the interview actually took place." In November 1937, Dodd attracted the attention of the NS regime. Goebbels noted on 25 November in his notes: "The son of ambassador Dodd held a mean agitatory speech against Germany. Dodd is withdrawn. An agriment [read: agreement] on his successor has already been reached." Cf. Elke Fröhlich (ed.), Die Tagebücher von Joseph Goebbels. Sämtliche Fragmente, Teil I: Aufzeichnungen 1924–1941, vol. 3: 1 Jan. 1937–31 Dec. 1939, Munich-New York-Paris 1987, 345. See on the National Socialist picture of America: Philipp Gassert, Amerika im Dritten Reich. Ideologie, Propaganda und Volksmeinung 1933–1945, Stuttgart 1997, in particular 247 ff.

38   Cf. Klaus Scholder, Die Kirchen und das Dritte Reich, vol. 1: Vorgeschichte und Zeit der Illusionen 1918–1934, Frankfurt a. M.-Berlin ²1986, 332 ff. See in detail Armin Boyens, Kirchenkampf und Ökumene. Darstellung und Dokumentation, vol. 1: 1933–1939, Munich 1969, 37 ff., text: 290. The American and British ambassadors in Berlin were empowered by their respective governments (USA: 3 March 1933) to meet the German foreign minister to investigate matters of excess against the Jews. An analogous letter from the president of the Federal Council of Churches of Christ, Albert W. Beaven on 24 March 1933 to the President of the *Deutscher Evangelischer Kirchenbund* (DEK, German protestant Church association), Hermann Kapler, was only answered by Hosemann on 7 June 1933, who included in his friendly letter a "Memorandum über die gegenwärtige Lage in Deutschland, insbesondere über die Judenfrage" from the same day [Memorandum on the current situation in Germany, in particular in relationship to the Jewish question] (printed in Boyens, Kirchenkampf und Ökumene, vol. 1, 299–308). Department of History, Presbyterian Church, Philadelphia (DeptHist PresbChurch, Phila.), RG 18–9–16. In August 1935 because of the statement from the American president on 15 November 1938 such diplomatic interventions repeated themselves, cf. Report from the American embassy: Action by the United States Government with Regard to the Excesses against the Jews in Germany, 24 Feb. 1940, NA Washington, RG 59, 862.4016/2162. In mid-May 1933, Samuel McCrea Cavert, the successor to Macfarland as general secretary of the FCC, reported to the Federal Council on his visit to Berlin at the end of April. He emphasised how important it is for the German Churches that they are supported by the American Churches, cf. Meeting of the Executive Committee of the Federal Council of the Churches of Christ in America, Friday, 19 May 1933, DeptHistPresbChurch, Phila., RG 18–1–7.

39   Macfarland claimed to have had interviews alongside Hitler with Bishop Müller, Minister of the interior Frick, Alfred Rosenberg, Friedrich von Bodelschwingh and Karl Barth, cf. Macfarland, The New Church (op. cit. note 37), VIII.

40   As recorded by Hitler's advisor Thomsen. The transcript was given to Macfarland, who quoted from it, cf. The New Church (op. cit. note 37), 145 f.

41   Cf. Scholder, Die Kirchen (op. cit. note 38), vol. 1, 689 f.

42   Macfarland, The New Church (op. cit. note 37), 143, 148. In June 1937, Macfarland addressed an open letter to Hitler, in which he sharply criticised the oppression of the Church in Germany, cf. Evangelisches Zentralarchiv (EZA) Berlin, 50/116/96 ff.

43   H. S. Leiper to Sam (probably Samuel McCrea Cavert) on 3 Sep. 1933, DeptHistPresb Church, Phila., RG 18–33–8. McCrea Cavert had visited Germany in May 1933 and published his impressions in an article in the "Christian Century" and elsewhere. His from the outset critical position in regard to the developments in Germany follows

from his letter to Schreiber on 13 Sep. 1933, cf. DeptHistPresbChurch, Phila., RG 18-9-16.

44   "It [i. e. the bringing into line] does mean trying to tune together, in the radio or musical sense, the various organs of social expression in the land. It comes from the electrical world as a symbol and means the search for like disposition, similar will, cooperative relations, and coordination of effort. In that sense it is not so evil a thing as it has been made to appear and we have some rather conspicuous examples of the same sort of thing in our own land just now! (God be thanked!)", cf. H. S. Leiper to Sam (op. cit. note 43).

45   Cf. Dietrich Bonhoeffer, Illegale Theologenausbildung: Sammelvikariate 1937–1940, ed. by Dirk Schultz (Dietrich Bonhoeffer Werke 15), Gütersloh 1998, 167 f., 177, 192.

46   Quoted from David H. Kelsey, 'Paul Tillich', in David Ford (ed.), Theologen der Gegenwart, Paderborn 1993, 127–142, 128.

47   Cf. Statement on the situation in Germany from 26 Jan. 1934, Meeting of Executive Committee of the Federal Council of the Churches of Christ in America, Friday, January 26, 1934, DeptHistPresbChurch, Phila., RF 18-1-8; see also Statement on the Church situation in Germany on the occasion of the ban by the German government to stop the delegates travelling to Oxford in 1937, Meeting of Executive Committee of the Federal Council of the Churches of Christ in America, June 4, 1937, DeptHist PresbChurch, Phila., RG 18-1-9.

48   Cf. Letter to the Confessional Synod of the German Protestant Church on 26 Oct. 1934, Meeting of Executive Committee of the Federal Council of the Churches of Christ in America, Friday, 26 Oct. 1934 (op. cit. note 47). On 17 October 1934, the German ambassador in Washington reported that Luther, the Methodist bishop Mac Dowell and the general secretary of the Federal Council, Cavert, had been to see him in order to express their apprehension about the "violent oppression of the confessional synod or its leading members". Such events would "influence the good relationship between the American and German protestant movement". Luther added: "Measures have been introduced in order to influence the Federal Council in the sense of omission, when possible." Cf. express note VLR. Roediger to the Reich ministry of the interior on 18 Oct. 1934, Pol AA, VI A 7,2.

49   The letter from German foreign minister von Neurath to minister of the interior Frick (with a duplicate sent to Lammers) on 18 June 1934 appears too much on the basis of this background information, in order to put an end to the reprisals against the Church. In any case Neurath's judgement that in the USA "through the abandonment of Protestantism recently a until now open hole of anti-German feeling had been closed" turned out to be wrong, cf. BA Koblenz, R. 43 II 161–164.

50   Cf. Leonore Siegele-Wenschkewitz and Carsten Nicolaisen (eds), Theologische Fakultäten im Nationalsozialismus (AKZG, B 18), Göttingen 1993; Kurt Meier, Die Theologischen Fakultäten im Dritten Reich, Berlin-New York 1996.

51   Protocol Rudolf Betz, employee of the American embassy, on the conversation between Leiper, Stahn and Dudzus on 31 Aug. 1935, NA Washington, RG 59, 862.404/ 146. As Leiper wrote in a series of articles for the Information Service on "The German Church Problem", the former associate Rector of the Ascension Memorial Church in New York heavily criticised him in a letter and a critical article. Cf. DeptHistPresbChurch, Phila., RG 18-33-4.

52   Cf. Meeting of Executive Committee of the Federal Council of the Churches of Christ in America, Friday, 27 Sep. 1935, DeptHistPresbChurch, Phila., RG 18-1-8.

53   Cf. Meeting of Executive Committee of the Federal Council of the Churches of Christ in America, 22 Nov. 1935, DeptHistPresbChurch, Phila., RG 18-1-8.

54   Cf. Robert W. Ross, So it was true. The American Protestant Press and the Nazi Persecution of the Jews, Minneapolis 1980, 104.

55   Text: Karl Zehrer, Evangelische Freikirchen und das "Dritte Reich" (AGK E 13), Göttingen 1986, 149–151. The Free Churches also signed the German protest against the "open letter" from the Americans. See Andrea Strübind, Die unfreie Freikirche.

Der Bund der Baptistengemeinden im "Dritten Reich" (HThSt 1), Neukirchen-Vluyn 1991; E. Earl Joiner, 'Baptists and the Holocaust', in Remembering the Future, 385–394. This illustrates among others the agreement of the American Baptists with the National Socialist regime after they had returned from the 1934 Baptist World Congress, which took place in Germany (ibid. 390). See also Meeting of Executive Committee of the Federal Council of the Churches of Christ in America, 25 Mar. 1938, DeptHistPresbChurch, Phila., RG 18-1-10.

56 See James Bentley, Martin Niemöller, Oxford 1984, 162 ff.; Matthias Schreiber, Martin Niemöller, Reinbek bei Hamburg 1997, 81 ff. Cf. on the British protest Andrew Chandler (ed.), Brethren in Adversity. Bishop George Bell, the Church of England and the Crisis of German Protestantism. 1933–1939, Suffolk 1997.

57 See Rolf-Ulrich Kunze, Theodor Heckel 1894–1867. Eine Biographie (KoGe 13), Stuttgart-Berlin-Cologne 1997.

58 See also the written correspondence between Long and Baron Ulrich von Gienanth, the attaché to the German embassy in Washington, in connection to the German letter of response, AELCA, Chicago, Best. NLC 2/3/1, Executive Director Ralph H. Long, General Files 1930–1947, Box 5. In a written correspondence with J. Sheatsly, who had also published an open letter on the situation of the German Church in the Lutheran Standard, Long explained why the Lutherans had refrained from making their position clear to the public: "Our German brethren, who are on the firing line, prefer that we do not engage in formal protests such as have been issued." (loc. cit.) On the denunciation of a supposedly communist pastor cf. Robert M. Müller, American Protestantism and Social Issues, 1919–1939, Chapel Hill 1958, 66 f., 79, 109 ff., 124 f.

59 Meeting of Executive Committee of the Federal Council of the Churches of Christ in America, September 23, 1938, DeptHistPresbChurch, Phila., RG 18-1-10.

60 Cf. Thomas E. Fitzgerald, The Orthodox Church (Denominations in America 7), Westport 1995, 64 ff.; Constance J. Tarasar (ed.), Orthodox America 1794–1976. Development of the Orthodox Church in America, Syosset 1975.

61 Note Haugg on 28 Sep. 1938 for the Reich Church Ministry, BstU ZA MfS HA XX/4-1870, Bl. 98.

62 Kirchliches Jahrbuch 60–71 (1933–1944), 284 f.

63 Kirchliches Jahrbuch (op. cit. note 62), 285. Cf. Boyens, Kichenkampf und Ökumene, vol. 1 (op. cit. note 38), 256. Marahrens signed a moderated version of the Godesberg Declaration in mid-May 1939, the "Principles for a New Order of the DEK According to Present Requirements", cf. Klügel, Landeskirche (op. cit. note 8), 363–370. Text: Kirchliches Jahrbuch (op. cit. note 62), 290 f.

64 Cf. The Lutheran from 3 May 1939; cf. Boyens, 'Luthertum im Zeitalter der Diktatoren' (op. cit. note 3), 251 f.

65 Cf. Nelson, The Rise of World Lutheranism (op. cit. note 4), 287.

66 Cf. Gerhard Besier and Eckhard Lessing (eds), Die Geschichte der Evangelischen Kirche der Union. Trennung von Staat und Kirche – Krise und Erneuerung kirchlicher Gemeinschaft, vol. 3, Leipzig 1999 (contains further references).

67 On the religious-sociological analysis of this phenomenon until present day see Roger Finke and Rodney Starke, The Churching of America 1776–1990. Winners and Losers in our Religious Economy, New Brunswick 1992; Donald E. Miller, Reinventing American Protestantism. Christianity in the New Millennium, Berkeley-Los Angeles-London 1997. From an historical perspective: Thomas C. Reeves, The Empty Church. The Suicide of Liberal Christianity, New York 1996; Hartmut Lehmann, 'The Christianisation of America and the Dechristianisation of Europe in the 19th and 20th Centuries', in KZG 11 (1998), 8–20; William R. Hutchison, 'The Emperor's old clothes. A comment on Hartmut Lehmann's "The Christianisation of America and the Dechristianisation of Europe in the 19th and 20th Centuries"', ibid. 137–142.

68 Cf. James H. Smylie, A Brief History of the Presbyterians, Louisville 1989, in particular 111 ff.

69 Cf. William Wilson Manross, A history of the American Episcopal Church, New York 1959, also see Sandra and Ronald Caldwell, The History of the Episcopal Church in America, 1607–1991. A bibliography, New York 1993.

70 Cf. J. William T. Youngs, The Congregationalists (Denominations in America 4), Westport 1990.

71 Cf. John G. McEllhenney (ed.), Proclaiming grace and freedom: The Story of United Methodism in America, Nashville 1982; Russel E. Richey, The Methodist Conference in America: A History, Nashville 1996.

72 Cf. William Henry Brackney, The Baptists (Denominations in America 2), Westport 1994.

73 Cf. William E. Tucker and Lester G. McAllister, Journey in faith. A History of the Christian Church (Disciples of Christ), Saint Louis 1975.

74 Cf. Robert A. Schneider, 'Voice of Many Waters: Church Federation in the Twentieth Century', in William R. Hutchison (ed.), Between the Times: The Travail of the Protestant Establishment in America, 1900–1960, Cambridge 1989, 95–121.

75 Cf. Martin E. Marty, Modern American Religion, vol. 2 (op. cit. note 7), 33 f.; Elias Sanford, Origin and History of the Federal Council of Churches of Christ in America, Hartford 1916.

76 Cf. George M. Marsden, Fundamentalism and American Culture: The Shaping of Twentieth-Century Evangelicalism 1870–1925, Oxford-New York 1982, in particular 179 ff.

77 Cf. Marty, Modern American Religion, vol. 3 (op. cit. note 31), 343 ff.

78 Cf. James DeForest Murch, Cooperation without Compromise: A History of the National Association of Evangelicals, Grand Rapids 1956, in particular 135 ff.

79 Cf. Louis Gasper, The Fundamentalist Movement, The Hague 1963, 119 ff.

80 On the National Council of Churches, which was established in 1950 and replaced the Federal Council, cf. Marty, Modern American Religion, vol. 3 (op. cit. note 31), 263 ff. The foundation was both ideologically and organisationally in close connection to the definitive establishment of the World Council of Churches after the Second World War, which was expressed from the very beginning by opponents of the National Council and the World Council. As an outlet for disapproving position towards the Geneva World Council of Churches, Carl McIntire from the fundamental "American Council of Christian Churches" established in 1948 the "International Council of Christian Churches". Cf. also the brochure from the National Association of Evangelicals: Billy A. Melvin, Answers to Your Questions About the National and World Councils of Churches, Wheaton 1990.

81 Also see A. R. Wentz, in Robert H. Fisher (ed.), Franklin Clark Fry. A Palette for a Portrait (The Lutheran Quarterly XXIV), Springfield 1972, 99–106.

82 Cf. Nelson, The Lutherans in North America (op. cit. note 7), 448 f.

83 Ibid. 444.

84 Cf. Marsden, Fundamentalism and Culture (op. cit. note 76), 194 f.

85 The positions were appointed as such: Chairman – S. Parker Cadman, Secretary – Henry S. Leiper, Treasurer – Henry L. Smithers, Executive Secretary – Robert A. Ashworth.

86 Ashworth to Long on 14 May 1934, AELCA, Chicago, Best. NLC 2/3/1, Executive Director Ralph H. Long, General Files 1930–1947, Box 3.

87 Long to Ashworth on 23 May 1934 (op. cit. note 86). However, in his letter to Rev. Wilson Long gave another reason; saying that to help Christians of Jewish descent through the committee "would complicate our relations with our German brethren", cf. AELCA, Chicago, Best. NLC 2/3/1, Executive Director Ralph H. Long, General Files 1930–1947, Box 3.

88 Cf. Working Agreement between the Lutheran Churches of America and the American Committee for Christian German Refugees, July 15, 1938, AELCA, Chicago, Best. NLC 2/3/1, Executive Director Ralph H. Long, General Files 1930–1947, Box 5. To the initially less successful attempts to establish a Protestant help programme for Ger-

man Christians of Jewish descent cf. P. W. Ludlow, 'The refugee problem in the 1930s. The failures and successes of Protestant relief programmes', in HER 90 (1975), 564–603; cf. also Wolfgang Gerlach, 'Zur Entstehung des Internationalen kirchlichen Hilfs-komitees für deutsche Flüchtlinge 1933–1936', in Hermann Delfs (ed.), Aktiver Friede, Festschrift F. Siegmund-Schultze, Soest 1972, 35–45.

89 Arther Schlesinger Jr., The Crisis of the Old Order, vol. 1: The Age of Roosevelt, Boston 1957, 3.

90 Cf. Nelson, The Lutherans in North America (op. cit. note 7), 453 ff.

91 See Ralph Lord Roy, Communism and Churches, New York 1960, 66 ff.; Miller, American Protestantism (op. cit. note 67), 66 f., 79, 109 ff., 124 f. On the Communist Party of the USA cf. Harvey Klehr, John Earl Haynes and Kyrill Andersen, The Soviet World of American Communism, New Haven-London 1998.

92 Cf. Robert S. McElvaine, The Great Depression: America, 1929–1941, New York 1984.

93 The Hoover-Stimson Doctrine of 7 January 1932, which confirmed the non-recogni-tion of the Japanese conquest in China, showed as expected no political consequences. Henry Lewis Stimson (1867–1950) was secretary of war between 1940 and 1945.

94 Cf. Herbert C. Hoover, The Challenge to Liberty, New York 1934, in particular 193. Here it is stated: "No nation can introduce a new social philosophy or a new culture alien to its growth without moral and spiritual chaos. I am anxious for the future of freedom and liberty of men."

95 Since 1935, the Institute of Public Opinion in Princeton, which was established by George H. Gallup, regularly carried out public opinion polls, cf. George H. Gallup, The Gallup Poll. Public Opinion, 1935–1971, 3 vols, New York 1972. The Roosevelt government acted very much in line with public opinion and sought to influence it through "information departments", which were established in the ministries and au-thorities, cf. Michael Leigh, Mobilizing Consent, Public Opinion and American For-eign Policy, 1937–1947, Westport 1976.

96 Cf. Erich Angermann, Die Vereinigten Staaten von Amerika seit 1917, Munich 1995, 167.

97 Cf. Melvyn P. Leffler, The Specter of Communism: The United States and the Origins of the Cold War, 1917–1953, New York 1994, 25. Roosevelt's work "Das neue Ameri-ka" (Luzern 1937) was on the Nazi's list of damaging and undesirable literature, 31 Dec. 1938. Cf. Liste des schädlichen und unerwünschten Schrifttums. Stand vom 31. Dezember 1938 und Jahreslisten 1939–1941, Vaduz/Liechtenstein 1979, 121. Also see Walter Wieland, Zwischen Freiheit und Sicherheit. Amerikanische Sozialpolitik im Widerstreit der Interessengruppen 1935–1954 (Nordamerikanische Studien 4), Hamburg 1995.

98 Cf. Roosevelt's letter to Morehead on 24 Sept. 1935, AELCA, Chicago, Best. LWC 1/2, Correspondence File 1921–47, Box 24. On Morehead cf. Nelson, The Rise of World Lutheranism (op. cit. note 4), 282. Morehead should have been nominated for a Nobel Prize according to the Lutherans. Cf. Roosevelt to Morgenthau from 15 Nov. 1935, cf. Edgar B. Nixon (ed.), Franklin D. Roosevelt and Foreign Affairs, vol. 3: September 1935–January 1937, Cambridge/Mass. 1969, 71 f.

99 Cf. e. g. Morehead's letter to Herbert Hoover from 23 July 1935, AELCA, Chicago, Best. LWC 1/2, Correspondence File 1921–47, Box 23.

100 Cf. Jürgen Heideking (ed.), Die amerikanischen Präsidenten. 41 historische Porträts von George Washington bis Bill Clinton, Munich 1995, 312.

101 Ibid. 306.

102 Ibid. 318.

103 Cf. Arnold A. Offner, American appeasement: United States foreign policy and Ger-many, 1933–1938, Cambridge 1969; Wayne S. Cole, Roosevelt and the Isolationists 1932–45, Lincoln-London 1983.

104 Cf. the statement to American-Japanese relations on 1 Mar. 1935, Meeting of Executive Committee of the Federal Council of Churches of Christ in America, Friday, March 1, 1935, DeptHistPresbChurch, Phila., RG 18-1-8.

105 Cf. the Statement presented to the President of he United States, 15 Feb. 1938, Meeting of Executive Committee of the Federal Council of the Churches of Christ in America, 25 Mar. 1938, DeptHistPresbChurch, Phila., RG 18-1-10.

106 Cf. Franz Knipping, Die amerikanische Russlandpolitik in der Zeit des Hitler-Stalin-Pakts 1939-1941, Tübingen 1974, 1 ff. Also see George F. Kennan, Soviet Foreign Policy, Princeton 1960, 80 ff., 170 ff.

107 Cf. Boe's letters to Morehead on 7 and 28 Mar. 1934, and Morehead to Boe on 16 Apr. 1934, AELCA, Chicago, LWC 1/2, Correspondence File 1921-47, Box 21.

108 "Is it possible for the Embassy of the German government in Russia to extend to Bishop [Arthur] Malmgren [Rector of the Lutheran Seminar in Leningrad] and to Lutheran Church interests in that country the large measure of un-official protection which was so helpfully extended by the diplomatic representatives of the German government in the past to the lamented Bishop Dr Meyer?", cf. Morehead's letter to Marahrens on 27 Aug. 1934, AELCA, Chicago 1/2, Correspondence File 1921-47, Box 21.

109 Cf. Wilhelm Kahle, Geschichte der evangelisch-lutherischen Gemeinden in der Sowjetunion 1917-1938, Leiden 1974; Wilhelm Kahle, Die lutherische Kirchen und Gemeinden in der Sowjetunion seit 1938/40 (Die lutherische Kirche, Geschichte und Gestalten 8), Gütersloh 1985; Wilhelm Kahle (ed.), Dokumente und Berichte zum Leben der lutherischen Kirchen und Gemeinden in der Sowjetunion seit 1939/40 (Die lutherische Kirche, Geschichte und Gestalten 9), Gütersloh 1988.

110 Cf. Morehead to Pehrsson on 24 Aug. 1934, AELCA, Chicago, Best. LWC 1/2 Correspondence File 1921-47, Box 21.

111 Cf. Morehead's letters from 12 Feb. 1935 and 26 Sep. 1935 to the members of the executive committee of the Lutheran World Convent, AELCA, Chicago, Best. LWC 1/2, Correspondence File 1921-47, Box 23. Also see Morehead's correspondence with different political organs, AELCA, Chicago, Best. LWC 1/2, Correspondence File 1921-47, Box 24.

112 Cf. Jens Holger Schjørring et al. (eds), Vom Weltbund zur Gemeinschaft. Geschichte des Lutherischen Weltbundes 1947 1997, Hanover 1997, 31. John S. Conway wrote: "The tone of such writings [on the part of the Federal Council and the British clergy] was unanimously and sharply critical of Nazi church policies, even though these authors had at first been prepared to be supportive of the wave of renewal inside Germany." Cf. Conway, 'The attitudes of English-speaking Churches to developments in German Protestantism 1933-1990. A personal assessment', in KZG 6 (1993), 149.

113 Jørgensen to Frederick H. Knubel (President of the ULCA), Long, Boe, Abdel Ross Wentz, Moe, Pehrsson and von Bonsdorff on 10 Mar. 1937, AELCA, Chicago, Best. LWC 1/3, Correspondence File 1936-47, Box 1. Cf. Jørgensen's letter to the same recipients on 29 Dec. 1937, loc. cit. It reads: "A big hope [for the situation of the Church] exists, in the Führer himself! A foreigner, who visits Germany has to wonder Hitler and all that he has achieved. And in ecclesiastical questions Hitler has always been cautious."

114 Cf. Lutherischer Weltkonvent zu Paris vom 13.-20. Oktober 1935, Denkschrift ed. p.p. of the executive committee, Berlin 1939 [printed as a manuscript]; Schmidt-Clausen, Vom Lutherischen Weltkonvent zum Lutherischen Weltbund (op. cit. note 3), 197; Nelson, The Rise of World Lutheranism (op. cit. note 4), 280; Record from Meiser in Hannelore Braun and Carsten Nicolaisen (eds), Verantwortung für die Kirche. Stenographische Aufzeichnungen und Mitschriften von Landesbischof Hans Meiser 1933-1955, vol. 2: Herbst 1935 bis Frühjahr 1937 (AKZG, A 4), Göttingen 1993, 49-59. See also the letter from Jørgensen to Richthofen on 16 Oct. 1934, Pol AA, Bonn, VI A 7,2. In it Jørgensen assures that the foreigners did not travel to Munich "in order to take part in the German Church struggle". With this statement he wanted to prevent foreigners from being forbidden to enter Germany.

115 Cf. Nelson, The Rise of World Lutheranism (op. cit. note 4), 284, 297.

116 See Verantwortung für die Kirche, vol. 2 (op. cit. note 114), 52, 285–313, in particular 307, 309. Cf. H. Lilje's autobiography: Hanns Lilje, Memorabila. Schwerpunkte eines Lebens, Nürnberg 1973.

117 Cf. Jørgensen to Long on 18 Nov. 1926, AELCA, Chicago, Best. LWC 1/3, Correspondence File 1936–47, Box 1. Cf. also Long's letter to Jørgensen on 7 Jan. 1937 and his answer on 10 Mar. 1937, loc. cit. The correspondence suggests that the Americans supported Lilje, whilst the North European Lutherans continued to harbour reservations due to Lilje's nationality. Cf. Nelson, The Rise of World Lutheranism (op. cit. note 4), 284. Only the American J. Michael Reu had doubts on Lilje's orthodox Lutheranism, ibid. 290.

118 According to Lilje in his declaration of willingness to take over the office in a letter to Long, 3 Dec. 1936, AELCA, Chicago, Best. LWC 1/3, Correspondence File 1936–47, Box 1. On the supposed rivalry between Lilje and Jørgensen cf. Nelson, The Rise of World Lutheranism (op. cit. note 4), 289 f.

119 Ibid. 285.

120 Cf. Schmidt-Clausen, Vom Lutherischen Weltkonvent zum Lutherischen Weltbund (op. cit. note 3), 199 ff.; Nelson, The Rise of World Lutheranism (op. cit. note 4), 298 f.

121 Cf. Knubel's official letter to Marahrens on 29 Jan. 1936, AELCA, Chicago, Best. LWC 1/3, Correspondence File 1936–47, Box 1. It states: "It was decided that our little group of four Americans [i. e. Boe, Long, Wentz and Knubel] should organise itself and as a result Dr Long was elected as secretary and treasurer of the American group and I was selected as the chairman."

122 Cf. Sydney E. Ahlstrom, A Religious History of the American People, New Haven-London 1972, 802 ff. Also see Sidney E. Mead, Das Christentum in Nordamerika. Glaube und Religionsfreiheit in vier Jahrhunderten, Göttingen 1987, 185 ff.; Paul A. Carter, The Decline and Revival of the Social Gospel. Social and Political Liberalism in American Protestant Churches, 1920–1940, Ithaca/NY 1956, in particular 134 ff., 163 ff.

123 Cf. Marty, Modern American Religion, vol. 2 (op. cit. note 7), 374 f. See also William Adams Brown, Toward a United Church: Three Decades of Ecumenical Christianity, New York 1946.

124 Cf. Smylie, A Brief History of he Presbyterians (op. cit. note 68), 115.

125 Rabbi Israel Goldstein, the president of the Synagogue Council of America, wrote on 3 Mar. 1943 to his friend Everett R. Clinchy, a Presbyterian pastor and president of the National Conference of Christians and Jews: "How can an organisation whose program is brotherhood, exclude from its sphere of concern ... the dying gasp of European Jewry?" Quoted from David S. Wyman, Abandonment of the Jews. America and the Holocaust 1941–1945, New York 1984, 101. On the stance of Roosevelt and the American government see Sean Dennis Cashman, America, Roosevelt and World War II, New York-London 1989, 308 ff.

126 Cf. Marty, Modern American Religion, vol. 3 (op. cit. note 31), 111.

127 Conrad Hoffman, Confidential Report Concerning the Conditions of Non-Aryans in Germany. With Suggestions for Possible Means of Assistance, New York, 1 Sep. 1935, AELCA, Chicago, Best. NLC 2/3/1, Executive Director Ralph H. Long, General Files 1930–1947, Box 3. Also the letter from Rev. Brevan (Pittsburgh) to Long on 20 April 1936 suggests an exact knowledge of the situation: "I have information that pastors and deaconesses have been ousted from their offices, to say nothing of thousands of lay-people, who are considered Christians by the Jews and Jews by the 'Christians.'" (loc. cit.).

128 See Marty, Modern American Religion, vol. 3 (op. cit. note 31), 111.

129 Cf. e. g. The Zion Society for Israel or the American Committee for Non-Aryan German Christian Refugees, which cooperated with the Lutherans of America, AELCA, Chicago, Best. NLC 2/3/1, Executive Director Ralph H. Long, General Files 1930–1947, Box 5. On the occasion of a concrete case (that of Pastor Hans Werner Jordan, Nuremberg), Long wrote to Reu on 8 June 1939: "In several similar cases

I have found that a letter from the National Lutheran Council to the American Consul usually is sufficient for the issuance of a visa", loc. cit., Box 6. In a letter to Long on 28 May 1939, Otto A. Piper (formally of the Universities of Göttingen and Münster, then in Princeton, N. J.) interceded on behalf of Pastor Paul Leo from Osnabrück. Long rather cautiously answered Piper on 5 June 1939. Cf. on the earlier Göttingen dispute regarding Piper Heinrich Assel, Der andere Aufbruch. Die Lutherrenaissance, Göttingen 1994, 25 f. See for the "case" Leo and other pastors of Jewish descent in Marahrens' Lutheran State Church in Hanover Gerhard Lindemann, "Typisch jü- disch". Die Stellung der Ev.-luth. Landeskirche Hannover zu Antijudaismus, Juden- feindschaft und Antisemitismus 1919–1949 (Schriften der Gesellschaft für Deutsch- landforschung 63), Berlin 1998. On 10 Sept. 1941, Long wrote to Freudenberg: "Thus far we have dealt with 1,458 Lutheran refugees of which 1,247 have been referred to our churches for their spiritual care and 916 have been placed in self-supporting po- sitions." AELCA, Chicago, Best. NLC 2/3/1, Executive Director Ralph H. Long, General Files 1930–1947, Box 6.

130 Cf. Long to Freudenberg on 10 Dec. 1941, AELCA, Chicago, Best. NLC 2/3/1, Executive Director Ralph H. Long, General Files 1930–1947, Box 6.

131 According to Freudenberg's estimation (World Council of Churches, Ecumenical Committee for Christian Refugees) in a letter to Long on 3 July 1941, loc. cit.

132 Cf. Stewart W. Herman's letter to Long on 21 June 1940 and the letter from Teller to Herman on 17 June 1940, loc. cit.

133 Cf. Marty, Modern American Religion, vol. 2 (op. cit. note 7), 131.

134 Ivan Lee Holt, The Search for a New Strategy in Protestantism, Nashville 1936.

135 Marty, Modern American Religion, vol. 2 (op. cit. note 7), 376.

136 Quoted from ibid.

137 Report on Conference with the President of the United States, Appendix B, Meeting of Executive Committee of the Federal Council of the Churches of Christ in America, November 22, 1935 DeptHistPresbChurch, Phila., RG 18-1-8.

138 Cf. Marty, Modern American Religion, vol. 2 (op. cit. note 7), 383.

139 Cf. e. g. Christian Century 55 from 23 Nov. 1938, 1422 f., 1456–1458; The Presbyterian 111 from 11 Dec. 1941, 2. Also see Ross, So it was True (op. cit. note 54).

140 See Gerald R. Sittser, A Cautious Patriotism: The American Churches and the Second World War, Chapel Hill 1997, 23 ff.

141 Cf. John S. Conway, 'Myron C. Taylor's Mission to the Vatican, 1940–1950', in Church History 44 (1975) 85–99; George Q. Flynn, Roosevelt and Romanism. Catholics and American Diplomacy, 1937–1945, Westport 1976, 102 ff. Roosevelt's actions began with a Christmas appeal to Christian and Jewish religious leaders including the Pope in 1939. In this appeal he showed for the first time his intention to send a special am- bassador to Rome, so as not to leave any stone unturned in the attempt to re-instate peace.

142 Cf. Official information from State Department (Pierrepont Moffat, Chief, Division of European Affairs) to Osborne Hauge (Publicity Secretary, The News Bureau of the NLC) on 8 May 1939, AELCA, Chicago, Best. NLC 2/3/1, Executive Director Ralph H. Long, General Files 1930–1947, Box 6.

143 Cf. Flynn, Roosevelt and Romanism (op. cit. note 141), 98 ff., in particular 102. Cf. Ralph F. de Bedts, Ambassador Joseph Kennedy 1938–1940. An Anatomy of Appease- ment, New York 1985; Michael R. Beschloss, Kennedy and Roosevelt: The uneasy al- liance, New York 1980; Richard J. Wahlen, The founding father. The story of Joseph P. Kennedy, Washington, D. C. 1993.

144 Cf. John Cooney, The American Pope. The life and times of Francis Cardinal Spell- man, New York 1984.

145 On Roosevelt's good relations to the Arch Bishop of Chicago, George Mundelein, and to the catholic moral theologian John Augustine Ryan cf. Michael Zöller, Washington und Rom. Der Katholizismus in der amerikanischen Kultur, Berlin 1995, 156 f. Both of them supported Roosevelts New-Deal-Liberalism.

146 The cooperation between Rome and the Catholic Church in the USA had proven itself twice in the field of foreign policy, concerning the "Policy of Neighbourliness"
with the majority of the catholic Latin-American states and in regard to the Spanish
Civil War. Cf. Flynn, Roosevelt and Romanism (op. cit. note 141), 14 ff., 29 ff.

147 Ibid. 21.

148 Cf. Zöller, Washington and Rome (op. cit. note 145), 172.

149 Cf. Marty, Modern American Religion, vol. 3 (op. cit. note 31), 108 ff. Also see Long's
critical description of Catholicism in a presentation from June 1939 with the title "The
State of the Church throughout the World", AELCA, Chicago, Best. NLC 2/3/1, Executive Director Ralph H. Long, General Files 1930-1947, Box 6. He commented
rather more harshly in a statement on 26 June 1940, loc. cit.

150 Cf. Sittser, Patriotism (op. cit. note 140), 167 f.

151 Cf. Robert T. Hardy, A History of the Churches in the United States and Canada,
Oxford 1976, 392 f.

152 H. Richard Niebuhr, The Kingdom of God in America, New York 1959 (1937). Partial
quotation from André Siegtried, America comes of Age, New York 1927, 33. Also see
R. Laurence Moore, Religious Outsiders and the Making of Americans, New York-
Oxford 1987, 48 ff.

153 Cf. Discussion, draft and final version of the Protest note: Minutes of the Executive
Committee of the Federal Council of the Churches of Christ in America, 26 Jan. 1940,
DeptHistPresbChurch, Phila., RG 18-1-11.

154 Cf. Letter of the President of the Federal Council, Buttrick, to Roosevelt on 27 Feb.
1940 and Roosevelt's answer on 14 Mar. 1940, Minutes of the Executive Committee
of the Federal Council of the Churches of Christ in America, March 29, 1940,
DeptHistPresbChurch, Phila., RG 18-1-11. The special ambassador remained in office until 1951. Cf. to the continuation of events Hansjakob Stehle, Geheimdiplomatie
im Vatikan. Die Päpste und die Kommunisten, Zurich 1993, 199 ff. Also see Taylor's:
Ennio Di Nolfo, Vaticano e Stati Uniti 1939-1952 (dalle carte di Myron C. Taylor)
[Ennio Di Nolfo, The Vatican and the United States 1939-1952 (from the papers of
Myron C. Taylor)]. On Taylor's interventions in the Vatican to stop Italy taking Germany's side in the war cf. Hearden, Roosevelt Confronts Hitler (op. cit. note 31), 145,
147.

155 Cf. The Protest telegram from the Federal Council to Roosevelt on 18 March 1941 on
the occasion of an article in the New York Times, which claimed that Roosevelt wanted to send a second representative to Rome, cf. Minutes of the Executive Committee
of the Federal Council of the Churches of Christ in America, 13 Jun. 1941, DeptHist
PresbChurch, Phila., RG 18-1-12.

156 Cf. the letter of Edward W. Schramm, who was the editor of the Lutheran Standard,
the official organ of the American Lutheran Church, to Roosevelt on 4 May 1934, in
Franklin D. Roosevelt and Foreign Affairs, vol. 2: March 1934-August 1935, ed. by
Edgar B. Nixon, Cambridge/Mass. 1969, 86-88. Due to a press report Schramm pro-
tested against "the proposed recognition on the part of our government of the Vatican
State" (ibid. 87) and attached a corresponding open letter from the Lutherans to the
President.

157 Cf. Flynn, Roosevelt and Romanism (op. cit. note 141), 13 f.

158 Ibid. On 21 May 1937 Goebbels noted: "Cardinal Mundelein from Chicago has insult-
ed the Führer, me and the Third Reich. He doubted the correctness of our clerical
processes. I let the German press loss on him." Cf. Die Tagebücher von Joseph Goebbels, 1/3, 149 [self-translation]. Cf. also 'Zwischenfall Kardinal Mundelein', Pol.
Archiv des Auswärtigen Amtes, Bonn, Pol III (HI. Stuhl), Po 2.

159 Jørgensen to Boe, Knubel, Long, Wentz, von Bonsdorff, Moe and Pehrsson on 29 Dec.
1937, AELCA, Chicago, Best. LWC 1/3, Correspondence File 1936-47, Box 1.

160 Jørgensen to Boe, Knubel, Long, Wentz, von Bonsdorff, Moe and Pehrsson on 5 Nov.
1938, loc. cit.

161 Michelfelder to Long on 22 Nov. 1938, loc. cit. On 31 January 1939, Jørgensen wrote to the Americans, who had requested him to invite Lilje to the Scandinavian countries to hold lectures: "The persecution of the Jews have created here in Scandinavia a public opinion, which is not favourable to a speaker from Germany. It has been said from many sides that it is desirable that the German bishops protest against the persecution of the Jews." [self-translation] AELCA, Chicago, Best. LWC 1/3, Correspondence File 1936–47, Box 2.

162 See Cashman, America, Roosevelt, and World War II (op. cit. note 125), 34 f. Cf. also Ingeborg Fleischhauer, 'Der deutsch-sowjetische Grenz- und Freundschaftsvertrag vom 28. September 1939. Die deutschen Aufzeichnungen über die Verhandlungen zwischen Stalin, Molotov und Ribbentrop in Moskau', in VZG 39 (1991) 447–470. Stalin was elected twice "Man of the Year" by the US magazine TIME: in 1939 (cf. TIME, January 1, 1940) and in 1942 (cf. TIME, January 4, 1943); cf. also Manfred Hildermeier, Geschichte der Sowjetunion 1917–1991. Entstehung und Niedergang des ersten sozialistischen Staates, Munich 1998, 590 ff.

163 Cf. Marty, Modern American Religion, vol. 2 (op. cit. note 7), 301.

164 Cf. Angermann, Die Vereinigten Staaten (op. cit. note 96), 217.

165 The Kellogg-Briand-Pact from 27 August 1928 in Paris, which was ratified by the American senate on 15 January 1929, formed the political basis of this attitude. Cf. Sittser, Patriotism (op. cit. note 140), 18, 24. Also see the letter from the National Peace Conference to Roosevelt on 27 Aug. 1935, Franklin D. Roosevelt and Foreign Affairs, vol. 2: March 1934–August 1935, 621 f. On behalf of the Federal Council its president Ivan Lee Holt signed the document.

166 Cf. Sittser, Patriotism (op. cit. note 140), 26.

167 Martin Dies, The Trojan Horse in America, New York, 1977, reprint of the edition from 1940.

168 Cf. Sittser, Patriotism (op. cit. note 140), 189 f.

169 Cf. Heather A. Warren, Theologians of a New World Order, Reinhold Niebuhr and the Christian Realists 1920–1948, New York-Oxford 1997, in particular 94 ff.

170 Cf. Ronald W. Pruessen, John Foster Dulles. The Road to Power, New York-London 1982; Anthony C. Arend, Pursuing a just and durable Peace. John Foster Dulles and International Organization, New York 1988; Richard H. Immerman (ed.), John Foster Dulles and the Diplomacy of the Cold War, Princeton, N. J. 1990; Frederick W. Marks, Power and Peace. The Diplomacy of John Foster Dulles, Westport, Conn. 1993.

171 Cf. Armin Boyens, 'Die Ökumenische Bewegung und die totalitären Ideologien des 20. Jahrhunderts', in Martin Greschat and Jochen-Christoph Kaiser (eds), Christentum und Demokratie im 20. Jahrhundert (KoGe 4), Stuttgart-Berlin-Cologne 1992, 19–44, in particular 25–28.

172 H. Lilje wrote: "Then followed the war years. It was unusually difficult to keep in touch. The highest praise is deserved for those who kept in touch throughout those difficult times. This primarily includes Stewart Hermann [.], the pastor of the American parish in Berlin." Cf. Memorabila (op. cit. note 116), 211. Also see Herman, It's Your Souls we want (op. cit. note 2); idem, American Church in Berlin, New York 1978, 48 ff. Between 1943 and 1945, Herman worked as Germany expert for the American secret Office of Strategic Services (OSS). Cf. Gerhard Besier, 'Ökumenische Mission in Nachkriegsdeutschland. Die Berichte von Stewart W. Herman über die Verhältnisse in der evangelischen Kirche 1945/46', in KZG 1 (1988) 151–187; cf. also Barry M. Katz, Foreign Intelligence. Research and Analysis in the Office of Strategic Service 1942–1945, Cambridge 1989; Jürgen Heideking, 'USA und die deutsche Kirchen, Beobachtung, Planungen und Besatzungspolitik 1942–1949', in Anselm Doering-Manteuffel and Joachim Mehlhausen (eds), Christliches Ethos und der Widerstand gegen den Nationalsozialismus in Europa (KoGe 9), Stuttgart-Berlin-Cologne 1995, 119–138; also see Jürgen Heideking and Christof Mauch (eds), USA und deutscher Widerstand. Analysen und Operationen des amerikanischen Geheimdienstes im Zweiten Weltkrieg, Tübingen-Basel 1993, in particular 200 ff.

173 On the situation of the Berlin embassy since the beginning of the war cf. George F. Kennan, Memoirs 1925–1950, London 1968, 105 ff.
174 Cf. various correspondence from S. W. Herman 1940, AELCA, Chicago, Best. NLC 2/3/1, Executive Director Ralph H. Long, General Files 1930–1947, Box 6.
175 Cf. e. g. Report from the embassy on 8 May 1935, NA Washington, RG 59, 862.404/119.
176 NA Washington, RG 59, 862.404/120.
177 Cf. Reports from the American embassy on 4 Jun., 21 Jul. and 27 Aug. 1936, NA Washington, RG 59, 862.404/184–187. See on the memorandum: Martin Greschat (ed.), Zwischen Widerspruch und Widerstand. Texte zur Denkschrift der Bekennenden Kirche an Hitler (1936) (Studienbücher zur kirchlichen Zeitgeschichte 6), Munich 1987. For a broader background on the indiscretion and denunciation in connection with the memorandum cf. Werner Koch, "Sollen wir K. weiter beobachten?" Ein Leben im Widerstand, Stuttgart 1982, 157 ff.; EZA Berlin, 50/260, 26 ff.; BstU ZA MfS-HA XX/4, 2481; MfS ZA AOP 518/59, 64 volumes; MfS AU 1310/58; MfS ZA SV 4–84; MfS ZA SV 14/74. The Ministry of state security (*Staatssicherheit* – Stasi) had achieved in the document storage of their main department IX/11 the documents of the Gestapo from Düsseldorf and Berlin from the years 1936/37. In this collection there are acts of the security office or rather the Reich's security office, which have been kept since the fifties in the NS archive of the Stasi of the GDR and are today either in the Bundesarchiv or in a temporary archive at Dahlwitz-Hoppegarten. See Dagmar Unverhau (ed.), Das "NS-Archiv" des Ministeriums für Staatssicherheit. Stationen einer Entwicklung, Münster 1998. Cf. Martin Greschat, 'Friedrich Weißler. Ein Jurist der BK im Widerstand gegen Hitler', in Ursula Büttner and Martin Greschat (eds), Die verlassenen Kinder der Kirche. Der Umgang mit Christen jüdischer Herkunft im "Dritten Reich", Göttingen 1998, 86–122. Gerhard Besier, Die Kirchen und das Dritte Reich. Spaltungen und Abwehrkämpfe 1934–1937, Berlin-München 2001, 482 ff.
178 Embassy report on 17 Feb. 1937, NA Washington, RG 59, 862.404/196. In the embassy report on 21 June 1937 it reads: "As has always been maintained by the Embassy, the Catholic opposition, owing to its close organization, appears of greater consequence to the State than that emanating from the Evangelical Churches, even though the latter may claim to embrace two-thirds of the population. Protestant opposition essentially derives from the small band of pastors in Prussia and in certain parts of West Germany who combat National Socialism in the sincere conviction that they are defending the Christian belief, while experience has shown that the large mass of Protestants represented by the Lutherans do not usually intervene until steps are taken by the Party or State against their Church organization." Cf. NA Washington, RG 59, 862.404/217.
179 Cf. American consulate in Bremen to the American embassy in Berlin on 14 Apr. 937, NA Washington, RG 59, 862.404/209.
180 In Dodd's report to the State Department on 23 March 1937 it reads: "The Catholics ... must be considered to have lost much ground doctrinally to the new religion of National Socialism which has swept Germany as a reaction to the long post-war years of depression and despair." Cf. NA Washington, RG 59, 862.404/201. Cf also Gerhard Besier and Eckard Lessing (eds), Trennung von Staat und Kirche (op. cit. note 66), 449–482.
181 Memorandum from 28 Dec. 1938 and telegram from the Berlin embassy on 20 Jan. 1939, NA Washington, RG 59, 862.00/3814.
182 Report from the Berlin embassy from 5 Dec. 1938, NA Washington, RG 59, 862.00/3806.
183 Cf. Telegram from the Berlin embassy from 20 Jan. 1939, NA Washington, RG 59, 862.00/3814.
184 Cf. Embassy report from Rome on 24 Sep. 1937, NA Washington, RG 59, 862.404/230.

185 Cf. Embassy report from Rome on 18 May 1938, NA Washington, RG 59, 862.404/ 273.
186 Cf. Carl J. Burckhardt, Meine Danziger Mission 1937-1939, Munich 1962.
187 Cf. Embassy report from Warsaw on 8 Dec. 1938, NA Washington, RG 59, 862.404/ 284.
188 Cf. Franz Scholz, Zwischen Staatsräson und Evangelium. Kardinal Hlond und die Tragödie der ostdeutschen Diözesen, Frankfurt a. M. ³1989.
189 Cf. Report from the American embassy on 30 Aug. 1938, NA Washington, RG 59, 862.404/323.
190 Cf. Report from the American embassy on 17 Feb. 1939, NA Washington, LM 193/ II, 48485-487.
191 Cf. John S. Conway, 'The Vatican, Britain and Relations with Germany', 1938-1940, in The Historical Journal 16 (1973) 147-167.
192 Cf. Telegram from the American embassy in Berlin on 9 May 1939 regarding the audience with the papal ambassador (the subject of the conversation was the visit to Hitler), NA Washington, RG 59, 862.404/292; see also the telegram from the American embassy on 24 May 1939, loc. cit., 293.
193 Cf. the speech to the House of Lords from the Arch-Bishop of Canterbury on 20 Mar. 1939, Boyens, Kirchenkampf und Ökumene, vol. 1 (op. cit. note 38), 256. Leiper, the associate secretary in the provisional committee of the World Council of Churches (in formation) sent on 6 April an appeal to the State Department. The appeal came from a high positioned German ("Mister X") and was to form the basis of an international protest against Hitler and Mussolini, cf. NA Washington, RG 59, 862.00/3842. A considerable difference between both documents was that the Arch Bishop of Canterbury even suggested the difficult cooperation with the USSR, while the German initiative suggested cooperation between the Italian people, who were lead by the Pope, England, France and the USA. "If such action is taken immediately, the world can reach the haven of enduring peace this year without being impelled to seek the aid of Russia."
194 A Statement on the American Churches and the European War, Minutes of the Executive Committee of the Federal Council of the Churches of Christ in America, 22 Sep. 1939, DeptHistPresbChurch, Phila., RG 18-1-10.
195 Minutes of the Executive Committee of the Federal Council of the Churches of Christ in America, 6 Oct.1939, loc. cit.
196 Cf. Letter from the Federal Council on 9 Oct. 1939 to Roosevelt. In the letter parts of the draft position of 22 September 1939 were used.
197 F. Willem A. Visser't Hooft, Die Welt war meine Gemeinde, Munich ²1971.
198 Cf. Boyens, Kirchenkampf und Ökumene, vol. 2: 1939-1945, Munich 1973, 78 f., text: loc. cit., 318 f.
199 Quoted from to the Minutes of the Executive Committee of the Federal Council of the Churches of Christ in America, May 17, 1940, DeptHistPresbChurch, Phila., RG 18-1-11. Keller was the leader of the Central Bureau for Relief of the Evangelical Churches of Europe in Geneva. In a memorandum on 13 April 1933 on "Facts and Meaning of the German Revolution as seen from a Neutral Point of View" Keller had written: "One of the most important features in the German revolution must be seen in the struggle against the disintegrating influences of Marxism and Bolshevism, which were leading the nation to civil war. As it cannot be denied that the Jewish element played an important role in Russian Bolshevism as well as in the growing of German communism and atheism, a good deal of the blamed anti-Semitism and hatred finds its explanation in what is called the destructive and more disintegrating influence of the revolutionary Jewish mind. The hatred against Jews is therefore not only to be understood as a form of blind race antagonism, which finds its parallel in the Negro problem of America or in the race difficulties of South Africa, but as a charge against a part of the foreign and recently immigrated Jewish element as being responsible for the lowering of moral standards in public life on which quite a series of re-

cent law-suits have thrown a gloomy light." Cf. DeptHistPresbChurch, Phila., RG 18-9-15.

200 A Statement on the Present Opportunity and Duty of Christians, 21 Jun. 1940, Minutes of the Executive Committee of the Federal Council of the Churches of Christ in America, 21 Jun. 1940, DeptHistPresbChurch, Phila., RG 18-1-11.

201 Report from the American embassy on 29 Feb. 1940, NA Washington, RG 59, 862.404/302

202 Loc. cit.

203 Cf. George F. Kennan, Russia and the West under Lenin and Stalin, London 1961, 349 ff.; Ralph B. Levering, American Opinion and Russian Alliance, 1939-1945, Chapel Hill 1976, 39 ff.

204 Cf. Levering, American Opinion (op. cit. note 203), 17-20. With regard to the "Great Terror" between September 1936 and November 1938 in the USSR, of which hundreds of thousands from the Party, the administrative elite and national minorities were victims, such preconceptions had a quite real background. Cf. Stéphane Courtois et al., Das Schwarzbuch des Kommunismus. Unterdrückung, Verbrechen und Terror, Munich-Zurich 1998, 206 ff. Cf. Also Hermann Weber and Ulrich Mählert (eds), Terror. Stalinistische Parteisäuberungen 1936-1953, Paderborn 1998.

205 Cf. H. L. Trefousse, German and American Neutrality 1939-1941, New York 1969, 46 ff. The author writes that not only isolationists, but "ironical enough, pacifist groups and causes" supported the German-American Bund.

206 Cf. Angermann, Die Vereinigten Staaten (op. cit. note 96), 231 f.; Gernot H. Graessner, Deutschland und die Nationalsozialisten in den Vereinigten Staaten von Amerika 1933-1939. Ein Beitrag zur Deutschtumspolitk des Dritten Reiches, Bonn 1973; Cornelia Wilhelm, Bewegung oder Verein? Nationalsozialistische Volkstumspolitik in den USA, Stuttgart 1998; Herbert Sirois, Zwischen Illusion und Krieg. Deutschland und die USA 1933-41, Paderborn 1998. Extensive material can be found in the Hoover Institution Archives, Stanford, Cal., Radical Right Collection 1907-1982 (Conservatism United States), in particular Folder 6, Christianity and Politics, and Folder 7, Fundamentalism. John E. Dolibois, the American ambassador to Luxembourg, wrote in his autobiography: "[In 1939] 'American Firsters' were demonstrating for non-involvement. President Roosevelt was urged to keep us out. A lot of neutralist sentiment was stirred up by members of Hitler's 'Fifth Column' operating in the United States and other countries." Cf. Pattern of Circles. An Ambassador's Story, Kent-Ohio-London 1989, 46.

207 Cf. Saul S. Friedman, No Haven for the Oppressed. United States Policy toward Jewish Refugees 1938-1945, Detroit 1973; Wyman, The Abandonment of the Jews (op. cit. note 125), 5 ff.

208 Cf. Catherine Wiedmann, Die amerikanische Außenpolitik des Jahres 1941 zwischen Isolationismus und Interventionismus: Der Einfluß der Interventionisten, Mag.-Arb., Konstanz 1997.

209 Under the leadership of General Robert E. Wood, the boss of the large mail order company Sears, Roebuck & Co., the isolationists established the American First Committee, who had prominent members such as Ex-president Herbert Hoover, General Hugh Johnson, the senators Gerald P. Nye and Burton K. Wheeler, the brothers La Follette, Charles A. Beard, Father Coughlin and the airman Charles A. Lindbergh. See Geoffry S. Smith, To Save a Nation. American Counter subversives, the New Deal and the Coming of World War II, New York 1973. See also Shirer, Berlin Diary (op. cit. note 18), 213, 220.

210 An important element for isolationism was the insular segmentisation of the American society according to class, race and ethnic groups. Cf. Cashman, America, Roosevelt and World War II (op. cit. note 125), 12 ff.

211 Cf. Marty, Modern American Religion, vol. 2 (op. cit. note 7), 90 ff.

212 Ibid. 262.

213 Jørgensen to the non-German members and deputies of the executive committee of the Lutheran World Convent on 27 Sep. 1939, AELCA, Chicago, Best. LWC 1/3, Correspondence File 1936–47, Box 2. On 27 February 1940 Helene Bursche, the daughter of Julius Bursche, addressed a letter of request to the American Lutherans, in which she told in detail of the fate of her father in a German prison, cf. AELCA, Chicago, Best. LWC 1/3, Correspondence File 1936–47, Box 3. In his letter to the Americans on 3 February 1940, Jørgensen had already expressed the request for Knubel to take on the case, loc. cit. See Bernd Krebs, Nationale Identität und kirchliche Selbstbehauptung. Julius Bursche und die Auseinandersetzungen um Auftrag und Weg des Protestantismus in Polen 1917–1939, Neukirchen-Vluyn 1993. At the end of February 1940, the American embassy in Berlin reported that the Vatican Radio has said that many Catholic Churches in areas occupied by the Germans had either been closed or converted into Protestant Churches, cf. Report of the American embassy from 29 Feb. 1940, NA Washington, RG 59, 862.404/302.
214 Long, World Lutheranism, 5 Sep. 1939, AELCA, Chicago, Best. NLC 2/3/1, Executive Director Ralph H. Long, General Files 1930–1947, Box 6.
215 Long, The State of the Church throughout the World. Prepared for the Convention of the Eastern District, American Lutheran Church, 26–29 Jun. 1940, AELCA, Chicago, Best. NLC 2/3/1, Executive Director Ralph H. Long, General Files 1930–1947, Box 6.
216 Hickersen (Department of State, Division for European Affairs) to Berle on 26 Feb. 1940, NA Washington, RG 59, 862.4016/2198.
217 Department of State, 23 Feb. 1940, loc. cit.
218 Letter from the Berlin embassy to the State Department on 22 Nov. 1940, NA Washington, RG 59, 862.1416/2183. Cf. also Callum MacDonald and Jan Kaplan, Prague. In the Shadow of the Swastika. A History of the German Occupation 1939–1945, Prague 1995. Also see George F. Kennan, From Prague after Munich. Diplomatic Papers 1938–1940, Princeton, N. J. 1968, particularly 42 ff.
219 Telegram from the American embassy in Berlin to the State Department on 22 Feb. 1941. It reads: "It is my own opinion that the furnishing of such information through the Foreign Service to a relief organisation is inappropriate and may cause embarrassment." Cf. NA Washington, RG 59, (862.4016/2192. On 22 February 1941, the state department wired its consent, loc. cit.
220 Cf. Telegram from the American embassy on 30 Sep. 1941, NA Washington, RG 59, 862.4016/2204. PS/BH.
221 Cf. Telegram from the Berlin embassy on 18 Oct. 1941, 22 and 28 Nov. 1941, NA Washington, RG 59, 862.4016/2206, 2213 and 2216.
222 Minutes of the Executive Committee of the Federal Council of the Churches of Christ in America, 19 Sep. 1941, DeptHistPresbChurch, Phila., RG 18-1-14.
223 Actes et Documents du Saint Siège Relatifs à la Seconde Guerre Mondiale, Città del Vaticano (ADSS), vol. 5, Vatican 1969, doc. no. 59, 179 f.; Myron C. Taylor, Wartime Correspondence between President Roosevelt and Pope Pius XII, New York [2]1975, 62.
224 Loc. cit.
225 Cf. Hearden, Roosevelt Confronts Hitler (op. cit. note 31), 199 f.
226 Cf. Otto Luchterhand, Der Sowjetstaat und die Russisch-Orthodoxe Kirche, Cologne 1976, 100 ff.; Dimitry Pospielovsky, The Russian Church under the Soviet Regime, vol. 1, Crestwood 1984, 193 ff.
227 Cf. Warren F. Kimball, The Juggler. Franklin Roosevelt as Wartime Statesman, Princeton, N. J. 1991, 34. Also see Robert Dallek, Franklin D. Roosevelt and American Foreign Policy, 1932–1945, New York 1979, 279.
228 Cf. ADSS, vol. 5, doc. nos 93 and 131. Also see David J. O'Brien, The Renewal of American Catholicism, New York, 127 f.
229 DH 3771–3774.
230 Cf. Raymond H. Dawson, The Decision to Aid Russia, 1941, Chapel Hill 1959, 265–268; Cf. Conway, Myron C. Taylor's Mission (op. cit. note 141), 90 f. In return,

on request of Pius XII, the USA was to stop the threatened bombing of Rome by the British.

231 ADSS, vol. 5, doc. no. 93, 240 f.

232 ADSS, vol. 5, doc. no. 131, 285–288, quote: 286.

233 Cf. Department of State Bulletin 5, 4 October 1941, 246.

234 Statement on religious freedom in Russia, Minutes of the Executive Committee of the Federal Council of the Churches of Christ in America, 28 Nov. 1941, DeptHist PresbChurch, Phila., RG 18-1-12, published in the Federal Council Bulletin 23 from November 1941, 6.

235 Cf. Knipping, Die amerikanische Rußlandpolitik (op. cit. note 106); Levering, American Opinion (op. cit. note 203), in particular 52 ff.

236 Cf. Petition on 21 Oct. 1941, in Protestant Digest, 25 Oct. 1941.

237 Cf. Minutes of the Executive Committee of the Federal Council of the Churches of Christ in America, December 30, 1941, DeptHistPresbChurch, Phila., RG 18-1-12.

238 Sittser, Patriotism (op. cit. note 140).

239 Cf. Marty, Modern American Religion, vol. 1: The Irony of it all 1893–1919, Chicago-London 1997, 38 f., passim.

240 Report from the American embassy on 29 Feb. 1940, NA Washington, RG 59, 862.404/302.

241 Cf. in comparison Conway, The Attitude of English-speaking Churches (op. cit. note 112), 149. He judges for the twenties and early thirties that "scholarly enquiry was downplayed and church history was tailored to serve the needs of each denomination, which effectively cut off any profound study of German conditions or even of Luther".

242 Cf. Georg Seide, Verantwortung in der Diaspora. Die russisch-orthodoxe Kirche im Ausland, Munich 1989.

243 For the latest research on massacres of religious groups cf. ENI Bulletin, no. 23, 26 Nov. 1997, 13 f. It reads: "In 1995, a Russian government commission found that more than 200,000 priests and nuns of various denominations had been killed, and half-a-million imprisoned or deported in Soviet purges of the 1920s and 1930s, a period now described as the worst persecution ever inflicted on Christians."

244 Cf. The Gallup Polls (op. cit. note 95), vol. 1, 3, 46, 54, 65, 120, 137, 141, 145, 149.

245 On 13 July 1934, Morehead wrote to Marahrens: "Above all the friends of the international understanding and good-will in America need to know the truth about what is taking place in Germany, supported by the authoritative evidence." AELCA, Best. LWC 1/2, Correspondence File 1921–1947, Box 21.

In Contradiction to the Grassroots?
The Stance of the Federal Council of the Churches
of Christ (FCC) towards the "Third Reich"*

1. The Federal Council, the basis of its ideas, and its opponents

1.1 The foundation of the FCC and the relationship towards its own institutions

In December 1908, a number of "mainline churches" founded the Federal Council of the Churches of Christ in America, "to manifest the essential oneness of the Christian Churches of America in Jesus Christ as their divine Lord and Savior". Finally, 33 churches comprising 18 million Christians were members of this Council. The purpose of this loose merger without any executive powers was to advise member churches in order to overcome conflicts, encourage further cooperation and put a Christian body of thought in "every relation of human life"[2]. The pillars of this Council were, above all, the descendants of the old colonial churches – Presbyterians[3], Episcopalians[4] and Congregationalists[5], but also Methodists[6], Baptists and Disciples of Christ[7]. The churches of non-English-speaking immigrants – such as Lutherans[8], Reformed Churches and others – were present on a much lower scale. The way the Council was perceived differed in the member churches. While some wanted to see it as a definite merger, other denominations only saw it as an advising body. It is interesting to note that among the main churches belonging to the church alliance were some who, in Europe, enjoyed the status of state churches or of privileged mainline churches, such as the Episcopalians or the Lutherans. Other member churches, though, were classical representatives of the so-called Free Churches in Europe, such as the Baptists or Methodists.

Despite the founding of the Federal Council, the US-American Protestants remained divided into different denominations until the end of World War I; there were not always religious reasons for this ecclesiastical individualism. The division was often based on cultural or national peculiarities of the immigrants.[9] Over generations, the church remained the stronghold of customs and traditions derived from the country of origin, meaning it had the function of preserving a community's identity. Still, in 1937, five of eight Protestant denominations asked, declined an ecclesiastical unification with other Protestant churches. The "separatist" denominations were led by the Southern Baptists (25 % yes- versus 75 % no-votes) and the Lutherans (33 % yes- versus 67 % no-votes).[10]

*   First published in *Kyrkohistorisk Årsskrift*, Lund 2003, 139–156.

1.2   Theological self-definition of the FCC and Christian opposition

Ideologically, the Federal Council was inspired by the "social gospel" movement, an awakening movement for social reform closely related to the rise of liberal Protestantism since the 1890s, which was influential until the Great Depression of 1929.[11] The "social gospel" gave a voice to the concepts of political and social reform of American Protestantism and documented its opening towards the modern branches of science, especially the theory of evolution, and towards the pressing social problems of those days. The Christianisation of social matters and their transformation caused an enormous change in the cultural climate of the United States at the beginning of the 20th century. The religious project of salvation became a "social matter", but soon lost its spiritual contents and became part of American consumer society.[12]

The most important opponent of the social gospel was pre-millennial Dispensationalism, which, with its theology of criticism of the churches, gave new impetus to the fundamentalist movement. The Dispensationalists taught that the Second Coming of Christ would take place before the turn of the millennium, after a period of growing godlessness.[13] Against the background of the horrors of World War I and a general disappearance of optimism, this doctrine spread fast.[14] Like Lutheran Confessionalism, it professed a gain of individual salvation through the process of becoming conscience of one's sins, changing one's ways, and being reborn.

Due to World War I and the following economic depression and catastrophic social consequences, a collective feeling of decline which took hold on the United States from the 1920s onwards, caused a new generation of mainline theologians to gradually dissociate themselves from the social gospel. Among them were personalities who would later decide on the course of the FCC – the General Secretary Samuel McCrea Cavert (1888–1976) being one of them.[15] The majority of these theologians had been educated at Union Theological Seminary in New York City, and a large number of them were teachers at this institute. With prophetic claims, these theologians criticised the validity of the liberal theology and social order. Similar to the developments in Europe, the former liberal optimism of their theology had collapsed during World War I and the crises of the 1920s and early 1930s. Thus, they made "excessive" liberalism relative by reintegrating supernatural elements and Christocentric visions, which led to a self-critical position regarding some manifestations of Christianity. According to their understanding of themselves, these informal discussion groups formulated a "neo-liberal" theology of "Christian realism"[16]. It included a rediscovery of sin, which was regarded as the real root of political and social evils in this world. "Sin made it necessary for Christians also to take political action to prevent regression into moral barbarism, whether fascism or communism."[17]

1.3   The relationship of Federal Council and Universal Christian Council

A decisive impulse was given to the "social gospel" theory as to neo-liberal "Christian realism" by the ecumenical movement. The movement was represented by the Universal Christian Council for Life and Work as well as by all endeavours based on it in connection with the long process of foundation of the World Council of Churches since 1937. The FCC and its theologians saw themselves as protagonists of this movement, which also emerged from the fact that they occupied leading posts in both councils.[18] It was Cavert who first suggested the name "World Council of Churches".[19] The Federal Council's Department of Relations with Churches Abroad served as the American Section of the Universal Christian Council.[20] The aim was to overcome confessional and national boundaries and to let the universal kingship of Christ become visible in this world.[21] These circles were ruled by a pacifist mentality and a strong aversion to political intervention in other countries.[22] This pacifist stance was looked upon most unfavourably by the conservative circle of the defence lobby. There were efforts within the Navy League to give the FCC the "red badge", in order to weaken their power.[23]

1.4   Differences within the Churches between Liberal Protestants,
        Fundamentalists, Evangelicals and Confessionalists

The ideas of liberal Modernists[24] did not remain unquestioned, though. In the 1920s, the controversies among them, and the fundamentalist movement[25], ensured a further return of mainline Protestantism to the common theological basis. The FCC intended to defend its claim of shaping the religious lifestyle of the Protestant "nation under God" against the explosive spreading of fundamentalist or evangelical piousness. The FCC's elaborate twenty-fifth anniversary celebration on 6 December 1933, where President Roosevelt gave a speech, was meant to emphasise this claim.[26] But the growing dissent of the large Protestant denominations stressed the force of the religious alternatives.

The institutional pressure towards unification within mainline churches, which were organised in the Federal Council, grew at the beginning of the 1940s, when Fundamentalist and Evangelical federations were founded. The neo-Evangelical "National Association of Evangelicals" (NAE), which provided the religious Conservatives with a new national identity, was founded in 1942.[27] In 1943, the Evangelicals opened an Office in Washington, D. C., in order to gain more influence over the US-American government.[28] Last, but not least, Liberal as well as Conservative Protestants felt more and more threatened by the strong Roman Catholic Church in America.[29]

On this theologically challenged, uncertain basis of discussion, which was contemporarily burdened with heavy economic disruptions in the United States followed by great political uncertainties[30], the FCC felt obliged to express its opinion on the changes taking place in Europe, and especially in Germany. Certainly the Church Officers of the FCC did not only find it necessary to observe European dictatorships. Together with their British colleagues, they understood that the totalitarian concept was a universal threat to religious freedom throughout modern nations. The situation in Turkey, Japan, and Mexico was also constantly observed and commented on.[31]

2.   Debates of the Federal Council with Churches and Christians on how to appraise the German situation

2.1   First disagreements between the FCC and German Protestantism

Already in mid-March 1933, Congregationalist minister Henry Smith Leiper[32], who, as Executive of the Commission of Relations with Churches Abroad, had been in charge of questions of the kind in the FCC (Federal Council of Churches) since 1930, wrote to August Wilhelm Schreiber. Schreiber was in charge of ecumenical questions at the German Federal Church Office. In his letter, Leiper informed the German church representative that the National Socialist attacks against American Jews "have had a very bad effect upon American sentiment generally"[33]. This letter, a further message by the President of the FCC, Albert W. Beaven, and a Resolution of the FCC, did not produce the expected declaration by the German churches, namely that German Protestantism also thought of anti-Semitism as being un-Christian. To the surprise of the Americans, they received complaints from Germany about the American reminders. The Germans clearly advised against interfering in their domestic affairs and told the Americans in no uncertain terms that ecclesiastical cooperation might be heavily disturbed by these procedures. Although the 1 April 1933 boycott against Jews confirmed rather than dispelled American fears, the situation seemed to calm down shortly afterwards[34], especially because within the FCC's Executive Committee there had been reservations against interfering in German domestic matters[35]. Charles Macfarland[36], general secretary of the FCC until 1930, his successor Samuel McCrea Cavert, and "foreign secretary" Henry Smith Leiper repeatedly travelled to Germany and, in 1933/34, reported quite positively about their experiences with the German dictatorship. Macfarland was – upon Wilhelm Schreiber's recommendation[37], among others – even received by Hitler at the end of October 1933 and misunderstood the church conflict in Germany, according to the constellation existing in the United States, as an argument between Liberals and Fundamentalists. He trusted that the now informed Hitler would re-establish the peace among the churches.[38] In early 1934, Macfarland sent Hitler his book "The New Church and the New Germany"[39]. He wrote in an accompanying note that he was convinced Hitler did not intend to instrumentalise the Church.[40] Although Macfarland came under much pressure from the American Church, due to his position on the matter[41], the Germans supported him[42]. The head of the Church's Foreign Department (*Kirchliches Außenamt* – KA) of the official German Evangelical Church (*Deutsche Evangelische Kirche* – DEK), Bishop Theodor Heckel, sent him a sincere letter of praise for his 70th birthday in mid-June 1936.[43] Only in mid-1937 did Macfarland give up his favourable attitude towards the NS regime and accused Hitler in an Open Letter of having deceived him, of mercilessly persecuting Jews, destroying churches and isolating Germany with his policy.[44]

Even the descriptions given by those German clergymen most loyal to the regime, could not conceal forever from the unbiased US-American visitors that Jews were being persecuted in Germany, and at least parts of the churches were being suppressed. From 1935 onwards, the officials of the Federal Council gained a more critical view of the situation in Germany, wrote corresponding letters and issued a number of appeals. These position papers are essentially well known.[45] Much less attention has been paid up to now to the opposing opinions of the FCC member churches and individual Christians, who tried through argumentation to change the FCC-course to a critical stance towards the NS regime. According to his position as "foreign secretary", Henry Smith Leiper had to face these attacks and accept the responsibility for the questionable course the FCC foreign policy pursued. On the other hand, it was Leiper himself who contributed considerably to the confrontational course of American Christendom towards the NS state. Leiper's decisive stance, when looking at the situation in Germany, was certainly influenced by a personal talk with German theologian Dietrich Bonhoeffer. This had taken place in August of 1934, and was the result of a meeting of the Universal Christian Council of Life and Work in Fanö.[46] During Leiper's travels within Europe, the first contact between Bonhoeffer and Leiper was established in London as early as in the summer of 1933.[47]

2.2   The opposition of American Lutheranism against FCC church policy

The greatest problem for the FCC was certainly that even the United Lutheran Church of America, the only Lutheran member church cooperating with the FCC[48], opposed any measure that might have been regarded as "anti-Hitlerist". Besides this, not only the American Lutherans, but also the Lutheran World Convention generally looked upon the national and international Christian Council Movement with great suspicion.[49] In it, they perceived the danger of a blurring of the differences among the Protestant confessions – of creating an indifferent unification (*Unionisierung*) of Protestantism. Deep scepticism was expressed by many American Lutherans on the question as to whether shattered American democracy would be able to solve the moral and economic problems within the country. An open sympathy for the National Socialist state developed out of this, which was openly expressed on several occasions especially by Lars W. Boe, one of the three representatives of the American National Lutheran Council.[50]

The Church's Foreign Department (KA) of the DEK, knew exactly how American Lutherans viewed the situation. Heckel's colleague in the KA, Friedrich-Wilhelm Krummacher, noted in his US travels in mid-1936, that one must strengthen ties with the Lutherans, who had been critical of the FCC. He considered the Lutheran Academy in Sondershausen an instrument to implement these politics. American Lutheranism was critical of Anglicanism. This tendency was to be welcomed "in view of the Anglican efforts with Scandinavian Lutheranism"[51].

When the Executive Committee of the Lutheran World Convention met at the end of September/the beginning of October 1936 in New York City[52], Frederick H. Knubel, vice president of the LWC und president of the United Lutheran Church in America, would have preferred for the Lutheran guests from Germany not to contact the representatives of the FCC at all[53]. When Cavert asked him, Knubel answered reluctantly that a meeting of the FCC with the delegates must not be limited to the German representatives alone, and delicate subjects such as the "'Confessional Synod' in Germany" must not be discussed.[54] In order not to waste a chance for a confidential conversation, Cavert directly addressed the German Hanns Lilje and invited him both to his own home and to the FCC Offices.[55] Knubel's aversion to Leiper's "nefarious activities"[56] was so strong that Leiper felt like a "persona non grata"[57] in Lutheran circles, and therefore felt unable to negotiate directly with Knubel and always asked Cavert to take charge of this task. Leiper wrote Cavert: "The one thing I am most anxious about is that we should get Lutherans to act."[58]

In mid-December 1937, Knubel criticised the appeals of the American Christian Committee for German Refugees[59], founded in 1934, saying that „the primary purpose of this movement was anti-Hitler, and that it was only secondarily humanitarian. It is because I do not care to engage in a primarily anti-Hitler movement, much as I deprecate many Hitler principles, that I feel it necessary to remain aloof."[60] Even bridging explanations saying that Hitler had doubtlessly done much for Germany, but that the un-Christian NS worldview made help for "non-Aryan" Christians necessary could not convince Knubel.[61]

2.3   The FCC and the Jews in America

On the other hand, Rabbi Stephen S. Wise, president of the American Jewish Congress, insisted with his friend Leiper (and thus the FCC), that they proceed more energetically against the misinformation spread by the Lutherans. After the Lutheran Henry Koch had claimed in front of 130 Lutheran ministers in Bronxville in spring 1937 that the Free Lutheran Church in Germany "enjoys more liberty now than it did in the days of the monarchy or the revolution after the war", Wise asked Leiper to organise a "great religious meeting against the atrocities of the Hitler regime against religion and race"[62]. Leiper refused, stating that he had no time to organise such a meeting, and that in view of the many meetings that had been held pertaining to this matter, a further one would hardly make sense. Despite this rejection, Leiper's opinion of (German) Lutheranism was negative: "I know no way to silence these Lutherans from Germany who go on with their pathetic bleating about how wonderful Hitler is and how he keeps helping the Church. If they can't see what that villain stands for by this time, they never will, no matter what we say to them."[63]

Wise had written a letter to Leiper already in mid-October 1935, reporting that the president of the Executive Committee of the *Reichsvertretung* (Reich representation) of the Jews in Germany, Otto Hirsch, was arrested in Berlin in connection with a Yom Kippur message issued to the Jews of Germany by the *Reichsvertretung* and was being interrogated by the Gestapo. "I cannot help feel, dear Henry", Wise wrote, "that it would be a fine thing if a group of Christian ministers, at your instance and under your leadership, were to express their horror at the conduct of the Nazi government."[64] As in similar cases, leading personalities sent a letter of protest to the German foreign ambassador, Hans Luther, in Washington, D. C. This letter states:

"The recent arrest of Dr Leo Baeck, Acting Chief Rabbi of Germany, and the eight day detention of Dr Otto Hirsch, President of the Central Body of German Jews, without legal charges or the privilege of communication with his friends, appears to us almost unbelievable. We have heard of no formal charges before, during, or since the period of their forcible detention. ... We would earnestly point out that any government which permits or condones such actions towards religious leaders – whether they be Jewish or Christian – cannot expect the leaders of religious life in other lands to take seriously its claims to be friendly to ethics, religion, and the standard of civilisation."[65]

Understandably, Luther did not appreciate such interventions. His successor, Hans Heinrich Dieckhoff[66], finally rejected passing on these letters of protest that criticised internal politics within Germany. He declared that he held the American ambassador responsible for the delivery of such messages.[67]

One month earlier, in mid-September 1935, Rabbi Morris Samuel Lazaron of the Baltimore Hebrew Congregation had published an appeal to the Christians of America in "The Churchman". Under the title "Can we learn from Germany?" Lazarus appealed to his fellow countrymen to defend the American values and show solidarity with the Jews. "The anti-Semitic propaganda which issues forth from Berlin to all parts of the world is a thing which Jews alone cannot meet. We need the understanding of our Christian friends. We need their cooperation."[68] He linked his request to the assurance that the Jews would keep their own house in order and "remove irritating factors in Jewish life"[69]. He defined the state-church system existing in Germany as an important factor for the Christians' loyalty to the National Socialist regime and complained about the lack of a common front of Catholics, Protestants and Jews. Lazaron's article revealed the fears of Jews living in America that anti-Semitism existing in Germany might break out in the USA, if influenced by German propaganda. Leiper, who corresponded with Lazaron[70], was also of the opinion that National Socialism should not be treated as a national problem, but as an international threat to humanity, which must be combated together.

Not only the American Jewish Congress, but also the American Jewish Committee, other Jewish Organisations and individual personalities continually provided Leiper with reports on the situation of Jews in Germany. Thus he was well-informed about all details and could hardly ignore the terrible news.[71]

American anti-Semitism reached its first peak in the 1936 presidential campaign. The burden of its propaganda was that "The New Deal is a Jew Deal" and the personnel of the Roosevelt administration was the object of the attack. A second wave began in 1939 regarding the 1940 campaign. In mid-June 1939, the FCC published an article on "Current Manifestations of Organized Anti-Semitism" in its Information Service.[72] The article said that, among the anti-Semitic organisations, some carried the term "Christian" in their names. Referring to an article in the "Saturday Evening Post"[73], seven groups were mentioned "as having 'a strictly evangelical front'". In contrast, the article cites many leading personalities of the Christian churches condemning anti-Semitism. Furthermore, the authors provided facts and data[74] in order to prove that public opinion in America was not dominated by Jews.

2.4   Protests against the policy of the FCC: By individual outsiders, or as the voice of the silent majority, the Grassroots Movement?

The Executive Secretary of the Federation of Churches of Rochester and Monroe County, C. Franklin Ward, accused Leiper of giving the Americans a wrong impression of the state-church relationship in Germany with his information policy. "It seems to me that what you are doing is to stir an uneasy feeling in the minds of thoughtful people as to the integrity of the Christian Church in Germany. ... Nothing displeases me more than the disposition here in America to be Pharisaical towards the peoples of other lands. ... What right have we as a Federal Council of Churches or as leaders in the field of religion to be hammering away at a problem which I think that the Christian people of Germany ought to meet in their own strength."[75] In other words, the American churches and the government would be better off minding their own business. Ward conveyed his opinion to the Senate Committee which was under the Chairmanship of Senator Gerald P. Nye. This special Senate Committee had not only denounced the American (munitions) industry's war profits; its accusations culminated with the indictment that the United States had entered World War I because of the machinations of bankers and munitions industrials.[76] According to Ward, the German churches were in perfect accordance with their history such as with Luther and his anti-Semitism. To the world's general surprise, Adolf Hitler solved the problems caused by the Treaty of Versailles in a peaceful manner. In his reply, Leiper referred, as in similar situations, to his frequent visits to Germany and his excellent contacts to German church personalities. Actually, he knew the details of the situation the church was in, better than his critic. But, his general assessments of the situation in Germany, such as his critique comparing the German and American circumstances, show quite a lack of understanding. For example, Leiper wrongly denied "that the present regime is supported ... by the vast majority of the German people"[77]. Following Ward's opinion, he acknowledged "that he [Hitler] has done many excellent things for Germany", and – referring to his own book "The Ghost of Caesar Walks – The Conflict of Nationalism and World Christianity"[78] – he stressed "the fact that we have here in America the same pernicious type of nationalism that has become such a problem in Germany". Furthermore, he prided himself on having spoken about the documents of the Nye Committee in many churches in Europe and having warned them that "the same pernicious influences which were at work in America" might also become effective under the European governments. Leiper did not deem it necessary to stress the fundamental differences existing between the American democracy and the National Socialist dictatorship.

Dampening the enthusiasm of many Baptists over the Fifth Baptist World Conference in Berlin at the beginning of August 1934 was no easy task for Leiper either.[79] He wrote to the General Secretary of the New York City Baptist Mission Society, Rev. Charles H. Sears, asking him to consider how small the number of Baptists in Germany was, and what a catastrophic effect for millions of Christians in Germany a far too positive reporting on the freedom of the Baptist Church in Germany would have had. "It is a good strategy for the Germans at the present time to point as they do to the freedom accorded Baptists and Methodists who after all constitute such a minute proportion of the church population."[80] Four years later, Rev. John Schmidt of the First German Baptist Church in New York City protested against the FCC information material. "After reading your literature and comparing your statements with my recent experiences and observations in Germany, I wish to protest emphatically against the misleading reports you are spreading in our country about Germany. This is a very poor way to serve the cause of Christ and His church."[81]

In addition to individual member churches or church parishes, various famous Christians also put critical questions to Leiper or asked for further information. The president of the Theological Seminary of the Reformed Church in Lancaster, Pennsylvania, did not agree with the draft version of Leiper's "Manifesto on the Religion of Race, Blood and Soil", and addressed the Chairman of the Department on Relations with Churches Abroad, William Adams Brown. The latter agreed: "My own feeling about that paper is that it is too polemic and not sufficiently objective."[82] The FCC booklet "American Churches to Hitler" stirred similar critiques. For example, Pastor W. Reinecke of the American Lutheran Church in Leola, South Dakota, wrote to Brown: "This booklet contains the same kind of lying propaganda against Germany that we were accustomed to before and especially during the World War. You are certainly doing your best to help the Jews incite the leaders of Christianity in our country to new hatred against the 'Hun'."[83] Leiper reacted very late and, as usual when dealing with Lutherans, rather irritably. "I pray your eyes may be opened that you may see yourself as you actually are, fighting on the side of the anti-Christ when you uphold Hitler and his program of the bastardisation and prostitution of Christianity"[84]. Reinecke replied to him that in his opinion it was anti-Christian "to fraternise with members of the Jewish religion"[85], and that, whether voluntarily or not, Leiper was serving those who wanted a new war. Leiper answered with quotes from Hitler's *Mein Kampf*, from Rosenberg's writings and Kerrl's speeches, in order to prove to the Lutheran minister that the aim of National Socialism was to destroy Christianity.

Pierre Jay Wurts, a layman from Englewood, New Jersey, told Leiper that his niece had been living three years in Potsdam, near Berlin. "As a result she is strongly pro-Nazi and anti-Semitic."[86] He went on saying that his niece thought the information on Germany spread in the United States was misleading and intentionally brought about by Jewish controlled newspapers. Regarding the situation of the churches, Wurts' niece referred to the description given by the German Christian professor of systematic theology and general religious studies at the

University of Breslau, Gajus Fabricius.[87] Fabricius had given a much idealised description of the situation of the churches in Germany in the apologetic essay "Germany in the Religious World Situation", which had appeared in English. Leiper's answer to Wurts stood out due to its firmness on one hand, and to a resigned tone on the other. He called Fabricius his "friend" with whom he had had several discussions, and who was unable to recognise the church's real situation.[88] On the other hand, he responded to Karl Barth and his writings, saying, "Personally, I think Karl Barth has seen the thing from the right angle from the beginning. Not many others in the earlier stages saw what was coming, and many don't even recognise it yet for what it is."[89] Even the press in the United States, said Leiper, informed its readership better about Germany than anybody reporting directly from Germany could have done. But then he conceded a certain enthusiasm to those who had seen National Socialist Germany: "Of course, I can easily understand why they become enthusiastic about certain aspects of National Socialism. ... All I can say is I am afraid she will discover that time will prove that she is mistaken." Fourteen days later, since he was apparently not satisfied with his own letter, Leiper sent a second one to Wurts.[90] In it, he contrasted eight fundamental statements of Hitler's *Mein Kampf* with Christian principles which must be preserved, if Christian civilisation should continue to exist in Germany.

Not only in their private correspondence, but also in many articles, journalists and pastors susceptible to National Socialism tried to prove that the FCC was circulating malicious lies regarding the situation of the churches in Germany. When Gerald Burton Winrod published such an article in the "Defender"[91], Leiper replied to him that his point of view was "in perfect accord with Nazi propaganda"[92]. He also sent him information material and invited him to his office in order to show him further documents, but Winrod did not seize this opportunity.[93] Winrod was the leading personality of the Convention of Fundamentalist Ministers and their Followers, a merger of fundamentalist pastors from the South and Midwest United States.[94] He was also the Chairman of an organisation called Defenders of the Christian Faith.[95]

The extremist German-American Bund[96] was also among the strongest opponents of the FCC. This organisation saw Jewish-Marxist powers in the FCC and considered these powers to be responsible for "all Atheistic Subversion in the Country today"[97]. The *Bund* was reinforced in this opinion by a pro-National Socialist "Christian Front", which gathered approximately 200 Protestant pastors at its inaugural meeting in 1934.[98] Another "Christian Front", also with anti-Semitic and anti-liberal aims, was founded after 1936 by the former Catholic radio preacher Charles E. Coughlin.[99] All these organisations, which were under observation by the House Committee on un-American activities of the US-American Parliament[100], and especially their leading personalities, were linked to the well-known car industry personality Henry Ford or to one of his closest collaborators of Ford Motor-Company[101]. Ford, who had expressed an undoubtedly anti-Semitic opinion in the 1920s, was still considered an anti-Semite in the 1930s and 1940s, although he had become more cautious and denied his attitude more than once in Open Letters addressed to famous personalities. Leiper, too, was in possession of one such letter, which stated: "I do not subscribe to or support, directly or indirectly, any agitation which would promote antagonism against my Jewish fellow-citizens."[102] It has never been proven that Ford financially supported the German-American Bund, although these rumours never vanished.[103] But it has been ascertained that Ford did support the equally anti-Semitic radio preacher Gerald L. K. Smith.[104]

2.5 The Niemöller case and the Reich pogrom night provide arguments for the FCC

During the continuing struggle for an adequate appraisal of the situation in Germany, an examination of clear acts of injustice was essential. The way pastor Martin Niemöller of Berlin was unjustly treated, who after a court proceeding, contrary to the sentence given, was not released[105] but committed to Oranienburg-Sachsenhausen concentration camp on 2 March 1938, had a high degree of symbolic meaning[106]. On 21 April 1938, Leiper sent Secretary of German Church Affairs, Hanns Kerrl, and the German ambassador in Washington, Hans Dieckoff, an ecumenical protest resolution against "the ruthless destruction of Christianity in Germany and the arrest and persecution of Martin Niemöller"[107]. It was signed by over 250 personalities of church life in the USA and thus constituted one of the few documents of unanimity.[108] But despite this, there were strong protests. After the issue of the FCC message to the churches of other countries of 11 February 1938[109], a Lutheran of Cleveland (Ohio) with the Germanic name Swenhagen reproached the FCC strongly. He reminded the FCC of its activities during the war, accused it of pursuing a leftist policy, and of supporting a "red Loyalist religion" from the pulpits in Spain.

"You claim in your propaganda message of 11 February that you are speaking for Christians of America. This is a distortion of fact. You know as well as 4,000,000 Lutherans of America know, they would not permit or ask you to represent them in any capacity whatever. You may be the mouthpiece of a dying church organisation with empty pews and lamenting preachers who cannot understand why people do not come to hear their modern political or propaganda sermons while Christ left through the back door. In this city, you have exchanged pulpits with the Jewish rabbis and I see no reason why you should not extend such invitations to them, the difference perhaps is only racial by this time and this may be the answer to your message of 11 February 1938, and also the answer to your support of a Communist Loyalist Spain."[110]

Leiper answered Swenhagen altogether calmly and asked him to produce proof to support his allegations against Spain. Only regarding the matter of Lutheranism in America did he react clearly impassioned. "It is a tragic fact that they seem for the most part more pro-Hitler than they are pro-Christ ... I am personally trying as hard as I can to get the Lutherans of America to open their eyes to the fact with respect to the situation of Germany."[111] He went on to say that the FCC had protested the Treaty of Versailles long before Hitler. Besides, in Hitler's book *Mein Kampf*, one could derive that the German dictator wanted to get rid of the Christian churches. Even Jesus Christ had preached in synagogues, so Leiper saw no reason why His successors should not. Swenhagen replied that Leiper's "modern broad religion" did not convince him, and that Leiper and the likes of him envied Germany for its ascent. After all, Hitler rejected the Jewish religion, instead of tolerating its blending with the Christian faith. "Many acts of Hitler prove that he himself is a religious man and not a foe of the church."[112] Swenhagen could not understand why the FCC took part in Jewish and Communist boycotts against Germany. He asserted that America was run by Communists, who, for their part depended on Jews and their money, and that political Catholicism was in agreement with them. Germany, on the contrary, had freed itself from these bonds. The League for Human Rights, according to Swenhagen, was an organisation dominated by Protestant pastors, Jews and Communists, which had recruited brigades for the Civil War in Spain and, in February 1938, had arranged a memorial service for Lenin in the Euclid Avenue Baptist Church together with Communists. These accusations, accompanied by a series of newspaper clips to prove them, peaked with the assertion "that your church is so broad that you could compromise even with Hitler if it were not for the fact that Hitler hits your co-religionaires, Jews and communists, between the eyes". Not even then did Leiper put an end to their communication – he sent some information material to Swenhagen, pointed out the fact that individual clergymen did not represent the FCC in general, and assured his critic that he personally, had always fought against Communism.[113]

Heckel perceived Leiper to be behind the FCC actions supporting Niemöller and asked at the Ministry of Foreign Affairs "whether something could be done to support the announced measures of the 'Reich' against foreigners spreading news of atrocities"[114]. On 9 March 1938, the Secretary of State in the Church Ministry of the "Third Reich", Hermann Muhs, demanded of the KA a "short, but effective rejection of the American Church Proclamation". On 16 March, Heckel wrote an explanation in response, and eight days later, a press release followed.[115] The situation culminated in the Church Ministry of the "Third Reich" distancing itself from writings that intended to make German protest public, even though Old Catholics, Methodists, and Baptists had supported and signed the writings. They stated that "the situation was not favourable" for these actions.[116]

In addition to the Niemöller case, the *Reichspogromnacht* (Reich pogrom night) of November 1938 caused a deep change in America's public opinion.[117] The massive attacks against German Jews and their belongings caused, for the first time, a "Joint Resolution Representing American Churches" to be taken in the United States, which was jointly signed by Protestants and Roman Catholics. In it, the churches expressed their abhorrence of the atrocities of the NS regime, and called upon Christendom to pray unitedly for the victims.[118] The last paragraph states: "We express the conviction that all political totalitarianism whether Communist or Fascist is incompatible with Christianity, usurping as it does loyalties which are due to God alone."[119] Preceding the "Resolution", there had been some discord, though, because several signatories had insisted that no Jews should join the statement, in order for it not to be "considered to be propaganda by them and for them"[120].

Some personalities were so shocked about the persecution of the Jews in Germany and so alarmed over "organised attempts to arouse race hatred in the United

States" that at the end of November 1938, they founded a "Council against anti-Semitism"[121]. Among the 52 distinguished persons who founded the Council, next to Jewish personalities like Stephen Wise, were again many leading Christian clergymen, such as Leiper and Reinhold Niebuhr.[122]

The FCC also organised the protests of American celebrities against German anti-Semitism over a nation-wide radio broadcast. Here, former President of the United States Herbert C. Hoover stated: "Americans are and should be indignant at the terrible outbreak of Jewish persecution in Germany and the attacks upon the Catholic Church."[123] Christian and Jewish papers such as "The National Jewish Monthly" confirmed the importance of a common action against anti-Semitism in the whole world. Many American Jews believed "that the strength of an alert and intrinsically liberal American Protestant Church is the best guarantee of Jewish security in this land"[124]. In the December 1938 issue of "Opinion", Leiper, Wise and others gave an impressive demonstration of religious unity of those struggling against National Socialist anti-Semitism and paganism. The contributors defined their viewpoint as strongly opposed to that of Nazi sympathisers in the USA, extending their critique to anti-Semitic Catholics. Their opinion on Father Charles Coughlin was: "For the Jew, Coughlin is a regrettable phenomenon. For the Catholic Church he is a disaster; above all, he is America's shame."[125] In his organ "Social Justice", Coughlin had published a series of excerpts from "The Protocols of the Learned Elders of Zion" until Thanksgiving 1938.[126] Leiper analysed the situation as follows: "The attack on the Synagogue and on the Church – Catholic and Protestant – is not a mere incidental affair in a confused situation. It is the most vivid evidence of the character of what is afoot. It is a deliberate and well advertised attempt to pervert what has been central in Western civilisation – namely, the Mosaic Law, the prophetic ideals, the Sermon on the Mount, the Cross and the universal Father God."[127] Wise demanded in his statement that the Jewish boycott of German products and German services must become a general boycott by all Americans. The Jewish boycott had included all Ford products since 1938.[128]

2.6   Diplomatic contacts of the FCC to the Foreign Office of the *Deutsche Evangelische Kirche* and the German embassy

Similar to the Church of England and other large churches, the FCC too – despite massive controversies – avoided breaking off its relations with Bishop Theodor Heckel's official German Church Foreign Office (*Kirchliches Außenamt* – KA). The latter received continuous information on the FCC from the so-called "Selberg Circle"[129]. This "Circle" was in constant contact with American theologians and their confidante Paul F. Douglass[130], who was a member of the Commission of International Justice and Goodwill (which belonged to the FCC)[131]. In addition to this, secret reports on FCC meetings were being passed on to the KA via Oberst (Colonel) von Herwarth.[132]

In autumn 1934, Leiper, in the name of the American Section of the Universal Christian Council (he was the Executive Secretary)[133], wrote a declaration entitled "Great Tribulation". Herein Leiper called for the collection of monetary funds for the Confessing Church. In response to this, the KA turned to the General Secretary of the Universal Christian Council, Henry L. Henriod. Henriod, however, informed the *Oberkonsistorialrat* Hans Wahl of the KA that he had no information on the American text.[134] Heckel used the meeting of the Universal Christian Conference for Life and Work in mid-August 1935 in Chamby to discuss the subject.[135] Heckel was right in theory: without consulting the Universal Christian Council in Geneva, the American Section should not be allowed to carry out such actions. Leiper expressed his regrets and left a handwritten note for Heckel before travelling on to Paris. It states: "I have been deeply aware of the problems which you forced and have greatly regretted personally that I must have appeared as an unfriendly critic."[136] Heckel thanked him for the short letter.[137] Leiper also sent an undated handwritten note to Wahl, who had also been in Chamby, saying that he had forgotten to inform him (i. e. Wahl) that two important aspects of "Great Tribulations" had been altered. "The statement that the church was destroyed was changed to greatly entangled."[138] Also, the addresser of the declaration had been changed from the Universal Christian Council to being the FCC. Wahl wrote on 29 August 1935 that the "Great Tribulation" had been sent to people "who, in Leiper's opinion had been too optimistic (!) about the state of the German Church"[139].

In mid-November 1935, Heckel's collaborator, Friedrich Wilhelm Krummacher, complained to Leiper about the large adherence of church circles to the boycott plans regarding the Berlin Olympic Games. "I can only say that from our point of view", Krummacher wrote, "we feel that such a struggle, especially if lead and supported by Christian churches, represents a purely political rejection of Germany."[140] Krummacher went on asserting that "the Protestant Church [was] also decisively involved in the extensive preparations of the Olympic Games". On the other hand, Krummacher did not mention any problems within the churches, or tensions between parts of the churches and the state.

The background of this complaint was an article written by the general secretary of the FCC, McCrea Cavert, in the "New York Times". The paper published it with the sensational title: "Olympic Boycott urged by Cavert"[141]. On 11 October, a further article appeared in the "New York Times", from which followed that Leiper was co-chairman of the Committee on 'Fair Play' in Sports. This committee had started a campaign to keep American athletes out of the Games.[142]

In early February 1935, Adolf Keller[143], who was the European FCC representative at the time, had denied an according statement by the Secretary of the Boycott Committee, Samuel Untermeyer. Untermeyer had "written Dr. Leiper a clear apology, which I was intended to receive, but has not arrived as yet. This writing conveys that the Federal Council has never in any way supported the Boycott-movement. Just the opposite, it has stood against it, and has tried to convince the leaders of the movement, that regarding this matter they will cause more harm than anything else."[144] In September 1935, the Executive Committee of the FCC officially dealt with this matter and declared that the question whether the USA participates in the Olympic Games or not is not only a matter of sports.

"But there is a moral issue in the situation which prompts the question and on this the Council feels that it is competent to pronounce judgment. That issue is whether a government, which deliberately excludes from full social and economic fellowship the members of one race on grounds of race alone is acting consistently with Christian principles. On this issue our judgment is clear and unequivocal that such a policy is inconsistent with Christian principles and we are glad to know that in this judgment we are supported by responsible sections of Christian opinion in Germany. Having on many occasions expressed our judgment on issues of social justice which have arisen in our own country, we feel more free to express our conviction on the present situation in Germany."[145]

Leiper took five months to answer Krummacher's complaint, and then pointed to the deep dissent dividing both churches.

"I have long intended to write you at length about a number of subjects concerning which we have had conversation and correspondence. My only reason for not having done it is that I have not wished to embarrass you by including in your correspondence a good many facts and views which I fear would be painful. If you really desire that I should write on these subjects in full frankness and detail I should be glad to do so. We constantly struggle to have it clear that our strong feeling of concern over many aspects of the policy of the German Government towards the Church and education is not based on anti-German feelings but quite the contrary. It is a genuine expression of our sense of fellowship in the Universal brotherhood of Christ's followers. We are at the same time highly critical of many aspects of the policy of our own Government which we are forced to regard as far from Christian."[146]

Despite the obvious disagreements with Heckel and his Church Foreign Office, the FCC was forced to collaborate with this Office in order not to risk the German Protestant Church leaving the ecumenical movement. Hans Schönfeld, a German, was director of the Research Department of the Universal Christian Council for Life and Work. On 21 June 1938, he wrote William Adams Brown, Chairman of the FCC Commission of Relations with Churches Abroad: "I must emphasise anew that the comprehensive carrying forward of such ecumenical work is ever and again being made possible through the fact that Bishop Heckel and his colleagues in the Foreign Office of the Church defend this ecumenical work against all attacks, in press and periodicals and in other ways, although such attacks have often been directed against the Foreign Office as well."[147] Schönfeld went on to say that the Confessional Church, on the contrary, was, neither according to its institution, nor to its personnel or its finances, able to take over the Foreign Office's place.[148]

The FCC presented itself as an ecumenical body independent of national interests. That is why Leiper and his colleagues almost always referred to the critical FCC attitude towards wrong developments within the American society and towards its own government.[149] But more and more, self-criticism lost importance, while accusations against the situation in Germany increased. On 11 February 1938, the FCC sent a letter to the Secretary of German Church Affairs, Kerrl, which focused on the anti-Christian propaganda and the persecution of Christians. The churches announced an end to cooperation between America and

Germany as a consequence of these conditions. "As you will realise, the basis of such understanding and good will is mutual confidence. That is now lacking."[150]

When, in St Matthew's Evangelical Lutheran Church in Hoboken, Hans Borchers of the German General Consulate in New York City had defended Hitler's policy and defined the information about Germany spreading in America as one-sided, Leiper wrote him a strong letter of protest. "It is impossible to believe that in your secret heart you can approve the atrocious and abominable actions of your Government with respect to Jews and Christians. ... I think one of the saddest of sights is the attempt of gentlemen of breeding and good-will to whitewash actions which everyone knows are beyond all human decency."[151]

2.7   Erwin Kraft and "Kulturkampf" Magazine

In order to give more resonance in the United States to his view of the situation in Germany, Leiper did not limit himself to writing reports for church periodicals or to asking colleagues such as Reinhold Niebuhr to express themselves critically on various subjects in "The Christian Century".[152] He, furthermore, passed on information to the "New York Times" and other papers with a large circulation and asked them to report on the case.[153] At the end of 1938, Leiper tried to establish an American edition of the "News Bulletin on the Religious Policy of the Third Reich". This magazine was published in London by a German emigrant, Erwin Kraft[154], under the title "Kulturkampf"[155]. It claimed to be "the only regular source of information as to the religious crisis in Germany"[156], and documented both Catholic and Protestant events. In spring 1939, the first issue of the American edition of "Kulturkampf"[157] appeared. Since the end of 1937/the beginning of 1938, Erwin Kraft had been in New York in order to facilitate his fortnightly Bulletins towards a good start in the United States. Through support from Leiper and his friends, Kraft finally attained a residence permit and organised the literary resistance against the Nazi regime within the community of German emigrants in New York.[158] In this way, Leiper had succeeded in establishing a periodical in the USA which widely documented the struggle of the NS worldview against Jews and Christians, and which could convince conservative American Christians. But just a few months after this success, the war started in Europe.

3.   The ambivalence of public opinion in the United States towards Nazi Germany

Considering the various endeavours of the FCC to influence public opinion in the USA against Hitler's anti-Semitism and his enmity towards the churches, the question arises as to how successful all these resolutions, appeals, radio speeches and newspaper articles actually were. The answer is ambivalent: on the one hand, the protests of the mainline churches and other groups in society led to mass demonstrations of up to 20,000 people, such as in Madison Square Garden on 21 November 1938.[159] When asked which European country they liked most, only eight percent of Americans chose Germany.[160] Then again, what the mainline churches reported of the atrocities taking place in Germany did not seem to move the Americans much. In addition, over a third of the Americans interviewed (namely 35 percent) said in a 1938 Roper poll that they did not like Jews.[161] Even in 1942, almost half of the Americans asked were of the opinion that the Jews had too great an influence in the USA, and almost 16 percent demonstrated their sympathy with the suppression of the power of Jews in Germany.[162] Support for the victims of German anti-Semitic policy would have immediately raised discussion on immigration policies having to be relaxed. This would have led to election losses in the United States, which was at that time shaken by economic crisis. Next to economic problems, the States suffered from a strong spiritual uncertainty. The rise of "un-American" Catholicism was perceived by Protestants as a threat to their dominant position.[163] This development, and debates within Protestantism, led to a kind of "religious depression"[164]. Therefore, the delimitation of Roman Catholic influence in Germany was, for many Conservative Protestants in the United States, no reason to despise National Socialism. The news on the situation of German Protestantism differed. Over a long period of time, German Lutherans assured their fellow believers in the United States that the situation in Germany had to be seen in a subtly differentiated way. Hitler's movement was also perceived as a moral, economic and social renewal for his shattered country, as a kind of self-liberation from the modernistic symptoms of decline of the 1920s. Secretly, many conservative Protestants in the United States longed for a similar development in their own country. In January 1937, the American magazine "Time" nominated Hitler Man of the Year. After all, for a long period of time, Hitler was seen as a bulwark against Communism, which, from the point of view of many Americans, threatened the USA as well. Finally, the churches (no matter what their denomination was) and the majority of their members, did not want a policy of intervention, and therefore urged their government not to interfere with German matters.[165] Under no circumstances did they want to risk a war for the so-called values of "western civilisation" the FCC mentioned so often. In this respect, the impressive evidence left by the FCC had, above all, a ritual function: it served to assure one's loyalty to the American system of values without taking the appropriate steps regarding the relationship between the churches or even seriously risking an open conflict with Nazi Germany. It was not until 1940 that some liberal theologians (gathered around Reinhold Niebuhr) founded the anti-isolationist magazine "Christianity and Crisis".[166] Regarding the situation in the period between 1934 and 1939, it can be concluded that the protests against FCC policy were not voices of outsiders, but represented the mood of a silent majority.

Notes

1   Cf. Martin E. Marty, Modern American Religion, vol. 2: The Noise of Conflict 1919–1941, Chicago-London 1991, 33 f.; Charles S. Macfarland, Christian Unity in the Making: The First Twenty-Five Years of the Federal Council of the Churches of Christ in America 1905–1930, New York 1948; H. George Anderson, 'Ecumenical Movements', in David W. Lotz et al. (eds), Altered Landscapes. Christianity in America, 1935–1985, Grand Rapids 1989, 92–105. On the history of the religious Council Movement in America, see also John A. Hutchison, We Are Not Divided: A Critical and Historical Study of the Federal Council of the Churches of Christ in America, New York 1941; William Adams Brown, Toward a United Church: Three Decades of Ecumenical Christianity, New York 1946; Ross W. Sanderson, Church Cooperation in The United States. The Nation-Wide Backgrounds and Ecumenical Significance of State and Local Council of Churches in their Historical Perspective, New York 1960.

2   Cf. Jean-Jacques Bauswein/Lukas Vischer (eds), The Reformed Family Worldwide. A Survey of Reformed Churches, Theological Schools, and International Organizations, Grand Rapids-Cambridge 1999, 516 ff.; Rick L. Nutt, Toward Peacemaking. Presbyterians in the South and National Security, 1945–1983, Tuscaloosa-London 1994, 3 ff.

3   Cf. Daniel G. Reid (ed.), Dictionary of Christianity in America, Downers Grove 1990, 949–951 (lit.).

4   Cf. J. William T. Youngs, The Congregationalists, Westport-London 1998.

5   Cf. Frederick A. Norwood, The Story of American Methodism, 355 ff.; James E. Kirby et al., The Methodists, Westport-London 1998.

6   Cf. as an overview: Frank S. Mead/Samuel S. Hill, Handbook of Denominations in the United States, Nashville [10]1995; Reid, Dictionary of Christianity in America (op. cit. note 3).

7   Cf. E. Clifford Nelson, The Lutherans in North America, Philadelphia 1980; see also Kenneth C. Barnes, 'American Lutherans and the Third Reich', in Betty Rubenstein/Michael Berenbaum (eds), What Kind of God? Essays in Honour of Richard Rubenstein, Lanham 1995, 187–199.

8   Cf. on German-American contacts Reiner Pommerin, Der Kaiser und Amerika. Die USA in der Politik der Reichsleitung 1890–1917, Köln 1987; Charles Thomas Johnson, Culture at Twilight. The National German-American Alliance, 1901–1918 (New German-American Studies 20), New York 1999; on Italian-American relations, see Michael Behnen, Die USA und Italien 1921–1933, Teilband 1: Demokratie, Dollars und Faschismus, Münster 1998; on Swedish-American influence see Scott E. Erickson, American Religious Influences in Sweden, Stockholm 1997. See also Ernst Benz, 'Über den Zusammenhang der europäischen und der amerikanischen Kirchengeschichte', in idem, Kirchengeschichte in ökumenischer Sicht (Ökumenische Studien 3), Leiden-Köln 1961, 75–111; Erich Beyreuther, 'Die Rückwirkung amerikanischer kirchengeschichtlicher Wandlungen auf das evangelische Deutschland im 19. und 20. Jahrhundert (1964)', in idem, Frömmigkeit und Theologie. Gesammelte Aufsätze zum Pietismus und zur Erweckungsbewegung, Hildesheim-New York 1980, 245–256.

9   Cf. The Gallup Poll. Public Opinion 1935–1971, vol. 1: 1935–1948, New York 1972, 53. The poll covered Northern Baptists (47 % yes, 53 % no), Southern Baptists (25 % yes, 75 % no), Methodists (43 % yes, 57 % no), Lutherans (33 % yes, 67 % no), Presbyterians (48 % yes, 52 % no), Episcopalians (40 % yes, 60 % no), Congregationalists (65 % yes, 35 % no), Reformed (52 % yes, 48 % no). On the shifts that took place in the 1938 poll, see ibid. 109. Only the Congregationalists still opted clearly for unification; among Presbyterians and Methodists, the relation had switched to 50:50.

10   Cf. Mark A. Noll, A History of Christianity in the United States and Canada, Grand Rapids (MI) 1992, 304–306.

11   Cf. S. A. Curtis, A Consuming Faith: The Social Gospel and Modern American Culture, Baltimore 1991.

12 Paul S. Boyer, When Time Shall Be No More: Prophecy Belief in Modern American Culture, Cambridge (Mass.) 1992; see also Stephen Hunt (ed.), Christian Millenarianism: From the early Church to Waco, Bloomington 2001 and the article on 'Dispensationalism', in Randall Balmer, Encyclopedia of Evangelism, Louisville-London 2002, 167 f. (including a bibliography).

13 Cf. Noll, History of Christianity (op. cit. note 10), 376–378.

14 Cf. William J. Schmidt, Architect of Unity: A Biography of Samuel McCrea Cavert, New York 1978, 211 ff. Cavert was, with Charles S. Macfarland, General Secretary of the FCC from 1921 to 1930, and then from 1930 to 1954 the sole General Secretary of the FCC or NCC, cf. ibid. 46 ff., 237 ff. See also on Henry Pitney Van Dusen (1897–1975): R. T. Handy, A History of Union Theological Seminary in New York, New York 1987, 211 ff.; D. K. Thompson, 'Henry Pitney Van Dusen, Ecumenical Statesman', Ph.D. Diss., Union Theological Seminary, Richmond, Virginia, 1974; on Reinhold Niebuhr (1892–1971): Paul Merkley, Reinhold Niebuhr. A Political Account, Montreal 1975, 181 ff.; Richard Wightman Fox, Reinhold Niebuhr. A Biography, San Francisco 1987; idem, 'The Niebuhr Brothers and the Liberal Protestant Heritage', in Michael J. Lacey (ed.), Religion and Twentieth-Century American Intellectual Life, Cambridge 1989, 94–115; Ronald H. Stone, Professor Reinhold Niebuhr. A Mentor to the Twentieth Century, Louisville 1992, 202 ff.; Robert H. Craig, Religion and Radical Politics, 177 ff. Charles C. Brown, Niebuhr and his Age. Reinhold Niebuhr's Prophetic Role in the Twentieth Century, Philadelphia 1992, esp. 124 ff.; Ursula M. Niebuhr (ed.), Remembering Reinhold Niebuhr. Letters of Reinhold and Ursula M. Niebuhr, San Francisco 1991, esp. 187 ff. For Niebuhr's theological view of political ethics, see above all his book Moral Man and Immoral Society. A Study in Ethics and Politics, New York 1960; on Niebuhr's understanding of history cf. Gordon Harland, The Thought of Reinhold Niebuhr, New York 1960, 90 ff.; Gary B. Bullert, 'Reinhold Niebuhr and The Christian Century: World War II and the Eclipse of the Social Gospel', JCS 44 (2002), 271–290; on John Coleman Bennett (born 1902): Edward L. Long, Jr./Robert T. Handy (eds), Theology and Church in Times of Change. Essays in Honor of John Coleman Bennett, Philadelphia (Pa.) 1970; David H. Smith, The Achievement of John C. Bennett, New York 1970; cf. Bennett, Christians and the State, New York 1958.

15 Cf. Martin E. Marty, Modern American Religion, vol. 2: The Noise of Conflict (op. cit. note 1), 303 ff.; Heather A. Warren, Theologians of a New World Order, New York-Oxford 1997. On Reinhold Niebuhr's view of liberalism, cf. Robert Song, Christianity and Liberal Society, Oxford-New York 1997, 55 ff. See also Schmidt, Architect of Unity (op. cit. note 14), 86 ff. (The Theology of Realism).

16 Warren, Theologians (op. cit. note 15), 6 f.

17 Leiper, for example, was also associate general secretary of the World Council of Churches from 1938 on.

18 Cf. Schmidt, Architect of Unity (op. cit. note 14), 104 f.; see also Samuel McCrea Cavert, The American Churches in the Ecumenical Movement 1900–1968, New York 1968.

19 Cf. the Reports of the Department of Relations with Churches Abroad, World Council of Churches' Library (WCCL), Geneva, WCC 24.002. Life and Work, American Section, Reports from Henry Smith Leiper and Charles Macfarland 1925–40.

20 Cf. the correspondence between Leiper and Schönfeld, UTS 1–2–1. On the analogous development of the idealist League of Nations idea and the US contribution to it, see John Allphin Moore, Jr./Jerry Pubantz, To Create a New World? American Presidents and the United Nations, New York 1999, 12 ff.

21 Cf., e. g., against the background of the Ethiopian crisis, the article published in FCB, January 1936, 7: 'Church Leaders Support American Neutrality'.

22 Cf. Federal Council Bulletin. A Journal of Religious Cooperation and Interchurch Activities (FCB), vol. XIX, April 1936, 1 ff.; The Christian Century, LIII (1936), 315 ff.

See also Besier, "'The friends ... in America need to know the truth ...'" The German Churches in the Opinion of the United States (1933–1941)', in this volume.

23 Cf. Randall Balmer, Religion in Twentieth Century America, Oxford-New York 2001, 28 f.

24 Cf. George M. Marsden, Fundamentalism and American Culture. The Shaping of Twentieth-Century Evangelism 1870–1925, Oxford-New York 1982, esp. 164 ff.; Clyde Wilcox, Onward Christian Soldiers? The Religious Right in American Politics, Boulder (Col.) 1996, 25 ff.; Martin E. Marty/R. Scott Appleby, Herausforderung Fundamentalismus. Radikale Christen, Moslems und Juden im Kampf gegen die Moderne, Frankfurt/M.-New York 1996, 48 ff.; Joel A. Carpenter, Revive Us Again. The Reawakening of American Fundamentalism, New York-Oxford 1997, 13 ff.; Derek J. Tidball, Reizwort Evangelikal. Entwicklung einer Frömmigkeitsbewegung, Stuttgart 1999, 108 ff. (an outline of the history of the Evangelical movement from 1740 to the present).

25 Text of Roosevelt's Address to the Churches: FCB, vol. XVII, no. 1, January 1934, 7 f. Adolf Keller, Director of the European Central Office of Inter-Church Aid in Geneva and Permanent Representative of the FCC in Europe, reported on the celebrations on 4 January 1934. Evangelisches Zentralarchiv in Berlin (EZA), Bestand Kirchliches Außenamt (5), Bd. 194. Reich Bishop Müller had sent the FCC a congratulatory letter dated 23 November 1933. Ibid. On Keller's organisation and his position within it, see idem, Amerikanisches Christentum – Heute, Zollikon-Zurich 1943, 367 ff.

26 Cf. Everett L. Cattell, 'National Association of Evangelicals and World Evangelical Fellowship', Christianity Today IX (1965), 432–434; David F. Wells/John D. Woodbridge (eds), The Evangelicals. What They Believe, Who They Are, Where They Are Changing, Nashville-New York 1975; Robert Wuthnow, The Restructuring of American Religion. Society and Faith since World War II, Princeton 1989, 173 ff. On the beginnings of the NAE, see also H. Shelton Smith, 'Conflicting Interchurch Movements in American Protestantism', Christendom 12/2 (Spring 1947) 165–176; for information on the members: Constant H. Jacquet, Jr. (ed.), Yearbook of American and Canadian Churches, Nashville 1986, 14. For the NAE perspective, see their brochure on NCC and WCC: Billy A. Melvin, Executive Director of NAE, Answers to Your Questions About NCC and WCC, Wheaton 1990. Cf. now also Robert H. Krapohl/Charles H. Lippy, The Evangelicals. A Historical, Thematic, and Bibliographical Guide, Westport-London 1999. On the engagement of the Evangelicals with modern science, cf. David N. Livingstone/D. G. Hart/Mark A. Noll (eds), Evangelicals and Science in Historical Perspective (Religion in America Series), New York-Oxford 1999.

27 Cf. James DeForest Murch, Cooperation without Compromise: A History of the National Association of Evangelicals, Grand Rapids 1956, esp. 135 ff.

28 "The Presidential Election of 1928 demonstrated the persistence of anti-Catholic bias among the nation's Protestants. Alfred E. Smith, governor of New York and the Democratic nominee for President, faced relentless attacks because he was Roman Catholic." Balmer, Religion in Twentieth-Century America (op. cit. note 23), 37.

29 Cf. Besier, The friends, in this volume. On the following, see also John S. Conway, 'The North American Churches. Reactions to the German Church Struggle', in Gerhard Besier (ed.), Zwischen "nationaler Revolution" und militärischer Aggression. Transformationen in Kirche und Gesellschaft 1934–1939 (Schriften des Historischen Kollegs. Kolloquien 48), Munich 2001, 259–270.

30 Cf. e. g. FCB, April 1935, 13 (Mexican Conflict); FCB, October 1935, 7 f. (Ethiopian Crisis); FCB, November-December 1935, 8 (Religion in Russia); FCB November-December 1935, 10 (Ethiopian Crisis). See also John Baillie, 'Christianity and the Totalitarian Claims of the Modern State', in The Churches in Action. News Letter of the Universal Christian Council for Life and Work and the World Alliance for International Friendship through the Churches no. 8, June 1935. The author writes: "It will be generally admitted that no greater problem confronts organised Christianity in our own time than that which emerges out of the claim put forward by so many modern states to exercise supreme control over all departments of human life."

31 Cf. William J. Schmidt/Edward Ouellette, What Kind of a Man? The Life of Henry Smith Leiper, New York 1986, esp. 146 ff.; William J. Schmidt, 'Ecumenist For Our Time: Henry Smith Leiper', Mid-Stream, vol. XXVIII, no. 1, January 1989, 173–182.

32 Quoted according to Armin Boyens, Kirchenkampf und Ökumene 1933–1939, Munich 1969, 38.

33 On 1 April 1933, Cavert and Leiper sent a telegram to William Adams Brown, then in Rome, urging him to go to Berlin and make it clear to Kapler that the appeal in favour of fair treatment for the Jews was in no way an unfriendly act towards the German nation (UTS 1-2-4). On 2 April 1933, Brown cabled a reply indicating that the journey to Berlin was impossible for the moment. Cf. also the correspondence between Schreiber and the President of the Universal Christian Council for Life and Work (American Section), S. Parkes Cadman, UTS 1-2-6; Gerhard Besier, Die Kirchen und das Dritte Reich, vol. 3: Spaltungen und Abwehrkämpfe (1934–1937), Berlin 2001, 897 f. Cadman (alongside Cavert, Leiper, Macfarland, R. Niebuhr and W. Van Kirk) was a member of the National Conference of Jews and Christians, which published a sharply worded statement opposing Hitler's persecution of the Jews on 8 May 1933. UTS 1-1-1.

34 Cf. Walter Van Kirk to Leiper, 20 March 1933, UTS 1-1-6. But on 26 May 1933, the New York Times published a protest resolution against the treatment of the Jews in Germany signed by 1,200 pastors from 26 denominations.

35 In early 1930, Macfarland had handed in his resignation for the end of the year. Alongside health reasons, his activity as church censor for the film industry was also an operative factor. The payments he received for this activity put him in a difficult position. Cf. Keller's report of 28 April 1930. EZA 5, 2860. See also Ev. Deutschland no. 18 of 4 May 1930. See also William J. Schmidt, Architect of Unity (op. cit. note 14), 72 ff.

36 On 22 September 1933, at the request of Adolf Keller, Schreiber asked Dr Mersaldt to arrange for a visit to Hitler by Macfarland. In response, senior government officer Thomsen of the Reich Chancellery asked Schreiber to visit him. At the subsequent meeting, Thomsen recommended that Macfarland should apply for the visit via the American ambassador. EZA, 5, Bd. 194.

37 Cf. Besier, The friends, in this volume. Cf. also Macfarland, 'The German Evangelical Church and the German Reich: A Tragedy of Errors', FCC Information Service, 28 April 1934. In a German memo dated 30 November 1933 on the exchange between Hitler and Macfarland on 30 October 1933, we read: "For the relations between the churches, the Aryan paragraph in the Old Prussian church is a decisive obstacle. This obstacle is not caused by the fact that the church is addressing the racial question in the first place, the American churches are also aware of the race problem. The idea that American Christians find unpalatable is that the regulation of this practical problem should have been elevated to the status of a principle and a value judgment." EZA 5, Bd. 194. See also the reports by William E. Dodds and J. C. Whites (US Embassy, Berlin) to the State Department of 8 November 1933 and 16 November 1933 on Macfarland's visit, National Archives [NA] at College Park, MD (Archives II).

38 New York 1934.

39 Macfarland to Hitler, 5 January 1934. EZA 5, Bd. 194. On the same day, Macfarland also wrote to Thomsen, explaining the motives for his article and suggesting its publication in German. Thomsen rejected this proposal in a letter dated 8 January 1934. Ibid. On 24 May 1934, Krummacher sent Macfarland a detailed response to the book. Ibid.

40 So Macfarland to Krummacher, 29 May 1934, ibid.

41 Wahl to Macfarland, 15 June 1934, ibid.

42 On 5 November 1936, Keller had reminded the members of the Executive Committee that Macfarland would be celebrating his 70th birthday on 12 December 1936. Thereupon, Heckel wrote the birthday letter already referred to (1 December 1936). EZA 5,

Bd. 195. In early 1936, Macfarland had informed Krummacher about his new book "Contemporary Christian Thought" (New York 1936). Ibid.

43 The letter was printed in the New York Times on 9 June 1937. On this and the following, see also G. Besier, Die Kirchen, vol. 3 (op. cit. note 33), 901. On 1 June 1937, Macfarland acquainted Krummacher with his Open Letter. EZA, 5, Bd. 195. Shortly afterwards, he sent him his new book "Trends of Christian Thinking" (New York 1937). On 9 October 1937, Wahl sent Macfarland's Open Letter to Fabricius, remarking that the church foreign department did not intend to reply to it. Macfarland, he said, need not be taken too seriously. Ibid.

44 Cf. on this point Robert W. Ross, So it was true. The American Protestant Press and the Nazi Persecution of the Jews, Minneapolis 1980; William Nawyn, American Protestantism's Response to Germany's Jews and Refugees 1933–1941, Ann Arbor 1981; Haim Genizi, American Apathy: the Plight of Christian Refugees from Nazism, Ramat-Gan 1983.

45 Cf. Schmidt/Ouellette, What Kind of a Man? (op. cit. note 31), 115 f., 152 f.; cf. also Eberhard Bethge, Dietrich Bonhoeffer, Theologe – Christ – Zeitgenosse, Munich 1967, 443; 626; 732 ff.; Dietrich Bonhoeffer Werke, Bd. 15, 177 f. passim.

46 This is evident from the list of persons interviewed by Leiper in Paris and London: 'Individuals interviewed while in Europe, summer of 1933'. WCCL, Geneva, WCC 24.002. Life and Work, American Section. Reports from Henry Smith Leiper and Charles Macfarland 1925–40.

47 On 14 March 1934, the American Lutheran Conference (made up of members of The Norwegian Lutheran Church of America, American Lutheran Church, The Evangelical Lutheran Augustana Synod of North America, The Lutheran Free Church and the United Danish Evangelical Lutheran Church in America) made the following communication to Leiper in response to an inquiry on his part: "It was resolved that in reply thereto the president inform this organization that the Executive Committee of the American Lutheran Conference is not authorized to accept a consultative membership in the American section of the Universal Christian Council for Life and Work." World Council of Churches' Library (WCCL), Geneva, WCC General Secretariat, General Correspondence, Leiper 1933–1957, German Church Struggle.

48 Cf. E. Clifford Nelson, The Lutherans in North America (op. cit. note 7), 440 ff.

49 Cf. Besier, The friends, in this volume; idem, Die Kirchen, vol. 3 (op. cit. note 33), 3 f., 895, 911 f. See also the 'Declaration of the Evangelical Lutheran Church in America to the Jewish Community' of 18 April 1994, published in Interfaith Focus 2 (1995): Luther, Lutheranism and the Jews, New York 1995, iii, and also available on the internet: www.elca.org/ea/interfaith/jewish/declaration.html. A German translation of the ELCA declaration has appeared in Hans Hermann Henrix/Wolfgang Kraus (eds), Die Kirchen und das Judentum, vol. 2: Dokumente von 1986–2000, Paderborn 2001, 499 f. See also Towards a New Day in Jewish-Lutheran Relations, New York 1999.

50 Note by Krummacher dated 7 July 1936 and report on his trip to America from 15 April to 20 June 1936, EZA 5, Bd. 195. On Sondershausen, cf. Besier, Die Kirchen, vol. 3 (op. cit. note 33), 476 ff.

51 Cf. Besier, Die Kirchen, vol. 3 (op. cit. note 33), 576 ff.

52 Cf. Cavert to Leiper, 18 September 1936, UTS 1-1-6.

53 Knubel to Cavert, 25 August 1936, UTS 1-1-6.

54 Cavert to Lilje, 14 September 1936, UTS 1-1-6.

55 So Leiper to Cavert, 21 September 1936, UTS 1-1-6.

56 So Leiper to Cavert, 19 October 1937, UTS 1-1-6.

57 Ibid. In a letter to the Bischop of Chichester, George Bell, dated 10 March 1938, Leiper compared the latter's problems with the Bishop of Gloucester and Chairman of the Church of England Council on Foreign Relations, Artur Cayley Headlam, with those he himself had with the Lutherans: "I am wondering whether our old friend the Bishop of Gloucester still is insisting that the view you and I take of the German

Church situation is a mistaken one. We are still struggling with this type of person in the Lutheran Churches in America. Their unwillingness to believe that Hitler can intend any harm to the Church would be ludicrous were not so pathetic. Tuesday of this week in Chicago – without benefit of Lutherans – we had an important luncheon meeting in the interests of the Christian Refugees." Lambeth Palace Library, Bell Papers, German Church 8, Bl. 148.

58 Cf. Nawyn, American Protestantism's Response (op. cit. note 44), 159 ff.

59 Knubel to R. K. Veryard, 10 December 1937, Union Theological Seminary (UTS), Henry Smith-Leiper Collection (HSLC), Correspondence 1-2-9.

60 Veryard to Knubel, 14 December 1937, ibid.

61 Wise to Leiper, 30 April 1937, UTS 1-2-7.

62 Leiper to Wise, 6 May 1937, UTS 1-2-7.

63 Wise to Leiper, 14 October 1935, UTS 1-1-1.

64 Leiper et al. to Luther, Oct. 22, 1935, WCCL, Geneva, WCC General Secretariat, General Correspondence. Leiper 1933–1957, German Church Struggle. On 17 October 1935 Reinhold Niebuhr wrote Leiper: "I am glad to sign your letter to the German Ambassador. I notice that Dr. Hirsch has been released but I think the letter, slightly altered, ought to go out anyway so that the people know that we are cognizant of what they are doing."

65 Dieckhoff became ambassador at the end of March 1937. Cf. Maria Keippert/Peter Grupp (eds), Biographisches Handbuch des deutschen Auswärtigen Dienstes 1871–1945, vol. I, Paderborn 2000, 420 f. One month after the assumption of his post, Ernst W. Meyer resigned as First Secretary of the German Embassy in the USA because of his inability to longer accept Nazi principles. The FCC gave a reception for him in February 1938, at which Meyer spoke on "Christianity and National Socialism – Two Conflicting World Philosophies". Both Meyer's resignation and the support he received from the FCC caused a major stir. Cf. FCB, April 1938, 7.

66 Dieckhoff to FCC, 23 February 1938, EZA 5, 95.

67 The Churchman, 15 September 1935, 10 f.

68 Ibid.

69 Cf. Leiper to Lazaron on 7 June 1935, UTS 1-2-4.

70 Cf. UTS 1-1-1.

71 Vol. XVIII, no. 23, part 2, 10 June 1939.

72 Stanley High, 'Star Spangled Fascists', Saturday Evening Post, 27 May 1939.

73 The authors mainly based themselves on a survey of "Fortune Magazine" of 1936, which was later published separately with the title "Jews in America".

74 Ward to Leiper, 3 June 1935, UTS 1-2-7.

75 Cf. Erich Angermann, Die Vereinigten Staaten von Amerika seit 1917, [9]1995, 205 f.

76 Leiper to Ward, 8 June 1935, UTS 1-2-7.

77 New York 1935.

78 See on this Karl Zehrer, Evangelische Freikirchen und das "Dritte Reich" (AGK.E 13), Göttingen 1986, 117 f.; Andrea Strübind, Die unfreie Freikirche. Der Bund der Baptistengemeinden im "Dritten Reich" (Monographien und Studienbücher 399), Wuppertal-Zürich [2]1995, 116 ff., 147 ff.

79 Leiper to Sears, 10 January 1935, UTS 1-2-6.

80 J. Schmidt to Leiper, 10 June 1938, UTS 1-2-6. Cf. Leiper's reply, 7 July 1938, ibid.

81 Brown to Richards, 17 December 1935, UTS 1-2-5. Cf. also Leiper to Richards, 31 December 1935, ibid.

82 Reinecke to Brown, 24 June 1937, UTS 1-2-5.

83 Leiper to Reinecke, 6 January 1938, UTS 1-2-5.

84 Reinecke to Leiper, 20 January 1938, UTS 1-2-5.

85 Wurts to Leiper, 30 March 1939, UTS 1-2-7.

86 On Fabricius, cf. Kurt Meier, Die Theologischen Fakultäten im Dritten Reich, Berlin-New York 1996, 427.

87 In a letter dated 2 October 1934, Fabricius had complained to Macfarland about an article by Leiper in The Federal Council Bulletin of May 1934 and demanded the publication of his corrective "Ten theses concerning church-situation in Germany". (UTS 1–2–3). Cf. also Fabricius to Leiper, 4 August 1934 and Leiper to Fabricius, 23 October 1934, ibid. See also Schmidt/Ouellette, What Kind of a Man? (op. cit. note 31), 151.
88 Leiper to Wurts, 3 April 1939, UTS 1–2–7.
89 Leiper to Wurts, 18 April 1939, UTS 1–2–7.
90 Winrod, 'Protestantism in Germany', Defender, March 1939.
91 Leiper to Winrod, 9 March 1939, UTS 1–2–7.
92 Cf. Leiper to Winrod, 23 March 1940, UTS 1–2–7.
93 For a list of the leading personalities in this convention, see UTS 1–1–1.
94 Cf. Balmer, Religion in Twentieth Century America (op. cit. note 23), 40.
95 Cf. Martin E. Marty, Modern American Religion, vol. 2 (op. cit. note 1), 259 ff.
96 Cf. Call of the German American Bund to a Mass Demonstration for true Americanism to take place on 20 February 1939, UTS 1–2–3.
97 Cf. Cornelia Wilhelm, Bewegung oder Verein? Nationalsozialistische Volkstumspolitik in den USA, Stuttgart 1998, 225.
98 Ibid. 226. Cf. also Karl Holl, 'Das deutschsprachige Exil in den USA seit 1933', in Jürgen Elvert/Michael Salewski (eds), Deutschland und der Westen im 19. und 20. Jahrhundert, part 1: Transatlantische Beziehungen, Stuttgart 1993, 323–339, here: 330.
99 The chairman of this committee set up in 1938 was the Texan deputy Martin Dies. In 1940, he published the report "The Trojan Horse in America". Most of this report is concerned with the "un-American" activities of the communists in the US. The chapters concerning fascist and/or National Socialist activities in the US were translated into German in 1942 by the "Schriftendienst Übersee" (Stuttgart-Hamburg).
100 Cf. Neil Baldwin, Henry Ford and the Jews. The Mass Production of Hate, New York 2001, esp. 268 ff.
101 Henry Ford to Sigmund Livingston, 7 January 1942, UTS 1–1–1.
102 Baldwin, Henry Ford (op. cit. note 100), 277.
103 Ibid. 306 f.
104 The court had sentenced Niemöller to seven months incarceration, which he had already served in investigative custody. Cf. Wilhelm Niemöller, Macht geht vor Recht. Der Prozeß Martin Niemöllers, Munich 1952; Jürgen Schmidt, Martin Niemöller im Kirchenkampf, Hamburg 1971, 433 ff.
105 To strengthen the opposition from the Confessional Church, the Eden Theological Seminary conferred in 1936 to the "outstanding figures in the resistance of German Protestantism to coercion by the State" Martin Niemöller, Otto Dibelius and Gerhard Jacobi, the honorary degree of Doctor in Divinity. Cf. FCB, April 1936, 10.
106 Leiper to Kerrl and Dieckhoff, 21 April 1938, UTS 1–2–4. Cf. Besier, The friends, in this volume. On the preparations for this protest action, see the telegrams, UTS 1–2–3. See also the positive responses to the letter by the FCC dated 19 February 1938 and addressed to the various churches of the world (with the exception of the US, Switzerland, England, Scotland, France, Mexico, and Canada), UTS 1–1–6.
107 On 12 April 1938, the Church of England and the United Church of Canada sent a joint letter to Hitler, in which they protested in the name of Christianity against the unlawful arrest of Niemöller. UTS 1–2–6. On 14 February 1939, the FCC called upon its members to commemorate Martin Niemöller in their religious services on 5 March 1939, UTS 1–1–6.
108 The FCC's letter on the trial of Martin Niemöller of 11 February 1938 was published in German by the Swiss Press Service on 23 February 1938. Text: Zehrer, Evangelische Freikirchen, 149. Heckel's reply cf. ibid. 149–151; McCrea Cavert's response to Heckel of 29 September 1938, UTS 1–2–4. In it, he states that as long as Heckel was unable to refute the quoted facts, the American statement must be regarded "as an accurate one". In a reply to Leiper dated 13 January 1939, Heckel replied: "With our letter we

had no intention of debating with you the correctness or otherwise of individual assertions made in your appeal – and it does indeed contain many objectively inaccurate assertions – but restricted ourselves to questioning an appeal of this nature as the
appropriate method." He went on to say that he did not consider public demonstrations to be a suitable way of establishing the truth about the situation of the German
church and that this appeal was an example of the futility of the various attempts in
this direction made by international churches. EZA 5, 195.

109 H. D. Swenhagen to Leiper, 20 July 1938, UTS 1–2–6.
110 Leiper to Swenhagen, 25 July 1938, UTS 1–2–6.
111 Swenhagen to Leiper, 15 September 1938, UTS 1–2–6.
112 Leiper to Swenhagen, 3 December 1938, UTS 1–2–6.
113 Heckel to German Foreign Office (*Auswärtiges Amt*), 28 February 1938, EZA 5, 195.
114 Ibid.
115 Note by Wahl of 5 May 1938, ibid. In his letter of 9 March 1938, Muhs had announced
    to the KA that he would be attempting to obtain these signatures.
116 Cf. Herbert Sirois, Zwischen Illusion und Krieg. Deutschland und die USA
    1933–1941, Paderborn 2000, 126 ff.
117 Cf. press release of the FCC of 23 December 1938, UTS 1–1–6; see also the article
    'The Churches' United Front', in The New York Times of 27 December 1938.
118 Quoted according The New York Times of 27 December 1938.
119 Thus the pastor of St Batholomew's Church, New York City, in a letter to Leiper dat-
    ed 7 December 1938, UTS 1–1–6.
120 Cf. telegram William Allen White to Leiper, 21 November 1938, UTS 1–1–1.
121 'Council Created to Fight Race Bias. Provisional Council against Anti-Semitism is
    formed by 52 Distinguished Persons', New York Times, November 1938.
122 Undated flysheet, UTS 1–1–1.
123 Henry W. Levy, 'Good Will To Men', The National Jewish Monthly, December 1938,
    128 ff.
124 Opinion. A Journal of Jewish Life and Letters, December 1938, 7.
125 Cf. Baldwin, Henry Ford (op. cit. note 100), 297. See also Hadassa Ben-Itto, "Die
    Protokolle der Weisen von Zion". Anatomie einer Fälschung, Berlin 2001.
126 Opinion. A Journal of Jewish Life and Letters, December 1938, 9.
127 Cf. Baldwin, Henry Ford (op. cit. note 100), 299.
128 Cf. reports of the Selberg Circle, EZA 5, 194.
129 About Douglass, cf. Schmidt, Architect of Unity (op. cit. note 14), 79 f.
130 Information by the Selberg Circle, 20 July 1934 (op. cit. note 128).
131 EZA 5, 195.
132 Cf. the note in The Christian Century, 7 November 1934.
133 Ibid.
134 Cf. report by Heckel, 30 October 1935, about a talk to Leiper on 30 October 1935,
    EZA, 5, 194. The Minutes of the Meeting of the Executive Committee Chamby s.
    Montreux (Switzerland), 18–22 August 1935, make no mention of the matter.
135 Undated handwritten communication, EZA, 5, 195.
136 Heckel to Leiper, 25 September 1935 (op. cit. note 134).
137 Ibid.
138 Ibid.
139 Krummacher to Leiper, 18 November 1935, UTS 1–2–7.
140 New York Times, 22 September 1935. Cf. also the article in FCB, November-December
    1935, 13.
141 Cf. Schmidt/Ouellette, What Kind of a Man? (op. cit. note 31), 157 ff.
142 On Keller, cf. Günter Gloede, 'Adolf Keller. Ein Pfadfinder zwischenkirchlicher Hilfs-
    arbeit', in idem (ed.), Ökumenische Gestalten. Brückenbauer der einen Kirche, Berlin
    (Ost), undated (1970), 118–124.
143 Keller to Heckel, 2 February 1935, EZA, 5, 195. Cf. also Leiper to Henriod, 11 January
    1935. UTS 1–2–4. The letter indicates that Cadman had written a rather unfortunate

article on the matter, which in Leiper's view was bound to create the impression that "the American Section of the Universal Christian Council was supporting the movement to boycott Germany. On the contrary, by articles, addresses, and personal conferences we have thrown our weight in the opposite scales."

144 FCB, November-December 1935, 13. Cf. also Minutes of the Executive Committee of the FCC, 27 September 1935. The Department of History Presbyterian Church (USA), Philadelphia. See also the article 'Move the Olympics', in The Christian Century, 7 August 1935.

145 Leiper to Krummacher, 16 April 1936, UTS 1-2-7.

146 Schönfeld to Brown, 21 June 1938, UTS 1-2-1. At the time, Schönfeld's salary was largely paid for by the FCC (cf. Leiper to Schönfeld, 21 July 1938, UTS 1-2-1).

147 On 28 July 1939, William Paton, who had been Secretary of the International Missionary Council since 1927 and associate Secretary General of the World Council of Churches, then in the process of formation, wrote to Bell, saying how passionately Schönfeld had taken Heckel's part in the Administrative Committee of the WCC. "We gave long and anxious thought to the problem of Bishop Heckel. Schönfeld made most moving and pathetic plea for some positive action to be taken along the lines of Heckel's desires, and I think he affected the Committee a good deal ... It was, on the whole, the general view of the Administrative Committee that we should try to maintain relations and not let them be broken and, if they were broken, the breach should come from Heckel's side. We cannot but stand at least with the view that we must keep in touch with all parts of the German Church." LPL, Bell Papers, German Church 9, Bl. 336. He concluded that a "no" to Heckel would mean the end of ecumenical relations. Cf. also Alphons Koechlin to Bell on 11 February 1938, in Andreas Lindt (ed.), George Bell – Alphons Koechlin. Briefwechsel 1933–1945, Zurich 1969, 354–357, esp. 355.

148 Cavert, for instance, wrote: "Many Germans defend the present trend by saying that it is no worse than the way Negroes are treated in the United States. There is enough truth in the report to make Americans hang their heads in shame, but there is one important difference: our unjust treatment of the Negro, indefensible as it is, is at least not a policy deliberately adopted by the Government." New York Times of 22 September 1935. Cf. also the statement by the FCC of 24 March 1933, New York Times, 25 March 1933, 10.

149 Letter of FCC to Kerrl, 18 February 1938, UTS 1-2-4.

150 Leiper to Borchers, 6 December 1938, UTS 1-2-3.

151 Cf. e. g. Leiper to Niebuhr, 16 December 1937, UTS 1-2-5. In this letter, Leiper asks the instructor at the UTS to reply to Matthes Ziegler's book "Protestantism between Rome and Moscow in CC". Ziegler was an associate of Rosenberg's. See also Leiper to Schönfeld, 16 December 1937, UTS 1-2-1.

152 Cf. letter of Leiper to Hon. James G. MacDonald, Editorial Department of the New York Times, 19 May 1937, UTS 1-2-5.

153 Leiper described Kraft, who died in New York in 1959, as "one of the main leaders in refugee work in England for Germans" (Leiper to Johnson, 2 November 1938, UTS 1-1-7). Kraft's wife Hettie was a Christian of Jewish origin. Cf. also Alfred Wiener, 'Untersuchungen zum Widerhall des deutschen Kulturkampfes in England (1933–1938)', in Max Beloff (ed.), On the Track of Tyranny. Essays presented by the Wiener Library to Leonard G. Montefiore, London 1960, 211–232, here: 213, 223. Kraft, a wool merchant in London, was a naturalised British citizen born in Germany. His wife and his two daughters, Margaret Helen (born on 11 December 1918) and Joan Vera (born on 8 March 1920), were native-born British citizen. Cf. National Archives, Washington, D. C., Record Group 59, General Records of the Department of State, Visa Division, Case File 811.111 Kraft, Irwin. During the war, Kraft worked for the so-called "Harrar Council", an organisation that proposed the creation of an autonomous Jewish Province comprising the Harrar territory of Ethiopia together with a small portion of British-Somalia. Ibid.

154 About the history of the journal and its dissemination also in a German, French and
    Spanish version see Heinz Hürten (ed.), Kulturkampf. Berichte aus dem Dritten
    Reich, Paris. Eine Auswahl aus den deutschsprachigen Jahrgängen 1936–1939,
    Regensburg 1988, esp. XIII ff. Cf. correspondence of Leiper and Kraft, UTS 1–2–4,
    and Leiper's letter to Bell of 6 December 1938, UTS 1–2–3. Leiper's exhortatory cir-
    cular to a number of leading churchmen in the US dates from 20 December 1938
    (UTS 1–1–7). On the correspondence between Kraft and the Bishop of Chichester,
    George Bell, cf. Lambeth Palace Library (LPL) London, Bell Papers, German Church
    9, Bl. 143 f., 149 f., 161 ff., 171, 174, 176, 178, 285. Among the members of the Lon-
    don committee responsible for the Kulturkampf were Hon. Treasurer Margrieta Beer,
    M.A. and Hon. Secretary H. Kraft, B.A. Also listed in the official *Kulturkampf* letter-
    head were Bell, the Dean of Chichester, Arthur Stuart Duncan-Jones, Rev. W. T. Elms-
    lie, M.A., Lady Winefride Elwes, John Epstein, Dr. Letitia Fairfield, Rev. Alfred E.
    Garvie, D.D., Dr. G. P. Gooch, Rev. L. O'Hea, S. J., MA, and Erwin Kraft. In a letter
    to Bell on 7 January 1938, Kraft comments on his concern and the composition of
    the Committee as follows: "It is still my hope that the *Kulturkampf* Association may
    grow into a movement capable of bringing home to the English-speaking world the
    true facts about Nazi-ism. You may have noticed that our committee, apart from Mrs.
    Kraft and myself, consists of six Protestants and six Catholics, and I hope it will be
    possible to obtain growing measure of support from the press. I feel that our Associa-
    tion is too immature to attempt by itself to organise public meetings in this country,
    but if a more powerful organization were to take this matter in hand, we could no
    doubt give some assistance." (LPL, Bell Papers 9, Bl. 121). Kraft also belonged to a
    "German Church Conference" in London, which numbered various dignitaries among
    its members, including (once again) Margrieta Beer and Dorothy F. Buxton. Cf. LPL,
    Bell Papers 9, Bl. 280 f.; Bell Papers 15, Bl. 49. See also Keith Robbins, 'Church and
    Politics: Dorothy Buxton and the German Church Struggle', in idem, History, Religion
    and Identity in Modern Britain, London 1993, 183–194, esp. 189.

155 Thus a circular by the *Kulturkampf* Association, signed by M. Beer Hon. Treasurer,
    UTS 1–1–7.

156 Cf. accompanying letter by Brown and Leiper of 20 March 1939, UTS 1–1–7.

157 Cf. H. M. Kallen to Leiper, 29 March 1939; Leiper to Brown, 11 April 1939, UTS
    1–1–7.

158 Cf. Thomas Reuther, Die ambivalente Normalisierung. Deutschlanddiskurs und
    Deutschlandbilder in den USA 1941–1955, Stuttgart 2000, 73.

159 Detlef Junker, Kampf um die Weltmacht. Die USA und das Dritte Reich 1933–1945,
    Düsseldorf 1988, 70.

160 Cf. Doris Kearns Goodwin, No Ordinary Time. Franklin and Eleanor Roosevelt: The
    Home Front in World War II, New York 1995, 102.

161 Michaela Hönicke, '"Know Your Enemy". American Wartime Images of Germany,
    1942–1943', in Ragnhield Fiebig-von Hase / Ursula Lehmkuhl (eds), Enemy Images
    in American History, Providence-Oxford 1997, 237.

162 Cf. Besier, The friends, in this volume.

163 Cf. Nelson, The Lutherans in North America (op. cit. note 7), 454. Though in 1938
    the respondents listed the Bible as the "most interesting book that they had ever read"
    ("Gone with the Wind" came second), in the following year 50 % of the respondents
    indicated that their parents had gone to church more frequently than they had, while
    40 % were of the opinion that religious interest had declined. The Gallup Poll (op. cit.
    note 9), vol. 1, 135, 146.

164 Cf. Besier, The friends, in this volume; Leo P. Ribuffo, 'Religion in the History of U. S.
    Foreign Policy', in Elliot Abrams (ed.), The Influence of Faith. Religious Groups and
    Foreign Policy, Lanham-Boulder-New York-Oxford 2001, 1–27, here: 12.

165 Cf. Warren, Theologians (op. cit. note 15), 94 ff.

Anti-Bolshevism and Anti-Semitism: The Catholic Church in Germany and National Socialist Ideology 1936/37*

In his essay "Judaism and Christianity in the ideology and politics of National Socialism"[1] Klaus Scholder outlined the basic principles of Hitler's worldview and examined his perception of the relationship between Christianity and anti-Semitism. According to Hitler, there could be no doubt that Christian leaders, given the nature of their beliefs, should be active exponents of anti-Semitism. He revived the old motif of the Jews as "Christ's killers" and described Jesus as "a leader of the people", who "opposed Jewry".[2] Jesus was thus murdered on the initiative of the Jews and the Jew Paul "refined, falsified and exploited the teaching of the Galilean for his own ends".[3] It is notable that although Hitler's basic beliefs can be proven to be unchanged from the 1920s to the 1940s, his view of Christianity was subjected to considerable alteration. The longer the Churches repudiated his racial anti-Semitism the more he considered they had been influenced by Judaism: "Those who did not support the National Socialist fight against Jewry must themselves have been contaminated by Judaism. That was true of Bolshevism, of capitalism and now of Christianity."[4] Thus, since Hitler was unable to transform the mainstream anti-Jewish tradition from a theological to a racial concept because Christianity, although divided in many ways, held to its Jewish roots, it seemed much more promising to use anti-Bolshevism to entice the Churches into lending their support to the National Socialist ideology. National Socialism and Christianity both viewed Bolshevism as an ideological threat. The fear of Bolshevism was for many churchmen more powerful than their long-standing religiously based antipathy towards Judaism. Moreover, as Klaus Scholder pointed out, "for both Hitler and for the Cardinal [Faulhaber] Bolshevism and Judaism were largely identical concepts".[5] Well-known Christians in their analysis of Bolshevism agreed with the National Socialists that the world Jewry was one of the basic ingredients of "red internationalism". This is illustrated more precisely by the example of the Catholic Church.

1936 was an important year in the National Socialist anti-Bolshevist campaign. One of the secrets of the success of the dictatorship and its propaganda was its ability to use convincing political principles to support its ideology. There was a realistic background to the anti-Bolshevist campaign because by January 1936 the Russian defence budget had more than doubled from 6.5 to 14.8 billion roubles. A popular front government was elected in Spain the following month and at the end of the month the governments in Paris and Moscow ratified the Franco-Soviet Alliance. Since 4 June Léon Blum had led a Popular Front government in France.

---

* First published in *The Journal of Ecclesiastical History* 43 (1992) 3, 447–456.

Hitler had already formulated an anti-Soviet policy. On 22 July 1936 he told the Japanese military attaché that "big block Russia" should "again [be] divided into its original, historical parts".[6]

Hitler probably feared a Bolshevist policy that was aimed at isolating Germany, as is evident in his well-known memorandum on the aims of the four-year plan in August 1936. This memorandum concluded: "Since the outbreak of the French Revolution the world has hurtled with increasing speed towards a new confrontation; the most extreme solution is Bolshevism, which desires to eliminate the leading social strata of mankind and replace it with internationally-spread Jewry."[7] This way of thinking explains why Hitler decided to comply with Franco's request for help so quickly on the evening of 25 July 1936. Even three years later when Hitler spoke to the returning Condor Legion his interpretation of the situation was the same: "In the summer of 1936 Spain seemed to be lost. International powers stirred up the fire of a revolution which was determined to reduce not only Spain but also Europe to rubble ... . I ordered military aid so that not only Europe but also our own Fatherland could be protected from a similar disaster later on ... . The international plutocracies did not understand or acknowledge these idealistic motives."[8]

Germany had to be a bulwark against Bolshevism because the fear of a Soviet-Bolshevik power bloc ought to bring all non-communist countries together. The Rome-Berlin Axis and the anti-Comintern Pact with Japan proved the success of this policy, though Hitler was unable to persuade Britain to join a similar anti-Soviet alliance.

In connection with the military conflict in Spain, the Nazi state promoted the idea of a Bolshevik enemy that had great influence throughout the world. To this end the state enlisted the help of the press and leading politicians under the instruction of the ministry of propaganda. German reports focused primarily on the anti-Church rioting of the Republicans. Stories of ruined monasteries and churches as well as acts of violence against priests, nuns and bishops were consistently highlighted in reports on the atrocities in Spain. The *Völkischer Beobachter* newspaper in Germany made it very clear that its reports on the disaster in Spain, which was caused by the "Jewish-Bolshevist revolution", were primarily intended for the readership of the German Churches. In the reports the Church should foresee the consequences of a "Jewish-Marxist invasion" for Germany, as well as for Europe, namely the destruction of Western Christian culture. Russian Bolshevism would negate the Western Christian culture and its crudeness would deny the most fundamental ethical principles, without which no civilisation could exist.[9]

The alleged close connection between Bolshevism and world Jewry was not only evident in the National Socialist press but also in the speeches of National Socialist leaders at party conferences. In September 1936, Hitler announced at the party conference in Nuremberg: "We German National Socialists were never afraid of Communism. We alone recognised this shameful Jewish doctrine of world aggression, we studied its diabolic methods and warned of its consequences."[10] National Socialism here appears as a reactive factor and Bolshevism as the real driving force. In his final speech at the party conference in September 1936 Hitler tried to define the difference between the National Socialist and the Bolshevik revolution. As he put it: "For this is the difference between the Bolshevik and the National Socialist revolution: the one reduces flourishing countries to an atrocious sea of debris. The other transforms a destroyed and impoverished Reich into a sound state and a flourishing economy."[11]

On this occasion Goebbels, the minister of propaganda, also attempted to show the close connection between Bolshevism and the world Jewry. He explained that Bolshevism was "a pathological, criminal madness, thought up and led by Jews for the annihilation of civilised European nations and the establishment of international Jewish world domination. Only Jews were able to develop Bolshevism ... . The Bolshevik reality with its horrible and bloody cruelties can only be imagined in the hands of Jews ... . In fact Bolshevism is the most extreme reign of blood and terror ever seen in the world. Jews thought it up to make their rule unassailable and Jews practise it today ... . Bolshevism has to be annihilated if Europe is to recover."[12]

Furthermore, Goebbels asserted the basic incompatibility of the Jewish-Bolshevik and Christian systems: "This is the real character of Bolshevik atheism, which dares to offer its co-operation with churches in other countries. The picture of nuns pulled out of their coffins in Barcelona is a symbol of Bolshevism's violation of everything sacred. When Andres Nin, one of the main agitators in Spain, declared 'we solved the church problem by destroying all the temples', we have to stress that this is godlessness personified and that it is the real face of Bolshevism."[13]

There can be no doubt that the tone of the propaganda machine had considerable influence on the formation of opinion among the German population and also abroad. Nevertheless, it cannot be supposed that the position of the Catholic Church towards the Spanish Civil War was decisively influenced by the mobilisation of public opinion. From the start there was no doubt about the Vatican's sympathies. But the Nazi attempt to use events in Spain to secure Catholic support for their anti-Bolshevik campaign was gravely compromised by their actions against the Catholic Church in Germany. By the summer of 1936 the German Catholic Church was aroused into opposition against the National Socialist "*Ent konfessionalisierung (secularisation)* of public life", which was the directive issued by the minister of the Interior in 1935. Behind this system was the ill-concealed plan of the state and party to systematically oust the Catholic Church from public life. Catholic associations and the Catholic press were to be disbanded, as were the Catholic schools. The German episcopate and the Holy See felt particular bitterness over the disbanding of the schools because the guarantee of denominational schools had been the most decisive gain from the Concordat and the most important reason for signing it. These measures were accompanied by a carefully prepared campaign of slander, which was carried out by means of court cases against priests, monks and nuns for breaches of exchange control regulations and in particular for alleged sex crimes.[14]

Despite the growing tension between the Catholic Church and the National Socialist state, Catholic Church leaders decided to co-operate with the dictatorship. One possible factor was the Nazi regime's skilful use of prominent international Catholic voices against Bolshevism in order to push German Catholic interests into the background. For example the *Völkischer Beobachter* carried on its front page the headline "Cardinal of Paris[15] warns France of Moscow" followed up with remarks from the cardinal:

"Cardinal Baudrilla[r]t pointed out that signs of a corrupting influence are clearly noticeable in contemporary France. There is real evidence of concrete preparations being made to undermine the political system. Moscow is already sending its messengers with orders to agitate. The Cardinal pointed out that he had been assured by personal sources three years ago, when the Spanish revolution first cast its bloody shadows, that sixty Russian Jews had arrived in Spain after crossing the Pyrenees. They had been sent by Moscow as Soviet agents to set churches and monasteries on fire, to plunder and to establish the movement of godlessness in the Spanish population. For France the same danger exists ... . State authority is increasingly undermined and the machinery of civil war is being set in motion ... . The messengers of Moscow are ready to act."[16]

At the same time the *Völkischer Beobachter* regretted that the stance of the Catholic Church in Germany against Bolshevism was not as resolute as that of the French cardinal.

The Austrian Bishop Hudal, who lived in Rome, achieved similar notoriety. No less a person than the Nazi chief ideologist, Alfred Rosenberg, was kindly disposed towards Hudal's ideas. The Austrian bishop saw in Bolshevism a "sign of nihilism and of decadent Jewry devoid of all religious commitments". He praised National Socialism as a great European ideology, "which opposes world Bolshevism in an uncompromising manner".[17] Catholicism in Germany should unite against Bolshevism as church leaders from abroad did. It is notable that the French cardinals and the Austrian bishop identified Bolshevism with world Jewry and were as such completely in accord with Nazi ideology.

In fact the German episcopate lost little time in joining the anti-Bolshevik campaign of the Nazi state. In August 1936, hardly a month after German auxiliary troops had been sent to Spain, the German bishops met for their annual plenary session in Fulda. In their pastoral letter they more or less reiterated the National Socialist analysis of the role of Bolshevism in foreign affairs and declared their solidarity with the Nazi state. This letter asserted: "We start from the obvious fact and conviction that Communism and Bolshevism are at present trying with diabolic determination and toughness to advance into the heart of Europe, thus putting it in grave danger. Therefore, German unity should not be sacrificed to religious antagonism, quarrels, contempt and struggles. Rather, our national power of resistance must be increased and strengthened so that not only Europe [may be] freed from Bolshevism by us but also that the whole civilised world may be indebted to us."[18]

Apart from the Catholic hierarchy's general approval of and support for the National Socialists in the struggle against Bolshevism, there was also another factor at work. The bishops demanded the restoration of religious peace because they thought this was the only possible way to successfully defend the nation against Bolshevism. The bishops' position was clear, they sought to stop the Nazi discrimination against church institutions and organisations in return for their co-operation against Bolshevism. In return the Catholic Church was willing to regard the

Spanish events from the Nazis' point of view. In a pastoral letter, it was asserted *inter alia*:

"We may be spared from going into the details of the crimes [of the Spanish Republicans G. B.] committed by a rabid mob, which had been incited by the mendacious promises of the Russian emissaries. These crimes are the horror of all civilised nations ... . In fact Russian and Spanish Bolshevism sees its enemy in the Catholic Church; in its clergy and religious orders they see their most irreconcilable and most dangerous enemies. Hence the hatred and will to annihilate, which goes to the bloodiest extremes ... . May the future not show that the Communist mob will make priests, monks, and nuns on the Iberian Peninsula its first target, to strike at them as the last bastion against its ideas and its advance. It is a fact: Bolshevism, as has been proved in Russia and Mexico, begins and is founded on a condemnation of religion as the opium of the masses and it can only advance if the belief in Christ and in a personal, metaphysical God and in a hereafter disappears from the hearts and consciences of all human beings."[19]

It is clear that in their respective interpretations of the Spanish situation there was no difference between the Nazi state and the Catholic Church. The Catholic Church believed the Republican side was controlled by Russian Bolshevism and this was a struggle between good and evil. The bishops adopted the virtually uncritical one-sidedness of the reports in the *Völkischer Beobachter*. The only difference was that it replaced the Nazi ideology with Christianity. In this way the Church seemed to be competing with Hitler to be the strongest bastion against Bolshevism. The bishops made it perfectly clear that they believed there was no "ideological substitute" capable "of defeating the ideological basis of Bolshevism".[20]

Through its relations with the National Socialists, the Catholic Church tried to represent itself as the guarantor of the successful fight against Bolshevism. However, in a pastoral letter, while stressing the common interest of the Catholic Church and the Nazi state, the Church also made it clear that it would allow nothing, not even the National Socialist ideology, to question its own role in the struggle against Bolshevism. The bishops protested cautiously against the treatment of the Catholic Church by the Nazi state. The Episcopal Conference apparently expected that its approval of the state and its anti-Bolshevism would be rewarded by concessions to the Catholic Church. But the state did not respond. Instead the subsequent pastoral letter and a speech by the Pope on 15 September along the same lines were not allowed to be published. The willingness of the Catholic Church to compromise had not paid off. Neither its loyalty to the state nor its support for anti-Bolshevism could persuade the Nazi state to accept protest or criticism of its own actions towards the Church.

A dialogue between Cardinal Faulhaber of Munich and Hitler on 4 November 1936 was of great significance for the later position of the Catholic Church regarding anti-Bolshevism. First of all, Hitler and Faulhaber discussed the "Bolshevik danger in foreign affairs". During this conversation Hitler said: "If National Socialism does not defeat Bolshevism, this will mean the end of Christianity and the Churches in Europe. Bolshevism is the mortal enemy of the Church as well as of Fascism ... . We have reports about these subhuman creatures, who, agitated by Jews, act in a bestial manner in Spain ... . It will not miss this historical hour."[21]

Faulhaber fully agreed with Hitler and referenced both his speech at the party conference in Nuremberg and the speech given by the Pope: "While the Führer's speech in Nuremberg impressively explained the general cultural and economic consequences of Bolshevism (it can only destroy, it is led by Jews, it destroys every national economy), the Pope on that very same day described atheism, godlessness and blasphemy as the root and essence of Bolshevism."[22] In drawing a parallel between the two speeches and their different emphases Faulhaber sought to stress that the two approaches were compatible. While Hitler emphasised the political, economic and racial aspects of the danger of Bolshevism, the Pope stressed the dangers to religion. This was the point of no return. Whereas the Episcopal Conference at Fulda had carefully avoided explicitly accepting the anti-Semitic element of Nazi anti-Bolshevism, it now accepted it implicitly and tacitly. In his dialogue with Hitler, Faulhaber agreed with Hitler's analysis of the Jewish-Bolshevik phenomenon and thus adopted the racial anti-Semitism of Nazi ideology in the context of defence against Bolshevism. The following extract from the conversation demonstrates to what extent Faulhaber adopted the National Socialist racial myth of blood and soil. When Hitler declared "We want to protect the German people from such congenitally afflicted criminals currently wrecking the most dreadful havoc in Spain. I see it as the will of God.",[23] Faulhaber replied "The Church, Mr Chancellor, will not refuse the state the right to keep these pests away from the national community within the framework of the moral law."[24] As in the pastoral letter of 19 August Faulhaber reiterated the protests of the Catholic Church against National Socialist church policy but this issue remained in the background. Hitler brushed the cardinal's complaints aside with vague promises and indicated that any change in church policy was dependent on the German bishops' willingness to issue an anti-Bolshevik statement: "You should consider, Cardinal, and discuss with other leaders of the Church, how you will support National Socialism in its great labour of fighting Bolshevism and how you will attain a peaceful relationship with the state. Either National Socialism and the Church will win together or they will both be destroyed. I promise you I will eliminate every minor irritant that disturbs peaceful co-operation, such as the cloister trials and the German religious movement. I do not want horse-trading. You know that I am opposed to any compromise but this should be the last attempt."[25]

These vague statements persuaded the cardinal to identify much more closely with the National Socialist ideology. As he was completely taken in by Hitler's statesmanlike behaviour and religious ideas, Faulhaber believed that "Without any doubt the Chancellor believes in God. He accepts Christianity as the architect of Western culture."[26] In the following weeks, Faulhaber became the key figure in the Catholic Church policy towards Bolshevism as a result of his three-hour conversation with Hitler. He immediately set to work to keep his promise of producing an anti-Bolshevik declaration by all Catholic bishops, but thought he needed time so that it would not seem to have been initiated by the Chancellor. Moreover, the pastoral letter from Cologne had recently been published and it protested strongly against National Socialist church policy without mentioning loyalty to either the state or Bolshevism.[27] In order to avoid the impression that the Church could go from one extreme to the other, Faulhaber published an "interim statement" of the Bavarian episcopacy, which included both complaints from the Catholic Church on suppression by the National Socialists and affirmation of loyalty to the state as well as support for the Führer "in his stance against Bolshevism, which is of great significance in world history".[28] But this carefully considered diplomatic action was not without contradictions. The Archbishop of Bamberg, for example, expressed serious doubts about publishing the Bavarian pastoral letter because he thought that the Nazi leadership would interpret it as a "toning down of the promise" of the common fight against Bolshevism and would see it as an opportunity to increase attacks on the Catholic Church.[29]

On 24 December 1936 Faulhaber wrote the final draft of the pastoral letter "On the Defence Against Bolshevism". It was preached from the pulpit of every Catholic Church in Germany. It read:

"Bolshevism has begun its march from Russia to the countries of Europe, especially to our country and its aim is to overthrow here, as everywhere else, every social system and every system of government, to destroy economic affluence and to annihilate religious life. Russian Bolshevism controls a large number of able-bodied men and raw material in abundance as in no other European nation ... . The fateful hour has come for our nation and for the Christian culture of the Western world ... . The Führer and Chancellor Adolf Hitler saw the march of Bolshevism from afar and turned his mind and energies towards averting this enormous danger for the German people and the whole Western world. The German bishops consider it their duty to do their utmost to support the leader of the Reich with every available means. Since Bolshevism is the mortal enemy of the system of government, since it is primarily the gravedigger of religious culture and always attacks the servants and sacred places of church life, as the Spanish events have recently proved, since it is a question of the survival of church order, it is thus clear that support for the struggle against this diabolic power must become an important task of the contemporary Church."[30]

In this letter the church leaders did not differentiate between the real danger and the National Socialist propaganda. Rather they adopted this propaganda *in corpore* and supported the National Socialist political-ideological assessment of the situation because they had identified Bolshevism as a satanic power since 1922. Thus, they demonstrated the importance of this confrontation for Christianity.[31] It is certainly correct that the bishops abstained from extreme anti-Semitic statements and did not list all the events the Führer "saw from afar". But in confirming their conviction that Hitler's worldview was generally correct, they necessarily approved this characteristic element of the National Socialist view of Bolshevism. Bolshevism as "the advance guard of the Anti-Christ" was the only way in which contemporaries could interpret the Catholic Statement, and this included world Jewry. The pastoral letter confirmed this interpretation because, as in all former statements, the Catholic bishops only criticised the damage done to the Catholic episcopate and did not protest against the assaults on human rights or the brutal oppression and persecution of minorities, in particular the German Jews. But even the complaints expressed in the most restrained manner at the end of the pastoral letter were enough for Hitler to be able to declare all previous

Catholic statements of solidarity in the common fight against anti-Bolshevism as insignificant. The Church either had to completely accept the National Socialist policy or it would be considered an opponent and treated accordingly.

The encyclical "With Burning Sorrow" of March 1937 exemplified the failure of the policy of co-operation between the Catholic Church and the Nazi state. The papal letter, which included a clear and unambiguous condemnation of Nazi ideology, was read from all Catholic pulpits. It asserted: "Whoever regards race or nation or the state or the type of state, the representatives of the state's authority or any other basic value of human community ... as the measure of all worth, including religious values ... reverses and falsifies the God-given order of life."[32] However, could this admirable clarification simply be the disappointed reaction of the rejected partner in an alliance, which four months previously and without reservation had confirmed the Church's absolute loyalty to Führer and Fatherland – the only condition being that the Church's right to life in the Nazi state was to be maintained? Cardinal Bertram provides an illustration of how little this encyclical reflected the wishes and ideas of many German bishops on church policy. On 20 April 1940, Hitler's fifty-first birthday, Bertram congratulated the "highly honoured Chancellor and Führer ... in the name of the spiritual leaders of all German dioceses ... in conjunction with the prayers being said at the altars for the people, army and the Fatherland, for state and Führer, by German Catholics on 20 April".[33] In autumn 1941, the draft of a pastoral letter was written. It referred in strong terms to all controversial themes with the exception of the Jewish question, which was intentionally left out.[34] Even so Bertram rejected this draft firmly so it was never published. It was left to the individual to raise his voice against the persecution and annihilation of the Jews. Thus, it turned out that the Catholic Church was more prepared to make compromises than the Protestant Church was.

It would be inappropriate to accuse the Roman Catholic Church of racial anti-Semitism. However, in regard to the broad anti-Jewish tradition of the Christian Churches in general, it was obviously not hard for the German episcopate to tolerate the racial anti-Semitism of Nazi ideology as part of the common defence of the country against Bolshevism. Thereby, it may almost have accepted it implicitly. In 1936, Hitler persuaded the Catholic Church by means of confidential talks, public statements and the example of the Spanish Civil War to make anti-Bolshevik statements, which in their political substance were totally based on Nazi ideology. In public, this gave the impression of the Catholic Church agreeing with the National Socialist interpretation of Bolshevism, i. e. the product of a Jewry intent on destroying the Christian European culture.

Notes

1   Klaus Scholder, 'Judaism and Christianity in the ideology and politics of National Socialism', in Otto Dov Kulka and Paul R. Mendes-Flohr (eds), Papers Presented to the International Symposium on Judaism and Christianity under the Impact of National Socialism (1919-1945), Jerusalem 1987, 183-195. Cf. idem, 'Politics and church politics in the Third Reich', in Karl Otmar von Aretin and Gerhard Besier (eds), Klaus Scholder: a requiem for Hitler and other new perspectives on the German Church struggle, London-Philadelphia 1989, 140-156.
2   Scholder, 'Judaism and Christianity' (op. cit. note 1), 194.
3   Ibid.
4   Ibid. 193 f.
5   Ibid. 189 f.
6   Klaus Hildebrand, Das Dritte Reich (Grundriss der Geschichte 17), Munich 1979, 28.
7   Hans-Henning Abendroth, Hitler in der spanischen Arena: die deutsch-spanischen Beziehungen im Spannungsfeld der europäischen Interessenpolitik vom Ausbruch des Bürgerkrieges bis zum Ausbruch des Weltkrieges, 1936-1939, Paderborn 1973, 33.
8   Paul Meier-Benneckenstein, Dokumente der deutschen Politik, vol. 7, part 1, Berlin 1940, 55.
9   Völkischer Beobachter [VB], 4 Sept. 1936, 1.
10 VB, 10 Sept. 1936, 2.
11 VB, 16 Sept. 1936, 3.
12 VB, 11 Sept. 1936, 6 ff.
13 Ibid.
14 Cf. Hans Günter Hockerts, Die Sittlichkeitsprozesse gegen katholische Ordensangehörige und Priester 1936/37: eine Studie zur nationalsozialistischen Herrschaftstechnik und zum Kirchenkampf (VKZG.F 6), Mainz 1971; Ludwig Volk (ed.), Akten deutscher Bischöfe über die Lage der Kirche (VKZG.Q 30), vol. IV: 1936-39, Mainz 1981; Ulrich von Hehl, Priester unter Hitlers Terror: eine biographische statistische Erhebung (VKZG.Q 37), Mainz 1985; Klaus J. Volkmann, Die Rechtsprechung staatlicher Gerichte in Kirchensachen 1933-1945 (VKZG.F 24), Mainz 1978; Joachim Maier, Schulkampf in Baden 1933-1945: die Reaktion der katholischen Kirche auf die nationalsozialistische Schulpolitik, dargestellt am Beispiel des Religionsunterrichts in den badischen Volksschulen (VKZG.F 38), Mainz 1983; Wilhelm Damberg, Der Kampf um die Schulen in Westfalen 1933-1945 (VKZG.F 43), Mainz 1986.
15 In fact Baudrillart was not the cardinal of Paris but had become cardinal-priest in 1935. V.-L. Saubeuler, s.v. Baudrillart, Dictionnaire de Biographie Française, vol. V, Paris 1985, 893-895.
16 VB, 17 Sept. 1936, 1.
17 VB, 18 Sept. 1936, 1. See also Alois C. Hudal, Römische Tagebücher: Lebensberichte eines alten Bischofs, Stuttgart 1976; Gerhard Besier/Francesca Piombo, The Holy See and Hitler's Germany, Basingstoke 2007.
18 Bernhard Stasiewski (ed.), Akten deutscher Bischöfe über die Lage der Kirche 1933-1945 (VKZG.Q 25), vol. III: 1935-36, Mainz 1979, 479.
19 Ibid. 480.
20 Ibid. 481.
21 Ludwig Volk (ed.), Akten Kardinal Michael von Faulhabers (VKZG.Q 26), vol. II: 1935-45, Mainz 1978, 185.
22 Ibid. The papal speech to Spanish refugees in Rome is published in Acta Apostolicae Sedis, Commentarium officiale, Rome 1936, 375 ff.
23 Volk, Akten Kardinal Michael von Faulhabers (op. cit. note 21), 190 ff.
24 Ibid. 191.
25 Ibid. 193.
26 Ibid. 194.

27 Wilhelm Corsten (ed.), Kölner Aktenstücke zur Lage der katholischen Kirche in Deutschland 1933–1945, Cologne 1949, 150 ff.
28 Volk, Akten Kardinal Michael von Faulhabers (op. cit. note 21), 233.
29 Ibid. 241.
30 Ibid. 245.
31 Ibid. It is also stated: "The essence and root of it [Bolshevism] is the negation of every kind of religion, it is state-directed atheism, it is a gateway to hell, a vanguard of the Anti-Christ, which in an epistle of Paul is called the secret of malice."
32 Dieter Albrecht, Der Notenwechsel zwischen dem Heiligen Stuhl und der deutschen Reichsregierung (VKZG.Q 1), vol. I: Von der Ratifizierung des Reichskonkordats bis zur Enzyklika 'Mit brennender Sorge', Mainz 1965, 409.
33 Walter Adolph, Hirtenamt und Hitlerdiktatur, Berlin (West) 1965, 161.
34 Volk, Akten Kardinal Michael von Faulhabers (op. cit. note 21), 833 f.

Confessional versus Ideological Convictions: The *Fliednersches Evangelisationswerk* and the Ecclesiastical Foreign Office of the German Protestant Church during the Spanish Civil War*

1. Introduction

Theodor Heckel, the leader of the *Ecclesiastical Foreign Office*, was appointed bishop in 1933 and was one of the most faithful executors of the National Socialist foreign policy as far as the Protestant Church was concerned.[1] He was credited with absolute loyalty in the area of the foreign parishes in his charge and regarding the ecumenical movement. He also took pains to defend the National Socialist domestic and foreign politics against any kind of criticism. The Spanish Civil War[2] is classed as a special conflict because both political contrasts and denominational differences clashed.

As a result the Protestant minority developed an ambivalent attitude towards the conflict between the republican government and the Franquists. While the one side rallied with great fury against Communism to help Spanish emigrants, the other was pervaded with anti-Catholic emotions. The latter probably resulted from the tendency of the Spanish and Italian clergy to hold not only Bolshevism but also Protestantism responsible for the Spanish disturbances.[3]

While the Catholic Church was persecuted, the Protestant Church experienced complete religious freedom and even slight patronage for the first time in Spain, which was now ruled by a republican government. Pastor Albricias of Alicante wrote: "Not one single Protestant, pastor or layman had to suffer even the slightest harassment. Our churches remained open as well as the Protestant schools."[4] On the other hand, the French pastor Jules Jézéquel testified "that on the part of the insurgents Protestant pastors and laymen have been killed, just because they were Protestants"[5].

From circles close to the *Fliednersches Evangelisationswerk* (Fliedner's Protestant missionary society) in Spain and the *Iglesia Evangélica Española*, which were both founded by Fritz Fliedner (1845–1901) and continued by his sons Georg (1875–1966), Theodor (1873–1938)[6] and Hans Fliedner (1878–1964),[7] one could read a certain satisfaction in a collection campaign: "This religious people declared war against the Catholic Church. Spain, the Vatican's pillar, no longer exists."[8] Theodor Fliedner senior wrote on 7 October 1936 from Madrid to the Protestant Consistory in Berlin: "It is very unfortunate to see Junker-airplanes with German crews fighting side by side with the rebels and the Moroccans!"[9]

---

*   First published in *KZG/CCH* 15 (2002), 509–518.

As a consequence the *Ecclesiastical Foreign Office* dissociated itself from the *Association to Promote the Gospel in Spain*[10] and declared that Fliedner was not able to see "the global connections, Moscow's influence and the attitude of the German Reich"[11]. Not even under the impression of the terror, which was caused by the "red militia", did Fliedner change his mind.[12] As quoted by the *Times* he claimed that the Roman Catholic Church had "declared itself an enemy of the republic" after the latter announced the separation of state and Church. As, he added, the Roman Catholicism had spread "the lie about Spanish Bolshevism, it had conspired against the republic in secret and public and it had falsely claimed to be persecuted, even though in reality the Roman Catholic Church had been granted complete freedom"[13]. Fliedner also claimed that Spanish Protestant pastors were being deported from areas controlled by the fascist troops, locked up or killed just because they were regarded as "half-socialists". In the fascist circles close to Franco the following claim resounded: "We have diminished Marxism, Protestantism and Freemasonry in Spain once and for all." The *Ecclesiastical Foreign Office* in Germany talked of a "detrimental behaviour" to the state and ensured that Theodor Fliedner senior did not receive financial support[14] and that his *Association to Promote the Gospel in Spain* alongside all its connected unions were with immediate effect dissolved and prohibited[15]. Thus, the policy of keeping its distance from Theodor Fliedner senior in autumn 1937 was of no use to the association.[16] After Franco's victory in 1939 the Protestant secondary school *El Porvenir* in Madrid, as well as the three further Protestant schools and nurseries were closed down.[17] The publication of *España Evangélica*, the weekly paper of Spanish Protestantism was also discontinued.[18]

2.   German Protestantism: A patriotic as well as a cultural mission in Spain since 1870

The *Association to Evangelise Among the Spanish People*[19], which since 1870 was represented by the German Protestant interior mission, was also a national and political affair.

This was obvious because the German consul general was a member of the *Presbyterium* (parochial church council) of the German Protestant community in Barcelona and because the German crown prince donated a Bible with a personal dedication for the altar.[20] In 1895 a pastor lamented that there was no protection against molestation during the services: "... the law only allows us to exercise our religion in secret, we are not even allowed to publish the times of our services."[21] At the laying of the foundation-stone of the church of Barcelona in March 1903 the consul general said: "In this house, which is under the protection of his Majesty the Emperor, may there always be peace, may true Christian love radiate in honour of God for the welfare of the community, in the glory of the German fatherland. May God grant all that!"[22]

Bishop Heckel was invited to celebrate the 50th anniversary of the German Protestant parish in Barcelona on 20 October 1935. However, he was unable to take part. The invitation emphasised especially how "important a day for German-hood in Spain" this was.[23] The German ambassador gave "a speech at the anniversary celebrations, marking the importance of the clerical work in preserving and strengthening German folklore abroad".[24]

During the nineteen-twenties and early thirties German Protestant communities, such as the *Fliedner's Evangelisationswerk*, received money not only from the Church (Gustav-Adolfs-Verein), but also from the German *Ministry of Foreign Affairs* for the "cultivation of ecclesiastical Germanhood abroad"[25] and also from the *Public Union for Germanhood Abroad.*[26]

In 1927 the *Evangelisationswerk,* established by Fritz Fliedner,[27] and the *Association to Promote the Gospel in Spain,* despite the association's severe financial problems[28], employed 48 persons in 10 communities and 15 schools, of which 37 were trained pastors or teachers[29]. The association's main goal was to support the approximately 15,000 Protestants living among 19.5 million Catholics. To mobilise donors the missionary society (*Missionswerk*) reawoke emotions connected with historical events, such as the persecution of the Protestants in the "land of the Inquisition".[30] In a donation appeal it claimed: "Without any human assistance a new Protestant springtime has awoken against all ecclesiastical and social opposition from a long and death-like silence in the Inquisition's home country. But our poor and scattered Spanish brethren in faith are in need of help. The Church of Rome is spreading everywhere in today's world; almost every Roman Catholic is an obedient soldier of his Church. We want Protestants in Protestant liberty more than ever to do the same and not be crushed. Attack is the best defence – the attack of love!"[31]

3.   The conflict between confessional interests and ideological
       fixations: 1931–1938

The Roman Catholic Church lost all its privileges as a state church when the Spanish constitution of 1931, which by the way was strongly influenced by the Weimar *Reich* constitution[32], came into force. For the first time in Spain the new constitution guaranteed freedom of conscience and freedom of religion.[33] All religious beliefs were treated equally, churches were regarded as private societies, thus privileges and support were abolished. Religious orders were not allowed to purchase property nor were they allowed to conduct business, perform trades or teach. They were subject to the general tax law and the Jesuit Order was completely outlawed. This secular legislation took all privileges away from the Roman Catholic Church and by doing so put the Protestants on equal footing.[34]

In May 1933 Gotthelf Conrad[35], a pastor from Kassel and the chairman of the executive board of the *Association to Promote the Gospel in Spain*, travelled to Spain. In his report of his travels he praised "the open door of unhindered proclamation of the word of God"[36] under republican conditions.

Despite the fundamental decision in favour of state schools the government was "not at all hostile towards Protestant schools"[37]. However, Conrad had the feeling that the gospel was being threatened from another direction: "The feeling has really imposed itself on me that a disastrous combination of religion and politics has occurred here and there in the Protestant parishes. All over Protestant local leaders have been dragged into the political life as loyal republicans. Their political work endangers the power of their Protestant preaching and the parishioners are confusing the marvellous liberty of the children of God with formal religious freedom."[38]

In the *Letter to the Friends of the Association to Promote the Gospel in Spain* the German national milieu was clearly opposed to the anticlerical Bolshevism that was said to be behind the radical change of 1931.[39] In Spain the revolution of 1931 was rather experienced as a national start "similar to the one that the German people experienced on 21 March 1933"[40]. The letter stated that reports on the alleged mistreatment of clergymen came from the realm of clerical atrocity propaganda, just as the new German government had to endure slander, which was caused by international Jewry. The very troublesome comparison between the democratic republican government in Spain and the totalitarian Nazi-government in Germany was intended to fill in the gap that had been opened by different interests. Although the Protestant clergymen working in Spain did not exactly hold dear any sympathies for the socialist government, they saw the opportunity under the new political conditions "to struggle, exactly like Luther had on his mind, for the soul of the Spanish people"[41]. However, to accomplish this they required the financial support of National Socialist Germany and the official German Church.

In a second report, which was written as an "expert opinion" in October 1933, Conrad once more underlined how favourable the developments in republican Spain were for Protestantism. "The local riots against the Protestant-minded, which happened so often before the revolution, have almost completely stopped."[42] The "new Spain" was "ready to hear the message of the Gospel"[43]. According to this report Rome had resisted the development and was preparing a "counter attack". Spanish Protestantism was said to "represent a moral outpost of the German influence" and to maintain the resistance against the "world lie".[44] That was why the *Association* must receive greater financial support from Germany.[45]

The victory of the right-wing parties in the parliamentary elections of November 1933 appeared to be a disaster from the denominational perspective of Spanish Protestantism and German Protestants in Spain. "In September [1933] the government of Manuel Azaña was overthrown, allegedly because the majority of the people did not correspond with the majority of the parliament. The elections in November [1933] brought an unexpected victory for the clerics, because the republicans were divided."[46] A Protestant teacher was accused by Roman Catholic priests of being the ringleader of farm hand strikes and was subsequently thrown into prison. The Protestant pastor of Granada was subjected to a body check.[47]

In August 1934, Theodor Fliedner senior remembered in the *Writings from Spain* (*Blätter aus Spanien*), the last victim of the Inquisition, the teacher Kajetan Ripoll, who was burned in 1826. He added "... that heretics were imprisoned until just a few years ago. Even nowadays very unpleasant things can happen to a

Protestant ... . 'You can breathe the air of the fifteenth century right here, right now', a pastor wrote to me"[48]. The Protestants' dread of the "clerical consequences" was also articulated in the *Writings from Spain* in the spring of 1935. The return of the Catholic predominance was visible everywhere.[49] Actually, Protestant services could no longer be held in all places because of the abolition of the freedom of assembly and Protestant pastors were once more arrested.[50]

An open conflict broke out among the Protestant pastors with the armed forces' rebellion of 18 July 1936 against the Spanish government, which had been elected in February of the same year. While the Fliedner family's Spanish missionary society, as member of the Spanish Protestant church, stood alongside the elected government (Theodor Fliedner even condemned the German intervention on the part of Franco), the Protestant communities in Barcelona and Madrid, which were subordinate to Heckel's foreign office, allied themselves with the Franquists. The pastor of the Protestant parish in Barcelona, Georg Gründler, accused the Spanish Protestant Church and the *Fliednerwerk* of holding sympathies with the political "left-wing movement" and pressed the German *Ecclesiastical Foreign Office* to make a clear and visible distinction between the German Protestant communities and the Spanish missionary society, led by the Fliedner brothers.[51] To emphasise his request, Gründler published an article in the *Deutsches Pfarrerblatt,* which claimed that the left-wing parties were anti-German and ideologically dangerous partners for Protestantism. He criticised Theodor Fliedner senior for misjudging the political situation and made a distinction between the "non-clerical" position of the missionary society and the clerical position of the German communities. In October 1936, Gründler expressed his hope that the military revolt might finally win.[52] In several letters to Heckel enclosing further documents he denounced the *Fliednerwerk* for cooperating with the *Popular Front Government,* which he claimed was "undermined and ruled by Bolshevism"[53]. He urged Heckel to dissociate himself from the Fliedner family in the name of the German Protestant Church. Heckel wrote a corresponding letter to the topmost authorities of the German Protestant national churches in order to avoid confusion between the Fliedners and the German parishes in Spain.[54] Even the *Association to Promote the Gospel in Spain* now dissociated itself from Fliedner's reports from Spain and claimed that the Fliedner family could not see the real situation "because of the psychological pressure that reigned near Madrid, where they lived"[55]. A letter of thanks, written by the Association's chairman Conrad to the *Ecclesiastical Foreign Office,* proves the existence of such close arrangements and consultations with Heckel in order to be able to make such statements. Enclosed in that letter there was also a note for the German embassy in Spain "as agreed upon"[56]. When several national churches asked whether they should transfer the previously collected donations to the *Association to Promote the Gospel in Spain,* Heckel advised against it.[57] The article, which Fliedner wrote for the *Deutsches Pfarrerblatt* reporting on persecutions of Protestants by the Franquists, remained unpublished.[58]

4.   The Fliedner Family sitting on the fence

Since almost all members of the Fliedner family were somehow engaged in the National Socialist movement, Gottfried Fliedner's name appeared on the so-called fascist-list of several anarchical left-wing groups in Spain and he only escaped from persecution by fleeing to Germany.[59] Nevertheless, not only the *Ecclesiastical Foreign Office* but also the National Socialists were incensed at Theodor Fliedner senior's positive attitude towards the clearly anti-Catholic and left-wing Protestantism in Spain.[60] With this attitude he was inevitably in conflict with the pro-fascist German politics concerning Spain. The Fliedner family now was sitting on the fence.

Theodor Fliedner's opposition to the Franquists and his option in favour of the elected republican government were of course not based on democratic convictions. As Conrad, he rather compared the political upheaval of 1931 in Spain with Germany in 1933. He was in favour of both. He experienced the second Spanish republic as a kind of liberation of his church from the burden of Catholicism and feared that the former conditions of a state-Church system would be re-established under Franco's rule. Considering this, he only judged the *Popular Front Government* from the churches' perspective and the possibilities of the Protestant Church to be realised in Spain. Bishop Heckel and the *Ecclesiastical Foreign Office* showed no consideration for such internal reflections. However, they supported the German foreign policy with almost every means[61] and even untruly claimed that the "red terror severely distressed their German comrades"[62].

Notes

1   Cf. Gerhard Besier, Die Kirchen und das Dritte Reich, vol. 3: Spaltungen und Abwehr-kämpfe 1934–1937, Berlin-Munich 2001, 431 f., 475 ff., 553 ff.; passim.
2   Cf. Wayne H. Bowen, Spaniards and Nazi Germany. Collaboration in the New Order, Columbia-London 2000, 13 ff.
3   Cf. Aldo Albonico, 'Dall'impegno originale all'allineamento. I cattolici milanesi e la "crociata" in Spagna' [From original commitment to alignment. The Catholics of Milan and the 'crusade' in Spain], in Giorgio Campanini (ed.), I cattolici italiani e la guerra di Spagna. Studi e ricerche (Biblioteca di storia contemporanea) [The Italian Catholics and the Spanish Civil War. Studies and researches (Library of Contemporary History)], Brescia 1987, 61–97, here: 66. Cf. also Walther L. Bernecker, Religion in Spanien. Darstellung und Daten zu Geschichte und Gegenwart, Gütersloh 1995, 85–100; Jean Grugel and Tim Rees, Franco's Spain, London-New York 1997, 128 ff.
4   Albricias of Alicante, 'The situation of the Protestant Church in Spain', in Ökumeni-sches Jahrbuch 1936–1937, 249–254, here: 250.
5   Ibid. 253. See also Juan-Bautista Vilar, 'La persecución religiosa en la zona nacional-ista durante la Guerra Civil. El caso de los protestantes españoles' [Religious perse-cution in the Nationalist zone during the Civil War. The case of the Spanish Protes-tants], in Universidad de Murcia, Academia Alfonso X el Sabio (ed.), Homenaje al profesor Juan Torres Fontes, Murcia 1987, 1749–1762. Only recently have Spanish historians discovered that the Franquists killed three times as many Republicans as the Republicans killed Nationalists. 150,000 "reds" were victims of the Franquists. See on this Julián Casanova, La Iglesia de Franco, Madrid 2001. Between 1936 and 1939

Franco's generals interned at least 367,000 political opponents in at least 104 concentration camps, subjected them to a religious and ideological "re-education" and forced them to labour. Cf. the article on a conference of Spanish historians in Frankfurter Allgemeine Zeitung (FAZ), no. 246 on 23 Oct. 2002.

6   In 1935 Theodor Fliedner senior applied for retirement. In 1936 his son, Theodor Fliedner jr. (1906–1970), took over the direction of Fliedner's Protestant Missionary Society in Spain. Cf. Gotthelf Conrad's circular letter, 22 July 1935; Minutes of the General Meeting of the Association to Promote the Gospel in Spain, 24 Oct. 1935 in Dresden, and the agreement with Theodor Fliedner jr. on 8 Nov. 1935. Archives of the Association to Promote the Gospel in Spain (AAPGS), Herford (Germany), File Spanish Civil War, 1936–1939.

7   Cf. Das deutsche Hilfswerk für die evangelische Kirche in Spanien, eine Darstellung seiner Wirksamkeit wie seiner Begründung bis zur Gegenwart, Nuremberg 1957, esp. 17 ff. and 58 ff.; Fritz Fliedner, Aus meinem Leben. Erinnerungen und Erfahrungen, vol. 2, Berlin 1903, 68 ff., 115 ff., 359 ff.; RGG, vol. 2, 978. Ref. the relationship between Fritz Fliedner and the founder and first Protestant minister of the Madrid parish Iglesia de Jesús, Francisco de Paula Ruet, cf. Theodor Fliedner jun., Calvatrava. Eine Stätte evangelischen Zeugnisses in der Hauptstadt Spaniens, Madrid 1962, 4 ff. See also epd ZA no. 77, 1 Apr. 1969, 5; epd Bavarian Regional Service 4/359, 1 Apr. 1969. See also Rodríguez Domingo (ed.), Memorias de la familia Fliedner, más de 100 años al servicio del protestantismo en España, Barcelona 1997.

8   Spanien erlebt eine große Stunde [without date, end of Oct. 1936], Evangelisches Zentralarchiv in Berlin (EZA) 7/4128.

9   Theodor Fliedner to the consistorial bank in Berlin, 7 Oct. 1936, ibid.

10   See: Heckel to the highest Church authorities of the German Protestant national churches, 9 Oct. 1936, ibid. The Association to Promote the Gospel in Spain, a union of different relief associations to help Protestants in Spain, was established in 1924. Cf. Das Deutsche Hilfswerk (op. cit. note 7), 58. See also Conrad's circular letter, 29 Oct. 1936, AAPGS, File Spanish Civil War, 1936–1939.

11   Note by Krummacher (Ecclesiastical Foreign Office), 9 Oct. 1936, EZA 7/4128. See also the minutes of the General Meeting of the Association to Promote the Gospel in Spain, 15/16 Sep. 1937 in Kassel. The protocol says: "An extensive statement is given on the position taken by the retired Pastor Theodor Fliedner senior at the Universal Christian Conference in Oxford, intimating during the following negotiations that the members of the Association regret the fact that retired Pastor Fliedner has ignored the request, reiterated several times since 1931, to refrain from any political statement in his reports." It is stressed several times "that the Association should refrain from making any political statement and focus on its ecclesiastical task instead. The same must be expected from the head of the organisation in Spain." AAPGS, File Spanish Civil War, 1936–1939.

12   Theodor Fliedner to Georg Fliedner on 22 Sep. 1936, EZA 7/4128.

13   The Times, 24 July 1937.

14   Muhs to DEK, DEKK and KA, 2 Aug. 1937, EZA 7/4128.

15   Circular letter from the Reichsführer SS, 7 June 1938, EZA 5/1880, fol. 399. Cf. Das Deutsche Hilfswerk (op. cit. note 7), 59. Only in 1951 could the Association be re-constituted. See also the correspondence between the members of the board of the Association to Promote the Gospel in Spain, esp. Conrad's circular letter to the board of the Association, 5 July 1938, AAPGS, File Spanish Civil War, 1936–1939. Not before the democratic constitution came into force in 1977 was the Iglesia Evangélica Española fully acknowledged by the state and from then on could work in a free manner.

16   Cf. Conrad's Report of Sep. 1937, AAPGS, File Spanish Civil War, 1936–1939.

17   Cf. Das Deutsche Hilfswerk (op. cit. note 7), 24 ff., 28, 34 ff. See also '90 Aniversario El Porvenir', Historia Viva, 31 Oct. 1897–1987, Madrid 1987, esp. 33 ff.

18   Cf. Das Deutsche Hilfswerk (op. cit. note 7), 33.

19 Quoted by: 1885–1925. Protestant Parish of Barcelona [Evangelische Gemeinde Barcelona], Festschrift zur 40–jährigen Jubelfeier der Gemeinde by Fritz Olbricht, pastor in Barcelona [without year], 4.
20 Ibid. 5.
21 Ibid. 11.
22 Ibid. 14.
23 EZA 5/1893, fol. 237.
24 Report by Köcher, German consulate general in Spain, 5 Nov. 1935, EZA 5/1893, fol. 385.
25 EZA 5/1893, fol. 103.
26 Ibid. fol. 184.
27 Cf. 'Fritz Fliedner (1845–1901)', in Biographisch-Bibliographisches Kirchenlexikon, vol. 2, 56 f.
28 Letter from Pastor G. Funcke (Association to Promote the Gospel in Spain, Barmen) to the General Superintendent Burghard on 26 July 1927, EZA 5/1880, fol. 2. According to a memorandum from 1935 on a plan to eliminate the debts of the Protestant missionary society in Spain the society needed 150,000 Swiss Gold-Francs to get out of its bank debts. AAPGS, File Spanish Civil War, 1936–1939.
29 Denkschrift des Verbandes zur Förderung des Evangeliums in Spanien from 9 June 1928, 18–27, here: 18.
30 Cf. August W. Schreiber, Deutschlands Anteil an der Evangelischen Bewegung in Spanien. Ein Gruß an die Leser der "Blätter aus Spanien" [no place, no year], 2.
31 Donation call (approximately from the year 1927), EZA 5/1880, fol. 56.
32 Cf. Walther Bernecker, Spanische Geschichte. Von der Reconquista bis heute, Darmstadt 2002, 161.
33 Cf. Theodor Fliedner, 'Politik und Evangelium in Spanien', in Evangelium in Spanien. Jahrbuch 1934, 3–6. See also 'Recopilación de textos del codigo penal sobre delitos contra la Religion' [Collection of texts from the penal code on offences against religion], in La Luz. Boletin de la Iglesia Española Reformada Episcopal (IERE), no. 1071, Mar.-Apr.-May 1972, 20–26.
34 Cf. Juan-Bautista Vilar, 'Los protestantes españoles ante la guerra civil (1936–1939)' [The Spanish Protestants before the Civil War (1936–1939)], Cuenta y Razon no. 21, Madrid 1985, 213–230.
35 Conrad was a member of the Wittenberger Bund. See Kurt Meier, Der Evangelische Kirchenkampf, vol. 2, Göttingen ²1984, 374.
36 Conrad, 'Bericht über meine Reise nach Spanien (1933)', EZA 5/1880, fols 123–128, quote: 123.
37 Ibid. fol. 124.
38 Ibid.
39 Letter to friends [no date, 1933], EZA 5/1880, fol. 129.
40 Ibid.
41 The secretary-general of the Association to Promote the Gospel in Spain, S. Meinhof, to Reich Bishop Müller on 19 Sep. 1933, ibid. fol. 134.
42 Expert opinion by Conrad, 17 Oct. 1933, ibid. fol. 137.
43 Ibid. fol. 138.
44 Ibid. fol. 139.
45 See also the note by Heckel on a conversation with Theodor Fliedner on 28 Sep. 1934, ibid. fol. 188. In it Heckel states that he told Fliedner that the means of the German Protestant communities abroad were earmarked, but he would support other means of clerical aid for the association.
46 Blätter aus Spanien, no. 189, Sep. 1934, 2995.
47 Ibid. 2998.
48 Ibid. 3006.
49 See Blätter aus Spanien, June 1935, 3030.
50 Ibid. 3035. See also Blätter aus Spanien, June 1935, 3041 ff.

51 Gründler to the Ecclesiastical Foreign Office on 15 Sep. 1936, EZA 5/1880, fols 232–234.

52 Deutsches Pfarrerblatt, no. 40, 6 Oct. 1936, 701 f.

53 Gründler to Heckel, 21 Oct. 1936, EZA 5/1880, fol. 239.

54 See Heckel's letter of 29 Oct. 1936, ibid. fol. 277.

55 Conrad to the German embassy in Spain, 29 Oct. 1936, ibid. fol. 252.

56 Conrad to the Ecclesiastical Foreign Office, 29 Oct. 1936, ibid. fol. 254. See also note by Krummacher on 29 Oct. 1936, ibid. fols 258–261.

57 National Bishop of Baden to Heckel, 1 Oct. 1936, and Heckel's negative response, ibid. fols 266–268.

58 See Deutsches Pfarrerblatt (Pastor Seiler) to Heckel on 23 Sep. 1936 and 19 Oct. 1936, as well as Heckel's response of 25 Sep. 1936, ibid. fols 272, 269.

59 See Theodor Fliedner to Gottfried Fliedner, 22 Sep. 1936, ibid. fol. 281. See also Conrad's Circular letter, 11 Nov. 1936, AAPGS, File Spanish Civil War, 1936–1939.

60 See NSDAP Support Committee for the Germans in Spain [NSDAP-Hilfsausschuss für die Spaniendeutschen] to Gründler, 14 May 1937; Gründler to the Support Committee, 22 May 1937, ibid. fols 299, 301. Theodor Fliedner's report on the situation of the Protestants in Spain, which he presented to the Universal Christian Council in Oxford 1937, caused much dismay. EZA 5/1880, fols 314–320.

61 See Heckel's propaganda campaign to support Franco, EZA 5/1867.

62 GBI. DEK no. 21, 1 Aug. 1936. See more reports in EZA 5/1866.

Neo-Pagan Religiosity and Protestantism in the National Socialist State: The Cathedral in Quedlinburg as a Cult and Consecration Site*

Introduction

In mid-October 1935, a conference took place on the initiative of the National Socialist committee for culture in Quedlinburg.[1] The subject of this meeting was the planning of the thousandth anniversary of King Heinrich I (919–936), who has ever since played a role in the formation of myths and – from the nineteenth century onwards – was the subject of Romantic national fantasies.[2] SS-Brigade-führer (Brigade Leader) Reischle, the head of the Race and Settlement Department of the SS, learned from his colleague SS-Unterscharführer (Junior Squad Leader) Alfred Thoss of the festival plans of the mayor of Quedlinburg and NSDAP member Karl Selig. Thoss had received the instructions to write a biography on King Heinrich[3] and had taken part in the meeting. The Quedlinburg millennium anniversary, which had been celebrated with many references to Heinrich I, had already been celebrated in 1922.[4] Therefore Heinrich's millennium celebration, which according to SS member Reischle was "propaganda that was absolutely a present sent from heaven", was well prepared. In Reischle's view, "... through the practical organisation of the festival we can achieve in one fell swoop, what otherwise could only arduously be forced in via other propaganda methods".[5] Reischle recommended that his superior urgently seek the influence of the SS in the preparation and organisation of the celebrations. The Quedlinburg collegiate church offered its services for the "development of the Germanic heritage" because Heinrich I, who was buried under the monastery, was claimed to be the ancestor of the National Socialist movement. The cathedral in Braunschweig with its memorial to Heinrich der Löwe (Henry the Lion) and the monastery church in Enger as the presumed burial site of Widukind, the eighth century leader of the Saxons baptised in 785, also made such claims. These myths came from a time that was stylised by the Middle Ages, which were not completely but nevertheless heavily influenced by Christianity[6], and placed in the ostentatious National Socialist calendar of festivals.[7]

Heinrich I, the founder of *regnum orientalis Franciae* (Eastern Frankish Kingdom), with his famous "house rules" from 929 did not only achieve the introduction of individual succession but also the establishment of the monarchy as an important integration factor for the unity of the Kingdom.[8] This dynastical new beginning[9] and the internal policy of alliances of Heinrich I[10] were actually part

---

*   First published in German as 'Neuheidnische Religiosität und Protestantismus im NS-Staat: Der Dom zu Quedlinburg als Kult- und Weihestätte der SS' in *RSG* 1 (2000), 145–188.

of a meaningful break with tradition on the road to the "developing unity of the German nation"[11]. That after his election to King[12], Heinrich I declined Arch Bishop Heriger of Mainz's offer of a blessing[13] may to some extent be explained by the fear that the Pope wanted to make his valid claims to collaboration with the King[14]. However, the Carolingian tradition was so strong that a "a concept of Kaiserhood without Rome" would have been unable to gain a foothold.[15]

Heinrich's *Königspfalz* (King's palatinate or court) in Quedlinburg[16], which is probably identical to the "villa quae dicitur Quitligaburg"[17], is a valley settlement[18]. The function of the chapel, which belonged to every royal court, was probably fulfilled by the old Church of St Wiperti.[19] Possibly around 929, Heinrich moved the King's seat to the sand stone cliffs north of the Wiperti Court, to the castle, which was already expanded.[20] There was also a church in this new fortified palace. It was named after her patron St Peter. After his death in Memleben in 936 the corpse of Heinrich "was taken by his sons to the town of Quedlinburg and buried in the Church of St Peter before the alter to the sound tears and lamentations from many tribes"[21]. Next to the Wigbert patronage in the valley there was also a Peter patronage on the *Pfalzburg* (palatinate castle), which with the foundation of the convent by Heinrich's widow Matilda was made into the patronage of Servatius and put the St Peter patronage in second place.[22] The convent on the mount, which the Queen lead as the abbess, had already existed as a canon monastery. It presence guaranteed constant prayers over the King's grave and as such provided an important precondition for the Heinrich's burial there.[23] The canons moved from the monastery in the King's court in the valley near to the old Wigberti church. This lead to a double patronage of the church by the Confessor Wigbertus and the Apostle Jacobus. Matilda's great grandson Otto III moved the palace once again from the mountain into a valley[24] and also gave the convent on the mountain the right to mint its own coins in addition to its market and customs rights.[25] Matilda's granddaughter, the daughter of Otto I, was also named Matilda and was introduced in 966 as abbess (966–999) by her grandmother.[26] She allowed work to begin on the building of a bigger convent church.[27] Her successor Adelheid I (999–1043) finished the new building and fitted the old convent church with a crypt. In 1021 the new church was consecrated. A blaze in 1070 destroyed all the buildings on the castle mountain, including the church. The new building, which was finished in 1129, included the old Heinrich Church as a crypt.[28] At various excavations and attempts at restoration in 1756, 1869 and 1877/78 only a few remains of Heinrich were ever found, whereas the sarcophagus of his wife Matilda was effectively preserved.

I.   From the Saint Servatii cathedral to the "King Heinrich Hall"[29]

Heinrich I appeared to be an ideal ancestor for "national Unity" for the National Socialist cultural activity and its cultivation of the "heritage of ancestors".[30] It was his kingdom that the "actions of Adolf Hitler" made possible once again.[31] On Heinrich's grave in the crypt of the so-called "cathedral" of the St Servatii Church in Quedlinburg "a grand memorial service" was to be held on 2 July 1936. It was, according to the wishes of local dignitaries, "to be held as a Reich event"[32]. As a result of this occasion the close-by Wiperti Court, the former royal estate of Heinrich I was to be declared as "Reich's hereditary court" and to be extended into a "national *Thingstätte*" (thingstead)[33]. Finally a festival theatre week was suggested, which was to be organised by the town of Quedlinburg. Otherwise the summer equinox, which occurred shortly before, was to be celebrated as an empire-wide prelude to the millennium celebrations and this opportunity was to be taken to light a permanent stove fire at the Reich's hereditary court. To put their ambitious project into practice the Reich propaganda ministry along with press, radio and film was to support the festivities. The culture planners in Quedlinburg needed urgent financial support from Berlin. Soon it turned out that the initiators had completely transferred their task over to the SS. Mayor Karl Selig, who contacted several times a SS-Obersturmführer (Senior Storm Leader), who came from Quedlinburg[34], "announced that, according to Reichsführer SS (Reich Leader) Himmler's orders the SS and the town of Quedlinburg ought to be the sole bearers of the costs of the Heinrich I millennium celebration"[35].

From a detail draft for a programme for 2 July 1936 can be seen that the thousandth anniversary of Heinrich I's death was initially to be celebrated with a state ceremony. Afterwards the town and the SS planned a rally in the market place of Quedlinburg. Finally the Wiperti Court, the old royal estate of Heinrich I, was to be converted by a celebratory declaration to an "SS settlement" and the St Wiperti Church, under its German name St Wigbert's Church was put into the "charge of the SS".[36] Additionally, the dilapidated farm had to first be bought[37] from its owner, ret. cavalry captain Ernst Baentsch[38]. On the evening of the first day the premiere of the celebratory play "Heinrich I" was planned, which at the time did not exist and thus still had to be written. The SS Main Security office favoured Eberhard Künig (1871–1949) as author. He was a well-known national author, who had made his name[39] with Germanophile heroic epics such as "Wielant der Schmied" (Wielant, the blacksmith)[40] and "Dietrich von Bern"[41]. However, Reichsführer (Reich Leader) Heinrich Himmler, who had very much enjoyed Bauer's theatre piece[42], saw to it that the poetic SS-Obersturmführer (Senior Storm Leader) Heinrich Bauer was given the task of writing the play[43].

The Leitmotif to be incorporated was Heinrich's actions to overcome the unimportant episode of the Carolingian and to bring together the biggest Germanic tribes in "a voluntary, i. e. blood-connected unity".[44] "As such the Nordic Kingdom of Heinrich stood against the Southern Oriental Empire."[45]

"A highlight of the celebratory play was *Der Bauer Heinrich* (Heinrich the farmer)[46], who was fluent in bird language and standing firmly on his *Odal* homestead, turned down the offer of a coronation from the Pope because he takes his rights and his job from a higher hand than the Pope's. Heinrich established and organised the *Wehrmacht* (*7 Heerschilde*). Matilda was not portrayed as a saint made in Rome but as a German woman. In view of her virtues the sequined gold of the halo, given by Rome becomes a meaningless nothing. The restless internal activity of Heinrich as a duke of the Germans (in the military and judicial); the purposeful freeing of the Empire outwards; the rule of the King over the Church. The state of the Germans, established in the cogitations blood and soil."[47]

The second day was to begin with an open-air concert from the SS band on the market place in Quedlinburg. On the afternoon, a ceremonial tournament was to be carried out by the SS, horse riders associations and the Reich defence forces of Quedlinburg. The crowning finale was to be a "good concert" (Händel, Haydn etc.).[48]

Since at the meeting between the town and the SS on 9 January 1936 only the deputy major and the cultural departmental head[49], Boisly, could take part, Mayor Selig wrote on 23 January to SS-Hauptsturmführer (Head Storm Leader) Weigel, who was working on the matter, and suggested a full week of festivities in the name of Heinrich, probably in order to remain in charge of the festivities. As a new element he named the opening of the *König-Heinrich-Brücke* (King Heinrich bridge, previously known as *Bahnhofsbrücke*, station bridge), a musical hour of consecration in the cathedral, a district role call of the NSDAP in the district of Magdeburg-Anhalt, as well as the meeting of the Land's farming community and the National Socialist teachers' association. Additionally, he wanted to organise the first Reich meeting for German folklore.[50] A note from Weigel in a file from 24 January 1936 proves that a whole host of important local figures, such as Carl Harke, the editor of the National Socialist *Landpost* weekly, wanted to distinguish themselves with the Heinrich celebrations and did not want the preparations for the event to be taken out of their hands.[51]

On 3 March 1936, the head of the Race and Settlement Department of the SS commanded the procurement of the "King's court of Heinrich I" to make it into a place of consecration and to be converted into a SS-settlement.[52] Besides, Himmler desired that discussions with the parish begin on the subject of the acquisition of Heinrich I's crypt.[53] A few weeks later Himmler ordered that it would be limited to the preparation of the Wipeti crypt and Heinrich's crypt and altogether give the Heinrich celebrations a smaller remit.[54] At the beginning of April, the SS discovered that Heinrich's crypt did not belong to the church but rather to the Prussian State. As a result it was decided, "to make an agreement with the state, that the care and cultivation of the burial place of King Heinrich would be entrusted to the SS instead of the church"[55]. In the middle of April, a meeting took place at Tegernsee, between Himmler, Hauptsturmführer (Head Storm Leader) Grau from the Main Armed Forces Personnel Section and the SS-Untersturmführer (Junior Storm Leader) Max Schmidt, who was in charge of the Race and Settlement Department. It was decided that Grau was to be responsible for the design of the celebration and Schmidt for the rearrangement of the two crypts.[56] Already on 30 April the SS work staff, which had been gathered together in the meantime, could report on the preparation of the Heinrich ceremony that the "negotiation for the repair work on the two crypts in Quedlinburg ... had achieved a very favourable result"[57]. In regard to the cathedral the SS, according to the report, had mutually negotiated with the responsible superintendent, Johannes Schmidt (1873–1954). A leashing contract on the Wiperti Crypt was signed with Baentsch for a period of thirty years.[58]

At the end of April 1936, the deputy major, Boisly, addressed Untersturm-führer (Junior Storm Leader) Schmidt and asked him to consider whether the small crypt of Heinrich was right place for the organisation of a state ceremony "with speeches and some musical frame"[59]. Upon which he suggested that state ceremony should take place inside the cathedral itself. "One cannot imagine a more beautiful royal hall from the early Germanic period than this mighty flat roofed construction with an amazing abundance of Germanic symbols on all capitals and wall ornamentation. The altar can be taken out without any problem."[60] After the ringing of the bells, a slow movement from the *"Kaiserquartett"* by Haydn, further musical performances, the recital from Paul Ernst's book on *"Die Sachsenkaiser"*[61] (the emperors of the Saxons) the official speech and a movement from Bach's "Brandenburg concerto" was to sound. "During this movement the Führer arises ... and proceeds into the crypt to the burial place of Heinrich I, whilst those present arise. After laying a wreath the Führer leaves the crypt through the Gothic gate."[62] Himmler's great interest in the proceedings is illustrated by the fact that during the renovation of the crypts Untersturmführer (Junior Storm Leader) Max Schmidt had to convey to the Land's curate privy "the special wishes of the Reich Leader of the SS"[63] and that in mid-May Himmler closely examined the planned redesign of the burial place.[64]

From the extensive plans for the festivities on 2 and 3 July 1936, there only remained the military presentation of SS units of altogether approximately 1,200 men, and the state ceremony.[65] The play, which was especially written for the occasion and gave a religious national interpretation of events, was omitted. However, the author of the play, Heinrich Bauer, was still ignorant as of 5 June 1936.[66] The superintendent of the church district of Quedlinburg, Johannes Schmidt, informed Untersturmführer (Junior Storm Leader) Schmidt on 27 June that the Church parish was to organise a celebratory service in the cathedral on the occasion of the King Heinrich memorial celebration and the chairman of the Prussian Church committee, Johannes Eger[67], would be present. Eger was to give the sermon.[68] Schmidt invited SS-Untersturmführer (Junior Storm Leader) Schmidt to the service as one of the guests of honour.

The Quedlinburg engineer, Erich Keil, who was first brought in on 7 May on the recommendation of Selig, judged everything about the renovation of the two crypts as well as various excavations until mid-May 1936. He claimed that the planned action has been "actually only a more or less confused churning up"[69]. Despite his disability, Keil had declared himself willing to work on an hourly wage because he had held an active interest in the history of Quedlinburg for years. One night a stone pillar in the Wiperti crypt was damaged and as a result Max Schmidt fired Keil with immediate effect, although it was not part of his duties to keep the building site under surveillance.[70] Despite his understandable anger Keil accurately judged the building measures of the SS: Until today the SS excavations are found to be "amateur-like".[71]

Since Hitler himself did not appear the centre of the Heinrich celebrations 1936, the main focus of the celebration was the commemorative speech by Himmler and the consecration of the flag by the Reichsjugendführer (Reich Youth Leader), Baldur von Schirach.[72] A decorated copy of Himmler's speech was printed afterwards and sold to the visitors of the Wiperti crypt. Opposite the title there was a photo featuring Party and State in the nave of the cathedral in front of the entrance to Heinrich's crypt. In the foreword of the SS-guide d'Alquen it read:

"It is no longer a church in the normal sense of the word, it is a house of God, a *festival hall of an almighty omnipresent Creator,* in which we upright and proudly enter. Down in the simple crypt ... SS-men stand like iron statues, like the loyal knights of the courageous Lord, with their helmeted heads bowed, in their hands the rifle to keep watch ... . And as an outward sign that the chain will never break from Heinrich, who laid the ground of the Reich from typical Germanic strength, above us ... the Youth Leader of the German Reich consecrates the banner of the forthcoming ... . They often want to simply label us heathens out of misunderstanding and foolishness. If they had wanted to see, the would have experienced true German devoutness, which corresponds to *our way* and *our* belief."[73]

Himmler presented Heinrich as a "Germanic personality", as the "generous farmer of his people"[74], who in his actions against the "Carolingian-Christian methods of government" had re-erected the "principle of loyalty to the duke and his followers to one another"[75]. Under this direction he was able to unite the Reich and win back the lost territories in the West and predominantly in the East. One of Heinrich's harshest critics in this reconsolidation work was the Church and "the Princes of the Church, who in their politicising did not shy away from assassination"[76]. "There were still the open wounds of the radical and bloody introduction of Christianity everywhere. The Reich was weakened on the inside by the ceaseless claims to power of the Prince Bishops and the interference of the Church in worldly matters ... . At his election to King ... he rejected the anointment from the Church and with it testified before all Teutons by the clever recognition of the current state of things that it was not his will to tolerate Church powers influencing political matters in Germany during his reign."[77]

Mathilde, who was "old Widukind's great-granddaughter"[78], represented in the eyes of Himmler "a prime example of German womanhood"[79] in so far that the "devout convictions" of the Queen did not "hinder" Heinrich I.[80] Himmler concluded that Heinrich would be best honoured in "that for Germany, for Germania we in thoughts, words and deeds loyally serve the man, who after a thousand years re-established the human and political heritage of King Heinrich, our Führer Adolf Hitler."[81] With this anti-Church interpretation and the emphasis on the continuity from Heinrich I to Hitler, not solely in relation to the "the re-germanisation of the Germanic *Lebensraum* in the East"[82] Himmler simply reiterated the basic message of the two officially supported works by Thoss and Franz Lüdtke.[83] Although contemporary medievalists[84] contradicted these two works, they determined the public image of Heinrich in the National Socialist State. Himmler's understanding of history as "ritually celebrated ... visualisation of historical examples"[85] in relation to Heinrich I, however, had a personally tainted religious tone: Against the backdrop of his belief in rebirth and Karma[86], Himmler saw himself as the reincarnation of Heinrich, which was constantly claimed by SS-Obergruppenführer (Senior Group Leader) Karl Wolff and other loyal followers from his inner circle.[87]

By the end of July 1936, the Quedlinburg SS units had taken over the care and surveillance of the chapel on the royal estate, which became evident by the provisional visiting rules, which were formulated by SS-Untersturmführer (Junior Storm Leader) Max Schmidt.[88] However, this caused the SS great difficulties, as they had to find suitable men among their ranks for the voluntary guarding and giving guided tours.[89] In the end, a new position for the planning of these posts had to be established in the Settlement Department, which SS-Hauptscharführer (Head Squad Leader) Gerhard Fischer was designated to after a period of indecision.[90]

On 10 July, Second Lieutenant Schmidt wrote to inform Superintendent Schmidt that the care of Heinrich's crypt was still not arranged and gave him provisional instructions on the "worthy" treatment of the memorial. The visitors to the cathedral should only be allowed in via the new wrought iron doors in front of the crypt, there should be no meetings held in the crypt and no lighting of candles. For the "maintenance of worth and order"[91] on the main days of visiting Schmidt offered Superintendent Schmidt a SS guard. A real or supposed complaint from the verger about the large amount of visitors and their "improper" behaviour was used by Schmidt as an occasion to instruct SS-Standortführer (Local Leader) Warch, "to have the church-cum-castle supervised during high season"[92].

The first dispute with the lord of the manor occurred when he in the company of guests and his hound, which ran after him, visited the Wiperti crypt. As a result the guard temporarily shut the entrance to the chapel from the estate.[93] The confiscation of memorial postcards of the Wiperti crypt from local book stores lead to further discrepancies.[94] In regard to the photographic images of Heinrich's crypt, the SS proceeded with more caution. However, even in this case they demanded that to take new photos a special permit must be acquired from the SS. The SS received some of the profit from the sale of the new pictures and written materials, which were authorised by the SS. Initially, there was a high number of visitors; 7,416 visitors to the old chapel in July, but this quickly subsided. In the first half of November only 174 people visited the "place of consecration of the German nation"[95].

Despite his not always pleasing experiences with the SS, Mayor Selig clearly wanted to establish further contact with the SS and had Untersturmführer (Junior Storm Leader) Max Schmidt ask Himmler, whether he would be so kind as to receive an honorary citizenship, that was offered to him by the town Quedlinburg.[96] At the beginning of May 1937, Selig received an answer in the affirmative[97], but on 11 May 1937 SS-Gruppenführer (Group Leader) Wolff informed SS-Obersturmführer (Senior Storm Leader) Rolf Höhne that Himmler was "not in agreement with the suggestion and requested that no further steps in this direction be made"[98]. In the end, Himmler was, nevertheless, happy to accept the award of an honorary citizen of the town of Quedlinburg.[99] The Heinrich celebration in 1937 had been chosen as the occasion of the bestowal of the honorary citizenship.[100] The document praised him as a "fighter for the new national evaluation of German history"[101]. Himmler had anyway intended to attend the midnight hour on 1 July 1937[102], in which the skeleton of Heinrich that was supposedly found during the excavation, was laid to rest next to that of the Queen in the cathedral crypt[103]. The head of the regional administrative district, Rudolf Jordan, promised to be willing to manage "a tremendous pilgrimage of the military formations"[104]. After the celebrations of 1936, the work staff department for the preparation of the Heinrich celebrations to Himmler was not disbanded. Instead it continued to make plans.

At the end of August 1936, the SS seized the convenient opportunity to purchase the royal estate.[105] The air force claimed 100 acres of the estate for the extension of the airfield in Quedlinburg, besides an aircraft production company, the *Junkerswerk* from Dessau, claimed a further 400 acres for the establishment of the planned propeller works. With the 1,000 remaining acres the estate could no longer economically function as a large enterprise. SS-Untersturmführer (Junior Storm Leader) Schmidt suggested to Himmler the rebuilding of the whole estate with a mortgage of 550,000 RM (*Reichsmark*) and afterwards the sale of 400 acres to the industrial plant for 320,000 RM (i. e. 800 RM per acre).[106] Schmidt had discovered from Mayor Selig that the *Junkerswerk* was said to be prepared to pay such a horrendous sum.[107] However, as there was no money for the project, Himmler ordered the developments to be watched further and at the right moment to induce the air force, "to also buy the remaining parts of the estate and then leave it to us, so that the royal estate can be acquired by us without the use of money"[108]. Yet it soon became clear that the *Junkerswerk* was not prepared to pay the price named by Selig so they built their factory near to Bernburg.[109] There was not enough money to fulfil the plans of the SS.

In the middle of October 1937, Max Schmidt reported to the Personal Staff (personal headquarters) of Himmler that the Reichsstatthalter (Reich Governor) Jordan supported the establishment of a *König-Heinrich-Gedächtnis-Stiftung* (King-Heinrich-memorial-foundation).[110] It was hoped that Hitler would be the founder of the foundation in the name of the NSDAP. At the beginning of November 1937, Rolf Höhne told Schmidt about *Ahnenerbe e. V.* (society for research and teaching of ancestral heritage).[111] It was the "culture department" of the SS and Himmler had transferred the handling of the *König-Heinrich-Gedächtnis-Stiftung* to it.[112] At the King Heinrich celebrations on 1 and 2 July 1938 the establishment of the foundation was made public[113], without the request for the approval of the foundation and the acquisition of its legal capacities having been submitted[114]. Himmler and the *Gesellschaft zur Pflege und Föderung deutscher Kulturdenkmäler* (society for the care and promotion of German cultural monuments) were to be the responsible bodies. The foundation should be secured as financially independent thanks to profits and donations. For this reason for the Heinrich celebration in 1939 all mayors from towns that had a special connection to Heinrich were invited. During the first meeting of the *König-Heinrich-Gedächtnis-Stiftung* on 1 July 1939, Selig revealed to the other town mayors, which had been admitted to the foundation, the fixed sum that each town should pay.[115] A number of towns, including Merseburg, were doubtful and in the following period either did not fulfil their imposed commitments or released themselves from the membership.[116]

In the spring of 1938, renovation work began on the cathedral.[117] According to the plans of the curator the renovations were to cost approximately 120,000 RM.[118] Before the end of 1940, the idealistic curator had spent 180,000 RM.[119]

All suggestions were taken from a focal point of history: "The most essential for us ... is," according to Höhne, "that from this church a King Heinrich cathedral will be created, which is there for all Germans, without them having to commit themselves to a denomination."[120] The architectural way towards this goal was envisaged both by the National Socialist ideologists and the monument conservator[121] as a re-romanisation of the complete church. Through the renovations, which continued until 1940, the interior received "the aesthetic effect of a dramatically strictness" and a "monumentality"[122].

In regard to the ritual organisation the Heinrich celebrations 1939 in the newly redesigned cathedral was without doubt the high point of the celebrations in the years between 1936 and 1944.[123] For the first time, Himmler's chief staff office (Adjudantur) had decided the order and content of the celebrations[124], to which 129 guests of honour were invited. The meticulously planned sequence of events consisted of meaningfully staged symbolic acts, in which military pomp prevailed. It also included the roll call of the concentration camp guards of the SS elite officers' training school in Braunschweig with the slogan "King Heinrich – Greater Germany!" and the parade of the guard. The standard, the party flag and the flags of the party's subdivisions took position and entered the cathedral lead by the guards. The cathedral had been redecorated as a Germanic royal hall: It was decorated with royal blue velvet, the seals of the towns in Lower Saxony and the coats of arms of the "Quedlinburg Lineage"[125], provisional plaques of lineage hung on the walls, the side transept was adorned with flowers and green ribbons, in the high choir gallery hung a Swastika flag flanked by two SS flags. Between Heinrich's court and the cathedral SS men formed a torched guard; as Himmler left the Wiperti chapel the bells began to ring and the organ began to play, which was transmitted outside of the church with the help of loud speakers. On the various places of memorial Himmler, Jordan and the mayors of the "Heinrich towns" laid oak or rather pine wreaths and oak branches. Simultaneous to the laying of wreaths, a gun salute was fired by the honorary company. "After the wreaths had been laid (quiet but audible) organ music leads into the National Socialist German national anthem and the Horst Wessel Song. While the songs of the nation play, everyone in the crypt should remain silent."[126] Since the lighting effects played a particular role, the cathedral was floodlit and a large part of the celebratory programme was postponed until the night. During the festivities in "King Heinrich's cathedral" large wood fires were lit on the heights around Quedlinburg and on the rim of East Harz Mountains. On the afternoon, the SS-liturgists integrated a celebration for the poet Klopstock in his house of birth. As such they also incorporated another son of Quedlinburg, born on 2 July 1724, into the ancestral heritage. In the castle the consecration of King Heinrich memorial room also occurred. A wall painting from Wilhelm Petersen (Elmshorn)[127], a specially painted image of King Heinrich hung in the memorial room. It showed Heinrich I on his royal estate Bodfeld, where his warriors handed over imprisoned Hungarian princes. Sketches by the artist were presented to Himmler and Jordan. In the anteroom of the memorial hall articles were exhibited that the director of the Quedlinburg museum, Karl Schirwitz, had collected during excavations. On 2 July, the festival was ended with a ceremonial tattoo in the evening.

After 1940, Himmler no longer personally took part in the ceremony in the Wiperti crypt and the cathedral. SS-Obergruppenführer (Senior Group Leader) Heißmeyer in 1940, SS-Gruppenführer (Group Leader) Panke between 1941–43[128] and in 1944 SS-Gruppenführer (Senior Group Leader) and chairman of the government (Regierungspräsident) Dietrich Klagges were present on his behalf.[129] Also due to the shortage in supplies because of the war, the celebrations became more modest and shorter. Selig received little help from outside, thus he always had to improvise.[130] On 29 July 1940, the foundation of *König-Heinrich I.-Gedächtnis-Stiftung,* which had its seat in Berlin, was approved by the decision of the Prussian state ministers.[131]

As a result of the war, the personal staff of Himmler were increasingly losing interest in the places of ritual worship; many of those responsible for them found themselves on the front. Only Mayor Selig, who in the meantime had been promoted to SS-Sturmbannführer (Storm Unit Leader) and was a bearer of the death's head ring that was bestowed on him by Himmler, unwaveringly continued to represent the interests of the Heinrich memorial and the Heinrich foundation, of which he was the acting manager.[132] The Land curate, assistant head of department Hiecke, also worked on the plans for the decoration of the cathedral.[133] However, it was not to the satisfaction of Selig, who critically commented that Hiecke had "established far too many correlations in relationship to the Church decoration"[134]. In comparison, Selig had completely engulfed himself in the Nazi worldview and asked for guidelines on the performance of marriage consecrations, funeral ceremonies and naming ceremonies.[135] However, the training office did not answer his request.[136] Therefore, there were still relatively few ritual ceremonies in the usurped church. Every year on 9 November, the NSDAP organised a ceremony for the fallen of the movement[137] and some district party group leaders used the cathedral as a ceremonial hall on the occasion of the promotion of boys from the German Youth (the junior division of the Hitler Youth) in the Hitler Youth.[138] At such enlistment ceremonies of duty the organisers of Hitler Youth sounded the bells, without contacting the superintendent beforehand. It was pointed out in a protest letter to Selig, "that the church bells and the sound mechanism are the property of the church parish"; therefore the organiser should have "contacted us ..., if the use of the church bells were desired."[139] In response, Selig wrote a harsh letter to the responsible Hitler Youth Leader, through which it came to be known that the Hitler Youth had already often been conspicuous in the form of disruption of services and the "independent use of church property"[140]. What Selig himself thought of the incident also became clear: "Alone from the party disciplinary viewpoint one must refrain from causing difficulties with the church in the current climate. Its representatives, in my opinion, exaggerate about unimportant things and attempt to use them for their own advantage and 'concerns'. How often must I in the interest of peace and safety as a political speaker keep my mouth shut in the face of the representatives of the church and swallow that which I am dying to say."[141]

In contrast, the NSDAP-district leader pointed out that in the past few years "the Party [had rung] the bells at all the ceremonies in the cathedral". The fact that only now the protest had been made, "is the best proof that our celebration of confirmation already decidedly causes some damage"[142]. When the Party with its subdivisions wished to celebrate in the cathedral, not only did it disregard the church's rights but it had also failed to inform the foundation.[143] For example the NSDAP, without the knowledge of the foundation, had celebrated the Führer's birthday on 20 April 1941. However, there was a negative consideration against a clarification of ownership in favour of the SS in case the Prussian state would not pay for the renovations.[144]

II.   The Usurpation of the cathedral by the SS

As Mayor Selig took the initiative for the King Heinrich celebrations and Major Boisly insistently encouraged the SS not only to use the crypt but also the inside of the church for the event[145], the difficulties on the part of the St Servatii Cathedral with its 6,000 souls were not taken account of. The parish church was prepared to provide the church for the Heinrich celebrations at the beginning of July in 1936 and 1937 without any problems. But what was the internal stance that the clergy and the lay members took regarding National Socialism?

A record from the pastors convent of the Church district Quedlinburg on 28 September[146] infers that the clergy, who met there, on the whole, i. e. Heinrich Rendtorff and Paul Althaus, sympathised[147] with the concept of the *christlich-deutsche Bewegung* (Christian-German movement)[148]. After the discussion following Pastor Büschel's (of Neinstedt) presentation entitled: *"Vor welche Aufgaben wird die Verkündigung des Evangeliums durch die völkische Bewegung gestellt?"* (What tasks does the preaching of the Gospel by the national movement face?) it was ascertained that the guiding principles, which were propounded in the presentation, found general support. This thesis claimed that the national movement turned with justification "against money and power greedy internationalism" and fought for the "rights and purity of the national traditions".[149] In contrast, a "cultivation of racial hatred" was rejected and the Bible was highlighted as being the centre of Christian belief. In connection to the coming Church elections those gathered welcomed that a "big political movement approved of the Church and allowed its organisations to take part in Church life" and that this movement wanted to place itself "in the service of the church". However, they also expressed their concern about the "politicising of the Church".[150] Even after the seizure of power by Hitler it did not appear as though a radicalisation of the pastors was occurring. Only Pastor Pipphardt (from Quedlinburg) proved to be very politically engaged as a member of the NSDAP, its advisor to the district Leader on church issues and the district Leader of the religious movement *Deutsche Christen* (DC, German Christians). His political commitments "caused a certain tension and irritation among the pastors of the church district"[151]. At the pastor's convent in mid-June 1933, the "joyful position of approval of the national revolution in fraternal circles" was assumed. However, it was also stressed that the Church did not undergo any change in terms of content as a result of it, and that a clear difference between the Church and the state concerns had to be maintained. Pipphardt held a presentation on the theme: "*Vor welche Aufgaben werden Kirche und Pfarrer durch die staatliche Neuordnung gestellt?*" (What tasks do the Church and the pastors face as a consequence of the state reform?) Those gathered agreed with the harsh criticism of Liberalism, which Pipphardt preached. However, they did not share the racial emphasis in German Christian theology on a heroic Christianity. In particular, they asked Pipphardt for "a more precise explanation of the much used expression "*artgemäße Verkündigung* (appropriate preaching)"[152].

The exact opposite position to Pipphardt was represented by Rudolf Hein[153] (1892–1955), the second pastor of the cathedral parish of Quedlinburg. He did not only belong to the Sydower Brotherhood, the *Pfarrernotbund* (the Pastors' Emergency League) and the extended provincial council of Brethren from the Confessing Church (CC)[154], but he also actively opposed the parish council which was dominated by German-Christians. Thus, after the German Christians' victory in the Church corporation, he decorated the church flag on the offices with mourning ribbons, directed attacks against the German Christians from the pulpit, handed out flyers after the services and formed a church house group. In his actions he judged, according to his own testimony, not only the secondary school teacher Krause but also the Bishops Hossenfelder and Peter as well as senior consistory councillor Wienecke to be "teachers of deceit"[155]. As a result, the German Christian fraction of the cathedral parish applied to the Church leadership in Magdeburg for Hein's transfer.[156] In both the case of Pipphardt and of Hein Superintendent Johannes Schmidt[157], who was a member, the provincial chairman, the head of the *Pfarrerkreis* (pastor's circle) (1938) and the chairman (1942) of the ecclesiastic mediation group *Wittenberger Bund*[158], tried to keep things on an even keel and attempted to settle the arguments. However, Hein continued with his opposition in 1934 and in the years afterwards[159]. He expressed criticism in front of both parish and party members on the "movement of 'modern paganism'"[160], to which leading National Socialists also belonged. He judged Rosenberg's "*Mythus des 20. Jahrhunderts*" (The Myth of the twentieth Century) as "dark mysticism". Some of the parish members found his statements to be "anything but German" and informed the consistory in Magdeburg of Hein's actions.[161] At the end of February 1936, the provincial church committee reacted to the complaints and summoned Hein to a discussion at the beginning of March at their offices in Magdeburg.[162] Hein told a member of the provincial church committee that he did not recognise the church committee as the leadership of the church and, therefore, he would not attend the arranged meeting.[163] A letter to the Prussian Protestant Church Board (*Preußischer Evangelischer Oberkirchenrat*, EOK) from the consistory of the province of Saxony described the "case" of Hein a year later. However, he made no recommendation that further measures should be taken. On the relationship between Superintendent Schmidt and Hein the letter read "that Pastor Hein, despite repeated annoyance from the parish and regrettable tactlessness could still retain his office, is thanks to the peaceful and calm manner of Superintendent Schmidt, who as Superintendent and as brother in service at the same church ... had consistently tried to settle misunderstandings and to bridge difficulties with often admirable patience".[164] In his strong official policy of neutrality Schmidt clung to the valid canon law of the official Church and allowed himself to be sworn to Hitler by Bishop Peter on 18 October 1934.[165] Schmidt, as the speaker of the *Wittenberger Bund* ecclesiastic mediation group, maintained good contact with the consistory of the Church Province of Saxony.[166] As the provincial *Bruderrat* (Council of Brethren) allocated Hein a verger, who had studied at the Church foreign seminary in Ilsenburg/Harz[167], Schmidt did not recognise the candidate.[168] The argument about Hein's Confessing Church stance smouldered on. Being the only pastor of the Confessing Church in the ecclesiastical administrative district, he was ever increasingly left out. That was clear for Mayor Selig, who wrote "that you, as a pastor of the Confessing Front, are working against the endeavours of the National Socialist State," and he forbade Hein to enter state schooling facilities.[169] Shortly after, he expanded the ban to all municipally owned property, institutes and organisations.[170] As a result the manager of the town and district hospital refused Hein entry to the clinic.[171] In a letter of complain to the consistory in Magdeburg, Selig explained that Hein's service were currently being observed by the Gestapo and the local police, in particularly because the collection of money for the Confessing Church infringed the *Sammlungsgesetz*.[172] Besides, he read aloud in the service the prayers of intercession of the Confessing Church. In a letter to the consistory Superintendent Schmidt verified Selig's statement.

"Thus, the church relations in Quedlinburg have escalated in an unbearable manner thanks to the unwise, clumsy and unaccommodating behaviour of Pastor Hein. The particularly regrettable thing in all of this is that there is an attitude of resistance against him in further parts of the population, which has negative consequences on the work and position of other clerics in the town. The numerous opponents of the church profit from this. Hein does not have many followers: the number of the total members of the 'Confessing Church' in Quedlinburg is hardly more than 100, of which the majority are women ... . I ask the consistory to take the actions currently possible, so that the work of the Church in Quedlinburg will not suffer great damage".[173]

On the advice of the provincial council of Brethren, Hein had brought a libel claim against Selig to the magistrate court in Quedlinburg because Selig had described him as an "enemy of the state" and as one of the "shady characters of the town" in front of the gathered SS storm troopers.[174] In the court's judgement it was explicitly recognised, "that the description of Pastor Hein as an 'enemy of the state' was accurate"[175]. Selig's harsh words on Hein in front of the storm troops were nevertheless so classified by the court "to have crossed the line of the conservation of justified interest". However, due to the amnesty law (*Amnestiegesetz*) Selig was also not punished in this case.

In November and December 1937, i. e. the time in which the disagreement between Selig and Hein worsened, the wrangle about the cathedral escalated. The parish council of the St Servatii Cathedral had previously allowed its church to be used[176] without any difficulty for the state ceremony on 2 July 1936 with many prominent guests from the state and the party.[177] This was a result of the appropriate applications from Sturmbannführer (Storm Unit Leader) Grau and Mayor Selig. It is true that after the ceremony the regional propaganda leader, Ihlenburg, wanted to persuade Superintendent Schmidt to do without the cathedral in the summer months and prevent the seating from being set out again. However, this suggestion was flatly rejected by Schmidt and he informed the provincial church committee that he feared the Ihlenburg would contact them. Schmidt wrote to the committee claiming "there would be a storm of indignation, should we relinquish the cathedral, be it only for the summer months"[178]. As a result, the Magdeburg consistory called for a report from Schmidt. Superintendent Schmidt complained about the impious treatment of candles, crucifixes and the Bible by the SS men, but realised that "apart from these lamentable events the week-long cooperation between the representatives of the Reich Leadership SS and the parish council was thoroughly unclouded. Neither attacks nor high-handedness had otherwise occurred".[179] All the same, Schmidt still appeared so alarmed by Ihlenburg's intervention and newspaper reports on the conversion of the cathedral into an old Germanic King's Hall that he reminded the consistory of the property rights of the church building.

The consistory addressed "with the consent of the provincial church committee" the Land church committee (*Landeskirchenausschuss* – LKA) of the Old Prussian united state Church (*Altpreußische Union* – ApU) and asked urgently for an "insistent idea from the Reich Leadership of the SS": "It will also be necessary to be extremely careful with the lending of houses of God in the future. In principle houses of God should only be used for religious ceremonies. On no condition may the crucifix or the Bible be removed again."[180] The Land's church committee decided against taking action for the time being.[181]

In summer 1937, everything went smoothly. On the orders of Himmler, Höhne asked Superintendent Schmidt on 20 June 1937 "to place the St Servatii cathedral on the *Schloßberg* in Quedlinburg at the disposal of the Reich Leader of the SS, Himmler, and to allow the church to be decorated as it was in 1936".[182] Due to the short amount of time before the event Höhne asked for a decision per telegram, which he received the following day from the chairman Schmidt of the parish council.[183]

At the time Schmidt informed the SS of the positive decisions of the parish council, he knew nothing of the supposed information, which was being spread by Obersturmführer (Senior Storm Leader) Höhne and Mayor Selig.[184] According to Höhne, Selig had already informed him in April 1937 that the church parish had come to terms with the loss of the cathedral, intended to use the St Blasii Church and it was general knowledge in Quedlinburg, "that with the 2 July [1937] ceremony the cathedral would be transformed into a King Heinrich Hall"[185]. Nevertheless, Höhne reckoned with "a very strong rebellion on the part of the Catholic Church" and asked "to arrange until further notice post surveillance" in the cases of Pastors Schmidt and Hein.[186] In mid-May 1937, Höhne informed the head of the Personal staff, Wolff, that an oral consultation in the Reich Church Ministry had taken place and Minister Hanns Kerrl was going to personally lead the negotiations on the handing over of the cathedral with Himmler. He urgently asked for such negotiations because the situation was extremely favourable at the time. The amount of visitors to the cathedral was so low that the *Gesellschaft zur Pflege und Förderung deutscher Kulturdenkmäler* could, with good reason, call for the handing over of the cathedral. Besides, the inhabitants were already prepared "that on 2 July the cathedral would find its historical acknowledgement thanks to the SS take-over"[187]. However, Himmler informed Höhne through Wolff that "under no circumstances [should] he take any action"[188]. Therefore, at the beginning of June, Höhne asked Mayor Selig to talk to Schmidt and encourage him to do without the cathedral. However, Schmidt rejected Selig's attempts to persuade him and informed him that it was up to the parish council to decide.[189] Due to the excavation work on the cathedral crypt the parish was presently using the St Blasii Church, much to the annoyance of the cathedral verger Sann.[190] When giving guided tours, Sann rebelled by determinedly describing the cathedral as a Christian building for devout Christians, "never spoke of Germanic but always of pagan culture" and left the listener with "the impression that he had been subjected to propaganda speech in the name of Christianity".[191] In the meantime, Selig's initial confidence had left him: he wrote to Höhne that "the whole affair would certainly be a very difficult birth".[192] As a result, Höhne established contact with Julius Stahn, the assistant head of department[193] from Reich Church Ministry and found him to be a willing cooperation partner. On 13 December, Obersturmführer (Senior Storm Leader) Höhne recorded, in a file note, a message from Stahn on 10 December. According to the message, Kerrl had "essentially given his consent to the plans prepared by Stahn and me"[194]. The cathedral could be cleared in the coming weeks.

On the same day the good news from Stahn arrived, Höhne applied to Schmidt for the loan of the cathedral for a ceremony on 18 and 19 December "on the occasion of the reception of the Italian consulate general Renzetti"[195]. He combined the message with this piece of information that, in agreement with the Reich Church Ministry, the pews would be definitively removed and in their place 200 chairs would be installed in the cathedral. Schmidt replied in an official machine written letter, that he had already negotiated with Lütcke, the manager of the *Klopstock-Gesellschaft*, and had given him permission to use the cathedral for a ceremony. However, the removal of the pews and the decorations in the cathedral, as was done for the King Heinrich celebrations was "to [his] regret impossible, in consideration of the service on the next day"[196]. Besides, Höhne pointed out that on question of seating in the cathedral the Protestant Church Board in Berlin was responsible, not the Reich Church Ministry. But Stahn, the expert from the Reich Church Ministry, had even personally spoken with him the day before[197] and he had not mentioned an instruction to permanently replace the pews with chairs. In view of the Christmas season, a change in the seating was not even to be considered. "We have proved that we are ready to enter every cooperation."[198] Enclosed with the official letter to Höhne was a hand written letter. It read: "I am very sorry that I cannot give you any other answer than the enclosed. Please be ensured that I also would have carried out the wishes of the SS, of which I have been a supportive member of for four years, if it were possible. Until now I have willing carried out your wishes, which has lead to reproaches on the part of certain people that I went too far."[199]

To Stahn, Schmidt referred to the small congregation that was expected guests and emphasised: "I see in the planned preparation the first step, of which more will follow, in order to render the decision on the cathedral a fait accompli."[200] At the same time, Schmidt drew attention to the church-political consequences of such measures: "If against the will of the parish something was carried out by the SS, that would bring about tremendous annoyance in church circles. As such it would both gravely endanger the promising beginnings of church peace, which I began in Quedlinburg, and give the confessing front a new impulse."[201]

As a result, Höhne retracted his latest demands and contented himself with a ceremony in the crypt[202]. However, he kept plans to take over the cathedral in the name of the SS. In addition, he developed a make-shift solution in the form of an eight point programme, which envisaged the conjoint use of the cathedral by the parish and the SS. The leadership of the cathedral, as well as the cathedral treasures, should be taken over by the SS and instead of pews moveable chairs should be acquired. A revised version of this agreement[203] was signed on 18 December 1937 by the Reich Church Ministry and Himmler, without the involvement of the St Servatii parish, the consistory or the Protestant Church Board of the Old Prussian united state Church.[204] In mid-January 1938, Stahn wrote to Höhne that due to the "implementation of the matter" there would "be a meeting between the church authorities and our ministry in the near future"[205]. However, Höhne did not wait for the meeting but informed Schmidt on 25 January 1938 that he was coming to Quedlinburg on 27 January "to receive the key and to take possession of the cathedral" and asked for them to have ready the "various inventory lists"[206].

Seven days earlier, Schmidt had taken part in a meeting with the consistory and the EOK.[207] As a result of the conclusions of this meeting he did not feel he had the right to fulfill Höhne's orders.[208] After receiving the letter from Höhne on 27 January 1938, Schmidt rang Werner. The EOK President explained that he did not know the exact details of the agreement between the Reich Church Ministry. However, Schmidt was not by any means empowered to hand over the key "without the instruction of the superior church authorities"[209]. In a further telephone conversation Werner aired "his personal opinion" in that he found it unthinkable to hand over the keys to the treasury and the crypt. Both rooms did not serve church purposes.[210]

Superintendent Schmidt claimed that he had not received the appropriate instructions from further up in the hierarchy and thus refused to hand over the key.[211] As a result, Höhne rang Stahn from the Reich Church Ministry, who immediately contacted the EOK.[212] The EOK President Werner telegraphed Schmidt without delay and ordered him to give Höhne the key to the crypt and the treasury. Because of the limitation of the parish's authority and to insure the continuation of services he arranged a meeting for 29 January.[213] On the very same evening Schmidt gave Fischer[214], who was engaged by Höhne, the relevant keys. However, they were not the keys to the main entrance of the cathedral.[215]

In the EOK Schmidt was given the task of producing a statement for the parish church council on the agreement between the Reich Church Ministry and the SS.[216] Despite of this, the disagreements in Quedlinburg continued, where SS-Untersturmführer (Junior Storm Leader) Fischer with the well-meaning support from Höhne in Berlin, caused the escalation of the conflict through an alarming report from the Quedlinburg "front".[217] He expressed his worries on the whereabouts of the cathedral treasures as well as other valuable objects and he denounced as provocative the sermons of Hein, the pastor from the Confessing Church. Part of Hein's "confessing parish Quedlinburg also belongs to cathedral parish". The parish sent a letter on 28 January 1938 to the president of the EOK, Friedrich Werner and the chairman of the parish council of St Servatii, Schmidt. In the letter they asked, "in the interests of the cathedral parish and protestant Christianity in Germany to fiercely resist [the intentions of the SS] to take the cathedral into its possession"[218].

Schmidt insisted on his position stating that in Werner's telegram there was no talk of the cathedral key and refused to hand it over.[219] As a result, Höhne arranged for Fischer to secretly make a soap copy of the cathedral key, in order to make a proper copy in Halberstadt.[220] In the end it did not get so far because on 6 February, a Sunday, Superintendent Schmidt finally gave Höhne the key to the cathedral "with reservations".[221] On the afternoon of the very same day, Höhne had the black SS flag hoisted up on the church tower.[222] A day later, Höhne told Schmidt that services could continue to take place in the cathedral "on the previous scale". The parish should be made aware of this in the next sermon.[223]

During the meeting on 2 February, the parish council once more emphasised its legal position, of which Schmidt had constantly reminded them since 1936. In its opinion a contract between the Prussian state and the Protestant parish of St Servatii had existed since 1854, which assured the church the sole management and use[224] that could only be annulled by a law but not by an agreement between the Reich Church Ministry and SS. With the exception of the crypt, the committee showed itself unwilling to accommodate the extensive concession in the SS's wishes for use and renovation. Alongside historical and legal grounds, they also argued with a "deep felt irritation ... in Protestant circles in the town"[225]. In his letter, which accompanied the protocol and he sent to Werner, Schmidt emphasised that the parish council did not ignore the realisation that: "also in the area of the notion of God new powers are at work and have been pushing for something new since the radical change [i. e. the Nazi seizure of power]. However, it held the conviction that solely the Führer controls the direction and speed of these developments and it must be up to him to enforce the laws, which he himself has proclaimed."[226]

The ascertainment that it concerned a contract from 29 April 1854 regarding a "defeated legal view" was not to be left to "individual positions or authorities". Hitler had repeatedly explained that the Third Reich was a state founded on the rule of law. Thus, a new legal development could only be decided "by the Führer through the legislation, which he commands". The following day, Schmidt again sent the presidency of the EOK a summary of the developments in the conflict. In it he countered above all the argument that the parish in the preceding years had voluntarily allowed the SS to use the cathedral and therefore it established a sort of customary law. Furthermore he had emphasised from the beginning that "a voluntary signing over of the cathedral was out of the question".[227]

The EOK joined the Reich Church Ministry in its statement of 11 February 1938, which partially incorporated the parish council's protocol[228]. The committee's conception of legality and precautionary explained, "that the parish council's ability to work has not been disturbed by the church political quarrels within the Protestant Church".[229] He went on to explain that it was "internally impossible [for the Protestant parish] to give up it sole right to use of a place of worship for the benefit of a '*Simultaneum*' [i. e. the simultaneous use by two different organisations] with an organisation that rejects Christian teaching, if not actually fights against it ... . The parish may not even give the guided tours through their house of God[230], this cannot be given to a third party, in this case representatives, who have an ideology that rejects Christianity."[231] In his answer on behalf of the Reich Church Ministry, State Secretary Muhs replied on 18 February 1938 that the declaration from the EOK gave him "no occasion to amend the agreement on the joint use of Quedlinburg cathedral, which had been settled with Himmler"[232]. In 1854, it was not a question of a contract but of an act of state sovereignty. In response to the information from the EOK about the incompatibility of the SS with Christianity ideology, Muhs used it as an impassioned laudatory in the SS's struggle against communism: "I must decidedly reject reports of this kind. Those men, who now claim the joint use of this German architectural monument are the very same men, who in the times of great German distress have also stepped forward with body and soul, that this and other German cathedrals have remained and still remain safe from a completely different 'concern', which has been granted to churches in other countries in the most dreadful way."[233]

A guided tour through a German architectural monument, just as a guide through a museum i. e. the treasury, is a matter of the state. Fischer, who in the meantime had been promoted to Obersturmführer (Senior Storm Leader), caused some criticism, even among the ranks of the party, due to his ideological overloaded but historical ignorant tours, which he performed in uniform and with constant references to Himmler.[234] During the cathedral tours, Verger Sann had to "remove all signs, which indicated the current use of the cathedral"[235].

Hans von Dippe, one of the four elders of the St Servatii parish[236] refused to take part in further meetings at the Magdeburg Consistory, which concerned the prevention of the take over of the cathedral by the SS. It appeared to him that "the legal side of the matter [is] now clear" and it "is no longer comparable with my previous opinion ... . I am also aware that a large number of the parish members agree with the use of the church in this way."[237]

In the meantime, Schmidt had organised a letter of solidarity to the consistory in Madgeburg, which had been signed by forty superintendents. In it, Superintendent Schmidt protested against the use of a Christian place of worship: "Even for national celebrations without a Christian character ... we find it incompatible with the honour and dignity of the Christian belief, that a Christian community should hold their service of worship in a space, in which it may have been spoken out against Christianity and the Christian belief on other occasions, where the holy symbols of Christianity are experienced as disturbing and must therefore be tidied away."[238] Shortly after, the mediation group of the *Wittenberger Bund*, which Schmidt belonged to, sent a petition to the EOK as well as the Consistory of the Church district.[239] The petition recommended to abandon all measures until a legally binding decision had been reached by a court. The contemplated changes meant ignoring the wishes which Heinrich I had stated in his last will. Besides, it ought also to be viewed as a disregard of the Christian belief, if during non-Christian ceremonies opinions against Christ and the Christian belief were expressed in a church.

On 26 February 1938, Superintendent Schmidt called on the Magdeburg Consistory and urgently recommended to obtain legal reports. The consistory followed suit and asked the EOK to urgently take the relevant steps.[240] Of the two legal reports which were thus sought by the EOK, the 55 pages long report from Ernst Forsthoff[241], which was in favour of the parish, was missing[242], whilst the paper from Berlin lawyer, Walter Hoepffner, reached the conclusion "with reservations" that the "use of the cathedral [by Himmler] ... fell exclusively within the frame of his sovereign authority, which he is entitled to"[243]. Forsthoff assumed the continuity of law "in the full relationship between the state and the Protestant Church"[244] and based this on article 3 of the constitution of the German Protestant Church (DEK) of 14 July 1933[245] and also Julius Stahn's referral in the introduction to the law on the safeguarding of the German Protestant Church on 24 September.[246] As far as the agreement between the Reich Church Ministry and the SS went, it was considered "an illegal infringement in the *iura in sacra* because they moved into a part of the building that was actually used as a place of worship". As a result of Hoepffner's statement, the superior consistory councilor from Berlin announced that he "not longer whole heartedly believed ... in the possibility of a process like course of action".[247]

On 23 April, Höhne had Fischer inform the owners of the cathedral keys to hand them over because new locks were being installed.[248] In the old locks box spanners were inserted so that the verger, the organist and the employee responsible for heating the church, as well as the two pastors, had to ask Fischer to open the cathedral every time they needed to enter. Fischer never let the key out of his hand again. It was under these circumstances that the parish had to use the St Blasii Church from Easter 1938 onwards. As in the previous years, with permission from Selig, the cantata singing during the children's service still took place on the castle court.[249]

Concerning the episode of the key the SS had acted beyond of the limits of the agreement, which they had made with the Reich Church Ministry. They explained the complete taking over of the Church to the outside world as a consequence of the planned construction works[250], which was backed up by a letter from the Reich Church Ministry[251]. The parish had to use the "dilapidated Blasii church"[252], which, according to Hein, was too small.[253] In May 1938, the ruins of the smashed cathedral pulpit and the cathedral alter turned up in the castle yard[254], where they remained for weeks.[255] Even the "table of honour, with the names of parishioners, who had fallen in the World War" had been removed by the SS.[256] Höhne and his henchman, Fischer, had carried out all the work. Despite his engagement, Himmler dropped Höhne, who gave up his post at *Ahnenerbe e. V.* on 1 August 1938.[257] Fischer and two of his SS helpers from the management of the memorial were conscripted to the *Wehrmacht* on 25 August 1939.

On 31 August 1938, Superintendent Schmidt reported to the consistory that it was no longer possible for him to enter the cathedral due to the missing key. Entry was only possible in the company of the SS.[258] A good year later, Schmidt informed the consistory that "from the previous course of the repair works[259] and from some statements from involved parties"[260] one was given the impression that it was no longer possible for the parish to use the cathedral. Even minor stipulations from the agreement in December 1937 such as a compensation for the parish for the loss of revenue from the guided tours[261] were not met by SS.[262]

Even the EOK did not highly regard the SS's respect for the law and the Nazi state. Since a follow-up of the course of legal action "was not presently recommended because of process and other reasons", the vice-president of the EOK, Loycke, wrote a year later to the Magdeburg Consistory: "The parish has no other option than to wait, whether and according to what circumstances and conditions the state will arrange for the use of the cathedral as a place of worship once the renovations are complete".[263]

In 1941, Schmidt had advised the consistory in a letter not to conscript Pastor Hein as a war pastor. It read: "It is true that he [Hein] is a loyal and enthusiastic pastor and would defiantly prove himself in the individual spiritual welfare, even in the *Wehrmacht.* But his manner of sermons is predominantly educational and less thrilling. It is prevailingly determined with a tone of penitence, it is lacking in the rallying and the joyfulness of the protestant proclamation, which is exactly what a soldier needs. The fluency of the sermon is also missing in certain parts. Apart from all of that, I find it unthinkable to recommend a man to be a war pastor, who as the chairman of the Confessing Church has had repeated conflicts with the secret state police and whose sermons are occasionally listened to by the criminal police."[264] Two and a half years later Hein was dismissed from military service.[265]

At the beginning of the war in 1939, the SS had the cathedral treasures placed to the safe room in the Quedlinburg *Sparkasse* (savings bank) and in July 1942 it was taken to the more bomb proof *Altenburg-Höhle*, a cave situated near the town. On 19 April 1945, the Americans reached Quedlinburg. The mayor led the troops to the cave. Despite being under American observation, it was ascertained on 20 April that in the intervening time the boxes had been opened and important pieces had been stolen from them.[266] An officer from 87 Artillery Battalion, First Lieutenant Joe Tom Meador (1916–1980) had taken some of the treasures and send them to Texas using the armed forces postal service. Thanks to laborious research and expensive legal battles with the inheritors, the treasure was finally returned to Quedlinburg in 1993.

It was not possible to hold Christian services in the Church until 3 June 1945, after the Church had been returned to the parish by the American military government.[267] A note from the EOK on 12 June stated that in the meeting of the Protestant consistory on the same day it was announced "that the cathedral of the Protestant parish of Quedlinburg was to be returned and services were already being to held in it"[268]. On 25 February 1948, the newly finished sarcophagus for the alleged skeleton of Heinrich I, which was made to match Matilda's coffin, was removed from the church, the mortal remains were taken out and were reburied a little later in the place, where they had originally been found. Cathedral verger Sann and Pastor Hein were present at the opening of the coffin and read Psalm 73. The new Superintendent J. Richer, who replaced Schmidt after his retirement on 1 April 1947, asked why the changes were being made. The town master architect answered that it concerned "the restoration to the earlier condition of the crypt and the removal of a Nazi memorial"[269]. Since the effort was not made to acquire an expert check of the results from the SS excavation, it may be assumed that especially the latter reason for the recent changes was the decisive factor: The removal of the National Socialist place of consecration was desired because it was still thought to be possible that former National Socialists and former members of the SS would come to Heinrich's grave as if it were a place of pilgrimage. Superintendent Richter agreed and critically wrote in his report: "The passionate love of the German history is not recognised with all the arbitrary constriction. However, the removal of those constructions, which were used by the Nazis, can never exorcise the historical concepts and the nationalistic feeling from these places. Were it only a question of an object, it would have only needed a simple covering of the apparent coffin."[270]

Conclusion

In the described conflict over the cathedral in Quedlinburg both "religions"[271] were strangely weak. It is true that through lighting effects, "solemn" music[272], "dignified" speeches, collective touched silences, military march-pasts of those in uniform and symbolic actions, such as the consecration of flags and the laying of wreaths, the SS managed to selectively create a civil religious experience of community. However, the basic myth of a German Empire (*Reich*), which was reactivated by Himmler, was not "understood" and "internalised" in its bizarre core as the myth of nation, race, blood and earth, but only in its generally striking cult-like manifestation, which was consumed by its ritual actions. Thus, this myth was incapable of leaving a lasting mental effect. It remained an emotionally moving spectacle, which nevertheless failed to convert three quarters of the SS men.[273] Furthermore, because of the polycentric structure, even in the field of ideology[274], it lacked in common will and probably also in material resources to powerfully drive on the project of the "National Socialist Religion". The eloquent complaints of Mayor Selig verify that the majority of the organisational work was left to him. He had become so involved with the National Socialist state that after the fall of the Third Reich he saw no reason to continue and shot himself during his imprisonment in the US headquarters.[275]

On the part of the Church the main actors were the pastors Hein and Schmidt, who found themselves in very different milieus. One was a stout pastor of the Confessing Church with rather small group of followers, should one believe Schmidt's judgement. He was regarded, probably correctly, as an opponent of the system and the complete opposite of Superintendent Schmidt. Schmidt was a supportive member of the SS, had no essential problem with the National Socialist state and even accepted the myth of the Führer, according to which Hitler had formal legislative power. Upon these facts, Schmidt formed a defence strategy, in that he emphasised that a new development in law could only come from Hitler, "via his order of legislation". An authoritative intervention on the part of Hitler in the case of the cathedral would have consequently been accepted by Schmidt. In contrast, his religious arguments and those from the *Wittenberger Bund* primarily appeared as a means in the struggle to protect the Church's assets. After Schmidt had let the SS use the place of worship in 1936 and 1937 without any religious reservations and according to his own expression they had taken part in "faultless ... cooperation over weeks"[276], the belatedly validated confessional reservations appear to be rather false. His hidden threats that a usurpation of the cathedral would cause considerable unrest among the population corresponded exactly to the fears of the mayor and his friends in the SS, however, in retrospect they proved to be completely unfounded. There was neither mass protests against the neo-pagan use of the church nor did the believers protest against the conversion of the cathedral to an old Germanic cult and consecration site.

In so far the process was not only an example of the spiritual weakness of the Church but it appears as if the Church had very little support among the people. Additionally the conflict verified once more the institutional weakness even in the official Church i. e. in cooperation with the National Socialist State. As a former member of the *Wittenberger Bund* Schmidt had close contact to the Magdeburg Consistory and through this he was capable of drawing the Prussian Church Board on to his side. Nevertheless the Reich Church Ministry simply disregarded the wishes of the thoroughly state-friendly and cooperation willing wing of the Church, whether it was out of conviction or because it shied away from conflict with the SS, remains an open question.

The population found great pleasure in the spectacular hustle and bustle of the SS and accepted the dual level of the celebrations. On the one hand it was an excessive religious celebration of the new elite, in which the population were only extras. On the other hand it provided, particularly during the day, many occasions with the character of a fairground without the "ceremonial" stage-managing in the narrow sense of the word. In contrast, the ceremony nights remained predominantly reserved as a dark mysterious ritual of the SS-elite.

Notes

1   Cf. Report on the conference for the thousand year festivities on 18.10.1935, town archive of Quedlinburg [StA Q], Vorakte XI 362/1, sheets 1–3.
2   Cf. on this as well as on the following (without using church archives): Albrecht Dubiel, König-Heinrich-Feiern in Quedlinburg 1936–1944, dissertation submitted to the history department at the University of Leipzig, Winter Semester 1997/98; Frank Helzel, Ein König, ein Reichsführer und der Wilde Osten, Bielefeld 2004, esp. 175 ff.
3   Cf. A. Thoss, Heinrich I. (919–936). Der Gründer des ersten deutschen Volksreiches, Goslar 1936.
4   Cf. Hermann Lorenz, Werdegang der 1000jährigen Stadt Quedlinburg, Quedlinburg 1925. See also Hans-Hartmut Schauer, Quedlinburg. Fachwerkstadt/Weltkulturerbe, Berlin 1999.
5   Confidential note from Reischle on 24.10.1935, StA Q, 363/I, V. Baul. Veränd., sheets 1–3.

6 Cf. Jan-Holger Kirsch, '"Wir leben im Zeitalter der endgültigen Auseinandersetzung mit dem Christentum." Nationalsozialistische Projekte für Kirchenumbauten in Enger, Quedlinburg und Braunschweig', in Stefan Brakensiek (ed.), Widukind. Forschungen zu einem Mythos (Stadt Enger, Beiträge zur Stadtgeschichte 9), Bielefeld 1997, 33–93. In this series the burial grounds of the Brandenburg Margrave (*Markgraf*) Albrecht the Bear in Ballenstedt is also mentioned. The inscription on his gravestone reads "Der Wegbereiter ins deutsche Ostland" [the trailblazer in the German East], see the illustration in Bernd Gerhard Ulbrich/Sebastian Kaps, Ballenstedt, Dessau 1995, 45. Cf. also Winfried Korf, Ballenstedt. Kloster, Schloß und Schloßbezirk, Munich ²1996, 9. Also see the instrumentalisation of the *Kaiserdome* in Speyer, Worms and Mainz during the Nazi period: Ursula Clemens, 'Deuter Deutscher Geschichte. Die Kaiserdome in Speyer, Worms und Mainz in der NS-Zeit', in Bazon Brock/Achim Preiß (eds), Kunst auf Befehl? Dreiunddreißig bis Fünfundvierzig, Munich 1990, 77–120.

7 Cf. Werner Freitag (ed.), Das Dritte Reich im Fest. Führermythos, Feierlaune und Verweigerung in Westfalen 1933–1945, Bielefeld 1997.

8 Wolfgang Eggert, Das ostfränkisch-deutsche Reich in der Auffassung seiner Zeitgenossen, Berlin 1973.

9 Cf. Gerd Althoff/Hagen Keller, Heinrich I. und Otto der Große, Göttingen ²1994.

10 Cf. Gerd Althoff, Verwandte, Freunde und Getreue. Zum politischen Stellenwert der Gruppenbindung im früheren Mittelalter, Darmstadt 1990.

11 Quoted from Walter Schlesinger, 'Die Grundlegung der deutschen Einheit im frühen Mittelalter', in idem, Beiträge zur deutschen Verfassungsgeschichte des Mittelalters, vol. 1, Göttingen 1963, 245–285, quote: 284.

12 Cf. Walter Schlesinger, 'Die Königserhebung Heinrichs I. zu Fritzlar im Jahre 919', in idem, Ausgewählte Aufsätze, ed. by Hans Patz/Fred Schwind, Sigmaringen 1987, 199–220.

13 Cf. Widukind, Rerum gestarum Saxonicarum, 1, 26. Cf. also Robert Holtzmann, Geschichte der Sächsischen Kaiserzeit, Munich 1979, 68 ff.

14 Cf. Horst Fuhrmann, 'Die Synode von Hohenaltheim (916) quellenkundlich betrachtet', in DA 43 (1987), 440–468

15 Cf. Martin Lintzel, 'Das abendländische Kaisertum im 9. und 10. Jahrhundert', in idem, Ausgewählte Schriften, vol. 2, Berlin 1961, 122–144; Karl Ferdinand Werner, 'L'Empire carolingien et le Saint Empire', in idem, Vom Frankenreich zur Entfaltung Deutschlands und Frankreichs. Ursprünge, Strukturen, Beziehungen, Ausgewählte Beiträge, Festgabe zu seinem 60. Geburtstag, Sigmaringen 1984, 329–376.

16 Cf. on this and on the following Ulrich Reuling, 'Quedlinburg. Königspfalz – Reichsstift – Markt', in Lutz Fenske (ed.), Deutsche Königspfalzen. Beiträge zu ihrer historischen und archäologischen Erforschung (Veröffentlichungen des Max-Planck-Institutes für Geschichte, 11/4: Pfalzen – Reichsgut – Königshöfe), Göttingen 1996, 184–147.

17 DHI 3.

18 Cf. Carl Erdmann, 'Beiträge zur Geschichte Heinrichs I. (IV-VI)', in idem, Ottonische Studien, ed. by H. Beumann, Darmstadt 1968, 83–20, here: 90.

19 According to Josef Fleckenstein, Pfalz und Stift Quedlinburg. Zum Problem ihrer Zuordnung unter den Ottonen (Nachrichten der Akademie der Wissenschaften in Göttingen I. Philologisch-Historische Klasse, 2/92), Göttingen 1992, 9–21, here: 12.

20 Cf. Fleckenstein, Pfalz und Stift Quedlinburg (op. cit. note 19), 13.

21 Widukind, Res gestae Saxonicae I, 41.

22 Cf. Fleckenstein, Pfalz und Stift Quedlinburg (op. cit. note 19), 15, 18.

23 Ibid. 16.

24 Ibid. 21.

25 Cf. Manfred Mehl, 'Die Münzprägung der Quedlinburger Äbtissinnen', in Zur Kultur- und Sozialgeschichte Sachsen-Anhalts. Protokoll der Wissenschaftlichen Konferenz

am 8. und 9. Oktober 1994 in Quedlinburg (Beiträge zur Regional- und Landeskultur Sachsen-Anhalts, 1), Halle/S. 1995, 188–193.

26 On the importance of proprietary monasteries in noble families in the Early and High Middle ages see Gerd Althoff, 'Gandersheim und Quedlinburg. Ottonische Frauen-klöster als Herrschafts- und Überlieferungszentrum', in Frühmittelalterliche Studien. Jahrbuch des Instituts für Frühmittelalterforschung der Universität Münster 25 (1991), 123–144.

27 Cf. on this and on the following Gerhard Leopold, 'Die Stiftskirche der Königin Mathilde in Quedlinburg. Ein Vorbericht zum Gründungsbau des Damenstifts', in Frühmittelalterliche Studien. Jahrbuch des Instituts für Frühmittelalterforschung der Universität Münster 25 (1991), 145–170.

28 Cf. Klaus Voigtländer, Die Stiftskirche St. Servatii zu Quedlinburg, Berlin 1989; Frie-demann Goßlau/Rosemarie Radecke, Die Stiftskirche zu Quedlinburg. Eine Führung durch den romanischen Sakralbau, Quedlinburg 1999; Wolfgang Hofmann, Die Kirchen in Quedlinburg, Wernigerode 1994.

29 Cf. 'Geschichtliche Weihestunde in Quedlinburg. Die feierliche Wiederbeisetzung der Gebeine des ersten deutschen Königs', in Germanien (1937), 25 f.

30 Cf. Micheal H. Kater, Das Ahnenerbe der SS 1935–1945. Ein Beitrag zur Kulturpolitik des Dritten Reiches, Stuttgart 1974.

31 Report on the meeting on 18.10.1935 for the thousand year celebration in Quedlin-burg, StA Q, Vorakte XI 362/I, sheet 1.

32 Cf. op. cit. note 31, sheet 2.

33 All in all, 23 such places of culture were planned to facilitate the Germanic traditions.

34 Cf. Letter from SS-Obersturmführer (Senior Storm Leader) Klumm to Reich Leader Himmler on 7.12.1935, StA Q, Vorakte XI 362/I, sheet 21.

35 Report on the meeting in Quedlinburg on 9.1.1936, op. cit. note 34, sheet 4. Cf. also Chief Adjutant of Reich Leader Himmler to Reischle on 22.12.1935, StA Q, 363/I, V. Baul. Veränd., sheet 5; SS-Obersturmführer (Senior Storm Leader) Klumm to Reischle on 7.1.1936, op. cit. note 34, sheet 4.

36 Report on the meeting in Quedlinburg on 9.1.1936, StA Q, Vorakte XI 362/I, sheet 4.

37 Cf. File note from Weigel on 24.1.1936, StA Q, Vorakte XI 362/I, sheet 14.

38 In 1831, a senior civil servant, Ludwig Baentsch, bought the estate from the Prussian state. Since then it remained in the Baentsch family.

39 Cf. Uwe Puschner et al. (eds), Handbuch zur "Völkischen Bewegung" 1871–1918, Munich-New Providence-London-Paris 1996, 669.

40 Ein dramatisches Heldengedicht [A dramatic heroic poem], Berlin 1906.

41 Bühnendichtung in drei Abenden [Stage poetry in three evenings], Leipzig-Harten-stein, 1921/22.

42 Letter from the staff manager of the race department to the head of the race depart-ment, SS-Brigadeführer (Brigade Leader) Reischle, on 13.1.1936, StA Q, Vorakte XI 362/I, sheet 20. Heinrich Bauer's novel 'Florian Geyer' appeared in 1935 in Blut und Boden Verlag [Blood and Earth publishers].

43 Heinrich Ferdinand Bauer was born 29 March 1896 in Helmstedt, married Lieselotte, née Wollenweber, and had two children. After studying history, art, literature and the-atre history in Göttingen and Munich, he obtained a doctorate in 1920. His published works include Oliver Cromwell (1932), Schicksalswende Europas (1939), Männer und Siege (1940), Freude schöner Götterfunken, Beethoven-Erzählung (1949), Kaiser Friedrich Barbarossa (1954) and Prinz Eugen (1955). After 1957, there is no available information about him.

44 Report on the meeting in Quedlinburg on 9.1.1936, StA Q, Vorakte XI 362/I, sheet 6.

45 Ibid.

46 On the national ideal of farming and Himmler's reception of this idea cf. George L. Mosse, Die völkische Revolution. Über die geistigen Wurzeln des Nationalsozialismus, Frankfurt/M. 1991, 130 ff.

47 Report on the meeting in Quedlinburg on 9.1.1936, StA Q, Vorakte XI 362/I, sheet 6. Alfred Thoss from the Race and Settlement Department in Goslar was asked by the Race and Settlement Department of the SS in Berlin on 23.1.1936 for the publication of his collection on Heinrich, however, he replied that he wanted to personally give the author of the piece on Heinrich some pointers. Cf. Thoss to Race and Settlement Department Berlin on 27.1.1936 (op. cit. note 44), sheet 10.

48 Report on the meeting in Quedlinburg on 9.1.1936 (op. cit. note 44), sheet 7.

49 Cf. Boisly to SS-Obersturmführer (Senior Storm Leader) Höhne on 6.11.1937, StA Q, XI63/II 2, sheet 162 f.

50 Cf. Selig to Weigel on 23.1.1936, StA Q, Vorakte XI 362/I, sheet 12.

51 Cf. File note of Harke, subj.: Quedlinburg, from 24.1.1936, StA Q (op. cit. note 50), sheet 13-16.

52 Order on 5.3.1936 (op. cit. note 50), sheet 25. See also the detailed plan from the head of staff of the settlement department, Untersturmführer (Junior Storm Leader) Schmidt, on the conversion of the estate and the creation of a place of consecration on 11.3.1936, ibid. sheet 12-27.

53 Cf. Note from SS-Untersturmführer (Junior Storm Leader) Schmidt on 31.3.1936 (op. cit. note 50), sheet 12-27.

54 Cf. SS-Untersturmführer (Junior Storm Leader) to the race department on 8.4.1936 (op. cit. note 50), sheet 36.

55 Report by Untersturmführer (Junior Storm Leader) Schmidt on the inspection of the Wiperti estate and Heinrich's crypt on 2./3.4.1936 in Quedlinburg (op. cit. note 50), sheet 41-48, quote: 43.

56 Cf. File note Grau/Schmidt from 13.4.1936 (op. cit. note 50), sheet 13-17.

57 SS-work head quarters on the preparations of the Heinrich celebrations to SS-Untersturmführer (Junior Storm Leader) Wille, building unit of the *Reichsnährstand* (Reich Agriculture Organisation), on 30.4.1936 (op. cit. note 50), sheet 40.

58 Text of the contract, which was concluded on 18.4.1936, as well as the declaration of permission and authorisation from Himmler on 5.5.1936, see op. cit. note 50, sheet 56-58, 62.

59 Boisly to SS-Untersturmführer (Junior Storm Leader) Schmidt on 30.4.1936 (op. cit. note 50), sheet 21-22, quotation: 21.

60 Ibid.

61 Paul Ernst, Das Kaiserbuch. Ein Epos in drei Teilen (6 vols), part 1: Die Sachsenkaiser (vol. 2), Munich 1923/1926.

62 Boisly to SS-Untersturmführer (Junior Storm Leader) Schmidt on 30.4.1936, StA Q, Vorakte XI 362/I, sheet 21-22.

63 File note from SS-Untersturmführer (Junior Storm Leader) Schmidt on 21.4.1936 (op. cit. note 62), sheet 19.

64 Note by SS-Untersturmführer (Junior Storm Leader) Schmidt on 11.5.1936 (op. cit. note 62), sheet 30-32. It is clear from Schmidt's report on the inspections on 2./3.2.1936 that also Reich Leader Rosenberg has inspected the Wiperti court (ibid. sheet 45). On Himmler see also Peter Longerich, Heinrich Himmler. Biographie, Munich 2007.

65 Cf. SS-Gruppenführer (Group Leader) Heissmeyer (Head of the SS-Headquarters) on 6.5.1936, StA Q, XI 362/I, 4, sheet 6 f.

66 Cf. Letter from Hilde Degenhardt to SS-Untersturmführer (Junior Storm Leader) Schmidt on 5.6.1936 (op. cit. note 65), sheet 8.

67 Cf. Gerhard Besier, 'Die Lenkung der APU durch die Kirchenausschüsse (1935-1937)', in idem/Eckart Lessing (eds), Die Geschichte der Evangelischen Kirche der Union, vol. 3: Trennung von Staat und Kirche: Kirchlich-politische Krisen. Erneuerung kirchlicher Gemeinschaft (1918-1992), Leipzig 1999, 305-368, esp. 313 ff., 350 ff.

68 Cf. Superintendent Schmidt to Untersturmführer (Junior Storm Leader) Schmidt from 27.6.1936, StA Q, XI 362/I, 4, sheet 9.

69 Keil to the deputy of the Führer on 1.6.1936, StA Q, XI 362/I, A 11, sheet 6–10, quotation: 7.
70 Cf. Schmidt to Sturmbannführer (Storm Unit Leader) Grau on 23.6.1936 (op. cit. note 69), sheet 12–15. In July 1940, an attempt was made to open the new door between the cathedral and Heinrich's crypt with force. Once again one of the builders was given the blame for the incident, in this case the stonemason Rudolf Striebig. Cf. Note from Selig on 23.7.1940; Letter from Selig to Striebig from 24.7.1940, StA Q, X/364/XI, A 11, sheet 33–35.
71 Fleckenstein, Pfalz und Stift Quedlinburg (op. cit. note 19), 10; cf. also Carl Erdmann, 'Das Grab Heinrichs I.', in idem, Ottonische Studien (op. cit. note 18), 31–52, here: 31 f., note 1. On 7.3.1938, Erdmann attended a tour of the cathedral in Quedlinburg. SS-Untersturmführer (Junior Storm Leader) Gerhard Fischer gave a report on Erdmanns's questions to his superior, StA Q, 363/IV 4, sheet 83 f. An exact report on the various excavations in Quedlinburg during the National Socialist regime was published after the war by Hermann Wächter, Der Bauberg in Quedlinburg. Geschichte seiner Bauten bis zum ausgehenden 12. Jahrhundert nach den Ergebnissen der Grabungen von 1938–1942, Berlin 1959.
72 Cf. on the flag as a religious National Socialist Symbol Hans-Joachim Gamm, Der braune Kult. Das Dritte Reich und seine Ersatzreligion. Ein Beitrag zur politischen Bildung, Hamburg 1962, 43 ff. See also Gerhard Besier, Die Kirchen und das Dritte Reich, vol. 3, Berlin 2001, 186, 241–249.
73 Himmler's speech in the Quedlinburg cathedral on 2.7.1936 [self translation], Nordland Verlag, Berlin 1936, 5 f.
74 Op. cit. note 73, 14, 16.
75 Ibid. 14.
76 Ibid.
77 Op. cit. note 73, 7 f. [self translation].
78 Ibid. 14.
79 Ibid. 19.
80 Ibid. 14.
81 Ibid. 20.
82 Thoss, Heinrich I. (op. cit. note 3), 96.
83 Cf. Franz Lüdtke, König Heinrich I., Berlin 1936.
84 Cf. Friedrich Schneider, Die neueren Anschauungen der deutschen Historiker über die deutsche Kaiserpolitik des Mittelalters und die mit ihr verbundene Ostpolitik, Weimar [6]1943, 41 f.; Carl Erdmann, Der ungesalbte König (1938), in idem, Ottonische Studien, ed. and introduced by Helmut Beumann, Darmstadt 1968, 1–30.
85 Frank-Lothar Kroll, Utopie als Ideologie. Geschichtsdenken und politisches Handeln im Dritten Reich, Paderborn 1998, 252, see also 238 f.
86 Cf. Claus-Ekkehard Bärsch, Die politische Religion des Nationalsozialismus. Die religiöse Dimension der NS-Ideologie in den Schriften von Dietrich Eckhart, Joseph Goebbels, Alfred Rosenberg und Adolf Hitler, Munich 1998, 166 f.
87 According to Walter Schellenberg, Memoiren, Cologne, 1956, 40; John M. Steiner, 'Über das Glaubensbekenntnis der SS', in Karl Dietrich Bracher/Manfred Funke/Hans-Adolf Jacobsen (eds), Nationalsozialistische Diktatur 1933–1945. Eine Bilanz (Schriftenreihe der Bundeszentrale für politische Bildung 192), Bonn 1986, 206–223, here: 207, note 5a; Robin Lumsden, Himmler's Black Order. A History of the SS, 1923–45, Gloucestershire 1997, 120–123. Others say that he thought he was the reincarnation of Henry the Lion (1129–1195), cf. Bracher/Funke/Jacobsen, ibid. Also see Josef Ackermann, Heinrich Himmler als Ideologe, Göttingen 1970, 60; Katharine Ruf, 'Der Quedlinburger Dom in Dritten Reich', in Kritische Berichte 12 (1984) 1, 47–59, here: 54. On other religious extravagancies of Himmler, for example his strange obsession with research on witches, see Sönke Lorenz/Dieter R. Bauer/Wolfgang Behringer/Jürgen Michael Schmidt (eds), Himmlers Hexenkartothek. Das Interesse des Nationalsozialismus an der Hexenverfolgung (Hexenforschung, 4), Bielefeld 1999.

See on the leading figures of the SS also Ronald Smelser/Enrico Syring (eds), Die SS: Elite unter dem Totenkopf. 30 Lebensläufe, Paderborn 2000.

88   Cf. Schmidt to Himmler from 26.6.1936, StA Q, XI 362/I, A 8, sheet 1 f.; Schmidt to the SS-Standortführer (Local Leader), SS-Untersturmführer (Junior Storm Leader) Warch on 3.7.1936, ibid. sheet 3; Provisional rules for visitors from 3.7.1936, ibid. sheet 4.

89   Cf. Letter from Schmidt to SS-Standortführer (Local Leader) Warch on 7.9.1936 (op. cit. note 88), sheet 68; Note SS-Hauptscharführer (Head Squad Leader) Sergent Fischer, no date, ibid. sheet 82 f.

90   Schmidt to Himmler's Chief Adjutant from 26.9.1936 (op. cit. note 88), 90; Schmidt to the personal department of the settlement department on 24.10.1936, ibid. sheet 115; Himmler to Darré (head of the Race and Settlement department) on 19.1.1937, ibid. sheet 176. In it, Himmler expresses his conviction that the cost for the post could be covered by the sale of the literature and art in the Wiperti chapel. Cf. also Schmidt to personal staff of Himmler on 9.2.1937, ibid. sheet 202 f.; Schmidt to Fischer on 7.5.1937, ibid. sheet 154–156.

91   Untersturmführer (Junior Storm Leader) Schmidt to Superintendent Schmidt on 10.7.1936 (op. cit. note 88), sheet 6 f.

92   Schmidt to Warch on 7.9.1936, ibid. sheet 64. Warch had to leave his post shortly after because he had not properly done the accounts of the collected monies and had thus been an unworthy representative of the SS. See Dubiel, König-Heinrich-Feiern (op. cit. note 2), 43.

93   Cf. SS-Standortführer (Local Leader) Warch to SS-Untersturmführer (Junior Storm Leader) Schmidt on 25.7.1936, StA Q, XI 362/I, A 8, sheet 37; Schmidt to Baentsch on 30.7.1936, ibid. sheet 43 f.; Baentsch to Schmidt on 3.8.1936, ibid. sheet 41.

94   Gestapo Berlin to SS-Obersturmführer (Senior Storm Leader) Höhne on 30.10.1936 (op. cit. note 93), sheet 137 f.; Schmidt to the Gestapo on 13.11.1936, ibid. sheet 134–141.

95   Warch to Schmidt on 23.11.196, ibid. sheet 150.

96   Cf. also the letter from Obersturmführer (Senior Storm Leader) Höhne to the head of the personal staff, Wolff, on 28.4.1937, StA Q, XI 363/IV, A 4, sheet 1.

97   Cf. Schmidt to Selig on 3.5.1937, StA Q, 362/1, A 8, sheet 142.

98   Wolff to Höhne on 11.5.1937, StA Q, 363/IV, A 4, sheet 2.

99   Cf. Höhne to Grau on 25.6.1937, StA Q, 363/IV, 4, sheet 5.

100 Cf. Letter from Selig to Höhne on 28.6.1937 (op. cit. note 99), sheet 19.

101 Quoted according to Dubiel, König-Heinrich-Feiern (op. cit. note 2), 33.

102 On the preference of the National Socialists nightly celebrations and the affinity to the cult of the dead, which sends shivers down ones spine, cf. Gamm, Der braune Kult (op. cit. note 72), 151 ff., 156 ff.

103 Cf. Höhne to the president of the government of the Province Magdeburg-Anhalt, von Jagow, on 26.6.1937, StA Q, 363/IV, 4, sheet 6. See Sabine Behrenbeck, Der Kult um die toten Helden. Nationalsozialistische Mythen, Riten und Symbole, Greifswald 1996. On the excavation and the internment of the skeleton see Dubiel, König-Heinrich-Feiern (op. cit. note 2), 45 ff.

104 Quoted from Höhne's letter to Grau on 25.6.1937, StA Q 363/IV, 4, sheet 5.

105 Letters from Untersturmführer (Junior Storm Leader) Schmidt to Himmler on 25.8.1936 and 18.9.1936, StA Q, XI 362/I, A 7, sheet 2 f., 10–12.

106 Cf. ibid.

107 Cf. Schmidt to Himmler on 18.9.1936, StA Q, XI 362/I, A 7, sheet 11; Schmidt to Selig on 20.3.1937, ibid. sheet 31; Schmidt to Selig on 8.3.1937, ibid. sheet 40.

108 Himmler to Untersturmführer (Junior Storm Leader) Schmidt on 17.3.1937, (op. cit. note 107), sheet 30. Cf. also the note from Schmidt on 5.4.1937, ibid. sheet 37 f.

109 File note from SS-Oberscharführer (Senior Squad Leader) Tostmann from 6.4.1937, ibid. sheet 39.

110 Cf. Schmidt to the personal staff of Himmler on 14.10.1937 with appendix, StA Q, XI 362/I, A 10, sheet 2–5; Schmidt to Höhne on 15.10.1937, ibid. 12.
111 The results of the research of the *Ahnenerbe e. V.* (Society for Research into the Teaching of Ancestral Heritage) were published in the house magazine "Germanien. Monatshefte zur Erkenntnis deutschen Wesens".
112 Cf. Höhne to Schmidt on 1.11.1937, StA Q, XI 363/III, A 3, sheet 241.
113 Cf. Draft programme for the Heinrich celebrations in Quedlinburg on 1./2.7.1938 from the press office of Himmler on 31.5.1938, StA Q, 363/IV, 4, sheet 22. A second highlight of the celebrations was the "consecration of the first table of lineage" in the cathedral by Himmler, ibid.
114 Cf. Letter from SS Sturmbannführer (Storm Unit Leader) Sievers to the head of the administration "V. u. W.", Himmler, on 7.5.1940, StA Q, XI 364/I, A 1, sheet 25–27; Statute of the *König-Heinrich I.-Gedächtnis-Stiftung*, ibid. 2 f. Cf. account of Himmler's speech: StA Q, X 363/1,1, sheet 5 f.
115 Cf. Report of the first meeting of the *König-Heinrich I.-Gedächtnis-Stiftung* on 1.7.1939, StA Q, X 363/1,1, sheet 1–7. Satzung der Stiftung: StA Q, XI 364/IV, A 4, sheet 17.
116 Cf. Reich manager of the *Ahnenerbe*, SS-Standartenführer (Regiment Leader) Sievers to Selig on 28.5.1940, StA Q, 364/IV, A 4, sheet 39 f.; personal staff of Himmler to Selig on 3.5.1940, ibid. 40.
117 Cf. Fischer to Höhne on 7.3.1938, StA Q, 363/IV, 4, sheet 83; Reich Church Ministry [RCM], Muhs, to the Protestant Church Board in Berlin [EOK] on 13.4.1938, Evangelisches Zentralarchiv Berlin [EZA], 7/9903, sheet 71.
118 Cf. Hiecke, explanation of the planned repair works in the Quedlinburg cathedral, April 1938, StA Q, 363/IV, 4, sheet 85–96.
119 See on the renovation work Kirsch, 'Zeitalter' (op. cit. note 6), esp. 59–63, here: 61.
120 Höhne to SS-Obersturmbannführer (Senior Storm Unit Leader) Diebitisch on 26.3.1938, StA Q X 363/I, 1, sheet 199 f.
121 Cf. the detailed correspondence between the governmental head of the planning department in the Prussian *Staatliches Hochbauamt II* Halberstadt, Kniese, and Hiecke from the Reich Ministry for Science, Education and National Training, Archive of the Protestant Church of the Church Province of Saxony, Magdeburg [AKPS], Rep A Spec. 6, No. A 2141.
122 Kirsch, 'Zeitalter' (op. cit. note 6), 59 f.
123 Cf. the report on the celebration in the newspapers Quedlinburger Kreisblatt on 3.7.1939; Der Mitteldeutsche on 2.7.1939 and Magdeburgische Zeitung on 8./9.7.1939. Also see the incoming descriptions of the 1939 celebration in Dubiel, König-Heinrich-Feiern (op. cit. note 2), 58 ff. Cf. but already to the celebration in 1938 the press clipping 'Nächtliche Feierstunde am Grab Heinrichs I.', EZA, 7/9903, sheet 268.
124 According to Selig in his letter to SS-Oberführer (Senior Leader) Müller on 23.1.1945, StA Q, X/364/VIII, A 8, sheet 44. Cf. also the SS command from Himmler on the organisation of the memorial celebration on 26.6.1937, StA Q, 363/IV, 4, sheet 21.
125 Quoted from Höhne in a letter to Superintendent Schmidt on 10.12.1937, StA Q, 363/I, Baul. Veränd. V, sheet 27; Parish archive of St Servatii [KGA StS], Act on the transfer of the cathedral to the SS, the restitution and reparation of the same, sheet 5.
126 Provisional minutes for the Heinrich celebration in Quedlinburg on 1./2.7.1939, StA Q, X/364/X, A 10, sheet 3–10.
127 Professor at the Nordische Akademie für bildende Kunst in Bremen.
128 Cf. Selig's letter to SS-Obergruppenführer (Senior Group Leader) Höfle on 12.6.1944, StA Q, X/364/VIII, A 8, sheet 66.
129 On Klagges' initiative the cathedral in Braunschweig was dedicated to "(Heinrich) Henry the Lion" and was renovated as a "Heinrich cathedral", one of the National Socialist places of memorial and consecration, cf. Karl Arndt, 'Mißbrauchte Geschichte: Der Braunschweiger Dom als politisches Denkmal (1933/45)', in Niederdeutsche Beiträge zur Kunstgeschichte 21 (1981), 189–223; Kirsch, 'Zeitalter' (op. cit. note 6), 66–71. Klagges, who since 1931 was the minister of the interior for the NSDAP of the

free state of Braunschweig, had awarded Hitler, who was stateless, German national-ity on 25.1.1932, cf. Holger Germann, Die politische Religion des Nationalsozialisten Dietrich Klagge, Frankfurt/M. 1995, 16.

130 Cf. note Selig on 27.6.1944, StA Q, X/364/VIII, A 8, sheet 70.

131 Cf. Note Selig to the mayors of the King Heinrich I towns on 23.8.1940, StA Q, X/364/VIII, A 4, sheet 15.

132 Cf. Selig's letter to the Reich manager of the *Ahnenerbe*, SS-Standartenführer (Regi-ment Leader) Sievers on 24.5.1943, StA Q, Vorakte XI 362/I, A 11, sheet 65 f. Also see the letter from SS-Untersturmführer (Junior Storm Leader) Montag, Hauptabtei-lung für Sonderaufgaben ('main department for special tasks'), Administration de-partment to Selig on 24.6.1941, StA Q, X/364/VIII, A 8, sheet 12. It is clear from it that the manager of the Main Department of Economy and Administration (W. u. V.-Hauptamt), SS-Gruppenführer (Group Leader) Pohl, functioned as the manager of the foundation.

133 Cf. Sievers to Selig on 24.7.1943 (op. cit. note 132), 70; Note from Selig on 26.8.1943, ibid.

134 Selig to Sievers on 21.7.1943, ibid. 68.

135 Cf. ibid.

136 Cf. Sievers to Selig on 24.7.1943, ibid. 70; Note Selig on 26.8.1943, ibid.

137 Cf. NSDAP, district leadership Quedlinburg-Ballenstedt to Selig on 20.10.1941, StA Q, X/364/VIII, A 8, sheet 1.

138 Cf. Note Selig on 10.3.1942 (op. cit. note 137), sheet 2.

139 Letter from Schmidt to Selig on 25.3.1942, ibid. sheet 3.

140 Selig to Hitler Youth Leader Pg. (*Parteigenosse*, party member) Scholz on 26.3.1942, ibid. sheet 4.

141 Ibid. There was no "fear ... of the church representatives" expressed in this letter, as Dubiel, König-Heinrich-Feier (op. cit. note 2), 101, assumed, but rather annoyance that in times of war he had uphold a truce with the Church.

142 Letter from the NSDAP district leadership Quedlinburg-Ballenstedt to Selig on 1.4.1942, StA Q, X/364/VIII, A 8, sheet 5.

143 Note Selig on a meeting with Sturmbannführer (Storm Unit Leader) Klein, Chief of the Main Department for Special Tasks, section administration, in Berlin-Lichterfelde West, and his assistant, Untersturmführer (Junior Squad Leader) Montag on 22.4. 1941 (op. cit. note 142), sheet 8 f.

144 Cf. Montag's letter to Selig on 24.6.1941, StA Q, X/364/VIII, A 8, sheet 12.

145 See above, 152.

146 Cf. Report of the official meeting of the pastors of the clergy of the diocese Quedlin-burg on 28.9.1932, KKA Q.

147 Cf. Pfarrstellenvermögen und Steuerleistungen der Kirchengemeinde Quedlinburg laut örtlichem Fragebogen II on 1.4.1926, Kirchenkreisarchiv Quedlinburg [KKA Q], no. 147.

148 Cf. Christoph Weiling, Die "Christlich-deutsche Bewegung." Eine Studie zum konser-vativen Protestantismus in der Weimarer Republik (AKZG B 28), Göttingen 1998.

149 Büschel, 'Vor welche Aufgaben wird die Verkündigung des Evangeliums durch die völkische Bewegung gestellt? Thesen' (op. cit. note 147).

150 Report of the official meeting of the pastors in the diocese of Quedlinburg on 28.9.1932, ibid.

151 Quoted from Superintendent Schmidt's letter to General Superintendent Eger on 27.5.1933, ibid.

152 Negotiation report of the official meeting of the pastors in the church diocese of Quedlinburg on 14.6.1933, ibid.

153 Personal file Hein: AKPS, Rep. A Spec. P, H 744 I.

154 Report of Pastor Hein on 8.1.1934, AKPS, Rep. A Spec. P, H 744, vol. 2; Martin Onnasch, Um Kirchliche Macht und Geistliche Vollmacht. Ein Beitrag zur Geschichte

des Kirchenkampfes in der Kirchenprovinz Sachsen 1932–1945, PhD. Theol. Halle/S. 1979, A 182. On Heins activity in the Confessing Church see also KKA Q, no. 624.
155 Report from Pastor Hein on 8.1.1934, AKPS, Rep. A Spec. P, H 744, vol. 2.
156 Cf. Letter from the German Christian Fraction of the cathedral parish of Quedlinburg to Bishop Peter on 19.12.193 (op. cit. note 155).
157 For futher information on his life cf. AKPS, Rep. A Spec. P., Sch 633 I; EZA, 7/9903, vol. 24 VR.
158 Cf. Besier, in Handbuch der EKU, vol. 3 (op. cit. note 67), 406–413. In Quedlinburg the group had 400 members. Cf. Consistory Magdeburg, Fretzdorff to Superintendent Spangenberg in Altenwedding, duplicate, EZA, 7/9903, vol. 417.
159 On 20.3.1934, Schmidt wrote to Pastor Bergmann: "At the same time, the emergency association of pastors with the exception of Pastor Hein have in no way have become ecclesiastically noticeable and have never thought of bringing the ecclesiastical agitation of their association into their parishes." KKA Q, Nr. 226.
160 Cf. Report from criminal assistant Göckel on Church surveillance from 20.11.1935, duplicate from duplicate, EZA, 7/9903, sheet 103 VR; Reich Ministry for Public Enlightenment and Propaganda to the Reich Church Ministry on 27.12.1935, ibid. sheet 102.
161 Letter from Friedrich Sackstedt on 16.10.1934; Report of Pastor Hein on 8.1.1934, AKPS, Rep. A Spec. P, H 744, vol. 2.; cf. also von Klewitz, Quedlinburg, to the chairman of the parish council of the cathedral parish of Quedlinburg on 9.6.1935, EZA, 7/9903, sheet 149 VR.
162 Cf. Provincial Church committee to Hein on 26.2.1936, AKPS, Rep. A Spec. P, H 744, vol. 2.
163 Cf. Hein to Müller on 29.2.1936 (op. cit. note 162).
164 Protestant consistory of the Province Saxony, superior consistory councillor Zippel to EOK Berlin on 1.4.1937, ibid.; EZA, 7/9903, sheet 163 f.
165 AKPS, Rep. A Spec. P, Sch 633 I.
166 Cf. Onnasch, Um Kirchliche Macht und Geistliche Vollmacht (op. cit. note 154), 213.
167 Cf. on this Ferdinand Schlingensiepen (ed.), Theologisches Studium im Dritten Reich. Das Kirchliche Auslandsseminar in Ilsenburg/Harz, Düsseldorf 1998; Besier, Die Kirchen (op. cit. note 72), 475–479.
168 Cf. note provincial church committee on 7.12.1936, AKPS, Rep. A Spec. 6, A 11208.
169 Selig to Hein on 19.10.1937, KKA Q.
170 Cf. Selig's orders to all institution heads, caretakers and tenants in state accommodation on 29.10.1937 (op. cit. note 169).
171 Cf. Naudé to Hein on 2.11.1937, ibid.
172 *Sammlungsgesetz*: the collection law, which forced Church members to contribute to Nazi party projects. Cf. Selig to the consistory on 4.11.1937, ibid.
173 Schmidt to the Magdeburg consistory on 8.11.1937, ibid.
174 Ibid.
175 According to Schmidt in his report to the consistory on 17.11.1937, AKPS, Rep. A Spec. P, H 744, vol. 1.
176 Letter from Superintendent Schmidt to the PKA (Provisional Church Committee) on 23.6.1936, AKPS, Rep. A Spec. 6, A 11208.
177 Reich ministers Darré, Frick, Frank and Rust took part, the Reich Leader of the labour service, Ley, Rosenberg, Baldur von Schirach, Bormann, Daluege, Heydrich, all *Oberabschnitts-* and *Abschnittsführer* of the SS, State council Eggeling, state secretary Körner representing Göring, Klagges, assistant head of department Bernd representing Goebbels and many others, cf. Quedlinburger Kreisblatt on 3.7.1936. Himmler's speech on 2.7.1936, which was also broadcast on the radio, was printed in Germanien. Monatshefte zur Erkenntnis deutschen Wesens, issue 8, 1936. See also text in Dubiel, König-Heinrich-Feiern (op. cit. note 2), 113–116, and Interpretation, ibid. 41 f., 81–84.
178 Schmidt to Pastor Jahnecke on 1.7.1936 (op. cit. note 176).
179 Schmidt's report to the consistory on 6.8.1936, ibid.

180 Letter from 17.8.1936, EZA, 7/9903, sheet 121 VR.
181 Cf. File note to the Reich church committee on the meeting of the Land church committee on 30.9.1936, EZA, 7/9903, sheet 126. The Magdeburg consistory learnt of this decision on 12.1.1937 only after making an inquiry on 1.12.1936. Cf. ibid. sheet 127 VR.
182 Höhne to Schmidt on 20.6.1936, StA Q, 363/IV 4, sheet 3.
183 Cf. Schmidt to Höhne on 21.6.1937 (op. cit. note 182), sheet 4.
184 Cf. here and to the following Willi Schulze, 'Der Quedlinburger Dom als Kultstätte der SS', in Jahrbuch für Wirtschaftsgeschichte der Deutschen Akademie der Wissenschaften zu Berlin. Institut für Wirtschaftsgeschichte, Berlin (East) 1966, 215-234. The author was the former town archivist in Quedlinburg, cf. list of authors, ibid. 316. His manuscript reached his colleague, Rogowski, via a Dr. Jonas (probably Wolfgang Jonas, acting director of the Institut für Wirtschaftsgeschichte der Deutschen Akademie der Wissenschaften zu Berlin) the state secretary for church affairs and was in 1965 examined by him. He judged that "a publication of the work in the form of a brochure would be of no use for our political convincing work on Christian orientated persons", however, he had nothing against the evaluation of the contribution in an academic magazine, cf. Bundesarchiv Berlin [BAB], DO-4, 485, Pers. Referent, Berlin 3.8.1965. For the publication of the essay in the Jahrbuch für Wirtschaftsgeschichte, Lotte Zumpe, the head of the department for Wirtschaftsgeschichte des Imperialismus in Deutschland am Institut der Deutschen Akademie der Wissenschaften zu Berlin (ibid. 316) wrote a foreword (ibid. 215-217), in which she justified the publication in various forms including the historical-political stance: "And besides, it is not only justified because today in West Germany the old members of these criminal organisation [read SS] publicly and with the blessing of the state demand rehabilitation, for should they eventually be brought to court, they are treated so leniently that it equals the mockery of the uncountable victims, and in exactly this the West German state sees no contradiction to its official proclaimed Christian Democratic Principles."
185 Höhne to Himmler's head of personal staff, Wolff, on 22.4.1937, StA Q, 363/I, Baul. Veränd. V, sheet 6. For a duplicate of the document see Schulze, Der Quedlinburger Dom (op. cit. note 184), 220 f.
186 Note Höhne on 28.4.1937, StA Q, 363/I, Baul. Veränd. V, sheet 7, duplicate of the document: Schulze, Der Quedlinburger Dom (op. cit. note 184), 221. Schulze tacitly corrected "*katholisch*" (Catholic) to "*kirchlich*" (Church), which actually better expresses the meaning.
187 Höhne to Wolff on 18.5.1937, StA Q, 363/I, Baul. Veränd. V, sheet 8.
188 Wolff to Höhne on 28.5.1937, ibid. sheet 9.
189 Cf. Letter from Selig to Höhne on 10.6.1937, ibid. sheet 10, duplicate of the document: Schulze, Der Quedlinburger Dom (op. cit. note 184), 222.
190 Cf. note of SS-Untersturmführer (Junior Storm Leader) Fischer on 15.7.1937, StA Q, 363/I Baul. Veränd. V, sheet 13.
191 Letter of complaint from Salzmann to Höhne on 6.8.1937 (op. cit. note 190), sheet 19. This letter was arranged by Höhne. Cf. Schulze, Der Quedlinburger Dom (op. cit. note 184), 224. On the stance of Sann cf. also note EOK on 8.4.1938, EZA, 7/9909, sheet 297 f.
192 Selig to Höhne on 24.7.1937, StA Q, 363/I, Baul. Veränd. V, sheet 16.
193 On Stahn see Heike Kreutzer, Das Reichskirchenministerium im Gefüge der nationalsozialistischen Herrschaft, Diss. Phil. Tübingen 2000, ch. III. 2, esp. 161 ff.
194 Note Höhne on 13.12.1937, StA Q, X 363/I, 1, sheet 193.
195 Höhne to Schmidt on 10.12.1937, StA Q, 363/I, Baul. Veränd. V, sheet 27.
196 Schmidt to Höhne on 11.12.1937 (op. cit. note 125), sheet 29; KGA StS, Act "Übereignung des Doms an die SS, Rückgabe und Wiederinstandsetzung derselben" [The assignment of the cathedral to the SS, the restitution and reparation of the same], vol. 4.
197 Report from Schmidt to Werner on 4.2.1938, EZA B, 1/C3/212. Stahn wanted to tie Schmidt down to the Wiperti Church and to its renovation with the promise of monies

from the Reich Church Ministry in this conversation on 9.12.1937, as Schmidt wrote, ibid. On 6.12.1937 Stahn had announced this to Schmidt and received a positive answer from him. Correspondence in KGA StS (op. cit. note 125), sheet 1 f. Through it Schmidt, according to his own information, had "not allowed the handing over of the cathedral to the SS for the annual King Heinrich celebrations without any questions". Letter to the EOK on 22.1.1938, EZA B, 7/9903, sheet 173; KGA StS (op. cit. note 125), sheet 8. Essentially the mentioned act on the St Servatii church parish supports the description in Franz-Reinhold Hildebrandt, 'Die gewaltsame Inbesitznahme der Stiftskirche I Quedlinburg durch die SS', in Walter Bauer et al. (eds), Ich glaube eine Heilige Kirche. Festschrift für Hans Asmussen zum 65. Geburtstag am 21.8. 1962, Stuttgart-Berlin-Hamburg 1963, 105–114.

198 Schmidt to Höhne on 11.12.1937, StA Q, 363/I, Baul. Veränd. V, sheet 29.
199 Handwritten letter from Schmidt to Höhne on 11.12.1937 (op. cit. note 198), sheet 30, duplicate of the document: Schulze, Der Quedlinburger Dom (op. cit. note 184), 226.
200 Letter on 12.12.1937, KGA StS (op. cit. note 125), sheet 6; EZA, 7/9903, sheet 175.
201 Ibid.
202 Cf. Höhne to Schmidt on 13.12.1937, StA Q, 363/I, Baul. Veränd. V, sheet 31; KGA StS (op. cit. note 125), sheet 7.
203 Text of the agreement: StA Q, 363/I, Baul. Veränd. V, sheet 37–39; EZA, 7/9903, sheet 170–172.
204 Letter from the EOK to the Reich Church Ministry on 11.2.1938, EZA, 7/9903, sheet 242–247; AKPS, Rep. A Spec. 6A 2351. After that, the EOK only learnt of the agreement between the Reich Church Ministry and the SS from a letter dated 17.1.1938. The short letter from the Reich Church Ministry to the EOK is found in EZA, 7/9903, sheet 169. Superintendent Schmidt pointed out on 22.1.1938 to the EOK: "If I had known that the Reich Church Ministry would present the EOK and the cathedral parish a fait accompli then of course I would have made a report on the state of affairs." At the start it reads: "I emphasise once more that I have never agreed to the taking over of the cathedral by the SS. It is just as unlikely to have come from the parish itself." EZA, 7/9903, sheet 173 VR.
205 Stahn to Höhne on 18.1.1938, StA Q, 363/I, Baul. Veränd. V, sheet 35.
206 Höhne to Schmidt on 25.1.1938 (op. cit. note 205), sheet 40; KGA StS (op. cit. note 125), sheet 9. On 24.4.1938 Superindent Schmidt asked the Staatliches Hochbauamt II Halberstadt "for a notification as soon as possible, detailing what on the inventory is state property". KGA StS (as note 125), sheet 58.
207 Cf. Journey report of Consistory councillor Schmidt, Magdeburg on 15.1.1938, AKPS, Rep. A Spec. 6A 2351.
208 Cf. also the letter from Schmidt to the Consistory in Magdeburg on 2.2.1938 (op. cit. note 207).
209 Account of the contents of the negotiations between Himmler's representatives, SS-Obersturmführer (Senior Storm Leader) Dr. Höhne and Superintendent Schmidt, who signed on 27 January 1938 at 4 p.m. in the office of the Superintendent, KGA StS (op. cit. note 125), sheet 10 f.; EZA, 7/9903, sheet 185 f.
210 Ibid.
211 Cf. ibid.; Höhne's report of his official trip to Quedlinburg on 26./27.1.1938, StA Q, 63/I, Baul. Veränd. V, sheet 40a.
212 Cf. Höhne's journey report (op. cit. note 211).
213 Cf. Telegram from Werner to Schmidt on 27.1.1938, KGA StS (op. cit. note 125), sheet 12 f.; also EZA, 7/9903, sheet 184; AKPS, Rep. A Spec. 6A 2351.
214 Cf. the hand written authorisation from Höhne on 27.1.1938, KGA StS (op. cit. note 125), sheet 14.
215 Cf. confirmation of receipt from Fischer on 27.1.1938, KGA StS (op. cit. note 125), sheet 15; account of the contents of the negotiations between Himmler's representatives, SS-Obersturmführer (Senior Storm Leader) Dr. Höhne and the signatory Superintendent Schmidt (op. cit. note 209), sheet 10 f. On 28.1.1938, Schmidt described to

the elders the events of 27.1.1938 and invited them to a parish council meeting on 2.2.1938. Cf. KGA StS (op. cit. note 125), sheet 16.

216 Cf. Schmidt to Werner on 3.2.1938, EZA B, 1/C3/212; KGA StS (op. cit. note 125), sheet 33 f. On 31.1.1938, Schmidt had informed the parish elders of the conversation with Werner: "During the conversation in the office of the president of the Protestant superior Church Council I met with deep sympathy and the assurance that we would still be supported ... task, to create an immediate decisive statement from the parish council. Only because of our decision can the superior church council take further steps." Cf. KGA StS (op. cit. note 125), sheet 21.

217 Cf. Fischer to Höhne on 30.1.1938 with three enclosed documents, StA Q, 363/I, Baul. Veränd. V, sheets 42–46, duplicate of the document: Schulze, Der Quedlinburger Dom (op. cit. note 184), 227 f.

218 Letter signed by the council of Brethren of the confessing parish on 30.1.1938, EZA B, 7/9903, sheet 189; Letter to Schmidt KGA StS (op. cit. note 125), sheet 17.

219 Cf. Schmidt to Werner on 7.2.1938, AKPS, Rep. A Spec. 6A 2351; KGA StS (op. cit. note 125), sheet 28 f.

220 Höhne to Fischer on 31.1.1938, StA Q, 363/I, Baul. Veränd. V, sheet 47, duplicate of the document: Schulze, Der Quedlinburger Dom (op. cit. note 184), 229.

221 Note Schmidt on 6.2.1938, KGA StS (op. cit. note 125), sheet 27; Letter from Schmidt to Werner on 7.2.1938, in which he confirmed the handing over of the key, StA Q, 363/I, Baul. Veränd. V, sheet 49; KGA StS (op. cit. note 125), sheet 30. Also see the letter from Höhne to Himmler on 7.2.1938, StA Q (op. cit in this note), sheet 51; File note from Heyer on 7.2.1938, EZA, 7/9903, sheet 202 f.

222 Cf. Letter from Schmidt to Werner on 7.2.1938, EZA B, 7/9903, 235 f.; file note from Heyer on 7.2.1938, EZA B, 7/9903, sheet 202 f.; cf. also the newspapers Mitteldeutschland/Saale-Zeitung on 21.2.1938, Der Evangelische Beobachter no. 20a and Deutscher Glaube, April edition 1938, 206.

223 Cf. letter from 7.2.1938, EZA, 7/9903, sheet 241.

224 Duplicate KGA StS (op. cit. note 125), sheet 20.

225 Record of the negotiations of the parish council of St Servatii on 2.2.1938, EZA, 1/C3/212; certified copy KGA StS (op. cit. note 125), sheet 35–38.

226 Accompanying letter from Schmidt to Werner on 3.2.1938 (op. cit. note 125).

227 Report from Schmidt to Werner on 4.2.1938, ibid. This report is identical to the one, which Schmidt also gave to the consistory (KGA StS, ibid. sheet 23–26); accompanying letter on 4.2.1938, ibid. sheet 22.

228 Cf. also Schmidt's note for the members of the parish council on 8.2.1938, KGA StS (op. cit. note 125), sheet 31 f.; EZA, 7/9903, sheet 239 f.

229 Statement of the EOK to the Reich Church Ministry on 11.2.1938, EZA, 1/C3/212.

230 Cf. on it Schmidt's letter to Werner already on 7.2.1938, EZA B, 7/9903, 235 f.

231 Statement from the EOK to the Reich Church Ministry on 11.2.1938, EZA, 1/C3/212. Schmidt came with well-founded worries about the behaviour of Werner, who rang him at midday on 12.2. and explained, "that he had been in a meeting with Dr. Höhne three hours ago and in it he had found out various information, which he had not known before". He promised to visit Quedlinburg with Höhne in the coming week. Cf. Letter from Schmidt to the superior consistory councillor (Heyer) on 13.2.1938, KGA StS (op. cit. note 125), sheet 43.

232 Muhs, Reich Church Ministry to the EOK on 18.2.1938, EZA, 7/9903, sheet 253 f.; also StA Q, 363/I, Baul. Veränd. V, sheets 56–61a.

233 Ibid. Schmidt sent this letter on 23.2.1938 to the consistory as well as to the council of elders and his colleague Hein. Cf. KGA StS (op. cit. note 125), sheet 46 f.

234 Cf. Fischer's report on 15.8.1938, StA Q, 363/I, Baul. Veränd. V, sheet 72 f., duplicate of the document in Schulze, Der Quedlinburger Dom (op. cit. note. 184), 232 ff.; File note from Schleif on 23.8.1938, op. cit. in this note. However, there were also positive voices. As reported the land's court councillor Haugg from the Reich Church Ministry that the Swedish professor of theology D. Gyllenberg from the Abo Academy in Turku,

Finland on the occasion of his visit to the 7th conference of higher education at the Luther-Akademie Sondershausen in Quedlinburg, "spoke positively of the SS-guide". Cf. Report from Haugg on 16.8.1938, BAB, R 5101–22543, sheet 212–217, quote: 213.

235 "Number tables for the song book, the hymn books themselves, the hanging display boxes and even the collection plate [were removed]." Note from EOK on 8.4.1938, EZA, 7/9903, sheet 297 f., here: 297 R.

236 The parish council of St Servatii was formed by the clergymen Schmidt (chairman) and Hein as well as the lay persons Giessmann, v. Dippe, Heinemann and H. Mette.

237 Letter on 23.2.1938, KGA StS (op. cit. note 125), sheet 50 f.; cf. also von Dippe to Schmidt on 1.3.1938, ibid. sheet 52. Von Dippe abstained in the vote on the decision of the parish council on 2.3.1938 (cf. note 240), "with consideration for his position as representative of patron council". Extract from the protocol EZA, 7/9903, sheet 262, here: R.

238 Resolution of the forty superintendents, which was passed on 10.2.1938 and sent to the Consistory on 4.3.1938, AKPS, Rep. A Spec. 6, A 2351. A less fiercely written draft KGA StS (op. cit. note 125), sheet 48.

239 Cf. Letter from Hermann Wagner from 9.3.1938 to EOK; to the Consistory of the KPD, with the text of the petition, EZA, 7/9903, sheet 259 f.; AKPS, Rep. A Spec. 6, A 2351.

240 Cf. Letter from the Consistory Magdeburg, Fretzdorff to the EOK on 2.3.1938, EZA B, 7/9903, sheet 258; AKPS, Rep. A Spec. 6, A 2351, also KGA StS (op. cit. note 125), 53 and R. According to the protocol, the parish council asked the committee of the Consistory on 3.3.1938, "at the Protestant Church Board to go there, to ask for legal meaning of the contract, which was completed between the parish of St Servatii and the then King of Prussia on 20 April 1854, from a recognised professor of national jurisprudence". Duplicate of the protocol to TOP 1 KGA StS (op. cit. note 125), sheet 55; cf. also AKPS, Rep. A Spec. A 2351; Schmidt passed on the decision from 4.3.1938 to the Consistory. Cf. KGA StS (op. cit. note 125), sheet 54. The exact step, which the cathedral parish wanted, was taken by the Consistory on 2.3.1938 in its letter to the EOK and recommended as expert "Professor Liermann in Erlangen, Solicitor Dr. Karl Horn in Berlin or the Profs Mirbt and Feine", cf. KGA StS (op. cit. note 125), sheet 75. Cf. also Consistory to the EOK on 17.3.1938, EZA, 7/990, sheet 261.

241 Cf. EOK to Forsthoff on 7.2.1938, EZA, 7/9903, sheet 256.

242 Forsthoff, Gutachten in Sachen Quedlinburger Dom [expert report concerning the cathedral in Quedlinburg] (op. cit. note 241), sheet 303–357.

243 Expert report on 21.6.1938, ibid. sheet 204–234, here 223. Cf. also Hildebrandt, Die gewaltsame Inbesitznahme (op. cit. note 197), 113.

244 Forsthoff, Gutachten in Sachen Quedlinburger Dom (op. cit. note 242), sheet 306, 334.

245 Article 3, paragraph 1 reads "The German Protestant Church controls the legal activity of the German Church" [English translation], quoted from Ernst Rudolf Huber/ Wolfgang Huber, Staat und Kirche im 19. und 20. Jahrhundert. Dokumente zur Geschichte des deutschen Staatskirchenrechts, vol. IV: Staat und Kirche in der Zeit der Weimar Republik, Berlin (West) 1988, 862.

246 Cf. Kurt Dietrich Schmidt, Dokumente des Kirchenkampfs II/1 (Arbeiten zur Geschichte des Kirchenkampfes, 13), Göttingen 1964, 9 f.; Pfundtner-Neubert, Das neue Deutsche Reichsrecht, I. d. IV 4, 15.

247 Document from 24.6.1938, KGA StS (op. cit. note 125), sheet 64.

248 Cf. Höhne to Fischer on 23.4.1938, StA Q, 363/I, Baul. Veränd. V, sheet 67.

249 Cf. Schmidt to the leader of the children's service on 5.5.1938, KKA Q, no. 95. See also Schmidt to Selig on 3.5.1938, ibid. In a connected decision the children's service was omitted, as had already happened on Reich singing Sunday 1937, ibid.

250 Cf. Schmidt to *Staatliches Hochbauamt II* in Halberstadt on 5.7.1939, KGA StS (op. cit. note 125), sheet 93 and Kniese's answer on 10.7.1939, KGA StS, ibid. sheet 94; AKPS, Rep. A Spec. 6, A 2351. In regard to the EOK, Muhs of the Reich Church Ministry stressed on 13.1.1938: "The wish of the Parish that the planned start of the

renovations should not be moved to the period of the passion. I would also like to assert that this wish has been complied with." EZA, 7/9903, sheet 271.
251 Muhs to the EOK on 13.4.1938, StA Q 363/I, 1, sheet 23. On the financing of the renovation work the RCM provided 60,000 RM. Cf. Muhs to Himmler on 13.4.1938, ibid. sheet 24.
252 Cf. Schmidt to EOK on 11.5.1938, EZA, 7/9903, sheet 287; KGA StS (op. cit. note 125), sheet 59; cf. also Schmidt to the parish council of St Blasii on 12.4.1938, KGA StS (op. cit. note 125), sheet 87.
253 Cf. note EOK on 8.4.1938, EZA, 7/9903, sheet 297 f., here: 298.
254 Cf. A photo by Schmidt with file notes on 25.5.1938, EZA, 7/9903, sheet 270.
255 Cf. Schmidt to the Consistory Magdeburg on 31.8.1938, KGA StS (op. cit. note 125), sheet 75.
256 Cf. Schmidt to *Staatliches Hochbauamt II* Halberstadt on 5.7.1939, KGA StS (op. cit. note 125), sheet 93; Schmidt to the Consistory in Magdeburg on 31.8.1938, ibid. sheet 75. The heating system, which belonged to the parish, was removed without their knowledge and "sold as scrap metal". Schmidt to the Consistory in Magdeburg on 31.8.1938, ibid. sheet 75.
257 Cf. Voigtländer, Die Stiftskirche zu Quedlinburg (op. cit. note 28), 49; Kater, Das Ahnenerbe der SS (op. cit. note 30), 81.
258 "Even when Küster has to ring the bells for a funeral ... a SS man is always present to supervise him." Schmidt to the Consistory Magdeburg on 31.8.1938, KGA StS (op. cit. note 125), sheet 75.
259 Cf. see on it briefly Schmidt to the finance department Magdeburg on 2.5.1939, KGA StS (op. cit. note 125), sheet 92. Schmidt found fault with the long duration of the building works and complained to *Staatliches Hochbauamt II* in Halberstadt on 5.7.1938. Cf. ibid. sheet 93.
260 Schmidt to the Consistory Magdeburg on 24.8.1939, KGA Sts (op. cit. note 125), sheet 95 f.: AKPS, Rep. A Spec. 6, A 2351.
261 Cf. Schmidt already to the finance department in Magdeburg on 5.4.1938, KGA StS (op. cit. note 125), sheet 56.
262 According to Schmidt to the Consistory Magdeburg on 25.8.1939, EZA, 7/9903, sheet 531; KKA Q. Cf. also KGA StS (op. cit. note 125), sheet 97, 102–107.
263 Letter from Ernst Loycke to the Consistory Magdeburg on 10.7.1940 AKPS, Rep. A Spec. b, A 2351. Also see Schmidt's report to the Consistory Magdeburg on 24.8.1939, KGA StS (op. cit. note 125), sheet 95 f., according to which the parish council decided on 9.5.1938 to receive no financial help for the structural changes. Cf. KGA StS, ibid. sheet 60; cf. also Schmidt to EOK on 11.5.1938, ibid. sheet 59. For the further exchange of correspondence on the matter see sheets 61–63, 74.
264 Schmidt to Consistory Magdeburg on 21.2.1941, AKPS, Rep. A Spec. P, H 744, vol. 3.
265 Cf. Schmidt's notification to the Consistory on 23.7.1943, KKA Quedlinburg, no. 626.
266 Cf. on the exact circumstances of the theft and repatriation of the treasures at the end of the 1980s and beginning of the 1990s, Siegfried Kogelfranz/Willi A. Korte, Quedlinburg – Texas und zurück. Schwarzhandel mit geraubter Kunst, Munich 1996; Friedemann Goßlau, Verloren, gefunden, heimgeholt. Die Wiedervereinigung des Quedlinburger Domschatzes, Quedlinburg 1996 (including the description and illustration of the cathedral treasures); William H. Honan, Treasure Hunt. A New Yorker Times Reporter tracks the Quedlinburg Hoard, New York 1997.
267 Superintendent Schmidt held the sermon on 1 Ki 8,57 f. In it was stated: "Only the flagrant arrogance and the fatal blindness of that movement of our times, which has now been overcome, intended to make from the place, which for a millennium was consecrated for the worship of the heavenly father, a place of pilgrimage at the grave of the earthly King for a further millennium ... had thought, that it could banish Christ from the heart of the German nation and made the work of the men of the Church in their service to the population difficult in every possible way." Schmidt called on the parish to repent and said: "We are all guilty, certainly not all in the same sense,

as our conquers believe, but in a much deeper sense as Christians." KGA StS (op. cit. note 125), sheet 109–111.

268 Note from 12.6.1945, EZA, 7/9904.

269 Protocol from Richter on the opening and removal of the so-called Heinrich Sarcophagus in the crypt of the Quedlinburg monastery church on 25.2.1948, KGA StS (op. cit. note 125), sheet 137 and R.

270 Ibid.

271 On whether one can recognise in Italian Fascism, Russian Communism and in German National Socialism a "religion-like phenomena" (Hans Maier, 'Politische Religionen. Ein Konzept des Diktaturvergleichs', in Hermann Lübbe [ed.], Heilserwartung und Terror. Politische Religionen des 20. Jahrhunderts [Schriften der Katholischen Akademie in Bayern, 152], Düsseldorf 1995, 94–112, here: 97; cf. Hans Maier, Politische Religionen. Die totalitären Regime und das Christentum, Freiburg/Basel/Wien 1995), whether it is a religion or a totalitarian ideology, there is no agreement between historians, theologians and social scientists. While Schoeps has no doubts on the matter, Hans Mommsen was of the opinion that a clear structured dogmatic doctrinal system belongs to a religion (cf. Hans Mommsen, 'Leistungen und Grenzen des Totalitarismus-Theorems: Die Anwendung auf die nationalsozialistische Diktatur', in Hans Maier [ed.], Totalitarismus und politische Religion. Konzepte des Diktaturvergleichs, Paderborn 1996, 201–300; cf. Julius H. Schoeps, 'Erlösungswahn und Vernichtungswille. Der Nationalsozialismus als politische Religion', in Micheal Ley/Schoeps [eds], Der Nationalsozialismus als politische Religion [Studien zu Geistesgeschichte, 20], Mainz 1997, 261–271 and the contribution by Hans Mommsen, 'Der Nationalsozialismus als Politische Religion', in Gerhard Besier, Zwischen "Nationaler Revolution" und militärischer Aggression. Transformationen in Kirche und Gesellschaft unter der konsolidierten NS-Gewaltherrschaft [Herbst 1934 bis Herbst 1939]. Forschungsstand und Fragestellungen, Munich 2000). These facts point to a unclear concept of religion (cf. Fritz Stolz, Grundzüge der Religionswissenschaft [Kleine Vandenhoeck-Reihe, 1527], Göttingen 1988, 10 f.; Hubert Seiwert, 'Das Spezifische religiöser Wahrheit. Diskursive und pragmatische Begründung religiöser Wahrheitsansprüche', in Walter Kerber [ed.], Die Wahrheit der Religionen: Ein Symposium [Fragen einer neuen Weltkultur, 10], Munich 1994, 15–72).

272 Cf. on National Socialist musicology and the care of the *Ahnenerbe*, Pamela M. Potter, Most German of the Arts. Musicology and Society from the Weimar Republic to the End of Hitler's Reich, New Haven 1998, esp. 131 ff.

273 Only 25 percent of the SS members declared that they were believers in the National Socialist sense, the rest continued to belong to the traditional denominations. Only in the SS death head association did the percentage of believers reach 90. In 1938, only 61,030 members of the SS bared witness to the Nordic National Socialist belief (cf. Steiner, 'Über das Glaubenbekenntniss der SS' [op. cit. note 87]). This drawn-out distancing from the traditional churches is even more surprising, as the SS from 1936 on promoted the secession from the church of SS members and their relatives. In a letter from the Prussian Land's Church committee to the Reich Church Ministry on 5.1.1937 it reads: "In the meantime, complaints from the most different parts of our Land's church are increasing. There is not only a mass exodus from the Church by the SS, but also that of those belonging to SS formations frequently have pressure put on them, which is tantamount to official orders the Church, or that SS men, who wanted to get married, were forbidden to take their marriage bands in Church via the threat of the committee in the case of violation." EZA, 1/C3/218.

274 Cf. Besier, 'Der Nationalsozialismus als Säkularreligion', in Handbuch der EKU, vol. 3 (op. cit. note 67), 445–478, here: 460.

275 According to Kogelfranz/Korte, Quedlinburg – Texas und zurück (op. cit. note 266), 29.

276 According to Schmidt's report to the Consistory in Magdeburg on 6.8.1936, EZA, 1/C 3/210.

Martin Dibelius – an Internationally Renowned German. New Testament Scholar under National Socialism*

Martin Dibelius[1] (1883–1947) became chair of the department for New Testament Studies in Heidelberg in 1915. He was an exception in numerous respects and this was also true of his reputation as a scholar. As a convinced democrat, Dibelius was highly regarded in both Europe and the United States. His theological works on the history of religion, the pre-literary and oral formation of Gospel material as well as the question of New Testament ethics, in particular his critical study *From Tradition to Gospel* (1919), had a formative influence on an entire generation of New Testament scholars. Indeed *From Tradition to Gospel* has had such a lasting influence on theology that even in 1981 Gerd Theißen refered to it as a "point of reference for current research".[2] Moreover, Dibelius was active in several branches of the ecumenical movement and was the deputy chairman of the Faith and Order Commission.[3] He was also well respected at his university. He held the position of rector in 1927/28 and in the summer of 1929. He also served as Dean of the Faculty of Theology in 1919/20, 1924/25 and 1945.[4] He became a full member of the Heidelberg Academy of Sciences in 1926[5], and in 1915 he was awarded an honorary doctorate by the Faculty of Theology in Berlin and in 1937 he was made an honorary doctor of theology by the University of St. Andrews in Scotland. Dibelius had always been interested in politics. He was deeply influenced by Friedrich Naumann's National-Social Association at the start of the century[6] and in 1917 he joined the Progressive People's Party. He invariably refused to make vituperative speeches, instead emphasising the citizen's responsibility for the whole. Alongside Otto Frommel he signed a nationwide appeal of the "People's League for Freedom and Fatherland" in February 1918 calling for a negotiated peace. Dibelius drew a parallel between the living conditions of Germans during the war and the prevailing social and spiritual-cultural situation in the Reich. He viewed war as a given fate whose historical and political causes can only be analysed once the archives have been opened. After the revolution he joined Naumann's German Democratic Party (DDP), which he held to be a "party of culture", in contrast to the more proletarian Social Democratic Party (SPD). However, he recommended that his party form a coalition with the Social Democrats. Dibelius worked for the state committee of the DDP in Baden and played a part in its cultural committee on the national level. In addition he published articles on contemporary political and church-related issues, which primarily appeared in the two major national newspapers, the *Vossische Zeitung* and the *Frankfurter Zeitung*. He maintained that professors, just as normal citizens, should avoid becoming too deeply engrossed in their field of specialisation. He, therefore, especially tried to encourage young people to become involved in political bodies and thus play a role in making informed judgements and in the formula-

* First published in *KZG/CCH* 17 (2004), 412–422.

tion of responsible democratic objectives. He openly supported the Weimar Constitution, which espoused a "culture-conscious democracy" and the cultivation of a national and social ethos. For Dibelius, the "idea of humanity", the "concept of the League of Nations" and "internationality" were the desirable aims of political education. In the framework of various ecumenical conferences he pleaded, in full agreement with the Pact of the League of Nations, for international disarmament. He actively campaigned for the DDP in the run-up to elections, viewed it as a "party of the spirit" and expected it, in principle expecting all parties, to make an effort to develop their political powers of judgement as well as to endeavour towards the constructive resolution of political disputes. In his view taking a firm stand against anti-Jewish propaganda was a prerequisite to raising the moral and spiritual level of politics. With one representative each from the SPD and the Center Party he actively promoted the Catholic candidate, Wilhelm Marx, in Heidelberg for the German presidential elections of 1925. He thereby exposed himself to the vehement criticism from "positive" (i. e. Evangelical) circles in the Church and from nationalist university instructors. Impressed by Hindenburg's unifying force he campaigned for the latter's re-election in 1930. Nevertheless, he did not wish to join the German State Party, which absorbed the DDP in 1930 and at the same time he was still unable to commit himself to the SPD. Dibelius made a political name for himself on numerous occasions during his terms as rector in 1927/28 and in the summer of 1929 by appealing for greater responsibility in contemporary affairs. Of particular importance were the addresses[7] he held on the occasion of German Foreign Minister Gustav Stresemann and U. S. Ambassador Jacob C. Schurman being awarded honorary doctorates in 1928, in which he declared his belief in the democratic state and the Western orientation of the German Reich. In July 1929, he issued a notice calling for the student body to commemorate the tenth anniversary of the Weimar Constitution. This along with his support for Günther Dehn earned Dibelius some hostility, which included boycotts of his lectures. Apart from domestic and foreign policy he had a keen interest in social policy. He deemed it the specific task of the Church to do its part in working for social equality. Against the prevailing signs of crisis as Dibelius construed them, the "deadening" and "atomisation" caused by mechanisation and superficial diversions, he offered a vision of a culturally conservative, educated-bourgeois and religious unity. Dibelius seldom made compromises following Hitler's rise to power. However, he generally kept a low profile in political affairs and in matters of church policy during that time. In his travels abroad he did not shy away from criticising the Nazi church policy and the disenfranchisement of Jewish citizens.[8] The liberal theologian did not take part in the struggle within the Protestant Church due to his rejection of or scepticism towards his adversaries, yet he did support the cause of "Confessing forces" in a local context.[9] Alongside Heidelberg's city Pastor Hermann Maas[10] he took part in aiding the escape of Jewish citizens and protested to the Heidelberg mayor about the deportation of Jewish inhabitants in October 1940.[11]

In the autumn of 1935, Dean Odenwald was requested by the rector[12] to ask his colleague Dibelius whether he could suggest the name of a foreign theologian or churchman worthy of receiving an honorary doctorate with a view to the university's anniversary celebrations the following year. Dibelius used the opportunity to write a six-page letter naming such prominent individuals as the Swedish Archbishop Erling Eidem (Uppsala) and Lord Bishop of Chichester, George Bell.[13] In it he underlined each candidate's particular merits and the splendid options available, only to reject them at length for political considerations and reasons of church policy.[14] In this manner he tried to make clear to German Christian (DC) theologian Odenwald that the official German theology had hopelessly isolated itself and for the reasons cited had become academically incapacitated. When the "Party's position" made it seem "out of the question" to award honorary doctorates to German nationals then there was no sense giving doctorates to foreigners: "As long as ... things are such that nearly every foreigner would have to ask himself upon receiving a doctorate (at least the theologian, who knows something of the struggle between Church and State [*Kirchenkampf*]): now which Germany is it that is honouring me and: can I accept the honour for my own sake? – as long as this is so, I would, as a matter of principle, prefer not awarding doctorates to foreigners *alone* and running the risk of rejection."[15] As a reaction to the creation of Protestant Seminaries [*Kirchliche Hochschulen*] in the autumn of 1935 and the boycott of certain DC theologians and faculties by adherents of the Confessing Church the German Ministry of Education (REM) proposed in the autumn of 1936 the removal the first theological examination from the Church's sphere of responsibility and instead introducing a uniform faculty-based exam at state universities.[16] This was then to be the sole prerequisite for acceptance into pre-service training in the religious profession. The plan was the subject of heated discussions among the members of the faculty senate. In Heidelberg it was not the relevant dean but a group of professors and instructors, who under the leadership of Dibelius had considerable misgivings. While Dean Odenwald kept out of things entirely, Dibelius informed him on 24 May 1937 of a letter to the chairman of the faculty senate, Hans Schmidt, in which he protested against the introduction of the faculty-based exam.[17] Dibelius' letter to Hans Schmidt from 24 May 1937, which was also signed by Campenhausen, Greeven, Hupfeld, Frommel, Hölscher and Thielicke, read as follows:

"To the National-Socialist state it must be much less a matter of indifference than to previous states, whether theologians are trained at specialist colleges or in the fellowship of the university. A National-Socialist cultural policy intent on bringing everyone possible into its sphere of influence can only 'free' theologians if it hopes for the rapid degeneration of the entire profession. We, at least, do not want to accuse the state of hoping for such. Since however, for the National-Socialist state the faculties are avowedly not merely an educational institution but training institutions having a direct impact on life, it must have an interest in trained students not landing in a void but, in fact, in the Church ... . [The] German Protestant Church must be placed in the framework of national-political reality ... . It then cannot be otherwise that trained theologians are handed over to the Church for the purpose of examination because the Church alone offers them the function cut out for them, which is not solely, but in certain respects, a function within national-political reality. Particular matters, e. g., whether examinations are exclusively or only partly to be conducted by professors, may be resolved in various ways; the fundamental right of the Church to conduct examinations should not be challenged."[18]

In 1941, Dibelius penned a study entitled "Why Theology? On the Work and Purpose of Theological Scholarship". The aim of this "commissioned work"[19] was to counteract the plans to close theological faculties by proving university theology to be the central point of reference of German science on the whole. Moreover, Dibelius attempted, in a not unproblematic language and style, to portray Christian theology as being a discipline bound to and serving the nation and state. Certainly, he maintained that the science of theology must always refer to Christianity. "Because even if the German majority were largely to turn away from Christianity, it would still be more fruitful and realistic to deal with the questions of religion and the history of religion from a standpoint within Christianity than from a standpoint in nothing or in an unhistorical modern religion."[20] The previous year he had been prepared to make considerable concessions to the Nazi state in regards to foreign policy. With his book *British Christianity and British World Power*, which appeared in the semi-official series "The British Empire in World Politics", Dibelius partook in the "propaganda efforts of German scholars against enemy countries".[21] According to the security service (SD) of the SS these works were meant to "show the deep historical causes of present conflicts".[22] Dibelius performed the task in his own fashion[23] and accused "the British" of "hypocrisy in the domain of political ethics", of "Puritanical pride" and "Puritanical law", which culminated in their purported self-image as "God's chosen nation". All of this led them to "that delusion, which among the Jews and the British has shown as the phenomenon we call Pharisaism."[24] It seems that with this work he revoked nearly all of the positive statements he had made in the preceding years about British Christianity and understanding among nations on both bilateral and ecumenical levels.[25] However, the author himself saw things in a different light, which is featured in his post-war reflections. In the latter he claimed that by agreeing to write such a work he had prevented the "vilification of England" and contributed to an understanding of the "links between Christianity and politics in England".[26] This is certainly a euphemism, even though it may be true that Dibelius' work was of a somewhat more moderate nature in comparison to say Gerhard Kittel's *The Roots of the English Belief in Divine Election*[27], which was published the following year. The stereotypes and clichés based on *the* British on the one hand and *the* "always struggling, always searching", Germans[28] on the other hand are exasperating. Such stereotypes were also employed by Dibelius at the height of Germany's confidence in victory and placed him close to Nazi terminology. What is more he seems to have eluded any criticism by the person or the body commissioning the work. The SD report on the propaganda campaign reads in a generalising way: "It has been shown that the scientists are open to this sort of collaboration on current events and are extremely grateful."[29] However, interest among students on the subject of his book was rather moderate with only 26 students attending the interdisciplinary lecture on "Anglo-Saxon Christianity", which Dibelius held in the second trimester of 1940.[30]

In 1935, the Heidelberg systematic theologian Jelke reported "his colleague, Dibelius, several times to official National-Socialist offices", so that "ultimately the university leadership itself had to explain himself at an official faculty meeting".[31] Jelke had long been a notorious informer[32], thus his interventions could hardly be called successful. Without stating the reason Dibelius' salary was re-duced[33], in 1933/34 he had to endure two house searches, which entailed the con-fiscation of his correspondences and in 1938 he had to temporarily hand over his passport.[34] Yet all the attempts to oust him from the Ruperta Carola through in-terrogation and defamation as well as the demands for his removal from his uni-versity position failed, not least of all because he invariably conducted himself correctly and had ardent admirers even among the Nazi student body.[35] Among Dibelius' most bitter opponents were the Bishop of the Palatinate, Ludwig Diehl[36] and various Palatine pastors from the DC milieu, who ultimately demanded his transfer in the summer of 1934. They threatened to otherwise cancel plans to cre-ate a clubhouse for Palatine theology students in Heidelberg and to steer clear of the faculty in general.[37] However, the Baden Ministry of Culture and Education shied away from radical measures and sought instead to marginalize Dibelius' po-sition at the faculty by promoting the New Testament scholar Wendland. "There was nonetheless unanimous agreement [scil. among the rector's 'staff'] that Dr. Wendland does not possess the bold kind of character that would enable him to assert himself next to a man with the intellectual stature of Professor Dibelius, though Professor Dibelius, openly admitting the failure of his earlier [sic!] poli-tical views has been utterly reserved in his behaviour."[38] Thus, they were looking for "a real personality", who was to be enticed, of all things, by the planned "church professorship". Wendland, who was well aware of the reasons for his pro-motion, did his utmost to secure his own chair along with a corresponding raise. However, he still wanted to remain in his previous teaching post for social ethics, "not only because I have close personal ties to the discipline but because objec-tively speaking the special treatment of the relations between Christianity, church, state and nation, etc. is absolutely and of particular importance for the theology student today with regard to the practical administration of his future profes-sion".[39] Although Wendland was entrusted with conducting an advanced New Testament seminar[40] and as a private lecturer had all the duties of a full profes-sor[41], he had to do without an increase in pay and status.[42]

Among experts in Germany and abroad three professors were of outstanding importance: Dibelius, Köhler and Hölscher. It is certainly not an coincidence that these three also played an "important role when it came to forming the 'inner life'" of the Heidelberg Academy of Sciences by introducing topics, "which hard-ly corresponded with the spirit of the times at all".[43] If the number of students were referred to as an indicator for the attractiveness of a faculty, then Heidelberg would have been among the least attractive.[44] In the winter semester of 1932/33 Dibelius[45] and Wendland gave three lectures open to the general public. Within that project Dibelius gave a two-hour overview lecture on "Religion and religions" and the field of New Testament studies Dibelius offered a four-hour lecture ex-plaining the Gospel of John. In the summer semester of 1934, Beer lectured to the general public on "The influence of Aryanism on Israel's history and culture", Dibelius on "The importance of the Old Testament for Christianity and the lim-its of its importance" (this was repeated in winter semester of 1937/38) and Wendland lectured on "The importance of Protestantism in the genesis of the German state" (which was attended by 31 students).[46] Considering the actual historical circumstances, those topics could have been explosive. At the end of March 1945, the preparation committee for the reopening of the faculty, which consisted of Dibelius, Hölscher, Hupfeld[47], Campenhausen and Rosenkranz[48], made personnel suggestions for the employment of a denazified academic staff.[49] The military authorities allowed Jelke to retain his position at the end of the war[50], which was against the repeated objections of the faculty, but he had been neither a member of the Nazi Party nor belonged to any other organisation.[51] The faculty now brought to bear the individual acts of denunciation and defamation committed by Jelke since 1931 and in its attempt to provide evidence of theses the faculty behaved, in structural terms, in a manner not unlike their despised colleague in the foregone years.[52] Jelke manoeuvred cleverly. "He adroitly mobilised the Catholics, of which a delegation appeared before Prof. Schnabel[53] that asserted that Jelke had always been the only one to support a dialogue between denominations (in contrast to Mr. Dibelius, the driving force in the case against Jelke ...)."[54] Jelke refused to be ousted, gave lectures at the newly opened university in the winter semester of 1945/46[55] and then filed an application for retirement[56] to take effect on 3 March 1946, only to revoke it shortly afterwards with the aid of an attorney.[57] At the same time he announced his plans to take legal action against Dibelius, whom he regarded as the instigator of his early retirement.[58] To best demonstrate Dibelius' "complicity" he submitted Dibelius' brochure "British Christianity" from 1940[59] to the military government. He characterised the work to the rector as "tendentious National-Socialist writing of the worst kind".[60] The affair dragged on until the beginning of 1949. On 31 December 1948, a good thirteen months after Dibelius' death, the faculty decided "unanimously ... in the case of Jelke ... to request that the rector [scil. Geiler] file a petition with the government to institute disciplinary proceedings".[61] The proceedings against Jelke, which were indeed petitioned in the early summer of 1949[62], were never opened.[63] Incidentally Jelke continued to lecture with growing success up to and including April of the summer semester of 1949.[64] Despite his serious illness, Dibelius played an eminent role in the renewal of Heidelberg's academic theology and moreover in the academic and educational political regeneration of the university in the first years after the war.[65] Alongside the philosopher Karl Jaspers and the physician Karl Heinrich Bauer Dibelius spoke in favour of purging of the university staff and made preparations for the first election of a new rector.[66] In radio talks and essays Dibelius theologically reflected on the past without losing sight of the appropriate shaping of the present. His essay on the relation of "Protestantism and politics" from 1946 received much attention. The necessity of evaluating incriminated colleagues, in which Dibelius participated through expertise and the therefore essential inquiries[67] led Dibelius just like Karl Jaspers, the first post-war Rector Heinrich Bauer[68] and others to considerations on the question of guilt.[69] In spring 1946 at the same time as Jaspers' famous lectures on "The question of guilt", Dibelius wrote an essay on the "German self-reflection". Due to delays in the printing caused by the French censorship authorities, which continued after Dibelius' death on 11 November 1947, the text remained unpublished for fifty years.[70] The church historian Heinrich Bornkamm (1901–1977)[71], who was appointed as a professor to Heidelberg in 1948, made use of the fortunate circumstance that in Heidelberg, for example in contrast to Göttingen[72] and Erlangen[73], famous theologians from the university were not close to the Nazi-State but had generally rejected it, whereas inferior scholars had been politically incriminated, for a "purge" in its own way. While writing about the Heidelberg Faculty of Theology in 1961, he mentioned Martin Dibelius, Gustav Hölscher and Walther Köhler[74], but not Odenwald, Jelke or the others.[75]

Notes

1   Cf. Jansen and Thierfelder, Martin Dibelius, Badische Biographien, NF vol. 4, Stuttgart 1996, 52–55; Merk, Dibelius, in RGG 4, vol. 2, 833; Wolfes, 'Schuld und Verantwortung. Die Auseinandersetzung des Heidelberger Theologen Martin Dibelius mit dem Dritten Reich', in ZKG 111 (2000), 185–209.

2   Theißen, 'Die "Formgeschichte des Evangeliums" von Martin Dibelius und ihre gegenwärtige Bedeutung', in Theologische Fakultät Heidelberg (ed.), Lese-Zeichen für Annelies Findeiß zum 65. Geburtstag am 15. März 1984 von dankbaren Benutzern der Bibliothek des WTS der Universität Heidelberg, Heidelberg 1984 (ms.), 137–152, here: 137.

3   Cf. Dibelius, 'Die Kirchen in der ökumenischen Bewegung. Zwischen Stockholm und Oxford', in Gerstenmaier, Kirche, Volk und Staat. Stimmen aus der Deutschen Evangelischen Kirche zur Oxforder Weltkirchenkonferenz, Berlin 1937, 183–200, esp. 186 f.

4   Cf. Wolfes, 'Schuld und Verantwortung' (op. cit. note 1), 187.

5   Cf. Wennemuth, Wissenschaftsorganisation und Wissenschaftsförderung in Baden. Die Heidelberger Akademie der Wissenschaften 1909–1949, Heidelberg 1994, 626, 350 f., 548 f.

6   On this and the following cf. Fix, Universitätstheologie und Politik. Die Heidelberger Theologische Fakultät in der Weimarer Republik, Heidelberg 1994, 93 ff.; Wolfes, 'Demokratiefähigkeit liberaler Theologen', in vom Bruch (ed.), Friedrich Naumann in seiner Zeit, Berlin-New York 2000, 287–314, here: 295 ff.; idem, 'Schuld und Verantwortung' (op. cit. note 1), 311 ff.; Geiser, Verantwortung und Schuld. Studien zu Martin Dibelius, Hamburger Theologische Studien 20, Münster 2001, 40 ff.

7   Dibelius, Um Kirche und Nation: aus Schriften und Reden, selected by Günther Harder, Berlin 1935, Reden, 5–7.

8   Graf (ed.), 'Martin Dibelius über die Zerstörung der Bürgerlichkeit. Ein Vortrag im Heidelberger Marianne Weber-Kreis 1932', in Zeitschrift für neuere Theologiegeschichte 4 (1997), 114–153, here: 120 f.

9   Cf. Hölscher, 'Gelehrter in politischer Zeit', in Ruperto Carola 29 (1976/77), 53–60, here: 58.

10   Cf. Moraw, 'Die nationalsozialistische Diktatur', in Czer, Geschichte der Juden in Heidelberg, Heidelberg 1996, 440–455, here: 516 f.

11   Cf. Jansen and Thierfelder, Martin Dibelius (op. cit. note 1), 54; Graf, 'Martin Dibelius über die Zerstörung der Bürgerlichkeit' (op. cit. note 8), 122 f.

12   On 21 Sep. 1935 the rector asked the dean to propose candidates for honorary doctorates by 1 Nov. The letter read as follows: "The provisional working committee for the preparation of the university's 550th anniversary celebration considers it necessary, despite some reservations, that at the ceremony scheduled for 30 June 1936 at municipal hall honorary doctorates should be awarded by the dean after the speech of the German minister of science because it is expected above all from abroad that this tradition is upheld." Universitätsarchiv Heidelberg (hereinafter cited as UAH), Theol. Fak., 169. On 7 Feb. 1936 the rector also informed the dean that Hitler had declared the 550-year celebration to be "important for the Reich". Ibid.

13   On the relationship between Bell and Dibelius cf. their correspondence: Lambeth Palace Library (hereinafter cited as LPL), London, esp. the letters on the occasion of Deissmann's death, the letter from Dibelius to Bell on 20 Apr. 1937 and from Bell to Dibelius on 29 Apr. 1937, LPL, Bell Papers 20 (German Church), 445, 448.

14   Letter from Dibelius to Odenwald on 26 Oct. 1935, UAH, Theol. Fak., 144.

15   Op. cit. note 14.

16   Cf. Meier, Die Theologischen Fakultäten im Dritten Reich, Berlin 1996, 297 ff.

17   UAH, Theol. Fak., 165. Cf. Meier, Die Theologischen Fakultäten im Dritten Reich (op. cit. note 16), 303.

18   Ibid.

19   Cf. Geiser, Verantwortung und Schuld (op. cit. note 6), 24, with reference to Kümmel from whom Dibelius received the "commission" in the first place remains unanswered. Cf. also Geiser's interpretation of the study, ibid. 25 ff.

20   Martin Dibelius, Wozu Theologie? Von Arbeit und Aufgabe theologischer Wissenschaft, Leipzig 1941, 78.

21   Cf. Boberach (ed.), Meldungen aus dem Reich. Die geheimen Lageberichte des Sicherheitsdienstes der SS 1938–1945, iii, Hersching 1984, 869 ff.

22   Op. cit. note 21, 870.

23   Cf. Geiser's interpretation: Verantwortung und Schuld (op. cit. note 6), 145 ff., 159 ff., 188.

24   Quote from: Dibelius, Britisches Christentum und britische Weltmacht, Schriften des Deutschen Instituts für Außenpolitische Forschung 36; Das Britische Reich in der Weltpolitik 21, Berlin 1940, 42 f.

25   Cf. Dibelius, 'Englische Eindrücke', ThBl 5 (1926), 137–143; idem, 'Fragen und Aufgaben der ökumenischen Bewegung. Vortrag, gehalten im Harnack-Haus in Berlin am 3. Februar 1933', Die Eiche 21 (1933), 41–49, esp. 46–49.

26   Quoted in Geiser, Verantwortung (op. cit. note 6), 160.

27   HZ 163 (1941), 43–81.

28   Dibelius, Britisches Christentum (op. cit. note 24), 66.

29   Boberach, Meldungen aus dem Reich (op. cit. note 21), 870. A further concession to the theology of the German Christians was the review by Grundmann, Jesus der Galiläer und das Judentum, Leipzig 1940. Here Dibelius generally agreed to a large extent with Grundmann's position that Jesus was a decided opponent to Judaism of his time. Cf. Martin Dibelius, 'Neue Deutungen und Umdeutungen des Evangeliums', Die Christliche Welt 55, 1941, 3–7, here: 5 f.

30   UAH, Rep. 27, 209.

31   Faculty report from July 1945, UAH, Theol. Fak., 180.

32   On the difficulties he caused Wendland as early as the nineteen-twenties cf. idem, Wege und Umwege. 50 Jahre erlebter Theologie 1919–1970, Gütersloh 1977, 135.

33   Cf. Jansen and Thierfelder, Martin Dibelius (op. cit. note 1), 54. In contrast Odenwald recieved a pay raise. Including seniority bonuses, as of 1 Apr. 1939 he earned 11,600 Reichsmarks per annum.

34   Cf. letter from Dibelius to Odenwald on 1 Aug. 1938, UAH, PA 241 (Dibelius). Cf. also Mußgnug, Die vertriebenen Heidelberger Dozenten. Zur Geschichte der Ruprecht-Karls-Universität nach 1933 (Heidelberger Abhandlungen zur mittleren und neueren Geschichte NF 2), Heidelberg 1988, 29; Geiser, Verantwortung und Schuld (op. cit. note 6), 99 ff., 129 ff.

35   Cf. Wolfes, 'Schuld und Verantwortung' (op. cit. note 6), 193 f.; Geiser, Verantwortung und Schuld (op. cit. note 6), 99 ff., 120 ff.

36   Cf. Reichrath, Ludwig Diehl. Kreuz und Hakenkreuz im Leben eines Pfälzer Pfarrers und Landesbischofs, Speyer 1995.

37   Cf. letter from Pastor Schmidt to Voges on 12 Aug. 1934 as well as from the rector to the Baden Ministry of Culture and Education on 31 Oct. 1934 and 7 Nov. 1934, GLA, 235, 3147. According to information from the Central Archive of the Protestant Church of Rhineland-Palatinate (Christine Lauer) on 19 July 2002 there are no doc-

uments pertaining to the project of building a clubhouse [Kameradschaftshaus]. On DC Pastor Schmidt (Kaiserslautern) and the places of study of Palatine theology students cf. Fandel, Konfession und Nationalsozialismus. Evangelische und katholische Pfarrer in der Pfalz 1930–1939 (VKZG B 76), Paderborn 1997, 88, 107 ff., 520.

38 Letter from the rector to Baden Ministry of Culture and Education on 31 Oct. 1934 and 7 Nov. 1934, GLA, 235, 3147.

39 Report from Wendland to the rector on 28 Sep. 1934, GLA 235, 3147.

40 Cf. letter from the Baden Minister of Culture and Education to the rector from 28 Apr. 1934, op. cit. note 39.

41 Cf. letter from Wendland to the rector on 16 Dec. 1934, ibid.

42 On 7 Jan. 1935, the rector informed the Baden Ministry of Culture and Education that Wendland was to conduct an advanced New Testament seminar and should therefore receive a higher wage. On 2 July 1935, the Baden Ministry of Culture and Education responded to the rector that the financial resources could not be made available to increase Wendland's income. GLA 235, 3147.

43 Wennemuth, Wissenschaftsorganisation und Wissenschaftsförderung in Baden (op. cit. note 5), 392 f.

44 On this and the following cf. Rainer Hering, Theologische Wissenschaft und "Drittes Reich", Pfaffenweiler 1990, 25.

45 Cf. the list of courses held by Dibelius, in Geiser, Verantwortung und Schuld (op. cit. note 6), 294 ff.

46 UAH, Rep. 27, 1429.

47 According to a report published in the Rhein-Neckarzeitung on 24 May 1947 there had been considerations for a short period of time on appointing Hupfeld as the Minister of Culture and Education in Baden.

48 In 1947 Rosenkranz was appointed extraordinary professor and in 1948 he was offered a chair as professor of theology of mission and ecumenical theology at the faculty of theology at the University of Tübingen (since 1962 known as the department for theology of mission and ecumenical theology). In 1949 he was awarded an honorary doctorate by the faculty of theology of the University of Heidelberg. Biographisch-Bibliographisches Kirchenlexikon, XXVIII, 2001, 1205 f.

49 On this and the following cf. Wolgast, 'Die Neubildung der Heidelberger Theologischen Fakultät 1945–1950', in Marggraf, Thierfelder and Wennemuth (eds), Unterdrückung, Anpassung, Bekenntnis. Die Evangelische Kirche in Baden im Zweiten Weltkrieg und in der Nachkriegszeit, Karlsruhe 2005; Schulte, 'Die Theologische Fakultät der Universität Heidelberg nach der Befreiung', in Theologische Fakultät der Universität Heidelberg (ed.), Kleine Geschichte der Heidelberger Theologischen Fakultät von Marsilius von Inghen bis Gottfried Seebaß. Festgabe des Dekanats zum 60. Geburtstag von Gottfried Seebaß, Heidelberg 1997, 85–87.

50 Cf. letter from the Theological Faculty to Major Powhida on 22 Aug. 1945, UAH, Theol. Fak., 180; Wolgast, "Neubildung" (op. cit. note 49), 13.

51 On 17 Feb. 1937, Hölscher wrote to the president of the Department of Culture and Education of the District of Baden, Thoma: "Mr. Jelke's influence was increasingly rejected by the theologically reliable, i.e., in practical terms, the antifascist segment of the student body. The reasons for this are to be found not in his teachings but in his personality. The faculty is therefore unanimously of the conviction that Mr. Jelke, however great or small his purely political incrimination may seem, should not be allowed to play a decisive role in the reconstruction, i. e., as an active professor." UAH, PA 4380 (Jelke).

52 Cf. letter from Hölscher to the military government on 18 Sep. 1945; from Hölscher to Huber (Government of Baden, Department of Culture and Education) on 11 Nov. 1945; report on Jelke's position in the case of Dehn 1931 sent from Dibelius to Huber on 12 Nov. 1945, cf. UAH, PA 248 (Jelke). Jelke lodged an appeal against the indictment submitted by the theological faculty on 31 Oct. 1935 and forwarded it to the sen-

ate commission of the university. Cf. the charge of attorney Ludwig from 8 Sep. 1948. UAH, PA 4380. On 21 Dec. 1948, Jelke's lawsuit was dismissed. Ibid.

53　On Schnabel, who was "retired" from his chair in Karlsruhe in 1936 and played a pivotal role in the reconstruction of the Baden school and educational system between 1945 and 1947, cf. Lönne, 'Franz Schnabel', Wehler (ed.), Deutsche Historiker, IX, Göttingen 1982, 81–101, esp. 95; Hertfelder, Franz Schnabel und die deutsche Geschichtswissenschaft, Schriftenreihe der Historischen Kommission bei der Bayerischen Akademie der Wissenschaften 60, 2 vols, Göttingen 1998. During his stint as a private scholar in Heidelberg, Schnabel became acquainted with Dibelius in the house of Marianne Weber. Cf. Hertfelder, Franz Schnabel und die deutsche Geschichtswissenschaft, 682.

54　Handwritten letter from Huber to Hölscher on 29 Nov. 1945, UAH, PA 248 (Jelke). Cf. letter from Jelke to Schnabel on 25 Mar. 1946, ibid., in which he complains that no mention was made of his lectures.

55　Heinrich Kraft, Damals nach dem Krieg, gives a lively account of the makeshift conditions, in which lectures and seminars were held, usually in the apartments of professors due to a lack of fuel and the situation of libraries. Cf. also Edmund Schlink, 'Laudatio', in Theologische Fakultät Heidelberg (ed.), Lese-Zeichen, 9–12.

56　Cf. Geiser, Verantwortung und Schuld (op. cit. note 6), 184 ff.

57　Cf. letter from attorney Ganzmüller to the president of the District of Baden, Dr. Thoma, on 26 Sep. 1946. UAH, PA 248 (Jelke).

58　Jelke wrote to Hölscher on 7 Apr. 1947 in an attempt to win his favour: "When I was dean in the winter semester of 1934/35 and in my capacity as such had to negotiate in Berlin with the advisor for Protestant theology, the latter (Mr. Mattiat) asked me if I couldn't put in a good word for you in Heidelberg or as the dean explain that no faculty is willing to have you and that you would have to be sent into retirement if Heidelberg, the only option remaining, did not accept you. Out of sheer loyalty to you as a colleague, I cleared the way for you to Heidelberg, at the price of incurring the antagonism of nationalist students here." UAH, PA 248 (Jelke).

59　Cf. UAH, PA 4380 (Jelke).

60　Letter from Jelke to the rector on 13 Dec. 1948, UAH, PA 4380.

61　Minutes of the faculty meeting, Protokollbuch, 193. UAH, Theol. Fak., 68.

62　Cf. the resolution of the senate select committee from 21 June 1949 to approve the request submitted by the theological faculty to the president of the District of Baden, Department of Culture and Education, calling for formal proceedings to be instituted against Jelke. UAH, PA 4380 (Jelke).

63　Cf. Geiser, Verantwortung und Schuld (op. cit. note 6), 187 f.

64　At least in the winter semester 1946/47 35 students attended his lecture. UAH, Rep. 27, 651.

65　Cf. Geiser, Verantwortung und Schuld (op. cit. note 6), 225 ff.

66　Cf. Wolgast, Die Universität Heidelberg 1386–1986, Berlin-Heidelberg-New York 1986, 167; idem, 'Karl Bauer – der erste Heidelberger Nachkriegsdirektor. Weltbild und Handeln 1945–1946', in Heß, Lehmann and Sellin with Junker and Wolgast (eds), Heidelberg 1945 (Transatlantische Historische Studien 5), Stuttgart 1996, 107–129; Wennemuth, Wissenschaftsorganisation und Wissenschaftsförderung in Baden, 548.

67　Cf. Tent, 'Edward Yarnall Hartshorne and the Reopening of the Ruprecht-Karls-Universität', in "Heidelberg 1945: His Personal Account", in Heß, Lehmann and Sellin, Heidelberg 1945 (op. cit. note 66), 55–74, here: 65.

68　Cf. Bauer, 'Was bedeutet uns die Universität?', in idem (ed.), Vom neuen Geist der Universität. Dokumente, Reden und Vorträge, Berlin-Heidelberg 1947, 15–18.

69　Cf. Besier and Sauter, Wie Christen ihre Schuld bekennen. Die Stuttgarter Erklärung, Göttingen 1985; Wolfes, 'Schuld und Verantwortung' (op. cit. note 6), 196 ff.

70　Cf. Graf, 'Martin Dibelius über die Zerstörung der Bürgerlichkeit' (op. cit. note 8).

71　On Bornkamm cf. Greschat, 'Die Evangelisch-Theologische Fakultät in Gießen in der Zeit des Nationalsozialismus (1933–1935)', in Jendorff, Mayer and Schmalenberg (eds), Theologie im Kontext der Geschichte der Alma Mater Ludoviciana, Gießen 1983, 139–166, here: 142 f., 148 f., 157; Lehmann, 'Muß Luther nach Nürnberg? Deutsche Schuld im Lichte der Lutherliteratur 1946/47', in idem, Protestantisches Christentum im Prozeß der Säkularisierung, Göttingen 2001, 64–80, here: 76 f.; idem, 'Heinrich Bornkamm im Spiegel seiner Lutherstudien von 1933 und 1947', in Kaufmann and Oelke (eds), Evangelische Kirchenhistoriker im "Dritten Reich", Gütersloh 2002, 367–380; Besier, Die Kirchen und das Dritte Reich, vol. 3: Spaltungen und Abwehrkämpfe 1934–1937, Munich-Berlin 2001, 181 f., 958; Wilfried Werbeck, Bornkamm, in RGG 4, i, 1698.

72 Cf. e. g. Robert Ericksen, Theologen unter Hitler. Das Bündnis zwischen evangelischer Dogmatik und Nationalsozialismus, Munich-Vienna 1986, esp. 167 ff.

73 Cf. e. g. Ericksen, 'Assessing the Heritage. German Prostestant Theologians, Nazis and the "Jewish Question"', in idem and Heschel (eds), Betrayal. German Churches and the Holocaust, Minneapolis 1999, 22–39; idem, 'Genocide, Religion and Gerhard Kittel, Protestant Theologians Face the Third Reich', in Bartov and Mack (eds), In God's Name. Genocide and Religion in the Twentieth Century, New York-Oxford 2001, 62–78; Hamm, 'Werner Elert als Kriegstheologe. Zugleich ein Beitrag zur Diskussion "Luthertum und Nationalsozialismus"', in KZG 11 (1998), 206–254.

74 On Köhler's works cf. his bibliography, published by the Zwingli Society in 1940.

75 Cf. Bornkamm, 'Die Theologische Fakultät Heidelberg', in Hinz (ed.), Aus der Geschichte der Universität Heidelberg und ihrer Fakultäten, Ruperto Carola, Sonderband, Heidelberg 1961, 135–162, here: 151, 153.

"Efforts to strengthen the German Church".
The Federal Council of Churches of Christ in America and the Representatives of the German Protestant Church after the Second World War (1945–1948)*

As a result of the Stuttgart Declaration of Guilt on 19 October 1945[1] the churches of the Western alliance[2] and also the Churches in countries, which had suffered under German occupation, renewed their ecumenical community with the Protestant Churches of Germany. Alongside the establishment of multilateral ecclesiastical relations through the World Council of Churches, which was in the process of being established, some individual national churches also sought to explore the situation in Germany and restore contacts with the representatives of the German churches.[3] At the Church Conference of Treysa in August 1945 it was decided that Martin Niemöller should "take over the care of the ecumenical relations for the Protestant Church in Germany"[4]. It was therefore inevitable that the Secretary General of the Federal Council of Churches of Christ in America[5], Samuel McCrea Cavert[6], invited Martin Niemöller to visit the United States when both German representatives of the German Protestant Church (*Evangelische Kirche in Deutschland*, EKD), Niemöller and Theophil Wurm[7], met with colleagues from the ecumenical churches in Geneva in February 1946 during the session of the Provisional Committee of the World Council[8]. A similar invitation to Great Britain was given shortly after by the bishop of Chichester, George Bell.[9]

These visits completely complied with Niemöller's own wishes and ideas. Already at his press conference in Naples on 5 June 1945 he had expressed the wish "to go to England and America in order to talk to the resident Christian leaders, for I need also to satiate a spiritual hunger"[10]. The day before leaving Naples he had already received an invitation[11] from the Executive Director of the National Lutheran Council (NLC)[12], Ralph H. Long, who asked Niemöller to come to the United States as a guest of the American Lutherans.[13] Public relations considerations in favour of their confession also played a role on the part of the Lutherans.[14] However, the Anglo-American Church representatives had not expected the various forms of opposition, which arose in their own countries.[15] These led to considerable annoyance and to Niemöller's temporary decision not to travel to Great Britain. On the other hand, Niemöller's first public comments also caused a certain abatement of the Americans' initial enthusiasm about the "good German". Niemöller's remark made to a *Mirror* correspondent that he

* First published in German as 'Efforts to strengthen the German Church. Der Federal Council of Churches of Christ in America und die Repräsentanten der deutschen evangelischen Kirche in der Nachkriegszeit (1945–1948)', in Gerhard Besier and Günter R. Schmidt (eds), *Widerstehen und Erziehen im christlichen Glauben. Festgabe für Gerhard Ringshausen zum 60. Geburtstag*, Holzgerlingen 1999, 206–238, notes 341–363.

would like to come to the United States, but that he thought it would be better to safeguard Germany's interests if not only the Lutherans but all religious forces were a party to this invitation[16], gave the Lutherans a possibility to withdraw. Long wrote on 6 June 1945 to the president of the Lutheran Synod of Virginia of the United Lutheran Church in America: "In the light of the news story, which appeared in this morning's *New York Herald Tribune* the question arises whether we will be wise in trying to get Niemöller here. Some of the statements, which he is reported to have made are of course not very satisfactory from an American point of view. If he insists on making statements like those he is reported to have made, he would do us more harm than good."[17]

On 8 March 1946, i. e. one month after the meeting of the Provisional Committee of the WCC in Geneva, the newspapers published the "Law for the Delivering of National Socialism from Militarism"[18], which gave the Council of the EKD the impression that it made an "understanding and pacification in the German people" and a "spiritual renewal as good as impossible"[19]. Denominational and Church political tensions within the EKD added to the trouble of difficulties in acceptance and backstrokes abroad. In order to support Niemöller and to prevent him from giving up, the WCC General Secretary, Willem A. Visser't Hooft, wrote to him on 25 July 1946 that "we of the World Council are hoping that you will remain the responsible man for foreign relations. ... From the point of view of ecumenical Christianity, it remains immensely important that Martin Niemöller and no one else pulls the strings for outside relations."[20] He asked him not to take "these rather fanatic Lutherans"[21] close to the Munich member of the Church assembly, Christian Stoll[22], too seriously because according to Hanns Lilje they did not determine the course of the Lutheran national churches.[23] Finally, Niemöller changed his opinion at the beginning of September 1946 and accepted the invitation to Great Britain, which had eventually been extended.[24] In the autumn of 1946 this journey came to be[25], however, it was declared to be a strictly private event. During the trip Niemöller also visited a German internment camp.[26]

In a letter to General Eisenhower from mid-March 1946, Cavert named the establishment of cooperative relations between the German and the American churches as the reason for inviting Niemöller to America. "I hope and believe that the outcome of these contacts will be a strengthening of the German Church along democratic lines."[27] Cavert expressed himself similarly towards the War Department, he hoped the visit of Niemöller and other German churchmen to the USA would promote other efforts to strengthen the Church and to "materially contribute to the rebuilding of a New Germany"[28]. The meeting with foreign churchmen in Geneva in February 1946 had already made a contribution, according to Cavert's statement to the visa department of the State Department. Niemöller would be given an understanding of the spirit and nature "of our western democracies" and his efforts "to bring the Church of Germany into line with our own point of view"[29] had been strengthened. Cavert added that the aim was to influence the Church by leading German churchmen in a way corresponding to the ideas of the western powers, so that it developed a corresponding effectiveness in the "rebuilding of German life"[30]. It is hard to determine who first expressed the idea of inviting Niemöller to the United States.[31] At any rate Paul Tillich was also among those who recommended Niemöller to the Federal Council. In mid-January 1946, Tillich wrote to Henry Smith Leiper[32], the acting WCC General Secretary, that "nobody could impress as strongly as he the American public opinion with the facts about the struggle of the Confessing Church against Hitler and about the present situation of German Protestantism"[33]. Admittedly, he added: "Arrangements should, however, be made to protect Niemöller from abuses by reporters and interviewers."[34] A situation like the one in Naples on 5 June 1945 should be avoided.[35]

Fourteen days later, Tillich's colleague at Union Theological Seminary[36], John C. Bennett[37], expressed great apprehension about the planned visit from Germany. A day earlier he had heard a lecture by Rabbi Stephen S. Wise, the president of the American Jewish Congress, who as Bennet referred had harshly attacked Niemöller because he had done nothing "to resist anti-Semitism"[38]. Rabbi Wise had said that he would deem it very unfortunate should Niemöller come to the United States and win over "a lot of women's clubs". Bennett expressed his fear "that an ugly situation may arise if there is a Jewish demonstration against him when he comes"[39], and of course a number of newspapers would join the campaign in this case. He asked Leiper to possibly publish proofs that Niemöller had opposed anti-Semitism in Germany.[40] Furthermore, he recommended a detailed consultation with the leading personalities of the Jewish organisations before Niemöller's arrival. Cavert compiled a white paper entitled "The Truth About Pastor Niemöller", which was intended to contribute to the correction of the misinformation.[41]

Although the resistance to the visit from Germany mounted when Niemöller's invitation became known in March 1946, Cavert worked unperturbedly for the realisation of his stay. Besides the known objections of Eleanor Roosevelt[42], the widow of President Franklin D. Roosevelt († 12 April 1945), a handful of rumours circulated, which were bound to disavow Niemöller. For example, Cavert was asked whether it was correct that Niemöller had converted to the Roman Catholic Church.[43] Cavert, who as Secretary-General of the Federal Council had apparently been uninformed of Niemöller's High-Church episode of 1940/41[44], replied that he considered the statement to be incorrect. He said that Niemöller had a high-ranking position in the EKD and enthusiastically accepted membership of the Provisional Committee of the WCC.[45] What was more important than all other objections was the fact that Franklin Clark Fry[46], the president of the United Lutheran Church in America and member of the executive committee of the National Lutheran Council, "is not keen about his [scil. Niemöller's] coming at the present time"[47].

Not only the misgivings from different sides, but also the problem of getting a visa for Niemöller[48], finally induced Cavert to postpone the visit planned for the summer of 1946 to the late autumn of that year. Furthermore, as he wrote to Visser't Hooft he hoped that in the autumn Fry "would not be so jittery about the Situation in the EKD and would therefore be more cooperative in welcoming Niemöller here"[49]. Therefore, the tensions between the Lutherans in Germany, who would have preferred the foundation of a Lutheran national church instead of a church association[50], and the advocates of the EKD had an effect on America[51]. The news hit the Wartburg Theological Seminary of the American Lutheran Church that the Barthians in Germany did everything in their power "to discredit Luther and Lutheranism"[52] and that the United Lutherans (*Unierte*) close to Niemöller wanted to swallow up Lutheranism. Thus, Niemöller, the protagonist of the Confessing Church from a supra-confessional Protestant Church in Germany, should not be received as the first German churchman in America. Michelfelder wrote to Long in a confidential report: "All of the Lutherans feel that the coming of Niemöller to America will give him a prestige, which is quite out of proportion to the place he should hold in the public estimation of the cause of the Church in Germany. It certainly would be most unfortunate if Niemöller publicly criticizes the Lutherans as he has in Germany."[53]

Karl Barth[54], Hans-Bernd Gisevius[55] and Niemöller tried to influence the military government against the Bavarian national Bishop Meiser. "They have created the opinion that Meiser is intensely nationalistic and that he is for the restoration of the pre-war State Church [tie]-up through the bishoprics, which is not true."[56] Since Cavert only named the bishop of Wuerttemberg, Theophil Wurm, as the second potential visitor from Germany, whose work for Church unification could practically be regarded as a precursor organisation of the EKD[57], the Lutherans on both sides of the Atlantic missed a genuine Lutheran representative from Germany. However, Michelfelder considered it unlikely that after several verbal lapses Wurm would get a chance to leave Germany.[58]

Therefore, the Lutherans concentrated their attention on Niemöller. Ralph H. Long wrote to the president of the American Lutheran Church, Walter E. Schuette: "Our American section of the Lutheran World Convention did not believe it would be advisable for him [read: Niemöller] to come over here alone because there would be a tendency on his part, when he returns to Germany, to make use of the prestige and the honour, which would be bestowed upon him."[59]

However, Hanns Lilje told the American Lutherans if the Federal Council should stick to its invitation to Niemöller and should he actually receive an entry authorisation, then it would be unwise to simply ignore him. "Niemoller and Asmussen must be kept in the Lutheran camp. If you folks ignore him when he comes to America you will certainly get him to pop off concerning the hierarchical tendencies of the Landesbischof. Niemoller can be influenced by the right people. Lilje knows how to handle him and has kept him from speaking hastily ... It would be a catastrophe if Niemoller were offended by the Lutherans of America. This would create a situation in Germany for the Lutherans like Lilje, which would split EKD. The effect would be identical as if Missouri should succeed in alienating Meiser and the Church of Bavaria."[60]

Stewart W. Herman[61], a Lutheran pastor from the USA and the assistant director of the reconstruction department of the WCC, told Cavert that according to his information Niemöller intended to remain in the United States for six months. Herman personally would deem it a good thing if somebody such as Hanns Lilje accompanied Niemöller.[62] Cavert immediately telegraphed Herman: "Please advise Niemöller Lutheran cooperation with his itinerary better if postponed until fall."[63] He wrote to Visser't Hooft that Fry hoped that Niemöller would not come. At his request he added the issue was probably discussed in the executive committee of the National Lutheran Council and the decision had been made that the Lutherans would not invite Niemöller. Of course, he concluded, the invitation of the Federal Council would be honoured. "It would however be too bad to have the official Lutheranism in this country taking a somewhat negative attitude toward his coming and I wonder whether he might not prefer to wait five or six months in the hope that in this way the American Lutherans would become much more enthusiastic about his coming and cooperate thoroughly."[64]

Cavert stated that if Niemöller really wanted to remain six months in the United States he would attract massive criticism for leaving his church alone so long in these difficult times. The best time for a visit in the USA would be at the beginning of December 1946 because the biennial meeting of the Federal Council was taking place in Seattle at this time. At the end of the letter Cavert asked Visser't Hooft to convey these messages to Niemöller. In another letter from Cavert to Visser't Hooft it reads: "I am sorry to have to say that there is still a good deal of criticism of him in some quarters in this country, particularly in the quarters where the general point of view is that there are no 'good Germans'. I think that this point of view does not prevail much in Church circles but I run into it in Jewish circles."[65]

At the beginning of June 1946, Niemöller wrote to Cavert that he would try to obtain the visa for the United States in mid-July, travel to Great Britain at the beginning of July and from there he would then arrive to the USA at the beginning of September.[66] Regarding Lutheranism he expressed the hope that an arrangement would be possible without him causing "feelings of embitterment"[67] with anybody. Niemöller's travel plans were delayed for about two months due to the visas, thus he did not return from Geneva until the beginning of September.[68] In the meantime Cavert, who had been the temporary representative of the Federal Council in Germany and Europe since July[69], had personally spoken to General Clay about Niemöller's planned stay in the USA. Clay had agreed to try to obtain an entry permit for Niemöller, "if we were prepared to invite two others at the same time", in order to avoid giving the impression that he was favouring "any one faction in Germany"[70]. Cavert made use of Clay's tip and in mid-August 1946 asked the Secretary of War, Robert P. Patterson, for an entry permit for a German delegation of three. Beside Niemöller, he now named the bishop of Berlin, Otto Dibelius, and the Stuttgart prelate, Karl Hartenstein.[71] However, he emphasised that Niemöller must be in time for the Biennial Meeting of the Federal Council opening in Seattle in December 1946, whereas the two other visitors might arrive somewhat later. Admittedly, he sent neither Dibelius nor Hartenstein a direct invitation until mid-September.[72]

In September 1946, changes in different fields began to emerge, which seemed to facilitate Niemöller's entry to the United States. The US government loosened its restrictive politics of delimitation against the Germans. The Federal Council's Executive Committee appointed the Lutheran, Julius Bodensieck, who until then had been president of the Wartburg Theological Seminary in Dubuque, Iowa[73], as the new permanent representative of the American churches for Germany and as contact between the American military administration and German Protestantism in agreement with the WCC[74] and Franklin Fry.

The Lutheran, Bodensieck, has hardly arrived in Germany when he sought to strengthen his denomination. On 20 November 1946 he wrote to Long: "I am distressed at the obvious attempts to calvinise Germany."[75] When American professors were, as planned, to be invited to Germany their denomination must be taken into account, "so that Lutheranism is given a fair hearing"[76]. Despite such alarming news Fry abandoned his resistance to Niemöller's USA visit, so that now the Lutherans also sent him invitations.[77] Only the American military government's authorisations for departure were still to arrive.[78]

After a conversation in the Pentagon with the secretary of war, Robert P. Patterson, on 23 October 1946[79] Cavert seemed to have guarantees that Niemöller could arrive in time in the USA for the Biennial Meeting[80]. However, he was mistaken. An internal memorandum from the US Government over a session of the G[erman]-A[merican]-Secretariat in the State Department on 25 October 1946 states:

"It was the consensus of opinion that it would be unfortunate for Niemöller to be one of the first Germans to visit this country, for the following reasons: (1) inaugurating the [exchange] program with any controversial figure is undesirable, since it is the object of the program to facilitate, rather than confuse, the German reorientation and to muster support for our efforts in the US, (2) while considered in some circles here to be a martyr to Nazism, Niemöller is known to large sections of the public, both here and in Germany, as a strong German nationalist. His selection for such a visit so early in the program would set a tone unjustified by our plans, (3) that Niemöller is particular undesirable as a choice at this time because he handles himself badly in press interviews ..., (4) that there is little to gain in Germany from Niemöller's presence here even should his visit pass without incident, since he has no substantial support in Germany today."[81]

Although generally agreeing on the matter the United States Government saw three possibilities of action. As there was no security threat but only political misgivings, the War Department might have granted entry to the country within the framework of the exchange programme, or unofficial contacts to the Federal Council might be used to convince it to withdraw the invitation to Niemöller and get a more suitable Church personality to visit the country. Finally, there would be the possibility not to allow Niemöller to enter the country, "until a number of more representative and less controversial Germans have visited the US".

When Cavert pursued the reasons of the further unexpected postponement he learnt that the acting secretary of state, Dean G. Acheson, in person had spoken out against granting a visa for entry to the USA because he had taken offence at some of Niemöller's remarks reported by the press.[82] Only on 14 November did the bishops G. Bromley Oxnam and Henry Knox Sherrill[83] as well as John Foster Dulles[84] succeed in making the top official change his mind[85]. Acheson had the content and effect of Niemöller's speeches and appearances in America reported to him at the end of January 1947.[86]

Regarding the invitations issued to two further Germans Cavert supposed that Bishop Dibelius would cancel his visit anyway, "since a bishop of the Russian Zone ought not to come to America at this time"[87]. He thought Asmussen[88] was not an especially good alternative but he was willing to invite him if Visser't Hooft could recommend no other. "Of course Asmussen cannot make a great impression because he does not speak English well enough but we could use him in small groups of leaders."[89] Herman, whose book "The Rebirth of the German Church" with a foreword by Martin Niemöller was due to appear a month later[90], advised Cavert to invite the ecumenically knowledgeable Lutheran, Hanns Lilje from Hanover or the systematic theologian Hans-Joachim Iwand instead of Asmussen[91]. The United Lutheran Church of America appeared particularly interested in Lilje because he was already intended to give lectures at Hamma Divinity School in the current academic year.[92]

A short time later, Cavert requested visas for Niemöller and also Hanns Lilje from the State Department's Visitors' Office, although Lilje lived in the British Zone.[93] At the beginning of November 1946, Cavert informed Visser't Hooft that he had also invited Asmussen and Dibelius and had received a letter from the latter saying that he could visit the United States at the beginning of 1947.[94]

In Geneva, as in the USA, church officials worried about the EKD's inner condition and hoped for Niemöller's mediation in the Church-political confrontations between Barthians and Lutherans. On 10 November 1946, the systematic theologian, John C. Bennett, reported to the Americans from Geneva.

"There is a standing problem that may at any time make matters worse, the drive of the extreme Barthians in Germany on the present German Church government and also on the extreme Lutherans. Wim [Visser't Hooft] does not take the extreme position here but he is often bracketed with Barth and what he says is resented by even the moderate Lutherans in Geneva. This is a terribly confused issue. Niemöller is now taking a mediating position compared with the extreme Barthians, who want to wreck the whole provisional government of the Church and start all over again on a sectarian basis, on the basis of a purely prophetic attitude toward the revival of the Church which is very intolerant of all who disagree. I think that Wim stands with Niemöller in this. The conflict is most tragic ... . This problem is going to test the leadership of the World Council almost as much as the Orthodox problem."[95]

Bennett's alarming letter therefore involved not only domestic German Church relations but this theologian also feared the problem was be passed on into the WCC. Thanks to Cavert's insistent efforts he succeeded literally at the last minute to have Niemöller and his wife flown into the country[96] for the Biennial Meeting of the Federal Council in Seattle[97]. As was to turn out the secretary general of the American Church Association had rightly assessed Niemöller's appearance in the USA. With the sermons and talks that he and his wife gave, but also with the interviews they gave, both won over the hearts of many Americans.[98] "They both made a significant impression", Cavert wrote enthusiastically to Visser't Hooft. "Niemöller is getting at wonderful reception from the general public, marred by occasional unfriendly criticism made by people like Mrs. Roosevelt ... . The net effect ... is certainly splendid."[99]

However, Cavert had hardly left anything to coincidence. Rev. Ewart Edmund Turner of the American Committee of the WCC carefully prepared the press conferences and the individual audiences as such trying to avoid negative headlines.[100] Nonetheless, he could not prevent some newspapers running the title

"Niemöller Criticizes American Occupation Policy". With this exception even Turner himself was surprised about the sparse criticism and the huge success of the American tour. Turner wrote passionately to Cavert: "If we do not make mistakes and if we open at way for the Lord's way the possibilities of this visit will have significance for American foreign policy and certainly for bettering the chances for ecumenical victory in our time."[101]

At the end of December 1946 E. Theodore Bachmann[102], the WCC's new liaison officer with the German churches[103], asked Cavert for information on the current stand of relations between German and American Protestantism as well as on the American Lutheran's stance towards Niemöller's visit to the USA[104]. Cavert answered him that Niemöller had not made gaffes until then and to the disappointment of the press, his messages were politically devoid and quite spiritual. Since American Lutheranism had placed less confidence in Niemöller than him (i. e. Cavert), they had been "rather lukewarm" in their estimation of the visit.[105] According to a dispatch of the Religious News Service the American section of the Lutheran World Convention had actually withdrawn its financial support for Niemöller's journey to America. However, Cavert commented that fortunately the press had hardly noticed this and Fry had confirmed that the reason for the withdrawal was only that the responsibility for Niemöller's journey should be taken on by the Federal Council alone. Fry was particularly intent on having Asmussen in the USA. He himself (i. e. Cavert) had undertaken nothing more on the matter of Asmussen's and Dibelius's journey. However, he worked with the dean of the Hamma Divinity School (Springfield, Ohio), Elmer Ellsworth Flack[106], to gain an entry permit for Hanns Lilje[107].

The personal and factual tensions between German Lutheranism and the representatives of the Barthian wing of the Confessing Church had therefore clear effects on the invitation politics of the American churches. While Cavert clearly expressed that he cared little for a visit from Asmussen and Dibelius, Fry favoured the visit of the leader of the EKD church chamber[108] and tried to ignore Niemöller's visit. However, this stand could not prevent the Niemöllers from going from city to city in a kind of "triumphal entry"[109]. "There is tremendous interest in them. Our people take them as a symbol of the fact that there was real resistance in the German Church to Nazism."[110]

Visser't Hooft did not report anything positive about Germany and the German churches after his stay in the destroyed country. "Unfortunately, the Church is not playing a very helpful role in this whole situation. At this moment it becomes specially clear that the German Church is lacking in wise leadership. In official cercles [sic] there has been considerable irritation concerning the rather demonstrative action of the Church for the sake of the liberation of prisoners of war. Instead of discussing this point at least informally with the authorities, before taking action, they created a *fait accompli*. I saw both General McNarney[111] and General Koenig[112] and both were very displeased, especially the latter."[113]

Regarding the situation of the personnel of the Protestant Church Visser't Hooft mentioned Niemöller's strong erratic mood swings, which made him "not an easy element" in the present situation. He hoped that Niemöller's sojourn in

America enhanced the constructive elements of his personality. Asmussen was wondering whether he had only been invited to America because Niemöller could not be invited alone or whether there was real interest in him.

"Asmussen is really a sick man and since he speaks no English, I am not sure that he is going to be very helpful in the situation. On the other hand, he would be rather unhappy if the invitation was simply dropped. The best thing might be to invite him not so much for much speaking but for a period of study and personal contact in some theological seminary ... . As to Dibelius he is also interested in coming to America but since he has just gone to England I think the matter might well be postponed a bit. His danger is of course that in the very delicate situation, in which he finds himself with regard to the Russians he may weaken his own position by spending too much time in the Western nations ... . My own impression is that Dibelius is not as constructive as he might be in his relations with the Russians. In this connection I want to mention another name, namely that of Fräulein Zernack. She has been quite wonderful in these last years and is still by all odds the outstanding Christian Women Leader in Germany. At the same time she speaks English very well. I think it would be a very good move to get her to visit America ... . Then again it would be very useful to have Lilje come over. The chances that he may become Bishop of Hanover within the next six months are again increasing."[114]

Cavert answered Visser't Hooft that Miss Zernack probably ought be invited by the YWCA rather than by the Federal Council. He said that the American government was still extraordinarily reserved about granting entry visas to Germans, albeit a precedent had now been created with Niemöller, so that further cases would probably make much less effort necessary. On the other hand, it also marked the border of willingness on the part of the Federal Council to invite even more Church personalities from Germany as intended. "In general, however, I have to say that I do not believe that we can effectively use more German leaders than the Niemöllers, Asmussen, Dibelius and Lilje this year so I am not inclined to issue further invitations and I certainly am not prepared to say that we can finance the coming of an additional one beyond those whom I have mentioned above."[115] Henry Smith Leiper asked John R. Mott, the grand old man of the ecumenical movement, to intervene in the State Department, in order to bring Lilje to the Provisional Committee of the WCC in Buck Hill Falls in the USA in mid-April 1947.[116]

While Niemöller travelled the USA, Dibelius also surprisingly seemed to be wanting to travel there.[117] Rev. L. W. Goebel, the president of the Evangelical and Reformed Church, responded to it with apprehension. "The appearance of any other German after the itinerary of Niemöller will definitely be anticlimactic"[118], he wrote to Cavert at the end of January 1947. Cavert completely agreed with him. "I hope to be able to make him see that there is an advantage in deferring his trip."[119]

If the other visits from Germany required just as much time to prepare as Niemöller's visit he added that he must free himself from all other obligations. Cavert reacted with consternation when he heard from Bodensieck that at the end of April 1947 Wurm accompanied by Asmussen also wanted to come to the United States in order to take part in the last session of the Provisional Committee of the WCC in Buck Hill Falls (Pennsylvania).[120] He wrote to Niemöller, who was in Washington, D. C.: "None of us had had any information hitherto about Bishop Wurm's coming."[121] Even more unpleasant than the arrival of the two Germans for Cavert was the massive presence of all three theologians with the corresponding consequences for the Federal Council. Therefore, he suggested that Niemöller leave the USA in mid-March. "Since Bishop Wurm is the Principal representing the German Church in the Provisional Committee probably you will not feel that you are under any obligation to remain for the meeting. Moreover, I cannot help thinking that it is doubtful whether you would be wise to remain away from Germany longer than the middle of March."[122]

After the mainly positive resonance on Niemöller's visit during the first weeks, the climate of public opinion was gradually changing. "It is becoming clear to me that the longer you stay the more criticism you will encounter from those persons, who assume that you are trying to carry out 'propaganda' for Germany"[123], Cavert told Niemöller, and continued bluntly: "If you stay much longer than three months, which is really a long visit for a European to make in our country, perhaps some people will begin to wonder whether you do not have some other purpose in visiting America than that of bearing your Christian testimony and strengthening the ties between the American and the German Church. This suspicion will probably be increased by the arrival of Cardinal von Preysing[124] yesterday and the coming of Bishop Wurm and Pastor Asmussen."[125]

Visser't Hooft informed Cavert that Niemöller admittedly intended to leave America in mid-March, but he wanted to return in April for the Provisional Committee of the WCC. "This is of course an impossible idea. He does not seem to realise what has happened in various offices in New York, Washington, Berlin and Geneva to get him across. No one wants a second headache of this kind."[126] Furthermore, in a letter to a friend Niemöller expressed his disappointment about the fact that he still had not met any influential American politicians, for example John Foster Dulles. Also he had been expecting to be able to raise funds in America for the ecumenical work in Germany. Cavert hurried to fulfil Niemöller's wishes about political contacts and financial support.[127] The latter wrote him he did not want to leave the representation of the EKD in the Provisional Committee of the WCC up to Bishop Wurm alone. If Wurm did not come to the USA then he would remain until mid-April, alternatively he had the intention of leaving the USA in March and returning in mid-April.[128]

At the end of January 1947, the not unexpected protest on the Jewish part escalated. The president of the American Jewish Congress, Stephen S. Wise, reproached the Federal Council for having done America a bad service by inviting Niemöller. He reminded them of the National Protestant behaviour of Niemöller, including his admission into the armed forces in 1939, and held against Cavert that such examples weakened the democratic forces in the world. He also believed Niemöller's appeals for the Americans to treat the Germans gently were completely unreasonable.[129] Wise had the core issues of his three-page letter published in the *New York Times* on the next day.[130] Several corrections and pieces of information displayed by the Federal Council[131], as well as a recommendation in favour of Stewart W. Herman's books[132], did not hush the protests[133]. For example, a

Methodist pastor wrote that he could not understand the hurry, with which the Federal Council had brought Niemöller to the United States, "to talk religion to the people of America"[134]. The Czechoslovak secretary of State, Jan Masaryk, complained to press representatives during a stay in Paris that Niemöller was able to make propaganda in favour of the Germans in the USA. He said that Eleanor Roosevelt[135] had called him and asked for an article of protest[136]. For Cavert it was a "considerable curiosity" that Niemöller's critics in America did not express the same criticism against Cardinal Preysing. However, Eleanor Roosevelt also criticised Preysing's presence in the USA "on the ground that these people 'naturally create sympathy for Germany, a country which twice has plunged the world into war'"[137]. Cavert believed there was a common suspicion in the USA that the Federal Council had only brought Niemöller into the country in order to influence public opinion in favour of the Germans.[138]

At the end of February, the situation relaxed as it became clear that a massive appearance of German churchmen would not occur in the USA. Both Bishop Wurm[139] and Hanns Lilje dropped their plans to visit America, the latter because it was almost certain that Marahrens would resign in March and a new bishop would be elected in April.[140] As a result, Visser't Hooft telegraphed Cavert to urge Niemöller to remain in the United States until April so that the German churches were represented.[141] The Federal Council officially ended Niemöller's America tour with a press release in mid-March 1947.[142] Two months later, Niemöller left the USA after staying there for nearly six months.[143] On the evening before his departure, Niemöller appeared very dejected because of the behaviour of Colonel Newman, the director of the American military government in Hesse. Newman had demanded the prosecution of black marketers, the enforcement of a strike prohibition from the German authorities and he threatened to impose martial law on the region.[144] As a result, Cavert proposed a resolution in the Federal Council, which was accepted on 20 May 1947. In this resolution the governor's heartlessness was condemned and thanks were expressed to General Clay for toning down the penalties threatened.[145] In this way Niemöller's American visit ended happily.

After his return there were still two "Niemöller-aftershocks" in the USA. In one case the General Synod of the Reformed Church in America reported that Niemöller had said during one of his appearances that he was "worried about the doctrinal and spiritual anaemia of the Federal Council"[146]. When questioned by Cavert Niemöller said that this diction was not part of his English repertoire and he had every reason to be grateful to the Federal Council.[147] In American Lutheranism a rumour circulated that Niemöller in a lecture had stated that the Lutheran churches of America were less alive than others and would not overcome didactics.[148] However, in contrast to Cavert Long did not investigate the matter. In a letter to Tillmanns of Wartburg College, he wrote that this remark was not known to him, but it was "probably true. ... Niemöller is somewhat discredited in Germany. I learned from Dr. Bodensieck while in Lund that the German church leaders are not too enthusiastic about his reports on America ... . We are hoping to bring some other German church leaders to this country before very long and think that that will offset the influence, which Niemöller is trying to exert."[149]

The second irritation was sparked off by an article in the *New York Times* on 19 August 1947 bearing the title "Niemöller joins with Marxists to combat influence of Vatican"[150]. Its author, Delbert Clark, had taken a meeting between Protestant churchmen and SPD politicians as the evidence for his story.[151] Reinhold Niebuhr wrote a reader's letter on 20 August[152] intending to correct the falsehood, however it was not printed. Cavert apologised to Niemöller for the misinterpretation "in one of our best American newspapers"[153]. Niemöller's long stay in America, contrary to some fears, had not seriously harmed him in Germany. At the end of September 1947, the Protestant church elected him as the Church president of Hesse and Nassau.[154] At the beginning of 1948 on Niemöller's instance[155] Cavert received an honorary doctoral degree of the Theological School of Georg August University in Göttingen[156].

During his stay in the United States Niemöller had communicated some of his observations in letters to Germany. For example, in a letter to the president of the Church chancellery of the EKD, Hans Asmussen, it reads: "The big halls could not be taken [for Niemöller's appearances] because of the race problem. The Negroes are not let in. So, America has its worries and needs, too. And it is not only about the Negro problem: anti-Semitism is also an open question, on which there would be a lot to say."[157]

On the other hand, he appeared deeply impressed by the great piety and Christian life in America's "practical everyday life". However, despite the Christian solidarity with Europe Niemöller believed he perceived a narrow viewpoint in the USA: "They simply don't see that there are still other problems than the Russia-America issue."[158]

Mistakenly, Asmussen ascribed the difficulties of his own and Dibelius's plans for an American visit to Niemöller's behavior in the USA. "What is being written there [scil. in the American press] is not very pleasant in general. There is also the fact that the way the matter of Dibelius's and my departure was treated reinforces the impression that through your visit they have become sensitive in the States."[159] Niemöller described the situation correctly in his letter of reply: "In the meantime I had heard from different sources about your planned trip with Wurm, but it could not be determined with precision what was true about it, so that I was undecided for a while because one does not like having several of us over there out of consideration for the public opinion, or what is called so. Already Bishop Preysing's visit had evoked a new contradiction by E. R[oosevelt]."[160]

In mid-March 1947 Niemöller wrote to Asmussen, who finally wanted to travel to the Provisional Committee of the WCC of Buck Hill Falls without Wurm, that Cavert had told him it would be better if he postponed his America-trip until the autumn.[161] Asmussen complained about a "very bitter muddle" as a result. Six times his trip had been imminent, but had always been postponed. "I have the strong impression that there are forces effective in ecumenical Christianity, which want to know only one excerpt of German church life and also only one excerpt of the Confessing Church. I cannot judge how far they are being influenced from Germany."[162]

Actually, Visser't Hooft had advised against inviting Asmussen as the German delegate to Buck Hill Falls. On 28 January 1947, he passed a damning judgment on the leader of the EKD church chancellery in a letter to Cavert:

"Asmussen has recently shown such complete lack of judgement that I have had to change my mind about him. Some months ago I was still inclined to defend him against what seemed to me rather exaggerated criticisms. But since I have been in Germany and have seen some of his most recent actions and utterances I have come to believe that he is very much the wrong man in the wrong place. And I am not alone in this attitude. Quite objective observers of the situation such as von Thadden or Colonel Sturm or Pastor Fricke all of whom I have seen recently feel the same way. This is probably largely due to the fact that Asmussen is really a nervous wreck. But even that only explains part of the problem. What must we think when Asmussen proposes solemnly that the Church of Germany must now declare a general absolution of all those who have really repented of their sins? I need not give you more examples, since Niemöller can tell you all about it. But the upshot of it is that I do not look with enthusiasm upon the idea of having him at the Provisional Committee for he would not really represent the best thought of the German Church ... . To sum up I put Lilje first, Dibelius second and put a very big interrogation mark behind the name of Asmussen."[163]

As a result, Cavert telegraphed Arild Olsen, the head of the Religious Affairs Office of the American military administration: "After careful consultation convinced that unwise to have three German church leaders here simultaneously. Fear it would create impression of too heavy pressure on American opinion and produce unfavourable reaction towards German Church. Stop. Strongly urge Dibelius Asmussen defer visits until Niemöller's return."[164]

The back and forth of invitations and cancellations of invitations to leading Church personalities in Germany caused, not only with Asmussen, mistrust and considerable irritation. Berlin bishop Otto Dibelius[165] wrote extremely indignantly to the Americans on 13 March 1947:

"Things happened rather irritatingly about my journey to America. Originally, Feb[ruary] was in prospect as the date in question. Then they said that, due to Niemöller's journey, a later point of time was better. I then kept the month of March free from commitments. Then they said the old Bishop Wurm, aged 78, was supposed to come to a meeting of the Federal Council in N. Y.; so I was asked to postpone my coming to the Fall. But now they cannot seriously treat a Protestant bishop this way, who has his obligations and must fix his schedule months in advance. It worked completely differently with the Catholics. 14 days after the Catholic bishop of Berlin was invited to America, he was already over there, is coming back right now and is standing there as the one whom they want in America and who has done something for the German population in America, while the Protestant bishop, whose planned journey had already been published in the press by the Americans, is standing there like the one who achieves nothing. I am therefore very annoyed with Dr. Cavert, so much the more since he never deemed it necessary to negotiate with myself, but always acted through the American Military Government. Wurm's journey will of course come to nothing. I myself will probably travel to America in the fall, but probably independently of the Federal Council."[166]

Due to the intercession of the president of the Evangelical and Reformed Church, Rev. L. W. Goebel, after a visit by Carl E. Schneider of Eden Theological Seminary[167], and different conversations with Bachmann[168] at the Berlin bishop's office, at the end of May the latter was finally ready to accept a new invitation from the Federal Council for the autumn of 1947, despite the past disappointments[169]. In reality it took until October 1947 for Dibelius to also be able to travel to the USA at the invitation of the Lutherans.

Only at the beginning of June 1947 did Visser't Hooft receive official authorisation to send out a WCC church liaison officer to the American occupation zone. According to Clay it was his serious hope that the WCC through this contact could "make a real contribution toward the religious and moral rehabilitation of the German people and toward the development of a peaceful and democratic Germany"[170]. Visser't Hooft was not very happy about Bodensieck, who had done this job since the autumn of 1946. "He does not really represent the kind of policy that the Federal Council or the World Council would like to see pursued in the German Church situation. One gets the impression that he has personalised the job to such an extent that he has just become a friendly American visitor seeing people in an individual rather than a representative capacity ... . Unfortunately, there are no signs that he plans to return soon to the U.S.A. One particular point to keep in mind in this connection is that as far as my information goes Bodensieck has practically no contact with the Free Churches, which are of course specially important from the Federal Council angle."[171]

The small German Free Churches such as the Baptists and the Protestant Folk Church played a key role in the economic support of Germany since they were sister churches of the wealthy as well as established American Free Churches.[172] Moreover, Bodensieck belonged to the restrained wing of the Lutheran National Council, wherein Lutheranism was united in the USA. According to this self-image, he warned Long against the relief activities of the conservative Missouri Synod.[173]

"I have the impression that Missouri is very active. In practically every place I hear that the Missourians have been there. At pastoral conferences, for instance, they make their appearance; they place a large can of tobacco and a box of cigars before the nicotine-starved preachers and say, help yourselves; it seems easier to convince the preachers, after this introduction, that the Missouri doctrine of predestination or election or what not is true; they see to it that the preachers receive CARE or other food packages and a little later their Brief Statement of 1932.[174] I feel that the ethics of this procedure is very reprehensible; but it helps make an impression on the men. It is true that the Missouri plan to unite all the Lutherische Freikirchen in one body, under Missouri Leadership, has failed; the only group which has fallen for the scheme, is the Old Lutheran Church (Breslau Synod); even this group will not go over to Missouri in its totality but only on part; at least some of the Bavarian members of this church will not go along; it is quite clearly felt that it is Missouri's money, its offer to build a nice theological school, and other financial inducements, which constitute the really persuasive force of their arguments. The Missourians see to it that their gifts are plainly labelled as to their origin so that some of our brethren here have the impression that they are the only Lutherans who are doing anything. Naturally, I do not approve of their methods; they probably do not realise that they are desecrating Christian charity by using it as a cloak for their church-political aspirations. Nevertheless, it may not be a bad idea to organise some very concrete help for the pastors, on the part of NLC."[175]

Therefore, not only German contrasts in Protestantism influenced the American church milieu, but the inter denominational tensions in American Lutheranism brought forth their effects on the situation of the German churches.

Since Bachmann wanted to leave his position in October 1947[176], Cavert proposed to make Bodensieck the WCC Liaison Officer for Germany in his place[177]. However, Visser't Hooft opposed it. Instead, he offered Danish theologian Hogsbrø the position and justified his election primarily because of the desolate church situation in Germany. "... the whole picture, which I get of the German situation through many recent contacts is that the chaotic tendencies are as bad as ever and that indeed unless something drastic is done the German Church will fall apart into a lot of separatist regional bodies and functions. The crisis of leadership is worse than ever."[178] Bodensieck was an ambassador of goodwill, however, in this serious situation a man must achieve real basis-work, like Hogsbrø, and represent the WCC's politics.[179]

It was only in the middle of October 1947 that Bishop Dibelius travelled to the USA. Hans Asmussen was expected in November 1947 because the National Lutheran Council had taken responsibility for his trip.[180] Actually, he did not arrive until 3 December 1947 and stayed approximately seven weeks. He arrived the week after Dibelius left the USA after a six-week stay.[181] Dibelius had refused the possibility, offered by Cavert, to travel the USA with Asmussen.[182] Long passed a judgment on the stay of the Berlin bishop: "I think it has done a great deal toward interesting our people in the situation over there to have men like this to come and tell their story."[183]

After the first half of his stay in the United States Dibelius had even considered breaking off the trip. In a handwritten letter to Cavert he thanked him for the manifold friendliness he had experienced, but then continued:

"But as a whole I think it was a failure, at all events for me and for my Church in Eastern Germany. To address day by day a couple of students or a very modest number of ministers, every young German minister would have been able to do. Nobody in Germany will ever understand, that the Bishop of Berlin, after being told by the Russians that they disagreed with him going to America, and so getting in rather earnest personal danger, was not allowed to do anything else than that. They can only think that either the Americans were terribly disappointed by the Bishop or that the Churches of America have already 'abgeschrieben' [i. e. written off] the East of Germany, so that their invitation to the Bishop was only a matter of courteousy [sic], no earnest intention being behind that, to do something more for this Russian colony. This impression will be strengthend [sic], when, as I understand, Bishop Lilje from Western Germany will come over in the spring because I do not doubt that the Lutherans here will make a rather big matter out of his visit."[184]

He added that in sleepless nights he had repeatedly thought about this situation, which would change his position in public life and particularly in the Church life of Germany. He saw no other way than to break off the trip, return home empty-handed and explain frankly that he had made a mistake because in the context of his trip there was nothing to inform, which reflected the hopes for the Church in the Russian zone. "The Russians will be satisfied by this end of my visit and my diocese, after having overcome the first disappointment, will understand my leaving the ecumenical work as a whole and limiting my work to my duties at home in future."[185] Cavert was as surprised as perplex about the letter. "I wish I knew what he really expects or wants", he wrote to Goebel and asked him to talk to Dibelius.[186] He then asked Dibelius to formulate his disappointed expectations about the visit more plainly so that he could make corresponding arrangements. In addition he told him that the echo of his appearances was extremely positive. "It indicates that you have been very successful in helping our church people to get a better picture of what conditions actually are in Germany. It seems to me that this is the most important thing that you can do. If our people come to a fuller appreciation of the conditions in Germany you can be sure that Church World Service (which includes practically all the bodies of the Federal Council) and other agencies, like the National Lutheran Council, will raise far greater sums for Germany and be able to transmit larger amounts to 'Hilfswerk'."[187]

In a personal conversation Goebel succeeded in convincing Dibelius that he had no reason to be disappointed about the results of his America journey. "After a helpful talk to Dr. Goebel I will go on", Dibelius telegraphed to Cavert on 17 November.[188] Goebel's secretary, E. W. Berlekamp, reported the following to Cavert on the reasons for the envisaged premature departure: "It would appear that Bishop Dibelius had hoped he might return to Germany with unmistakable evidence (such as perhaps an order for one thousand CARE Packages) of the success of his trip. Dr. Goebel has assured him, I believe, that a goodly number of such packages will be forwarded to persons whose names and addresses will be given either him or our World Service Committee."[189]

On returning Dibelius reported on his transatlantic experiences in the Protestant weekly magazine *Die Kirche*, without mentioning his mid-November crisis. The journey he made by airplane "costs much money, much time, much strength. Can one answer for this expenditure at a moment when the home country requires the use of all strength?" Exactly for the "need of the home country", Dibelius continued that he could "refuse no longer ... the constantly repeated, urgent and cordial invitation of the American churches". Although Niemöller's journey was certainly more effective it was necessary "that once in a while also somebody from the German East goes over there and expresses a word of gratitude to the American communities[190], also telling them how very much we will still need such help, especially in the coming winter"[191].

Due to his delayed arrival as a result of a pilots' strike and a forced stay of some days in London[192] Dibelius could not attend the meetings and church services intended for him in New York City. Therefore, the journey started with visits to theological departments "in order to get in touch with the young generation of theologians there". He saw the training centres, which were independent from the churches, like the Union Theological Seminary in New York City, as "impressive facilities", in which "not at all primarily soccer [was] played", but also serious academic work was done. For a German "the excess of physical strength, which one meets in the studentship" was especially impressive.

The helpfulness of the relief organisations of the larger churches, which he also made early contact, was "marvellous" even if as Dibelius emphasised at the same time, the sums advanced in planning were "not at all always reached". He pointed it out to his readers that the financial sacrifices were "not always easy" for the middle class: "One cannot continuously send Care parcels to Germany. At any rate, the average American cannot."[193]

The twenty-minute reception with President Truman, which Dibelius, according to his report had not sought himself[194], was an important moment of his trip. The German churchman was impressed by the "absolute simplicity, in which it proceeded. ... We shook hands without any solemn ceremony. And then one sat at his desk, face to face, in friendly conversation. ... And the inconspicuous, open and sober manner of the president. It was truly like quickly saying hello to a friend in his office."[195]

In the main Sunday church service Dibelius preached in the Washington cathedral of the Episcopalian Church. The bishop reported on the display of the American ensign in church services[196] and concluded that, in the United States, the differences between "individual churches [played ...] not all too big a role"[197]. In his last letter Dibelius wrote among other things about "the meaning of the American churches for the life of the nation", which was growing like the number of church-members. He noted the large amount of service participants and the great number of weekly events, describing them as "fields of force ... which exert an influence on the whole life of the nation"[198]. Not quite unselfishly the bishop also generally commented on the existence of church schools in the United States. Regarding the American attitude in contrast to Germany, he merely reported that "outside the churches still very much bitterness ... exists"[199].

After completing his exhausting journey[200] Dibelius once again appreciated the American churches' strong helpfulness[201], which "may gladly be strengthened through a personal message from Germany". In this respect the churches differed from the American "masses", who were not interested in Germany or the forces hostile to Germany.[202] Regarding the American stance towards the political situation in Europe or the world, Dibelius was more sceptical: "Regarding political decisions, one generally trusts the government will get whatever is possible out of the present situation, for America, of course. And America needs a political Europe with a viable, politically harmless Germany. No new war! Details do not matter too much. After all, who should expect that an office employee at his desk or a worker in his automobile-factory should consider what a division of Germany means for Europe and whether the East German border is sustainable?"[203]

Dibelius responded sceptically on the strengthening of the state in America[204], by which "also the influence ... on the intellectual life and on the life in the churches" grew. "However, the Christian who comes from Germany and has experienced what we all have experienced, does not feel comfortable with it. The new state-concept, which we need if humanity is not to sink into a sea of blood and tears, cannot be developed in America. It must come from a world, which has grasped the apocalyptic character of the present time. It must probably come from a Germany, which is completely shattered on the outside, in order to be serious about the Gospel. The parting from America ... would be depressing if the country, to which one returns, this destroyed Germany almost hopelessly bleeding to death, did not also have a big task ahead of her. At any rate the Germany, which stands by the Gospel of Jesus Christ."[205]

At the Annual Meeting of the Friends of the WCC in New York in mid-December 1947 Asmussen held the main lecture. He talked about "The Meaning of the Idea of Ecumenism for the German Churches". In it he explained that the ecumenical thought was widespread in Germany among theologians and laypersons alike and they were trying to obtain an organisation, which included not only state churches but also the free churches. He expressed his conviction that Christianity must set out to become Christ's body across all denominations and religious confessions.[206] As Cavert had predicted, Asmussen did not find nearly as much resonance as his native antipode, Niemöller, had evoked.[207] Joseph Krenek from Prague[208], the president of the Czech citizens' community, spoke after him. He received as much attention as Asmussen. Moreover, Asmussen had to hear the Executive Secretary of the Canadian church council, William J. Gallagher, define Niemöller and his wife's visit as a "highlight" and an important event in the life of the Canadian Church.[209] Apart from Krenek, Asmussen did not take part in the meeting of the American Committee of the WCC either, although this took place on the same day and in the same place as the Annual Meeting of the Friends of the WCC.[210]

During his stay in America Asmussen gave eight sermons, five lectures in places of Lutheran theological education and nine speeches to meetings of pastors. Furthermore, he spoke at the American Bible Society and the Federal Council. Finally, he had the opportunity to speak to officials of the State and War Departments. While he himself was "extremely pleased" with the large number of contacts, the report of the US-American National Committee of the Lutheran World Association formulated a sobering balance: "It was unfortunate that the period spent in our country included the Christmas holidays, which limited his engagements to a great degree ... . It was unfortunate that the limited time, in which to plan his schedule and our uncertainty of his use of English language prevented us from a better planned itinerary."[211]

Asmussen had only just returned to Germany when he wrote a report, which he read on 24 February 1948 in St Mark's Church (*Markuskirche*) in Stuttgart. He judged the "nature of the American churches" that "for decades a liberal Gospel ... of human joy and social justice" had been announced. "Nobody can resent the people in general for mistaking the missionary consciousness of the government for this type of gospel. Thus it happens often enough that democracy appears as a religious ideal."[212] The Americans understood their democracy often as a sound Christian doctrine of salvation and in so far as an appropriate method against Communism's atheistic doctrine. Lutheranism was different. "I was a guest of the Lutheran Church in America. For the sake of gratitude I must say that with it [i. e. Lutheranism] the concrete answer to all political doctrines of salvation is the teaching of the cross of Golgatha."[213]

He heard many voices in America demanding that the Germans opt "for the east *or* the west". He had always refused this request and could only confirm "that the German people are free from Hitler"[214]. However, he prayed for Communism not to reach any further. The Germans had every reasons to thank the American people for their great helpfulness. "I have not yet thanked for another world starting behind the Iron Curtain, though."[215] Nevertheless, he refused any political religion. Three months later, the news-office of the American Lutheran Council reported that Asmussen had been forced to give up his office as president of the EKD Church chancery on 1 June 1948.[216] "The move to oust Dr. Asmussen was launched earlier this year while he was visiting the United States under auspices of the U.S.A. Committee for the Lutheran Federation. He lectured here from early December until late January."[217]

At last one of the prominent German churchmen, who were considered as German guests from the start[218], Hanns Lilje, now the Land bishop of the Protestant-Lutheran State Church of Hanover, visited the United States on the invitation of the National Lutheran Council from mid-April to mid-June 1948[219]. On behalf of the Federal Council Samuel McCrea Cavert gave a festive dinner in honour of the German bishop.[220] To the War Department the National Lutheran Council justified Lilje's journey as follows: "The purpose of this visit is to contact Lutheran Church leaders, visit Church institutions and attend conferences in order to learn American Church methods and to understand our thinking. He will then be better able to interpret American Church life in his own diocese and in Germany."[221]

During his visit from mid-April to mid-June 1948 Lilje not only gave lectures at Hamma Divinity School, but also visited other theological education facilities and numerous communities, as well as representatives of several Lutheran churches and the Missouri Synod Church. Having obviously been well-prepared by the Lutherans from the National Lutheran Council, he accused the Missouri Synod in St. Louis of having used its charity work in Germany in order to make propaganda for Free Churches. Lawrence Meyer denied this intention and repeated his rejection once again in writing: "... it has ever been farthest from our mind to use our relief work to proselytise. The Missouri Synod has no interest whatsoever in building up a Missouri Synod Church in Europe. Our one and only interest in helping the churches of Europe is to be of service, wherever we can in helping the churches to help themselves and to rebuild their own organisation. Whenever and wherever our relief work has been used for the purpose of making propaganda either for the Free Church of Germany or for the Missouri Synod, it has happened without our knowledge and certainly without our approval."[222]

However, the last sentence hinted that collaborators of the Missouri Synod had indeed used charity offerings for proselytising advertisement. This impression was further supported by an open letter, which the Missouri Synod had published in its publication *The Lutheran* that was also distributed in Germany in 1947. It expressly pointed out that it did not want to proselytise with charity offerings.

Lilje was received by President Truman in mid-May 1948. "He thanked him for the American help on behalf of the German people and emphasised in the discussion that indications of a mental renaissance were already recognisable in Germany, particularly among youngsters."[223] Lilje succeeded, like probably only Niemöller before him, in asking for support for the Germans through his lectures, interviews and sermons in the United States.

Conclusion

The efforts of American Protestants to give the Protestant Church in Germany support through a programme of mutual visits proved to be altogether beneficial for ecumenism. However, the difficulties concerning the personnel stressed on both sides the fact that only very few persons appeared truly suitable for the communication programme. For this reason, an important mediating and clearing function came up to the still developing WCC in Geneva and especially its General Secretary Willem A. Visser't Hooft. The Federal Council, as the WCC, wanted a united "Protestant Church in Germany" and therefore rather tried to hinder both Lutheran special endeavours and ideas representing a staunch Confessing Church stance. It thus supported the "middle" course of Württemberg Bishop Wurm. Conflicts occurred on this matter between the Federal Council and the National Lutheran Council in the USA, since the American Lutherans were afraid that their denomination would become marginalised in Germany and America in favour of Unionist tendencies. However, also the inner-Lutheran American competition between the National Lutheran Council and the fundamentalist-oriented Missouri Synod intensified over the support deliveries for German Lutherans. The latter awakened the impression as if it wanted to procure itself an advantage with the Germans through a massive supply of goods. Whether the visits of German churchmen in America actually enhanced the democratic renewal in Germany, as was repeatedly emphasised to the American Government, sure enough also for tactical reasons, may be questioned. Rather, the Germans noted also some critical aspects regarding Church and social circumstances in America. An inclination towards an intellectual transfer across the Atlantic can, at any rate, hardly be ascertained. On the other hand, Niemöller's and Lilje's appearances in America and the reports of the Americans Bodensieck, Bachmann, Cavert and others from Germany contributed to depict the Germans in a milder manner and to give material support to the defeated people. This was exactly what some circles in the United States had been fearing. How strong an effect in favour of the Germans the mutual church contacts had, became clear when American churchmen and theologians, often against public opinion in the United States, massively criticised the activity of their government regarding Germany. This should become evident once again plainly in 1949 in connection with the war criminal trials.[224]

Notes

1   Cf. Gerhard Besier and G. Sauter, Wie Christen ihre Schuld bekennen. Die Stuttgarter Erklärung 1945, Göttingen 1985.

2   On German-American church relations until 1941 cf. Gerhard Besier, 'The friends ... in America need to know the truth ...'. Die deutschen Kirchen im Urteil der Vereinigten Staaten (1933–1941)', in this volume. On the response from the Federal Council of Churches of Christ in America to the Stuttgart Declaration of Guilt (*Stuttgarter Schulderklärung*), cf. the Council's Minutes of the Executive Committee of

15 January 1946, DeptHistPresb Church, Phila., 18-1-16. See also Heather A. Warren, Theologians of a New World Order. Reinhold Niebuhr and the Christian Realists 1920-1948, New York-Oxford 1997, esp. 94-115.

3   From 28 November to 7 December 1945 an official American church delegation visited Germany. Their report is published in Clemens Vollnhals, Die evangelische Kirche nach dem Zusammenbruch. Berichte ausländischer Beobachter aus dem Jahr 1945 (AKZG.A 3), Göttingen 1988, 263-266. The preparatory memorandum for this visit states: "The purpose of this visitation was outlined to President Truman on 13 September 1945. The President stated he heartily approved the idea of a delegation representative of the Protestant communions visiting Germany." Cf. Memorandum Concerning Visit of a Delegation of The Federal Council of the Churches of Christ in America to the Protestant Churches of Germany, no date, Herman Papers, Shelter Island Heights, N.Y.

4   Niemöller in a letter to Adolf Keller on 3 September 1945, Library of the WCC, Geneva, General Correspondence, Niemöller, Martin, 1937-1948. Cf. on Treysa: Gerhard Besier, H. Ludwig and J. Thierfelder (eds), Der Kompromiß von Treysa. Die Entstehung der Evangelischen Kirche in Deutschland (EKD) 1945. Eine Dokumentation, Weinheim 1995.

5   Cf. on the Federal Council during this time Martin E. Marty, Modern American Religion, vol. 3: Under God, Indivisible 1941-1960, Chicago-London 1996, 95 ff., 434 ff.

6   Cf. William J. Schmidt, Architect of Unity: A Biography of Samuel McCrea Cavert, New York 1978, 181-211, esp. 191, 200.

7   There was a controversial correspondence between Franklin Clark Fry and Samuel McCrea Cavert about Niemöller and Wurm's invitation as representatives of the EKD to the WCC. Fry did not find it suitable to speak of the EKD as a "church", and thought Lutheranism was not well represented on the personal level. Furthermore, he criticised Visser't Hooft's statement that Marahrens had been the German representative, and Wurm and Niemöller had taken over his place. Cf. Fry to Cavert on 9 February 1946, AELCA Chicago, NLC 2/3/2, Box 3. See also Visser't Hooft's paper "Can E.K.D. be considered as a Church in the sense of the constitution of the World Council of Churches?" of 26 November 1945 and Niemöller's Memorandum of 28 November 1945, Visser't Hooft assumed in his explanations that the EKD formed a "spiritual unity" against the background of the Barmen, Dahlem and Augsburg declarations. On 11 February 1946, Asmussen sent a comment to Visser't Hooft carrying the title 'Was ist die EKD?' [What is the EKD?], in which he too dealt with the question "whether the EKD [was] a church in theological sense". Cf. General Correspondence, Asmussen, Hans, 1936-1952, Library of the WCC, Geneva. See also Visser't Hooft's letter of reply to Asmussen on 15 March 1946.

8   Cf. Willem A. Visser't Hooft, Die Welt war meine Gemeinde. Autobiographie, Munich 1972, 235 ff. Published in English as Memoirs, Geneva 1987; Hannes Karnick and Wolfgang Richter (eds), Protestant. Das Jahrhundert des Pastors Martin Niemöller, Darmstadt 1992, 206 f. See also Gunnar Heienne, Eivind Berggrav. Eine Biographie, Göttingen 1997, 207 ff.; Heather A. Warren, Theologians of a New World Order (op. cit. note 2), 117 f. Also see Armin Boyens, in Gerhard Besier, A. Boyens and G. Lindemann, Nationaler Protestantismus und Ökumenische Bewegung. Kirchliches Handeln im Kalten Krieg (1945-1990), Berlin 1999. On the negotiations of the EKD Council regarding the WCC Preparatory Committee in Geneva (20-23 February 1946) cf. Carsten Nicolaisen and Nora Andrea Schulze (processors), Die Protokolle des Rates der Evangelischen Kirche in Deutschland, vol. 1: 1945/46 (AKZG.A 5), Göttingen 1995, esp. 32, 403 f.

9   Cf. James Bentley, Martin Niemöller. Eine Biographie, Munich 1985, 220. Published in English as Martin Niemöller, London 1986. See also Edwin Robertson, Unshakable Friend. George Bell and the German Churches, London 1995, esp. 116 ff.

10   Quote from J. Bentley, Martin Niemöller (op. cit. note 9) 193 ff., quote: 218.

11   Long's telegram on 29 May 1945 was sent to General Mark Clark and read: "May we ask you kindly to convey to Pastor Martin Niemöller earnest request of National Lutheran Council that he make visit at his convenience to United States as guest of American Lutherans for purpose of conferring on post war rehabilitation of European Churches and other mutual problems." AELCA Chicago, NLC 2/3/1, Box 9.

12   Cf. Frederick K. Wentz, Lutherans in Concert: The Story of the National Lutheran Council 1918-1966, Minneapolis 1968; Frost, Golden Visions, Broken Dreams: A Short History of the Lutheran Council in the U.S.A., New York 1987.

13   Cf. Niemöller to Long on 9 July 1945, AELCA Chicago, NLC 2/3/1, Box 9. See also the letter of Vicar David L. Ostergren to the president of the National Lutheran Council, Peter O. Bersell, of 28 August 1945. In it Ostergren describes Niemöller's ambivalent state. "He [scil. Niemöller] can be a tremendous help to the work of Christ in Germany. However, his eight years imprisonment have made him rather nervous. This nervousness has made him very sensitive. Such a sensitiveness can easily be fanned into resentment. Especially is this true if the actions of Americans in Germany do not keep in harmony with the ideals of democracy."

14   Cf. on this W. P. Elson to Long on 11 May 1945, and the memorandum by Elson to Long on 2 June 1945, AELCA Chicago, NLC 2/3/1, Box 9.

15   On 15 June 1945, the War Department wrote to Long "that under the existing military regulations no travel is authorized for German civilians". AELCA Chicago, NLC 2/3/1, Box 9.

16   Cf. Memorandum by Elson to Long on 2 June 1945, AELCA Chicago, NLC 2/3/1. Box 9.

17   Long to Scheerer on 6 June 1945, AELCA Chicago, NLC 2/3/1, Box 9.

18   Cf. Vollnhals, Entnazifizierung. Politische Säuberung und Rehabilitierung in den vier Besatzungszonen 1945-1949, Munich 1991.

19   Niemöller to Visser't Hooft on 23 March 1946, Library of the WCC, Geneva, General Correspondence, Niemöller, Martin, 1937-1948. Published in C. Nicolaisen and N. A. Schulze (processors), Die Protokolle des Rates der EKD, vol. 1 (op. cit. note 8), 527 f. Cf. also the discussion on de-nazification at the EKD Council meeting on 1/2 May 1946, and its according resolution, 471 ff., 501 ff. Visser't Hooft wrote to Cavert on 17 May 1946: "I am personally convinced that this resolution is justified. If, therefore, the occupation authorities take a negative attitude to it, I believe it to be our duty to defend the German Church .... Stewart Herman has come out of Germany very much worried about that a new church struggle may begin, if the occupation authorities react negatively to this resolution of the German Church." DeptHistPresbChurch, Phila., 18-23-2. See also Visser't Hooft to Cavert on 12 June 1946.

20   Visser't Hooft to Niemöller on 25 July 1946, General Correspondence, Niemöller, Martin, 1937-1948, Library of the WCC, Geneva.

21   Ibid.

22   On Stoll's position and Niemöller's comments about that, cf. C. Nicolaisen and N. A. Schulze (processors), Die Protokolle des Rates der EKD, vol. 1 (op. cit. note 8), 583, 624, 635.

23   Visser't Hooft reports on the talk with Hanns Lilje in London, in a letter to Cavert of 17 May 1946, DeptHistPresbChurch, Phila., 18-23-2. Already in the handwritten notes of Ralph H. Long, the Executive Director of the National Lutheran Council, on his European travels at the end of February/beginning of April 1945, it reads regarding the General Secretary of the Lutheran World Federation, Lilje: "1. Can You come to America? 2. If not can we have a second message; 3. What about L.W.C.; 4. Relations to World Council; 5. United Luth. Ch. in Germany; 6. White Book." Long, European Trip Notes, 1945. AELCA Chicago, NLC 2/3/1, Box 9. Cf. also Clifford Nelson, The Rise of World Lutheranism. An American Perspective, Philadelphia 1982, 352 ff.; idem, The Lutherans in North America, Philadelphia 1980, esp. 487 ff.

24   Cf. Bentley, Martin Niemöller (op. cit. note 9), 224.

25   Ibid. 224 ff.

26   Cf. Klaus Loscher, Studium und Alltag hinter Stacheldraht. Birger Forells Beitrag zum theologisch-pädagogischen Lehrbetrieb in Norton Camp (1945–1948), Neukirchen-Vluyn 1997.

27   Cavert to Eisenhower on 19 March 1946, DeptHistPresbChurch, Phila., 18-15-24. On the following see also Schmidt, Architect of Unity (op. cit. note 6), 201 ff.

28   Cavert to Kenneth C. Royall, Acting Secretary of War, on 22 January 1946, DeptHist PresbChurch, Phila., 18-15-24.

29   Cavert to Howard K. Travers, Chief of Visa Division, Department of State, on 8 April 1946, DeptHistPresbChurch, Phila., 18-15-24.

30   Ibid.

31   On Paul Tillich's political activities against the National Socialist state, cf. Stone and Weaver (eds), Against the Third Reich. Paul Tillich's Wartime Radio Broadcasts into Nazi Germany, Louisville (Kentucky) 1998. See also Ursula Langkau-Alex and Thomas M. Ruprecht (eds), Was soll aus Deutschland werden? Der Council for a Democratic Germany in New York 1944–1945. Aufsätze und Dokumente (Quellen und Studien zur Sozialgeschichte 15), Frankfurt/M. 1995.

32   Cf. William J. Schmidt, 'Ecumenist for Our Time: Henry Smith Leiper', in Mid-Stream 28 (1989), 173–182; idem and Ouellette, What Kind of a Man? The Life of Henry Smith Leiper, New York 1986.

33   P. Tillich to H. S. Leiper on 14 January 1946, DeptHistPresbChurch, Phila., 18-23-2.

34   Ibid.

35   Cf. on this Bentley, Martin Niemöller (op. cit. note 9), 193 ff.

36   Cf. Robert T. Handy, A History of Union Theological Seminary in New York, New York 1987.

37   Cf. E. L. Long, Jr. and Robert T. Handy (eds), Theology and Church in Times of Change. Essays in Honor of John Coleman Bennett, Philadelphia 1970.

38   Bennett to Leiper on 31 January 1946, DeptHistPresbChurch, Phila., 18-15-24.

39   Ibid. See also Shlomo Shafir, Ambiguous Relations. The American Jewish Community and Germany since 1945, Detroit 1999.

40   Cf. on this 'Testifies Niemöller not an Anti-Semite', in The Christian Century 64 (1947), 1477.

41   Cf. Schmidt, Architect of Unity (op. cit. note 6), 201 f. Thomas Mann had already given a testimony in favour of Niemöller in his preface for the Niemöller-book God is my Führer. Being the Last Twenty-Eight Sermons, New York 1941. Cf. the German version of the preface in Thomas Mann, Gesammelte Werke in dreizehn Bänden, vol. XII, Frankfurt/M. 1974, 910–918.

42   Cf. Dietmar Schmidt, Martin Niemöller – eine Biographie, Stuttgart 1983, 173, 189; Bentley, Martin Niemöller (op. cit. note 9), 229 f. Cf. Roosevelt and Black, Casting Her Own Shadow. Eleanor Roosevelt and the Shaping of Postwar Liberalism, New York 1996. However, her attacks against Preysing are not mentioned.

43   Cf. telegram R. A. Park, The living Church, Milwaukee (Wis.) to Cavert on 28 March 1946, DeptHistPresbChurch, Phila., 18-15-24.

44   Cf. Gerhard Besier and Eckhard Lessing (eds), Die Geschichte der Evangelischen Kirche der Union, vol. 3: Trennung von Staat und Kirche – Politische und konfessionelle Krisen – Erneuerung kirchlicher Gemeinschaft (1918–1992), Leipzig 1999, 441. On 24 June 1947, i. e. immediately after his return from the United States, Niemöller wrote to Asmussen: "I know very well that for some time (and quite a long time as to that), I showed – taking this position regarding myself and others – a much stronger 'Catholicising tendency' than has ever been pronounced at the heart of our brethren's council and of our circle of friends … . I am convinced still to the present day that the dogma of justification, as we have it, has its theological flaws; but it stands at any rate closer by the truth, as we once testified in Barmen, than the *tridentinum* and the canon of mass. Thus in Dachau, when living with the priests, I was lead to the realisation that indeed I had had my 'hours of weakness' in Sachsenhausen. I really do not feel ashamed about them, but about trying to free myself from this weak-

ness by criticising the dogma mentioned above. If I had to choose today between the Roman Church and, e. g., Congregationalism, I know I would never decide in favour of the Roman Church." Cf. ZEKHN Darmstadt, 62/2000b. See also H. Asmussen, Zur Jüngsten Kirchengeschichte. Anmerkungen und Folgerungen, Stuttgart 1961, 54.

45 Cf. Cavert to Park on 28 March 1946, DeptHistPresbChurch, Phila., 18-15-24.

46 Cf. Jens Holger Schjørring et al. (eds), Vom Weltbund zur Gemeinschaft. Geschichte des Lutherischen Weltbundes 1947-1997, Hanover 1997, 386 ff.

47 Cavert to Visser't Hooft on 29 March 1946, DeptHistPresbChurch, Phila., 18-15-24.

48 Cf. Travers to Cavert on 12 April 1946, DeptHistPresbChurch, Phila., 18-15-24.

49 Cavert to Visser't Hooft on 29 April 1946, DeptHistPresbChurch, Phila., 18-15-24. In a writing, addressed to Stewart Herman, on 18 June 1946 (Herman Papers, Shelter Island Heights) Fry tried to justify the position on Lutheranism upheld by Cavert. "Our American group did unanimously, with the concurrence of [Abdel Ross] Wentz and [Peter O.] Bersell [president of NLC and the Augustana Synod], come to the conviction that a visit by Niemöller last spring would have been unfortunate. You may be surprised at the reasons .... We felt first that excessive American adulation of Niemöller might have unwholesome repercussions in Germany when he returned. In a word, I was afraid that they would make him look like a Quisling. If I wanted to compromise him, there would have been no shrewder device that I could recommend. It is because we emphatically did not want to compromise him that we cautioned delay. Our second reason has been that we hope that Niemöller will not go to South America. That is blunt and it is equally true. If we are still the friends that I hope that we are, I am sure that you will not embarrass me by repeating it in just that bald a fashion. The German churches in South America are in the process of achieving an evolution, which has been artificially delayed for far too long a time already. They are at last becoming indigenous churches and we earnestly do not want anything to intervene which would impede that transition. Because of Niemöller's official position, a visit of his to Brazil and Argentina might prove to be exactly that frustrating factor. I regret that Doctor Cavert apparently did not make it explicit that others in America objected quite as strenuously as the Lutherans."

50 Cf. Besier, Ludwig and Thierfelder, Der Kompromiß von Treysa (op. cit. note 4), 21 ff.

51 Cf., on the contrary, the correspondence between Rev. K. L. Engstrom (Gwinner, North Dakota) and Long of mid-April 1946, AELCA Chicago, NLC 2/3/1, Box 9. When Engstrom asked worriedly, Long answered taking the position that a United Lutheran Church in Germany would not endanger the EKD merger. Cf. Long to Engstrom on 17 April 1946.

52 Expression used in a letter by John C. Mattes, Wartburg Theological Seminary, to Long of 29 November 1946, AELCA Chicago, NLC 2/3/2, Box 2. Mattes was referring to a letter by Bodensieck, from which he quoted extensively. See also Long's letter of response on 6 December 1946.

53 Michelfelder to Long on 12 June 1946. AELCA Chicago, NLC 2/3/2, Box 3.

54 The Karl Barth implored Niemöller "*not*" to go "to America now". "What can you have lost and be looking for over there, which would not find a much more important counterpart in the German sorrows? ... I dread at the thought of all that might happen without your disturbing control, or controlling disturbance, in the EKD Council and originating from the 'Schwäbisch Gmünd' [scil. Asmussen!], while you are being photographed, interviewed and maybe even filmed over there." Barth to Niemöller on 29 June 1946, ACDP St. Augustin, Best. I-398 NL Asmussen, X, 48 b.

55 Cf. on C. Gisevius, C. Nicolaisen and N. A. Schulze (processors), Die Protokolle des Rates der Evangelischen Kirche in Deutschland, vol. 1 (op. cit. note 8), 79, note 92.

56 Michelfelder to Long on 12 June 1946, AELCA Chicago, NLC 2/3/2, Box 3.

57 Cf. Besier, Ludwig and Thierfelder, Der Kompromiß von Treysa, 32 ff.

58 Cf. Michelfelder's confidential report to Long and the collaborators of the Executive Committee of the American Section of the Lutheran World Conference on 12 June 1946, AELCA Chicago, NLC 2/3/2, Box 3. According to Michelfelder's assessment,

Wurm's mistakes were his letter to the Archbishop of Canterbury, the interview with Reuters in Geneva and his efforts to get his son out of prison in Wiesbaden.

59 Long to Schuette on 26 September 1946, AELCA Chicago. NLC 2/3/1, Box 9. In this letter Long affirmed his ambivalent judgement on Niemöller: "I have said in a number of instances that Dr. Niemöller is an exceedingly dynamic man and by that same token will become a dangerous man unless his course is properly chartered ... . I should say in conclusion that Dr. Niemöller is a consecrated man and a man of great force. It is merely a question of directing his energy into the right channel."

60 Michelfelder to Long on 30 May 1946 with reference to a talk with Lilje, AELCA Chicago, NLC 2/3/2, Box 3. On 17 May 1946, Michelfelder had written Long: "... if the Lutherans of America keep Niemöller out of America, that very thing will help to widen the gap within Germany." He warned Long that Cavert and other representatives of the Federal Council passed on all information on the stance of the American Lutherans to Niemöller, a wrong assumption.

61 Cf. G. Besier (ed.), 'Ökumenische Mission in Nachkriegsdeutschland. Die Berichte von Stewart W. Herman über die Verhältnisse in der evangelischen Kirche 1945/46', in KZG 1, 1988, 151.

62 Herman to Cavert on 3 May 1946, DeptHistPresbChurch, Phila., 18-15-24. See also: Stewart W. Herman, Wanted: An American Lutheran Foreign Policy, 4 June 1946, Herman Papers, Shelter Island Heights, N.Y.

63 Quoted from a letter of Cavert's to Visser't Hooft on 10 May 1946, DeptHistPresb Church, Phila., 18-15-24.

64 Cavert to Visser't Hooft on 10 May 1946.

65 Cavert to Visser't Hooft on 22 May 1946, DeptHistPresbChurch, Phila., 18-23-2.

66 Cf. Niemöller to Cavert on 2 May 1946, DeptHistPresbChurch, Phila., 18-15-24.

67 Ibid. Cf. also Cavert to Niemöller on 4 June 1946, DeptHistPresbChurch, Phila., 18-15-24.

68 Cf. Niemöller to Cavert on 2 September 1946, DeptHistPresbChurch, Phila., 18-15-24.

69 Cavert had received an invitation by the head of military chaplains to perform a visitation to them. Cf. Schmidt, Architect of Unity (op. cit. note 42), 194 ff. See also Cavert to Visser't Hooft on 10 June 1946. DeptHistPresbChurch, Phila., 18-23-2. After, in December 1945, an agreement had been reached with General Clay to send a permanent American church representative to Germany (cf. Herman to Cavert on 2 July 1946, DeptHistPresbChurch, Phila., 18-23-2), the Federal Council looked desperately for such a representative, but met only with refusals from the envisaged candidates. Stewart W. Herman also declined the Federal Council's offer. Cf. Cavert to Visser't Hooft on 22 May 1946, DeptHistPresbChurch, Phila., 18-23-2. On Cavert's sojourn in Germany in the Summer of 1946, cf. his Report of A Mission to Germany, published by the Federal Council, DeptHistPresbChurch, Phila., 18-33-8. See also Clay to Cavert on 7 August 1946, DeptHistPresbChurch, Phila., 18-1-16. It states: "The development of a peaceful and democratic Germany is a task, which will require the use and coordination of all material and spiritual resources. May our efforts in this endeavour to reach our common objectives be successful and your services to the church in this important mission be fruitful."

70 Memorandum by Leiper for Barnes on 21 August 1946, DeptHistPresbChurch, Phila., 18-15-24.

71 Cf. Cavert to Patterson on 13 August 1946, DeptHistPresbChurch, Phila., 18-15-24. In a handwritten document Asmussen's name precedes Dibelius's. See on Hartenstein, Wolfgang Metzger (ed.), Karl Hartenstein. Ein Leben für Kirche und Mission, Stuttgart, 2nd ed., 1954, 74 ff. Hartenstein did not come to America before 1947 as a German delegate for the Fourth World Mission Conference in Whitby near Toronto (Canada).

72 Cf. Cavert to Visser't Hooft on 19 September 1946, DeptHistPresbChurch, Phila., 18-23-3.

73 See Clifford Nelson, The Rise of World Lutheranism (op. cit. note 23), 362. Contemporarily, the American Lutheran E. Theodore Bachmann was appointed WCC Liaison Officer for the German churches (ibid.). On this, see also Herman to Cavert on 25 September 1946, DeptHistPresbChurch, Phila., 18–23–3, and Cavert's answer of 4 October 1946. On 17 January 1946, the president of the Federal Council, Bishop G. Bromley Oxnam, had written to President Truman regarding the Liaison Officer between the American military government and the German churches and sent him a memorandum on this. He justified this suggestion with the experience that a delegation of American churchmen had during their visit in Germany at the beginning of December 1945. Oxnam defined his suggestion for a Liaison Officer as "a significant contribution to the democratization of Germany", cf. DeptHistPresbChurch, Phila., 18–21–7. On the history of this position and the question of its continuation, cf. the documents in DeptHistPresbChurch, Phila., 18–10–3.
74 Cf. Visser't Hooft to Cavert on 13 September 1946 and Cavert to Visser't Hooft on 19 September 1946, DeptHistPresbChurch, Phila., 18–23–3.
75 Bodensieck to Long on 20 November 1946, AELCA Chicago. NLC 2/3/2, Box 2.
76 Ibid.
77 Cf. memorandum by Roswell P. Barnes of 8 August 1946, DeptHistPresbChurch, Phila., 18–15–24.
78 Cf. Clay to Cavert on 15 October 1946, DeptHistPresbChurch, Phila., 18–15–24.
79 Cf. Cavert to Patterson on 23 October 1946, NA Washington, RG 59, 811.42762/10–2846.
80 Cf. telegram by Cavert for Visser't Hooft of 25 October 1946, DeptHistPresbChurch, Phila, 18–15–24.
81 Office Memorandum United States Government from O'Sullivan to General Hilldring, 28 October 1946, Subject: Visit of Niemöller to the United States, NA Washington, RG 59, 811.42762/10–2846.
82 Cf. New York Times, 6 June 1945.
83 Cf. on this, the correspondence between Acheson and Sherrill at the end of November 1946, DeptHistPresbChurch, Phila., 18–15–24. According to it, Acheson still took Niemöller for someone with a preference for anti-democratic, "authoritarian and militaristic concepts"; "his views are hostile to our occupational objectives"; "... we had hoped that the first few Germans selected under this program would be indisputably representative of democratic and peace-loving forces within Germany". See also Acheson to Cavert on 27 November 1946. On 16 December 1946, Cavert wrote to Acheson and by displaying the relevant documents called his attention to the fact that he had been duped by "some very serious misinformation". Finally, he offered that the Under Secretary of State could meet Niemöller, cf. DeptHistPresbChurch, Phila., 18–15–24.
84 Cf. on Dulles, Anthony Clark Arend, Pursuing A Just and Durable Peace. John Foster Dulles and International Organization, New York-Westport-London 1988; Frederick W. Marks III, Power and Peace. The Diplomacy of John Foster Dulles, Westport-London 1993; Manfred Görtemaker, 'John Foster Dulles und die Einigung Westeuropas', in Martin Greschat and Wilfried Loth (eds), Die Christen und die Entstehung der Europäischen Gemeinschaft (KoGe 5), Stuttgart 1994, 159–187.
85 Cf. Cavert to Visser't Hooft on 15 November 1946, DeptHistPresbChurch, Phila., 18–23–3. See also O. P. Echols, War Department, to Cavert on 1 November 1946, DeptHistPresbChurch, Phila., 18–15–24.
86 Cf. Ernest A. Gross to Acheson on 31 January 1947 with an enclosed three-page report of 28 January 1947, NA Washington, RG 59, 862.20200/1–3147. The report states: "Niemöller's reception has been mixed ... . In limited editorial comment, criticism of Niemöller and of his U.S. trip comes from a small group of liberals and from some spokesmen for the Jewish and Episcopalian faiths. Church groups, including his sponsor, the Federal Council of Churches, defend the Pastor."

87 Cavert to Visser't Hooft on 19 September 1946, DeptHistPresbChurch, Phila., 18–23–3.

88 Cf. on Hans Asmussen, Enno Konukiewitz, Hans Asmussen. Ein lutherischer Theologe im Kirchenkampf (LKGG 6), Gütersloh 1984; Wolfgang Lehmann, Hans Asmussen. Ein Leben für die Kirche, Göttingen 1988. Neither book mentions Asmussen's American visit. See also Gerhard Besier, 'Hans Asmussen, Karl Barth und Martin Niemöller im "Kirchenkampf". Theologie und Kirchenpolitik in "Schülerschaft", Partnerschaft und Gegnerschaft', in Josef Außermair (ed.), Hans Asmussen im Kontext heutiger ökumenischer Theologie, Münster 2001, 46–78.

89 Cavert to Visser't Hooft on 19 September 1946, DeptHistPresbChurch, Phila., 18–23–3.

90 Cf. Stewart Herman, The Rebirth of the German Church. With an Introduction by Martin Niemöller, London 1946.

91 Cf. telegram by Herman to Cavert of 24 September 1946, DeptHistPresbChurch. Phila., 18–23–3.

92 Cf. on this, Cavert to the Acting Secretary of State, Dean G. Acheson, on 15 October 1946, DeptHistPresbChurch. Phila., 18–15–24. Cf. also F. E. Mayer, systematic theologian at Concordia Seminary in St. Louis, to Lilje on 1 October 1946 (LKA Hanover, L 3 Nr. II 24). In this letter Mayer asks whether Lilje had accepted the Hamma Divinity School's invitation; if so, he would like to introduce Lilje to the community life of the Missouri Synod. Cf. also C. S. Meyer, Log Cabin to Luther Tower. Concordia Seminary during one hundred and twenty-five years toward a more excellent ministry 1839-1964, St. Louis 1965.

93 Cf. Cavert to Howard K. Travers on 10 October 1946, DeptHistPresbChurch, Phila., 18–15–24.

94 Cf. Cavert to Visser't Hooft on 4 November 1946, DeptHistPresbChurch, Phila., 18–23–3. Cf. also Cavert to Niemöller on 7 October 1946, DeptHistPresbChurch, Phila., 18–15–24. On 1 October 1946, Cavert wrote Goebel (Chicago): "To tell the truth, I hardly thought that either of them [Asmussen and Dibelius] would be able to come, but I thought that by thus inviting them and so meeting General Clay's point of view, I might at least secure Niemöller! I now hear that Bishop Dibelius has hopes that he may be able to come to this country sometime in the early part of 1947 – perhaps in February. I do not imagine that he will be a popular figure like Niemöller, but it seems to me that it would be well worth while for us to set up an itinerary for him, which would bring him into touch with church leaders."

95 Letter from Bennett on 10 November 1946, DeptHistPresbChurch, Phila., 18–23–3. Cf. also Cavert to L. W. Goebel on 21 November 1946, DeptHist PresbChurch, Phila., 18–15–24. From this letter it emerges that Cavert took Bennett's assessment very seriously.

96 Since Visser't Hooft also held reservations about a ship passage for the Niemöllers, this had to be paid for eventually. Cf. on this, Northam to Cavert on 10 March 1949, DeptHistPresbChurch, Phila., 18–23–8.

97 Cf. on this, Federal Council Meets in Seattle, in The Christian Century 63 (1946), 1528 f.

98 See on this and the following, Howard Schomer, 'Martin Niemöller in Amerika', in Hanfried Krüger (ed.), Bis an das Ende der Erde. Ökumenische Beiträge. Zum 70. Geburtstag von D. Martin Niemöller, München 1962, 75 f.

99 Cavert to Visser't Hooft on 17 December 1946, DeptHistPresbChurch, Phila., 18–23–3. On this, also see the reports in the Christian Century 63 (1946), 1524, 1574; Christian Century 64 (1947), 50, 70–72, 92, 100, 121, 181–184, 186, 211 f., 218–220, 240 f., 244, 373, 378, 436, 538, 633, 644.

100 Cf. on this, Ewart Edmund Turner, 'Memorandum Regarding Pastor Niemöller's Visit'; Turner's letter to Erwin R. Koch of 9 December 1946, and Turner's writing to Cavert of 8 December 1946, DeptHistPresbChurch. Phila., 18–15–24.

101 Turner to Cavert on 8 December 1946, DeptHistPresbChurch, Phila., 18–15–24.

102 Bachmann was only officially appointed in mid-June 1947. Cf. on this Minutes of the Meeting of Available Members of the Administrative Committee, 18 June 1947, DeptHistPresbChurch, Phila., 18–23–5. Already in October 1947 Bachmann decided to return to the United States. "Stewart [Herman] thinks that Bachmann has not understood how to handle the military." Visser't Hooft to Cavert on 28 August 1947, DeptHistPresbChurch, Phila., 18–23–5.

103 Since April 1945, Bachmann had been pleading for a cross exchange of German and American theologians. Cf. Bachmann to Long on 23 April 1945, AELCA Chicago, NLC 2/3/1, Box 9.

104 Cf. Bachmann to Cavert on 23 December 1946, DeptHistPresbChurch, Phila., 18–15–24.

105 Cavert to Bachmann on 27 December 1946, DeptHistPresbChurch, Phila., 18–15–24.

106 Cf. Cavert to Flack on 25 November 1946, DeptHistPresbChurch, Phila., 18–15–24.

107 Cavert-Flack correspondence: AELCA Chicago, NLC 2/3/1, Box 10. In his letter to Cavert on 7 January 1947, Flack took the position that it was only worth financing Lilje's travel and accommodation costs if he staid in the country for at least two months.

108 Cf. Gerhard Besier, 'Die Kirchenversammlung von Eisenach (1948), die Frage nach der "Entstehung einer vierten Konfession" und die Entlassung Hans Asmussens. Zugleich eine Erinnerung an den ersten Leiter der EKD-Kirchenkanzlei', in idem, Die evangelische Kirche in den Umbrüchen des 20. Jahrhunderts, Ges. Aufsätze, vol. 2, Neukirchen-Vluyn 1994, 57–87.

109 Cavert to Visser't Hooft on 26 December 1946, DeptHistPresbChurch, Phila., 18–23–3.

110 Ibid.

111 This means Joseph T. McNarney, who was replaced in the spring of 1947. Cf. John H. Backer, Die deutschen Jahre des Generals Clay. Der Weg zur Bundesrepublik Deutschland 1945–1949, Munich 1983, 193 f.

112 On the French occupation policy towards the churches cf. Martin Greschat, 'Die Kirchenpolitik Frankreichs in seiner Besatzungszone', in ZKG 109 (1998), 216–236, 363–387.

113 Visser't Hooft to Cavert on 3 December 1946, DeptHistPresbChurch, Phila., 18–23–3.

114 Ibid. On Bishop Marahrens's, who was Lilje's predecessor, cf. G. Besier, "Selbstreinigung" unter britischer Besatzungsherrschaft. Die Evangelisch-lutherische Landeskirche Hannovers und ihr Landesbischof Marahrens 1945–1947, Göttingen 1986.

115 Cavert to Visser't Hooft on 26 December 1946, DeptHistPresbChurch, Phila., 18–23–3.

116 Cf. Leiper to Mott on 15 January 1947, DeptHistPresbChurch, Phila., 18–23–4.

117 Dibelius does not mention his journey plans for America and his stay in America in Autumn 1947 in his autobiography Ein Christ ist immer im Dienst (Stuttgart 1961). Neither does Robert Stupperich (Otto Dibelius. Ein evangelischer Bischof im Umbruch der Zeiten, Göttingen 1989) mention Dibelius's journey to the United States.

118 Goebel to Cavert on 21 January 1947, DeptHistPresbChurch, Phila., 18–16–1.

119 Cavert to Goebel on 24 January 1947, DeptHistPresbChurch, Phila., 18–16–1.

120 Cf. Cavert, The American Churches in the Ecumenical Movement 1900–1968, New York 1968, 199.

121 Cavert to Niemöller on 14 December 1947, DeptHistPresbChurch, Phila., 18–16–1.

122 Ibid.

123 Ibid.

124 Cf. on Preysing's journey to America, Wolfgang Knauft, Konrad von Preysing – Anwalt des Rechts. Der erste Berliner Kardinal und seine Zeit, Berlin 1998, 255 ff.

125 Cavert to Niemöller on 14 February 1947, DeptHistPresbChurch, Phila., 18–16–1.

126 Visser't Hooft to Cavert on 14 February 1947, DeptHistPresbChurch, Phila., 18–16–1.

127 Cf. Cavert to Visser't Hooft on 17 February 1947, DeptHistPresbChurch, Phila., 18–23–4; Cavert to Niemöller on 17 February 1947, DeptHistPresbChurch, Phila.,

18–16–1; Leiper to Visser't Hooft on 21 February 1947, DeptHistPresbChurch, Phila., 18–23–4.

128 Cf. Niemöller to Cavert on 20 February 1947, DeptHistPresbChurch, Phila., 18–16–1. See also Cavert's reply on 21 February 1947.

129 Cf. Wise to Cavert on 24 January 1947, DeptHistPresbChurch, Phila., 18–16–1. See also Cavert's answer to Wise of 20 February 1947.

130 Cf. The New York Times on 25 January 1947. Cf. also Wilhelm Levinger's – a German Jew emigrated in 1937 – in contradiction to his letter to Cavert on 25 January 1947, DeptHistPresbChurch, Phila., 18–16–1.

131 Cf. e. g. Samuel McCavert's article 'The Truth About Pastor Niemöller', DeptHistPresb Church, Phila., 18–16–1, and Reinhold Niebuhr's Editorial in Christianity and Crisis on 17 February 1947.

132 Cavert referred both to the book It's Your Souls We Want (1942, German edition: Eure Seelen wollen wir. Kirche im Untergrund, Munich-Berlin 1952) and to The Rebirth of the German Church, published in 1946.

133 For example, The Witness on 13 February 1947 published an article with the title 'Niemöller Supported Hitler'. See also Cavert's letter to Bishop Frank W. Sterrett, Bethlehem (Penna.) on 17 February 1947, DeptHistPresbChurch, Phila., 18–16–1.

134 Letter from W. Maylan Jones on 24 January 1946 (meaning 1947), DeptHistPresb Church, Phila., 18–16–1.

135 Thus reported by the New York Sun of 11 February 1947.

136 Cf. Cavert to John Haynes Holnies, New York, on 17 February 1947, DeptHistPresb Church, Phila., 18–16–1.

137 Cavert in his letter to Visser't Hooft on 25 February 1947, DeptHistPresbChurch, Phila., 18–23–4.

138 Ibid.

139 From Buck Hill Falls, Cavert invited Wurm again on 22 April 1947, which he declined on 8 April 1947, but suggested Asmussen for an invitation, DeptHistPresbChurch, Phila., 18–9–21.

140 Cavert to Niemöller on 25 February 1947, DeptHistPresbChurch, Phila., 18–16–1. From letters from Oliver Tomkins (WCC, London Office) on 9 January 1947 and Sigrid Morden (WCC, Geneva) on 5 February 1947 to Lilje it emerges that Lilje had also initially intended to take part at the Meeting of the WCC Provisional Committee in April 1947, and had been invited by the president of the WCC General Secretariat. LKA Hanover, L 3 Nr. II 24. On the preparations of the EKD Council for the 1948 World Conference of Churches, cf. C. Nicolaisen and N. A. Schulze (processors), Die Protokolle des Rates der EKD, vol. 2: 1947/48 (AKZG.A 6), Göttingen 1997, 63, note 34. The question of a German representation at the last meeting of the WCC Provisional Committee in Buck Hill Falls in the Spring of 1947 was not treated, according to the notations – in contrast to the preparations for the WCC Provisional Committee in February 1946.

141 Cf. telegram from Visser't Hooft to Cavert in February 1947, DeptHistPresbChurch, Phila., 18–23–4.

142 Cf. 'Pastor Niemöller's Visit', DeptHistPresbChurch, Phila., 18–16–1.

143 Cf. Niemöller's letter of thanks to Cavert on 18 May 1947, DeptHistPresbChurch, Phila., 18–16–1.

144 Cf. Frank Schmidt, Christian Stock (1884–1967). Eine Biographie (Quellen und Forschungen zur hessischen Geschichte 113), Darmstadt-Marburg 1997, 307 f. Newman's threat was contained in the rough draft of his radio speech on 16 May 1947 but he did not read it aloud. The daily newspaper Frankfurter Rundschau had received the entire manuscript text, printed it in its edition on 17 May 1947 and sparked a wave of indignation, protests and official denials. The discussion even reached the United States, cf. New York Herald Tribune on 19 May 1947.

145 Cf. Cavert's letter to Visser't Hooft on 21 May 1947 with the enclosed resolution, DeptHistPresbChurch, Phila., 18–23–5.

146 Cavert to Niemöller on 10 June 1947, DeptHistPresbChurch, Phila., 18–16–1.
147 Cf. Cavert's letter to on 10 June 1947 and Niemöller's reply on 21 June 1947, DeptHistPresbChurch, Phila., 18–16–1.
148 Cf. W. G. Tillmanns to Long on 2 August 1947, AELCA Chicago, NLC 2/3/1, Box 10.
149 Long to Tillmanns on 19 August 1947, AELCA Chicago, NLC 2/3/1, Box 10.
150 Cf. New York Times on 19 August 1947.
151 Cf. Martin Möller, Kirche und sozialdemokratische Partei in den Jahren 1945–1950. Grundlagen der Verständigung und Beginn des Dialoges, Göttingen 1984.
152 Cf. letter from Reinhold Niebuhr to the New York Times editor on 20 August 1947, DeptHistPresbChurch, Phila., 18–16–1.
153 Cavert to Niemöller on 5 September 1947 and Niemöller to Cavert on 2 September 1947, DeptHistPresbChurch, Phila., 18–16–1.
154 See in detail Karl Dienst, 'Martin Niemöllers Berufung zum Kirchenpräsidenten der Evangelischen Kirche in Hessen und Nassau', in IBW-Journal, January/February 1997, 3–12.
155 See Niemöller to Cavert on 6 February 1948, DeptHistPresbChurch, Phila., 18–10–1.
156 Letter of Dean Wolfgang Trillhaas to Cavert of 9 February 1948 and letter of thanks by Cavert to Trillhaas on 22 March 1948.
157 Niemöller to Asmussen on 11 February 1947, ZEKHN Darmstadt, 62/2000b. On the relation between Niemöller and Asmussen, cf. Besier, Die Kirchenversammlung von Eisenach (1948) (op. cit. note 108).
158 Niemöller to Asmussen on 6 May 1947, ZEKHN Darmstadt, 62/2000b.
159 Asmussen to Niemöller on 26 February 1947. Dibelius expressed similar assumptions in a letter to the head of the Regional Office of the American Military Administration, Arild Olsen. See, on this, Olsen's letter to Cavert on 6 January 1947, DeptHistPresb Church, Phila., 18–7–22.
160 Niemöller to Asmussen on 7 March 1947, ZEKHN Darmstadt, 62/2000b.
161 Cf. Letter of Niemöller to Asmussen on 16 March 1947.
162 Asmussen to Niemöller on 21 March 1947. See also Asmussen to Niemöller on 29 March 1947.
163 Visser't Hooft to Cavert on 28 January 1947, DeptHistPresbChurch, Phila., 18–7–22. Cf. also Cavert to Visser't Hooft of 21 January 1947.
164 Quote after the explanatory letter by Cavert to Olsen on 29 January 1947, DeptHist PresbChurch, Phila., 18–7–22.
165 Cf. also Bodensieck to Cavert on 3 February 1947, DeptHistPresbChurch, Phila., 18–7–22. According to this letter Dibelius hat insisted on travelling to America in March or April. Otherwise, he would not come at all. Nevertheless Cavert adhered to his decision to postpone the journey. See, on this, his letter to Visser't Hooft on 18 February 1947. See also Cavert to Dibelius on 11 June 1947.
166 Dibelius to Rev. O. Wotklo, Camden N. Y., on 13 March 1947 (Abschrift), AELCA Chicago. NLC 2/3/2. Box 5.
167 See also letter of Dibelius to Schneider on 9 April 1946, Library of the WCC, Geneva, General Correspondence, Dibelius, Otto, 1945–1961.
168 Cf. Visser't Hooft to Dibelius on 29 March 1947.
169 Cf. on this Cavert to Acheson on 20 January 1947, DeptHistPresbChurch, Phila., 18–7–22; see also Goebel to Cavert on 20 May, 3 and 16 June 1947. Goebel had already taken up a correspondence with Dibelius on 18 January 1946, Library of the WCC, Geneva, General Correspondence, Dibelius, Martin, 1945–1961.
170 Clay to Visser't Hooft on 2 June 1947, DeptHistPresbChurch, Phila., 18–23–5.
171 Visser't Hooft to Cavert on 30 May 1947, DeptHistPresbChurch, Phila., 18–23–5.
172 Cf. Andrea Strübind, 'Freikirchen und Ökumene in der Nachkriegszeit', in KZG 6 (1993), 187–211. See also 'Free German Churches and State Group Plan to Cooperate', in The Christian Century 64 (1947), 1370.
173 Cf. F. D. Lueking, Mission in the Making. The Missionary Enterprise among Missouri Synod Lutherans, 1846–1963, St. Louis 1964; C. S. Meyer, Moving Frontiers. Readings

in the History of the Lutheran Church Missouri Synod, St. Louis 1964; M. L. Rudnick, Fundamentalism and the Missouri Synod. A historical study of their interaction and mutual influence, St. Louis 1966.

174 Cf. E. Clifford Nelson, The Lutherans in North America (op. cit. note 23), 461.

175 Bodensieck to Long on 8 October 1946, AELCA Chicago, NLC 2/3/2, Box 2. In a confidential report on 12 June 1946, also Michelfelder, Long and the Executive Committee of the American Section of the Lutheran World Convention had warned against the activities of the Missouri Synod. It stated that the "Missouri Brethren" had already heavily influenced Meiser's and Sasse's thinking and given the impression they were the leading American Lutheranism. AELCA Chicago, NLC 2/3/2, Box 3.

176 Cf. on Bachmann's assessment of the situation in Germany after his return The Christian Century 64 (1947), 1312, 1315. See also Bachmann's articles 'Wilderness of Want', 1482 f. and 'Self-Help in German Churches', 1609 f.

177 Cf. Cavert to Visser't Hooft on 3 October 1947, DeptHistPresbChurch, Phila, 18–23–5.

178 Visser't Hooft to Cavert on 8 October 1947, DeptHistPresbChurch, Phila., 18–23–5.

179 Cf. also World Council of Churches, 'Minutes of a Meeting of Available Officers and Staff' on 11 October 1947, Point 6, DeptHistPresbChurch, Phila., 18–23–5.

180 Cf. Cavert to Visser't Hooft on 24 September 1947, DeptHistPresbChurch, Phila., 18–23–5. See also Cavert's letter to Asmussen on 3 July 1946. AELCA Chicago, NLC 2/3/1, Box 10. He suggested that Asmussen attune his visit with Dibelius's in such a way that both of them are in the USA at different times, "for this would make it possible for us to arrange more satisfactory itineraries for you both".

181 In his report 'Was ich in Amerika sah und hörte' [What I saw and heard in America] on 24 February 1948, Asmussen wrote: "It was a special pleasure for me when I met Bishop Dibelius in New York City, who was spending his last days there before his voyage home," cf. ZEKHN Darmstadt, 62/2000 b.

182 Dibelius to Goebel on 11 July 1947, DeptHistPresbChurch, Phila., 18–7–22.

183 Long to Chaplain H. W. Reinke on 4 December 1947, AELCA Chicago, NLC 2/3/1, Box 10. Cf. the rare reports on Dibelius's appearance in den USA in The Christian Century 64 (1947) 1350, 1464, 1493, 1531.

184 Letter of Dibelius to Cavert on 9 November 1947, DeptHistPresbChurch, Phila., 18–7–22.

185 Op. cit.

186 Cavert to Goebel on 10 November 1947, DeptHistPresbChurch, Phila., 18–7–22.

187 Cavert to Dibelius on 10 November 1947, DeptHistPresbChurch, Phila., 18–7–22.

188 Telegram by Dibelius to Cavert on 17 November 1947, DeptHistPresbChurch, Phila., 18–7–22.

189 Berlekamp to Cavert on 12 November 1947, DeptHistPresbChurch, Phila., 18–7–22.

190 Also said in 'Das kirchliche Leben in den USA. Bischof Dibelius über seine Reiseeindrücke' [Church Life in the USA. Bishop Dibelius On His Travelling Impressions], in Neue Zeit, no. 298, 16 December 1947.

191 D. Dr. Dibelius, 'Briefe aus Amerika', in Die Kirche. Evangelische Wochenzeitung, vol. 2, no. 50, 9 November 1947, 1 f., here: 1. According to information given by the archive of the Protestant Church in Berlin-Brandenburg on 21 June 1999, a "Bishops' registrar" was not kept. A file on 'Dibelius, American Journey' ['Amerika-Reise Dibelius', or similar] could not be found.

192 On a remark allegedly made by the bishop, cf. 'Es ist nichts so fein gesponnen ...', in Märkische Volksstimme, 13 November 1947; 'Die Evangelische Kirchenleitung Berlin-Brandenburg an die Redaktion "Märkische Volksstimme", Potsdam, vom 25. November 1947' [The Protestant Church leadership of Berlin-Brandenburg to the editorial office of the Märkische Volksstimme, Potsdam, on 25 November 1947], Landeskirchliches Archiv [Church Archives] Berlin-Brandenburg, B 14; Excerpt from Dibelius's Declaration from 26 November 1947; Märkische Druck- und Verlags-GmbH to the Protestant Church leadership Berlin-Brandenburg of 15 December 1947; 'Was Bischof Dr. Dibelius wirklich gesagt hat. Ein Interview und seine Richtigstellung' [What

Bishop Dr. D. really did say. An interview and its rectification], in ENO, no. 14, 8 November 1947, 2.

193 'Hat die Kirche in Deutschland jemals in diesem Stil etwas für andere Völker und Kirchen getan?' Dibelius, Briefe aus Amerika ['Has the Church in Germany ever done anything of this kind for other peoples and churches?' Dibelius, Letters from America] (op. cit. note 191), 1 f.

194 The reception was initiated by Myron Taylor. Cf. Dibelius to Cavert on 16 September 1947, DeptHistPresbChurch, Phila., 18-7-22; Bodensieck to Cavert on 13 September 1947; Taylor to Cavert on 8 December 1947.

195 Dibelius related less about the contents of the talk: "We spoke about how much the spiritual and moral forces mean in the lives of the peoples and how necessary it is to create some unobstructed space for these forces right now, in order that not all of human life loses its sense and value. We spoke about which tasks the Sermon of the Mountain posed to the people these days, if rightly understood and rightly used – all questions, which move the hearts of all Christian among us as well and about what a bishop likes to talk with a politician about. It would not be right to say more about this conversation." Dibelius, 'Briefe aus Amerika', 1 f., here: 1.

196 Cf. on this also D. Dr. Dibelius, 'Abschied von Amerika', in Die Kirche. Evangelische Wochenzeitung, vol. 3, no. 6, 4 January 1948, 1 f., here: 2: "But it was by no means harmless in the First World War. And neither is it in the age of totalitarian developments."

197 Cf. op. cit., 1 f., quote: 2.

198 In this context Dibelius referred briefly to Reinhold Niebuhr's critical stance – "very similar to the way Karl Barth fought against it over here". Dibelius, 'Briefe aus Amerika', 1 f., here: 1.

199 Op. cit., 2.

200 "And also a foreign visitor is expected not to bother about spending the nights in the sleeping car and talking all along during daytime, about preaching and accounting to the press or to circles of a specially interested audience." Dibelius, 'Abschied von Amerika' (op. cit. note 196), 1.

201 See also Dibelius's letter to Cavert on 7 February 1948, in which he expresses his thanks for all his helpfulness and asks the American for black cloth for sewing robes and dark suits for his pastors, DeptHistPresbChurch, Phila., 18-10-1.

202 Dibelius expressed himself similarly regarding the question of war guilt, which was considered done in Christian circles, during a press conference in the Berlin Consistory after returning from the United States. Outside church circles the Germans still raised bitter feelings. "If my impression is right, public opinion is not very interested in the question how the frontier will be drawn in East Germany and whether Germany will be divided." 'Dibelius über seine USA-Reise', in Die Welt, no. 149, 16 December 1947. But there was no talking about hatred against Germany as after the First World War, Dibelius told the Neue Zeitung. 'Kein Haß gegen Deutschland'. Bischof Dibelius berichtet über seine Reise nach USA', in Berliner Blatt/Neue Zeitung München, no. 99, 13 December 1947.

203 Dibelius, 'Abschied von Amerika' (op. cit. note 196), 1.

204 Cf. also Bishop Dibelius on his journey to America. 'Angst vor der Depression – Entwicklung zum totalen Staat', in Tägliche Rundschau, Berlin, 16 February 1947: "Finally, Bishop Dibelius [in the presence of members of the press] pointed to the development of a totalitarian state, which was visible in the United States. The continually growing power of the state in all spheres public life involved a huge expansion of bureaucracy, a fact to which the due attention must be paid, especially so in connection with the Marshall Plan." Cf. also 'Dibelius über USA', in Tribüne, no. 293, 16 December 1947.

205 Dibelius, 'Abschied von Amerika' (op. cit. note 196), 2.

206 Cf. Minutes of the Annual Meeting of the Friends of the World Council of Churches, Inc., 16 December 1947, DeptHistPresbChurch, Phila., 18-23-5.

207 Cf. the brief report in The Christian Century 65 (1948), 156.

208 Ibid. 254.

209 Cf. Minutes of the Annual Meeting of the Friends of the World Council of Churches, Inc., 16 December 1947, DeptHistPresbChurch. Phila., 18–23–5.

210 Minutes of the Meeting of the American Committee for the World Council of Churches, 16 December 1947, DeptHistPresbChurch, Phila., 18–23–5.

211 Carl E. Lund-Quist, Division of Public Relations, Dr. Hans Asmussen's Visit to the United States (3.12.1947–21.1.1948), Report to the U.S. National Committee Lutheran World Federation, 21 January 1948, AELCA Chicago, NLC 2/3/2, Box 5.

212 Hans Asmussen, 'Was ich in Amerika sah und hörte', 24 February 1948, ZEKHN Darmstadt, 62/2000b.

213 Ibid.

214 Ibid.

215 Ibid.

216 Cf. Besier, 'Die Kirchenversammlung von Eisenach' (op. cit. note 108).

217 National Lutheran Council, 31 May 1948, quoted from ACDP St. Augustin, Best. I 398, X; 107.

218 Eugen Gerstenmaier, who had not been nominated as a possible church representative suitable for an invitation, was likewise in America in March 1948, on the invitation of the Missouri Synod and other Lutheran churches. Cf. the report in the May issue of the Kirchliches Monatsblatt 5 (1948), which was published in Philadelphia. See also E. Gerstenmaier, Streit und Friede hat seine Zeit. Ein Lebensbericht, Frankfurt/M.-Berlin-Wien 1981, 262–272, who stresses that the "Missouri Synod ... was one of our main donator churches from the beginning" (ibid. 263). Gerstenmaier was even received by Truman. Cf. Johannes Michael Wischnath, Kirche in Aktion. Das Evangelische Hilfswerk 1945–1957 und sein Verhältnis zu Kirche und Innerer Mission, Göttingen 1986, esp. 155. As emerges from a correspondence between Hans Schönfeld and the Associate General Secretary of the Federal Council, Roswell P. Barnes, the former had already suggested inviting Gerstenmaier to the USA on 20 October 1947. Barnes answered cautiously and explained the problem that German churchmen should not appear in great numbers in the United States, DeptHistPresbChurch, Phila., 18–9–21. See also Schönfeld to Barnes on 7 January 1948, DeptHistPresb Church, Phila., 18–10–1.

219 Cf. the correspondence with the British and American military governments about country exiting formalities: LKA Hanover, L 3, Nr. II 24. Official invitation letter of the National Lutheran Council president, Rees Edgar Tulloss, to Lilje on 6 January 1948. See also Lilje's article 'The Crisis of Modern Man', in The Christian Century 64 (1947), 1394 f.

220 Cf. Cavert to Lilje on 14 April 1948, LKA Hanover, L 3 III 1461.

221 Carl E. Lund-Quist to Capt. C. C. Axvall, War Department, of 3 February 1948, LKA Hanover, L 3, Nr. II 24.

222 Meyer to Lilje on 4 June 1948, LKA Hanover, L 3, Nr. II 24.

223 Hannoversche Neue Presse on 20 May 1948.

224 Cf. the documents in the DeptHistPresbChurch, Phila., 18–22–12. See also Asmussen's letter of request in this matter to Cavert on 14 December 1948, DeptHistPresb Church, Phila., 18–10–1.

The GDR and the State Churches (1958–1989)*

The role of Protestantism in the German Democratic Republic (the GDR) has been strongly disputed since the so-called *Wende* (turning point in German history related to the fall of the wall) and the reunification of 1989/90. Many of the disagreements derive from different interpretations of the relationship between State, Church and Society in the GDR. This paper first describes the state institutions which formulated and executed church policies for the Communist Party of the GDR (the SED), and then surveys relations between Church and State, offering an explanation for actions and motivations on both sides. The thesis advanced is that the decisive phase of the transformation of a "bourgeois" Church into a "Church within socialism" took place between 1958 and 1978, and that the preceding and subsequent periods merely had a character of "past history" and "epilogue".

A variety of institutions influenced Church-State policies in the GDR. First, at government level, there was until 1957 a department for ecclesiastical affairs controlled by the deputy prime minister; after that date, there was an official secretary for church affairs, answerable to the chairman of the government (*Ministerrat*). At party level in the SED, there was a working group for church affairs which was part of the secretariat of the SED's central committee, answerable to the first secretary or the secretary-general of the central committee. The central committee office included a member with specific responsibility for church affairs, generally the second in line after the the party chairman. In the Ministry for State Security (MfS), those involved were the head of the so-called "main department for social superstructure", together with a representative of the minister or the minister himself, and the heads of administration in individual *Länder* or districts.

Collaborators with the MfS's church policy were placed in other departments, where they could influence the procedures to suit the MfS. For example, the former leader of the MfS Leipzig department (BV\Leipzig\XX\4) moved to the sector of ecclesiastical affairs in the council of Leipzig district. In addition to this, the MfS employed in the secretariat for ecclesiastical affairs, officers in special deployment (*OibE*) and unofficial collaborators (*Inoffzielle Mitarbeiter* or *IM*). Although the East German Christian Democratic Union Party (the CDU) accepted the "leading role of the SED" in the fields of both Church and State, its own influence on the fate of the church is not to be underestimated.[1] Apart from the fact that the CDU chairman Otto Nuschke presided over the main department for "contact with the churches" up to 1957, the SED had assigned tasks to its allied party which influenced policy-making in the SED and MfS. The CDU wrote a huge number of letters, and created a climate designed to influence the clergy,

---

*   First published in *Journal of Ecclesiastical History* 50 (1999) 3. For explanatory notes on terms and abbreviations used in this article please see the appendix.

church employees and leading church officers. In addition, it provided material for the SED and its security service. "Thus the CDU, as regards the churches, degenerated into an instrument for procuring information for the SED and MfS, and into an instrument of influence at their service."[2]

Up to 1969, the Protestant state churches (*Landeskirchen*) in the Soviet zone (and later the GDR), were also members of the German Protestant Church Federation (EKD), formally established in 1948, and – depending on their denomination – members of either the United Lutheran Church in Germany (VELKD), or the German Evangelical Church of the Union (EKU, or APU until 1953). For this reason, in the view of the government in the East, they represented a constant gateway to western imperialism. It was a fact that the eastern member Churches were well aware of their ties to the west, and that they tried, in spite of all the difficulties, to maintain a close relationship with their western sister Churches. While the "Potsdam Agreement" of 1945 offered the possibility of German reunification, the Churches in East and West Germany made a further contribution towards holding the entire German territory together, the socio-political importance of which can hardly be overrated.

The repeated snubbing of the Soviet zone by the bishop of Berlin-Brandenburg, Otto Dibelius, had an inflammatory effect on the development of Church-State relationships. From 1949, Dibelius was also the chairman of the EKD. From the point of view of the Soviets, he was at the head of those church circles which stood in the way of the positive development of the Soviet Zone and which slandered the government of East Germany. At Whitsun-tide in 1949 Dibelius issued a pastoral letter which denounced, among other things, the secret police (the K5), political trials and the election procedure in the Soviet Zone. He also opposed the socialist drive to collectivise agriculture.[3]

With this Stalinist transformation of Eastern Germany, begun in 1949 and directed by the Soviet Union, the communists' mild church policy had come to an end. The Churches described the period as a second *Kirchenkampf*. Religious education in schools became nearly impossible, state subsidies to the churches were cut back and then terminated, church meetings were hindered and church diaconal institutions were in many cases confiscated by the state. The pastors of church youth work in the youth parishes and Protestant student parishes, as well as members of those parishes, were persecuted and imprisoned.[4]

The churches replied to this persecution with proclamations from the pulpit, protests and a letter to the chief state prosecutor of the GDR. At the peak of the persecutions and probably as a result of the new direction ordered for the GDR after the death of Stalin, a summit meeting took place. This was fixed at short notice for 10 June 1953, and Prime Minister Otto Grotewohl as well as the minister for state security, Wilhelm Zaisser, took part. In the communiqué issued at the end of the meeting, the state pledged to "guarantee the Church's existence according to the provisions of the constitution of the GDR", and the Church agreed to "avoid unconstitutional attacks and influences on political and economic life".[5]

The half-hearted and incomplete de-Stalinisation of the following period resulted in continuous conflict between Church and State. One twist in the SED's church policy was the reintroduction, on 12 November 1954, of the youth consecration ceremony (*Jugendweihe*) abolished in 1950.[6] From this time onwards it was a matter in dispute in both Church and State. This atheistic ceremony, which took place at the age of fourteen, included a promise to become a true citizen of the socialist state and was intended to supplant the traditional Church's confirmation ceremonies. Those who refused to take part in the ceremony offered by the state had to endure disadvantages in their school career. School officials were obliged to participate in it. Because of the *Jugendweihe*'s implicit atheistic and materialist world view, the Churches took a firm line against it, maintaining that a decision regarding confirmation versus *Jugendweihe* was a question of belief, not of political loyalty, and they prevented those taking the *Jugendweihe* from being confirmed by the Church.

The churches had to endure accusations of being a refuge for agents of imperialism. Soon, the "military chaplaincy agreement" was regarded as a main justification for this reproach: the Protestant Church in Germany had offered it to both German governments, but only the West Germans accepted. The conclusion of an agreement with the West German government on 22 February 1957, led to a further deterioration in the already strained relations between the communist state and the Church.[7] From the point of view of the MfS, the military chaplaincy agreement was the "decisive wedge, a charter for breaking German church unity"[8].

In November 1956, the Churches heard for the first time of the SED regime's intention of establishing a new intermediary between State and Churches: Otto Nuschke's department was to be replaced by a state secretariat of church affairs. In April 1957, Werner Eggerath, who had been ambassador to Romania, was appointed to this office. The EKD's emissary to the GDR, Provost Heinrich Grüber, knew him as a former fellow concentration camp inmate.

From 1958 to the construction of the Wall on 13 August 1961

On 17 May 1958, GDR Prime Minister Otto Grotewohl informed Grüber, as the authorised representative of the EKD, that its representation with the GDR government would no longer be recognised. Grotewohl would, nevertheless, be prepared to receive a delegation from the Protestant Churches of the GDR, whose members, however, would have to be citizens of the GDR. In response, on 2 June 1958, the Churches sent a delegation of the required composition to Grotewohl. The discussion was designated a good "new start" by the Thuringian bishop Moritz Mitzenheim[9], and – after further negotiations at a lower level – another meeting took place three weeks later. After a third discussion on 27 June, a communiqué was issued on 21 July, which for a long time formed the essential basis for the relationship between Church and State. While the State merely affirmed the general provisions of freedom of faith and conscience, the Church once more made several political concessions. It abandoned its charge that the state had violated the constitution, and, in an effort to deflect the state's criticism of the military chaplaincy agreement with the West German government, declared that the churches in the GDR were not bound by it. Moreover, it gave an indirect vote of confidence to the state's foreign policy, claiming that "with the means available to it, the Church serves peace between peoples and thus agrees with the efforts for peace of the GDR and its government". Finally, in the most definite statement yet of the Church's position, its representatives proclaimed that they "respect[ed] the development of socialism and contribute[d] to the peaceful construction of the life of the people". In return for these declarations, the Church received the state's pledge to check complaints regarding the educational system and to clarify outstanding problems.[10] The 1958 communiqué engendered intense debate in the Churches, both in the east and west, and led to criticism of the concessions made to the state for which Bishop Mitzenheim was held responsible as head of the delegation. In retrospect, it can be seen as a milestone on the way towards the Church's self-definition as a "Church within socialism".

Shortly after the summit meeting on 27 August 1958, the so-called Eastern Conference of the Church Leadership of the EKD decided to create its own church office for EKD member Churches in the east.[11] The SED reacted to this with deep scepticism. The decision was taken "not to recognise the new office as a negotiating partner and not to receive representatives of this office unless it could guarantee by its structure and personnel that it was acting independently of the western church offices as central office for the state Churches in the GDR"[12]. This office would become the first symbol of an institutional separation of the EKD from the west. After the talks of July 1958, there was a slight détente between State and Church. However, in the November 1958 edition of the magazine *Einheit* ("Unity"), edited by the central committee of the SED, Willi Barth (head of the department of church questions in the secretariat of the central committee) and Rudi Bellmann (his deputy, and successor in 1977), published "The justification of imperialistic plans for a nuclear war by politically-minded clergy", one of the most significant articles concerning the SED church policies.[13]

Bishop Dibelius, probably prompted by a collection of essays which Martin Fischer had compiled under the title *"Obrigkeit"* ("Authorities") in 1959 and which contained severe criticism of the western Churches, used the imminent sixtieth birthday of Hanns Lilje, bishop of Hanover, to write an open letter of congratulation, with the headline "Obrigkeit?". In this letter he interpreted the Greek word *exousia* ("authority") in Romans xiii, as "legal authority of the state". He pointed out that Luther's word *Obrigkeit* ("authorities") would no longer be regarded as an adequate translation for *exousia,* since neither modern democratic states nor totalitarian states were "authorities" in the original sense of the word. The bishop of Berlin wrote: "It is not true, though it has been repeatedly maintained, that minimum rights are protected equally in an anti-Christian sphere of influence. In a totalitarian state there are no rights in the Christian sense of the word. Neither maximum nor minimum rights. It is no coincidence that in the GDR the word rights is increasingly disappearing. There is only legality, which means a number of requirements that the rulers accept in the interest of their power and which they push through using the instruments of their power."[14]

Dibelius moderated the affront in this and other paragraphs in the following "discourse about authorities", but he left no doubt that in his opinion the government of the GDR was not in accordance with Romans xiii. The EKD synod of February 1960 in Berlin-Spandau also dealt with this controversial question; after tough debating, they emphasised that the declaration of the EKD synod of 1956 would remain in force:[15]

"The Gospel is inconsistent with any attempt to maintain a special human social order as absolute and to impose this order as the final objective by using violent methods ... The Gospel puts the state under the merciful order of God, which has validity independent of the rise of state-power or its political form. The Gospel gives us the liberty to say no to any totalitarian pretension of human power, to stand up for those who have been deprived of their rights by it [i. e. by the totalitarian use of human power] and for those who have been tempted by it; and to prefer to suffer than to obey ungodly laws and orders ... The Gospel is the great hope from God that the coming Lord will have the last word in heaven and on earth."[16]

Despite the fact that the EKD synod dissociated itself from the views of its chairman, Dibelius, the SED government viewed its discussions with great hostility. Moreover, they were apparently filled with consternation at the presence of western German politicians (Lemmer and Brandt), who took part in the EKD synod's opening service in the *Marienkirche* in East Berlin.[17] According to Erich Mielke, chief of the security service, it was "not a divine service but a Cold War rally" and required a reaction from the GDR government.[18] Preliminary proceedings against Dibelius were therefore begun by the chief state prosecutor – relations between State and Church were permanently affected.

From its point of view, the SED regime was bound to suppose that the GDR Churches entirely supported the EKD's pro-western line – in spite of some concessions to the GDR government. The socialists feared that the Church's way endangered political development in the GDR. The state meant to stop at nothing in dealing with anyone who allowed themselves to be used as an instrument of the enemy. Countering EKD church politics, actually or allegedly hostile to the GDR, the SED paid special attention to those church circles in east and west that opposed the majority of the EKD synod, which was loyal to the west. So the security service was gratified to report that during the nuclear debate of 1958 in the EKD synod – regarded as the main point of attack against the GDR[19] – opposition movements were very much in evidence for the first time.[20] Although the security service could not exploit strained political relations within the EKD synod to the state's advantage, it agreed to provide material and financial support to opposition circles in the western Churches.[21] The security service achieved some success in these years: in 1958 the "Bund Evangelischer Pfarrer in der DDR" (Association of Protestant Ministers in the GDR) was founded,[22] and in the same year the Prague Christian Peace Conference (CPC) was established, which was meant as an ecumenical counter-movement to the western-oriented World Council of Churches (WCC).[23]

As the SED regime could not decisively influence the entire EKD, it sought instead to establish the absolute independence of GDR Churches from all western institutions. Only in this way – under the existing political circumstances – could a "normalisation" of Church-state relations in the GDR be achieved, and the SED was very interested in this solution. To reach this goal the so-called

"Thuringian way" was of some importance to the SED. During the Third Reich the Thuringian Church was entirely under the influence of the German Christians, and soon after the war adopted a policy of supporting the SED. But at first observers misunderstood what was going on: criticism of Bishop Moritz Mitzenheim's concessions during the 1958 summit had already been mentioned. Mitzenheim appeared to be a conservative Lutheran who construed the Lutheran "Two Kingdoms Doctrine" as justifying active support for the state, in order to maintain the *Volkskirche* in Thuringia. The state used the example of the Thuringian Church to exert political pressure on the other *Landeskirchen*. Granting it many privileges, Ulbricht "differentiated" between Thuringia and the other *Landeskirchen*.[24] In 1993, a report was found that was made by a GDR security officer who fled to the west just before the erection of the Berlin Wall in 1961. He revealed the working structures of the GDR security service to the American and West German security services. When he started to describe how the security service had infiltrated the Thuringian Church, the agents sent him to Bishop Hermann Kunst, the EKD's emissary to the Federal Republic of Germany in Bonn. Kunst thus learnt that a couple of church officers were employed as "unofficial collaborators" by the Stasi.[25] However, the Churches did nothing about it, perhaps because they did not know what to do. The principal unofficial collaborator was Gerhard Lotz, a high-ranking church lawyer. He received goods as well as money for his work and he tried to shape church policies along the lines of SED expectations until his retirement in the early 1970s.[26]

From 1961 to the founding of the Kirchenbund in 1969

The construction of the Berlin Wall on 13 August 1961 on the one hand isolated the GDR Churches from the west, but on the other gave them a high degree of independence in many fields. Simultaneously, they came to realise that the unloved SED state had a higher life expectancy than they had thought. The new situation established a "relation between State and Church"[27] of a new kind. From now on, the SED no longer objected to the entire Church, but only to "negative forces" within it. This meant that officials singled out as enemies those Christians who did not want to adapt themselves to the GDR or who even criticised the system in public. This "double strategy" – "being determined and uncompromising on one side and yet prepared for communication and concessions on the other" – which had been further developed after the third congress of the SED in March 1956, was "not without effect on the Protestant Churches' leadership in the GDR"[28]. In particular, Bishop Beste of Schwerin, Bishop Krummacher of Greifswald and Bishop Mitzenheim of Eisenach were paid special attention by the SED because of their wish for "new points of view"[29]. The policy of selective dialogue, derived from the 1958 communiqué, reached its peak in the meeting between Ulbricht and Emil Fuchs, Professor of Theology at Leipzig, on 9 February 1961, and in the Wartburg conversation between Ulbricht and Mitzenheim on 18 August 1964. The meeting with Fuchs, a Christian socialist and father of Klaus

Fuchs, the atomic scientist and spy, was held shortly before GDR participation in the EKD synod was blocked and the Wall ended travel between East and West Berlin. Fuchs presented a letter supportive of the GDR signed by 32,000 theologians, church officers and church members. Today we know that many of these signatures had been forged by the security service.[30] Of course the talks had little resonance in the Protestant Church. Thus – in spite of the Church's ideological rapprochement to the SED regime – Church-state relations remained unstable.

In the face of the increasing political constraints imposed by the GDR following the construction of the Wall in 1961, the EKD made some practical accommodation, although it remained nominally unified across the new border. The so-called Eastern Conference became more formal: its chairman, Bishop Krummacher, served as spokesman for GDR members in the council of the EKD, and it became the real locus of decision on matters affecting the GDR Churches. In spite of Mitzenheim's opposition, Krummacher employed the son of his personal driver, a young lawyer, as secretary of the Eastern Conference's office, established in 1962. Later this young man, Manfred Stolpe, would become both the most important administrator in the GDR church federation and also the most important unofficial *Stasi* collaborator.[31]

"The intense process of social change taking place in the GDR led many East German church leaders to feel that the all-German EKD had become less relevant to the social context of the GDR Churches. Many also felt that they were being ignored by its West German majority."[32] Nevertheless Bishop Krummacher, chairman of the Eastern Conference, resisted such critical voices from within the Church while also rejecting the state's demands, maintaining that the Gospel of Christ had given the Church a mission to transcend borders and that the unity of the EKD served as an example to other Churches of the primacy of ecumenism over secular divisions. He maintained this point of view during the Fürstenwalde Eastern regional EKD synod in 1967.[33] He stated that separation from the EKD would only be necessary if there were false teaching and disobedience to God, which was not the case. In its final section the Fürstenwalde declaration stated: "We must give each other enough room to allow us to fulfil our task in the part of Germany in which we live. This requires of all churches in the EKD to always take the others into consideration in their decisions."[34]

This synod on the one hand granted the regional synods the right to act independently, but on the other hand the two regional synods elected the new EKD council as a united synod. This arrangement made the creation of two independent regional councils impossible, and was therefore in sharp contradiction to SED church policy. The "progressive" Thuringian *Landeskirche* pressed for separation by rejecting Thuringian nominations for the EKD council and the presidium of the EKD synod which had previously been agreed, and by proposing to regionalise both institutions.

The churches' stance on EKD unity was inhibited and weakened by the formulation and approval in 1968 of a new GDR constitution to replace that of 1949. This – in the view of the GDR government – effectively made the EKD leadership illegal since it was composed of ecclesiastical representatives of both German states.[35] Mitzenheim formulated the decisive sentence – apparently arranged in advance – at a citizens' meeting in Weimar on 29 February 1968 which was supposed to seal the separation: "The state borders of the German Democratic Republic also form the border of an ecclesiastical organisation."[36] Ulbricht also took part in that meeting. The GDR Churches were pressed for time because the state leadership intimated that it might begin separate negotiations with the individual Protestant Churches.[37] The Thuringian *Landeskirche* gave in to the state's demands. In the so-called letter from Lehnin of 15 February 1968, signed by all bishops except Mitzenheim, the church leaders declared their loyalty to Ulbricht but petitioned the state to restore the specific references to freedom of belief and conscience and the rights of the Church to the Constitution: "As citizens of a socialist state, we accept the task of realising socialism as the structure for a more just way of living together."[38]

Whereas Krummacher tried to preserve the unity of the German Churches, the three Lutheran Churches of Saxony-Dresden, Thuringia and Mecklenburg left the United Lutheran Church in Germany (VELKD) and formed their own Lutheran confessional organisation within the GDR. They did not give any hint of their intentions in advance, so their decision took the other Churches completely by surprise.[39] Since Lutheranism's identity as a Church derived essentially from its common theological confession, there remained no reason for the EKD, as merely a church federation, to insist on its unity.

In strong opposition to the president of the chancellery of the Evangelical Church of the Union (EKU), Franz-Reinhold Hildebrandt[40] and Albrecht Schönherr, the bishop-administrator of Berlin-Brandenburg in East Germany, proposed the founding of a new organisation, authorised by the *Landeskirchen*, and based on the Eastern Conference.[41] He was supported by, among others, Manfred Stolpe, secretary of the Eastern Conference office.[42] By late May 1968, support for this view had grown to the point, where the churches formed two commissions; a structure commission, mandated to propose new forms of organisation for the eight GDR *Landeskirchen*, and a negotiation commission, mandated to conduct any negotiations with the state. As against the Fürstenwalde declaration of 1967, Schönherr argued that: "Church agencies must serve the witness of the Church. When they can no longer do this, they must be changed. The witness of the Church takes priority over its form of organisation."[43] Schönherr accepted separation because, in his view, only thus could the Church carry on its work.

The charter of the incipient GDR church federation contained an EKD "clause", which was rejected by the Thuringian Church as well as by the SED. The clause spoke of "confessing the particular community of Protestant Christianity in Germany", thus stressing that the ties to the EKD were doctrinal in character. Nevertheless, against the strong opposition of the GDR government, this sentence forms part of the definitive version and is officially known as article 4.4.[44]

How far the SED state had already called the tune on the Churches' political duty can also be seen by the fact that – in spite of the World Council of Churches' request in August 1968 for protest against the occupation of Czechoslovakia by troops of the Warsaw Pact states[45] – there was no common "announcement from the pulpit" or statement by the GDR Churches.[46] However, a circular letter from

Albrecht Schönherr, on 5 September 1968, created some alarm in the central committee of the SED. In that letter pastors were asked to announce in their next service a statement of solidarity from the Brandenburg church leadership, addressed to the Churches of the Czechoslovak Socialist Republic.[47] The letter criticised the GDR's actions and expressed solidarity with the Czechs. Nevertheless the state reacted very mildly to this act of disobedience, because it knew through its security service that the "progressive" Schönherr had himself opposed the letter and had advised his Brandenburg Church to oppose it, too, but he had been voted down by conservatives.[48] When the church federation was founded, Schönherr was able to re-establish good relations with the state representatives.

The GDR Churches tried to comply with the process of separation sought by the SED and the ecclesiastical leadership, and tried also to provide theological reasons for a step which had been forced upon them by political circumstances. During the third conference of the first synod of the *Kirchenbund* in Eisenach in 1971, Bishop Schönherr stated: "A community of preaching and worship of the Churches in the GDR will have to think carefully about its location: within this society as it is, not alongside nor against it."[49] In his statement the phrase "Church within socialism", originally used by Mitzenheim, was interpreted in diverse ways and kept ambiguous until the end. In April 1971, Bishop Schönherr said that the phrase "Church within socialism" should signify to the Church its readiness to get involved with "the problems and achievements of society" and also "to contribute responsibly to its development".[50] Viewed in retrospect, the formation of the *Kirchenbund* in June 1969 represented a watershed in the postwar relationship between Church and state in the GDR. From that point the Churches' rapprochement with socialist society could advance faster. But at first this process seemed to be delayed by the state: its initial response to the *Kirchenbund* reflected an ambivalent, wait-and-see attitude.

From 1969 to the 1978 summit

In spite of the organisational division between the EKD and the *Kirchenbund*, the "particular community" between both federations as well as between the individual regional partner churches continued to exist. EKD and *Kirchenbund* appointed two mixed committees in order to maintain the "particular community" between them: the first was an advisory group with some fifteen from each side for the discussion of general political and ecclesiastical east-west affairs, founded just after the split. The other was the consultative group, founded in 1980, consisting of six from each side for the discussion of special ecclesiastical east-west affairs.[51] The consultative group above all developed common declarations and liturgies for peace services which were then issued to both German states.

In the meantime, the *Stasi* had gained many unofficial collaborators in key positions within the Churches' leadership. An example is Ingo Braecklein, former officer in the German army of the Third Reich, German Christian and member of the NSDAP. In 1965, he was recruited as an unofficial collaborator by the security service; in 1971, he became bishop of Thuringia and some time later received a prestigious GDR decoration.[52] Nevertheless, the security service did not manage to destroy article 4.4. of the Church's charter, nor did "progressive" churchmen and politicians succeed – in spite of intensive political work before the church conferences.[53] This "particular community" brought about – as the *Stasi* noticed during the Dresden synod in 1972 – a "considerable orientation of forces in the church government of the GDR which possesses an attitude of social democratic ideology in parallel to the EKD".[54]

In the late 1960s and the first half of the 1970s, the Social Democrats in West Germany under the Brandt government began to pursue a more open approach towards eastern Europe, the so-called *Ostpolitik*. This was also initiated by the EKD's eastern memorandum of 1965 and its peace memorandum of 1 March 1968.[55] At first, the GDR intensified its campaign of *Abgrenzung*, demanding nothing less than full diplomatic recognition as a state in its own right, independent of the Federal Republic. Increasingly, however, this ran counter to Soviet policy. The Soviets showed an increased interest in ratifying the postwar European *status quo,* in particular in stabilising their sphere of influence in Eastern Europe. They also sought closer economic ties with the FRG. Thus, they were more receptive to its initiatives in 1969. Perhaps that is one of the reasons why Ulbricht had to resign in 1971.[56] Under Ulbricht's successor, Erich Honecker, the two policy goals of recognition and special inter-German relations were brought into a new semblance of balance. Although internally the GDR propagated *Abgrenzung* even more intensively, externally it became more open in inter-German negotiations, which led to the Transit Agreement and the Basic Treaty in 1971 and 1972, respectively.

During this process the GDR had to open up towards the western world, a process which brought numerous new problems in the field of internal affairs. In the long term, a creeping liberalisation undermined the leading position of the official state party in ideological and cultural matters, in spite of the fact that its dominance was enshrined in the GDR constitution.[57] Although now as ever SED church policy suffered from a "lack of judgement regarding internal church affairs, and deficits in analysis",[58] the GDR decided on 24 February 1971 to approve the Federation of Protestant Churches as the official central representative of the GDR *Landeskirchen* with the state.

The degree to which the SED was ambiguous in its attitude towards the centralisation process of the Protestant churches in the GDR can be seen clearly in the regime's reaction to the so-called Eisenach recommendations of 1979. These, put forward by a delegates' conference of the *Kirchenbund*, suggested the creation of a centralised unified Protestant Church in the GDR and the dissolution of the *Landeskirchen*.[59] Such a development would have put an end to the policy of divide and rule which the state pursued with success in its handling of the *Landeskirchen*. On the other hand a centrally organised Church mirrored the centralist state structure. An SED outline memorandum commented: "Regarding domestic politics, one single Church is nearer to the principle of democratic centralism of the state than a great variety of church unions and leaderships. A merger into one single Church, provided with wider jurisdiction than the present *Kirchenbund*, could pursue this policy with more power. Provided the state could influence the leadership of this single Church, this construction could have positive effects."[60]

From the 1970s, the main goals of SED church policy were increasingly to induce the Churches to show their solidarity with the GDR's peace policy and to mobilise their co-operation in the further development of socialism. Despite several mistakes – as for example the decree published in November 1970, which obliged Bible studies to be registered,[61] and the continual discrimination against Christians in the educational system[62] – which resulted in tensions in Church-State relations, the SED made considerable progress in aligning the Churches with socialist guidelines and recognised that they showed a growing attachment to the GDR.[63] A growing number of bishops, church presidents and members of the church assembly could be won over to a "realistic" policy towards their state. The SED thought that they could above all count on three bishops (Ingo Braecklein of Eisenach, Horst Gienke of Greifswald, and church president Eberhard Natho of Dessau), together with the secretary of the BEK, Manfred Stolpe[64]; furthermore, three church officers (Günter Krusche, Ulrich von Brück and Christa Lewek) were regarded as reliable at that time.[65]

In August 1971, the new Thuringian bishop and president of the *Kirchenbund* synod, Ingo Braecklein, was decorated with the *Vaterländischer Verdienstorden* (patriot's order of merit) in gold, like his forerunner Moritz Mitzenheim in 1961. On the other hand, Schönherr's election as bishop of Berlin-Brandenburg on 4 November 1972 demonstrated the weakness of his grassroots support. Only on the third ballot did he succeed in receiving two-thirds of the votes; about forty members of the synod voted against him. This not only demonstrated criticism of his church politics in general, but also a rejection of an independent episcopate in the eastern region of Berlin-Brandenburg. In a declaration which he made after his election, Schönherr confirmed his political point of view: "It would be unrealistic to conclude from the fact of détente and the programme of peaceful coexistence, which includes a certain measure of cooperation and a neighbourly relationship, that uncontrolled contact across state borders and even a disregard for them, could occur. Under these circumstances, détente corresponds to a political and ideological demarcation (*Abgrenzung*)."[66]

At that time the regime was experiencing noticeable opposition from some church leaders, especially from Bishop Hans Joachim Fränkel of Görlitz, who was causing problems for the secretariat for church affairs (*Kirchenfragen*) in the SED's central committee. On 21 November 1973, in the course of state-sponsored efforts to isolate and to marginalise Fränkel, the chairman of the council in the district of Dresden tried to obtain Bishop Hempel's (of Dresden) condemnation of a lecture given by Fränkel on 8 November 1973 entitled "What did we learn from the *Kirchenkampf*?"[67]. According to the official state report, Hempel replied that the "government of the church could not dissociate itself from Fränkel's lecture", but stressed that such a lecture would never be given again in his Church in Saxony. During the course of the conversation he expressed his own opinion (different from Fränkel's) so clearly that the summary memorandum states: "In this conversation, we succeeded in creating [sic] a certain personal gulf between Hempel and Fränkel."[68]

On 23 November, Albrecht Schönherr is said to have declared to Seigewasser that "Fränkel had become a burden to the BEK", and Bishop Gienke is also said to have talked of provocation, referring to Fränkel's lecture.[69] "It was in accordance with the measures to isolate Fränkel that requests from the Church of Görlitz to enter or leave the country for ecumenical meetings were not processed and that, in events organised by the 'National Front', Christians in the district talked of their own engagement in the socialist society, clearly distancing themselves from their bishop".[70] The strategy obviously had an effect. In his report to the EKU synod of June 1976, Fränkel signalled a perceptible "change in the view of the SED". In a meeting with a representative of the state secretariat of ecclesiastical affairs, the bishop gave him to understand that if he had not acted as he did, pressure would have been put on him by his own Church and by the *Landeskirche* in Saxony.[71]

The greater involvement of the Churches in the process of peace and the Conference for Security and Co-operation in Europe (CSCE), as well as Schönherr's support of this development, should have had disadvantageous effects for the SED. After the conclusion of the CSCE final resolution in August 1975 at the latest, GDR citizens gained a basis for an appeal on fundamental human rights. According to these, the party, the government, but also the church could be judged. As the Churches took the resolution more seriously than did the SED, again the dictatorship felt forced to employ repressive measures against the call for human rights coming from the Church.

There was a pragmatic differentiation in policy: "realism" was rewarded and "reactionary behaviour" was attacked – if possible within the Churches and with the participation of unofficial collaborators within the administration of the Churches. Measures of self-discipline and obedience were to replace a missing constitution as well as a juridical interpretation of the position of the Churches within socialist society. An appropriate and constitutional consideration of the Churches was out of the question for ideological reasons. In the view of those in power in the GDR, Churches were dying institutions which they wanted to make use of for the time being. In a speech on 22 July 1976, the SED functionary Paul Verner expressed these facts unambiguously: "None of us assumes that religion is going to die in the next five years or in the near future or that it could be extinguished in an unnatural way. We proceed until within socialism the most important social causes for the production of religious ideologies are removed. In our situation the impulse towards religious studies steadily decreases. But this is a long and contradictory process. In the phases of social development marked by the party platform, Churches will still exist and will continue to work. We take this fact into account in our policy and in our practical work."[72]

Gerhard Lewerenz, later sector director for church affairs in the Dresden district council, provided a resumé of this position in his doctoral dissertation: "The Church is the only institution in socialism that does not correspond to the character of the socialistic social order, does not arise from it and is unnecessary for its development."[73]

The summit meeting of Erich Honecker and the leadership of the Kirchenbund, 6 March 1978

In spite of the fact that in 1971 the GDR recognised the *Kirchenbund* founded two years before in East Germany, grave conflicts between Church and state did not cease. In 1976, a spectacular event took place in the East German town of Zeitz, near Halle. The Protestant Reverend Oskar Brüsewitz set fire to himself in front of St Michael's Church and died four days later in hospital of severe burns. His act of desperation was a protest against discrimination against Christians under the communist regime as well as against the attitude of his church leaders who, in his view, conformed too much to the state system.[74] His funeral turned into a mass demonstration against the East German communist regime. The state, fearing foreign political repercussions, tried to play down the scandal. It was supported in this by high-ranking church officials like Manfred Stolpe, secretary of the *Kirchenbund*, and Bishop Albrecht Schönherr, its head.

Conflict between Church and State in the GDR was endemic in the socialist educational system, which discriminated not only against the Christian religion but also against pupils who belonged to a Christian denomination. The Church tried to be a loyal ally in the foreign policy of the communist state – for example on the question of GDR citizenship – and expected therefore to be treated as a real "partner" in internal affairs, especially in cultural questions. But the ideological claims of the SED forbade co-existence with the Church in the socialist society. The only role for the Church in this society would be to act on the periphery of society without any political relevance. Nevertheless, the Church continuously urged the regime to enter dialogue with it to find a new relationship, one which would enable the Church to work more freely in society. The Church had had unfortunate experiences with summit meetings in 1953 and 1958, but they seemed to be the only way ahead, because the constitution of the GDR did not define the status of the Churches and there were no laws guaranteeing the Church a secure place under the communist regime.

Consequently, after Bishop Schönherr (whom the state viewed with favour) had been re-elected as head of the *Kirchenbund* during the synod of September 1977, Manfred Stolpe asked an employee of the state secretary for church affairs, who was present at the church assembly, to make arrangements for a meeting between Erich Honecker and the executive board of the *Kirchenbund*. There were long discussions in the central committee of the SED on how to deal with this request. Finally Paul Verner, responsible for church affairs in the central committee, recommended the meeting. In November 1977, Erich Honecker signed the minutes himself and had the paper circulated.[75] The very same month, the head of the secretariat for church affairs of the central committee of the SED, Rudi Bellmann, began negotiations with Manfred Stolpe on the topics to be considered at the summit meeting.

They quickly agreed not to discuss subjects upon which they could not find a common position prior to the meeting. Hence all controversial matters were excluded. Stolpe suggested that they deliberate on basic questions but made no suggestions. However, he mentioned some points which he called useful: the celebration of the 500th anniversary of Martin Luther's birth in 1983; religious television broadcasts; some property questions concerning farmland in state hands but not paid for; the acceptance of pastors and other people working for the Church into state social insurance and old-age pension schemes, and the education of pastors in the GDR.[76]

On the basis of his conversation with Bellmann, Stolpe drew up a draft agenda for the summit meeting, which was accepted by the executive board of the *Kirchenbund* in November 1977. The draft included the following points: the shared responsibility of Church and State for shaping social conditions; the expansion of travel opportunities for important family matters in selected cases; equality of opportunities for all inhabitants irrespective of world view and religious belief; gratitude for the increased frankness of the dialogue between Church and State and the encouragement of constructive criticism; church reconstruction in the form of building projects alongside a recognition of the new buildings which the state had provided in the past; radio and television broadcasts on religious subjects; nursery schools run by the Church; the Luther anniversary in 1983; religious services for prisoners; the payment of rent to the Church for property confiscated by the state; privileges for farming and timber enterprises belonging to the Church equal to those enjoyed by the socialist farming and timber industry and rights for the Church to improve graveyards in its care. Subjects kept aside for future clarification were: old-age pensions for church employees; study of theology at university (the shaping of and possible participation by the Church); the import of literature and journals, and permission to print theological books.[77]

At the end of November, Stolpe suggested to Bellmann that a meeting between Schönherr and Paul Verner to agree on the agenda for the summit meeting would be useful. This discussion took place and at the beginning of December, Verner emphasised to the bishop that some of the questions included in Stolpe's draft had already been dealt with by laws and regulations. It was the wrong time to pose other questions, and some could not justifiably be asked. Verner pointed out in his speech the importance of the socialist struggle for peace and disarmament in view of the dangers posed by NATO. He stressed the achievements of the GDR in the fields of education and full employment. In the GDR, in comparison to western countries, there were no drug addicts or young people with no prospect. Therefore, he could not understand the demands of the Church for equal opportunities and more possiblity to travel to non-socialist states. He ended the speech with a harsh condemnation of the bishop of Magdeburg, Werner Krusche, who had attacked education on defence in East German schools. After this statement, Verner rejected most of the issues which Stolpe had proposed for discussion. Only four issues remained: the quincentenary of Luther's birth in 1983; religious broadcasts on radio and television on public holidays such as Easter and Christmas; payments for farmland exploited by the state and old-age pensions for church employees with the assumption that the western Churches would pay the benefits.[78]

Despite this rough reception, the bishop was so anxious to talk to Honecker that he accepted the conditions and told Verner how grateful he would be if he could meet him. He stressed that his political position of co-operation with the state was still very controversial in church circles and that the meeting with Honecker would greatly help to strengthen the links between Church and State.

At the end of December, Stolpe told Bellmann that he would give him a revised version of his draft for January which would omit the points of dispute. He promised that his partner would express the position of the Church within the socialist society in a clearer manner. Christa Lewek, a Berlin church official and Stolpe's close assistant, asked Bellmann to request Honecker to repeat his earlier declarations on the good relationship and the atmosphere of trust between Church and State. Bellmann in turn demanded a statement from the Church affirming that in the GDR the people enjoyed freedom of religion and that possibilities existed for the Church to work there. Bellmann sent the record of this conversation to Honecker, who signed it, which means that he had accepted the line taken.[79] The revised version of the draft was accepted by the state. Its experts said that there were no problems, except the Church's desire to participate in the development of society according to its own agenda.

During the bishops' conference in mid-January 1978, there was only a brief reference to the planned summit meeting and afterwards a confidential discussion on it. This was designed to maintain secrecy. The minutes of the meeting only refer to it in half a sentence.[80] In contrast, the *Stasi* knew exactly what had occurred during the bishops' meeting. The *Stasi's* comprehensive records refer to information from a so-called unofficial collaborator with the cover name *Sekretär*, the title of Stolpe's position in the *Kirchenbund*.[81] There are fifteen such reports on the summit meeting. They illustrate the extent of the state's knowledge on every step the Church took.

On 14 February 1978, the *Kirchenbund* received the official invitation to a meeting with Honecker on 6 March 1978 at 10.30 a.m. The executive board accepted this invitation. On 27 February, Stolpe sent a draft of the churchmen's proposed contributions to Bellmann. They came to an understanding on seating arrangements and other such matters. Again the information of the security service shows how detailed the preparations were. Every participant in the summit meeting on the part of the Church was required to specialise in a certain field and make a contribution. The *Stasi* knew which role each participant was intended to play and say. Thus the state was not surprised by the churchmen's opinions on 6 March 1978.[82]

The day, long awaited by the churchmen, finally arrived.[83] Honecker's welcome speech contained some of the catchwords which the executive board had expected, i.e. that the state esteemed the work of the Church; that there was common responsibility for the people and its future; that the Church had done much for peace in the world and for the ecumenical movement against racism and neo-colonialism. He promised co-operation between Church and State concerning human affairs and the development of the socialist society. Then he declared the positive decisions, which were exactly the points that the state had previously approved, i.e. the co-operation on the Luther quincentary in 1983, religious transmissions on radio and television on public holidays such as Easter and Christmas, payment for farmland exploited by the state, old-age pensions for church employees with the assumption that the western Churches would pay for them, worship for prisoners and in old people's homes, support for kindergartens run by the Church and fewer restrictions on importing literature and journals.

Then Schönherr gave his speech, its content well-known to the state because Stolpe had passed it on to Bellmann on 27 February 1978. Schönherr stated that the Church fully agreed with the political aims of the GDR, not only in foreign affairs, but also in home affairs. As a result of this crucial sentence all further potential criticism was undermined. Furthermore, he declared that the Church under socialism would be a Church, which would help people to find their way in socialist society. The sentence, which would later be repeatedly used, went: "The relationship between Church and State is as good as the individual citizen experiences it in his local situation."

The other members of the executive board spoke about the disadvantages suffered by Christian citizens in school and places of work, asked for an easing of travel restrictions to West Germany and pleaded that people, who wanted to leave the GDR for good, should be allowed to emigrate. Finally, Honecker gave reasons for his policies claiming that if the Federal Republic of Germany acknowledged the GDR as a foreign state, then travel from the GDR to the Federal Republic would be possible. Moreover, he had to protect the people of the GDR against the drug scene and the militant anti-communism in West Berlin and West Germany. Finally, the GDR had to protect its high technical standard because the Federal Republic would try to entice experts away from the GDR in order to ruin the socialist state. Once more he guaranteed the churchmen freedom of belief and religion in the GDR. Schönherr and the other members of the executive board were extremely impressed by Honecker's friendliness and the good atmosphere. A day later Schönherr wrote him a letter full of gratitude.[84]

A few hours after the meeting the unofficial collaborators, *Sekretär* and *Lorenz*, who had been members of the executive board which numbered only six people, gave a first report to the security service. *Sekretär* met his *Stasi* officer in a secret location called *Wendenschloss*. The collaborators reported that the other participants had been enthusiastic about the meeting, especially about the human qualities and statesmanship of Erich Honecker.[85] The security service thus learned that the initiative had been a complete success. They repeated this success time and again, because they differentiated between those in the Church, who demonstrated "realism" and those who showed "reactionary behaviour".

Many church officers disapproved of what had happened and accused those responsible, especially Schönherr, of betraying the Church and becoming an ally of the totalitarian state. Superintendent Reinhard Steinlein, for example, resigned from his role in ecclesiastical guidance.[86] But Schönherr and Stolpe were able to suppress such voices. The official Church as well as the state soon celebrated the meeting as the greatest Church-State event since 1949. Bishop Braecklein of Thuringia stated that it was the consummation of Bishop Mitzenheim's "Thuringian way".[87] However, the problems of the Church in the GDR did not change. On the contrary they worsened, for example with regard to the introduction of a special defence education curriculum in the schools, aiming to give pupils paramilitary training and to teach them that their country must be defended from the aggressive West.

There was another effect of the summit meeting: Stolpe received a decoration from the state. The documents seem to suggest that he was awarded the medal by the *Stasi* because he was the unofficial collaborator *Sekretär* and he informed the service about ecclesiastical affairs. But his file was destroyed in mid-December 1989. Stolpe himself denies that he received his medal from the *Stasi* and asserts that he was awarded it by the secretary of state for church affairs.[88]

This essay has described specific stages in the ecclesiastical division of east and west and the integration of the Protestant regional Churches into the "socialist" community system. The process was aided from the late 1960s onwards by the global détente, which gave socialism a better reputation.

After the construction of the Berlin Wall, Germany's neighbours feared the potential threat to peace posed by a united Germany more than they were interested in a solution to the problem. At the same time the World Council of Churches in Geneva became involved in the new concept of "change by rapprochement",[89] especially as the churches in the eastern bloc took care to nip any protest against human rights violation in the "second world" in the bud. The World Council of Churches began the global strategy of looking away, glossing over, hiding, perceiving only socialist achievements as well as one-sidedly emphasising the defects of western societies.[90]

After the GDR had succeeded in obtaining increasingly unequivocal statements of loyalty from the Churches, the state successfully tried to make them work in favour of greater international appreciation and a more positive evaluation of the regime. At the Prague Christian Movement, which was a Soviet-influenced ecumenical movement, they even succeeded in gaining approval for the three-state theory of German territory: GDR – Federal Republic – West Berlin. In 1969, under the leadership of Albrecht Schönherr, and with Manfred Stolpe working in the background, the *Kirchenbund* was founded as an independent body and a theologically qualified "new beginning". The foundation of a new kind of national Church, against which the Protestant Church had fought for so long, became a reality, even if in such a peculiar way. From then on there were few important events or decisions on personnel at a federal level, which had not been previously debated by an SED functionary.

With deep regret the all-German church federation was forced to tolerate this forced separation. From 1969 onwards, there was a deep mistrust between the "Church within socialism" and the western Church, which was termed the NATO Church by the SED. On the other hand both Churches claimed that there was a "special relationship" between them. At the time of the "summit talks" of 6 March 1978, the Church-State relationship in the GDR was better than ever before or since, while the relationship between the EKD and the *Kirchenbund* was worse than ever or since. During the 1980s, despite several attempts,[91] this high level of co-operation between Church and State was never achieved again. On the contrary, co-operation between the EKD and the *Kirchenbund* intensified once more. In view of growing internal problems, in contrast to an increasingly successful foreign policy,[92] the GDR expected the Protestant Church to soothe opposition movements.[93] Although the leadership of some individual member Churches and the leadership of the *Kirchenbund* took pains to fulfil these expectations, they did not succeed in controlling opposition at the grass roots level. An atmosphere of irritation and mutual mistrust followed, and the state fell back upon measures such as those of the period before 1978. Nevertheless, a majority among the leadership of the churches kept to the vision of an improved socialism, which is why after German reunification they only accepted with strong opposition and harsh criticism the integration of the new federal states (i.e. the former GDR states as they had existed before 1952) into the Federal Republic of Germany and the accession of the eastern *Landeskirchen* to the EKD.

The following terms and abbreviations are used in the text to this article:

Abgrenzung	cultural and legal demarcation of East from West Germany
APU	*Evangelische Kirche der Altpreussischen Union* Old Prussian united state Church; the predecessor of the EKU
BEK/BEKDDR	*Kirchenbund/Bund der Evangelischen Kirchen in der DDR* from 1969 to 1990, the Federation of Protestant Churches in the GDR
CDU	*Christlich-Demokratische Union* Christian Democratic Union Party
EKD	*Evangelische Kirche in Deutschland* German Protestant Church Federation (nowadays the only umbrella organisation, comprehending, among others, the Churches belonging to the VELKD and EKU federations, which in their turn were joined by the Churches formerly belonging to the *Kirchenbund*)
EKU	*Evangelische Kirche der Union* Evangelical Church of the Union; the former Prussian state Church (nowadays composed of seven autonomous regional member churches)
FRG	Federal Republic of Germany *Bundesrepublik Deutschland*: West Germany
GDR	German Democratic Republic *Deutsche Demokratische Republik*: East Germany
IM	*Inoffizielle Mitarbeiter* unofficial collaborators (with the *Stasi*)
Jugendweihe	atheist youth consecration ceremony
Kirchenkampf	"Church struggle". This expression describes the debates within the Protestant Church in Germany in the 1930s about what position to take towards the Nazi state, while the state heavily interfered in church affairs; later on a similar situation arose in the GDR

Land (pl. *Länder*)	one of the sixteen member-states of the Federal Republic of Germany
Landeskirche	state/regional Church (established Protestant Church in some *Länder*)
MfS	*Ministerium für Staatssicherheit* Ministry for State Security
Ostpolitik	"new Eastern policy", introduced by the Brandt government
SED	*Sozialistische Einheitspartei Deutschlands* Socialist Unity Party
Stasi	*Staatssicherheit* GDR security service
VELKD	*Vereinigte Evangelisch-Lutherische Kirche in Deutschland* United Lutheran Church in Germany; the federation of (most) Lutheran Protestant Churches in Germany
Volkskirche	mainstream Church; traditional nationally established Church

Notes

1   See H. Wentker, 'Ost-CDU und Protestantismus 1949–1958: die Partei der fortschritt-lichen Christen zwischen Repräsentationsanspruch und Transmissionsaufgabe', in Kirchliche Zeitgeschichte 6 (1993), 349–78; G. Besier, 'Auf der kirchenpolitischen Nebenbühne des SED-Staates: Evangelische Kirche und Ost-CDU', in idem., Die Evangelische Kirche in den Umbrüchen des 20. Jahrhunderts: Gesammelte Aufsätze, vol. II: Von der ersten Diktatur in die zweite Demokratie, Neukirchen-Vluyn 1994, 190–270.

2   M. Richter, Die Ost-CDU 1949–1952: Zwischen Widerstand und Gleichschaltung, Düsseldorf ²1991, 329.

3   See W. Dittmann and W.-D. Zimmermann (eds), Otto Dibelius: so habe ich's erlebt: Selbstzeugnisse, Berlin (West) 1980, 265–70.

4   See G. Besier, Der SED-Staat und die Kirche, vol. I: Der Weg in die Anpassung (1945–1969), Munich 1993; idem, vol. II: Die Vision vom 'Dritten Weg' (1969–1990); idem, vol. III: Höhenflug und Absturz (1983–1991), Berlin 1995, 66 ff.

5   Quotation from Kirchliches Jahrbuch [KJ] lxxx (1953), 178.

6   See D. Urban and H. W. Weinzen, Jugend ohne Bekenntnis? 30 Jahre Konfirmation und Jugendweihe im anderen Deutschland 1954–1984, Berlin (West) 1984, 22 ff.

7   See J. Vogel, Kirche und Wiederbewaffnung: die Haltung der Evangelischen Kirche in Deutschland in den Auseinandersetzungen um die Wiederbewaffnung der Bundes-republik 1949–1956, Göttingen 1978; K. Herbert, Kirche zwischen Aufbruch und Tradition: Entscheidungsjahre nach 1945, Stuttgart 1989, 253 ff.

8   Schlippes and Weissleder, 'Kirche und Politik in der BRD – analytische Dokumenta-tion zur Fundierung der politisch-operativen Arbeit des MfS', Potsdam 1983, BStU, VVSoOO1 MfS JHS 122/83, 254.

9   G. Köhler (ed.), Pontifex, nicht Partisan: Kirche und Staat in der DDR von 1949 bis 1958: Dokumente aus der Arbeit des Bevollmächtigten des Rates der EKD bei der Regierung der DDR, Stuttgart 1974, 175.

10   KJ lxxxv (1958), 144 f.

11   See Besier, Der Weg in die Anpassung (op. cit. note 4), 288 ff.

12   Working group for church affairs in the central committee of the SED (W. Barth), 22 Sept. 1958, to W. Ulbricht, quoted in G. Besier and S. Wolf (eds), 'Pfarrer, Christen

und Katholiken': das Ministerium für Staatssicherheit der ehemaligen DDR und die Kirchen, Neukirchen-Vluyn ²1992, 218 f.

13 Einheit xiii (1958), 1564 ff.
14 M. Dibelius, 'Obrigkeit?: eine Frage an den 60jährigen Landesbischof', quoted in R. Stupperich, Otto Dibelius: ein evangelischer Bischof im Umbruch der Zeiten, Göttingen 1989, 546.
15 Decision 'Zur Frage der Obrigkeit', KJ lxxxvii (1960), 82 f.
16 KJ lxxxiii (1956), 18; cf. KJ lxxxvi (1959), 135.
17 Cf. MfS, 'Bericht über die gesamtdeutsche Synode der EKD vom 5.3.1960', in Besier and Wolf, Pfarrer, Christen und Katholiken (op. cit. note 10), 225.
18 Mielke to Beater, 22. Feb. 1960, in ibid. 221 f.
19 MfS, Beater, 'Informationsmaterial der Linie V/4 (ev. und kath. Kirche) vom 4.7.1958', BdL 789/58 101 608, If., in ibid. 210.
20 'Einschätzung der Lage im demokratischen Sektor von Gross-Berlin vom 21.6.1958', in ibid. 209.
21 MfS, 'Bericht über die Gesamtdeutsche Synode Nr. 188/60 vom 5.3.1960', in ibid. 222–227.
22 See Besier, Der Weg in die Anpassung (op. cit. note 4), 291 ff.
23 Ibid. 441 ff.
24 See idem, 'Aus der Resistenz in die Kooperation: der "Thüringer Weg" zur "Kirche im Sozialismus"', in G. Heydemann and L. Kettenacker (eds), Kirchen in der Diktatur: Drittes Reich und SED-Staat, Göttingen 1993, 182–212.
25 Ibid. 203 ff.
26 See C. Vollnhals, 'Oberkirchenrat Lotz und das Ministerium für Staatssicherheit: zur IM-Akte "Karl"' (lecture given for the survey commission of the German parliament on 14. Dec. 1993), Deutschland Archiv 27 (1994), 332–336.
27 Telex from Leipzig local administration, 28 May 1968, in Besier and Wolf, Pfarrer, Christen und Katholiken (op. cit. note 12), 271.
28 J. Heise, Das Ringen der SED um die Mitarbeit von Gläubigen und um verfassungsmäßige Staat-Kirche-Beziehungen in der Übergangsperiode vom Kapitalismus zum Sozialismus in der DDR, Diss. Phil. B, Berlin (East) 1986, 43.
29 Ibid.
30 See Besier, Die Weg in die Anpassung (op. cit. note 4), 344 ff.
31 See M. Stolpe, Schwieriger Aufbruch, Berlin 1992, 111 ff.; R.-G. Reuth, IM "Sekretär": die 'Gauck-Recherche' und die Dokumente zum 'Fall Stolpe', Frankfurt am Main-Berlin 1992.
32 R. F. Goeckel, The Lutheran Church and the East German state: political conflict and change under Ulbricht and Honecker, Ithaca-London 1990, 64.
33 KJ 99 (1967), 1–177 and esp. 23–27.
34 Translated from ibid. 29.
35 See the statements of W. Ulbricht and G. Götting, ibid. 95 (1968), 167 f.
36 Quote from R. Henkys (ed.) Der Bund der evangelischen Kirchen in der DDR: Dokumente zu seiner Entstehung, Witten 1970, 116. Ulbricht's answer is found on p. 117. See also the interview with Mitzenheim in Neue Zeit, 4. Feb. 1968.
37 See H. Dohle, Grundzüge der Kirchenpolitik der SED zwischen und 1968 und 1978, Diss. Phil. B, Berlin (East) 1988, 48 ff., esp. 58 f.
38 KJ 95 (1968), 181.
39 See G. Besier, Die Vision vom "Dritten Weg" (op. cit. note 4), 29 ff.
40 See idem, 'Spaltung als "Regionalisierung"?: die Evangelische Kirche in Berlin-Brandenburg 1961–1972', in Gerd Heinrich (ed.), 1000 Jahre Kirchengeschichte Berlin-Brandenburg, Berlin 1999.
41 See A. Schönherr, ... aber die Zeit war nicht verloren: Erinnerungen eines Altbischofs, Berlin 1993; Besier, 'Spaltung als "Regionalisierung"?' (op. cit. note 40).
42 Cf. idem, Der Weg in die Anpassung (op. cit. note 4), 667–670.
43 KJ 95 (1968), 242.

44 See R. Henkys, Die evangelischen Kirchen in der DDR: Beiträge zu einer Bestandsaufnahme, Munich 1982, 183 f.

45 Ökumenischer Pressedienst 30/68, 12.

46 See KJ 95 (1968), 266.

47 Ibid. 267; cf. Besier, Der Weg in die Anpassung (op. cit. note 4), 684 ff.

48 Ibid.; cf. idem, Die Vision vom "Dritten Weg" (op. cot. note 4), 24 ff.

49 Quote from J. J. Seidel, Christen in der DDR: zur Lage der evangelischen Kirche, Bern 1986, 55.

50 Ibid. 57; cf. W. Krötke, 'Dietrich Bonhoeffer als "Theologe der DDR": ein kritischer Rückblick', in Zeitschrift für Evangelische Ethik 37 (1993), 94–105.

51 Jürgen Schmude, SPD politician and president of the EKD synod, was the last chairman of both groups. On the consultative group see Besier, 'Zur Geschichte des "Wortes zum Frieden" des Bundes der Evangelischen Kirchen in der DDR und des Rates der evangelischen Kirche in Deutschland vom Mai 1985', in idem., Von der ersten Diktatur in die zweite Demokratie (op. cit. note 1), 271–294. See also W. Hammer and U.-P. Heidingsfeld (eds), Die Konsultationen: ein Ausdruck der "besonderen Gemeinschaft" zwischen der Evangelischen Kirche in Deutschland und dem Bund der Evangelischen Kirchen in der DDR in den Jahren 1980 bis 1990: die Sitzungsniederschriften, ergänzendes Material und Erläuterungen, Frankfurt am Main 1995.

52 Cf. Besier and Wolf, Pfarrer, Christen und Katholiken (op. cit. note 10), 31, 277.

53 W. Albinus, P.-J. Heildberg and A. Bendel, 'Die Entwicklung der evangelisch-lutherischen Landeskirche Sachsens und ihre Stellung im kirchenpolitischen Bereich', Potsdam 1985, BStU, VVS JHS oOO1–325/85, 58.

54 Schlippes and Weissleder, 'Kirche und Politik in der BRD' (op. cit. note 8), 111.

55 'Die Lage der Vertriebenen und das Verhältnis des deutschen Volkes zu seinen östlichen Nachbarn: eine evangelische Denkschrift', in Die Denkschriften der Evangelischen Kirche in Deutschland, vol. I, part 1: Frieden, Versöhnung und Menschenrechte, Gütersloh 1978, 77–126; 'Friedensaufgaben der Deutschen: eine Studie', in ibid. vol. I, part 2, 15–33.

56 The main reasons for the end of Ulbricht's rule in East Germany are reportedly his independent attitude vis à vis the Soviet Union and differences on ideology, economic policy, his vision of a united albeit socialist Germany, his interest in improving economic relations between East and West Germany, his assessment of the West German Social Democratic Party (SPD) and his emphasis on East Germany's superior scientific standard in comparison to the Soviet Union: D. Staritz, Geschichte der DDR: Erweiterte Neuausgabe, Frankfurt am Main 1996, 266–275.

57 See Wörterbuch des Wissenschaftlichen Kommunismus, Berlin (East) 1982, s. v. 'politische Organisation (politisches System) der sozialistischen Gesellschaft'.

58 Dohle, Grundzüge (op. cit. note 37), 96.

59 See the recommendations in epd-Dokumentation 19/79, 29–33.

60 'Einflussnahme auf den Prozess der Bildung der Vereinigten Evangelischen Kirche' [the influence on the process of the formation of the united protestant Church] (outline from early 1979), SAPMO-BA ZPA IV B2/14/15.

61 'Verordnung über die Durchführung von Veranstaltungen vom 16. November 1970', KJ 98 (1971), 233–236.

62 See, for example, ibid. 240–247.

63 Dohle, Grundzüge (op. cit. note 37), 123.

64 See Stolpe, Schwieriger Aufbruch (op. cit. note 31), 111 ff.; Reuth, IM "Sekretär" (op. cit. note 31).

65 Dohle, Grundzüge (op. cit. note 37), 145–147.

66 See ibid. 123, 155.

67 H.-J. Fränkel, 'Was haben wir aus dem Kirchenkampf gelernt?', KJ 100 (1973), 161–167.

68 AG Kirchenfragen [working group on church affairs], 'Zum Gespräch mit Bischof Hempel, 28 Nov. 1973', SAPMO-BA ZPA IV B2/14/134, 120 f.

69 Dohle, Grundzüge (op. cit. note 37), 137.
70 Ibid.
71 Ibid. 160 and 473.
72 Translated from ibid. 158 f.
73 G. L. Lewerenz, Das Selbstverständnis evangelischer Landeskirchen in der DDR von Kirche im Sozialismus, Diss. Phil., Güstrow 1983, 31.
74 See the controversial works on the Brüsewitz case: H. Müller-Enbergs, H. Schmoll and W. Stock, Das Fanal: das Opfer des Pfarrers Brüsewitz und die Evangelische Kirche, Frankfurt am Main-Berlin 1993, and H. Schultze (ed.), Das Signal von Zeitz: Reaktionen der Kirche, des Staates und der Medien auf die Selbstverbrennung von Oskar Brüsewitz: eine Dokumentation, Leipzig 1993.
75 Verner to Honecker, 27 Oct. 1977 (with an attachment), in Frédéric Hartweg (ed.), SED und Kirche: eine Dokumentation ihrer Beziehungen, vol. II: 1968–1989, arranged by Dohle, Neukirchen-Vluyn 1995, 319–322.
76 Information from Bellmann, 8 Nov. 1977, about the discussion with Stolpe on 8 Nov. 1977, SAPMO-BA ZPA IV B2/14/7. See also Besier, Die Vision vom "Dritten Weg" (op. cit. note 4), 100 ff.
77 Stolpe to Bellmann, 25 Nov. 1977, SAPMO-BA ZPA IV B2/14/81.
78 Information from Hüttner, 8 Dec. 1977, about discussion between Verner and Schönherr, 6 Dec. 1977, in Besier, Die Vision vom "Dritten Weg" (op. cit. note 4), 323–326.
79 Bellmann notes, 28 Dec. 1977, about discussion between Stolpe and Lewek, 22 Dec. 1977, ibid. 327 f.
80 Remark by Schönherr, 16 Jan. 1978 on the bishops' convention in Bad Saarow, EZA Berlin, 101/1190, vol. 2.
81 See Reuth, IM "Sekretär" (op. cit. note 31), 161.
82 Ibid. See also 'Informationen über die Vorbereitung seitens der KKL des BEK zum Gespräch beim Generalsekretär der SED am 6.3.1978', BStU Berlin, ZAIG 2796.
83 See notes, 10 Mar. 1978, about discussion with head of conference and the president of council state [Staatsrat], 6 Mar. 1978 (13 ff.), EZA Berlin, 101/342.
84 Schönherr to Honecker, 7 Mar. 1978, ibid.
85 BStU Berlin, MfS HA XX/4, 1005, 6–8.
86 See R. Steinlein, Die gottlosen Jahre, Berlin 1993, 120 ff.
87 See Besier, Die Vision vom "Dritten Weg" (op. cit. note 4), 110 ff.
88 Ibid. 115.
89 The expression "change by rapprochement" ("Wandel durch Annäherung") was used as early as 1963 by the social democratic politician Egon Bahr to define what was in his opinion the only way to reunite Germany: Zu meiner Zeit, Munich 1996, 156.
90 See P. Abrecht, 'From Oxford to Vancouver: lessons from fifty years of ecumenical work for economic and social justice', Ecumenical Review 40 (1988), 147–168, and 'The predicament of Christian social thought after the cold war', ibid. 53 (1991), 318–328. See also R. M. Preston, Confusions in ecumenical social ethics, London 1994.
91 See, for example, the co-operation between the church and the state in the Luther anniversary year of 1983 or the formulation often used in 1984 by Bishop Hempel of a "basic trust" between Church and State Church: Besier, Höhenflug und Absturz (op. cit. note 4), 44 ff., 64 ff., 71 ff., 94 ff.
92 Especially the recognition of a sovereign GDR-citizenship seemed to have moved within close reach after the mid nineteen-eighties, alongside the FRG's renunciation of its claim to be the only representative of the German people: ibid. 56 ff., 187 ff.
93 See E. Neubert, Geschichte der Opposition in der DDR 1949–1989, Berlin 1997.

The "Church Struggle" during the Third Reich as a Subject of GDR Historiography. On the Conflict between Contextuality and Ethics of Profession*

In this paper, I would like to examine the question how far specific paradigms of research, given local constraints like contextual phenomena, forced patterns of attitude, and behaviour influenced the view of the "Church Struggle" in GDR historiography.[1] Former SED historian Horst Dohle and emeritus professor of church history Kurt Meier of Leipzig will serve as examples.

Due to his professional curriculum and his scientific-political functions exerted in the apparatus of state in GDR, Horst Dohle, whose last position was that of a leading employee in the State Secretariat of Church Questions[2], plays an essential role.[3] His expert reports regarding the question whether a certain book on the historiography of church history should be reprinted, and in what version, were of vital importance.[4] In 1963, Dohle presented his doctoral dissertation on "The Position of the Protestant Church towards Anti-Semitism and the Persecution of the Jews".[5] Although the manuscript never appeared in print, this work provided a central paradigm for judgement in the field of "the Church in the NS state" in the SED state.

Dohle describes "the Church and anti-Semitism" as a special form of "anti-fascist resistance of bourgeois circles"[6]. But in his opinion, the Church's resistance can only be understood when seen against the "background of a resistance movement of the German people motivated by reasons of political class, and as an addition to it"[7]. So, without the resistance of the working class, church resistance appears inconceivable as a movement within the bourgeois class. In spite of this hierarchisation, Dohle acknowledges its "own motivation" to the "ecclesiastical resistance movement"[8]. Dohle strictly differentiates between the "class position" of "church bureaucracy" and individual church members: "When later some individual leaders of the Church found the courage for anti-fascist activity, they did this because they knew they were being supported by their anti-fascist parish."[9]

As the second factor for the anti-fascist potential of the Church to be taken in consideration, Dohle names Karl Barth and his school as well as the representatives of Religious Socialism. He stresses the fact that Barth, whilst working as a minister in Switzerland, "kept in closest possible touch with the Religious Socialists" and the Social Democratic Party.[10] Due to the ecclesiological opposition between Barth and Otto Dibelius, in whose anti-bolshevist understanding of authority expressed between 1930 and 1959 Dohle perceived a clear line of continuity, Barth was rewarded with the remark that he had been able to "mobilise possible anti-fascist forces in the Church"[11]. Equally positive, he described Bonhoeffer as a "theological opponent of Künneth's and Dibelius's theology of war"[12].

---

* First published in *KZG* 14 (2001) 1, 71–76.

Following Marxist historiography, Dohle distinguishes between Luther before and after the Peasant Wars. "The reformer's later turning away from the 'predatory and murderous peasant mobs' and his turning towards the historically long doomed class of nobility was the cause of his development towards anti-Semitism."[13] Via this distinction, the possibility was given to integrate Luther and Lutheranism in a specific way into modern history. Gerhard Ritter, introduced by Dohle as the "west German pope of historiography", had in Dohle's opinion praised the later and therefore Capitalist and anti-Semitic Luther as the "eternal German"[14].

With his dissertation, Dohle paved the way for GDR historiographers at theological schools to deal with the 'German Christians' (*Deutsche Christen*, DC). Because of the anti-Semitic past history of the Protestant Church, he stated, it was not possible to "treat the DC as if they were 'possessed by the Devil' and send them to the desert, not considering them as part of the Protestant Church at all, and claim that in this Church, everything had been all right"[15]. Investigating the DC showed clearly that nothing was all right with this Church.

Regarding the theology of universities during the 'Third Reich', Dohle cautiously aligned himself alongside Baumgärtel and the latter's opinion, that discerning between Barthians and others, and accusing the latter wholesale of betraying the Gospel was an over-simplification.[16] Finally, with his "braking factor" thesis, Dohle gave a reason to legitimise research in the field of church history within so-called real socialistic research on fascism. The essential sentence reads: "The churches offered room for an orientation towards the next world to many people, they [the churches] distracted the thoughts of the people from war service, thus acting as 'braking factors'."[17] And a little later he states: "Our knowledge about the courageous acts of these individuals enables us to speak of a spontaneous Protestant-Christian resistance to fascism."[18]

Against a background of united Communist resistance, it seemed opportune to describe the essentially positive behaviour of the Protestant church towards national socialism and to point to the exceptions. "The resistance put up by Church members must be held in so much higher consideration when compared to the failure of the Church itself ... . This resistance is undeniably a part of the whole anti-fascist resistance movement in Germany and thus supported the unification of all democratic forces after 1945."[19]

Dohle even defends the employment of "former leading Fascists"[20] in the state churches in GDR provided they had changed their political position. So he judges Walter Grundmann: "When such a man speaks of the 'wrong point of view' of his former attitude, which now has been 'corrected', this must be respected."[21] The Darmstadt statement (*Darmstädter Wort*) of 8 August 1947, belongs – as a cornerstone of ecclesiastical historiography within real existing Socialism – right at the heart of a self-revision by the church.[22] It is considered to be "the most promising beginnings of a real understanding of the situation"[23]. Dohle's acknowledgement provided a yardstick for historiographical endeavours in East and West Germany. Theologians Otto Dibelius and Eugen Gerstenmaier, who were influential in the West, and about whom the SED regime had pronounced a devastating judgement through so-called 'documentations'[24], were rejected in this historiography. Moreover, "the leaders of the Protestant church of West Germany had actively cooperated in large measure in shaping clerical Fascism"[25].

When Dohle evaluated and revised Meier's three-volume opus *Der evangelische Kirchenkampf* for publication in the GDR, Dohle's historiographic measures played a role.[26] Especially in volume three, Meier raised his major digression about "The Protestant Church Struggle as a Problem of the Resistance"[27] to the rank of the core piece of his method, thus giving it the appearance of a research project in anti-fascist resistance. Meier had already acknowledged the important role played by the Religious Socialists and the workers' movement in volume one. The *Darmstädter Wort* of 1947, too, held an important position at the end of volume three and, from a real socialist perspective, the brief interpretation it deserved. "In the field of probation when re-establishing the Church, it [the *Darmstädter Wort*] was received quite differently in the Zones of Occupation, which had different socio-political structures, and in accordance with its political value, especially in the German Democratic Republic it later pointed the way ahead regarding the ecclesiastical concept and social orientation of the Protestant Church within a socialist country."[28] The so-called Peoples' Church (*Volkskirche*) appeared in essentials as a 'source of friction' in Meier's work. This was a parallel approach to Dohle's definition of the role played by the church as a 'braking factor'. Both definitions pointed to the church's functional role within society.

The reason why, despite Meier's toeing the historical line indicated by Dohle, a fierce debate followed the printing of Meier's book, is partly due to Rosemarie Müller-Streisand (Berlin). Her model of Marxist church historiography rivalled Dohle's (and Meier's). Parallel to her husband Hanfried Müller's systematic-theological position, which represented an extreme Barthian leftist position, she tried to define the small, radical wing of the Confessing Church as the predecessor of a 'Church within Socialism'. But her view lost ground in the 1980s, since it appeared 'sectarian' to the SED, and therefore not suitable as a majority position.

In West Germany, only Müller-Streisand's view was perceived as based on genuinely Marxist premises, while Meier's method was acknowledged as historical-liberal, and was supported both by liberal cultural theology[29] and modern social history. In the spring of 1989, Jochen-Christoph Kaiser wrote: "It is doubtless the merit of the 'Leipzig school' of modern church historiography associated with Kurt Meier and Kurt Nowak to have overcome this narrow perspective [a specific theologically orientated church history] by including the *structures* of a Peoples' Church which made resistance possible in the first place."[30]

There is no way to prove that Meier had ever read Dohle's dissertation. Even in Meier's later work *Kreuz und Hakenkreuz. Die evangelische Kirche im Dritten Reich*[31], Dohle's dissertation is not mentioned. But the fact that Meier quotes extensively from Dohle's postdoctoral thesis (1988) on the essential features of church policy of the SED[32] in his own contribution to the series on the History of Christianity[33], does attract attention.

Meier, who had been working as a so-called 'Unofficial Collaborator' (*Inoffizieller Mitarbeiter*) with the Department of State Security of GDR since 1957 (as *IM* 'Werner')[34], published a work on the theological university schools in the Third Reich (*Die theologischen Fakultäten im Dritten Reich*) in 1996, which looks extraordinarily empathic when treating the affinity of German professors of theology with the Third Reich: "The apologetic perspective on the politics of theology under National Socialism may let the suppression of a critical public opinion in GDR look justified", was Friedrich Wilhelm Graf's comment on this perspective.[35] And Graf went on, "Meier constructs patterns of interpretation for Protestantism under the first German dictatorship which are intended to explain his own role in the second German dictatorship. By writing about the history of theology under National Socialism at a state school in GDR, this church historian [Meier] implicitly speaks about himself and the state policy of theology under real existing Socialism"[36]. It looks similar to his three-volume "Protestant Church Struggle", written entirely from the perspective of a Peoples' Church, which was completely in line with National Socialism. Because of the decline of the 'theology of God's word alone' (*Wort-Gottes-Theologie*) in the 1970s, Meier received only little critique for this.[37] Heike Kreutzer expressed her assumption that some inaccurate sources given in Meier's three-volume description of the Church Struggle may not be due to slips of the pen. "It seems more appropriate to see a form of secrecy when [Meier] gives a reference instead of a file number. Meier was allowed to work with stock R 5101 [Reich's Church Department, in the period when Meier wrote, it was kept in the GDR Central State Archive in Potsdam] on orders of the secret service. This is why in several cases, he renders a critical checking of his own statements, allegedly supported by sources, impossible."[38] When considering Meier's numerous correct proofs provided by the same source material, this interpretation may seem too negative.

Notes

1   On this, see also the information given in Gerhard Besier, 'Widerstand im Dritten Reich. Ein kompatibler Forschungsgegenstand für gegenseitige Verständigung heute? Anfragen aus historisch-theologischer Perspektive (1988)', in idem, Die Evangelische Kirche in den Umbrüchen des 20. Jahrhunderts. Gesammelte Aufsätze, vol. 1: Kirche am Übergang vom Wilhelminismus zur Weimarer Republik. Von der Weimarer Republik ins "Dritte Reich" – der "Kirchenkampf", Neukirchen-Vluyn 1994, 243–261, esp. 244 f., 247 f., 252 f.; idem, 'Evangelische Kirche und Widerstand', in Kerygma und Dogma 42 (1996), 3–21.

2   Moreover, Dohle had been registered as a so-called 'Unofficial Collaborator' (*Inoffizieller Mitarbeiter*) with the Department of State Security of GDR since 1973 (as *IM* 'Horst'). Cf. Gerhard Besier, Der SED-Staat und die Kirche, vol. 3: Höhenflug und Absturz, Berlin 1995, 916 passim; Clemens Vollnhals, 'Die kirchenpolitische Abteilung des Ministeriums für Staatssicherheit', in idem (ed.), Die Kirchenpolitik von SED und Staatssicherheit. Eine Zwischenbilanz, Berlin [2]1997, 79–119, here: 96.

3   Cf. Siegfried Bräuer/Clemens Vollnhals (eds), "In der DDR gibt es keine Zensur". Die Evangelische Verlagsanstalt und die Praxis der Druckgenehmigung 1954–1989, Leipzig 1995, 358 ff. et al.

4   On the importance of Dohle's expert report regarding Kurt Meier's description of the *Kirchenkampf* see Meier's autobiographical account 'Kirche und Drittes Reich. Zeiterfahrung und Forschungsschwerpunkt', in Dietrich Meyer (ed.), Kirchengeschichte als Autobiographie. Ein Blick in die Werkstatt zeitgenössischer Kirchenhistoriker (Schriftenreihe des Vereins für Rheinische Kirchengeschichte 138), Düsseldorf 1999, 143–228, esp. 201 f.

5   Horst Dohle, Die Stellung der evangelischen Kirche in Deutschland zum Antisemitismus und zur Judenverfolgung zwischen 1933–1945, Diss. Phil., Berlin (East) 1963 (Ms.).

6   Dohle, Die Stellung (op. cit. note 5), 1 (introduction).

7   Ibid. 3.

8   Ibid.

9   Ibid. 34.

10 Ibid. 39.

11 Ibid. 41.

12 Ibid.

13 Ibid. 46.

14 Ibid. 47. Dohle relies on Hans Leube, 'Die deutsche Reformation', in ZThK 18 (1937), 9. See also Gerhard Ritter, Luther. Gestalt und Symbol, Munich 1925, 151.

15 Dohle, Die Stellung (op. cit. note 5), 58.

16 Ibid. 79; Friedrich Baumgärtel, Wider die Kirchenkampf-Legenden, Neuendettelsau 1958, esp. pp. 13, 15, 17.

17 Dohle, Die Stellung (op. cit. note 5), 198.

18 Ibid. 207.

19 Ibid. 210.

20 Ibid. 217.

21 Ibid. 216 f. Here Dohle refers to Grundmann's preface in the latter's book "Die Geschichte Jesu Christi", Berlin 1956.

22 About W. Grundmann after 1945, see Walter Schilling, 'Die "Bearbeitung" der Landeskirche Thüringen durch das MfS', in Vollnhals (ed.), Kirchenpolitik (op. cit. note 2), 211–266, here: 218–220; Gerhard Besier, 'Politische Reifeprozesse. Zum Engagement des MfS an den theologischen Fakultäten bzw. Sektionen', in Vollnhals (ed.), Kirchenpolitik (op. cit. note 2), 267–297, here: 269; Susannah Heschel, 'When Jesus was an Aryan. The Protestant Church and Anti-Semitic Propaganda', in Robert P. Ericksen/idem, Betrayal. German Churches and the Holocaust, Minneapolis 1999, 68–89, esp. 82 f.

23 Dohle, Die Stellung (op. cit. note 5), 213.
24 Cf. as the most recent Hubertus Knabe, Der diskrete Charme der DDR. Stasi und Westmedien, Berlin 2001, 247 f., 250 ff.
25 Dohle, Die Stellung (op. cit. note 5), 225.
26 Cf. Gerhard Besier, Der SED-Staat und die Kirche, vol. 2: Die Vision vom "Dritten Weg", Berlin 1995, 552 f.
27 Kurt Meier, Der evangelische Kirchenkampf. Gesamtdarstellung in drei Bänden, Halle/Saale-Göttingen 1984, 587 ff.
28 Meier, Kirchenkampf (op. cit. note 27), 586.
29 Cf. Trutz Rendtorff, 'Die Religion der Moderne – die Moderne in der Religion. Zur religiösen Dimension in der Neuzeit', in ThLZ 110 (1985), 561–574, and Hans Moritz, 'Religion und Gesellschaft in der DDR', in ibid. 574–588.
30 J.-C. Kaiser, Sozialer Protestantismus im 20. Jahrhundert, Munich 1989, 456.
31 Munich 1992.
32 H. Dohle, Grundzüge der Kirchenpolitik der SED zwischen 1968 und 1978, Diss. Phil. B, Berlin (East), Akademie für Gesellschaftswissenschaften beim Zentralkomitee der SED, 1988.
33 Cf. K. Meier, 'Deutschland und Österreich', in Jean-Marie Mayeur (ed.), Erster und Zweiter Weltkrieg – Demokratien und totalitäre Systeme (1914–1958) (Geschichte des Christentums 12), Freiburg-Basel-Vienna 1992, esp. 746–755.
34 Cf. Besier, 'Politische Reifeprozesse' (op. cit. note 22), 278.
35 'Jesu arische Herkunft. Deutungsmuster des Protestantismus in deutschen Diktaturen', in Frankfurter Allgemeine Zeitung no. 270, 19 Nov. 1996, 11.
36 Ibid.
37 Cf. Gerhard Besier, Kirche, Politik und Gesellschaft im 20. Jahrhundert (EDG 56), Munich 2000, esp. 64–66, 82.
38 H. Kreutzer, Das Reichskirchenministerium im Gefüge der nationalsozialistischen Herrschaft (Schriften des Bundesarchivs 56), Düsseldorf 2000, 118 f., note 87.

American Liaison Officers to Churches in Germany and Eastern Europe during the 1970s and 1980s*

After the GDR's governments recognition of the Federation of Protestant Churches in the GDR (FPC) in 1972 the FPC began developing intense activity in foreign church policy.[1] It did so, whether voluntarily or not, in close consultation with the GDR state secretary for church affairs and other institutions of the GDR government, in particular the office for foreign affairs. Alongside the countries of the so-called "Third World", another country played a very special role: the United States of America, the supreme power of the West and the symbol of western capitalism and imperialism. The foreign-relations officials of the FPC took advantage of the fact that the National Council of the Churches of Christ in the USA (NCC)[2] often took a position, which was in contrast to the internal and foreign policy of the government[3]. The disagreements on domestic issues between the NCC and the US governments concerned the insufficiency of social legislation, relief measures for the poor and the issue of racism, which still existed in the United States. In foreign policy the NCC criticised the Vietnam War and other military interventions, particularly those in South America, and the NATO rearmament programme. It regarded the arms race as part of the strategy of deterrance and the policy of strength.

The GDR government was primarily interested in attained diplomatic recognition from the USA. It, therefore, permitted all the FPC's activities, i. e. mutual visits of delegations and the exchange of opinions during conferences, if the subjects and probable results of the bilateral church consultation converged with the political aims of the Eastern Bloc. Among the favourite subjects of discussion were peace, disarmament, racism, poverty and the exploitation of the "Third World", as well as the equal acceptance of socialist dictatorships and pluralist democracies by the West. Naturally, there was no talk of dictatorships but of "socialist states" on the one hand and "capitalist states" on the other hand. Nor did the GDR government ever relinquish its authority to make the final decision on the meetings. Before every bilateral church conference the government was to be consulted to reassess the situation every time anew, thus keeping the right to express its permission or prohibition in every single case.

The government took advantage of the fact that the FPC, which was only established in 1969, strove desperately for foreign contacts and accepted almost every condition, simply to make contacts. It was part of the political tactics of the GDR government that due to the unclear diplomatic relations between the USA and the GDR, the first two American liaison officers received no permanent permit of residence and had to enter the country on visitor's visas. As a result they could use neither the apartment nor the office prepared for them in East Berlin[4]

*   First published in *KZG/CCH* 17 (2004), 245–253.

but had to live in and work from West Berlin. The fact that the third liaison officer received a repeatedly renewed residence permit from the GDR in 1986 illustrates that his predecessors' work was considered positive by the GDR government.

When they began their relationship, the FPC and the NCC were able to call on
the long-standing special friendship between the United Church of Christ and the
German Evangelical Church of the Union (i. e. the former Prussian Union).[5]
Since the 1960s, Reverend Peter Johan Meister of the United Church of Christ
(UCC) worked as the church liaison officer in West Berlin, where the chancery of
the Evangelical Church of the Union (*Evangelische Kirche der Union, EKU*) (western sector) was situated.

The visit by NCC representatives to the GDR and a return visit by FPC representatives to the USA in the mid-seventies were the occasions, upon which bilateral relations were established. More visits followed, during which the NCC often
gave the impression of being the FPC's political ally in its struggle against US imperialism and the oppression of civil rights movements in the United States. The
Church assembly member and FPC Ecumenical Revered Walter Pabst[6] had already worriedly asked Edwin Espy in 1971: "Please allow me today to ask about
the fate of arrested civil rights activist Angela Davis. May I openly ask you: are
you confident in her facing a fair process or must we fear that her colour and party affiliation will have a priori a detrimental effect? ... Has it [the NCC, *G. B.*] tak-
en measures in order to prevent the defendant getting an unfair judgment?"[7] He
then requested advice from Espy on "what further helpful actions we can carry
through in this matter"[8]. Since in view of GDR's circumstances there were no
similar requests made by the US churches the impression of a world turned up-
side down arises. In these church papers it was not the GDR but the USA that appeared as an undemocratic state exercising un-legitimised sovereignty.

The establishment of official church relations between the NCC and FPC took
place through the mediation of Rolf-Dieter Günther, the youth pastor of the *Mark
Brandenburg*.[9] During Günther's stay in the United States in May 1971, NCC President Bishop Sterling Cary (UCC) invited him for lunch. During the meal he said
he was "interested in a direct establishment of contacts [between the NCC and
the FPC] and would be pleased to accept an invitation to the GDR in the summer of 1974".[10] On his return Günther informed the FPC chairman, Bishop
Albrecht Schönherr, of Cary's wish and advised him to "take advantage of the
favourable situation given by the very independent and engaged political position
of the NCC."[11] On 23 January 1974, Schönherr invited the NCC president to the
GDR.[12] It took another two years before this visit was realised. Between 22 and
29 March 1976 the new NCC President William B. Thompson, Sterling Cary, the
NCC General Secretary Claire Randall and Peter Meister came to the GDR as
guests of the FPC.[13] The only state representative to take part was the GDR state
secretary for church affairs. Claire Randall "observed that, although the sources
of secularisation are different in our two countries, we face similar problems and
the churches in the GDR have learned to deal critically with problems that we also face, such as the message and role of the Church in a society, which no longer
accords it the same place it once held".[14] Even before the beginning of the jour-

ney, in mid-March 1976, Claire Randall had invited Schönherr, his wife and other leading figures of the church for a return visit to the USA in October or November of the same year.[15] During the course of this visit to the United States, the agreement was reached to place a liaison officer in Berlin.

The first appointee was Barbara Green from the United Presbyterian Church in the USA (UPCUSA). She took up the position in February 1977.[16] Her stay was at first limited to a probationary period of three months, which was then extended to four years. Pastor Green, who at that time was 27 years old, had studied for two years in Heidelberg (1972–1974) and, therefore, spoke good German. She was given a job at the Ecumenical Mission Institute (*Ökumenisch-Missionarisches Institut*) in West Berlin. Bé Ruys of the Dutch Ecumenical Parish in West Berlin and pastor Horsta Krum of the French Reformed Parish in West Berlin were asked to provide "personal and spiritual support and contacts" for Barbara Green.[17] Both pastors were distinctly sympathetic towards socialism. Krum had been recruited as an unofficial collaborator by the Ministry of State Security.[18] In order to cover Green's office and travel expenses, Bishop Schönherr asked the EKU church chancery (western area) for an annual subsidy of 3,000 to 5,000 DM. He considered it "very useful if she could also see other socialistic countries".[19] The general responsibility of the Federation for the supervision and the coordination of the representative was delegated to Schönherr's wife, Rev. Annemarie Schönherr, and a direct line of accountability was established to her. At the beginning of April 1978 a conference took place in Chorin between representatives of the NCC and the FPC. In the joint report fears about the progress of the arms race were articulated, for which the USA was one-sidedly blamed. "A reason for these fears is the news that the USA intends to start mass production of the neutron bomb and to introduce new weapon systems."[20] The NCC delegation did, however, suggest that the Warsaw Pact had stationed large numbers of tank units in Central Europe. The FPC delegation pointed out that the reason for this concentration of arms was the "need for security in the socialistic states, especially in the Soviet Union, which is substantiated by historic experience".[21] At the same time the USA was openly condemned because of the construction of the neutron bomb and the arms build-up on the part of the USSR was excused by the superpower's fear of new German aggression. In contrast the USA did not rearm out of fear of external opponents but for economic reasons. "An important drive of the rearmament is the so-called military-industrial-technological complex, which originated in the USA. Research institutions and large-scale enterprises work closely together with the military leadership and increase profit, power and prestige."[22] These so-called "peace-dialogues"[23] took place alternately in the GDR and the USA (1979 in Stony Point, 1982 in Ferch, 1985 in Oak Brook and 1989 in Erfurt).[24] Barbara Green took part in these and other dialogues until 1982. She also enjoyed a close personal relationship with the Schönherr family.[25] She was succeeded on 1 February 1982 by Charles Yerkes (1932–1993), an African American, who held this post until 31 December 1983.

Before returning to the United States, Yerkes talked to the German Church Officers Gerhard Linn and Maria Herrbruck about his impressions of the GDR. The note on this conversation reads: "The fact that he [*Yerkes, G. B.*], as a Christian, confesses to Marxism was one of the reasons why he was sent to the GDR even if there were voices in the NCC, who did 'not want to expect this of the Federation of the Protestant Churches' in the GDR. Ch. Yerkes came with great expectations in order to learn about real existing socialism and the Church's work in this society. He was disappointed in many ways. He met Christians and non-Christians from different groups, who suffer in this society. In the Church he met people who stressed that, as a Christian, one could not adhere to Marxism. Others, on the other hand, told him they would be glad to commit themselves more socially, but had to show consideration for the community."[26]

With his reports from the GDR, Yerkes faced the difficult problem that positive accounts would be advantageous to those social forces that believed that the NCC was infiltrated by communists. On the other hand critical reports would reinforce the prejudice that Christians in the GDR had fallen on hard times. "Regarding the role of the Church within socialism, Yerkes says that Christians would have to work more actively so that the socialist social order offers answers as well as alternatives to the solution of the fundamental questions of the present-day world situation. Capitalism will ruin the world with its great scientific-technological progress. The political prerequisites for the creation of an alternative economy are given in the socialist society, but not the human ones." One cause, in which Yerkes saw a lack of commitment by the Christians in the GDR, was the absence of a "confession of the Church for its failure towards the working class in the nineteenth century".[27] Apparently in agreement with his two German dialogues, Yerkes believed that the US churches could learn from this experience: "that 'being a Christian' in the GDR has its costs, that Christians think that they do so with dedication and engage themselves with motivation (why not also for the realisation of socialism), that the churches and individual Christians engage themselves intensively and concretely for peace, that values and judgments are influenced by life in a socialist society, that self-assertive Americanism is put in question and that the affiliation and cooperation with the WCC is very important for our ecumenical work."[28] From New York, Charles Yerkes wrote to Herrbruck on 20 April 1984, saying that he had in the meantime completed his dissertation and mentioning his anger over the "ideological captivity" of the American people "as well as over their shallowness". He wrote, "some of our best Christian fellow citizens are in Nicaragua as members of a 'peace mission' now, where from time to time they take turns at the Honduran border, in order to make sure peace over there is observed. Certainly you have already read something about it in your press".[29]

Yerkes' stance was even more orientated to the left than that of the "highly progressive" Church bureaucracy of the GDR church. He was bitterly disappointed about in the lack of commitment to socialism from the "church within socialism". It would seem that it were less the circumstances in the GDR but rather those in the USA that influenced his judgment. Yerkes, who had worked as a pastor with people on the fringes of society in New York City, was highly critical of the social system of his country and thought that he had found an alternative in the GDR. Coming from this background he could not understand how he met with scepticism and lethargy in the GDR churches regarding the construction of socialism.

It is also not surprising that Yerkes' commitment to the study on the "Roots of Racism", which was conducted by the FPC's theological studies department, was especially intense.[30]

Despite their mixed experiences with Yerkes, both the NCC and the FPC wanted to keep him employed. However, there were considerable financial problems on the part of the NCC, which gave rise to the expectation that the FPC or its affiliated church facilities of the EKU and the United Evangelical Lutheran Church in the GDR or the National Committee of the Lutheran World Federation (*Evangelisch-Lutherische Kirche in der DDR/Nationalkomitee*, VELK/NK) would share the expenses of the liaison officer's stay.[31] The FPC wanted to rename the "Liaison Officer" as "Fraternal Worker" or "ecumenical co-worker".[32] The report of the visit of an NCC[33] delegation to the FPC at the end of May 1984 includes a discussion about the influence of the churches on their respective societies. The representatives of the NCC made it "quite clear that the work of the churches in the USA has prevented worse developments regarding Reagan's policy in Central America. Furthermore, the overcoming of anticommunism was emphasised as a further task [in the USA, G. B]".[34] James Cogswell, the executive secretary of the Division of Overseas Ministry from the NCC, reported in the presence of Hermann Kalb, the acting GDR State Secretary for church affairs, that the churches in Latin America had "asked the NCC for help in order to make efforts against the current Reagan policy (i. e. the mining of harbours)".[35] Kalb asked the Americans to support the USSR and its efforts to maintain peace. "The S[oviet] U[nion] would immediately be ready to disarm, if the other side also showed willingness. The Warsaw Pact could immediately be disbanded if the NATO was disbanded too. ... The important aspect is the influence of public opinion. There, the churches have great possibilities and tasks."[36] When in a smaller circle the NCC representatives asked during an academic debate what they should campaign for regarding Europe, their GDR contacts answered: "Not enough has been done to prevent the deployment [of the US Pershing II and Cruise Missiles, G. B.]. It is important that individual human rights questions are not constantly misused as anticommunist propaganda."[37]

The close contacts of the NCC to the FPC as well as to the Russian-Orthodox Church soon yielded results, Yerkes reported. For example, the Presbyterian Church in the USA passed a resolution in mid-1983 to revise its stand towards communism. When an NCC delegation came back from the USSR the same year the delegation leader asked the General Assembly of the Presbyterian Church to give up "its idolatrous concept of good and evil empires: the idea that total repression exists in the East and total freedom in the West".[38] A talk with the NCC on the current relevance of the Theological Declaration of Barmen (*Barmer Theologische Erklärung*) and the state-church relationship was planned for Chicago in May 1985. Christa Lewek, a functionary of the FPC, wrote in the context of the preparations of the talks: "When choosing this topic, the experiences of Reagan's pseudo-religious grounds for his politics of strength and superiority are decisive, i. e. references to the Book of Revelations, the last days and the struggle between light and darkness."[39]

In mid-June 1986, after a vacancy of two and a half years, the NCC elected Rev. Stephen Johns-Boeme (Christian Church Disciples of Christ) and his wife Gratia Ann as the new liaison officers, now renamed "ecumenical co-worker".[40] The couple began service at the start of May 1987 and remained in the post until September 1989. In contrast to their predecessors the Johns-Boemes received a GDR residence permit for one year, which was then repeatedly extended. Thus, they could live in East Berlin.[41] The FPC made a small car, a used *Trabant*, available for the two Americans. However, like their predecessors, the Johns-Boemes experienced a difficult teething-period, which was not least due to the vagueness of their job description. There are no remarks on the political inclinations of the couple in the final assessment made by the FPC officials.[42] Due to the fall of the Berlin wall and the reintegration of the eastern affiliated churches into the EKD, no further liaison officers were appointed.

Conclusion

The liaison officers Barbara Green and Charles Yerkes belonged to the left wing of the mainstream churches in the USA. They sympathised openly with "real existing socialism" in the GDR and were heavily critical of the social conditions in the United States. The Reagan era was especially criticised. On the basis of the work done by them within the framework of the bilateral church relationships, the Christians in the GDR were exposed to a highly negative view of the United States. They learned that it was actually not them but the US citizens, who lived in servitude and suppression. In addition, it must be assumed that the liaison officers also gave the wrong impression of the GDR and its Christians to the Americans i. e. the romanticised view of a poor community with strong beliefs, trying to make its way in a socialist society. Politically this created the picture of a GDR which appeared at least as an acceptable alternative to the western systems, because, contrary to the western societies, social justice was supposed to be practised there.

Notes

1   Cf. Gerhard Besier, 'The GDR and the State Churches (1958–1989)', in this volume; idem, 'Seventy Years after "Machtergreifung". The German Churches' Political Stance 1933–2003', in this volume; John Arthur Emerson Vermaat, 'Soviet Manipulation of "Religious Circles", 1975–1986', in Ladislav Bittman (ed.), The New Image-Makers. Soviet Propaganda & Disinformation Today, Washington, D. C. 1988, 201–219.
2   Cf. Gerhard Besier, 'In Contradiction to the Grassroots? The Stance of the Federal Council of the Churches of Christ (FCC) towards the "Third Reich"', in Kyrkohistorisk Årsskrift (KHÅ) 2003, 139–156, in this volume.
3   Cf. on this and the following Gerhard Besier, 'Protestantismus, Kommunismus und Ökumene in den Vereinigten Staaten von Amerika', in idem/Armin Boyens/Gerhard

Lindemann, Nationaler Protestantismus und Ökumenische Bewegung. Kirchliches Handeln im Kalten Krieg (1945–1990), Berlin 1999, 323–652; here: 522 ff.

4   Cf. notes from a conversation with Rev. Dr. Schomer of the Board of World Ministries of the UCC/USA on 11 Nov. 1975. Evangelisches Zentralarchiv (EZA) Berlin, 101/1510.

5   Cf. Frederick Herzog/Reinhard Grosscurth (eds), Kirchengemeinschaft im Schmelz-ticgcl – Anfang einer neuen Ökumene? Anfragen und Dokumente aus der United Church of Christ (USA), Neukirchen-Vluyn 1989, 9 ff.

6   On Pabst's mainly negative impressions of the USA, cf. his report on his journey to the United States in July 1970: Amerikanische Erinnerungen, EZA Berlin, 101/1512.

7   Pabst to Espy on 9 Sep. 1971, ibid.

8   Ibid. See also Espy's grateful answer to Pabst on 22 Nov. 1971.

9   The GDR Ministry of State Security registered Günther as "IMB (*Inoffizieller Mitarbeiter Beobachtung*) 'Wilhelm'" in its files.

10 Günther to Pabst on 19 Nov. 1973, EZA Berlin, 101/1509.

11 Ibid.

12 Cf. Schönherr to Cary on 23 Jan. 1974, ibid.

13 Cf. programme for the visit. EZA Berlin, 101/1511.

14 National Council of Churches News. News and Information Service, 14 OGS 4/1/76.

15 Cf. Randall to Schönherr on 16 Mar. 1976. EZA Berlin, 101/1511. Besides the Schönherrs the Unity Director, Gill (of the *Evangelische Brüder-Unität*) and church assembly member, Walter Schulz from Schwerin, were involved.

16 Cf. Besier, Protestantismus, Kommunismus und Ökumene in den USA, (op. cit. note 3), 596 ff. Barbara Green as a minister of the Presbyterian Church (PC, USA) held the position of a Policy Advocate, Washington Office (PA USA) from 1983 to 1998. She is now the executive director of the Churches' Center for Theology and Public Policy, Washington, D. C. Her previous position before coming to Germany was that of an assistant to the director of the College of Wooster's study-travel programme in Germany. (Biographical information sent by the NCC, Office of the General Secretary, 17 Nov. 2003). On 23 Jan. 2004, Barbara Green wrote to the Landeskirchliches Archiv Berlin-Brandenburg: "So schön es war, habe ich leider nie etwas Zusammenfassendes darüber geschrieben." [As lovely as it was, I have never written anything to sum it up].

17 Pabst to NCC on 28 Apr. 1977, EZA Berlin, 101/1512.

18 Cf. on Horsta Krum epd-Dokumentation 16/94: 'Aus der Akte IM "Helena". Die Westberliner Pfarrerin Horsta Krum und die Stasi'.

19 Schönherr to EKU church chancery (western area) on 6 May 1977, EZA Berlin, 101/1512.

20 Common report on the dialogue between representatives of the NCC and the FPC as well as the Union of Evangelical Free Churches in the GDR in Chorin (GDR) on 5–7 Apr. 1978, EZA Berlin, 101/4056.

21 Ibid.

22 Ibid.

23 Cf. on the way of ecumenical Christianity from confrontation to "dialogue with communism", John Arthur Emerson Vermaat, 'Die Ökumenische Bewegung und die Ideologien (1925–1975)', in Peter Beyerhaus (ed.), Ideologien – Herausforderungen an den Glauben, Bad Liebenzell 1979, 37–54; idem, 'Links confessionalisme en vredenspolitiek', in Militaire Spectator 150/11 (1981), 483–495 [Links about confessionalism in world politics].

24 Cf. excerpt from the 'Protokoll der 79. Sitzung des Koordinierungsausschusses der Gemeinsamen Einrichtung Ökumene am 3.5.1990 in Berlin', EZA Berlin, 101/4056.

25 Cf. Albrecht Schönherr, ... aber die Zeit war nicht verloren. Erinnerungen eines Altbischofs, Berlin 1993, 323.

26 Note by Herrbruck on 23 Jan. 1984 on the evaluation by Ch. Yerkes on his stay in the GDR from 29 Dec. 1983, EZA Berlin, 101/4057.

27 Ibid.

28 Ibid.

29 The letter ends with regards to "Martin" [Ziegler, *G. B.*] and the other colleagues in the Auguststraße, EZA Berlin, 101/4057.

30 Cf. excerpt from 'Protokoll der 43. Sitzung des Koordinierungsausschusses der Gemeinsamen Einrichtung Ökumene [GEÖ] am 15.3.1984', EZA Berlin, 101/4057.

31 Cf. Eugene L. Stockwell, Associate General Secretary of the NCC, to Maria Herrbruck on 4 Oct. 1983, EZA Berlin, 101/4056; excerpt from 'Protokoll über die 162. Sitzung des Vorstandes am 2.4.1984', ibid.

32 Cf. excerpt from 'Protokoll der 43. Sitzung des Koordinierungsausschusses der Gemeinsamen Einrichtung Ökumene [GEÖ] am 15.3.1984', (op. cit. note 30).

33 Bishop Philip Cousin of the African Methodist Episcopal Church and president of the NCC, Claire Randall of the Presbyterian Church and general secretary of the NCC; James Cogswell, the adjunctive general secretary of the NCC and executive secretary for the Division of Overseas Ministry and Ms Margaret Cogswell were part of the NCC delegation.

34 Report from Herrbruck on the visit on 24 and 25 May 1984 of a NCC delegation with the FPC (*Bund der Evangelischen Freikirchen in der DDR*), EZA Berlin, 101/4057.

35 Ibid.

36 Ibid.

37 Ibid.

38 'Informationsrunde des BEK, 9.8.1983. Beitrag des Verbindungsbeauftragten des NCC, Charles Yerkes', EZA Berlin, 101/4057.

39 Note from Lewek on 13 Nov. 1984, 'Betr.: Fortsetzung des NCCC/USA-Dialogs zu Friedensfragen', ibid.

40 Cf. James A. Cogswell to Maria Herrbruck on 16 June 1986, EZA Berlin, 101/4058.

41 Cf. Grengel to Martin Kramer on 27 Nov. 1987, ibid.

42 Cf. note from Irene Koenig on 11 Oct. 1989 on 'Auswertungsgespräch über den Aufenthalt von Gratia und Steven Johns-Boeme am 22.9.1989', ibid.

Peace – Human Rights – International Understanding. An Examination of the Terminology*

Introduction

Too often today the terms "Peace", "International Understanding", and "Human Rights" have become little more than popular slogans, which are even held to have a kind of magical aura about them. They have long been emptied of any real concrete content, and instead are given an almost unlimited positive connotation, being used as symbols for a world filled with harmony, liberty and justice, as guarantees of a condition of general human happiness. They have become associated with widely propagated and believed utopian visions even though there is little evidence that those who disseminate and receive such vague notions have reached any clear consensus of what they mean by such terms, which are frequently presented in pseudo-religious forms. Any fruitful discussion must therefore first of all establish definite and clear criteria for evaluation of such evocative concepts.

This is particularly true for the term "Peace". It is both the oldest and the most all-encompassing idea, if one recalls its significance throughout history. It can be seen as the most significant of the three concepts to be dealt with here, since "Human Rights" and "International Understanding" are really subordinate themes of the same complex. The achievement of "Peace", both internally and internationally, it can be claimed, is a necessary precondition both for "International Understanding" and for the establishment of any enduring code of human rights and its actual implementation.

1.   Pax – Peace – Paix – Frieden[1]

The concept of peace, which always presupposed a form of human social organisation, originally included two particular meanings: a continuing condition of love and respect arising out of a situation of mutual obligation, or a more limited condition of the absence of force and violence. Under the influence of Christian theology, the Latin word *pax* was elucidated and developed as an all-encompassing term, which fully eclipsed the Germanic word *fridu*, and came to have a common meaning throughout the western world.

Because of this singular Christian interpretation of the word *pax*, the political and social concept of peace was for a long time outweighed by the more "moral" or "eschatological" definition of "Peace", understood as a cosmological principle of order. Such a rendering differed notably from the communal understanding

*   First published in *KZG* 4 (1991), 13–28.

consistently normative in the Old Testament (i. e. Shalom). It also can be seen as a change from the New Testament understanding of peace (εἰρήνη), which consciously strove to resolve the apparent tensions and contradictions between the idea of peace as a divine gift of salvation on the one hand, and as a vocation to minister to the existing political, legal and social situations on the other. One consequence of these contradictions can, for example, be seen in the fact that the early church members, following the commandment to love their enemies, were led to refuse military service for themselves, but would nevertheless pray for the monarch and his military victories.

St Augustine (AD 354–430), in the 19th book of "De civitate Dei", gave much more precision to the concepts of *pax*, and can thus be regarded as the father of Christian ideas of peace.[2] On the basis of his division of the world's condition between "the City of God" and "the earthly city under the power of the devil", Augustine made a sharp distinction between the secular realm, in which peace and security are to be preserved through power and might, and if necessary a "just war", and the realm of eschatological expectations of peace, which can only be fulfilled by God. These forms of governance have to be seen as separate, even though they are intertwined in the course of history. For Augustine, Peace and Justice are fundamental principles of the world's order, whereby Justice assigns everything its due place in a hierarchically constructed ranking. Earthly peace and earthly justice are, in the best of cases, *pax et justitia temporalis*, imperfect and incomplete images of the *pax aeterna, pax perfecta*. Any peace not built upon justice would be an evil or a false peace in contrast to the true peace. St Thomas Aquinas (1225–1274) followed Augustine in speaking of a peace based on an evil or imposed system of government as being no more than a *pax apparens*.

Berthold von Regensburg (1210–1272) described peace in three ways: Peace with God, peace with thyself, and peace with thy neighbour. Peace in the social and political realm was only one form of the *pax specialis*, of a more inclusive ideal. In the Middle Ages, the *pax temporalis*, as a means of securing earthly peace was highly valued and was seen as contrasting with spiritual peace, the *pax spiritualis*. Earthly peace kept "the natural man" in order or should seek to do so. It offered the prospect, in the understanding of those days, of achieving the values of *unitas*, *securitas*, and *tranquillitas*, which not only allowed for the development of human capabilities, but opened the way for reaching the *pax spiritualis* and the *pax aeterna*. "For mediaeval thinkers, the *pax temporalis* in the realm of earthly organisation, could be regarded as overarching and absolute, but yet as only of provisional or temporary value when compared with the true 'eternal city' commanded by God."[3]

This mediaeval synthesis of *christianitas, pax* et *justitia* was thrown in doubt by the religious divisions of the sixteenth century. From then on, the question was no longer the restoration of a world order of peace based on a recognised system of law, as in the case of a local feud, but rather the idea of a recognised system of law was itself disputed. The result of the denominational civil wars was to replace the idea of a *justa pax* with that of *pax civilis*, a settlement between the states. The overthrow of the concept of a unified Christian-theological world opened the way for a new idea of the unity of mankind in place of the unity of Christendom. The essential character of the *pax civilis* was the recognition of the *securitas pacis*, whereby, as in Hobbes, the counterparts of peace were seen as insecurity and fear. The concepts of peace and justice now became separated, since it was exactly the disputes over the nature of true justice which had caused the denominational civil wars to break out. From then on, the notion of *justitia* in connection with *pax* became limited to the concept of the kind of legal arrangement which would effectively guarantee security.

In the teachings of Martin Luther (1483-1546) a strict separation was made between the inner spiritual peace *pax spiritualis* and worldly peace. Since "peace in our time" is "the greatest good on earth, comprehending all other mortal goods"[4], so its maintenance is not only the task of the secular authorities but required the responsibility of each individual Christian.

Following this tradition, peace came to be regarded as the highest and most absolute reason of state. Law and Truth ought not to be pursued to the extreme, in order to preserve the *pax civilis*. Rather, the nation's peace rested upon effective use of force.

With the successful assertion of doctrines of natural law in the seventeenth and eighteenth centuries, the concept of justice again came to be more highly prized in relation to *pax* or *justitia*, even though no change took place in the priority given to the value of peace as secured by the state. The ideas of the state and of "inner" peace were seen as being closely related, but the civic view of peace outweighed the moral one.

After the successful establishment in the eighteenth century of the modern state's concept of providing the means of security for its own citizens, attention was diverted away from the internal organisation of the state towards consideration of how peace should be secured in the international arena. Internally, peace was to be guaranteed by the functions of law and order, but internationally no such system of legal jurisdiction existed. War was the only arbiter in situations of conflict. The idea of a "just war" replaced the notion of a just peace. As such peace between states was subordinated to the needs of maintaining peace within the nation; indeed, on occasions, securing internal peace appeared to justify war between the states (Bodin, Richelieu).

In the seventeenth century, increasing significance was given to the idea of making legally binding treaties of peace as a means of regulating relations between the nations. Both Hobbes (1588-1679) and Spinoza (1632-1677) regarded peace between the states as only possible on the basis of a *pactum pacis*, regardless of whether such plans were based on concepts of the natural state of peace, as Pufendorf and his school affirmed, or on those of the natural state of war, as Hobbes and his followers claimed.

For the thinkers of the Enlightenment, the notion of peace within the state based on force became more and more problematical. For this reason, the moral categories of values once more returned to the forefront in the interpretations given to the ideas of *justitia* and *pax*. True peace should be based on true law, not on unjust force. Inner and outward peace therefore belonged together, since a just internal order was a precondition for peace abroad (Kant). But if the notion of law was to be based on true moral reason, so the idea of peace must be regarded as universal and eternal. War is therefore the ultimate refusal of practical reason. Kant's view was that peace was the result of a legally established rule of law based on reason. And the connections between Reason-Law-Peace, as built up by Enlightenment thought, remained essential for liberal thinkers in the nineteenth century. But, in contrast to the English-speaking tradition, which stressed the utilitarian value of peace, continental writers followed Kant in emphasising its moral qualities. This notable difference remains clear even into the present century.

The eighteenth century Enlightenment philosophers were persuaded by their view of practical reason that opposition to a *pax perpetua* was not brought about by any devilish inspiration or inherently natural evil in mankind (*malice des hommes*), but by clear and correctable abuses in the social, economic, political or in part also the religious (Voltaire) circumstances of the day. Instead they fully believed that the *pax perpetua* could be guaranteed by encouraging the spirit of commerce (*esprit de commerce*) and thereby closely associated the idea of peace with economic progress (Mercantilism). Freedom of trade would lead to increased harmony of interests in the secular world, and could therefore be regarded not merely as useful but also as moral in tendency. Peaceful intercourse could therefore be seen as the condition of morality in practice, whereas war was dismissed as actively immoral. Only in limited circumstances could war be interpreted as justified, above all in cases of civil war. Since the Enlightenment believed that a *pax perpetua in terris* was realisable, it regarded an "unjust war" as a crime. The idea of a "just war" could no longer apply to conflicts between states, but only to those between the oppressed and the oppressors, the good and the evil.

But the semi-religious authentication given to the idea of "eternal peace" by the Enlightenment thinkers produced a counter-movement of "Bellicism", which asked whether this eternal peace might not become a nightmare, and war a blessing. Kant took over from the French Enlightenment this idea of "eternal peace", but did not endow it with notions of utopianism, regarding it rather as a direct result of practical reason. Legally established regulations, he believed, would best secure peace. He had little sympathy for the idea of the "natural" brotherhood of all men.

In the nineteenth century, however, we can see the growth of a new mood, which spurned the idea of eternal peace as being too negative and not dynamic enough. For many of the romantics, war was itself a sign of the cathartic moment of a people's identity, out of which arose new and higher developments. The dream of an eternal peace, on the other hand, was regarded as unworthy, flat and lacking in inspiration (for example, Treitschke 1879). War came to be looked on as a necessary refining process, indispensable for the regeneration of a people's moral forces. On the other side, the optimistic hopes for the future of mankind had become muted after the experiences of the Napoleonic Wars. Liberals became more cautious about their confident assertions that, through progress in education, reason and humanity would become the dominant characteristics of mankind. For their part, the more radical thinkers began to place their faith in the new ideas of socialism. Instead of trusting in the power of education, these men sought to bring about eternal peace by transforming existing political and social conditions. Peace and harmony among men would surely be achieved once these deformities in social life were removed. Moritz von Prittwitz (1796–1885), for example, in his poem composed in 1838, expressed this utopian vision:

> Once the walls of error are o'erthrown
> Then peace shall reign on earth
> Brother joins the hand of brother
> And Eden's bliss will shine again.

In this romantic phase, as a result of the stress laid on concepts of peace and the natural harmony of interests, the traditional idea of justice was neglected. The notion of peace as the result of legally binding engagements – *pactum pacis* – was hence overshadowed by the idea that peace could be achieved solely by freedom of thought and trade. Indeed, so widespread did this newer idea of peace through social reformation become that it, too, began to take on a pseudo-religious significance, and thereby became turned into an ideological crusade for the realisation of a future Kingdom of Peace.

Only in the most recent years since 1945 has awareness grown that, due to the indiscriminately destructive power of modern weapons, and the possibility of their employment throughout the globe, it is no longer possible to justify the use of such weapons as a means of securing justice and peace. To be sure, earlier in this century, attempts were made to obtain the renunciation of war as a means of implementing international systems of law. In the development of ideas of international law, we can trace the first attempt to establish laws for the prevention of war to the Covenant of the League of Nations, which was ratified in January 1920. This partial prohibition of war was extended by the Geneva Protocols of 1924, and made more explicit still in the Briand-Kellogg Pact of 1928, which condemned war as an instrument of international politics, and can therefore rightly be regarded as an attempt to outlaw war altogether.

The Charter of the United Nations, signed in 1945, extended the Briand-Kellogg Pact's prohibition of war with a still more general prohibition of the use of force, as a result of which the teachings of international law came to promulgate a universal duty to ensure peace. This in turn has become accepted as the norm for all international law systems, and also dictates the choice of means to effect it. Peace is only to be sought and maintained by peaceful means.

On the other side, the idea of peace was often misused in the period of the Cold War. The Soviet Union, for example, liked to regard itself, and was so regarded by its satellites, as a "mighty bulwark for peace". Hostilities between the nations, it was claimed, were primarily caused by the western powers whose class antagonisms not only led to internal conflicts but to international tension. Peace was threatened by "imperialistic forces" which sought "by all means to prevent the historically-conditioned triumph of the socialist and communist concepts of humanity through their policies of thwarting the victory of socialism and of the forces of national liberation". By contrast, peace was "an integral part of the nature of socialism and communism" and the "guiding principle for the international relations of peoples and states".[5] In the former East Germany, for example, the Socialist Unity Party proclaimed for forty years its dedication to "struggle for the maintenance of peace" and defended its "peace borders" against imperialist aggressors.[6]

Johannes Schwerdtfeger believes that the multiplicity of these concepts, experiences and expectations makes impossible any all-inclusive definition of the ideas of "peace".[7] While on the one hand this means there is an opening for further development, on the other we should beware of the danger of turning the idea of peace into an unlimited and vague idea of salvation, overloaded with mythology. In order to guard against this tendency, especially in the light of the above discussion, it is of great importance to stress the centuries-old connection between Peace and Justice. Any conceivable concept of peace worthy of the name must include the establishment of and respect for both law and justice. This is especially true for the maintenance of human rights.

2.   Human Rights – Droits de l'homme – Menschenrechte[8]

Human rights are today understood as covering those fundamental rights inherent to all persons independent of their belonging to defined groups or classes. This idea of human rights, like the concepts of peace, has developed historically as part of the growth of western civilisation.

The English *Magna Carta Libertatum* of 1215 has long been seen as having special significance in the growth of concepts of human and basic rights, as an early example of the process of securing the liberty of the individual as against his ruler, whereby the ruler was bound by treaty to make promises to uphold the *jura et libertates* of his subjects. Of course, such "liberties" were in fact corporative assurances to groups of subjects, and at the time were not seen as conferring individual rights. No direct connection between each individual subject and the ruler was created or envisaged in such treaties. On the other hand, these treaties do contain early on such individualistic concepts as "the right of choosing one's domicile", or the "inviolability of the person". But since these concepts did not draw distinctions between corporative and individual freedoms, but rather included both under general definitions of "Rights", "Freedoms" and "Liberties", it would seem difficult to trace any direct connection between fundamental human rights and these mediaeval "Freedoms".

So too, the notion propounded at the end of the sixteenth century of *leges fundamentales* did not mean individual human rights but rather was used as a collective term for the series of treaties organised between the rulers and the various estates of the realm. At the same time, however, the use of the term *lex fundamentalis* demonstrated the beginnings of thought about a constitution, which opened the possibility for the individual to achieve a certain status in his relation to the community or state. For this to happen, it was however necessary to go through the historical development allowing for the idea to emerge of a vertical connection between the state and its subjects (or citizens), replacing the former notion of there being solely rulers and estates, which would represent the individual. Jean Bodin (1529/30–1596) in his work published in 1576 argued that the state should be sovereign over all its subjects and should no longer be bound by these semi-sovereign estates. To be sure, Bodin was not primarily interested in individual rights, but rather in the maintenance of the unity of the state at a time of turbulent conflicts between the monarchy, the estates, and the various religious factions.

In the Peace of Augsburg of 1555, rulers asserted the right to determine the religion of their subjects. But this was soon followed by demands for religious toleration, which can be seen as an attempt to limit the powers of the state through the affirmation of the individual's right to religious freedom. To begin with, however, this led only to the granting of the right of religious dissenters to emigrate.

In the seventeenth century, new theories about the state took up the issue of the individual's place in society, though these were primarily designed not to enhance but to limit the ideas of natural freedom and equality of mankind. Thomas Hobbes, for example, asserted the principle of equality of freedoms in the natural state, and believed that the individual could not be deprived of such rights through the establishment of the social contract. But these natural freedoms had to become subordinate to the prior need of the state to enhance security, so that the freedom of each citizen must be at the disposition of the ruler. The natural freedom of the individual did not confer on him any right *against* the power of the state. But Hobbes did stress the idea of "inalienable" rights, even though these were not spelled out in concrete form. Spinoza, on the other hand, did not allow for such individual rights, since by joining the social contract these had been transferred to the society as a whole. For Spinoza, the individual could retain only his private right to think and judge as an actual, though not normative, limit to the power of the state.

Pufendorf (1632–1694) believed that each citizen was a partner in the social contract. Rulers were bound both by the purpose of securing the good of society and by natural laws. Citizens' rights were conferred only as the result of the obligations of the rulers, and were not conceived as intrinsic but only as subsidiary to the ruler of the state.

Christian Wolff (1679–1754) recognised equality and freedom as belonging to the natural being of man, which gave rise to "inborn duties" (*obligata connata*) and "inborn rights" (*jura connata*) – specifically *aequalitas, libertas, jus securitatis, jus defensionis, jus puniendi*. Such prime rights were however to be limited by the much more significantly explicit purposes of the state.

In Germany the main theoretical conceptions on the subject of natural rights did not seek to achieve the enunciation of the rights of the citizen in society.

The individual was considered basically free and equal, but equality and freedom were regarded as being limited to the primitive state of nature, and were not seen as placing demands on the state. The individual citizen was not regarded as possessing subjective rights, but rather was the object of the ruler's benevolence, which could be interpreted and realised on the basis of reason.[9]

John Locke (1632–1704) developed a contrary view of the basis of natural law. For him man's intrinsic nature was the foundation of the development of the rights of the citizen in society. The individual members voluntarily came together to form a social contract over equality, liberty and executive power, so that freedom and property would be secured for each person, rather than his being partially deprived of such goals.

Even before the first constitutions were drawn up on the continent of Europe, we find attempts being made, under the influence of the Enlightenment, to draw up codifications of the legal relationships between the state and its citizens. For example, we should note the General Civil Code of the Prussian State issued in 1791, and above all its first draft of 1784. Because of the impact of the French Revolution many of its more famous criteria found no place in the General Land Law of 1794. Yet the use of such terms as "natural freedoms" or "rights of the citizen" meant their acknowledgement in the system of law, whereby the power of the state was to be limited by the rights of the citizens. It is true that the term "natural freedom" was used only as a description of the human condition, but it served as an orientation point for future legislative programmes by the state. The establishment and maintenance of freedom was now seen as a major purpose for the state's existence and as such constrained the lawmaker, even though it did not limit the scope of his judgment.

Carl Gottlieb Svarez (1746–1798) was another writer who addressed the notion of equality. He understood the political prerogatives of the individual estates as duly acquired privileges, which were at the disposition of the lawmaker. But, for him, equality, as distinct from civil freedoms or property, did not constitute a claim or even an obligation on the lawmaker but was treated only as a possibility.

So too, in the political Code for Austria, produced in 1791, the idea of human rights was touched on with circumspection. Leopold II was determined not to use one of the slogans of the dreaded Revolution and therefore adopted the formula of the "rights of the citizen", not of the "rights of man".

The earliest positive approach to human rights in constitutional legal form is to be found in the Virginia Bill of Rights of 1776.[10] The roots of the American Declaration of Rights are to be found in the concepts of the intrinsic nature of freedom of religion and conscience, in the English declarations of freedom, particularly the Agreement of the People dating from 1647, in European ideas of natural rights, as well as in the revolutionary situation in the American colonies. But it is notable that the terminology of natural rights is uppermost in this declaration. The ideas of natural freedom and equality as being intrinsic and inalienable are here connected with John Locke's triad of life, liberty and property. The pursuit of happiness and security as the chief ends of human endeavour are ideas also drawn from continental European sources. The intrinsic right to religious liberty and freedom of conscience was placed beyond the scope of law and derived from the impossibility of using force to compel man to adopt any one religion or to pay respect to the Creator. A further premise to be enunciated was the sovereignty of the people. Other rights were here adumbrated as the means of guaranteeing the previously enunciated fundamental rights, such as Montesquieu's earlier suggestion for the separation of powers or freedom of the press. But these societal rights were regarded as subsidiary to the personal and individual rights to freedom. Human rights were thereby given concrete constitutional form and became the basis of the new community which existed to serve the people.

The French Declaration of Rights of 26 August 1789 also regarded the *droits de l'homme* as natural, inalienable and sacred, that is pre-existing the state. The state's purpose was to preserve and enhance these rights: freedom, property, security, resistance against oppression. Both the power of the state and the constitution makers themselves are to be bound by these human rights, which only underlined their character as transcending the existence of the state, or even as religious in nature. In contrast to the American declarations, the French ones did not claim any constitutional validity and were more abstract in form. The task of turning such principles into concrete realities was left to the constitution makers. At the same time, this broader interpretation of the Declaration of the Rights of Man and of the citizen means that the French people saw itself as proclaiming universal rights valid for all men and states. As such they went beyond the particular local circumstances – again in contrast to the American Declaration. "The French National Assembly promulgated in this *Declaration des droits de l'homme et du citoyen* a model not merely for the French but for every constitution. Thereby the declaration became the expression of an expansionist ideology, in whose service the French nation could enlist."[11]

However, the French Constitution of 1799 made no mention of human rights. At the beginning of the *Charte Constitutionelle Française*, issued on 4 June 1814, the chapter of France's Public Law includes a catalogue of rights which acknowledged "civic freedoms", but without making any reference to intrinsic or pre-existing rights as such. This catalogue of rights undoubtedly influenced the early movements in Germany seeking to achieve constitutions, even though in both the Federal Act of 8 June 1815, and in the majority of individual German states, the notion of "civic rights" was avoided. Instead the term "the rights of subjects" was used. Apparently the excesses of the French Revolution had discredited both the justification and the idealisation of intrinsic natural rights. Therefore no appeal at all was made to the notion of human rights. In most of the German states, the rights of subjects were to be guaranteed and secured, but they were not seen as existing prior to or superior to the state. Rather, in opposition to the principle of the "divine rights of kings", a dualistic framework for the estates of the realm was proposed, in which the local estates would now represent all of the subjects of every class.

In 1848, the Declaration of the Basic Rights of the German People proclaimed the whole people as the constituent body, but this was clearly more influenced by the idea of national unity than of the sovereignty of the people as such. In the pre-Parliament of that year, the concept of human rights as being both intrinsic and inalienable enjoyed a considerable renaissance and clearly made use of both the French and American Declarations. But the German Reich Constitution of 1871 dispensed with any codification of human rights, pointing instead to the guarantees for such rights in the individual states. The Weimar National Constitution of 1919 included for the first time a comprehensive codification of all basic rights (Articles 109–165), which spelled out not only the usual rights of the individual but also socially based rights and even the determination of cultural goals. By contrast the Basic Law issued in West Germany in 1949, in its Article 1, went back beyond the 1849 Constitution to the French Declaration of 1789, and

confirmed the concept that "inviolable and inalienable human rights are the basis of every state community"[12]. Such human rights consequently cannot be altered in any changes to the constitution. The Basic Laws are to be regarded – as
was the case in the French Constitution of 1791 – as giving expression to these
human rights for all areas of law in the life of the state.

It is a notable fact that until the 1940s the major churches of Europe decisively rejected these concepts of human rights, in contrast to their contributions to
the developments in the ideas of peace. The Roman Catholic Church, for example, repeatedly stated its opposition in various papal declarations from Pius VI
(1775–1799) to Leo XIII (1878–1903). The notion of human rights was always interpreted as a product of the subversive spirit of anarchy, of the French Revolution, or of the liberal-enlightenment movements touched off by such forces. The
secular demands for freedom as an intrinsic human right were seen as a threat to
the Christian understanding of man's nature, and, so the critics believed, were
signs of the spirit of secularism, indifferentism, naturalism and unrestrained individualism. A change only took place under Pope Pius XII (1939–1958) under
the impact of the threat by the totalitarian systems to all human values during
the Second World War. But the first Roman Catholic declaration on the question
of human rights only appeared in April 1963 when Pope John XXIII (1958–1963)
issued his Encyclical "Pacem in terries", in which the most important rights enunciated in the United Nations' Declaration of Human Rights of 1948 were adopted and justified as being based on respect for human individuality. These notions
were carried forward to the Second Vatican Council and were expressed in the
Pastoral Constitution on the Church and the Modern World and in the Declaration on Religious Freedom, both of which appeared in December 1965. Man is
here regarded as a being "endowed with dignity and freedom in consequence of
his creation in the image of God"[13]. It is particularly notable that the Catholic
ideas of human rights are not limited to the individual's right to freedom, but
rather raised the issues of the social and economic conditions necessary for men
to be able to live in dignity. This was especially stressed in the Message of the
Roman Bishops' Synod of October 1974, entitled "On Human Rights and Reconciliation".

In 1976, the Papal Commission Justice and Peace, and especially its working
paper "The Church and Human Rights", gave specific theological legitimation to
human rights. The theological argument pointed to the following features: God's
image and likeness in Man; the liberation of all men through Christ's redemptive
act, which calls for universal brotherly solidarity; and finally the divine commission to carry out Christ's act of liberation in the future. In the spirit of its prophetic mission, the Church should demonstrate a new and decisive commitment to
the poor and oppressed through support of their fundamental rights.

The major Protestant churches on the continent of Europe also adopted a negative view of human rights, at least until the 1940s. This attitude was based on
the close connection between the rulers and national Protestantism, as for example in Germany, a similar aversion to the liberal-enlightenment tradition adopted from Catholicism, and as well anti-western, above all anti-French sentiments.
In place of such western liberal ideals, these churches sought to propagate a more

genuinely Christian basis for society. After the military defeat of France in 1870/71, the idea was even noised abroad that the "French spirit" in men's hearts should be erased.

The shock of the Nazi and Stalinist crimes and atrocities against humanity, however, had the effect of forcing a re-valuation of this stance. Only then did these European Protestant churches recognise that a quite different view of human rights had developed in other branches of Protestantism, particularly in the more liberal branches of the church in the English-speaking world. Thanks to the energetic work of the World Council of Churches in making these views known, German Protestants after 1945 remarkably quickly adopted a more positive view of human rights.[14]

In the theological tradition of the Reformed Churches, the universal character of human rights is seen as being based on "God's Law for Man". "Such an argument pushes both the secular development of human rights and their legal character into the background. Instead the attempt is being made to inquire into the parallels between human rights and the foundations of Christian faith. Thereby the justification for Christian engagement for support of human rights could be clarified."[15]

The three parallel components were recognised as freedom, equality and participation. These were the notes most recently stressed, on the ecumenical level, by the World Council of Churches' Message of the World Assembly for Justice, Peace and the Integrity of Creation, issued in Seoul, Korea in March 1990, which affirmed the view that human rights are given by God and that "their promotion and safeguarding are decisive preconditions for Freedom, Justice and Peace"[16].

3.   Reconciliation between the Nations

The terms "reconciliation between the nations" or "international understanding" are not in themselves technical ones. They arose in the context of the efforts of the League of Nations to find a basis of mutual accommodation after the First World War. They were to be widely used at the well-known Stockholm Conference of 1925, when the attending churchmen undertook strenuous negotiations to find a new basis on which the nations could relate to one another.[17] But at Stockholm and thereafter, the topic was to prove highly controversial, both politically and theologically. The Germans refused to accept the Third Preparatory Commission's report on this matter, which in particular stressed the need to outlaw war and to give unreserved support to the League of Nations as "the only organisation at present capable of promoting a sure foundation upon which permanent international peace can be built"[18]. The German Lutherans' political criticism of the League of Nations was closely linked to their theological declarations. Whereas Britons and Frenchmen saw the work of the League of Nations as being in accordance with "God's Will", and Elie Gounelle (1865-1950) even believed that here was to be perceived "one of the milestones on the road to the Kingdom of God"[19], the German church leader Klingemann (1859-1946) argued that he could see in

the League of Nations in 1925 neither "any religious force" nor "any kind of inner connection with the Kingdom of God".[20] Walter Wolff (1870–1931) was another theologian who opposed the idea of regarding the League of Nations as a
"divinely-desired" example of international harmony.[21] After the conference, similar criticisms were made by the Archbishop of Finland, Gustav Johansson
(1844–1930), who regarded the "eagerness to unite all peoples in some artificial
or external manner" as a "great blunder which would divide the nations and cause
their downfall". The Stockholm Conference, he believed, had only increased the
gap between the Anglicans who were fully in agreement with the rationalist view,
and the Lutherans. "The core of Lutheran belief was faith in Christ as God's Son,
and in a Kingdom not of this world, just as Christ was not of this world."[22]

The German term *Verständigung* subsumed these theological reservations, in
that it still presumed the continued existence of separate national identities and
interests. Lutherans were particularly sceptical of any idea that such characteristics could be reconciled in this world, and therefore did not set their sights on
anything more than a balancing between divergent purposes and desires. They
failed to see that the English term "Reconciliation" included overtones of a more
far-reaching sense of "expiation and forgiveness". Only in later years was this bar-
rier overcome, as for example in 1978 when the members of the German Evangelical Churches' Commission for Public Responsibility issued a collection of this
Church's Declarations entitled "Peace, Reconciliation and Human Rights".[23]

In summary, let us return once again to the problem inherent in all three of
these terms. If, on the one hand, the immanent nature of these idealistic values,
as explicit throughout history, is over-stressed, there is a danger that the reason
for achieving them gets lost, and they become pseudo-religious or secularised
utopian notions. On the other hand, if the transcendent realisation of, for example, what peace is supposed to be, is overly accented, then secular efforts to
achieve peace run the risk of appearing too limited and insignificant compared
to such higher expectations.

All three of these terms belong to an ideological spectrum arising from the human desire for Cosmopolitanism. Peter Coulmas describes the present state of
this as yet unrealised utopia: "Today we are living in a world, interdependent, tech-
nically and economically unified, but politically insufficiently ordered. Above all,
we lack genuinely binding rules for living with and relating to one another.
Nowhere are there to be found new, powerful and universal ideals or a vision for
the civilised intercourse between the states. All the suggestions made in this direction during the last fifty years have been shown to be particularly barren, lacking in contour or without appeal."[24]

Instead of developing new, attractive and convincing concepts, there is now a
strong tendency to mystify the old images and the concepts which lie behind
them. Alternatively all sorts of irrationalisms are pursued, when, by the use of
moralistic slogans, established concepts are either elevated as being beyond discussion or ruthlessly rejected. One of the main tasks of scholarship today is to be
concerned about such a state of affairs.

Notes

1   Cf. on this and the following F. S. Northedge, art. 'Peace, War and Philosophy', in The Encyclopedia of Philosophy, vol. 6, London 1967, 63–67; Johan Galty, art. 'Peace', in International Encyclopedia of the Social Sciences, vol. 11, London 1968, 487–496; R. L. Ottley, art. 'Peace', in Encyclopedia of Religion and Ethics, vol. 9, 700 701; Wilhelm Janssen, art. 'Friede', in Geschichtliche Grundbegriffe. Historisches Lexikon zur politisch-sozialen Sprache in Deutschland, vol. 2, Stuttgart 1975, 543–591; Hans-Werner Gensichen/Hans Heinrich Schmid/Werner Theißen/Gerhard Delling/Wolfgang Huber, art. 'Friede', in TRE, vol. XI, Berlin 1983, 599–646; G. Mathon, art. 'Paix', in Catholicisme. Hier, aujourd'hui, demain, vol. 10, Paris 1985, 417–452; Johannes Schwerdtfeger/Wolfgang Lienemann, art. 'Frieden', in EKL, vol. 1, [3]1986, 1372–1382; Hans Maier/Otto Kimmenich/Franz Böckle/ Ernst-Otto Czempiel, art. 'Frieden', in StL, vol. 2, [7]1986, 745–757; Erwin Wilkens, art. 'Frieden', in EStL, vol. 1, [1]1987, 999–1007; Hans-Jürgen Schlochaner (ed.), Die Idee des ewigen Friedens. Ein Überblick über Entwicklung und Gestaltung des Friedenssicherungsgedankens auf der Grundlage einer Quellenauswahl, Bonn 1953; Hans Schmidt, Frieden, Stuttgart-Berlin 1969; Fritz Dickmann, Friedensrecht und Friedenssicherung. Studien zum Friedensproblem in der neueren Geschichte, Göttingen 1971; Jost Delbrück, Völkerrecht und Weltfriedenssicherung, in Dieter Grimm (ed.), Rechtswissenschaft und Nachbarwissenschaften, vol. 2, München 1976, 79–101; Knud Krakau, Friedensforschung und Völkerrecht, in op. cit., 192–204; Franz-Martin Schmölz (ed.), Christlicher Friedensbegriff und europäische Friedensordnung, München-Mainz 1977; Donald F. Durnbaugh (ed.), On Earth Peace. Discussion on War/Peace Issues Between Friends, Mennonites, Brothers and European Churches 1935–1975, Elgin/Ill. 1978; Thomas A. Shannon (ed.), War or Peace? The Search for New Answers, Maryknoll/N. Y. 1980; Rainer Steinweg (ed.), Der gerechte Krieg: Christentum, Islam, Marxismus, Frankfurt/M. 1980; Wolfgang Huber, Der Streit um die Wahrheit und die Fähigkeit zum Frieden. Vier Kapitel ökumenische Theologie, München 1980; Gustav W. Heinemann, Der Frieden ist der Ernstfall, ed. and introduced by Martin Lotz, München 1981; Ev. Kirchenamt für die Bundeswehr (ed.), Was können die Kirchen für den Frieden tun?, Gütersloh 1981; Peace and Disarmament. Documents of the World Council of Churches on International Affairs, and the Roman Catholic Church. Presented by the Pontifical Commission "Justitia et Pax", Genf 1982; Franz Alt, Frieden ist möglich. Die Politik der Bergpredigt, München-Zürich 1983; Eberhard Jüngel, Zum Wesen des Friedens. Frieden als Kategorie theologischer Anthropologie, München 1983; Eckehart Lorenz/Theodor Strohm, Das Wagnis engagierter Friedensarbeit. Internationale christliche Friedensorganisationen im Spannungsfeld zwischen christlichem Glauben und politischer Wirklichkeit. Eine kritische Analyse, Waldkirch 1985; Carl Friedrich v. Weizsäcker, Die Zeit drängt. Eine Weltversammlung der Christen für Gerechtigkeit. Frieden und die Bewahrung der Schöpfung, München-Wien 1986; Burkhard Haneke, Kriegsbegriff und Friedensdiskussion. Die Nutzanwendung einer ideengeschichtlichen Betrachtungsweise, in ZPol (NS) 33 (1986), 164–173; Hartmut Lenhard (ed.), Versöhnung und Frieden mit den Völkern der Sowjetunion. Herausforderungen zur Umkehr. Eine Thesenreihe, Gütersloh 1987; Friedhelm Solms/Marc Reuver, Welchen Frieden wollen die Kirchen? Beiträge zur ökonomischen Diskussion, Heidelberg 1988; Dietrich Goldschmidt (ed.), Frieden mit der Sowjetunion – eine unerledigte Aufgabe, Gütersloh 1989; Frieden in Gerechtigkeit. Die offiziellen Dokumente der Europäischen Ökumenischen Versammlung 1989 in Basel, ed. by the Konferenz Europäischer Kirchen und die Rat der Europäischen Bischofskonferenz, Basel-Zürich 1989; Götz Planer-Friedrich (ed.), Frieden und Gerechtigkeit. Auf dem Weg zu einer Ökumenischen Friedensethik. München 1989; Hans Diefenbacher/Bernhard Moltmann (eds), Zum Verhältnis von Frieden und Sicherheit, Heidelberg 1991; Gennadios Limouris (ed.), Justice, Peace and Integrity of Creation. Insights from Orthodoxy, Genf 1990; Wolfgang Huber/Hans-Richard Reuter (eds), Friedensethik, Stuttgart 1990.

2   Cf. Jüngel (op. cit. note 1), 25 ff.
3   So W. Janssen (op. cit. note 1), 552.
4   WA 3011, 538, 8.
5   Kleines Wörterbuch der Marxistisch-Leninistischen Philosophie, Berlin (Ost) 1975, 104 f.
6   Cf. on this terminology e. g. Joachim Heise, Die Politik der SED zur Einbeziehung der Gläubigen in den Aufbau des Sozialismus und in den Kampf um den Frieden. Von der Gründung der DDR im Oktober 1949 bis zur 2. Parteikonferenz der SED im Juli 1952, Diss. (A) phil. Berlin (Ost) 1982 (unprinted). Cf. also Heinrich Fink, Zur Herausforderung der Kirchen durch den realen Sozialismus, in Horst Dohle et al. (eds), Beiträge zur Theorie und Geschichte der Religion und des Atheismus, Heft 5, Berlin (Ost) 1989, 42–46.
7   Schwerdtfeger (op. cit. note 1), 1372.
8   Cf. on this and the following G. Jacquement, art. 'Droits de l'homme et du citoyen', in Catholicisme. Hier, aujourd'hui, demain, vol. 3, Paris 1952, 1124–1125; Ernst Friesenhahn, art. 'Menschenrechte', in Wörterbuch des Völkerrechts, vol. 2, Berlin [2]1961, 503–511; Stanley I. Benn, art. 'Rights', in The Encyclopedia of Philosophy, vol. 7, London 1967, 194–199; Ernst Friesenhahn, art. 'Grundrechte. Menschen- und Bürgerrechte', in Geschichtliche Grundbegriffe. Historisches Lexikon zur politisch-sozialen Sprache in Deutschland, vol. 2, Stuttgart 1975, 1047–1082; Alexander Hollerback/ Gerhard Luf/Jochen Abr. Fronein/Wolfgang Huber, art. 'Menschenrechte', in StL, vol. 3, [7]1987, 1104–1118; Fritz Hartung, Die Entwicklung der Menschen- und Bürgerrechte von 1776–1946, Berlin 1948; Roman Schnur (ed.), Zur Geschichte der Erklärung der Menschenrechte (WdF 11), Darmstadt 1964; Wolfgang Heidelmeyer, Die Menschenrechte, Paderborn 1972; idem (ed.), Menschenrechte – eine Herausforderung der Kirche, München-Mainz 1979; Gerd Kleinheyer, Grundrechte – Zur Geschichte eines Begriffs, Graz 1977; Die Denkschriften der Evangelischen Kirche in Deutschland, vols 1/I and 1/II: Frieden, Versöhnung, Menschenrechte, Gütersloh 1978; Martin Honnecker, Das Recht des Menschen. Einführung in die evangelische Sozialethik, Gütersloh 1978; Gerhard Oestreich, Geschichte der Menschenrechte und Grundfreiheiten im Umriß, Berlin [2]1978; Johannes Schwartländer (ed.), Menschenrechte. Aspekte ihrer Begründung und Verwirklichung, Tübingen 1978; Die Menschenrechte im ökumenischen Gespräch. Beiträge der Kammer der Evangelischen Kirche in Deutschland für öffentliche Verantwortung, Gütersloh 1979; Helmut Quaritsch (ed.), Von der ständischen Gesellschaft zur bürgerlichen Gleichheit, Berlin 1980; Karl Dietrich Bracher, Geschichte und Gewalt. Zur Politik im 20. Jahrhundert, Berlin 1981, 28–50; Günter Birtsch (ed.), Grund- und Freiheitsrechte im Wandel von Gesellschaft und Geschichte. Beiträge zur Geschichte der Grund- und Freiheitsrechte vom Ausgang des Mittelalters bis zur Revolution von 1848, Göttingen 1981; Eckehart Lorenz (ed.), "... erkämpft das Menschenrecht". Wie christlich sind die Menschenrechte?, Hamburg 1981; René Coste, L'église et les droits de l'homme, Paris 1983; Jack Donnely, The Concept of Human Rights, Oxford 1985; Günter Birtsch (ed.), Grund- und Freiheitsrechte von der ständischen zur spätbürgerlichen Gesellschaft (Veröffentlichungen zur Geschichte der Grund- und Freiheitsrechte, 2), Göttingen 1987; Ernst-Wolfgang Böckenförde/Robert Spaemann (eds), Menschenrechte und Menschenwürde. Historische Voraussetzungen – säkulare Gestalt – christliches Verständnis, Stuttgart 1987; Martin Heckel, Die Menschenrechte im Spiegel reformatorischer Theologie, Heidelberg 1987; Warren Lee Holleman, The Human Rights Movement. Western values and theological perspectives, New York 1987; Ludger Kuehnhardt, Die Universalität der Menschenrechte. Studie zur ideengeschichtlichen Bestimmung eines politischen Schlüsselbegriffs, München 1987; Wolfgang Huber/ Heinz Eduard Tödt, Menschenrechte. Perspektiven einer menschlichen Welt, München 1988; Martin Kriele, Freiheit und "Befreiung". Zur Rangordnung der Menschenrechte, Frankfurt/M. 1988; Hans Küng/Jürgen Moltmann (eds.), The Ethics of World, Religious and Human Rights (Concilium 1990/2), London 1990; Gerhard

Robbers, 'Menschen- und Bürgerrechte', in EKL, vol. 3, [3]1991, 361–365; Valentine Rothe, Die Auswirkung der Menschenrechtsdiskussion auf die deutsche Frauenbewegung, in Marieluise Christadler (ed.), Freiheit, Gleichheit, Weiblichkeit. Aufklärung, Revolution und die Frauen in Europa, Opladen 1990, 141–153.

9   Kleinheyer (op. cit. note 8), 1975, 1060.

10 Cf. Sidney E. Mead, Das Christentum in Nordamerika. Glaube und Religionsfreiheit in vier Jahrhunderten, Göttingen 1987, 36 ff.

11 Kleinheyer (op. cit. note 8), 1975, 1069.

12 Bundesgesetzblatt 1, 1949, 1.

13 Quoted from Karl Rahner/Herbert Vorgrimmler, Kleines Konzilskompendium. Alle Konstitutionen, Dekrete und Erklärungen des Zweiten Vaticanums in der bischöflich genehmigten Übersetzung, Freiburg-Basel-Wien 1966, 467.

14 Cf. on this e. g. Stellungnahme zu dem Entwurf der UN-Kommission für Menschenrechte für einen Convenant on Human Rights from March 1950, compiled in January 1950 by a commission of theologians and lawyers set up by the Kirchliches Außenamt of the EKD (Evangelisches Zentralarchiv Berlin, Bestand 6 [Kirchliches Außenamt der EKD], no. 2139, fol. 146–148 [German text]; fol. 139–141 [English version]. Documents and correspondence also in WCC Geneva, CCIA Country Files, Germany, 1946–1950).

15 Huber (op. cit. note 8), 1987, 1116. Cf. also Wolfgang Lienemann, Zur theologischen Begründung der Menschenrechte, in OR 39 (1990), 307–317; Christa Lewek/Manfred Stolpe/Joachim Garstecki (eds), Menschenrechte in christlicher Verantwortung, Berlin (Ost) 1980.

16 Quoted from JK 4/51 (1990), 245.

17 Cf. on this and the following Adolf Deißmann (ed.), Die Stockholmer Weltkirchenkonferenz. Vorgeschichte, Dienst und Arbeit der Weltkonferenz für Praktisches Christentum 19.-30. August 1925. Amtlicher Deutscher Bericht, Berlin 1926; Hanns Kerner, Luthertum und Ökumenische Bewegung für Praktisches Christentum 1919-1926, Gütersloh 1983 (lit.!).

18 Deißmann (op. cit. note 17), 77.

19 Ibid. 431 ff., 462.

20 Ibid. 460.

21 Ibid. 533.

22 Quoted from H. Kerner (op. cit. note 17), 485 f.

23 Cf. on the field of foreign policy also Ingeborg Koza, Völkerversöhnung und Europäisches Einigungsbemühen. Untersuchungen zur Nachkriegsgeschichte 1945–1951, Köln-Wien 1987.

24 Peter Coulmas, Weltbürger. Geschichte einer Menschheitssehnsucht, Hamburg 1990, 501 f.

The World Council of Churches' Programme to Combat Racism (PCR), the African Peoples' Republics and the German Churches*

1. The PCR as a means of drawing attention to shortcomings in the Western world

Since the ecumenical movement came into being[1] Christians throughout the world have condemned racial prejudices, racial discrimination and human rights violations at conferences and on committees.[2] Because the appeals and resolutions remained unfruitful, the General Meeting of the World Council of Churches (WCC) in Uppsala in 1968 called for a forcible action programme in the WCC to combat racism.[3] Meeting in Canterbury in August 1969, the Central Committee (CC) decided on a five-year plan, with a mandate that emphasised the connection between racism, economy and social system:

"In our ecumenical fellowship there are churches from all parts of the world, some of which have benefited and some of which have suffered from these racially exploitative economic systems. What is needed is an ecumenical act of solidarity, which would help to stem the deterioration in race relations. To do this, our action must cost something and must be constructive, visible and capable of emulation. ... We call upon the churches to move beyond charity, grants and traditional programming to relevant and sacrificial action leading to new relationships of dignity and justice among all men and to become agents for the radical reconstruction of society."[4]

In September 1970, the Executive Committee of the WCC in Arnoldshain took a resolution on the part of the programme, which triggered off the real dispute among the world churches: it was the Special Fund.[5] This fund, which was to implement the mandate, began with US $ 500,000. It was to be used for supporting organisations of the oppressed and victims of oppression. In 1970, a total of US $ 200,000 was distributed to nineteen organisations including liberation movements in Southern Africa. In 1972, the WCC replenished the Special Fund to US $ one million[6] and in 1974, the minimum annual amount was fixed at US $ 300,000.[7] At the subsequent meetings of the WCC Central Committee, the member churches from South Africa and the so-called First World repeatedly questioned certain aspects of the programme.

The PCR sought to improve the living conditions of Latin American Indians, ethnic minorities in the USA, Australia, New Zealand and the majority of blacks in Southern African countries.[8] This also affected the trading partners of those countries in Western Europe.[9] However, most countries in the former so-called

---

* First published in German as 'Das Programm des Ökumenischen Rates der Kirchen (ÖRK) zur Bekämpfung des Rassismus (PCR), afrikanische Volksrepubliken und die deutschen Kirchen' in *KZG* 9 (1996), 251–306. Revised.

Second and Third World were not only economically independent of America and Southern Africa, but also had close contacts with various liberation movements in Zimbabwe (Rhodesia), South Africa, Namibia, Angola and Mozambique.[10] Most of these movements were communist in orientation.

In the context of the entire discussion it could not be ignored, at least as background information, that the World Council of Churches was virtually entirely funded by the churches in West Germany and the United States. The 1977 financial report of the WCC showed that the contributions from the West German Protestant Church to the general funds of the WCC reached thirty-nine per cent (SFr 2,082,000) and that of the US churches amounted to thirty-seven per cent (SFr 1,937,000). The churches from all other countries together thus contributed a mere twenty-four per cent (SFr 1,279,000). The membership contribution from the East German Protestant Church, for instance, was approximately SFr 30,000.[11] The large-scale events alongside the Central Committee and general meetings of the WCC incurred further costs.[12] In order to pay for the General Meeting in Vancouver in 1983, including the organisation, the travel and accommodation expenses of delegates from the churches of poor countries[13] – not counting East Germany – the West German Protestant Church contributed DM 1.2 million.[14] In fact the sum was one million short of the expectations of the Geneva headquarters.

As for the issue of combating racism in its historical, social and economic contexts in as far as people were aware of them, a paradoxical situation arose whereby the contributing churches often found themselves in the dock. It was a court, which they themselves had funded. Moreover, they were expected to donate money to a cause that served not only to combat racism but was ultimately geared to bringing about drastic changes in the social order of the countries, from which they benefited. Oddly enough, the fact that the WCC owed its existence above all to the Western social system and its enormous economic power was never discussed. Rather, the ecumenists in the Eastern bloc states saw themselves as independent mediators in the "harsh polarity" between First and Third World Christians. The East German Church wanted to help "overcome this tension" by describing "what it means to be a church in a socialist environment because this is an issue which concerns many church representatives from developing countries with a view to their own future".[15] In mid-1974 Reverend Michael Knoch gave a talk to the East German delegates of the 1975 WCC General Meeting. It was subsequently described as "vividly controversial"[16], while at the same time being published in the *Ecumenical Review* as a quasi-official preliminary East German contribution.[17] To quote: "The social liberation brought about by socialism was bound to cause a crisis in the Protestant Church. ... Today we are confronted by the urgent task of liberating ourselves from the 'Constantine era' during which the Church for centuries exercised unquestioned spiritual power and was respected as a political force linked to the power of the state. ... Cooperation is increasing between the Church and the new society, although very cautiously and with many internal difficulties ... . When such a complex development is taking place it is inevitable that internal conflicts should arise which occasionally explode openly."[18]

During the Central Committee Meeting of the WCC in Addis Ababa in 1971 it was decided that the East German Church should become a member in its own right.[19] The question was also discussed as to whether movements that "are driven to violence as the only way left to them to redress grievance"[20] should be supported. In Utrecht (1972) investments were considered whereby racist regimes would be supported.[21] The Council of the West German Protestant Church proposed that all steps should be taken to "bring about the equality of all sections of the South African population in the area of economic development"[22]. However, the majority followed the original proposal of the Anti-Racism Committee and thus voted for non-cooperation and withdrawal of investments in companies trading with Southern Africa.[23] The WCC published lists and documents of companies and banks that granted loans or had business links with Southern Africa.[24]

The purpose of the PCR was not just to eliminate oppression motivated by racial discrimination but also to change socio-political and economic structures in the Western world. This can already be seen in some of the earlier texts. The report from the East German Church on the meeting of the WCC Central Committee at the end of August 1973 in Geneva includes the following: "It has been obvious for some time now that the issue of withdrawing investment from the territories governed by racist governments has assumed even greater significance than financial support for liberation movements. The withdrawal of investment casts considerable doubt on the very basis of the social, economic and political structures of the West and South Africa."[25]

At the Central Committee meeting in Geneva, it had also become obvious that the Eastern-bloc churches were taking a one-sided anti-Western stance in their treatment of the issues of violence, non-violence and social justice. The Council of the West German Protestant Church expressed this in the minutes of a meeting in September 1973: "Controversies arose as to whether the situation in the Eastern bloc should be taken into account. (At the passionate request from the Romanian Metropolitan and from Patriarch Nikodim, the Eastern bloc was not mentioned in the final statement of the Central Committee)."[26]

When the five-year mandate ended in 1974, the Central Committee discussed the continuation of the programme in West Berlin.[27] The PCR was included in the WCC work as a continuous project unit. At the same time a request by the West German Protestant Church was met by way of compromise, whereby the combating of racism was placed in the wider context of human rights.[28] In 1975, the General Meeting in Nairobi voted for the continuation of the PCR by a large majority and accepted the human rights catalogue[29], which was drawn up at a consultation in St Pölten (Austria).[30] In 1976, the Central Committee in Geneva decided to redefine the criteria for the Special Fund to Combat Racism.[31] It reads: "The situation in Southern Africa is recognised as a priority due to the overt and intensive nature of white racism and the increasing awareness on the part of the oppressed in their struggle for liberation."[32] The Soweto uprising of 1976 and the prohibition of anti-apartheid organisations in South Africa in 1977 led to a concentration of WCC efforts on South Africa.[33]

In 1978, the Patriotic Front of Zimbabwe received support from the WCC and the PCR once again came under vehement criticism.[34] Meeting in Kingston,

Jamaica at the beginning of January 1979, the Central Committee agreed that the member churches should undergo an eighteen-month consultation process on combating racism.[35] Following a number of regional conferences[36], the process was concluded with a world consultation in Noordwijkerhout, the Netherlands in 1980. It was agreed that the PCR should "remain an integral but distinct part of the work of the WCC" during the nineteen-eighties. The programme also included an item entitled "Racism and Church Structures" (Study Group 2).[37] In 1981, the WCC discontinued business links with three banks, which were involved in South Africa. It was the same year in which the PCR Committee met in Zimbabwe. The director of the PCR, the Dutchman Baldwin C. Sjolleman, had considerable influence on the anti-racism programme during his nine years of service. He was succeeded by the Pakistani Anwar M. Barkat in 1981.[38]

The preparatory programme for the General Meeting in Vancouver in 1983 focused particularly on combating racism.[39] At the Sixth General Meeting the importance of all the previous measures was emphasised and there was an appeal for far-reaching sanctions.[40] In late July and early August 1985 the Central Committee of the WCC published a memorandum in Buenos Aires with recommendations about Southern Africa.[41] Referring to the resolution of the national conference of the South African Council of Churches (SACC)[42], the WCC called upon its member churches to pray for an end to the unjust rule in South Africa, not to recognise the transitional government in Namibia, to step up pressure on the South African government through economic and other sanctions and to give solid support to the liberation movements. A month later, one hundred and fifty South African theologians published the so-called Kairos Document.[43] In early December 1985 an extraordinary meeting of the WCC took place in Harare, where the so-called Harare Declaration was issued.[44] It contained the demand for comprehensive and effective sanctions against the RSA by the international community, the resignation of Botha's government, the abolition of all forms of apartheid and the legalisation of all liberation movements that had been banned in the RSA. In addition they called for free and democratic elections in the RSA. The tenth anniversary of the Soweto uprising (16 June 1986) was declared a day of remembrance and of prayer for the termination of apartheid.[45] This was followed in May 1987 by the Lusaka Declaration (Zambia), where the churches re-confirmed the commitment they had declared in Harare.[46] The meeting was above all an exchange of ideas with the liberation movements of South Africa and Namibia.

By the time of the General Meeting of the WCC in Canberra in 1991, the world had not only witnessed the breakdown of the Eastern bloc and thus the strengthening of the Western social system but the end of the apartheid regime in South Africa was also in sight. Logically this meant that the WCC started to change its policy and began to advocate acts of reconciliation.[47] In January 1994, the WCC met in Johannesburg, where it celebrated the end of apartheid with the proclamation of the end of all sanctions.[48]

2.   The East German Protestant Church and the PCR

When the five-year mandate of the PCR was over, the head of the East Berlin Academy, Elisabeth Adler, gave a report in her country's *Die Kirche* (a Protestant weekly) in mid-October 1974. Ms Adler had just returned from several months work as part of the anti-racism division of the WCC. Referring to the PCR she wrote:

"It has set an example because through it the churches have overcome their inherent tendency to issue cautious statements ... . The East German Churches have support-ed this programme ever since it started. Two appeals for donations have brought in quite considerable sums. Many churches have made the effort to obtain information on the situation in Guinea-Bissau, Angola, Mozambique, Namibia, Rhodesia and South Africa and discussed the problems of those countries ... . It is still true, to some extent, that the Programme to Combat Racism is seen as 'controversial'. This is also the case in our churches ... . As the programme also supports liberation movements ... that are involved in a violent struggle, it is considered to be dubious ... . This is no doubt due to the strong impression made on churches by the non-violent struggle of Martin Luther King. It is a path, which has become an ideology in people's minds and indeed the only option that is open to Christians. At the same time, a different Protestant 'saint' is often forgotten – Dietrich Bonhoeffer, who supported the violent overthrow of Hitler because he was against a rule of violence ... . The programme has always been especially controversial in Western Europe, particularly in West Germany, Switzerland and the UK ... . These countries have close economic, political and mili-tary links [to Southern Africa] and what plays an important role is good investment opportunities, high profits through cheap (black) labour and NATO's strategic inter-est in maintaining a white bridgehead in Southern Africa. The churches do not usu-ally give reasons for their negative attitude. At the most, they accuse the WCC of be-ing one-sided in its assessment of the political situation in the world. This was done, for instance, in a recent statement[49] issued by the West German Protestant Church."[50]

The article did not mention the important reservations of the East German Protestant clergy and church members towards the PCR, thus it caused vigorous protest. In an indignant letter to *Die Kirche* Reverend Luckau from Buckow com-plained about Adler's insinuation. Apparently she claimed that the critical atti-tude of the Western European churches towards the anti-racism programme was entirely due to economic interests and that they were trying to hide this attitude behind other arguments. Luckau quoted from a discussion he had had with Theo-dor Schober, the president of the *Diakonisches Werk,* which is the West German Protestant welfare and social work organisation. Schober had said, "there seem to be some people, who have nothing better to do than to constantly attack West German churches"[51]. At the same time, Luckau wrote to Walter Pabst and point-ed out that "Ms Adler's biased article" might have negative consequences on the relationship between the churches in the two Germanys and on ecumenical dia-logue.[52] After a preliminary message, he received a reassuring letter.[53]

After taking part in one of the dissemination conferences[54], which were organ-ised by the East German Church on the anti-racism programme, Giselher Hickel summed up the problem with Elisabeth Adler and Christa Lewek, who was a member of the High Consistory: "I doubt that any consensus is tenable or even desirable between those who see East Germany as 'yet another unconstitutional state', against which a 'second front' should really be set up, and those who see this state as a suitable partner because important parts of its foreign policy can be useful to the interests of the affected nations."[55]

At the dissemination conference in 1971, Günter Krusche[56] gave a talk, in which he advanced the "theological reasons" why churches should take part in political struggles and demanded that churches should be "prepared to accept their guilt".[57] Part of the group discussion, which followed Krusche's talk was summarised as follows: "Solidarity means working with non-Christians. For us, solidarity cannot be separated from the fact that we live in a socialist country. (Solidarity is an important term in the workers' movement.) Socialist countries support the liberation movements, which means we have a partnership with communists."[58]

Not only did this "partnership" affect the sphere of foreign and East-West German politics but it also had an economic side. A large percentage of PCR donations that the churches collected was paid to the Afro-Asian Solidarity Committee of the GDR (AASK). Of the 900,000 East German marks collected in a campaign in the summer of 1971 the AASK was given 500,000 marks.[59] The AASK also submitted "proposals for the involvement of the charity organisation *Brot für die Welt* (*Bread for the World*) in solidarity aid for liberation organisations in Portuguese colonies".[60] This programme was adopted by the churches and *Bread for the World* organised a number of special collection campaigns for this anti-racism programme.[61] The secretary of the AASK, a certain Dr Scharf, was invited to the relevant church conferences as if it was a matter of course and was sent a friendly letter, which thanked him for his participation.[62] Dr Scharf also chaired East Germany's solidarity committee, into which the East German Churches and *Bread for the World* paid 1,637,500 East German marks towards projects in Africa, Vietnam and Chile from 1972 to 1975.[63] The Ecumenical Commission tried to find a common theological and political denominator for this cooperation: "What does our cooperation with the Afro-Asian Solidarity Committee mean for the implementation of the Programme to Combat Racism? To put it differently, can the socialist idea of solidarity make any practical contribution to the theory and practice of welfare and social work at the WCC?"[64]

The cooperation between Church and State, which was based on a mutual agreement at the highest level, did not take account of the conflicts between the denominational leadership and individual ministers. Reverend Manfred Hertel from Neukirchen wrote to Bishop Schönherr explaining that he had taken the liberty to change the appeal for donations that was issued in February 1971:[65] "All we need now is an 'action call for anti-class struggle activities and an anti-class hatred programme'. ... By class struggle and class hatred we understand man's suppression of people, who hold different worldviews, in particular the presumptuous conviction of superiority and privileges held by those preaching this struggle and hatred."[66]

Schönherr replied: "Unlike racism, one cannot dispute the fact that the class struggle is justified ... . Neither can it be denied that there is a connection between racism and exploitation ... . Although it is understandable if a person is annoyed at certain peculiar phenomena, I believe that one should not ignore the historical justification of the class struggle. After all, our workers did not achieve their rights through sympathetic Christian understanding or brotherly love but thanks to the massive class struggle of the trade unions and they need to make use of this class struggle again and again, as can be seen in numerous strikes in many areas throughout the world."[67]

When the Executive Committee of the WCC met in Bad Saarow in 1974, the East German Protestant Church asked the secretary of state for Church Issues if he would consent to at least ten per cent of all PCR donations being transferred directly to Geneva.[68] However, because East Germany was suffering from a shortage of hard currency funds he continued to insist that financial help should be channelled through East German institutions. This serious limitation gave the East German Protestant Church, against its will, the advantage that it did not have to discuss the Special Fund in the local churches thus avoiding any direct confrontation with the West German Protestant Churches, who were supporting the fund financially.[69]

Even the disseminators from the churches, who had successfully gone through the "necessary thinking and learning process"[70] at the anti-racism conferences of the East German Protestant Church could not prevent a number of lay people and clergy asking critical questions about their own country. However, they twisted the argument into the exact opposite: "Solidarity does not mean escaping from our own situation. It helps us see that a 'cold' in East Germany is nothing compared with the 'ulcer' in Southern Africa."[71]

This comparative interpretation is also interesting from a psychological point of view, as it contains an important element of exoneration in view of the oppressive situation in East Germany. By comparing their own life with the conditions of the black population in the white apartheid states, any observers who were also living under oppression would feel that the human rights violations in East Germany were trivial and not worth mentioning. Compared to South African racism, East Germany seemed to progressive Christians like a humane state with high ideals.

The State Department for Church Issues did not fail to notice the critical voices of Protestant clergy within the anti-racism programme. Its functionaries, therefore, expressed their views to the head of the Church's ecumenical relations division, Pabst: "Alien ideas are systematically being infiltrated among the clergy from outside." According to Pabst's own file memo he denied that this was the case: "I said that a minority of clergy and local churches were reserved about the anti-racism programme and that, so far, we had not received donations from all churches. However, I pointed out that I was not aware of any explicit counter-movement against the official political line of the Church or of any systematic propaganda against the activities of the WCC."[72]

However, at the beginning of 1974, Bishop Werner Krusche of Magdeburg in the Protestant diocese of Saxony, wrote to Ms Lewek, a councillor of the East German consistory. He pointed out that "there was no small number of clergymen who have questions about the anti-racism programme of the World Council of Churches. The clergy we sent to the Dissemination Conference in 1972 ... came home with critical questions that had not been answered."[73] The bishop offered to send about fifteen clergy from his diocese to a conference with specialists, so that they could form their "own well-founded views". The Catechetical Seminary in Naumburg and the ecclesiastic college of the diocese of Saxony had already formed their own view. In summer 1973, it set up a petition as part of its movement "Freedom for Nelson Mandela" and asked East and West German Protestant Churches to support its efforts.[74]

In summer 1973, the PCR Commission asked Elisabeth Adler to assess the work that had been done until then.[75] Her analysis was to help prepare the recommendations for the future mandate of the PCR, which were due to be made by the Central Committee in 1974.[76]

At the thirty-first conference of the Governing Bodies of Protestant Churches in East Germany on 12 and 13 July 1974, the draft proposal of the WCC Commission for an extension of the PCR mandate was accepted without any discussion.[77] The speed of this resolution was surprising as a day before the conference, the Protestant consistory of Görlitz had written a letter to the secretary-general of the WCC, which stated that although in principle they would support the continuation of the mandate they wanted to press for considerable modifications:[78]

"We feel that it is right to extend the mandate. As regards the question of implementation, we believe that a distinction needs to be made concerning the issue of violence. The issue cannot just be ignored. It needs to be asked whether the whole struggle against racism should not be put into the wider horizon of speaking out for the enforcement of human rights in general, throughout the world, so that certain serious and depressing issues are not left aside. We would also like to point out that our governing body has passed a resolution whereby 'the donations contributed by our local churches should only be given to movements that do not use the method of taking or killing hostages, who can be expected by the WCC not to replace one tyranny by another, but who want to create a fairer and more free social order than the one currently in existence in their country'. We have been given the undertaking that this request would be taken into account."[79]

In its publication entitled *Information on the Anti-Racism Programme of the WCC*[80], which was aimed at local churches, the East German Protestant Church justified its involvement in the PCR by giving information on the liberation movements it supported, which included those from block party sources.[81] It also printed the resolutions of the Central Committee. Another information brochure entitled *Live Together and for One Another*[82] (in early 1975) gave details to local churches on the struggle of the churches against apartheid. In these publications, Christian and "real socialist" concerns were continually mixed. The bibliography included a work by the East German CDU (Christian Democratic Union) on *Anti-Racism and Anti-Imperialism*[83] as well as a book issued by the East German publishing company *VEB Deutscher Verlag der Wissenschaften* entitled *African National Leaders and Their Opponents*.[84]

On 10 and 11 January 1975, the conference of Governing Bodies unanimously approved a third appeal for PCR donations during Passion Week.[85] The money was to be channelled through the welfare and social work organisations of the member churches to the Church's headquarters in East Berlin.[86] As parts of the clergy continued to harbour critical attitudes, the East German Protestant Church also used visits from the Geneva headquarters in its endeavour to change people's minds. When Reverend Alexander Kirby visited East Berlin in October 1976, he was taken to a Christian teaching seminar in Ludwigsfelde by Althausen and Adler because "when a visit had been made to the church district of Zossen ... there had been criticism of the anti-racism programme"[87]. Adler felt that Kirby's talks and assessments in Ludwigsfelde and elsewhere had done the East German Protestant Church "an important service in the creation of greater awareness ... . It was Kirby's first visit to member churches of the WCC since he had started to work for them and it was also his first visit to a socialist country. He met covert opponents of the anti-racism programme and people who were sceptical. Above all, however, he met people who were very open-minded and prepared to find things out and to learn."[88]

In September 1975, six years after the launch of the PCR the WCC held a consultation on "Racism in Theology – Theology against Racism".[89] According to the Ecumenical Study Group on Welfare and Social Work[90] of the East German Protestant Church this was the first "thorough treatment of theological issues raised by the Programme to Combat Racism".[91] In its paper, which was written with the PCR in mind, the Study Group proposed new theological reflections on the understanding of sin, the commission to bring about reconciliation, suffering and solidarity. The section of the consultation entitled "What kind of community?" (III, 2) was criticised by the East German Protestant Church: "We are surprised that this section contains no constructive ideas. In essence it distances itself from Marxist ideas and presents a limited acceptance of Marxist analysis."[92]

Following the Soweto uprising on 16 June 1976, the Ecumenical Missionary Centre in East Berlin intensified its anti-racism activities. A Southern Africa Study Group under the centre's director Heinz Blauert issued an informative circular[93], discussed a manuscript by Albrecht entitled *Churches in Southern Africa*, reviewed publications on "black theology" and put together bibliographical overviews of South Africa and its churches. The centre served as a forum not only for African and European theologians but also for Marxist scholars, such as Dr Alfred Babing[94] from the Institute of International Politics and Economics. In his talk to the churches he said: "From the very beginning the GDR has pursued anti-imperialist and anti-racist principles. Once the anti-imperialist principle is recognised and followed, then any discrimination against other races is excluded. The history of the GDR gives evidence that this is true: within three decades racism has been exterminated in the GDR. Fascism and racism developed out of colonialism, which is based on class structures. Class structures presuppose capitalist groups of private companies. The GDR has no private capitalist involvement in the socialist states and class structures and racism were exterminated in the GDR. So there are no longer any conditions for expansion or exploitation."[95]

In anticipation of the publication of his book on Namibia, Babing also reported on the "SED-Swapo agreement on long-term collaboration in vocational training and specialised management".[96] As soon as the Ecumenical Missionary Centre became involved, Adler, who also belonged to the centre, pointed out that any overlaps in content or target group should be avoided if possible.[97] Like all activities in this area the work of the centre met with criticism among the local churches. The minutes of the Study Group meeting of 8 June 1977 contains the note: "Critical questions from the local churches about the involvement of the Ecumenical Missionary Centre in the combating of racism are to ... be taken into account."[98] On another occasion the minutes read: "So far we have not succeeded in motivating local churches to take any substantial interest in supporting the churches in Southern Africa."[99]

From 1976 onwards, the East German Protestant publication *Information on the Anti-Racism Programme of the WCC* began to give a considerable amount of coverage to the situation in the United States. In-depth documentation was provided about Reverend Benjamin Chavis and the *Wilmington Ten,* the civil rights movement that fought for the rights of black Americans as guaranteed by the US Constitution. It also gave information on the fate of civil rights activists and the attitude of the WCC and published the life stories of those affected and interviews with their relatives.[100] By reprinting a 1977 *Time* magazine article on America's working class, the Ecumenical Study Group on Welfare and Social Work of the East German Protestant Church confirmed the Marxist theory that there is a connection between racism, capitalism and class structure.[101] In comparison, the deficits of a "socialist" society were seen as minor and reparable. Not a word was said about human rights violations in the Eastern bloc, the suppression of ethnic minorities and cases of unlawful incarceration. It was also not taken into consideration that the legal scandals in the USA and elsewhere in the Western world achieved so much publicity because of the free press.

A memo from Lewek to Stolpe in May 1978 shows how carefully the East German Protestant Church chose its foreign representatives and that some of the criteria were political. In coordination with von Brück and Adler, it was decided that Detlef Peter should be appointed a member of the East German Peace Delegation at the World Conference for the Elimination of Racism and Racial Discrimination in Basle. Not only was he knowledgeable but he was also "fully aligned with the Protestant Church" and Lewek said she would be giving him "political and ecclesiastical assistance".[102] Once again this world conference dealt with the relationship between racism, fascism, imperialism and colonialism.[103]

During the sixty-second conference of Governing Bodies of Protestant Churches in East Germany on 6 and 7 July 1979, Christa Lewek, Götz Planer-Friedrich[104] and Christoph Demke explained the assessment of the WCC background paper "South Africa today – hope at what price?"[105], which was prepared by the Ecumenical Study Group. An intensive discussion followed with the "participation of Dr Fränkel, Haberecht, Große, Dr Schönherr, Dr Planer-Friedrich, Dr Falcke, Dr Zeddies, Lewek, Dr Demke, Cieslak and Dr Krusche".[106] Falcke, Lewek and Demke were asked to submit a revised paper during the conference. The modified assessment[107] was accepted with one abstention and sent to the WCC. In the covering letter the study group said the paper contained a description of "the current state of our thoughts on the issue of using violence in the struggle against racism in South Africa", which formed "a first contribution to the consultation process ... initiated by the Kingston resolutions".[108] Konrad Raiser replied on behalf of the WCC secretary-general: "I have read the text closely and find it in many ways excellent. In particular, it seems to me that section two about theological aspects on the issue of using violence in South Africa is a very important contribution."[109]

The director of the PCR programme, Baldwin Sjollema, was also very pleased with the assessment from the East German Protestant Church and its information booklet no. 13 on the anti-racism programme. In a letter, he asked Lewek if he could duplicate and distribute the booklet as "information for the many German-speaking groups, who come to the Ecumenical Centre here".[110] Lewek replied that it would be the pleasure of the East German Protestant Church.[111] In its assessment the East German Protestant Church did not exclude the use of violence as a means to achieve social justice. Being aware that all Christians are involved in a web of guilt due to difficult living conditions around the world, it demanded discernment and solidarity with those among the oppressed, who chose to use violence to eliminate the injustice they have suffered.

In January 1979, the WCC Central Committee passed a resolution in Jamaica, whereby the member churches should initiate a consultation process on possible forms of church-based anti-racism work. This was followed by a regional consultation in Sigtuna, Sweden, at the beginning of March 1980. The conference of Governing Bodies of Protestant Churches in East Germany decided to send Elisabeth Adler, Ludwig Große, Götz Planer-Friedrich and Wolf-Dietrich Gutsch[112] as representatives of the Protestant churches.[113] When the Central Committee in Geneva decided to continue prioritising the PCR in August 1980[114] the Governing Bodies replied that they would also continue helping to combat racism throughout the 1980s and that they again would make a special appeal for funds to fulfil their pledge.[115]

At their 76th conference on 13 and 14 November 1981, the Governing Bodies decided that another appeal for donations for the victims of racism was to be held during Passion Week 1982[116] and invited the East German free churches[117] to join in the campaign.[118] However, the Association of Free Evangelical Churches replied with one single sentence, which simply declared "it would not participate in the donation appeal".[119]

Sjollema's circular of February 1981, which included programme categories for 1981, contained an interesting note: "One result of the consultation process is the realisation that combating racism at an international level is inseparably linked to combating it within our countries and that we need to be equally involved at both levels if the activities of the churches are to remain credible."[120]

At the end of 1981, the chief representative of the African National Congress in East Germany, Antony Mongalo, informed the East German Protestant Church that the ANC would be celebrating its seventieth anniversary on 8 February 1982. Bishop Werner Krusche, the chairman of the Governing Bodies of Protestant Churches, replied that until now the East German Protestant Church had "taken a very active part" in combating racism in South Africa until present day and that this had "led to our representatives attending good talks at your residence, where we obtained important information about your situation".[121] Moreover, he enclosed a copy of his denomination's donation appeal for 1982, which particularly mentioned "an ANC project – the Morogoro School".[122] In mid-March 1982,

Lewek thanked Mongalo for the "good meetings at your residence, where you gave us such valuable information, both verbal and visual on the situation of the ANC".[123] With her letter she enclosed the East German Protestant information material on combating racism. She also sent this material to the secretary-general of the East German Peace Council, Werner Rümpel. She says, among other things: "Our participation in the anti-racism programme of the World Council of Churches forms an important part of the East German Protestant Church's commitment to peace and justice, in fact the relationship between them is inseparable."[124]

In October 1983, the Theological Studies Division of the East German Protestant Church submitted an internal study on the "Roots of Racism". Götz Planer-Friedrich summed up the results in an essay, in which he commented on the mutual understanding between his denomination and the political aims of the GDR on the issue of anti-racism, while at the same time he rejected all allegations of "political opportunism".[125] Instead, he emphasised that the impetus for their involvement came from the WCC, as did the theological endeavour to identify guilt and to bring about a desire for change. In his further argument Planer-Friedrich moves into the realm of multi-factor arguments, in which he makes use of both "bourgeois" and Marxist approaches. In addition to socio-psychological, sociological and economic factors, which are of empirical sociological provenance, he incorporated elements of Marxist-Leninist ideology particularly in regard to the concept of ownership.

Following the memorandum on South Africa from the WCC Central Committee in Buenos Aires the Synod of the East German Protestant Church responded in September 1985 with a statement on the escalation of violence in South Africa. It called upon people to "pray ... for the victims of apartheid and for those fighting for their liberation, to express solidarity in word and deed ... and to support the anti-racism programme of the WCC in East Germany with renewed and deliberate effort".[126]

At the conference on 3 and 4 July 1987, the Governing Bodies of Protestant Churches in East Germany supported an appeal to the churches, in which they reconfirmed their unity with the WCC on the issue of racism. They also underlined the WCC's resolutions, called for the release of Nelson Mandela and asked church members to remember the people and churches in Southern Africa in various ways.[127]

3.   The Lessons of Mozambique and Angola

On 6 August 1975, a good month after the former Portuguese colony of Mozambique had gained her independence, Bishop Schönherr wrote a letter to the National Christian Council of Mozambique.[128] When he immediately contacted the churches of the young state, this was in accordance with the priorities of the GDR's foreign policies because Mozambique was one of the African "focus countries", to which the SED regime paid special attention. As Schönherr was probably unaware of the Christian institutions and their dignitaries in Mozambique he did not address his letter to the National Christian Council but to the president of the Synod Council of the Presbyterian Church, Isaias Funzamo. The Presbyterian churches in Southern Africa traditionally were rather reserved in matters of political theology.[129] In his letter, Schönherr reminded the Christians in Mozambique of the help the East German churches had given to the liberation movement. Donations in the form of material aid, which had been channelled through East Germany's official Solidarity Committee, had reached the former Portuguese colony via various church organisations.[130] For example, the WCC covered half the costs of a school maths book published in 1971, which was regarded a "prestige object of East German solidarity" and a "symbol of the solid political alliance between the GDR and the liberation movements".[131] In actual fact the book was "profoundly political" and "closely linked with the experiences and events of the armed liberation struggle".[132] In his letter to Isaias Funzamo, Bishop Schönherr expressed his desire to be in continuous contact with the Christian Council and to initiate mutual visits:

"We are moved when we think of Eduardo Mondlane, the former leader of Frelimo[133], who gave his life in the struggle for your country's independence and the just and peaceful togetherness of its people. We met him at the World Council of Churches ... . We have been following all the news from Mozambique with great solidarity. During the last few years our churches in East Germany have done what they could, under their circumstances, to give practical help to those people in your country who were fighting in the liberation movement as well as to humanitarian needs in the liberated areas."[134]

After the sixth general meeting of the Lutheran World Federation in Dar-es-Salaam in June 1977[135], the East German Protestant Church wanted to send the delegates Elisabeth Adler and Ulrich von Brück to Mozambique. However, this met with unexpected disapproval from the SED regime. In a memo, the Church's head of ecumenism, Pabst, commented on a discussion he had had with the secretary of state for Church Issues: "I pointed out that one would be risking a certain consequence for our Church colleagues and Church members if it became known that we were now not permitted to visit the churches in this country, which enjoys good relations with ours."[136]

However, Lewek and Stolpe did not give up but staunchly continued to try to obtain permission for the visit through various channels. The hand-written correspondence between Lewek and Pabst shows that the two were somewhat irritated by each other. Lewek apparently felt that Pabst had not even read the church politics draft strategies and that he had either lost or mislaid them.[137] Sjollema advised Lewek to abandon her contacts with the Presbyterians in Mozambique and to cultivate links with the National Christian Council. Schönherr then wrote to Mahlalela on 21 March 1977 asking for an official invitation.[138] To the Presbyterian, Funzamo, who had written on 11 May saying that he would like to travel to East Germany, the East German Protestant Church wrote in its turn on 6 and 27 June 1977 stating that it was "not currently in a position ... to be visited by your representatives [from Mozambique] here".[139]

On 27 July 1977, Lewek wrote to Secretary of State Seigewasser reminding him that Schönherr's letter of 1 June about Mozambique had been left unanswered for two months. She said it was impossible to explain to local churches "why the commitment they showed in supporting the WCC's anti-racism programme should not find its logical continuation in the form of direct contacts with the National Christian Council in the now independent Mozambique."[140] She pointed out that Geneva was in favour of the intended visit and that some lively mutual visits at political level between the two countries had long since been practiced. As early as 1975, East Germany began to train 110 Frelimo leaders at its Department of State Security, while 140 guerrillas were trained by the Ministry of the Interior and GDR border guards.[141] By 1983, 1,200 East German citizens were working in Mozambique.

As Lewek still had not received a response by mid-September 1977, she rang Horst Dohle at Seigewasser's department. He apologised and told her the letter had been forgotten over the holiday period.[142] Lewek visited the department on 15 September and the conflict was resolved. Both parties reassured each other that the delay had been caused by various slip-ups and misunderstandings. The East German government had no reservations about Adler and von Brück travelling to Mozambique[143], especially because they "fully trusted ... the two people".[144] Nevertheless, the two East German ecumenists were still not given a visa to enter the friendly socialist country. Neither were theologians from Mozambique permitted to enter East Germany, for the time being.[145]

However, the root of the problem was neither a misunderstanding between State and Church in East Germany nor a deliberate harassment of the Protestant Church on the part of the German Socialist State. In fact the churches in Mozambique had refrained from applying to the Communist regime in Maputo for an entry visa for the East German delegates, which was probably intended to demonstrate their independence. As a result the "comrades in Mozambique" asked the East German Foreign Ministry "to strengthen their position towards the churches by ... not granting an exit visa to the East German Protestant representatives for as long as the Mozambican churches were unwilling to cooperate with the relevant state authorities in international relations". This issue was apparently of considerable importance to the Mozambique government.[146]

After a government reshuffle in Mozambique in 1978, the new minister of the interior even rejected all visits from foreign church dignitaries to the new People's Republic.[147] On the personal initiative of President Machel, the communist regime began to pursue a ruthless strategy of subjugation against the churches, which was reminiscent of the Ulbricht era in East Germany.[148] The churches lost all the "privileges they had enjoyed during colonial times"[149], became subject to the Ministry of Justice and had to coordinate all intended activities with the state. All missionary schools were put under state control. The various religious denominations were completely ousted from the educational system. In this process, the Roman Catholic Church turned out to be the "toughest organised opponent of the Frelimo party and the People's Republic within the country, both ideologically and at a practical political level". The Roman Catholic clergy were "apparently not willing to work together with the people's government".[150]

The PCR gifts from the East German Protestant Church had, therefore, unwittingly helped to place in power a regime that pursued an uncompromising policy of suppression towards religious groups. Alongside the Eastern bloc, the WCC had toppled a colonial regime, only to have it replaced by a Communist dictatorship. For the churches in Mozambique the political change from one dictatorship to another clearly meant a deterioration in their freedom to work and to be influential because under the new regime the relationship between state and Church followed the pattern of the Communist dictatorships in the Eastern bloc.

Once the small Protestant denominations of Mozambique had unconditionally submitted to the new political situation, the president of the National Christian Council, Isaac David Mahlalela, was eventually permitted to visit East Germany in June 1980[151] and November 1983. He was accompanied by Elisabeth Adler and Maria Herrbruck, the head of the Ecumenical Division of the East German Protestant Church, on his visit to the State Department for Church Issues. He explained that "all problems had been clarified amicably" in a discussion with Machel at the end of 1982 and that church representatives would now be "invited to all the important political events".[152] Until 1985, East Germany, which was the fourth biggest trading partner of Mozambique and had considerable influence on the country's leadership[153], continued to do nothing to ease the oppressive religious policy of the regime. However, the nationalisation of church property, in particular hospitals, led to a marked deterioration in medical provision, the educational system suffered considerable damage and less and less charitable help was provided for the needy. No doubt partly due to the decline in the country as a result of the civil war[154] from 1984 onwards, Frelimo felt compelled to change its policy towards the churches and sought advice from the East Germans in East Berlin and the GDR embassy in Maputo. This was no mere coincidence. In 1984, Job Mabalane Chambal had been appointed head of the Religious Affairs Division of Mozambique's Ministry of Justice. From 1970 to 1975, Chambal had attended the Karl Marx Party College of the GDR state party, after which he worked as the principal of the Frelimo Party College, headed a rural development programme and was made a "Hero of the People's Republic of Mozambique". In 1985, he studied "State-Church relations" in East Germany, Hungary and the USSR and reported to the delegates of his former ideological training ground for new cadres about the state of affairs in the German "workers and peasants state":[155] "Apparently they were now facing the different task of toning down, balancing or where possible correcting these attacks [against the church]. However, there is currently no central policy on this matter. Some see this as resignation or weakness and are resisting such a line ... . In all, it has turned out to be impossible to isolate the church as a political factor or to push it out into a position of insignificance. The party leaders agree that it is now necessary to invest as much as possible in the development of society. This is to be done, above all, through the 'Mozambication' of the church."[156]

However, in this statement the Mozambican communists were primarily thinking of Roman Catholicism. As for the smaller Protestant denominations, Chambal felt that they had turned into willing helpmates of national reconstruction without having cultivated their own agenda during the preceding twelve years. "When working with the various reformed churches, which were organised in the Christian Council of Mozambique (CCM), one might make use of the relatively active social involvement of these churches ... . An agreement has been concluded between the government and the CCM, allowing the tax-free import of products [food, etc.]. Some of these products are sold. The profit is used by the CCM in those regions to improve the social infrastructure (schools, nursery schools and hospitals), in accordance with the focal areas specified by the government. There are no problems at all, as the CCM is making no claims with regard to the actual contents, e.g. the syllabus, etc."[157]

According to the state documents, the People's Republic of Mozambique wanted to adopt the State-Church system of East Germany as much as possible. They sent a functionary of their Religious Affairs Division to East Germany to become familiar with the work done by the secretary of state for Church Issues and sent a party college graduate to East Berlin to study theology at the Humboldt University. Moreover, "progressive" East German theologians were to help establish a faculty of theology in Mozambique.[158] At the East German embassy in Maputo, twenty-five Mozambican church representatives of different denominations attended lectures and were shown films on the positive model of "Church-State Relations in East Germany".[159]

Until the end of August 1989, the SED regime made further efforts to explore all "options to implement GDR policies in Southern Africa by working together with the churches".[160] When Chambal visited Salzer, the chargé d'affaires at the East German embassy in Maputo, in mid-August 1989, one subject of discussion was that the East German State Department for Church Issues should examine the Mozambican parliamentary bill on religious freedom to assess whether it was suitable. In the course of the discussion, Salzer declared "our interest in promoting the cooperation between the East German and Mozambican churches, in coordination with the government of Mozambique".[161] The East German Protestant Church was already well prepared. Chambal took this opportunity to thank the East German Church for the delivery of twenty-seven tonnes of clothes and one hundred tonnes of cement, which had arrived in May and August that year.

During the 1980s, it was not only clergy but also numerous Mozambicans from other walks of life, who visited East Germany as a showcase socialist country in order to learn how to achieve industrial victories. Moreover, the value of their labour was offset against the large debts, which by then Mozambique owed East Germany,[162] in other words a modern slave system. The workers were put up in remote hostels and during their spare time did not even have the opportunity to take part in local church events. These severe restrictions of the visitors' movements prompted East German theologians in early February 1988 to raise the matter at the State Department for Church Issues. "The Mozambicans are still having problems with the racial prejudices of their German colleagues at work and there is also an alcohol problem among the Mozambicans."[163] They suggested that the concerns of the Mozambicans should be specially emphasised to the church representatives responsible for counselling non-Germans. At the same time, they asked that the Mozambicans should always have "opportunities to go to church services" and to permit their "participation in retreats during their holidays and in their spare time".

The director of religious affairs at the Ministry of Justice in Mozambique, who was alarmed by such reports from East Germany, asked the East German ambassador to shed some light on the attitude of the East German Protestant Church. This was the end of September 1989. An East German church delegation was expected in early October and in view of the country's own State-Church problems there were concerns that one might be importing "counter-revolutionary" aspirations.[164]

East Germany also tried to gain influence over the Christian churches in Angola and supported the further training of Angolan theologians at East German colleges.[165] The East Berlin theologian and university lecturer, Carl-Jürgen Kaltenborn, researched the situation of the Angolan churches between 1978 and 1986 through a number of study trips to Cuba and Angola, which he also undertook on behalf of the Christian Peace Conference (CPC) in Prague.[166] According to Kaltenborn, the Angolan Council of Evangelical Churches (Conselho Angolano de Igrejas Evangélicas – CAIE)[167], which was established in February 1977, was greatly interested in East German churches in order to "learn from the experiences in a socialist society how the Angolan churches could build up a socialist society in Angola".[168] In October 1983, the East German ambassador to Angola, Johannes Schöche, sent a telegram from Luanda to East Berlin, which stated that the secretary-general of CAIE, Daniel Ntoni Nzinga, had expressed his "gratitude for the good working relationship with partner churches and state institutions in East Germany and for the amicable reception of their delegations and church figures travelling to East Germany."[169]

The CAIE also turned out to be very willing to learn. In October 1984, it submitted a memorandum on issues of "peace, justice and development in the People's Republic of Angola", which was met with the undivided approval of its East Berlin mentors.[170] Until that year, religious affairs had come under the auspices of the Ideology Division of the MPLA-PdA (*Movimento Popular de Libertaçao de Angola – Partido Democratico de Angola*) Central Committee. However, in 1984, they were placed in the hands of a newly created National Office for Religious Affairs, which was a branch of the State Department of Culture.[171] In the same year Daniel Ntoni Nzinga became president of the Ecumenical Association of Third World Theologians (EATWOT). In 1985, he passed his office as CAIE secretary-general to a relative of his wife's, Josè Belo Chipenda, and went to East Germany with his wife to study there for a number of years.[172]

As early as 1983, Daniel Ntoni Nzinga said to the East German ambassador in Luanda: "He said the trip of the last delegation in September in particular gave them some extremely interesting experiences and insights into the life of Christians in socialism, into ways in which Christian and Marxist forces could work together for the good of the working population. The commemorative events on Luther showed them how the common heritage of a nation's revolutionary forces can and should be used for the present and the future. This was also relevant to Angola."[173]

In the years to come, Kaltenborn intensified his contacts with Angola through trips and sought to extend the ecclesiastical links between the two countries.[174] At the end of August 1989, embassy secretary Hußner spoke to Lisboa Santos, who had been the national director of Religious Affairs since 1987, about the church policies of the MPLA-PdA and the role of the churches in Angola. "Since the armed liberation struggle, the MPLA had enjoyed a largely constructive relationship with the Protestant churches, which then developed mostly without problems. They were actively committed to MPLA-PdA policy and propagated the aims and the essence of the policy of mercy and national harmony in a variety of ways. It can be assumed that the churches were aware of general national aims and contributed to the development of Angolan identity."[175]

The relationship with the Roman Catholic Church was far more difficult. Having lost its status as the country's state religion, it was now branded as the official colonial Church. Jehovah's Witnesses and Muslims were not permitted in Angola. Where Hußner had problems was the fact that the person responsible for church issues in the Central Committee of the MPLA-PdA, Roberto Almeida, took an orthodox Marxist position.

On 14 February 1990, the Methodist bishop, Emilio de Carvalho, hosted a discussion with the East German ambassador, Bernd Hüttner, on the bishop's request. Carvalho expressed his concern that "the over-hasty unification of East and West Germany would endanger many social achievements, which the churches in East Germany had also supported. Knowing of the existing social conditions in developed capitalist countries, including the USA, he felt that the capitalist system could not offer any future to mankind and assumed that in a few years' time socialist ideas would arise from capitalism itself and from the developing countries and would, in turn, contribute to overcoming capitalism."[176] If we assume that the bishop actually said this, then his words provide positive feedback that the ideological endeavours of the Communist countries had borne fruit in Angola.

East Germany pursued similar interests not only in Mozambique and Angola but also in other parts of the region.[177] In a memo of 20 April 1989, the East German Foreign Ministry developed a number of ideas on how foreign policies towards Namibia[178] and South Africa could be implemented through the churches. "As the churches have a considerable amount of influence on the masses both in Namibia and in South Africa and are involved in the liberation struggle as in no other African country, it could be very beneficial for the foreign policies of the GDR if East German churches were to have contacts with these churches."[179]

In addition to the Christian Peace Conference (CPC), it was planned that the Gossner Mission and Study Group III of the East German Protestant Church should play an important role. In matters of African policy, the CPC had good connections to the Gossner Mission. As early as 1977, Reverend Schülzgen and Reverend Heyroth had reported on their trip to Zambia and on the liberation struggle in Zimbabwe. "The [two] clergymen emphasised their impression that Zambia was strongly westernised and that it was taking its cue very clearly from Western patterns of development. (Schülzgen mentioned Tanzania as a counterexample, a country he had visited in 1974.)[180] Everyone he spoke to had shown great solidarity with the liberation movement. In this context the Zambian church representatives had asked about the attitudes of Christians and the churches to the liberation movement ... . The churches in East Germany were asked to support the movement on an ecumenical level."[181]

However, once the independence process had started in Namibia on 1 April 1989 (UN Resolution 435), East Germany did not manage to proceed further than writing extensive memos on the situation of "Churches and Religious Groups in Namibia".[182] The breakdown of the East German government eventually prevented any implementation of its far-reaching plans. Namibia celebrated its independence on 21 March 1990 and although the GDR opened an embassy in Windhoek, which was incidentally its last embassy, there was no time left for the accreditation of its ambassador. The plan had been to use the Protestant Church as a springboard for culture and politics: "The development of contacts between East German and Namibian churches might lead to a much broader sphere of action in the bilateral relationship between the two countries. The Swapo representation in East Germany has repeatedly shown great interest in establishing contacts between East German and Namibian churches. So far contacts at church level have only been sporadic (in 1983, for example, Bishop Dumeni attended the Luther celebrations in East Germany)."[183]

This assessment was largely the result of a discussion between Zeise, from the East German embassy in Zimbabwe, and Bishop Kleopas Dumeni on 6 April 1989.[184] On 8 May 1989, the chairman of the Governing Bodies of Protestant Churches in East Germany, Bishop Leich, sent a letter to the secretary-general of the Christian Council of Namibia, Abisai Shevajali.[185] This was the first time that the East German Protestant Church had contacted the Namibian Christian Council since 1 April 1989. In the letter the East German Protestant Church assured the Namibians of their support and confessed their historical responsibility for the cruelties of German colonial policy.

Where military aid was concerned, East Germany had invested in the victorious liberation movements since 1967. As well as civilian goods, it had been supplying Zapu (Southern Rhodesia), the ANC and Swapo with "weapons and equipment ... [from] the East German army, police force and secret service. From 1971 onwards, 'cadres' from developing countries and liberation movements were trained at the Institute for International Relations, part of the Law College of the Department of State Security in Potsdam-Eiche."[186] A large part of the training programme of the liberation movements took place in East Germany. Between 1976 and 1979, East Germany alone gave payments in kind (including paramilitary items), which totalled 21.1 million East German marks to Zapu, 10 million marks to the ANC and 12.2 million marks to Swapo. Representatives of the military wing of the South African ANC, Umkhonto weSizwe ("Spear of the Nations" military cadre), recall that the continuous military training of their members had started in East Germany as early as the nineteen-sixties ... . By 1986/87, East Germany only came second to the USSR in training the largest number of military cadre guerrillas. East Germany offered the ANC six-month courses for 40 men at a time. This started in 1976 and continued for a period of twelve years. According to estimates made by ANC members over a thousand guerrillas were trained in East Germany.[187]

The training took place at secret camps of the Department of State Security near the small town of Teterow, in Mecklenburg. In addition to the "general training", special training was also provided for small groups and individuals. "Ronnie Kasrils, the former head of the ANC's military secret service and today's deputy minister of defence, stressed the very flexible character of the East German training, compared with other Eastern European states."[188] One can easily imagine how much intensive contact has continued between the East German trainers and their grateful students from Southern Africa to the present day, despite the political events that have occurred since then.

4.   The problem of sufficient WCC representation of the Eastern bloc churches (excursus)

Although from the very beginning the East German Protestant Church had enjoyed considerable social standing in Geneva, its representatives felt that it was not sufficiently represented at the various levels of ecumenical activities, in other words on the committees, commissions and in the WCC staff. Thus they tried to think of ways in which the situation might be remedied. Alongside the Ecumenical Commission, the head of the Ecumenical Institute in Berlin, Althausen (a one time member of the Office of Education in Geneva) drafted a memorandum on the "representation of East German churches in standing ecumenical committees", which recommended that the following should be covered: "Programmes in the World Mission and Evangelism Department, greater representation in the Programme to Combat Racism, the Commission of the Communications Department, editorial groups of the magazines and perhaps the Christian health commission."[189]

The East German Protestant Church was also seeking permanent representation in the programmes of the Section for Church and Society. "As things are at the moment (i. e. too much Western European-American orientation of the programmes), it would probably only be beneficial, for the time being, if we participated vigorously and at the same time very critically in the work on the issues at hand." Moreover, he felt it was "desirable to have a suitable representation of the GDR churches on the nomination committee of the General Meeting. This will be particularly difficult. We should, therefore, try all the more to keep up contacts with the secretary-general and David Gill, the secretary of the General Meeting." He said it was vital, during the preparations for the Fifth General Meeting of the WCC "to try to invite Dr Konrad Raiser, the deputy secretary-general for Programme Planning, and the secretary for the General Meeting, Reverend David Gill, to extensive visits to East Germany".[190]

The Governing Bodies of Protestant Churches in East Germany were extremely well informed about the Ecumenical Commission[191], had obtained lists of "East German members on ecumenical world committees" from Pabst[192] and apparently supported the staffing policy aims.[193] The meeting of the Ecumenical Commission on 9 August 1973 was recorded in the minutes as follows: "At the next

Ecumenical Commission we wish to discuss which representatives from the East German churches should be proposed to participate in which WCC committees. For this purpose we suggest contacting the most important WCC member churches in the socialist countries."[194]

The September minutes contained the following: "During her current trip to Geneva, Ms Adler has been officially given the task of enquiring as to whether representatives of the East German Protestant Church could serve on the WCC staff. The greatest attention is to be given to the preparation of ecumenical cadres in East Germany. For this purpose an overview of selection criteria and qualification features should first be developed."[195]

The East German Protestant Church wanted particularly to be represented on the Central Committee of the WCC, which was to be re-elected after Nairobi. Again and again the Church proposed the Bishop of Saxony Johannes Hempel and the district catechete, Ms Peper, to the leadership of the WCC.[196] Together with the WCC European Affairs secretary, Piet Bouman, and the deputy secretary-general, Konrad Raiser, the representatives of the East German Protestant Church vigilantly kept an eye open for any vacancies on the staff. With Raiser's help Pabst even compiled a list of vacancies. Raiser recommended concentrating on the sections of evangelism, worship renewal, upbringing and the family, and the European secretariat for Inter-Church Aid.[197]

To give more force to its request the secretariat of the East German Protestant Church made a detailed list, which proved that the sixteen WCC commissions employed "a total of 448 members, of which fifty-three are from churches in socialist countries".[198] In other words, the East German Protestant Church felt that "churches in socialist countries" were clearly under-represented. This was subsequently confirmed at a number of meetings between leading members of the WCC and representatives of Eastern bloc churches, thus the WCC promised to do something about it.[199] According to a file memo the GDR secretary of state for Church Issues was also interested in the endeavours of the East German Protestant Church.[200] The problem was that the WCC continually found itself in financial difficulties and the Western churches were in a position to pay the staff out of their own pockets, whereas churches from the Second and Third Worlds expected their Geneva staff to be paid by the WCC. The East German Protestant Church was a convenient exception as Pabst once pointed out in a letter to the president of the Magdeburg Consistory, Krause: "Finally, I would like to add that, according to Althausen, Schwerin and Adler the WCC does not have a single Swiss franc left to fund the fixed-term employment of a church employee from East Germany. The financial situation in Geneva has become rather worse during the last few years. So we may have to apply Article 4 (4) of the Church statutes."[201]

As the strategists from the East German Protestant Church preferred the level of personal communication in order to place their requests for employment at the WCC, they intensified their endeavours to invite Geneva staff members to their country. However, when Potter visited East Germany in mid-April 1975 his visit caused considerable annoyance. The official news agency AND, which reported on the meeting between Potter, the WCC secretary-general and the East German secretary of state for Church Issues, gave the impression that Potter unreservedly supported the socialist regimes in the Eastern bloc. Considering that Stolpe and other representatives of the Protestant Church had been part of this, Potter felt personally deceived as he had apparently expected the churchmen to see to it that a joint communiqué would be written. At best press coverage was careless. This impression was reinforced by the fact that the state bulletin was even printed in church publications because the Protestant East German news agency *ena* had failed to report on the meeting quickly enough.[202] Potter's comments on the issue were the strongest that have ever come from the pen of a WCC secretary-general. One reason, and not the least one, was that he thought his treatment was due to his "Third World origin" and that he was therefore considered to be naive.[203] He wrote:

"The Bund [the East German Protestant Church] must know that people in the GFR [meaning FRG, West Germany, *G. B.*] are always keen to find things to say or write against me, and they regard me as approving the East European régimes. At least that is the image made on me. Sometimes it is downright rude, at other times the attitude seems to be that I am a naive Third Worlder easily taken in by the communist authorities. So far as I know, the Bund has done nothing to redress this image. I have now reached the point where I will refuse to visit the DDR [GDR], unless I can have the assurance that this sort of thing will not be allowed to happen again. This is all the more necessary because the church people in the DDR have been encouraged to have the same image that the West Germans have of me."[204]

Whereas Raiser was "very agitated" about the paper[205] the East German Protestant Church responded extremely coolly and basically left it to the deputy secretary-general to remove the communication problem.[206] Raiser did so with success[207] and ensured that a surprisingly large number of the East German wishes were fulfilled regarding WCC positions.[208] From then on, the East German Protestant Church and individual dioceses continually invited him to their country where they treated him as a special guest of honour.[209] It was probably part of this endeavour to solve the conflict that Stolpe suggested to Raiser in January 1978 that he might invite the secretary of state for Church Issues and his head of department, Weise, to Geneva.[210]

In March 1976, the Eastern block delegates from the fifth General Meeting of the WCC in Nairobi met for an appraisal conference in Budapest.[211] As a result of their discussions, they wrote a letter to Potter and Scott, which contained harsh accusations and the demand for better representation on the ecumenical committees:

"We had the impression that it was not taken seriously enough at the General Meeting that the Socialist Revolution was the beginning of a new period in history and that the churches and Christians in socialist societies have been going along new paths of faith in their existence and in the fulfilment of their commission. We regret that those who criticise this reorientation apparently did not or did not want to understand what our intentions are. This is what led to the hasty and unbrotherly comments and accusations against leading churchmen and theologians in socialist countries ... . We are very much concerned that in Nairobi there was such unbrotherly behaviour towards churches from socialist countries, especially towards the Russian Orthodox Church and the Evangelical Baptist Church in the Soviet Union ... . The course of the discussion on the CSCE gave rise to resentment. We are also aware that some delegates deliberately tried to use this particular point on the agenda to attack the socialist societies in which our churches live and that they also wanted to discredit our churches ... . We see it as a requirement that the work on the programme units and sub-units, the organisation of seminars, consultations, conferences, meetings etc. should involve representatives of churches from socialist countries to a greater extent, in particular in leading positions and in the work on specific issues. We believe it is important to warrant an adequate contingent of church representatives from socialist countries in the appointment of members of the leading bodies of the WCC (Central Committee), the Executive Committee and the committees of the programme units and sub-units. We feel that the identification of the member churches from socialist countries with the aims of the WCC and their theological and practical experiences in ecumenical work provide a basis for serving in leading positions in the WCC, such as deputy secretary-general. This should also be taken into account in the composition of the staff."[212]

It was no doubt partly due to this compelling letter that the Geneva ecumenists met with church representatives from Eastern bloc countries in Budapest a year later.[213] According to the state records, Raiser spoke to the East German secretary of state for Church Issues in mid-September 1977 and emphasised that Geneva wanted to have "real working relationships with churches from socialist countries, so that there would be stronger stimuli not only from the churches but also from socialist societies".[214] For a conference of the WCC Commission "Church and Society" in East Germany he asked for a "Marxist expert on issues of economic and foreign aid".[215]

5. The Different responses to the PCR in the West and East German Protestant Churches

On 24 September 1970, the Council of the West German Protestant Church issued a critical statement on the resolution of the WCC Executive Committee to give several racially oppressed groups a total of US $ 200,000 as part of the Programme to Combat Racism.[216] The WCC secretary-general responded to the criticism on 6 October 1970 with a detailed statement, in which he largely reported on the process whereby the decision had been reached and the democratic way in which it was passed by the relevant committees.[217] Finally, at its conference in February 1971 in Spandau (West Berlin), the Synod of the West German Protestant Church acknowledged its support for the "ecumenical Programme to Combat Racism, as defined in Addis Ababa" and recommended that "the Council, the member churches and the local churches" should "take note".[218] Only a few weeks later Blake thanked the umbrella organisation of East Germany for the statement on the PCR by the Governing Bodies of Protestant Churches in East Germany, which had been issued as early as 9 January 1971.[219] To quote: "In my opinion, this is an excellent analysis of the situation, which as I have learnt has not failed to have an effect outside the borders of East Germany ... . However, we were slightly irritated by several comments, which suggested that we have changed our approach completely since Addis Ababa. The statement issued by the East German Protestant Church is therefore doubly beneficial because it shows unambiguously that this is by no means the case."[220]

Here it is obvious that Blake is criticising the West German Protestant Church and the other Western European churches which only reluctantly supported the Special Fund. The East German Protestant Church included this criticism in its press release.[221] With their different statements, the two Churches fulfilled their images: the rich, self-satisfied Western Church on the one hand and the poor Eastern Church, which was always prepared to act out of solidarity, on the other.

At a closed meeting of the Council of the West German Protestant Church on 20 and 21 May 1971, the relationship with the WCC was discussed on a broad basis. Werner Simpfendörfer, the director of the Study Group for Education and Communication at the Ecumenical Centre in Geneva, gave the group an insight into the work of the WCC since the structural reform from Addis Ababa. Simpfendörfer commented on the general situation:

"Compared to the nineteen-fifties and early sixties the face of the WCC has fundamentally changed because the Orthodox and coloured churches now form the majority of member churches. This is not only reflected in the composition of the decision-making committees and in the structure and priorities of the programmes, but also in the divergence of theological arguments. Moreover, the positions in Geneva are increasingly filled by representatives of non-white churches. This has led to a situation, in which the majority of WCC programmes are determined by the southern hemisphere, whereas the money continues to come from the northern hemisphere. The problem arises as to how one should define an order of priorities and distribution of funds that is balanced, in other words corresponds to the different interests, and to do so without putting a strain on the community of churches ... . The criticism expressed by the West German Protestant Church that the horizontal structure of the WCC should be strengthened, is therefore justified. The dispute about the anti-racism programme of the WCC is only one root of a communication crisis, which already existed."[222]

Simpfendörfer listed a number of factors, which in his estimation were putting pressure on the communication between the WCC and the West German Protestant Church. Finally, he asked the members of the Council: "What can the West German Protestant Church do to avoid the impression that it has developed into a church of the German nation that it is too closely interlinked with the interests of industry and politics and is therefore no longer able to act on an ecumenical level? ... Regarding the relationship between the WCC and the West German Protestant Church it is vital that we should regain the natural trust of the Visser't Hooft era, even under the new conditions. Moreover, we need to bear in mind that the coloured delegates see all church decisions in a political context."[223] Bishops Herrmann Kunst and Hermann Dietzfelbinger basically rejected the WCC's image of the West German Protestant Church and declared that anyone who passed such judgments was inadequately informed.

At that time, the West German Protestant Church was apparently not yet willing to submit to the new ecumenical rules of communication, which is illustrated by the fact that it did not hesitate to accuse the Eastern bloc churches of human rights violations a few months later. At its meeting in mid-September 1971, the Council of the West German Protestant Church felt it was "right that when the Protestant Church of Württemberg met with the Moscow patriarch, they should mention that, in the Soviet Union, people are being persecuted and put in psychiatric hospitals for their faith. That they are treated with drugs that destroy their personalities."[224] The available incriminating evidence was also to be submitted to Federal Chancellor Willy Brandt and the CDU chairman, Rainer Barzel.

Three years later, a discussion took place between representatives of the Württemberg Church and the WCC in Geneva. It focused mainly on Rolf Scheffbuch's questions to the WCC's contextual way of thinking and working. He felt that they improperly made God's Word dependent on the situation.[225] No satisfactory answers were given to Bishop Class's open questions on the unsolved issue of the relationship between text and situation, the Gospel and ideology or between Word and Spirit. Instead, the WCC warned the Württemberg group that their way of thinking was in "danger of turning German theology into something absolute".[226] Early in June 1974, a meeting took place in Geneva between the Council of the West German Protestant Church and WCC staff members.[227]

The WCC did little to bridge the widening gulf between the Western churches and the increasingly obvious Eastern and Southern orientation of its theology and politics. According to the minutes, the WCC delegate Leopoldo Niilus from Argentina expressed himself as follows on the occasion of his visit to the East German State Department for Church Issues in mid-October 1973: "He [Niilus] said in turn that one should be aware that the human rights declaration has so far often been interpreted in a Western way and thus used as a cold war instrument, so that a new approach must be found for the treatment of human rights, an approach that is objective and can be justified in international and ecumenical terms. In particular, this must mean learning to judge situations according to their development and within their context. He said this was especially true of the judgments passed in Western ecumenical circles on what is going on in socialist countries."[228] It was not surprising that the party official Weise expressed his appreciation, stating that "this fundamental approach" was "quite remarkable" and a "new basis for discussion".

On 29 and 30 August 1975, an informal meeting took place between the West and East German Protestant delegates to Nairobi.[229] In addition to other questions, the delegates exchanged ideas on their different attitudes towards the PCR. The East Germans described the PCR as a "model case that is directly linked to the issue of human rights. Therefore the East German churches have unanimously voted for this programme".[230] However, they felt that the "process of creating greater awareness" was progressing extremely slowly in the local churches.

It was also recognised that the political interest of the states in this programme may well be a hindrance. Moreover, it was pointed out that there are Christians in East Germany, who insist that if one draws attention to discrimination and recrimination in South Africa and advocates their elimination, one should also do the same within East Germany. Interestingly, there were people in East Germany, who did not support the Programme to Combat Racism or its Special Fund on the grounds that this would be tantamount to approving socialist movements and they would then be supporting something they would not want to support in their own country.[231] Representatives of the West German Protestant Church criticised that neither the Council nor the Synod of the West German Protestant Church had made the PCR an issue for the churches.[232] When asked by representatives of the East German Protestant Church, their West German counterparts did not deny that considerations of economic policy were responsible for the reaction to the Special Fund. However, not all resistance to the PCR could be attributed to this single factor. The sore point was the issue of using violence. It is worth noting that the theological argument also was often picked up by people, who had economic interests. Over and above this, there was a substantial number of people with no vested economic interest in the matter but who were concerned about the issue of violence.[233] As well as approval for the PCR there were also Christians both at the level of local church leadership and "among the full-time church staff" in the West German Protestant Church, who were indifferent towards the programme or even rejected it.

In the following discussion on the relationship between church politics and theology, there was a clear tendency not to make the Church's action dependent on prior theological reflections. The East Germans saw the PCR as a "test case" as to whether the Church was a "variable that can be taken seriously on a worldwide scale or not".[234] By describing themselves in this way, the two delegations had not only named the sore points between their respective churches in relation to the PCR but also of the friction in their relationship, which resulted from these disagreements. However, the East German delegates to Nairobi were not only subject to a serious altercation with their West German brothers and sisters. The GDR Secretary of State, Seigewasser, told Pabst that he wanted to talk to all the East German delegates before their departure and that this talk would be attended by an "expert on Kenya from the Foreign Ministry".[235]

Unlike in East Germany, where the Protestant Church showed unanimous approval of all the programmes of the PCR, there was at first only one regional church federation in West Germany, the Protestant Church of Hessen-Nassau, which contributed to the Special Fund. Following its resolutions of 24 October and 7 December 1970, it sent the sum of DM 100,000[236] although the United Protestant Lutheran Church in Germany regarded this as a danger to the unity of the West German Protestant Church.[237] The payment had also gained the disapproval of Hermann Dietzfelbinger (Munich), the chairman of the West German Protestant Church, as it prejudiced a joint decision.[238] The PCR work was promoted in West Germany not so much by the church leadership and the synodal bodies, but rather by various groups within the political left wing of the denominations. As they often distanced themselves from the social order within the Federal Republic they found it easier than the established church leadership to support revolutionary liberation movements in Southern Africa which, among other methods, used military force in their struggle. The different attitudes towards the use of violence led to conflicts. For instance, when Helmut Class, the bishop of Württemberg, was promoting the nineteenth appeal of *Bread for the World* in mid-November 1977, he felt compelled to prevent any misunderstandings among the clergy and laity of his region:

"Does it need mentioning that *Bread for the World* rejects terror and violence and re-fuses to fund them? I would like to point this out quite explicitly, as no rumour seems to be absurd enough not to be propagated again and again. With the Special Fund of the Programme to Combat Racism, in particular – a programme that also awards lump sums to the humanitarian work of liberation movements – the World Council of Churches (WCC) has embarked on a path, which we on the whole cannot support. The German churches and *Bread for the World* have repeatedly expressed their concern. Apart from a few well-known exceptions regional churches do not provide church funds for the Special Fund because we feel that this type of solidarity with the op-pressed would lead to misunderstandings, both theologically and politically. It would therefore be wrong to accuse the German churches or even *Bread for the World* of sup-porting militant liberation movements. The West German Protestant Church has pointed out again and again that it refuses to accept violence as a way of achieving po-litical aims and has refused to support liberation movements. The same is true for *Bread for the World*".[239]

This prompted Erdmut Fröhlich (Stuttgart) to write to Class:

"Your indiscriminate wording [in other words the use of 'we'] can easily give the im-pression that you are speaking for all members of the Protestant Church. I object to this and I would hereby like to have it recorded that – together with many members of the Protestant Church in Württemberg and in West Germany in general – I approve of the path taken by the majority of the WCC member churches regarding the Programme to Combat Racism and its Special Fund. It is equally inaccurate to say that 'the German churches ... have repeatedly expressed their concern'. As far as we are aware the churches in East Germany have not done so. Moreover, I believe it is wrong to talk indiscriminately of 'terror and violence' when it is obvious from your text that you are merely referring to liberation movements that have opted for the armed struggle."[240]

When Class replied that "the Protestant churches in East Germany" were "in a different situation ... from the churches in West Germany"[241], he once again touched on a sore point. Fröhlich replied immediately: "If we assume that the Protestant Church in East Germany also consists of mature Christians ... then the 'different situation' which you suggest exists in East Germany apparently refers to the political situation, in other words you are saying with a view to the author-ities that the East German Protestant Church had no option but to speak out in favour of the PCR Special Fund ... . However, their majority decision to support the Special Fund was a 'Yes' to ecumenism and was by no means based on the desire to appear in a favourable light with the authorities or because they had no option because of the interest of the state."[242]

In the summer of 1978, the Executive Committee of the West German Protes-tant Church accepted the offer of the president of the Foreign Affairs Division of the West German Protestant Church, Hans Joachim Held, to give a report[243] on his visit to South Africa.[244] Class and Held had travelled together on the invita-tion of the SACC, with whom they had also discussed their church report on the problem of mutual economic involvement between West Germany and South Africa.[245] In the East-West Church Dialogue of autumn 1978, which was record-ed by Planer-Friedrich, Held announced that "the influence of the ANC is very small. It bears the advantages and also the dangers of an opposition in exile". Following the line of the West German Protestant Church in its entirety[246] he advised the adoption of a policy of small steps:

"Rather than breaking diplomatic relations, there should be rationally dosed pressure. Neither the dogma of 'justified rebellion' in general (apparently Sjollema had overlooked the gradual development in South Africa) nor the condemnation of violent resistance. No clear-cut distinction between politics and religion (the SACC has seemingly declared all political welfare activities as religious!). No severing of relations but continuous insistence without moral condemnation. We should promote solidarity and protest against the codification of injustice ... . As Held sees it the Special Fund has achieved its aim: an awareness of the problem, a keener conscience and debates within the churches. It should now be discontinued because the allocation criteria are becoming more and more difficult to define with any clarity and we should avoid any intensification of the conflict."[247]

Schönherr, who according to the transcript added a few comments, said: "South Africa is at the stage of a 'slave-owning society'. The question about 'afterwards' may only be solved through the education of the blacks and raising their standard of living ... . Schönherr again pointed out the relationship between theology and politics and said it was something, upon which we would have to work 'theologically'. In addition we should support activities, in which people dare to take new steps."[248] In this German-German discussion on Southern Africa, no mention seems to have been made of the attitude of the United Protestant Lutheran Church in South West Africa to the political formation of the country. Its attitude touched on the different social systems in the two Germanys. The official report on their trip by the two West German churchmen reads:

"The joint statement by the three Lutheran church leaders on the domestic politics of the country in February 1978 shows the opportunities and problems involved in joint statements by church leaders. The statement contained a clear rejection of racial discrimination as well as a warning of the danger of submitting to the Marxist dictatorship of a Marxist ideology, which is just as disastrous and against freedom as slavery under the spirit of racism. ... [It was a matter of] not giving the black church leaders the impression that with this statement the church might be speaking out against the political independence movement Swapo in a one-sided and biased way. After all despite an unmistakable Marxist influence on Swapo many blacks feel that it expresses most clearly their desire for independence and for an uncompromising victory over a racist social order."[249]

Neither was it mentioned in the German-German discussion that there had been a report from the general administrator of South West Africa, Steyn, whereby after a South African military campaign the Swapo secretary-general had asked the Soviet Union for a new supply of arms.[250]

Elisabeth Adler, who regularly reported on the latest developments in the PCR at meetings of East German delegates participating on committees of the WCC and the Conference of European Churches, always emphasised why she felt that the work of the East German Protestant Church was particularly suitable in this area. At the end of 1979, she reported: "The opportunities of the East German Protestant churches to give effective support to this programme are, due to their distance from any mutual economic or political involvement, more uninhibited in providing genuine solidarity and help. Obstacles can be found wherever one is too concerned with one's own problems or not open to information and where one does not have the courage to take sides, fearing that any involvement might lead to discredit."[251]

Reporting on her work at the third meeting in April 1982: "Her involvement (as a white person) required great sensitivity and was a matter of listening and mediating. What helped her in her work was that she represented a church in a socialist country. For this reason and in view of the importance of the programme in our churches, we recommend the continuation of her work on this commission even after the general meeting."[252]

No details are given in these notes on the pernicious ambiguity of the East German Protestant Church, particularly regarding its ecumenical involvement. The ecumenical influence of the Church was partially based on the fact that, although it was seen as a church from the "socialist" East, it was economically very much dependent on its Western sister church. Without this constellation it could hardly have played a more significant role in the ecumenical arena than the Protestant churches of Hungary.

6.   The ecumenical church policies of the SED as domestic and foreign policies of the East German State

The GDR government had always viewed the ecumenical activities of the East German Protestant Church with the question in mind as to whether "their" Protestant Church could be used as a tool to propagate their foreign policies. After a church delegation had visited the UK in November 1970, the Secretary of State Seigewasser invited the bishop of Saxony, Noth, as well as the Church council, Pabst, to the *Unter den Linden* Hotel. Pabst reported on the consultation with the British Council of Churches: "The secretary of state was especially interested in the attitude of the British churches towards the issue of recognising East Germany under international law. The secretary of state said that Reverend Oestreicher had requested to visit him again in the near future."[253]

On 17 July 1970, the SED produced a "detailed concept" for the "strengthening of the role of the churches from socialist countries in the activities of international religious organisations in the interest of peace"[254], which showed the approaches chosen by the East German government in their intervention. It was felt that the Nordic-German Convention of Churches could be used "for our Scandinavian policy (i. e. the Baltic as a Sea of Peace)" and a "systematic, preferably planned coordination between our state offices" on church issues would warrant a united stance of church representatives from the Eastern bloc on the ecumenical committees.[255]

The "behaviour" of East German theologians abroad was monitored very closely by the SED, the State Department of Church Issues and the Department of State Security.[256] They were apparently satisfied with the visit by two delegations from the East German Protestant Church to Geneva and Berne that were headed by Schönherr and Braecklein[257] in March 1972:

"Throughout their stay in Switzerland, both the delegations expressed a clear position, particularly on the issue of East German peace policies, to leading representatives of ecumenism as well as to the press, foreign radio and television stations. Regarding the basic political questions the Bishops Schönherr and Braecklein repeatedly explained in Geneva that the leading committees of the East German Protestant Church and the United Lutheran Churches in the GDR supported the implementation of a European security conference and the involvement of East Germany on equal footing. Because of their responsibility for the world as a whole East Germany would have to become a member of the United Nations and its special organisations such as the World Health Organisation. They said it was imperative that East Germany should take part in the Stockholm conference on environmental protection with equal rights."[258]

Both church delegations apparently behaved in such a way that "groups with right-wing leanings in Geneva and the capitalist world" noted with deep disappointment "this discredits your testimony and gives rise to the suspicion that the churches are integrated into socialist society".[259]

Right from the beginning, the East German government saw the potential of the PCR for morally discrediting the Western countries and raising the international standing of the Eastern bloc within the "Third World" at the same time. To do so they needed the help of the East German Protestant Church.

"[The] development of the churches' anti-racism programme, which is based on resolutions of the UN and the OAU (Organisation for African Unity) and in particular the conflicting nature of domestic and foreign policies are a considerable moral danger to the imperialist monopolies that are interested in exploitation and ruling structures ... . As we pointed out at the beginning functionaries of the East German Protestant Church in all the international church organisations are now officially 'taking part in the extensive, opinion-forming, decision-making and organising of the ecumenical bodies'. This imposes a commitment and a responsibility on the state authorities to influence even more effectively the ecumenical behaviour of the various regional churches and their dignitaries in accordance with the agreed peace policy of the socialist community of states ... . We recommend envisaging certain clear long-term aims together with the small circle of church representatives who have ecumenical functions and over and above this, training young progressive clergy for ecumenical offices."[260]

Before and after each trip to an ecumenical conference, the delegation from the Protestant Church was invited to a discussion with representatives of the State Department for Church Issues and the International Relations Division of the East German Foreign Office. The meeting was usually accompanied by a festive programme. The state functionaries would emphasise the main features of East German foreign politics and impress it upon the church cadres so that they took them to heart.[261] In most cases this was not crude indoctrination. Instead principles were prepared, which were also likely to be found in the hearts of the churchmen. The amazing cynicism was that these principles were not upheld by the dictatorship itself. For example, in preparing for the meeting with the delegates of the Sixth General Meeting of the Lutheran World Federation in Dar-es-Salaam[262], the secretary of state for Church Issues had written a note for himself on the "strong emphasis of *fundamental human rights*"[263] being of primary interest to East Germany. The debriefing meeting after the ecumenical trips offered an opportunity to praise or criticise individual delegates and it was always made quite clear that the approval to go on the next trip was dependant upon that person's "behaviour" during the previous one.

Due to the internal dynamic within national delegations, delegates would check and monitor each other. An example of this was the relevant GDR embassy looking after East German citizens. In addition to the national element, there was a larger unit that required commitment, in other words considerable emphasis was placed on cultivating a sense of belonging to the "churches of the socialist countries". For each ecumenical conference there was a special Eastern bloc preparatory and follow-up meeting, with differing contingents of delegates. The purpose was to strengthen the feeling of belonging, to establish mutual monitoring mechanisms and to agree on joint approaches on important political issues.[264] If, for instance, a representative of the Russian Orthodox Church was criticised then all other delegates from the Eastern bloc were obviously expected to rush to his assistance. Not only central committees and events but also subunits, such as the Ecumenical Youth Council of Europe (Eyce) were carefully monitored for their politics and staffing, and suitable intervention was agreed upon.[265]

In 1985, the International Relations Division of the East German Foreign Office produced a 34-page study on "The attitude of the churches towards racism and apartheid in the Republic of South Africa (RSA) and Namibia":

"During the first half of the nineteen-seventies, the East German churches alongside churches from the Netherlands donated the largest amount of money to the anti-racism fund. From 1970 to 1975 they gave a total of 1.8 million East German marks, whereas the West German churches gave DM 540,000 during the same period.[266] The governing bodies of Protestant Churches in East Germany made its first appeal for special donations in 1971. The governing bodies declared their unanimous support for the PCR. Since then they have held appeals at roughly two-year intervals. For the East German Protestant Church the attitude towards racism is an important part of a 'church under socialism'. The ideological discussion of South African racism is in particular suitable for combining Christian/humanist positions with anti-imperialist partisanship and anti-imperialist solidarity because nowhere else is the connection between profit-seeking, imperialist policies and brutal racist oppression as obvious as in the RSA. The connection between NATO policies and racism is unmistakable. The nature of the policies of those in power in West Germany is very clear in this context. The core of the so-called North-South divide can easily be seen here. The image and the inhumane character of the current imperialism are transparent here in all their starkness as something that contradicts Christian/humanist principles. Anti-racist positions, which are in part connected to anti-fascist traditions, can promote a constructive basic attitude among the churches in East Germany to our country's foreign policy towards developing countries and young national states, especially if the anti-imperialist aspects of anti-racism are emphasised. For East German churches to gain a profile in ecumenism as well as in connection with its active role on the issue of human rights it is certainly possible to open up political potential. Even if the practical opportunities for affecting the development in the RSA may be relatively small, the discussion of the racism issue should have a political identification value for the churches in East Germany, which should not be underestimated, especially because, in the present phase, the struggle against apartheid has reached a new climax and a situation similar to civil war is beginning to emerge, showing up all the conflicts and deficits of the system even more clearly."[267]

This shows that it was of immense ideological value to the East German government that the churches, particularly the Protestant Church, should become involved in the PCR. Different from the situation in the First World, it was felt that the conditions in South Africa were such a harsh reflection of class antagonism and imperialist structures that the analysis of these conflicts must necessarily speed up the learning process and the development of socialist awareness in the churches.

Right until the end, the German Democratic Republic continually sought to use the religious institutions on its territory for an "increase of the international authority of the GDR". A strategy paper of September 1988 specified the following objectives: "To use the international contacts of the churches and religious communities of East Germany to impart information on positions of East German domestic and foreign policies. Such information is to be aimed at representatives of national and international religious institutions and also at political forces. To channel and use the contacts, especially on the foreign trips of church leaders, for the purpose of giving information to the rest of the world. To use the international relations of the churches and religious communities for the development of political awareness among East German church representatives."[268] The "problem areas" that could be used for this purpose were seen as the "struggle for peace and disarmament", "anti-imperialist solidarity" and "social justice". The PCR touched upon all three "problem areas" and was therefore ideal ground for East Germany's domestic and foreign policies.

Notes

1   See Willem A. Visser't Hooft, 'Ursprung und Entstehung des Ökumenischen Rates der Kirchen', in Ökumenische Rundschau 44 (1983); Wolfram Weiße, Südafrika und das Antirassismusprogramm. Kirchen im Spannungsfeld einer Rassengesellschaft, Berne-Frankfurt/Main 1975, 25 ff.; Armin Boyens, 'Die Ökumenische Bewegung und die totalitären Ideologien des 20. Jahrhunderts', in Martin Greschat and Jochen-Christoph Kaiser (eds), Christentum und Demokratie im 20. Jahrhundert (Konfession und Gesellschaft 4), Stuttgart-Berlin-Cologne 1992, 19–44; Gerhard Besier, Der SED-Staat und die Kirche. Der Weg in die Anpassung, Munich 1993, 139 ff., 434 ff.; idem, Der SED-Staat und die Kirche 1969–1990. Die Vision vom "Dritten Weg", Berlin-Frankfurt/Main 1995, 153 ff.; Martin Greschat, 'Verantwortung für den Menschen. Protestantische Aktivitäten für Menschenrechte und Religionsfreiheit im und nach dem II. Weltkrieg', in Bernhard Jendorff and Gerhard Schmalenberg (eds), Politik – Religion – Menschenwürde, Gießen 1993, 103–122.

2   Study and compare, e. g. 'Beschlüsse zu den politischen und rassistischen Weltspannungen', III: Gegen die Rassentrennung, in Heinrich Grüber and Gerhard Brennecke (eds), Christus – die Hoffnung der Welt. Ein Bericht über die zweite Weltkirchenkon-

ferenz. Evanston, August 1954, Berlin 1955, 22 f.; 'Report of the working group B. Theological issues in social ethics', in WCC (ed.), Christians in the Technical and Social Revolutions of Our Time. World Conference on Church and Society, Geneva, July 12–26, 1966, Geneva 1967, 195 ff. See also Armin Boyens, 'The South African Issue and the World Council of Churches in Geneva', in ibid. 232 ff. Factual articles and documentation from 1937–1967: Klaus-Martin Beckmann (ed.), Die Kirche und die Rassenfrage, Stuttgart-Berlin (West) 1967. See also idem (ed.), Rasse, Kirche und Humanum. Ein Beitrag zur Friedensforschung (Veröffentlichungen des sozialwissenschaftlichen Instituts der EKD 1), Gütersloh 1969; Hans Wilhelm Florin (ed.), Gewalt im Südlichen Afrika. Ein Bericht, Frankfurt 1971; Zolile Mbali, The Churches and Racism. A Black South African Perspective, London 1987. The International Relations Division of the East German State Department for Church Issues wrote a 34-page study in 1985 entitled: "Zur Haltung der Kirchen gegenüber Rassismus und Apartheid in der Republik Südafrika (RSA) und Namibia", Bundesarchiv, Abt. Potsdam, O-4, 4903.

3 Ans J. van der Bent (ed.), Breaking down the Walls. World Council of Churches Statements and Actions on Racism 1948–1985, Geneva [2]1986, 34 f.; see also Zeichen der Zeit 23 (1969), 138.

4 Van der Bent (ed.), Breaking down the Walls (op. cit. note 3), 39; on the attitude of churches in Southern Africa see Peter Randall (ed.), Power, privilege and poverty (SPRO-CAS publication, no. 7), Johannesburg 1973; Weiße, Südafrika und das Antirassismusprogramm (op. cit. note 1), 54; Marjorie Hope and James Young, The South African Churches in a Revolutionary Situation, Maryknoll [2]1983; Charles Villa-Vicencio, Trapped in Apartheid. A Socio-Theological History of the English-Speaking Churches, Maryknoll-Cape Town 1988; Stefan Rothe, Kirchen in Südafrika, Hamburg 1986; idem, Der Südafrikanische Kirchenrat (1968–1988): Aus liberaler Opposition zum radikalen Widerstand, Erlangen 1990.

5 The disputed decisions taken at Arnoldshain were partly based on suggestions made at the Notting Hill Conference in May 1969. For a further discussion on this issue see Klaus-Martin Becker, 'Zur Frage des institutionalisierten Rassismus. Interpretation eines ökumenischen Programmes', in Ökumenische Rundschau 19 (1970), 174–180; idem (ed.), 'Rasse, Entwicklung und Revolution. Der Notting-Hill-Report und zugehörige Dokumente', in Ökumenische Rundschau B 14/15, Stuttgart 1971, esp. 104 ff. On the assessment of the Arnoldshain decisions by the East German State Department for Church Issues, see the note by Weise on 16 Dec. 1970, 'Betr. Haltung des ÖRK und des Rates der EKD in Westdeutschland zu Fragen des Rassismus', Bundesarchiv, Abt. Potsdam, O-4, 487.

6 See the circular from the secretary-general of the WCC, Eugene C. Blake, to the member churches of the WCC on 11 Sept. 1972, Evangelisches Zentralarchiv [EZA, Protestant Central Archives] in Berlin, 101/1094. Also see item 5 of the minutes of the meeting of the Council of German Protestant Churches on 14 and 15 Dec. 1972 on the WCC decisions on the PCR, EZA Berlin, 101/1170.

7 Van der Bent, Breaking down the Walls (op. cit. note 3), 47.

8 When Zionism was condemned as a form of racism by a committee of the United Nations in 1975, Second World Christians also commented on the issue. Compare the statement of the leading East German Protestant clergy on Zionism from 27 Nov. 1975 with Kirchliches Jahrbuch (1975), 266 f., the 'Thesen zur Zionismusfrage' of the Christian Peace Conference Study Group called "Friede im Nahen Osten", EZA Berlin 101/1096, and the articles by the East German Protestant Church, entitled 'Israel im Nahen Osten', in Kirche als Lerngemeinschaft. Dokumente aus der Arbeit der BEKD-DR, East Berlin 1981, 239–249. See also Philip Potter's statement on the UN Zionism resolution, of which parts were printed by Ecumenical Press Service, 33, 42nd year, on 13 Nov. 1975, 5 f. See also Karin Kulow, 'Israel, SED und DDR. Zur Geschichte eines tragischen Beziehungskonfliktes', in Reinhard Renger (ed.), Die deutsche "Linke" und der Staat Israel, Leipzig 1994, 183–196; Michael Wolffsohn, Die Deutschland-Akte.

Juden und Deutsche in Ost und West. Tatsachen und Legenden, Munich 1995. Adler wrote in her summary of the WCC Committee meeting on the PCR of 17 to 23 April 1977 in Egham (UK): "In Western Europe racism is present in the treatment of the 11 million migrant workers." EZA Berlin, 101/1097. This meant that the entire Western world, including West Germany, had a racism problem. In 1976, the PCR core group logically demanded "a study of racism, class structure, sexism and capitalism as a contribution to finding a new form of society" (Adler's summary).

9   See also Reinhard Rode, Die Südafrikapolitik der Bundesrepublik Deutschland 1968–1972, Munich 1975.

10   See Richard Gibson, African Liberation Movements. Contemporary Struggles against White Minority Rule, London-New York-Toronto, 1972.

11   Compare the letter from Stolpe to Weil on 22 Dec. 1978 and Walter Pabst's extract from the WCC Financial Report, EZA Berlin, 101/1138.

12   On the subsidies for the meeting of the Central Committee in West Berlin in 1974, see the notes on the 78th session of the Council of German Protestant Church on 10 and 11 May 1973 in Munich and the 4th session of the Council on 1 and 2 July 1973 in Bonn, EZA Berlin, 101/1170. According to these documents the German Protestant Church paid the accommodation expenses of foreign delegates.

13   In a letter on 3 Oct. 1982, the East German Protestant Church asked the Special Committee of the West German Protestant Church to use the amount of DM 35,000 for accommodation expenses of East German delegates in Vancouver from the 1983 West German Auxiliary Fund. The West German Church President Walter Hammer was rather reserved at first and suggested applying to Geneva. The East German Church then played its ecclesiastical trump card of a "special relationship". ("Is it in the spirit of Article 4.4 to introduce a new procedure?", to quote Koch's discussion memo after speaking to Demke on 3 Nov. 1982.) After receiving a letter from Demke on 30 Nov. 1982 Hammer finally gave in. Demke wrote: "If we choose this path [requesting money from Geneva] our request may be handed on to the West German Church by the WCC anyway, which would completely distort the impression given by the relationship between our Churches in the ecumenical community." (All letters from EZA Berlin 101/1147).

14   See the file memo on the discussion between Koch and Hammer on 4 Nov. 1982.

15   Report on the first meeting of the advisory committee from 8 to 11 Feb. 1974 to prepare for the fifth General Meeting of the WCC in Jakarta in 1975, EZA Berlin, 101/1143. The continuous and uncommented use of the word "socialist" in church minutes, reports and memorandums to characterise the social order in the Eastern bloc states is matched by an equally unquestioned description of the Western social order as "capitalist". Take, for instance, a report by Garstecki and Ziemer on the Consultation of the Conference of European Churches on the issue of "Die KSZE und die Kirchen" ["The CSCE and the Churches"] from 27 to 31 Oct. 1975 in Buckow, East Germany: "Die sozialistischen und kapitalistischen Länder waren auf der Konsultation sehr ungleich vertreten." ["There was rather a discrepancy in the numeric representation of socialist and capitalist countries at the consultation."] EZA Berlin, 101/1339. Inappropriately (and falsely) using such semantic labels, perceived political facts were thus turned into common coinage and treated as though they were real.

16   Cf. the letter from Pabst to the members of the Executive Committee of the East German Church on 10 Dec. 1974 and his file memo of the same day, EZA Berlin, 101/1144. See also Grengel and Pabst's minutes of the Fourth Preparatory Discussion on the Fifth General Meeting of the WCC in East Berlin on 28 February and 1 March 1975, EZA Berlin 101/1155. These documents indicate that there was not only criticism but also approval. Commenting on action groups, the Nairobi delegate, Hinz, noted the "interest in Jesus, partial criticism of the Church and partial identification with Socialism. Marx opted for the real man." Ibid.

17   Michael Knoch, 'Jesus Christ Frees and Unites – in a Socialist Society', Ecumenical Review 26 (1974), 439–452.

18 Ibid. 440 f.
19 See also the reports of the East German ecumenical speaker Walter Pabst on the Central Committee Meeting of the WCC, EZA Berlin, 101/1169. On the decision of the various regional churches and church associations in Eastern Germany to be ecumenically represented abroad by the East German Protestant umbrella organisation, see the letter from the Lutheran Church Administration on 15 Jan. 1971, EZA Berlin, 101/903. See also Walter Pabst, 'Ökumene in der DDR', Ökumenische Rundschau 20 (1971), 330–333.
20 Van der Bent, Breaking down the Walls (op. cit. note 3), 42; see also Zeichen der Zeit 25 (1971), 146 f.
21 Van der Bent, Breaking down the Walls (op. cit. note 3), 45 f. The resolutions of the Central Committee of the WCC in Utrecht were described as "very satisfactory" by the East German Secretary of State, Hans Seigewasser, cf. Pabst's file memo on a talk at the State Department for Church Issues on 29 Aug. 1972, EZA Berlin, 101/1170. Virtually at the last minute an embarrassing mistake had to be ironed out in the Utrecht reports because it read "East Germany" after each of the delegates instead of the official "German Democratic Republic" (see also the correspondence between Martin Conway and Pabst on this issue in October/November 1972, ibid.).
22 Quoted from Pabst's report on the 25th Meeting of the Central Committee of the WCC in Utrecht from 13 to 28 Aug. 1972, 30.
23 See Pabst, op. cit. note 22, 32. See also 'Niederschrift der 68. Sitzung des Rates der EKD am 21./22.9.1972 in Hannover', EZA Berlin, 101/1170. At this meeting, Bishop Hermann Dietzfelbinger reported on the response of the South African Prime Minister, Vorster, who replied to queries by the German Protestant Church about torture and industrialists with subsidiaries in South Africa. On the responses of the East German authorities to the Utrecht meeting, see the paper of the International Relations Main Division of the State Department for Church Issues, dated 18 Sept. 1972, on 'EKD – Antirassismusprogramm des ÖRK und Revisionismus', Bundesarchiv, Abt. Potsdam, O-4, 4994.
24 See WCC, 'First List of Corporations Directly Involved in Investment in or Trade with South Africa, Namibia, Zimbabwe, Angola, Mozambique and Guinea-Bissau, December 1972'; 'Second List (Revised) of Corporations directly involved in Investment in or Trade with South Africa, Namibia, Zimbabwe, Angola, Mozambique and Guinea-Bissau, October 1973', Hoover Institute Archives, Stanford (USA), South African Subject Collection. Also: WCC, Apartheid und unsere Schuld, Geneva 1975; The WCC and Bank Loans to Apartheid, Geneva 1977. See also Frank Kürschner-Pelkmann, Sanktionen gegen Apartheid, Frankfurt am Main 1988, 129 ff.
25 Report from Oberkirchenrat Pabst (Head of Ecumenism in the East German Protestant Church) on the meeting of the Central Committee of the WCC 22 to 29 Aug. 1973, EZA Berlin, 101/1170.
26 'Niederschrift über die 6. Sitzung des Rates der EKD am 28./29.9.1973 in Hannover' [Protocol on the sixth conference of the council of the German Protestant Church on 28./29.9.1973], EZA Berlin (op. cit. note 25).
27 Van der Bent, Breaking down the Walls (op. cit. note 3), 47. At the end of July 1976, Philip Potter handed a copy of the correspondence between the WCC and the banks to the East German Protestant Church, see EZA Berlin, 101/1096. Disregarding the "reservations expressed by the East German Protestant Church" (Pabst's file memo on a discussion with Groscurth, a member of the High Consistory, on 17 Jan. 1973 – EZA Berlin, 101/1170) the West German Protestant Church as the inviting body decided that West Berlin should be the conference venue; see also Groscurth's memo to Stolpe on 30 Aug. 1972; letter from Pabst to Groscurth on 13 Nov. 1972; Pabst's memo after a discussion with Groscurth on 17 Jan. 1973 (EZA Berlin, 101/1170) and the comments by Karl-Alfred Odin in Frankfurter Allgemeine Zeitung on 22 and 28 Aug. 1972; Pabst's file memo on a discussion at the State Department for Church Issues on 10 May 1973 (EZA Berlin, 101/1170); see also Besier, Der SED-Staat und die

Kirche 1969–1990 (op. cit. note 1), 147. According to a file memo made at the State Department for Church Issues on 16 Aug. 1973, on the same date Stolpe gave a detailed report to the state authorities on the positions of the West German bishops and Church President as well as Potter's position on West Berlin as a venue. He promised to do his very best to persuade the West German Protestant Church and Geneva to choose a different venue. See also Bundesarchiv, Berlin-Lichterfelde, DO-4, 488. Before travelling to Geneva in August 1973, the two East German members of the WCC Central Committee, von Brück and Scholz, were urged by the International Relations Division of the State Department for Church Issues to do everything they could to prevent the choice of West Berlin as the venue (see Schöpe's file memo on 27 Aug. 1973 on a discussion with von Brück and Scholz before their departure, ibid.). Ulrich von Brück was listed by the East German Department of State Security as an unofficial informer under the name of "Zwinger"; see also note 256.

28   See also Kurt Scharf's statement to epd (evangelische Pressedienst), the German Protestant Press Service, on 9 Aug. 1974 and the epd special editions no. 2 (11 Aug. 1974), no. 3 (12 Aug. 1974), no. 4 (13 Aug. 1974) and no. 5 (14 Aug. 1974). The East German authorities saw this as an attempt to "give an imperialist profile to the issue of human rights in the context of the anti-racism issue" and to avoid the political commitment of the WCC to any "orientation of an anti-imperialist tendency" (information from Weise/Berger on 14 Aug. 1974 regarding the WCC Central Committee Meeting in West Berlin from 11 to 18 Aug. 1974, Bundesarchiv, Berlin-Lichterfelde, DO-4, 488). The East German Department of State Security was represented in large numbers at the Central Committee Meeting in Berlin. The state security division HA XX/4, which was responsible for church affairs, had set up a plan of action on 5 Aug. 1974, whereby the secret service sent out sixteen unofficial informers and one contact person. According to the plan of action two informers were to take part in the "internal meetings of the Central Committee", in other words they were among the delegates, cf. Der Bundesbeauftragte für die Unterlagen des Staatssicherheitsdienstes der ehemaligen DDR, Zentralarchiv [BStU, ZA; Federal German Department for State Security Documents of the Former GDR, Central Archives in Berlin], MfS-HA XX/4, 1197, 187–189. On this development see also Eckard Krüger, 'Kirchen, KSZE und Menschenrechte. Entstehung, Umfeld und Verlauf des Menschenrechtsprogramms der Kirchen', Ökumenische Rundschau 36 (1987), 289–302.

29   See Section V: 'Structures of Injustice and Struggles for Liberation', in David M. Paton (ed.), Breaking Barriers. Nairobi 1975. The Official Report of the Fifth Assembly of the World Council of Churches, Nairobi, 23 Nov. – 10 Dec. 1975, London-Grand Rapids (Michigan) 1976, 97–119; esp. 117 f. See also Christoph Hinz, 'Christliche Gemeinde in der DDR und das Thema von Nairobi', Ökumenische Rundschau 24 (1975), 455–465; Gerhard Thomas, 'Nairobi 1975 – von der DDR aus gesehen', Ökumenische Rundschau 25 (1976), 160–167.

30   Cf. Paton (ed.), Breaking Barriers (op. cit. note 29), 118.

31   Cf. van der Bent, Breaking down the Walls (op. cit. note 3), 62 f.

32   Ibid. See also Ellen Hellman and Henry Lever (ed.), Race Relations in South Africa 1929–1979, London-Basingstoke, 1980.

33   See the 1978 PCR Project List, EZA Berlin, 101/1098.

34   See also the WCC factual paper on the allocation of US $ 85,000 from the WCC Special Fund to Combat Racism to humanitarian programmes run by the Patriotic Front of Zimbabwe, which was announced by the WCC leadership on 11 Aug. 1978, EZA Berlin, 101/1100; Hermann Dietzfelbinger, 'Kritische Rede für den ÖRK', Ökumenische Rundschau 27 (1978), 303–314; 'Memorandum zum Verhältnis der EKD zum ÖRK – unter besonderer Berücksichtigung des PCR', (a resolution taken by the Council of the German Protestant Church on 6 Nov. 1978), Ökumenische Rundschau 28 (1979), 43–51. See also Wolfgang Lienemann, 'Widerstandsrecht und Menschenrechte. Überlegungen zur Fragen einer "Just Rebellion" in der ökumenischen Diskussion', Ökumenische Rundschau 29 (1980), 147–168.

35 Cf. van der Bent, Breaking down the Walls (op. cit. note 3), 67 f. See also the East German perspective in 'Kurzinformation Münchow vom 1.2.1979 über die Ergebnisse der Tagung des ÖRK in Kingston/Jamaika. 1. bis 11. Januar 1979', Bundesarchiv, Berlin-Lichterfelde, DO-4, 488. It was after this that the East German Protestant Church refused to take part in the ballot meeting of Eastern bloc church representatives in Prague, which had already been announced.

36 These conferences took place in Cleveland, Panama, Nairobi, New Delhi and Stockholm. See also Münchow's memo on 23 Feb. 1979 on his discussion with Ludwig Franke (Apolda), op. cit. note 35.

37 Van der Bent, Breaking down the Walls (op. cit. note 3), 74 ff.

38 Cf. Barkat's letter to the member churches on 15 June 1981, EZA Berlin, 101/1101; Sjollema's letter of farewell on 16 Dec. 1981, EZA Berlin, 01/1102. After having worked for the WCC for twenty-five years Sjollema now moved to the International Labour Organisation (ILO) in Geneva.

39 See 'Issues for the Churches and the WCC 3.6: Struggling for Justice and Human Dignity', in David Gill (ed.), Gathered for Life. Official Report. VI Assembly. World Council of Churches. Vancouver, Canada 24 July – 10 Aug. 1983, Geneva-Grand Rapids (Michigan) 1983, 83 ff. See also Eberhard Natho, 'Vancouver – seine Bedeutung für die Kirchen in der DDR', Ökumenische Rundschau 33 (1984), 151–164; Gerhard Thomas, 'Wie Christen in der DDR es mit der Ökumene halten: Zum Beispiel Vancouver', Ökumenische Rundschau 32 (1983), 192–200.

40 See also Gill (ed.), Gathered for Life (op. cit. note 39), 155 f. On the PCR between 1983 and 1988 read Thomas F. Best (ed.), Vancouver to Canberra 1983–1990. Report of the Central Committee to the Seventh Assembly of the World Council of Churches, Geneva 1990, 178 ff.

41 Cf. van der Bent, Breaking down the Walls (op. cit. note 3), 96 ff.

42 Literature on SACC: Stefan Rothe, Der südafrikanische Kirchenrat (1968–1988): Aus liberaler Opposition zum radikalen Widerstand, Erlangen 1990. The text of the resolution taken by the National Conference of the SACC on 28 June 1985 can be found in Ecunews 8/1985, 18 f.

43 See also Rudolf Hinz and Frank Kürschner-Pelkmann (eds), 'Christen im Widerstand. Die Diskussion um das südafrikanische KAIROS Dokument', in Texte zum Kirchlichen Entwicklungsdienst 40, Stuttgart 1987.

44 Text: op. cit. note 43, 99 f.

45 Cf. the East German embassy report from Harare on 10 Dec. 1985, Bundesarchiv, Berlin-Lichterfelde, DO-4, 4904.

46 Text: Hinz and Kürschner-Pelkmann (eds), 'Christen im Widerstand' (op. cit. note 43), 101–104.

47 See Assembly 1991. Reports and Statements relating to PCR from the WCC Seventh Assembly Canberra 1991 (PCR information no. 29 [1991]), Geneva 1991, 38.

48 See epd-Dokumentation 19/94, 16.

49 See the comment by the Council of West German Protestant Churches, 12 July 1974, on the extension of the mandate for the Programme to Combat Racism, in Kirchliches Jahrbuch 1974, 262–266, here: 264.

50 Elisabeth Adler, 'Ein umstrittenes Programm?', in Die Kirche. Evangelische Wochenzeitung, year 29, no. 41, 13 Oct. 1974.

51 Letter from Luckau to Gerhard Johann, chief editor, 14 Oct. 1974, EZA Berlin, 101/1094.

52 Luckau to Pabst, 14 Oct. 1974, op. cit. note 51.

53 See Pabst to Luckau, 27 Jan. 1975, ibid.

54 See the agendas and minutes of the Dissemination Conferences, EZA Berlin, 101/1093.

55 Letter from Hickel to Lewek and Adler, 1 Nov. 1972, op. cit. note 54.

56 Krusche was listed by the East German Department of State Security as an unofficial informer under the name of "Günther". See also Tina Krone and Reinhard Schult

(eds), Seid untertan der Obrigkeit. Originaldokumente der Stasi-Kirchenabteilung XX/4, Berlin 1992, 121 ff.

57 'Bericht über die Multiplikatorenkonferenz zu Fragen des Antirassismusprogramms des Ökumenischen Rates der Kirchen am 11./12. 10. 1971', EZA Berlin 101/1093.

58 Ibid.

59 See 'Protokoll der 14. Tagung der Konferenz der Ev. Kirchenleitungen [KKL] in der DDR am 10./11. 9. 1971', op. cit. note 57.

60 Appendix 3 of Dr Scharf's letter to von Brück, a member of the High Consistory, on 16 Aug. 1972, ibid. See also Lewek's memo on a discussion by the Afro-Asian Solidarity Committee [AASK] on 18 Dec. 1973, EZA Berlin, 101/1094; Lewek's memo on a discussion with Dr Scharf of AASK on 27 Feb. 1974, ibid.

61 Cf. 'Protokoll der 21. KKL-Tagung am 10./11. 11. 1972', EZA Berlin, 101/1093.

62 Cf. letters from Lewek to Dr Scharf on 16 Oct. 1972 and 6 Dec. 1972, op. cit. note 61.

63 Cf. 'Vermerk von Brück/Lewek über ein Gespräch mit Vertretern des Solidaritätskomitees der DDR am 4. 3. 1976 im BEK-Sekretariat', EZA Berlin, 101/1096.

64 'Zur Sitzung der Ökumenischen Kommission am 24. 9. 1973. Betrifft: Bericht über die Genfer Tätigkeit', EZA Berlin, 101/1135.

65 Text in Die Kirche. Evangelische Wochenzeitschrift, general edition, year 26, no. 9, 28 Feb. 1971, 1.

66 Hertel to Schönherr on 1 March 1971, Besier archives.

67 Schönherr to Hertel on 18 March 1971, op. cit. note 66.

68 See Althausen's letter to Lewek on 26 Feb. 1974, EZA Berlin, 101/1094; Lewek's draft letter to Seigewasser on 17 June 1974, ibid. During a discussion with Seigewasser on 7 Dec. 1977, Sjollema also tried to persuade the Secretary of State to consent to a 'direct financial contribution to the "anti-racism fund"'. [Aktenvermerk Münchow vom 21. 12. 1977 über Gespräch Seigewasser-Sjollema im Beisein von Lewek, Bundesarchiv, Berlin-Lichterfelde, DO-4, 488.]

69 See Demke's letter to Lingner of 10 Jan. 1980. When asked by the Foreign Relations Division of the West German Protestant Church on 30 Nov. 1979, Demke finally replied – after he had been sent a reminder: "The realisation [transfer of the collected money] can only take place in the form of material assets. In this we work together with the East German Solidarity Committee and the Red Cross of East Germany." EZA Berlin, 101/1101.

70 This was the wording used in the church appeal "Aufruf zur Sonderspende für das Antirassismusprogramm" during Passion Week, 1973, EZA Berlin, 101/1094 [self translation].

71 'Bericht über die Multiplikatorenkonferenz zu Fragen des Antirassismusprogramms des Ökumenischen Rates der Kirchen am 11./12. 10. 1971', EZA Berlin 101/1093.

72 Pabst's file memo on a discussion at the State Department for Church Issues on 5 Dec. 1972, op. cit. note 71.

73 W. Krusche to Lewek on 8 Jan. 1974, EZA Berlin, 101/1094; see Lewek's reply on 7 Feb. 1974, ibid.

74 Letters from Wolfgang Schenk, the principal of the seminary, on 6 July 1973 to the East German Protestant Church (G. Linnenbrink) of the West German Protestant Church Office, EZA Berlin, 101/1094. On Mandela's life, cf. Mary Benson, Nelson Mandela. The Man and the Movement, Reprinted with revisions and new material, Harmondsworth et al. 1994.

75 See Potter's circular to the member churches of the Central Committee of the WCC on May 1974, EZA Berlin, 101/1094.

76 Read A Small Beginning – An assessment of the First Five Years of the Programme to Combat Racism, Geneva 1974. This publication contains a detailed overview of the donations given by the West German Protestant Church to the PCR.

77 See also the 'Protokoll der 31. Tagung der KKL in der DDR am 12./13. 7. 1974', EZA Berlin, 101/1094.

78 See also Besier, Der SED-Staat und die Kirche 1969–1990 (op. cit. note 1), 153 ff.

79   Bunzel (Görlitz consistory) to the Secretary-General of the WCC on 11 July 1974, EZA Berlin, 101/1094.
80   German title: Informationen zum Antirassismusprogramm des ÖRK, 7 Jan. 1975.
81   See the reprint of the article from the East German CDU publication Neue Zeit on 5 Nov. 1974.
82   German title: Miteinander leben, für einander da sein, EZA Berlin, 101/1095. See also further brochures on the PCR mentioned in Informationen (see note 80).
83   Union Verlag, East Berlin, 1971.
84   Propheten – Partisanen – Präsidenten. Afrikanische Volksführer und ihre Widersacher, VEB Deutscher Verlag der Wissenschaften, Berlin (East) 1973.
85   See the 'Protokoll der 34. Tagung der KKL am 10./11.1.1975', EZA Berlin, 101/1095. See also Baldwin Sjollema's letter of thanks to Schönherr on 31 Jan. 1975, ibid. "The organisations of the racially oppressed in Latin and North America as well as in Australia and Asia continually require more help." The PCR Special Fund allocation report for 1975 only mentioned Asia once in the form of a Japanese national committee to combat discrimination against ethnic minorities. Second World countries and their political allies in the Third World were not mentioned.
86   See the 'Protokoll der 35. Tagung der KKL am 7./9.3.1973', EZA Berlin, 101/1095. See also Lewek to von Brück, 30 Dec. 1974 and the enclosed draft appeal for donations, ibid.
87   Adler's file memo from 12 Nov. 1976 regarding the visit of Reverend Alexander Kirby, EZA Berlin, 101/1096.
88   Ibid.
89   See epd-Dokumentation, 48a/75.
90   On the function and composition of the "Facharbeitskreis Ökumenische Diakonie" [Ecumenical Study Group on Welfare and Social Work] see the relevant draft of the 'Arbeiten zur Geschichte des Kirchenkampfes' on 18 June 1976, EZA Berlin, 101/1096. The basic ideas of the Study Group that were approved by the Protestant Governing Bodies on 9 July 1977 were printed in Kirche als Lerngemeinschaft, 225–228.
91   An assessment of the Study Group on the report of the WCC consultation 'Rassismus in der Theologie – Theologie gegen Rassismus', Lewek, EZA Berlin, 101/1096.
92   Assessment of the Study Group.
93   Compare circulars and minutes, EZA Berlin, 101/1540.
94   In the minutes of the 18th meeting of the Southern Africa Study Group on 30 Aug. 1979 [Protokoll der 18. Sitzung des Arbeitskreises Südliches Afrika am 30.8.1979] the name of the speaker is wrongly quoted as "Barding". EZA Berlin, 101/1541.
95   Appendix to the minutes of the 18th meeting of the Southern Africa Study Group on 30 Aug. 1979, op. cit. note 96.
96   Op. cit., see Alfred Babing, Namibia: ein Report, Berlin (East), 1979. The SED was the East German communist party: Sozialistische Einheitspartei Deutschlands [United Socialist Party of Germany].
97   See 'Protokoll der 9. Sitzung des Arbeitskreises Südliches Afrika beim Ökumenisch-Missionarischen Zentrum am 4.10.1976', EZA Berlin, 101/1540.
98   'Protokoll der 11. Sitzung des Arbeitskreises Südliches Afrika am 8.6.1977', op. cit. note 97.
99   'Protokoll der 14. Sitzung des Arbeitskreises Südliches Afrika am 12.10.1978', EZA Berlin, 101/1541.
100 See EZA Berlin, 101/1098.
101 Ibid.
102 Note from Lewek to Stolpe, 9 May 1978, EZA Berlin, 101/1098. See also invitation from the president of the East German Peace Council, Günther Drefahl, to Schönherr on 7 April 1978; note on a phone call from Kraja (Peace Council) to Stolpe; Lewek's note from 19 April 1978 on the conditions of participation, ibid.
103 Cf. the programme of the preparatory conference in January 1978, op. cit. note 102.

104 See G. Planer-Friedrich's report, 'Die Beteiligung der evangelischen Kirchen in der DDR an der Ökumene' [The Participation of the East German Protestant Churches in Ecumenism], which was written for the German parliamentary committee enquiring into the "history and consequences of the SED dictatorship in Germany" and his criticism of Heike Schmoll's observations on 'Die ökumenische Arbeit der Kirchen in der DDR unter politischen Aspekten', in Deutscher Bundestag (ed.), Materialien der Enquete-Kommission "Aufarbeitung von Geschichte und Folgen der SED-Diktatur in Deutschland" (12. Wahlperiode des Deutschen Bundestages), vol. 1, Baden-Baden 1995, 76–102.

105 WCC background paper 'South Africa today – hope at what price?'; the German edition 'Südafrika heute – Hoffnung um welchen Preis?' is to be found in Zeichen der Zeit 11 (1978), 407–419. See also the statement of the WCC Central Committee, Jamaica, 1979, in van der Bent, Breaking down the Walls (op. cit. note 3), 67 f.

106 'Protokoll der 62. Tagung der KKL am 6/7.7.1979', EZA Berlin, 101/1100.

107 Published in Kirche als Lerngemeinschaft, 228–239.

108 Letters from Lewek to Potter on 31 July 1979 and 28 Aug. 1979, EZA Berlin, 101/1100. On 10 Aug. 1979, Olaf Lingner (Berlin branch of the West German Church Office) was sent two copies of the assessment, ibid.

109 Konrad Raiser's reply to Lewek, 21 Sept. 1979, op. cit. note 108.

110 Sjollema to Lewek, 24 Oct. 1979, ibid.

111 Lewek to Sjollema, 5 Nov. 1979, ibid; see also Sjollema to Adler on 15 Jan. 1981, EZA Berlin, 101/1101.

112 Since 1970 Gutsch was listed by the East German Department of State Security as an unofficial informer called "Dietrich", cf. East German secret service files: BStU, ZA, MfS AIM 11870/85, I/1 and II,1–3. In addition to financial rewards he received the silver award of the NVA (Nationale Volksarmee, the East German Army) from Mielke in 1976 and in 1979 the "Order of Merit of the GDR". He died in March 1981. According to Major Kullik's report at a meeting on 24 March 1980 Gutsch provided abundant information on the regional consultation in Sweden. To quote the report: "A scrutiny of the WCC financial awards was called for. The WCC was accused of providing money for arms purchases of developing countries with a Marxist orientation. The Norwegian delegate [who asked this question] was supported by a number of West German Protestant delegates. The East German delegates were consistent and principled in issues of racism. Reverend Grosse (GDR) gave a long speech, showing that there is no racism in East Germany, that its roots have been eliminated and that East German statesmen had suffered under racism themselves (under the inhumane system of fascism). He said it was impossible to accuse the socialist countries of racism. The elimination of racism and its roots as a condition for a new social order had cost many people's lives and this must not be forgotten ... . The informer 'Dietrich' reported that a paper containing anti-Soviet propaganda had been smuggled into the conference material. It was a paper (in English), which dealt with the issue of the Tatars in the Soviet Union. A Baptist from the USSR condemned the paper as slander against the USSR ... . The informer 'Dietrich' feels that a number of delegates with anti-communist leanings tried to associate the issue of racism with the socialist countries under the heading of 'persecution of Jews and Tatars in the Soviet Union in connection with the human rights issue'. The church delegates from the socialist countries consistently opposed the attempts to falsely accuse these countries of racism." East German secret service files: BStU, ZA, MfS AIM 11870/85, I/1, I,3, 220–222. Gutsch also reported on the quarrels among the West German Protestant delegates on the PCR and recommended leading a "progressive West German Protestant delegate towards the Christian Peace Conference".

113 'Protokoll der 65. Tagung der KKL am 11./12.1.1980', EZA Berlin, 101/1101.

114 Cf. van der Bent, Breaking down the Walls (op. cit. note 3), 70–74, esp. 71 f.

115 See BEK-Informationen zum Antirassismusprogramm des ÖRK Nr. 15, East Berlin, 1981, 3 f.

116 See 'Protokoll über die 76. Tagung der KKL am 13./14.11.1981', EZA Berlin, 101/1101; the fourth appeal for PCR donations by the East German Protestant Church with a covering letter from Demke (11 Jan. 1982) to the leading administrators of the member churches, EZA Berlin, 101/1102.

117 See Ulrich Materne et al. (eds), Erlebt in der DDR. Berichte aus dem Bund Evangelisch-Freikirchlicher Gemeinden, Wuppertal-Kassel 1995.

118 Cf. Lewek's letter to the Arbeitsgemeinschaft Christlicher Kirchen [Christian Churches Study Group], 23 Dec. 1981, EZA Berlin, 101/1101.

119 Head office of the Federation of Free Evangelical Churches in East Germany to Lewek, 20 Jan. 1982, op. cit. note 118.

120 Sjollema to the WCC member churches, February 1981, ibid.

121 Mongalo's letter to the East German Protestant Church; Krusche's reply to Mongalo on 9 Jan. 1982, EZA Berlin, 101/1102.

122 Ibid.

123 Lewek to Mongalo, 17 March 1982, op. cit. note 121.

124 Lewek to Rümpel, 17 March 1982, ibid.

125 Götz Planer-Friedrich, 'Wurzeln des Rassismus – Zu einer Studie der Theologischen Studienabteilung beim Bund der Evangelischen Kirchen in der DDR', Ökumenische Rundschau 34 (1985), 200–207.

126 Quoted from 'BEK-Informationen zum Antirassismusprogramm des ÖRK Nr. 16', 1 Dec. 1985, 4, EZA Berlin, 101/93/1371.

127 Text: Christoph Demke et al. (eds), Zwischen Anpassung und Verweigerung. Dokumente aus der Arbeit des BEKDDR, Leipzig ²1995, 427–429.

128 It is partly due to a recommendation made by Potter that the East German Protestant Church concentrated on the Protestant denominations of Mozambique. See also the summary of a working discussion between representatives of the WCC and the East German Protestant Church on 23 April 1975, item 5, EZA Berlin, 101/1136. When Sjollema visited East Germany in early December 1977 he asked the Secretary of State for Church Issues to give support to requests by Church representatives to travel to Mozambique (cf. Münchow's file memo on 21 Dec. 1977 on a discussion between Seigewasser and Sjollema on 7 Dec. 1977, Bundesarchiv, Berlin-Lichterfelde, DO-4, 488).

129 According to Rothe, Kirchen in Südafrika (op. cit. note 4), 106.

130 Cf. also Ilona Schleicher, 'Das Solidaritätskomitee der DDR und Mosambik: Unterstützung des Befreiungskampfes und Entwicklungshilfe', in Hans-Georg Schleicher et al. (eds), Die DDR und Afrika. Zwischen Klassenkampf und neuem Denken, Münster-Hamburg 1993, 192–208, esp. 200 f.

131 Cf. Schleicher, Die DDR und Afrika (op. cit. note 130), 200.

132 Ibid. 201. See Joachim Kindler, Manual do Profesor, Matematica 1a classe.

133 On Frelimo (Frente de Libertação de Moçambique) see Gibson, African Liberation Movements, 276 ff.

134 'BEK-Informationen zum Antirassismusprogramm des ÖRK Nr. 8', 1975, 19 f., EZA Berlin, 101/1152. On 14 Nov. 1975, Isaias Funzamo replied in a letter of thanks: "Our churches have noted with great joy that the Protestant churches in your country, in particular the Presbyterian Church, are endeavouring to have contact with Frelimo and to extend this contact at church level. May God grant that personal contacts between our two churches will be possible one day.", cf. EZA Berlin, 101/1104. I. D. Mahlalela from the Council of Churches in Mozambique wrote on 17 Aug. 1976 that they were pleased to have these contacts but that they did not have enough money to travel within their own country and not to mention a different continent. See also the reply from the East German Protestant Church to Mahlalela, 26 Oct. 1976, ibid.

135 See the telegram sent by Weitz (East German embassy in Dar-es-Salaam) on 22 June 1977 regarding the general meeting of the Lutheran World Federation, Bundesarchiv, Berlin-Lichterfelde, DO-4, 4903. Cf. Arne Sovik (ed.), In Christ, a New Community.

The Proceedings of the Sixth Assembly of the Lutheran World Federation, Dar-es-Salaam, Tanzania, June 13–25, 1977, Geneva 1977.

136 Pabst's note on a discussion at the State Department on 25 April 1977, EZA Berlin, 101/1104.

137 See file memos Pabst/Lewek on Mozambique, spring 1977 (op. cit. note 136).

138 Cf. draft letter from 14 March 1977 (op. cit. note 136). Reply from Mahlalela on 27 May 1977, ibid. On the occasion of the Central Committee meeting in Geneva the chairman of the National Christian Council in Mozambique, Archbishop Sengulane, confirmed that entry visas for Adler and von Brück were available (cf. Lewek's note on 19 Sept. 1977, ibid.).

139 Pabst to Funzamo, 27 June 1977 (op. cite note 136).

140 Lewek to Seigewasser, 27 July 1977, ibid.

141 See also Hans-Georg Schleicher and Ulf Engel, 'DDR-Geheimdienst und Afrika-Politik', Außenpolitik. Zeitschrift für internationale Fragen 47 (1996), 399–409, here: 404.

142 Cf. Lewek's note on 19 Sept. 1977 (op. cit. note 136).

143 However, there were further problems, which continued until February 1978; see 'Protokoll der 52. KKL-Tagung am 11./12.11.1977' and Schönherr's letter to Bellman on 14 Feb. 1978, ibid.

144 Ibid.

145 See the letter from Schönherr to Seigewasser on 1 June 1977 with the appendix: "Warum ist die weitere Intensivierung der Beziehung zu den Kirchen in Mozambique jetzt durch einen Besuch dort nötig?", and Schönherr's letter to Gysi on 5 Aug. 1981, Bundesarchiv, Berlin-Lichterfelde, DO-4, 4903. Mahlalela travelled to Europe including East Germany in mid-1980; cf. Weise's file memo on 2 July 1980 regarding Mahlalela's visit to Gysi on 23 June 1980, Bundesarchiv, Berlin-Lichterfelde, DO-4, 4904.

146 Münchow's notes on phone calls with General Schleicher on 6 July 1977 and 14 Sept. 1977, Bundesarchiv, Berlin-Lichterfelde, DO-4, 4905; Münchow's note on 15 Feb. 1978, Bundesarchiv, Berlin-Lichterfelde, DO-4, 4903.

147 See Münchow's file memo on 27 June 1978 (op. cit. note 146).

148 Gero Schmidt's note entitled 'Zur Haltung der Partei- und Staatsführung der VR Moçambique gegenüber religiösen Glaubensgemeinschaften' on 3 Jan. 1983, Bundes-archiv, Berlin-Lichterfelde, DO-4, 4905.

149 Ibid.

150 Greif's file memo on a discussion with the head of the Religious Affairs Sector of the Central Committee of Frelimo, 27 May 1982 (op. cit. note 146).

151 See Weise's file memo from 2 July 1980 regarding Mahlalela's visit to Gysi on 23 June 1980, Bundesarchiv, Berlin-Lichterfelde, DO-4, 489.

152 Weise's note on 21 Nov. 1983 regarding a discussion with Secretary-General Mahlalela, Bundesarchiv, Berlin-Lichterfelde, DO-4, 4905. Kleinig's memo on the discussion between Gysi and Mahlalela on 18 Nov. 1983, Bundesarchiv, Berlin-Lichterfelde, DO-4, 490.

153 See Gessner's information about the consultation on the People's Republic of Mozambique at the East and Central Africa Division of the East German Ministry of Foreign Affairs on 23 Jan. 1984, Bundesarchiv, Berlin-Lichterfelde, DO-4, 4905 and 4903. On the economic relations between the two countries see also Hannelore Butters, 'Zur wirtschaftlichen Zusammenarbeit der DDR mit Mosambik', in Schleicher et al. (eds), 165–173.

154 Cf. Butters, 'Zur wirtschaftlichen Zusammenarbeit ...' (op. cit. note 153), 170 f.

155 Cf. Heyne's report from 23 Oct. 1985 on the fact-finding visit of General Job Chambal, the director of Religious Affairs to the Ministry of Justice of the People's Republic of Mozambique between 14 and 20 Oct. 1985 in East Germany, Bundesarchiv, Berlin-Lichterfelde, DO-4, 4905. See also Chambal's letter of thanks to Gysi on 28 Oct. 1985, Bundesarchiv, Berlin-Lichterfelde, DO-4, 4904.

156 Note taken by the second embassy secretary, B. Weidlich, on a discussion with Job Chambal, the Director of Religious Affairs at the Ministry of Justice of Mozambique, 24 Feb. 1987, Bundesarchiv, Berlin-Lichterfelde, DO-4, 4905. See also Weidlich's note from 29 April 1988 on a discussion with Chambal on 20 April 1988, Bundesarchiv, Berlin-Lichterfelde, DO-4, 4904.

157 Weidlich's note on 24 Feb. 1987 (op. cit. note 156).

158 See Heyne's report from 23 Oct. 1985 on the fact-finding visit of General Job Chambal, the director of Religious Affairs to the Ministry of Justice of the People's Republic of Mozambique from 14 to 20 Oct. 1985 in East Germany (op. cit. note 156). See also information from 27 Oct. 1988 on a two-year stay of a representative of the Youth Division of the Mozambican Council of Christians to East Germany, Bundesarchiv, Berlin-Lichterfelde, DO-4, 4904. Report by Giselher Hickel (East German Protestant Church) from 20 Jan. 1988 on the one-year stay by a representative of the Youth Division of the CCM in East Germany, ibid.

159 Weidlich's information on 7 Sept. 1987 regarding an event at the East German embassy in Maputo on 1 Sept. 1987, Bundesarchiv, Berlin-Lichterfelde, DO-4, 4905.

160 Salzer's note on 21 Aug. 1989 on a discussion with General Job Chambal on 15 Aug. 1989 (op. cit. note 159).

161 Ibid.

162 Cf. Butters, 'Zur wirtschaftlichen Zusammenarbeit ...' (op. cit. note 153), 172 f.

163 Will's note from 10 Feb. 1988 on a discussion with Berger (Ecumenical Missionary Centre) and König (East German Protestant Church) on 9 Feb. 1988, Bundesarchiv, Berlin-Lichterfelde, DO-4, 1047.

164 See Salzer's telegram to Löffler on 28 Sept. 1989, Bundesarchiv, Berlin-Lichterfelde, DO-4, 4904.

165 Cf. Will's file memo from 6 June 1979 regarding a discussion between Kalb and the bishop of the United Methodist Church in Angola, Emílio Julio Miguel de Carvalho, on 28 May 1979 in Berlin. Bundesarchiv, Berlin-Lichterfelde, DO-4, 483.

166 On 21 Oct. 1981, Kaltenborn's colleague Bernhardt, who was also East Germany's CPC chairman, invited the Secretary-General of CAIE, Daniel Ntoni Nzinga, and two other theologians to take part in the CPC conference "On the Issue of Peace" in East Berlin on 4 and 5 Dec. 1981. Bundesarchiv, Berlin-Lichterfelde, DO-4, 4905. Bernhardt was used as an unofficial informer with the cover name "Jäger" [hunter] and "Förster" [forester] by the East German Department of State Security. See below, note 256.

167 Cf. information from Juhl (East German embassy in Luanda) on churches and religious groups in the People's Republic of Angola, Bundesarchiv, Berlin-Lichterfelde, DO-4, 4904.

168 Information from Kaltenborn, 31 May 1984, on his work and study trip to Angola, Bundesarchiv, Berlin-Lichterfelde, DO-4, 4905. See also Kaltenborn's plans for the study trip to Angola on 25 Sept. 1979, ibid.; telegram from Schoen, 28 April 1980, on Kaltenborn's stay in Luanda, ibid.; Will's report from 23 July 1980 on Kaltenborn's stay in Angola, Bundesarchiv, Berlin-Lichterfelde, DO-4, 489; note taken by Bethge on 6 July 1983 regarding a discussion with Kaltenborn on the conclusion of his stay in Angola 28 June 1983, Bundesarchiv, Berlin-Lichterfelde, DO-4, 4905; Kaltenborn's report on his trip to Angola from 15 to 29 June 1983 with the appendix: 'Zur künftigen Kooperation zwischen CFK und CAJE', Bundesarchiv, Berlin-Lichterfelde, DO-4, 4903; overview of the International Relations Division at the East German State Department for Church Issues, 16 Sept. 1983, on the Angolan Council of Evangelical Churches (CAJE), Bundesarchiv, Berlin-Lichterfelde, DO-4, 4905; information from Juhl, 23 Jan. 1985, on Kaltenborn's trip to Angola, 2 to 9 Jan. 1985, ibid.

169 Schöche's telex from 26 Oct. 1983 to Comrades Gysi, Sieber, König, Bayerlacher and Neugebauer, op. cit. note 168.

170 Cf. Mörker's letter to Will, 29 Jan. 1985, Schöche to Sieber, 29 March 1985, ibid.

171 Ibid.

172 Cf. information from Juhl on 23 Jan. 1985 regarding Kaltenborn's trip to Angola, 2 to 9 Jan. 1985 (op. cit. note 168). See also his assessment of the current church situation in the People's Republic of Angola, March 1987, ibid. Cf. Bleskin's telegram to Will from 14 Oct. 1988 and information from Will on 3 Nov. 1988 regarding the visit of a delegation from the National Office for Church Issues of the People's Republic of Angola to East Germany in 1989, Bundesarchiv, Berlin-Lichterfelde, DO-4, 4904.

173 Schöche telegram to Gysi et al. on 26 Oct. 1983, Bundesarchiv, Berlin-Lichterfelde, DO-4, 4905.

174 Cf. Juhl's letter to Will, 21 Nov. 1986, Bundesarchiv, Berlin-Lichterfelde, DO-4, 4904; Kaltenborn's file memo from 10 July 1986 and 2 Dec. 1986 on medical aid to Angola, ibid.

175 Hußner's note from 28 Aug. 1989 regarding a discussion with Comrade Lisbõa Santos, 25 Aug. 1989 (op. cit. note 174). See also note by Schulze (East German embassy in Luanda) on 27 Feb. 1989 regarding Archbishop Desmond Tutu's visit to Angola from 18 to 23 Feb. 1989, ibid.

176 Note by Rauch, 15 Feb. 1990, regarding a discussion between Hüttner and Carvalho on 14 Feb. 1990 (op. cit. note 175). See also Juhl's information from 2 Feb. 1987 on a discussion with Carvalho on 29 Jan. 1987, ibid. Here, Carvalho expressed considerable anti-American sentiments.

177 The contact between the East German government or rather the East German Protestant Church and the ANC or the SACC [South African Council of Churches] was mostly cultivated through friendly neighbouring African states and during international church conferences outside of the RSA (op. cit. note 174). Cf. in particular Will's note to Gysi on 30 Oct. 1987, ibid. Here, the letter of solidarity from the East German Protestant Church to Winnie Mandela (March 1987) and the appeal of the Governing Bodies of Protestant Churches in East Germany (4 July 1987) are emphasised. Cf. Demke et al. (ed.), Zwischen Anpassung und Verweigerung (op. cit. note 127), 427 ff. Cf. Will's information from 23 April 1980 regarding the question of ecumenical relations between the East German Protestant Church and the churches in sub-Sahara Africa, Bundesarchiv, Berlin-Lichterfelde, DO-4, 489; Will's file memo from 12 March 1980 on a discussion between Münchow/Will and von Brück about his trip to Ethiopia, ibid.

178 On the developments in Namibia cf. Siegfried Groth, Namibische Passion. Tragik und Größe der namibischen Befreiungsbewegung, Wuppertal 1995.

179 Details of the discussion between Comrade Will and Comrade Schleicher from the Foreign Ministry, OZA Division on East Germany's position regarding Namibia and RSA, Bundesarchiv, Berlin-Lichterfelde, DO-4, 1011; cf. also Will's information on churches and religious groups in Namibia (undated), Bundesarchiv, Berlin-Lichterfelde, DO-4, 4904.

180 On the relationship between the East German authorities or the East German Church to the Church in Tanzania cf. Bundesarchiv, Berlin-Lichterfelde, DO-4, 4903; Ambassador Schädlich (Tanzania) to Bayerlacher at the East German Foreign Ministry on 12 Oct. 1982, ibid. Information on the relationship between the East German Protestant Church and the churches in Tanzania (no author, no date), Bundesarchiv, Berlin-Lichterfelde, DO-4, 4904. See also Will's note on 31 July 1981 regarding Bishop Gienke's planned trip to Iringa, Tanzania between 24 Sept. and 10 Oct. 1981, Bundesarchiv, Berlin-Lichterfelde, DO-4, 490.

181 Will's note on 16 Nov. 1977 regarding a discussion with Schülzgen and Heyroth on 11 Nov. 1977, Bundesarchiv, Berlin-Lichterfelde, DO-4, 488. Cf. also Will's file memo from 15 April 1988 on a discussion with Reverend Wolff (from Magdeburg) at the Department for Church Issues on 14 April 1988, Bundesarchiv, Berlin-Lichterfelde, DO-4, 4904. The discussion was to "evaluate" Wolff's trip to Lesotho, Botswana and Zimbabwe in March 1988.

182 See for example Will's memo from 13 April 1989 on 'Churches and Religious Groups in Namibia', Bundesarchiv, Berlin-Lichterfelde, DO-4, 1047.

183 Ibid. See also the strictly confidential secret service information no. 2227/87 from 12 June 1987 on the planned activities of the ANC and Swapo offices in East Germany and church activities (East German secret service files: BStU, ZA, MfS HA XX/ 4-1537, 15).

184 Cf. Zeise's note on 7 April 1989 regarding a discussion with Dumeni on 6 April 1989, Bundesarchiv, Berlin-Lichterfelde, DO-4, 4904.

185 Published in Demke et al. (eds), Zwischen Anpassung und Verweigerung (op. cit. note 127), 431 f.

186 Hans-Georg Schleicher and Ulf Engel (ed.), 'DDR-Geheimdienst und Afrika-Politik', Außenpolitik. Zeitschrift für Internationale Fragen 47 (1996), 405 f.

187 Op. cit. note 186, 407.

188 Ibid.

189 Althausen memorandum, as of 1 Nov. 1973, EZA Berlin, 101/1135. As early as 1967 Sokolovski, a Soviet specialist in religion from the secret service, recommended in an internal paper that staffing policy modifications should be made according to the "Blake Line". His plan stated "the churches from socialist countries should demand a larger number of seats both on the Central Committee and at the staff headquarters of the World Council of Churches in Geneva". He made a number of concrete staffing proposals and urged "the development of contacts between churches in the socialist countries and the most influential church dignitaries in the developing countries in particular, while at the same time aiming to weaken the influence of the Anglo-American block and Blake himself". Cf. East German secret service files: BStU, ZA, MfS XX/4, 1162, 392-407.

190 Althausen memorandum, 1 Nov. 1973, EZA Berlin, 101/1135. Cf. also Weise's file memos from 11 March 1975 on a talk with the executive secretary of the WCC, Gill, on 28 Feb. 1975 at the Department for Church Issues, Bundesarchiv, Berlin-Lichter-felde, DO-4, 488. On the early relationship between the USSR and the Ecumenical Movement see Klaus Spennmann, Die ökumenische Bewegung und der Kommunis-mus in Russland 1920-1956, Ph.D. thesis in theology, Heidelberg 1970.

191 See 'Protokoll über die 26. Tagung der KKL am 7./8.9.1973', EZA Berlin, 101/1153.

192 Cf. 'Protokoll der 21. KKL-Tagung am 10./11.11.1972', EZA Berlin, 101/1135.

193 Cf. leadership meeting of the governing bodies of Protestant Churches in East Ger-many: minutes of 25 April 1973, op. cit. note 192.

194 Cf. 'Protokoll über die Sitzung des LÖK am 9.8.1973', ibid.

195 Cf. 'Protokoll über die Sitzung des LÖK am 25.9.1973', ibid. See also Adler's hand-written note to Pabst on 14 Oct. 1973, ibid.

196 Cf. Pabst to Potter, 11 Feb. 1975, EZA Berlin, 101/1136; Pabst's memo for a discus-sion between leading members of the WCC and the East German Protestant Church (undated), ibid.

197 Cf. Pabst's note on a discussion with Raiser on 1 Aug. 1977, EZA Berlin, 101/1137.

198 List made by the secretariat of the East German Protestant Church on 22 Aug. 1977, op. cit. note 197.

199 'Programmaktivitäten des ÖRK in Zusammenarbeit mit Kirchen in osteuropäischen Ländern seit der Tagung des ZA im Jahre 1977'; aide-mémoire of a friendly discus-sion between leading dignitaries of the WCC and representatives of member church-es in the socialist countries of Eastern Europe, Budapest, 29 to 31 March 1977; Pabst's note on a meeting between leading members of the WCC and Eastern European del-egates to the Central Committee on 10 Jan. 1979 in Kingston; Herrbruck's note on the meeting of East German members on committees of the WCC and the Conference of European Churches on 3 Nov. 1979, EZA Berlin, 101/1138.

200 See Pabst's note on a discussion at the Department for Church Issues on 9 Sept. 1976, EZA Berlin, 101/1137.

201 Pabst to Krause, 16 Oct. 1978, EZA Berlin, 101/1138.

202 See Gerhard Horstmeier's comment in the church report from 16 May 1975, which Potter refers to.

203 On 17 and 18 March 1982 Potter was awarded an honorary doctorate by the Department of Theology of East Berlin's Humboldt University. See 'Protokoll der 3. Zusammenkunft der Vorbereitungsgruppe für die VV des ÖRK in Vancouver am 22.1.1982', EZA Berlin, 101/1146.
204 Potter's memorandum to P. Bouman, D. Epps and J. Hilke, 4 Aug. 1975, EZA Berlin, 101/1136.
205 Note by the interpreter, Ms Bauer, for Stolpe on 16 Sept. 1975, op. cit. note 204.
206 Cf. Bosinski's file memo for Lewek on 13 Jan. 1976, Lewek's comment from 14 Jan. 1976 on this subject, EZA Berlin, 101/1137 and Schönherr's note to the Secretariat of the East German Protestant Church, 19 Feb. 1976, ibid. Gerhard Bosinski was listed by the East German Department of State Security as an unofficial informer under the name of "Specht", cf. BStU, ZA, MfS AIM 15716/79,I,1; II,1.
207 Cf. Raiser's memorandum to Potter on 12 Feb. 1976; cf. EZA Berlin, 101/1137.
208 Cf. Pabst's memo on a discussion with Raiser on 1 Aug. 1977, op. cit. note 207; Pabst's letter to Raiser on 3 May 1978 and Raiser to Pabst on 22 May 1978, EZA Berlin, 101/1138. Also, Raiser to Pabst on 21 Feb. 1978 and 22 May 1978; Raiser to Hempel in September 1979; Herrbruck's 'Protokoll der 15. Referentenbesprechung der GEÖ am 26.9.1979', ibid. See also 'Protokoll über die 81. Tagung der KKL am 2./3.7.1982', EZA Berlin, 101/ 1147.
209 See for example Raiser's letter to Pabst on 4 May 1976, EZA Berlin, 101/1137; letter from Stolpe and Pabst to Raiser on 27 Sept. 1977, ibid.
210 Cf. Stolpe to Raiser on 23 Jan. 1978, EZA Berlin, 101/1138. Potter had invited Seigewasser in 1979 and repeated the invitation when he spoke to him in person (Pabst's note on a discussion between Raiser and Seigewasser on 22 June 1979, ibid.). However, due to Seigewasser's death it was not until late May 1981 that his successor, Klaus Gysi, could visit Geneva (see Lewek and Zeddies's report from 30 June 1981 on Gysi's visit to the Ecumenical Centre, 25 to 29 May 1981, EZA Berlin, 101/1139 and Gysi's report from 11 June 1981 on his visit to the WCC, Bundesarchiv, Berlin-Lichterfelde, DO-4, 489). See also epd Geneva on 27 May 1981.
211 Following the suggestion made by Bishop Bartha from Hungary a similar conference with a similar composition of delegates took place in Budapest in October 1975 in preparation for Nairobi. The East German Protestant Church had made its participation dependent on the condition that no uniform line should be agreed upon for the churches from socialist countries and that the WCC would not invite CPC representatives (see Hilke's memorandum to Potter on 6 Aug. 1975 [WCC General Secretariat, Country Files, Eastern Europe/GDR, volume: Eastern Europe General 1979–85]).
212 Letter from the delegates of European socialist countries at the Fifth General Meeting of the WCC to Dr Potter and Dr Scott. The letter was written at the appraisal conference in Budapest on 23 and 24 March 1976, Bundesarchiv, Berlin-Lichterfelde, DO-4, 488. Cf. Weise's memo from 21 Jan. 1976 regarding a discussion with Pabst on 13 Jan. 1976 about the Fifth General Meeting of the WCC in Nairobi and its results, ibid.
213 Cf. WCC activities in cooperation with churches from Eastern European countries since the Central Committee conference in 1977; aide-mémoire on a friendly discussion between leading dignitaries of the WCC and representatives of the member churches from the socialist states of Eastern Europe, Budapest, 29 to 31 March 1977; Pabst's note on a meeting of leading members of the WCC with Eastern European delegates from the Central Committee meeting on 10 Jan. 1979 in Kingston; Herrbruck's note on the meeting of East German members of the WCC and the Conference of European Churches on 3 Nov. 1979, EZA Berlin, 101/1138.
214 Dohle's file memo from 12 Sept. 1977 regarding a discussion between Seigewasser, Weise, Dohle, Raiser, Pabst and Borgmann on 12 Sept. 1977, Bundesarchiv, Berlin-Lichterfelde, DO-4, 488.
215 Op. cit. note 214.

216 Text: 'Anti-Rassismus-Programm der Ökumene. Dokumentation einer Auseinander-setzung', compiled and commented on by Klaus-Martin Beckmann, with an epilogue by Hans Thimme, Dokumentation Evangelischer Pressedienst, 5, Witten, Frankfurt am Main-Berlin 1971, 71–74. For further details see Christel Meyers-Herwartz, Die Rezeption des Antirassismus-Programms in der EKD, Stuttgart-Berlin-Cologne-Mainz 1979; for a chronology of the discussion within the West German Protestant Church and in the public arena see ibid. 357–359. See Reinhard Groscurth, 'Die Evangelische Kirche in Deutschland und der Ökumenische Rat der Kirchen. Versuch einer Zwi-schenbilanz nach 40 Jahren', Ökumenische Rundschau 37 (1988) 271–285; Roger Williamson, 'Die Evangelische Kirche in Deutschland, die Ökumene und das "insti-tutionelle Dilemma"', ibid. 285–300.

217 Cf. the comment of the WCC Secretary-General on 6 Oct. 1970, EZA Berlin, 101/1135.

218 Quoted from 'Anti-Rassismus Programm der Ökumene' (op. cit. note 216), 251 f.

219 See Blake's letter to Schönherr on 9 March 1971, EZA Berlin, 101/1135. Seigewasser also expressed his appreciation on 2 March 1971 in a discussion with Noth and Pabst: "The main interest of the secretary of state was in the resolutions on the anti-racism programme. He expressed his surprise at the unanimity that had been achieved and he spoke with appreciation of the letter from the Governing Bodies to Secretary General Dr Blake on 9 Jan. 1971." Pabst's draft memo of a discussion on 2 March 1971 about the trip by East German church delegates to the UK in November 1970 and the conference of the Central Committee of the WCC in Addis Ababa, EZA Berlin, 101/1169.

220 Blake to Schönherr, 9 March 1971, EZA Berlin, 101/1135. [This letter was written in German.]

221 Cf. press statement from the secretariat of the East German Protestant Church on Blake's letter of 29 April 1971 (op. cit. note 220).

222 Private meeting of the Council of the West German Protestant Church on 20 and 21 May 1971 at the Evangelische Sozialakademie Schloss Friedewald (the Friedewald Palace Protestant College of Social Sciences), ibid.

223 Ibid.

224 'Niederschrift der 55. Sitzung des Rates der EKD am 15./16.9.1971', EZA Berlin, 101/903. See also Aleksandr Solzhenitsyn, The Gulag Archipelago, Glasgow 1973.

225 Cf. Althausen's comment on 13 Dec. 1974 regarding the documentation of the dis-cussion between representatives of the Württemberg church and the WCC in Geneva, EZA Berlin, 101/1136. See also Rolf Scheffbuch, 'Anfragen an den Ökumenischen Rat der Kirchen', in idem, Frag-Würdige Ökumene, Stuttgart 1974, 46–82; idem, 'Vergebliche Liebesmühe?', Ökumenische Rundschau 24 (1975) 359–370.

226 Cf. Althausen's comment on 13 Dec. 1974, EZA Berlin, 101/1136.

227 See also Ernst Lange, 'Bericht über die Begegnung des Rates der EKD mit Mitgliedern des Stabes des ÖRK in Genf am 7.6.1974', Ökumenische Rundschau 23 (1974) 375–384.

228 Althausen's memo from 15 Oct. 1973 on the visit of Niilus and his wife to the State Department for Church Issues on 10 Oct. 1973, EZA Berlin, 101/903. See also the gov-ernmental note on 13 May 1977 regarding a talk with Niilus in East Berlin on 12 May 1977, Bundesarchiv, Berlin-Lichterfelde, DO-4, 488.

229 See also Besier, Der SED-Staat und die Kirche 1969–1990 (op. cit. note 1), 174 ff.

230 See 'Vertraulicher Protokoll-Entwurf über ein Treffen zwischen Nairobi-Delegierten aus der EKD und dem BEK vom 29./30.9.1975', EZA Berlin, 101/1155.

231 Ibid.

232 Ibid.

233 Ibid.

234 Ibid.

235 Pabst's note regarding a discussion at the State Department for Church Issues on 4 Nov. 1975, EZA Berlin, 101/1152. See also the information from the SED Study

Group on Church Issues on 6 Feb. 1976 regarding the Fifth WCC General Meeting in Nairobi, Kenya and its results, Bundesarchiv, Berlin-Lichterfelde, DO-4, 488. It was noted that there were attempts to "fight certain anti-imperialist tendencies in the policies of the World Council of Churches" and to assert "anti-Communist and anti-Soviet positions", but these attempts failed.

236 'Anti-Rassismus-Programm der Ökumene' (op. cit. note 216), 100 ff. and 161 ff.

237 Ibid. 104.

238 Ibid. 105.

239 Helmut Class to the clergy of the Protestant Church in Württemberg on 15 Nov. 1977, EZA Berlin, 101/1097.

240 Fröhlich to Class, 11 Dec. 1977, op. cit. note 239.

241 Class to Fröhlich, 14 Dec. 1977, ibid.

242 Fröhlich to Class, 18 Dec. 1977, ibid.

243 See 'Protokoll über die 91. Sitzung des BEK-Vorstandes am 25./26. 7. 1978' (39 pages), ibid.

244 Cf. report on the visit by the council chairman of the West German Protestant Church, Class, and the president of the Foreign Affairs Division of the West German Protestant Church, Hans Joachim Held, to South West and South Africa between 5 and 18 July 1978, EZA Berlin, 101/1541.

245 The West German study was in response to the study from SACC's Department for Justice and Reconciliation on the issue of foreign economic links with South Africa, which was published in the second half of 1977. See texts on economic relations with South Africa, in Texte zum Kirchlichen Entwicklungsdienst, XVIII, Frankfurt am Main 1978.

246 Cf. 'Memorandum zum Verhältnis der EKD zum ÖRK – unter besonderer Berücksichtigung des PCR', [resolution of the Council of the West German Protestant Church on 6 Nov. 1978], Ökumenische Rundschau 28 (1979), 43–51.

247 Transcript of the discussion between Held, Ziemer (chairman), Berger, Brückner, Gutsch, H. Schultze, Schönherr, Moderow, Planer-Friedrich, Romberg, Demke, Lewek and Gienke (part of the time) in autumn 1978 (undated, but initialled by Pabst to certify the accuracy of the transcript on 8 Nov. 1978).

248 Ibid.

249 Report on Class and Held's visit to South West and South Africa, EZA Berlin, 101/1541.

250 Cf. ibid.

251 Herrbruck's note on the meetings of the East German delegates of the committees of the WCC and the Conference of European Churches on 3 Nov. 1979, EZA Berlin, 101/1138.

252 Herrbruck's note on '3. Zusammenkunft von DDR-Mitgliedern in ÖRK-Gremien am 2. 4. 1982', EZA Berlin, 101/1139.

253 Pabst's draft file memo regarding a discussion on 2 March 1971 that concerned the visit of a delegation of East German churches to the UK in November 1970 and also a conference of the WCC Central Committee in Addis Ababa in January 1971, EZA Berlin, 101/1164. See also Weise's file memo from 10 Feb. 1978 on Weise and Will's discussion with Oestreicher at the State Department for Church Issues on 10 Feb. 1978 (Bundesarchiv, Berlin-Lichterfelde, DO-4, 488), which reads: "Oestreicher explained that the West German government and Protestant Church were still very much behind in their political attitudes to Southern Africa ... . Oestreicher, who was promoting his own personality and supposed influence, tried to give the impression that he held a decisive position in relation to the churches in England. He withdrew immediately and changed the subject as soon as he realised that his attempts to talk about issues of 'human rights' in socialist countries and the affairs of Amnesty International were countered by suitable arguments on our own part. It became obvious in the course of the conversation that Oestreicher is continuing to value contacts with the

authorities in socialist countries." See also Oestreicher's letter to Seigewasser on 20 Sept. 1979, ibid.

254 Bundesarchiv, Berlin-Lichterfelde, DO-4, 487.

255 Ibid. The Scandinavian members of the Nordic-German Convention of Churches, which was established in 1950, issued a declaration of confidence in the former GDR churches in the summer of 1996 (cf. Das Sonntagsblatt, no. 30 from 26 July 1996).

256 On the general way in which the Department of State Security "accompanied" the ecumenical activities of the East German Protestant Church see BStU, ZA, MfS HA XX/4, 140; 304; 496; 1104; 1162; 1163; 1197; 1198. These files contain numerous internal minutes of WCC staff meetings and other meetings, either in German or English. Those in the church, who were listed by the department as unofficial informers, as far as is known were used specially for the "Ecumenism" line of the Department of State Security: Gerhard Bassarak (alias "Bus"), Bernhardt (alias "Jäger" or "Förster"), Ulrich von Brück (alias "Zwinger"), Günther Donath (alias "Paul Pfalz", BstU; ASt. Halle, VIII-1603/82), Heinrich Fink (alias "Heiner"), Hans-Georg Fritzsche (alias "Fritz"), Dietrich Gutsch ("Dietrich"), "Kiesel", Eberhard Klages (alias "Ehrlich"), Günter Krusche (alias "Günther"), Ernst-Eugen Meckel (alias "Prinz"), "Tulpe", Joachim Rogge (alias "Ferdinand"). On the situation of the files in general, see Gerhard Besier and Stephan Wolf (eds), "Pfarrer, Christen und Katholiken". Das Ministerium für Staatssicherheit der ehemaligen DDR und die Kirchen (Historisch-Theologische Studien zum 19. und 20. Jahrhundert, Quellen 1), Neukirchen-Vluyn ²1992; Krone and Schult (eds), Seid untertan der Obrigkeit; Walter Schilling et al. (eds), Die "andere" Geschichte, Erfurt 1993; Dietmar Linke, Theologiestudenten der Humboldt-Universität. Zwischen Hörsaal und Anklagebank. Darstellung der partei-politischen Einflussnahme auf eine Theologische Fakultät in der DDR anhand von Dokumenten (Historisch-Theologische Studien zum 19. und 20. Jahrhundert, Quellen 3), Neukirchen-Vluyn 1994; Besier, Der SED-Staat und die Kirche 1969–1990 (op. cit. note 1); Gerhard Besier, Der SED-Staat und die Kirche. Höhenflug und Absturz, Berlin-Frankfurt am Main 1995; Roland Brauckmann and Christoph Bunzel, Rück-blick. Die evangelische Kirche des Görlitzer Kirchengebietes, die Einflussnahme des MfS und der DDR-Staat 1970–1994, Görlitz 1995.

257 Ingo Braecklein, the bishop of Thuringia, was registered under the name of "Ingo" by the Department of State Security between 1959 and 1987, BStU, ZA, MfS AIM 24028/91, I.1; II,1.

258 Information from 4 April 1972 regarding the behaviour of the delegation from the East German Protestant Church and the United East German Protestant Lutheran Church in Switzerland 14 to 24 March 1972, Bundesarchiv, Berlin-Lichterfelde, DO-4, 488.

259 Ibid. See also Information no. 9/72 from the secretary of state for Church Issues on 10 Oct. 1972 on regarding the ecumenical activities of the East German Protestant Church i. e. trips to the Soviet Union, Indonesia and the Netherlands as well as a number of problems involving the PCR, Bundesarchiv, Berlin-Lichterfelde, DO-4, 4994.

260 Ibid.

261 See Weise's note on 6 Jan. 1971 concerning a talk with von Brück, a member of the High Consistory, about a trip to Tanzania to visit the Evangelical Lutheran Church of Tanzania on 5 Jan. 1971, Bundesarchiv, Berlin-Lichterfelde, DO-4, 487.

262 Sovik, In Christ (op. cit. note 135).

263 Memo from 5 July 1977 on the secretary of state's meeting with the GDR delegates to the Sixth General Meeting of the LWF in Dar-es-Salaam, Bundesarchiv, Berlin-Lichterfelde, DO-4, 488.

264 See Weise's information from 12 June 1981 regarding a preparatory meeting for the conference of the WCC Central Committee in Dresden from 6 to 8 June 1981 in Sofia, Bulgaria, Bundesarchiv, Berlin-Lichterfelde, DO-4, 489. This was a meeting between the WCC Deputy Secretary-General Sabev, the state church authorities of Bulgaria and the GDR. Sabev reported on this occasion that Raiser had said in Geneva, "that

the development of the relationship between state and church in East Germany since 1978 had been proceeding quite positively. Information would have to be put together on this and provided to all delegates of the Central Committee meeting ... . Sabev said 80 % of all staffing matters in the WCC were prepared by Potter, Raiser and Sabev ... . Great disappointments were unlikely in staffing matters." Weise also wrote that Sabev was "concerned that the Afghanistan issue might be brought up again". The meeting with Sabev in Sofia had been planned in East Berlin (see Malina's note from 17 Feb. 1981, on a discussion between Gysi and the Bulgarian ambassador Valcho Naidenov on 16 Feb. 1981, ibid.). According to information on 10 Aug. 1981, the Department of State Security provided "security" for the meeting of the WCC Executive and Central Committee in the form of ten full-time East German State Security officers, sixteen unofficial informers from the district authorities and eleven from the State Security Division HA XX/4. In addition, there was "direct support through the use of Chekists" from the USSR, Czechoslovakia, Hungary and Cuba. A number of full-time officers were employed as WCC interpreters, BStU, ZA, MfS HA XX/4, 304, 72–77. On "Dresden" see also Gerhard Grohs, 'Kirche im Sozialismus – Weltfrieden – Vancouver 1983. Schwerpunkte auf der Zentralausschusssitzung des ÖRK in Dresden vom 16.-26.8.1981', Ökumenische Rundschau 30 (1981) 473–479.

265 See Will's information from 6 June 1978 regarding the political situation in the Ecumenical Youth Council of Europe (EYCE) and possible measures to strengthen its anti-imperialist stance (Work Schedule for 1 half of the year, item 31), Bundesarchiv, Berlin-Lichterfelde, DO-4, 488.

266 For these figures the division used an article from Frankfurter Rundschau, 9 Sept. 1978.

267 Bundesarchiv, Berlin-Lichterfelde, DO-4, 4903.

268 'Religiöse Einrichtungen und die Erhöhung der internationalen Autorität der DDR', preparatory work for a talk by the secretary of state to leading staff at the East German Foreign Office on 26 Sept. 1988, Bundesarchiv, Berlin-Lichterfelde, DO-4, 1011.